The Law of the Church in Wales

THE LAW OF THE CHURCH IN WALES

NORMAN DOE

Professor of Law, Cardiff University
Director of the Centre for Law and Religion
Member of the Legal Advisory Commission of the Church of England
Deputy Chancellor of the Diocese of Manchester

UNIVERSITY OF WALES PRESS
CARDIFF
2002

© Norman Doe, 2002

British Library Cataloguing-in-Publicaton Data.
A catalogue record for this book is available from the British Library.

ISBN 0–7083–1748–0

www.wales.ac.uk/press

The right of Norman Doe to be identified as author of this work has been asserted by him in accordance with the Copyright, Designs and Patents Act 1988.

Typeset by Mark Heslington, Scarborough, North Yorkshire
Printed in Great Britain by Bookcraft, Midsomer Norton, Avon

For Edward Doe, and the people of St Edward's Church, Roath, Cardiff, All Saints' Church, Trealaw and St Paul's Church, Porth, Rhondda

CONTENTS

Part IV: The Doctrine, Liturgy and Rites of the Church

FOREWORD

The Most Revd Dr Rowan Williams, Archbishop of Wales

It is a rare scholar who can manage to make unfashionable subjects fascinating and inspiring. Since Canon Law has tended often to be the kind of subject that makes eyes glaze rather rapidly, people will be surprised to learn that Professor Doe has caught the imagination of a wide range of audiences with his teaching and writing in this area. The courses on Canon Law which he has developed in Cardiff are recognized as setting standards of excellence for the whole English-speaking world and beyond. In the worldwide Anglican Communion, he has initiated one of the most constructive projects now in hand to consolidate the unity of the Communion through the study of the common principles at work in the various systems of law and discipline in local Anglican churches.

In this latest of a list of very distinguished publications, he not only provides a comprehensive and clear guide to the existing law of the Church in Wales, but also sets in context the development of that law, tracing the ways in which the legacy of establishment still shapes some of our practice and clarifying the wider legal framework in which it operates. His references to the practice of other provinces will be of great help and interest. Above all, Professor Doe never loses sight of what Canon Law, in Wales or anywhere else, is for: the advancing of God's Kingdom and the holiness of God's people.

This is an excellent and most welcome book, which will, I hope, find its place on the shelves of all involved in the ministry and management of the Church in Wales.

+ Rowan Cambrensis

PREFACE

The aim of this book is to provide a systematic and practical statement of the law of the Church in Wales. Like many other major institutions in society, the Church in Wales operates within the context of both its own domestic regulatory system and the law of the State. The variety and pervasiveness of legal rules, rights and duties, are self-evident: they impact on the life of the church in its government, ministry, doctrine, liturgy, ritual, property and ecumenical relations. The book describes the domestic, enacted ecclesiastical law of the Church in Wales. This provincial law is found in its constitution, canons, schemes, rules, regulations and liturgical norms created by the church since its institutional foundation in 1920. The study embraces too the received ecclesiastical law of the church: those instruments pre-dating the disestablishment of the Church of England in Wales (in 1920) which continue to apply to the Church in Wales unless and until abrogated by it. The book also examines ecclesiastical quasi-legislation, extra-legal norms (in guidelines, policy and other documents) increasingly made by a wide range of provincial and diocesan bodies, and designed to supplement the formal law of the church. The wider perspective necessitates inclusion of the law of the State applicable to the Church in Wales: living as it does in the secular environment, the church is governed in key areas by civil law, of which the Welsh Church Act 1914 is a fundamental text. The likely impact of the Human Rights Act 1998 is important in this regard, being today the legal basis of freedom of religion for the Church in Wales. So too is the National Assembly for Wales: this has many functions relevant to the activities of the Church in Wales. Finally, the book compares, where appropriate, legal arrangements in the Church in Wales with those operative in other churches of the worldwide Anglican Communion.

This book engages the law of the Church in Wales simply on the descriptive level. Any critical comment in it is confined to observations about lack of clarity, internal inconsistency, or gaps in the law. The enacted ecclesiastical law is highly developed with respect to the institutional organization of the church, ecumenism, property and finance. However, often the enacted law is silent on a particular matter, and then it is necessary to consult the received pre-1920 ecclesiastical law, much of which is ancient, inaccessible and uncertain; and this book does not attempt an exhaustive statement of it. Yet, this received law is especially active in areas such as ministry and liturgy. Equally, the impact of civil law is felt keenly by the church in relation to marriage, burial, the sharing of church buildings and other property matters. Commonly, too, the church relies directly on the State without having its own internal law or standards applicable to (for example) church trustees, facilities for the disabled, or provision for church employees. When the domestic law of the Church in Wales appears to be unclear, internally inconsistent, or silent, material is included from the legal systems of fellow Anglican churches in order to indicate possible alternative approaches to similar issues and problems. Indeed, whilst most Anglican churches embarked on radical revision of their canon law in the 1960s and 1970s, the law of the Church in Wales has developed in a largely piecemeal fashion, from case to case, with much of the enacted ecclesiastical law today the same as it was in the 1920s. As a result of these revisions, most Anglican churches have a modern, accessible canonical statement of (for instance) the functions of ordained and lay ministers. But the Church in Wales has no modern body of canon law. Instead, rules on such single subjects have to be culled from a diversity of materials found in enacted ecclesiastical law, received ecclesiastical law (including sometimes pre-Reformation law), liturgical texts, and policy documents.

In recent years, there has been a real renewal of interest in church law. This is not surprising. From the religious perspective, rules are a normal function of any ecclesial society, and canon law itself may be conceived as applied ecclesiology: law is a means to an end and aims to serve the purposes for which the church exists (though this book does not attempt to uncover theological ideas underlying the domestic law of the Church in Wales). From the secular perspective, there are persistent questions about the meaning and scope of religious freedom, and the posture of the State towards religious affairs. In turn, this renewal of interest has led in the international arena to conferences on religious freedom, ecumenical colloquia on comparative canon law, societies devoted to the study of church law, and the introduction of courses on law and religion. Indeed, 1987 saw the establishment of the Ecclesiastical Law Society, and, closer to home, in August 2001 the foundation of Cymdeithas Cyfraith Grefyddol Cymru, an ecumenical society promoting the study in Wales of law in religion. Recent years have also seen, globally, an astonishing increase in books and journals on church law. In the Welsh context, Philip Jones's *The Governance of the Church in Wales* (2000) (in part updating C. A. H. Green's *The Setting of the Constitution of the Church in Wales* (1937)) carries an abundance of historical material and critical comment on current arrangements in the church.

I have relied heavily on the kindness of many in writing this book. To David Lambert, legal adviser to the Presiding Officer at the National Assembly for Wales, and registrar of the Diocese of Llandaff, I owe a special debt of gratitude in reading draft chapters. For their expertise, suggestions and encouragement, I thank also my colleagues at the Centre for Law and Religion, Cardiff Law School: Anthony Jeremy, the Revd Gregory Cameron, Javier Garcia Oliva, the Revd Paul Davies, Roger Ruston and Joanna Nicholson. An award from the Isla Johnston Trust, managed by the Representative Body of the Church in Wales, to set up a research fellowship at the Centre for Law and Religion (held by Anthony Jeremy) provided me with much-needed space to work on the book. The law is, needless to say, in a perpetual motion of change. For providing suggestions and up-to-date materials from within the Church in Wales, I am equally grateful to David McIntyre (former Secretary General), John Shirley (current Secretary General), Charles Anderson, David Llewellyn, Julian Luke, John Richfield, Robin Greenwood, Tim Davenport, the Revd Jeffrey Gainer, the Very Revd John Davies, Kay Powell and the Revd Irving Hamer. I should also like to thank the Revd Gareth Powell (from the Methodist Church) and Fr Gareth Jones (from the Roman Catholic Church) for their encouragement in this project, and, for help with proof-reading, Susan Mansell. Any errors in the book are, of course, solely my responsibility.

Special thanks are owed to my colleague Sharron Alldred for tireless and cheerful assistance with word-processing and production of the typescript. Similarly, I wish to thank staff at the University of Wales Press for their patience with and painstaking scrutiny of the typescript, especially Ceinwen Jones. It was several years ago that I first mooted with Susan Jenkins, Director at the Press, the possibility of a book such as this. To her I am deeply indebted for her continued faith in and commitment to the project. Finally, I should like to thank, for their constant kindness and support, my family: my mother, father, brother Martin, my parents-in-law, and above all my wife Heather and our children Rachel, Elizabeth and Edward.

C.N.D.
Cardiff
1 May 2002

ABBREVIATIONS

Complete references to the following are to be found in the Bibliography. For the purposes of footnotes, normally the abbreviations listed below are used, unless the context is not obvious in which case, for the sake of clarity, the full title is given. Resolutions of the Lambeth Conference are to be found in E. Coleman (ed.), *Resolutions of the Twelve Lambeth Conferences 1867–1988* (Toronto, 1992).

ACC	Anglican Consultative Council
Acts of Convocation	A. F. Smethurst, H. R. Wilson and H. Riley (eds), *Acts of the Convocations of Canterbury and York* (London, 1961)
AMEW	*Anglican Marriage in England and Wales: A Guide to the Law for Clergy* (1999)
AO	Alternative Order
Art.	Article
Australia	Anglican Church of Australia
BCP	Book of Common Prayer
Bermuda	Anglican Church of Bermuda
BGR	Burial Grounds Rules
Brazil	Episcopal Anglican Church of Brazil
Burundi	Church of the Province of Burundi
CA	Court of Appeal
CACCR	Cathedrals and Churches Commission Rules
Can(s).	Canon(s)
Canada	Anglican Church of Canada
CDCPC	Constitution of Diocesan Churches and Pastoral Committees
Central Africa	Church of the Province of Central Africa
CFR	Church Fabric Regulations
Ch.	Chapter
Chile	Anglican Church of Chile
CLAC	Norman Doe, *Canon Law in the Anglican Communion: A Worldwide Perspective* (Oxford, 1998)
COFC	Composition of Committees (October 2001)
Const.	Constitution
CPC	*The Care and Protection of Children: Statement of Policy and Guidance for Implementation* (1997)

CS	*The Cure of Souls: The Calling, Life and Practice of Clergy* (1996)
CSB	The Scheme of the Cathedral Church of Brecon
CSBG	The Scheme of the Cathedral Church of Bangor
CSL	The Scheme of the Cathedral Church of Llandaff
CSSA	The Scheme of the Cathedral Church of St Asaph
CSSD	The Scheme of the Cathedral Church of St Davids
CSM	The Scheme of the Cathedral Church of Monmouth
CSR	Regulations Governing the Application of the Proceeds of Sale of Churches, Church Sites and Churchyards (commonly known as the Church Sales Regulations)
CWAR	Church in Wales Accounting Regulations
CYR	Regulations for the Administration of Churchyards (commonly known as the Churchyard Rules)
DB	Diocese of Bangor
DL	Diocese of Llandaff
DM	Diocese of Monmouth
DSA	Diocese of St Asaph
DSAB	Diocese of Swansea and Brecon
DSD	Diocese of St Davids
Dioc.	Diocese
ECHR	European Convention on Human Rights
ECUSA	Protestant Episcopal Church in the United States of America
ELJ	*Ecclesiastical Law Journal*
England	Church of England
Governance	P. Jones, *The Governance of the Church in Wales* (Cardiff, 2000)
GBSO	Standing Orders of the Governing Body
GS	General Synod
Halsbury	Halsbury, *Laws of England*, vol. 14, *Ecclesiastical Law* (4th edn, London, 1975)
HCt.	High Court
HL	House of Lords
HLE (1910)	Halsbury, *Laws of England* (London, 1910)
Indian Ocean	Church of the Province of the Indian Ocean
Ireland	Church of Ireland
Japan	Holy Catholic Church in Japan (Nippon Sei Ko Kai)
Kenya	Church of the Province of Kenya
Korea	Anglican Church of Korea
LC	Lambeth Conference
Melanesia	Church of the Province of Melanesia
Mexico	Anglican Church of Mexico
MMS	Maintenance of Ministry Scheme
New Zealand	Anglican Church in Aotearoa, New Zealand and Polynesia
Nigeria	Church of the Province of Nigeria
North India	United Church of North India

NT	New Testament
PA	*Parochial Administration Handbook for Use in the Church in Wales* (2002 edn)
Papua New Guinea	Anglican Church of (the Province of) Papua New Guinea
Philippines	Episcopal Church in the (Province of the) Philippines
Phillimore	R. Phillimore, *The Ecclesiastical Law of the Church of England*, 2 vols. (2nd edn, London, 1895)
Portugal	Lusitanian Church (Portuguese Episcopal Church)
PRRMG	Preamble to the Regulations Relating to the Removal of Monuments and Gravestones
r.	Rule or Regulation
RCR	Redundant Churches Regulations
Re	Concerning (or in the matter of)
Res.	Resolution
RODC	Rules of the Diocesan Court
ROPC	Rules of the Provincial Court
RRMG	Regulations Relating to the Removal of Monuments and Gravestones (commonly known as the Gravestones Regulations)
RTOM	Regulations to Provide for Training for the Ordained Ministry of the Church in Wales (commonly known as the Training Regulations)
Rwanda	Church of the Province of Rwanda
s.	Section
Sched.	Schedule
Scotland	Scottish Episcopal Church
Setting	C. A. H. Green, *The Setting of the Constitution of the Church in Wales* (London, 1937)
SI	Statutory Instrument
SO	Standing Order
South East Asia	Church of the Province of South East Asia
South India	United Church of South India
Southern Africa	Church of the Province of Southern Africa
Southern Cone	Anglican Church of the Southern Cone of America
Spain	Spanish Reformed Episcopal Church
SR	Supplementary Regulations
Tanzania	Church of the Province of Tanzania
Uganda	Church of the Province of Uganda
West Africa	Church of the Province of West Africa
West Indies	Church of the Province of the West Indies
YB	Year Book
Zaire	Church of the Province of Zaire

TABLE OF STATE LEGISLATION

ACTS OF PARLIAMENT

SECONDARY LEGISLATION

TABLE OF ECCLESIASTICAL LEGISLATION

THE CONSTITUTION OF THE CHURCH IN WALES

References to the Chapters and Sections within them, are styled as follows: (e.g.) Chapter XI, Section 47 is cited as XI.47.

THE CANONS OF THE CHURCH IN WALES

In the following, the citation indicates the Canon, its date of promulgation and, in brackets, a short statement of its subject-matter.

Part 1

The Canons listed in this part do not involve amendment of Chapters of the Constitution or the Book of Common Prayer.

1. Can. 30-9-1937 (Old Catholics)   282
2. Can. 29-9-1955 (Experimental Use of Proposed Revisions of BCP)   222, 223
3. Can. 28-9-1961 (Irregularity of Birth and Holy Orders)   146
4. Can. 29-9-1966 (Philippine Independent Church)   282
5. Can. 29-9-1966 (Spanish Reformed Episcopal Church)   282
6. Can. 29-9-1966 (Lusitanian Church)   282
7. Can. 26-4-1973 (Church of South India)   282
8. Can. 27-9-1973 (Church of North India)   282
9. Can. 27-9-1973 (Church of Pakistan)   282
10. Can. 1-5-1974 (Covenant for Union in Wales)   206, 233, 283–5
11. Can. 2-5-1974 (Bible Version)   228
12. Can. 24-9-1975 (Mar Thoma Syrian Church)   283
13. Can. 23-9-1976 (Church of Bangladesh)   282
14. Can. 21-9-1977 (Covenant with Baptist Churches)   283
15. Can. 16-4-1980 (Women Deacons)   145
16. Can. 21-4-1982 (Incapacitated Incumbents)   15, 158, 161, 169, 348–50
17. Can. 15-9-1982 (Days of Ordination)   146
18. Can. 19-9-1985 (Ecumenism and Marriage)   285
19. Can. 19-4-1990 (Clerical Disabilities)   174–7
20. Can. 19-4-1990 (Age for Ordination)   145
21. Can. 26-9-1991 (Local Ecumenical Projects)   84, 143, 286–90
22. Can. 28-9-1995 (Porvoo Declaration)   9, 134, 145, 206, 233, 245, 290–7
23. Can. 19-9-1996 (Women Priests)   121, 144, 145, 215
24. Can. 13-9-1998 (Divorce and Ordination)   146
25. Can. 27-4-2000 (Reuilly Agreement)   9, 292

Part 2

The Canons listed in this part amend Chapters of the Constitution or the Book of Common Prayer. This book makes reference to only some of these Canons, since, in the case of the majority, the text refers only to the affected Chapters of the Constitution. They are included in this Table for the sake of completeness.

1. Can. 28-9-1949 (Resignation of Incumbents)   170
2. Can. 25-9-1968 (Clerical Manpower)   351
3. Can. 8-4-1970 (Baptism and Confirmation)   237
4. Can. 27-9-1973 (Burial of the Dead)   273
5. Can. 2-5-1974 (Holy Matrimony)   265
6. Can. 26-9-1974 (Miscellaneous Constitutional Amendments)   142
7. Can. 28-9-1978 (Calendar, Tables and Rules)   222
8. Can. 27-9-1979 (Thanksgiving for Birth or Adoption of a Child)   222

RULES

REGULATIONS

SCHEMES

CANONS ECCLESIASTICAL 1603/4

SERVICE BOOKS

OTHER INSTRUMENTS

In so far as they contain regulatory norms, the following are included in this table for the sake of convenience.

TABLE OF CASES

PART I

THE LEGAL REGULATION OF THE CHURCH

1

THE NATURE AND SOURCES OF CHURCH LAW

The Church in Wales is an autonomous province of the worldwide Anglican Communion, its legal foundation following the disestablishment of the Church of England in Wales by Parliament in 1920. The Church in Wales is regulated by two broad categories of law: the law of the church and the law of the State. The internal law of the Church in Wales is the product of continuous historical development, theological reflection and practical action. It expresses, in a concrete way, ideas which the church has about its own nature, identity, mission, standards and organization. As applied ecclesiology, the law of the church is found in instruments which the church has created for itself since disestablishment, and in a host of sources pre-dating but inherited by the church at disestablishment. At the same time, like any other major institution in society, the Church in Wales lives in the wider legal environment of the external law of the State. Whilst its religious freedom, and that of its members, is protected by the Human Rights Act 1998, the church operates within the framework of a wide range of State laws, including statute, the common law and, increasingly, the law of the European Union.

THE HISTORICAL CONTINUITY OF CHURCH LAW IN WALES

The law of the modern Church in Wales has a long and evolutionary history. Like the contemporary Church in Wales itself, with its ancient and rich history traceable to the very beginnings of Christianity in the British Isles, the law of the church is the product of almost 2,000 years of continuity and change in the institutional church.

The Origins and Development of Church Law: An Outline

The embryonic formation and use of standards and norms in the ecclesial communities of New Testament times sought to enable, guide and order the life of the Christian faithful.[1] In the post-apostolic era, the early Councils

[1] For juristic features of the NT see e.g. J. A. Coriden, *An Introduction to Canon Law* (London, 1990), 7ff.

undertook to systematize these standards and norms in the form of canons. These were designed in both practical and idealistic ways to serve the purposes for which the church exists, and, in so doing, elucidated the identity of the church itself. This formative period, together with the subsequent inception in the Western church of a centralized system of papal government, generated a complex of regulatory instruments, operating in concert with local ecclesiastical customs. To this growing body of rules was soon attached the title *canon law*, partly through the pervasive influence of Roman law, and partly through the development of the notion of the church as an institution. From the mid-twelfth century the canon law was subjected to systematic organization and application throughout the Western church.[2]

It was from the medieval period that the four Welsh dioceses of Bangor, Llandaff, St Davids and St Asaph came under the jurisdictional control of Canterbury and, progressively, of Rome.[3] Alongside local law, the Welsh church was regulated by Roman canon law, sometimes the subject of study by Welsh canonists of international standing, until the Reformation.[4] The Henrician legislation of the 1530s terminated papal jurisdiction and resulted in the establishment of the Church of England, its formal and legal connection with the State effected through the royal supremacy. However, by parliamentary statute, pre-Reformation Roman canon law was to continue to apply unless it was contrary to the laws of the realm. The Canons Ecclesiastical 1603/4 were promulgated by the Convocations of York and of Canterbury, of which bishops and clergy from the Welsh dioceses formed part. It was by these canons, along with those elements of Roman canon law which survived the Reformation, and the decisions of the church courts that the institutional church was regulated. In addition, particularly in the nineteenth century and as a feature of establishment, Acts of Parliament represented a significant source of law applicable to the Church of England in Wales.[5]

---

[2] For historical overviews, see generally J. A. Brundage, *Medieval Canon Law* (London, 1995); see also C. A. H. Green, *The Setting of the Constitution of the Church in Wales* (London, 1937), Ch. V.

[3] See generally D. Walker (ed.), *A History of the Church in Wales* (Penarth, 1976; reissued 1990).

[4] See E. P. Roberts, 'The Welsh church, canon law and the Welsh language', in N. Doe (ed.), *Essays in Canon Law* (Cardiff, 1992), 151; for discussion of Welsh awareness and observance of canon law, and for the contribution of Welsh canonists (such as Johannes Galensis or Walensis, writing 1210–15), see generally H. Pryce, *Native Law and the Church in Medieval Wales* (Oxford, 1993); for William Lyndwood, bishop of St Davids, who completed his celebrated *Provinciale c.* 1433, see B. E. Ferme, *Canon Law in Medieval England* (Rome, 1996).

[5] For a historical overview, see P. Jones, *The Governance of the Church in Wales* (Cardiff, 2000), 1–8; see also e.g. M. Hill, *Ecclesiastical Law* (2nd edn, Oxford, 2001), Ch. 1.

Church Law and Disestablishment

The extensive constitutional readjustment of church–State relations throughout Europe during the nineteenth century was echoed in the British Isles in 1869 with Parliament's enactment of a statute for the disestablishment of the Church of Ireland, resulting in the dissolution of its constitutional union with the Church of England. This was a period of intense development in church law. In 1917, the Roman Catholic Church codified for the first time its canon law in the *Codex Iuris Canonici*, replaced by another code in 1983. In 1919, Parliament empowered the laity for the first time to legislate for the Church of England through the creation of the Church Assembly, later (in 1970) reconstituted as the General Synod. Above all, this period marked the legal foundation of the modern institutional Church in Wales. Through the Welsh Church Act 1914, Parliament effected the disestablishment of the four dioceses of the Church of England in Wales. The statute was enacted in 1914,[6] but its implementation was postponed, due to the First World War, until 31 March 1920, the date of disestablishment.[7] Until that time, 'the Church of England and the Church of Wales were one body established by law.'[8]

The Welsh Church Act 1914   The Welsh Church Act 1914 has two basic purposes. First, the statute provides for disestablishment: it deals with the constitutional effects of disestablishment on the relations between church and State, the legal severance of the Welsh dioceses from the Church of England, and the reconstitution of the Welsh church on a new legal basis. Secondly, the statute provides for the disendowment of the four Welsh dioceses, making arrangements for the distribution of funds arising from disendowment, including the partial re-endowment of the Church in Wales amongst other objects.[9] On the day of disestablishment, the Church of England, so far as it extended to and existed in Wales and Monmouthshire, ceased to be 'established by law'.[10] Terminating the royal supremacy for the purposes of the Church in Wales,[11] the Welsh Church Act 1914 provided that no person was to be appointed or nominated by the monarch or by any person, by virtue of any existing right of patronage, to any ecclesiastical office in the Church in Wales; every cathedral and ecclesiastical

---

[6]   It was enacted without the consent of the House of Lords by means of the procedure contained in the Parliament Act 1911, and received royal assent on 18 September 1914.
[7]   The date was fixed by the Welsh Church (Temporalities) Act 1919, s. 2.
[8]   *Re Clergy Orphan Corporation Trusts* [1933] I Ch 267 *per* Farwell J.
[9]   See the excellent study by R. Brown, 'The disestablishment of the Church in Wales', 5 *ELJ* (1999), 252.
[10]   Welsh Church Act 1914, s. 1.
[11]   See, however, P. Jones, *Governance*, 68, for the argument that 'all churches in Britain, not just the Church of England, are subject to the royal supremacy'.

corporation (sole and aggregate) was dissolved; bishops of the Welsh dioceses ceased to be members of the House of Lords; bishops and clergy ceased to be members of and represented in the Convocation of Canterbury; but bishops and clergy were no longer disqualified from election to the House of Commons.[12] The University of Wales, the National Library of Wales and Welsh local authorities were notable beneficiaries of the disendowment provisions of the statute, a process administered by the Welsh Church Commission.[13]

Ecclesiastical Law   The Welsh Church Act 1914 provides that, as from the date of disestablishment, 'the ecclesiastical law of the Church in Wales shall cease to exist as law' for the Welsh church.[14] Under the pre-existing establishment, the ecclesiastical law,[15] applicable to the Church of England in Wales, had formed part of the law of the land, being the law of the established church.[16] However, this ecclesiastical law (found in both State and church-made law) was not to lose all its authority for the Welsh church. The Welsh Church Act 1914 prescribes that pre-1920 ecclesiastical law is to continue to apply to the Church in Wales as the terms of a contract to which the members of the church are party. In so doing the statute ensures the continuity of the canonical tradition, as well as of the fundamentals of faith and order. The statute provides that, as from the date of disestablishment, pre-1920 ecclesiastical law, previously applicable to the Church of England, and the pre-1920 articles, doctrines, rites, rules, discipline and ordinances of the Church of England, are to continue to apply to the Church in Wales. These pre-1920 sources continue to bind the church as if its members had agreed to be bound by them. However, under the statute, they continue to apply unless and until modified or altered by the Church in Wales.[17]

Self-government   At the same time, the Welsh Church Act 1914 provides for the church's power of self-governance, the freedom of the Church in Wales to organize its own internal life, and to establish its own system of

---

[12]   Welsh Church Act 1914, ss. 1, 2 and 3(5).
[13]   Ibid., Part II; see Brown, 'Disestablishment', at 254; see also P. Jones, *Governance*, 9–24.
[14]   Welsh Church Act 1914, s. 3(1).
[15]   See below for definitions of ecclesiastical law.
[16]   *Mackonochie v Lord Penzance* (1881) 6 App Cas 424 at 446 *per* Lord Blackburn.
[17]   Welsh Church Act 1914, s. 3(2): as from the date of disestablishment, 'the then existing ecclesiastical law and the then existing articles, doctrines, rites, rules, discipline, and ordinances of the Church of England shall, with and subject to such modification or alteration, if any, as after the passing of this Act may be duly made therein, according to the constitution and regulations for the time being of the Church in Wales, be binding on the members for the time being of the Church in Wales in the same manner as if they had mutually agreed to be so bound.'

government and law. Nothing in any Act of Parliament, law or custom is to prevent the bishops, clergy and laity of the church from holding synods or electing representatives to these, nor from framing in such manner as they think fit 'constitutions and regulations for the general management and good government of the Church in Wales' and for its property and affairs.[18] The power of making (by means of a constitution and regulations) alterations and modifications in the inherited ecclesiastical law, includes the power of altering and modifying such law so far as it is embodied in any Act of Parliament forming part of pre-1920 ecclesiastical law.[19] Whilst the church was empowered to establish church courts, such courts are to exercise no coercive jurisdiction.[20] The current Constitution, an organic document which has been amended and added to from time to time since, originated in the work of a lay and clerical Convention held in Cardiff in 1917,[21] and is the product of influences from other Anglican legal systems, notably of the church in England and Ireland.[22]

The Canonical Tradition in Context

Not only does the law of the Church in Wales enjoy historical continuity with its own pre-disestablishment heritage, through the tradition of the institutional church to employ rules for its self-government, the legal history of the Church of England, and the persistent susceptibility of the church to treatment by secular legislative activity. The canonical tradition too links the Church in Wales to other Anglican churches and to other ecclesial communities: the Roman Catholic Church, the Eastern Catholic Churches, and some Anglican churches, recognize formally, and in so doing live out, in their juridical orders, the canonical tradition.[23] Moreover,

---

[18] Welsh Church Act 1914, s. 13(1).
[19] Welsh Church Act 1914, s. 3(4): this provides for a power to alter or modify the pre-1920 ecclesiastical law as embodied in the Church Discipline Act 1840, the Public Worship Regulation Act 1874, the Clergy Discipline Act 1892, the Ecclesiastical Dilapidations Acts 1871 and 1872, 'or any other Act of Parliament'; see now Const. XI.47 (discussed below) for the current list of statutes which the church has disapplied since disestablishment.
[20] Welsh Church Act 1914, s. 3(3).
[21] See *Official Report of the Proceedings of the Convention of the Church in Wales* (Cardiff, 1917); the basic structures were approved by the Governing Body at its first meeting on 8 January 1918; see generally R. Brown, 'What of the Church in Wales?', 3 *ELJ* (1993), 20.
[22] For contrary views about the respective influences of C. A. H. Green and Viscount Sankey, see: A. J. Edwards, 'Building a canon law: the contribution of Archbishop Green', in Doe (ed.), *Essays in Canon Law*, 49; and J. T. Gainer, 'John Sankey and the constitution of the Church in Wales' (LLM dissertation, University of Wales, Cardiff, 1994).
[23] N. Doe, 'The principles of canon law: a focus of legal unity in Anglican–Roman Catholic relations', 5 *ELJ* (1999), 221.

whilst there is no formal binding canon law globally applicable to all churches in the Anglican Communion, there are profound similarities between the actual laws of each particular Anglican church.[24]

From these similarities, many shared principles may be induced, a process of induction which indicates an unwritten common law of the Anglican Communion, its *ius commune*. The collective effect of similarities between individual canonical systems is the Anglican *ius commune*. It is a common law which grows from the similarities between Anglican legal systems, the Church in Wales like all other Anglican churches, through its own legal system, contributing to the common law.[25] The fundamental principles of the law of the Church in Wales – representative government, episcopal oversight, canonical ministry, the participation of the laity in church life, and access to the ministrations of the church – aim towards the pastoral values of facility and order, and provide an essential focus of unity in the characteristics they have in common with all other churches of the worldwide Anglican Communion.[26]

THE LEGAL NATURE AND POSITION OF THE CHURCH

The legal nature and position of the Church in Wales may be approached from two perspectives: the ecclesiastical and the secular.

The Ecclesiastical Perspective

According to the teaching of the Church in Wales, the church universal is 'the family of God and the Body of Christ', it is 'One, Holy, Catholic and Apostolic', and its members enter it by baptism. The mission of the church is 'to be the instrument of God in restoring all people to unity with God and each other in Christ'. The church carries out this mission, through the ministry of all its members, in prayer and worship, in proclaiming the Gospel and 'in promoting justice, peace and love in all the world'.[27] The visible church of Christ is 'a congregation of faithful men, in which the pure Word of God is preached, and the sacraments duly administered according to Christ's ordinance in all those things that of necessity are

---

[24] Doe, *Canon Law in the Anglican Communion* (Oxford 1998), hereafter CLAC.
[25] See N. Doe, 'Canon law and communion' (unpublished paper delivered to the Meeting of the Primates of the Anglican Communion, Kanuga, North Carolina, USA, 6 March 2001).
[26] See Const., Prefatory Note. In contrast to the Church in Wales, the vast majority of churches in the Anglican Communion have undertaken in recent years a radical and extensive revision of their constitutional and canonical systems: see Doe, CLAC, 383–5.
[27] BCP (1984), 690–1 (Catechism).

requisite to the same'.[28] The Church in Wales defines itself as 'the ancient Church of this land, catholic and reformed', proclaiming and maintaining 'the doctrine and ministry of the One, Holy, Catholic and Apostolic Church'.[29] In turn, the law of the Church in Wales acknowledges that the church belongs 'to the One, Holy, Catholic and Apostolic Church of Jesus Christ and truly participating in the apostolic mission of the whole people of God'.[30] In the church 'the Word of God is authentically preached', 'the sacraments of baptism and the eucharist are duly administered', and the apostolic faith is genuinely confessed.[31] The calling of the Church in Wales is 'to nurture men and women in the faith of Jesus Christ and to aid them to grow in the fellowship of the Holy Spirit'.[32] It is usually the case in other Anglican churches that such definitions are contained in the constitutional law of the church.[33]

In a wider ecclesiastical context, the Church in Wales is also a member of the Anglican Communion, 'a fellowship, within the One Holy Catholic and Apostolic Church, of those duly constituted dioceses, provinces and regional Churches in communion with the See of Canterbury'.[34] According to the Lambeth Conference, in its resolutions about the nature of the Anglican Communion, 'the true constitution of the Catholic Church involves the principle of the autonomy of particular Churches based on a common faith and order'.[35] The member churches 'uphold and propagate the Catholic and Apostolic faith and order as they are generally set forth in the Book of Common Prayer [1662]', and they 'promote within each of their territories a national expression of Christian faith'; they are 'bound together not by a central legislative and executive authority, but by mutual loyalty maintained through the common counsel of the bishops in

---

[28] Thirty-Nine Articles of Religion, Art. 19; for the Articles of Religion as a doctrinal document in the Church in Wales, see below, Ch. 9.

[29] BCP (1984), 692.

[30] Can. 28-9-1995: the Church in Wales, in this canon (designed to implement the Porvoo Declaration: see below, Ch. 12), indirectly claims these features for itself – the statements appear in the First Schedule to the Porvoo Declaration; see also Can. 27-4-2000 (a canon to implement the Reuilly Agreement).

[31] Can. 28-9-1995.

[32] Constitution, Prefatory Note.

[33] See e.g. New Zealand, *Constitution and Canons* (1995), Preamble: 'the Church is the body of which Christ is the head'; 'the Church (a) is One because it is one body, under one head, Jesus Christ; (b) is Holy because the Holy Spirit dwells in its members and guides it in mission; (c) is Catholic because it seeks to proclaim the whole faith to all people to the end of time and (d) is Apostolic because it professes the faith of the apostles and is sent to carry Christ's mission to all the world.'

[34] LC 1930, Res. 49; for the Church in Wales, 'The Anglican Communion is a family of Churches within the Catholic Church of Christ, maintaining apostolic doctrine and order and in full communion with one another and with the See of Canterbury' (BCP (1984), 692). For inter-Anglican relations, see below, Ch. 12.

[35] LC 1930, Ress. 48, 49.

conference'.[36] Consequently, unlike some Anglican churches which are national (their territory coincident with that of a State), united or extra-provincial, but in common with many,[37] the Church in Wales is a particular church,[38] organized on the basis of a province,[39] consisting of six dioceses.[40] In short, the Church in Wales is an autonomous, self-governing church, 'a fellowship of dioceses within the Holy Catholic Church, constituted as a Province of the Anglican Communion'.[41]

The Secular Perspective

The law of the State contains five different ideas about the nature and position of the Church in Wales. First, in civil law, a 'church' is the aggregate of the individual members of a religious body or a quasi-corporate institution carrying on the religious work of the denomination whose name it bears.[42] Secondly, the Church in Wales is sometimes classified as a disestablished church.[43] This is not technically the case, however. The legal foundation of the contemporary institutional Church in Wales was the result of the Welsh Church Act 1914.[44] The effect of this statute was the partial disestablishment of the Church of England on 31 March 1920. It was the Church of England, not the Church in Wales, that was

---

[36]   Ibid.

[37]   Doe, CLAC, 9.

[38]   For discussion of the national role of the Church in Wales, see Brown, 'What of the Church in Wales?', 20.

[39]   ACC-4, 1979: a province is 'a self-governing Church composed of several dioceses operating under a common Constitution and having one supreme legislative body'. See P. Jones, *Governance*, 31: the province of the Church in Wales was neither created by the Welsh Church Act 1914, nor by the Constitution, but by a declaration of the Archbishop of Canterbury, Randall Davidson, on 10 February 1920, 'the last act of English ecclesiastical law to bind the Church in Wales'.

[40]   The dioceses existing at disestablishment were St Davids, Llandaff, St Asaph and Bangor; the creation of two new dioceses followed: Monmouth (1921), and Swansea and Brecon (1923).

[41]   Const., Prefatory Note.

[42]   See *Re Barnes, Simpson v Barnes* (1922) [1930] 2 Ch 80 and *Re Schoales, Schoales v Schoales* [1930] 2 Ch 75. See also *Free Church of Scotland (General Assembly) v Lord Overtoun* [1904] AC 515, in which the HL defines a church as: an associated body of Christian believers, having a common interpretation of its source of belief, and acknowledging its collective belief thereby establishing their membership of it; for a discussion of this case, see P. Jones, *Governance*, 44–9.

[43]   *Representative Body of the Church in Wales v Tithe Redemption Commission and Others* [1944] 1 All ER 710 at 711: Viscount Simon speaks of 'the disestablishment and partial disendowment of the Church in Wales' and of 'the Representative Body which represented the disestablished Church'; see also 718, *per* Lord Porter, who speaks of the 'disestablished Church of Wales'; see also *Wallbank and Wallbank v PCC of Aston Cantlow and Wilmote with Billesley* (2001), CA Case No: A3/20000/0644.

[44]   See generally T. G. Watkin, 'Disestablishment, self-determination and the constitutional development of the Church in Wales', in Doe (ed.), *Essays in Canon Law*, 25.

disestablished.[45] As the Welsh Church Act itself provides, this was 'An Act to terminate the establishment of the Church of England in Wales and Monmouthshire'.[46] Moreover, insofar as the contemporary institutional Church in Wales was founded in direct consequence of a legislative act of the civil power, and given the notorious difficulties which exist in defining establishment,[47] there is modest judicial support for the view that the Church in Wales is a re-established church.[48] Indeed, two notable vestiges of establishment remain today in the duty of clergy of the Church in Wales to solemnize the marriages of parishioners and the right of parishioners to burial in the churchyard.[49] These and other incidents of establishment may suggest the view that the Church in Wales is a quasi-established church, being treated for these purposes as if it were established.[50]

Thirdly, the law of the State treats the Church in Wales as a consensual society classified in law, like other non-established religious organizations,[51] as an unincorporated voluntary association whose members are organized and bound together as a matter of private contract.[52] Since

---

[45] *Re MacManaway* [1951] AC 161 at 165, *arguendo*: 'the Welsh Church Act, 1914, did not disestablish the Welsh Church, but only disestablished the Church of England in so far as it then existed in Wales.'

[46] Welsh Church Act 1914, long title; see, however, s. 1: 'the Church of England, so far as it extends to and exists in Wales and Monmouthshire (in this Act referred to as the Church in Wales), shall cease to be established by law.'

[47] See e.g. *AG (Victoria), ex rel Black v Commonwealth* (1981) 146 CLR 559; and N. Doe, *The Legal Framework of the Church of England* (Oxford, 1996), 8f.

[48] *Powell v Representative Body of the Church in Wales* [1957] 1 All ER 400 at 403 *per* Wynn-Parry J: the object of the 1914 statute was 'to re-establish the Church in Wales on a contractual basis'. As is discussed elsewhere in this Chapter, through the Welsh Church Act 1914 (being the formal *legal* parent of the Church in Wales), the State provides the church with a statutory contract (consisting initially of pre-1920 ecclesiastical law), and with the statutory power to make its own constitution and regulations; the statute also provides for the power to alter and modify Acts of Parliament which formed part of the statutory contract provided for the church by the State (ss. 3(4), 13).

[49] See T. G. Watkin, 'The vestiges of establishment: the ecclesiastical and canon law of the Church in Wales', 2 *ELJ* (1990), 110; see also below, Ch. 11.

[50] For this concept, see M. H. Ogilvie, 'What is a church by law established', 28 *Osgoode Hall Law Journal* (1990), 179; for the application of this idea to the Church in Wales, see N. Doe, 'Disestablishment and the legal position of the Church in Wales' (unpublished paper delivered at a seminar to mark the Eightieth Anniversary of Disestablishment (1920–2000), Cardiff, 29 March 2000): see also below, Ch. 8 for the provision under the Prison Act 1952 of clergy of the Church in Wales as prison chaplains.

[51] *Forbes v Eden* (1867) LR 1 Sc & Div 568.

[52] *Powell v Representative Body of the Church in Wales* [1957] 1 All ER 400 at 403; for criticism of the applicability of the contract idea, see P. Jones, *Governance*, 51f.: this suggests that 'the notion of the Church in Wales as based on a contract . . . is flawed . . . because a church exists on the basis of shared religious belief', not contract; 'It would be better to speak of the governance of the Church in Wales as based on consensus rather than contract.'

disestablishment in 1920, the Church in Wales has been recognized by the courts of the State as having existed as 'a voluntary organisation of individuals, held together by no more than the contract implied by such mutuality'.[53] Consequently, 'the Church in Wales is a body whose legal authority arises from consensual submission to its jurisdiction'; the church has 'no statutory (*de facto* or *de iure*) governmental function', but is, rather, 'analogous to other religious bodies which are not established as part of the State'.[54] Like other religious voluntary associations, the Church in Wales is a consensual religious community,[55] operating its own largely self-regulatory system of governance, distinct from the State and its institutions.[56] Similarly, being an unincorporated association, the church has no separate legal identity; it is not treated as a juridic person and cannot sue or be sued,[57] though institutions within it may enjoy legal personality or identity in secular law.[58]

Fourthly, being in civil law a consensual body, the Church in Wales may enjoy the status of a voluntary organization for the purposes of dealings with the National Assembly for Wales. The Government of Wales Act 1998 provides a mechanism to enable relevant voluntary organizations to be consulted by the Assembly in the exercise of its functions. Relevant voluntary organizations are defined as those bodies whose activities are carried out otherwise than for profit and directly or indirectly benefit the whole or part of Wales.[59] Finally, whilst the matter has as yet not received

[53]   *R v The Dean and Chapter of St Paul's Cathedral and the Church in Wales, ex parte Williamson* (1998) 5 *ELJ* 129 *per* Sedley J.
[54]   *R v The Provincial Court of the Church in Wales, ex parte Reverend Clifford Williams* (1999) 5 *ELJ* 217 *per* Latham J.
[55]   *Re Clergy Orphan Corporation Trusts* [1933] I Ch 267 *per* Farwell J: the Church in Wales is organized 'as a matter of agreement between those persons who are members of that body'.
[56]   *R v Chief Rabbi of the United Hebrew Congregations of Great Britain and the Commonwealth, ex parte Wachmann* [1992] WLR 1036: for State court intervention, the test is that of 'government interest': 'to attract the court's supervisory jurisdiction there must not be merely a public but potentially governmental interest in the decision making power in question.'
[57]   See *Baker v Jones and Others* [1954] 2 All ER 553; *R v Jockey Club, ex parte RAM Racecourses Ltd* (1991) 3 Admin LR 265.
[58]   The Representative Body, for example, is incorporated by royal charter (see below Ch. 13); and the Governing Body is recognized as an 'appropriate authority' for the purposes of the Sharing of Church Buildings Act 1969 (Sched. 2).
[59]   Government of Wales Act 1998, s. 114. The Assembly is under a duty to make a scheme setting out how it proposes 'to promote the interests of relevant voluntary organizations'. Whether the Church in Wales is a voluntary organization, and therefore eligible for membership of a scheme, would be for the Assembly to decide. The scheme must specify how the Assembly proposes to consult relevant voluntary organizations about the exercise of its functions affecting, or of concern to, those organizations. Provision exists to keep the scheme under review, to remake and revise it, and to publish it. The Assembly must consult such organizations as it considers appropriate before making, remaking or revising the scheme.

judicial consideration, the Church in Wales may be classified as a religious organization, its members enjoying freedom of religion under the European Convention on Human Rights,[60] for the purposes of the Human Rights Act 1998.[61] As a general principle, it is unlawful for any public authority, including the National Assembly for Wales,[62] in carrying out its functions, to act in a way which is incompatible with Convention rights, such as the right of freedom of religion.[63]

DOMESTIC CHURCH LAW: THE FORMS OF ECCLESIASTICAL REGULATION

The Church in Wales is regulated by two bodies of law: one external, the other internal. The law of the State applicable to the Church in Wales is found in: primary legislation, statutes enacted by the Sovereign in Parliament, which may be addressed to the church indirectly or directly;[64] secondary legislation, such as that made or deemed to be made by the National Assembly for Wales;[65] European law;[66] and the decisions of the courts of the State, that is, decisions on the meaning of legislation and in

---

[60] ECHR, Art. 9: (1) 'Everyone has the right to freedom of thought, conscience and religion; this right includes freedom to change his religion or belief and freedom, either alone or in community with others and in public or private, to manifest his religion or belief, in worship, teaching, practice and observance'; (2) 'Freedom to manifest one's religion or beliefs shall be subject only to such limitations as are prescribed by law and are necessary in a democratic society in the interests of public safety, for the protection of public order, health or morals, or for the protection of the rights and freedoms of others.'

[61] Human Rights Act 1998, s. 13: 'If a court's determination of any question arising under this Act might affect the exercise by a religious organisation (itself or its members collectively), of the Convention right to freedom of conscience, thought and religion, it must have particular regard to the importance of that right'; in this section 'court' includes a tribunal.

[62] Government of Wales Act 1998, ss. 107, 153(2).

[63] Human Rights Act 1998, s. 6: acts include omissions.

[64] For direct applicability see e.g. the Welsh Church (Burial Grounds) Act 1945; for indirect applicability see e.g. Ecclesiastical Courts Jurisdiction Act 1860.

[65] Under the Government of Wales Act 1998, the Assembly is competent to exercise all those ministerial functions, which touch the Church in Wales, including the making of secondary legislation, contained in Acts of Parliament listed in Transfer of Functions Orders, and under Acts passed since devolution. Secondary legislation directly or indirectly affecting the Church in Wales which has already been made under statutory powers will continue to apply to the church as the law of the Assembly, unless and until altered by it: see e.g. the Ecclesiastical Exemption (Listed Buildings and Conservation Areas) Order 1994, SI 1994/1771, made under the Planning (Listed Buildings and Conservation Areas) Act 1990. The Church in Wales is party to the Laws Committee of CYTUN (Churches Together in Wales), a function of which is 'to review the effect of legislation on faith communities in Wales' enacted by the National Assembly.

[66] E.g. the Data Protection Act 1998 which gives effect to the requirements of Directive 95/46/EC of the European Parliament.

the common law. The internal or domestic law of the Church in Wales is found in a host of regulatory instruments which fall into four broad categories: the Constitution of the Church in Wales; pre-1920 ecclesiastical law; extra-constitutional legislation; and ecclesiastical quasi-legislation.[67] Each source is, in turn, composed of several forms of ecclesiastical regulation. In most Anglican churches, the law is to be found, simply, in a constitution and a code of canons.[68]

The Constitution

The *Constitution* of the Church in Wales, which applies throughout the province, is composed of chapters (and further chapters), 'all canons of the Church in Wales', and 'all rules and regulations made from time to time by or under the authority or with the consent of the Governing Body'.[69] The Governing Body is empowered 'to add to, alter, amend, or abrogate any of the provisions of the Constitution'.[70] The power to create *chapters* (or *further chapters*) is vested in the Governing Body,[71] their enactment, and alterations and additions to them, being effected commonly by means of the making of a canon. The *canons* of the Church in Wales are made, repealed and amended by the Governing Body, acting in accordance with bill procedure.[72] On promulgation by the President of the Governing Body, a canon becomes 'a law of the Church in Wales'.[73] *Rules* and *regulations* may be made by the Governing Body,[74] which may also authorize or

---

[67]   The domestic law of the church sometimes distinguishes between the 'received' ecclesiastical law, and the 'enacted' ecclesiastical law, the received being that which was inherited at disestablishment, and the enacted that which has since been made by the church; see e.g. the Scheme of the Cathedral Church of Llandaff, II.1; see also below.

[68]   The Constitution most commonly consists of fundamental declarations and principles: see e.g. the Church of the Province of Southern Africa, *Constitution and Canons* (1994). Others simply have a code of canons: see e.g. Scottish Episcopal Church, *Code of Canons* (1996). The canons of the Church of Ireland are incorporated in the Constitution (*The Constitution of the Church of Ireland*, Ch. IX). The law of the Church of England includes Measures (enacted by General Synod and approved by Parliament), and Canons (made by General Synod and assented to by the Monarch).

[69]   Const., I.1(1)(a)–(d); the English and Welsh versions of the Constitution have 'equal validity' (I.1(2)), though, for 'the purpose of interpretation and for the resolution of any ambiguity, the English version shall be the definitive text' (I.1(3)).

[70]   Const., II.43; see also II.33(1): the Governing Body may make constitutions and regulations for 'the general management and good government of the Church'; this is declaratory of the Welsh Church Act 1914, s. 13(1).

[71]   Const., I.1(a) and (b).

[72]   See below, Ch. 2; *Wallbank and Wallbank v PCC of Aston Cantlow* (2001), unreported, *per* Sedley LJ: 'The term canon law is properly applied to the law made by the churches for the regulation of legal matters within their competence.'

[73]   Const. II.42(2).

[74]   Const. I.1(1)(d); the terms are not defined, and the constitution seems to provide no procedure for their creation, alteration or repeal. See e.g. the Hardship Regulations,

consent to their creation by others, such as the Representative Body.[75] Regulations may operate under the authority of a canon,[76] but it is assumed that they cannot repeal or amend those elements of the constitution which may be repealed or amended only by bill procedure.[77]

Whilst the constitution does not include them in its formal list of sources,[78] the following are considered to be included in the constitutional law of the church. *Schemes* made by the Governing Body,[79] and by the Representative Body,[80] are treated as a matter of ecclesiastical convention as part of the Constitution. *Motions* and *resolutions* may be passed by the Governing Body, in accordance with prescribed procedures, and the latter may effect temporary amendments to the constitution.[81] Liturgical *rules*, *rubrics* and *general directions* are forms of ecclesiastical regulation: 'The law of worship of the Church in Wales is contained in the Book of Common Prayer' (1984),[82] itself authorized by the Governing Body by means of canon and, therefore, having constitutional authority. Finally, *ecclesiastical custom*, or long-standing and continuous usage, though a minor source of regulation, has been recognized by the Constitution as having binding authority.[83]

Pre-1920 Ecclesiastical Law

Although the ecclesiastical law, applicable to the Church of England prior to its disestablishment, has ceased to exist for the Welsh church as the law

---

made by the Governing Body to alleviate hardship arising from the promulgation of the canon enabling women to be ordained as priests.
[75]   See e.g. Rules made under the Welsh Church (Burial Grounds) Act 1945, s. 4(2).
[76]   See e.g. Regulations (relating to payments to incapacitated incumbents) made under Can. 21-4-82 as amended by the Incapacitated Incumbents (Amendment) Canon 1985 (they are found in the First Schedule to the canon).
[77]   See Chancel Repair Regulations: these regulations also describe the provisions in them as 'rules'; r. 11: 'Nothing in these rules shall affect the provisions of Chapter III of the Constitution.'
[78]   The following instruments are not explicitly listed in Const. I.1(1) (for which see above).
[79]   The six Cathedral Schemes are included in vol. II of the Constitution.
[80]   The Maintenance of Ministry Scheme, consisting of 'Regulations prescribed by the Representative Body', is included in vol. II of the Constitution.
[81]   Const. II.34 and 35; for the procedures see below, Ch. 2.
[82]   BCP (1984), v.
[83]   See e.g. Const. VI.17(1), (2); cathedral schemes too preserve the customs of cathedrals if they are not inconsistent with the terms of those schemes and, sometimes, under cathedral schemes, cathedral clergy are obliged 'faithfully to observe all the Customs of the cathedral' (see below, Ch. 7). See also *Ridsdale v Clifton* (1876) 1 PD 316 at 331: 'Usage, for a long series of years, in ecclesiastical custom especially, is entitled to the greatest respect; it has every presumption in its favour; but it cannot prevail against positive law, though, where doubt exists, it might turn the balance.'

of the land,[84] it continues to apply to the Church in Wales as part of the church's statutory contract; and sometimes the domestic law of the church distinguishes between the received and the enacted ecclesiastical law.[85] Its application is by virtue of the Welsh Church Act 1914, and it is operative unless and until altered or modified by the Church in Wales.[86] With the exception of those parliamentary statutes, and other elements of pre-1920 ecclesiastical law, which the Church in Wales has disapplied since disestablishment,[87] the constitution provides that the 'ecclesiastical law as existing in England', at the date of disestablishment, 'shall be binding on the members (including any body of members) of the Church in Wales'. This pre-1920 ecclesiastical law must be 'applied to the determination of any question or dispute' between the members of the church, 'in so far as it does not conflict with anything contained in the Constitution'; the church's post-1920 constitutional law prevails over pre-1920 ecclesiastical law.[88] However, whilst pre-1920 ecclesiastical law continues to bind the members of the church (unless altered by the church), the courts of the Church in Wales are 'not to be bound by any decision of the English Courts in relation to matters of faith, discipline or ceremonial'.[89] The post-1920 law of the Church of England forms no part of the law of the Church in Wales.[90]

The Welsh Church Act 1914 does not define the expression 'ecclesiastical law'.[91] However, a variety of definitions appear in judicial decisions – some are wide, others narrow: '[t]he term "ecclesiastical law" ... means

---

[84] With the exception of rights to prison chaplains, marriage, burial: see Chs. 8, 11.

[85] See e.g. Scheme for the Cathedral Church of St Davids, II.1: the governance of the cathedral is 'subject always to the ecclesiastical law received or enacted by the Governing Body of the Church in Wales'.

[86] Welsh Church Act 1914, s. 3(2); see also above.

[87] Const. XI.47 lists the following disapplied statutes: the Clergy Ordination Act 1804; the Church Discipline Act 1840; the Ecclesiastical Commissioners Act 1840; the Clerical Subscription Act 1865; the Clerical Disabilities Act 1870; the Colonial Clergy Act 1874; the Public Worship Regulation Act 1874; the Sales of Glebe Lands Act 1888; the Clergy Discipline Act 1892; the Benefices Act 1898; the Pluralities Acts and the Incumbents Resignation Acts.

[88] Const. XI.47. Moreover, it does not apply if in conflict with anything contained 'in any special contract as to glebe [land] between the Representative Body and an Incumbent' (Const. XI.47).

[89] Const. XI.47.

[90] The point is well made in P. Jones, *Governance*, 29f.

[91] Whilst canon law is commonly understood as the law which churches create for themselves (see above, n. 72), ecclesiastical law is understood as the law of the State applicable to churches. As will be apparent from the discussions in this Chapter, however, these definitions may not readily be applied to the Church in Wales. See also A. T. Denning, 'The meaning of "ecclesiastical law"', 60 *LQR* (1944), 235; in the HL in *Representative Body of the Church in Wales v Tithe Redemption Commission* [1944] 1 All ER 710 at 720, Lord Simonds considered, for the purpose of that case, that it was not 'necessary to determine the exact scope of that "ecclesiastical law of the Church in Wales" which by sect. 3 of the Act is to cease to exist as law'.

the law relating to any matter concerning the Church of England administered and enforced in any court', temporal or ecclesiastical; alternatively, it
is 'the law administered by ecclesiastical courts and persons', in the Church
of England, 'and not by the temporal courts'.[92] Some definitions appear to
be contradictory. On the one hand, 'The ecclesiastical law of England . . . is
part of the general law of England – of the common law – in that wider
sense which embraces all the ancient and approved customs of England
which form law.'[93] On the other hand, 'ecclesiastical law' has been distinguished from the common law.[94] For practical purposes, therefore, the
ecclesiastical law enjoying continuing authority in the Church in Wales,
encompasses all law, consistent with the constitution of the church, which
was before disestablishment applicable to the Church of England in Wales,
whether it was created by the State or by the English Church, and whether
it was enforceable in the courts of the State or in those of the Church.

Consequently,[95] sources of pre-1920 ecclesiastical law which continue to
bind the members of the Church, to the extent that they do not conflict
with the constitution or have not been disapplied or abrogated since
disestablishment, include: Acts of Parliament;[96] judicial decisions of the
ecclesiastical and secular courts;[97] the Canons Ecclesiastical of 1603/4;[98]
and the pre-Reformation Roman canon law, provided it is consistent with

---

[92]   *AG v Dean and Chapter of Ripon Cathedral* [1945] Ch 239; this was cited in
Wallbank and Wallbank v PCC of Aston Cantlow (2001) unreported CA *per* Sedley LJ:
'Ecclesiastical law is a portmanteau term which embraces not only the canon law but
both secular legislation and common law relating to the church.'
[93]   *Mackonochie v Lord Penzance* (1881) 6 App Cas 424 at 446 *per* Lord Blackburn;
see also *R v Millis* (1844) 10 Cl & Fin 534 at 678: 'the general canon law', which is 'no
doubt the basis' of ecclesiastical law, has been 'modified and altered from time to time by
the ecclesiastical constitutions of our archbishops and bishops, and by the legislature of
the realm, and . . . has been known from early times by the distinguished title of the
King's Ecclesiastical Law'.
[94]   *Representative Body of the Church in Wales v Tithe Redemption Commission*
[1944] 1 All ER 710 at 713: Viscount Simon distinguishes ecclesiastical law from 'the
common custom of England' (i.e. the common law); compare *Evers v Owen's Case*
(1627) Godb 431: 'There is a common law ecclesiastical, as well as our common law, *jus
commune ecclesiasticum*, as well as *jus commune laicum*.'
[95]   *Kemp v Wickes* (1809) 3 Phillim 264 at 276 *per* Sir John Nicholl: 'The law of the
Church of England and its history are to be deduced from the ancient general canon law,
from the particular constitutions made in this country to regulate the English church,
from our own canons, from the rubric, and from any acts of parliament that may have
been passed on the subject; and the whole may be illustrated also by the writings of
eminent persons.'
[96]   See e.g. the Sacrament Act 1547.
[97]   See e.g. *Argar v Holdsworth* (1758) 2 Lee 515 (concerning the right to marry in the
parish church). However, the *courts* of the Church in Wales 'are not bound by any
decision of the English Courts in relation to matters of faith, discipline or ceremonial'
(Const. XI.47).
[98]   For the difficulties in determining which of these canons continue to apply, and the
effect of non-usage or desuetude, see G. K. Cameron, 'The Church in Wales, the canons

the royal prerogative, the laws, statutes and customs of the realm, and has been incorporated as custom (through recognition and continuous usage) into the ecclesiastical law.[99] Moreover, the principles and maxims of canon law, rooted in the canonical tradition, also contribute to the law of the Church in Wales. These may be understood as overarching all individual canonical systems, expressing the Church's underlying values and traditions, distinctive by virtue of their theological content, and giving meaning and coherence to hosts of individual rules.[100] Finally, in accordance with canonical tradition, the learned works of pre-disestablishment jurists are of continuing persuasive authority.[101]

Extra-constitutional Legislation

The Constitution of the Church in Wales, its provincial law, empowers various church bodies to create regulatory instruments. These instruments enjoy a constitutional authority, insofar as they are made under powers conferred by the Constitution, but may best be understood as species of secondary, subordinate or delegated legislation not strictly forming part of the constitution. *Standing Orders* of the Governing Body, which must be consistent with the constitution and which the Governing Body may make, rescind, suspend or vary, are designed for the regulation of its own procedures.[102] Cathedral *constitutions*, *statutes*, *ordinances* and *customs* regulate cathedral life and administration,[103] and, the bishop may, with the consent of the cathedral chapter, abrogate, alter, enlarge, interpret and add

---

of 1604 and the doctrine of custom' (LLM dissertation, University of Wales, Cardiff, 1997). For historical antecedents to the Canons Ecclesiastical 1603, see G. Bray, *The Historic Anglican Canons: 1529–1947* (London, 1998).

[99]   Submission of the Clergy Act 1533, s. 3; *R v Millis* (1844) 10 Cl & Fin 534; *Bishop of Exeter v Marshall* (1868) LR 3 HL 17 at 53–6: according to a 'rule of practice', to be operative as custom, it must have been 'continued and uniformly recognised and acted upon by the bishops of the Anglican Church since the Reformation'; *Bryant v Foot* (1867) LR 2 QB 161: custom must have operated from time immemorial.

[100]   See Doe, 'The principles of canon law'; some Anglican churches refer to these in their constitutions and canons: see e.g. the Province of Southern Africa, *Constitution and Canons* (1994), Can. 50: 'if any question should arise as to the interpretation of the Canons or Laws of this Church, or of any part thereof, the interpretation shall be governed by the general principles of Canon Law thereto applicable'; see also the *Code of Canon Law* (1983) of the Roman Catholic Church (c. 19).

[101]   See *Kemp v Wickes* (1809) 3 Phillim 264 at 276 *per* Sir John Nicholl: ecclesiastical law may be 'illustrated also by the writings of eminent persons'; see e.g. R. Phillimore, *The Ecclesiastical Law of the Church of England*, 2 vols. (2nd edn, London, 1895).

[102]   Const. II.47.

[103]   See e.g. the Scheme of the Cathedral Church of St Davids, s. I.1: 'The Constitution, Statutes, Ordinances and Customs of the cathedral church of St Davids which are operative at the present time are hereby confirmed and continued, save only in so far as they may be contrary to or inconsistent with the following.'

to these, and may abolish cathedral custom.[104] Furthermore, the cathedral schemes of the Church in Wales empower cathedral authorities to make orders, regulations and by-laws, and to revise, annul or add to these.[105]

Rules may be made by the Representative Body for the regulation of its own procedures,[106] and it may make *regulations* for the powers and procedures to be followed by any of its committees.[107] Some rules made by the Representative Body require the approval of the State and have, therefore, the authority of secondary legislation in civil law.[108] Rules may also be made by the Rule Committee to put into effect provisions of the constitution concerning the administration, practice and procedure of the courts of the church.[109] *Diocesan decrees* may be made by a diocesan bishop with regard to prescribed matters;[110] an *act* of a Diocesan Conference binds 'the Conference and all other members of the Church in the diocese',[111] as does a *resolution* of a conference, when expressly approved by the provincial Synod.[112] Finally, *rules* and *regulations* may be made by a Parochial Church Council for its own procedures, and for the procedures of its committees, but these may be overriden by the Diocesan Conference.[113]

Ecclesiastical Quasi-legislation

Any description of the sources of the domestic law of the church should have regard to what is often styled ecclesiastical quasi-legislation which is a developing source of governance and regulation in the Church in Wales, as it is in other Anglican churches.[114] There is a fine line between regulatory instruments which are 'legislation', properly so-called, and quasi-legislative administrative regulatory instruments which contain informal administrative rules. The formal constitution sometimes makes reference to some of these forms of administrative regulation, but usually it does not. The constitution of the Church in Wales sometimes empowers ecclesiastical

---

[104] Ibid., s. III.7.
[105] Ibid., s. VI.4: 'The Chapter shall make such orders, regulations and bye-laws as may be necessary to give effect to this Scheme, and also shall have the power to revise, annul or add to the said orders, regulations and bye-laws.'
[106] Const. III.30.
[107] Const. III.32(5).
[108] Welsh Church (Burial Grounds) Act 1945, s. 4(2): to be operative they must be approved by the National Assembly.
[109] Const. XI.41; see also XI.28.
[110] Const. IV.34, 35.
[111] Const. IV.32.
[112] Const. IV.33.
[113] Const. VI.27(a) and (b); however, the Diocesan Conference may 'control, alter, repeal, or supersede any regulation made by the [Deanery] Conference, the Vestry Meeting and the Parochial Church Council' (IV.43).
[114] N. Doe, 'Ecclesiastical quasi-legislation', in N. Doe, M. Hill and R. Ombres (eds), *English Canon Law* (Cardiff, 1998), 93.

authorities, at various levels of the church, to make administrative rules, in the form of binding orders and directions. The Representative Body is empowered to raise and apply money 'subject to any *directions* to the contrary which may from time to time be given by the Governing Body'.[115] The Diocesan Conference is under a duty to 'conform to and carry out any *order* or *direction* of the Governing Body'.[116] 'Subject to the direction and control of the Governing Body . . . the Conference shall manage its own affairs and its own property' (if any) 'subject always . . . to any regulations of [the] Representative Body'.[117] The Diocesan Parsonage Board 'shall conform to the directions and be under the control of the Representative Body'.[118] A Parochial Church Council is under a duty to propagate and implement any provision made by the Governing Body, the Representative Body, the Diocesan or Deanery Conference (but without prejudice to its own powers).[119]

Regulation is also effected in the church by means of instruments to which the formal constitution makes no reference. Typically, in secular government, quasi-legislation is to be found in non-statutory 'directives', 'directions', 'resolutions', 'blanket resolutions', 'circulars', 'codes of practice', 'good practice', 'policy documents', and 'guidelines', designed to supplement and to interpret the formal law. The secular courts have treated quasi-legislation as binding on its makers until changed: provided the instrument in question is lawful and does not fetter legal discretions, and unless there are good reasons in particular cases for departing from it, quasi-legislation may contain rights and duties and foster legitimate expectations of compliance with it.[120] Similar practices, common in the Church of England,[121] have made their appearance in the Church in Wales in the form of a 'memorandum', 'guidance', a 'policy document' or a 'practice'. *The Cure of Souls* (1996), commended by the Bench of Bishops, is a typical example: it is a policy document which, though not of itself having the force of law, provides for good practice amongst clergy; it contains general statements and interpretations of the law of both the State and the church, and its terms are often presented in prescriptive language.[122]

---

[115] Const. III.24.

[116] Const. IV.29.

[117] Const. IV.22.

[118] Const. IV.21.

[119] Const. VI.22(3)(c).

[120] See R. Baldwin and J. Houghton, 'Circular arguments: the status and legitimacy of administrative rules', *Public Law* (1986), 239.

[121] See Hill, *Ecclesiastical Law*, 17.

[122] *The Cure of Souls: The Calling, Life and Practice of Clergy* (1996), being the Report of a Working Party set up in 1995 by the Archbishop of Wales; the document contains rights and duties which do not obviously appear in the formal law (eg: the duty of clergy to collaborate one with another; 'Failure to collaborate with fellow clergy and ministers is a breach of duty' (p. 7)). Indeed, reference is made to *Parochial Administra-*

THE PURPOSE, STATUS AND AUTHORITY
OF DOMESTIC CHURCH LAW

This final section explores ideas about the purposes for which the internal law of the church exists. It also examines the status and enforceability of the internal law of the church in the wider legal environment of the civil law, and the binding effect of the domestic law on the members of the Church in Wales, particularly the devices which the church employs to ensure compliance with the various forms of ecclesiastical regulation.

The Purposes of the Domestic Law of the Church

Regulation in the church is seen by many as restrictive and coercive: ecclesiastical life ought to be governed by the Holy Spirit, the faithful living under grace rather than under a series of humanly made commands and prohibitions.[123] Yet the purpose of law in the church is the same today as it was in the early church: to facilitate and to order the life of the people of God. These two ideas, of law as facility and as order, reflect the juristic tradition of the Church in Wales which it shares with other canonical churches.

Facility   The primary function of the law of the church is to serve the purposes for which the church exists, to enable the people of God to fulfil their mission to society. As such, ecclesiastical regulation is seen as dynamic and programmatic. The Church in Wales itself has adopted the idea that: '[t]he Constitution which regulates the Church in Wales exists to serve the sacramental integrity and good order of the Church and to assist its mission and its witness to the Lord Jesus Christ.'[124] The law exists to promote the church's 'purpose as an institution for the help of [individuals] in their following of our Lord', and, to this end, 'in its legislative activities the Church is guided by the criterion of utility . . . to have such laws in force as to assist it in its work of training up the followers of the Lord.'[125]

The notion of facility, largely neglected by Anglicans,[126] has been

---

tion (2002) in the formal law of the church: CWAR, r.6. See also above, Table of Ecclesiastical Legislation, under Other Instruments, for further examples of Guidelines.

[123]   Rudolf Sohm (1841–1917), for example, saw a fundamental antithesis between law and the church as a community bound together by love: for Sohm's *Kirchenrecht* (1892), see A. V. Dulles, *Models of the Church* (Dublin, 1976); compare Adolf Harnack's response in *The Constitution and Law of the Church in the First Two Centuries*, trans. F. L. Pogson (London, 1910). For a critical appraisal of modern Welsh church law, see A. T. Lewis, 'The case for constitutional renewal in the Church in Wales', in Doe (ed.), *Essays in Canon Law*, 175.

[124]   Const., Prefatory Note.

[125]   *The Canon Law of the Church of England*, Report of the Archbishops' Commission on Canon Law (London, 1947), 3–5.

[126]   See, however, N. Doe, 'A facilitative canon law: the problem of sanctions and forgiveness', in Doe (ed.), *Essays in Canon Law*, 69; and Doe, *Legal Framework*, 33ff.

particularly developed in relation to Roman Catholic canon law: for Pope Paul VI, '[t]o limit ecclesial law to a rigid order of injunctions would be to violate the Spirit who guides us toward perfect charity in the unity of the Church'; the first concern is 'to deepen the work of the Spirit which must be expressed in the church's law' which itself 'responds to a need inherent in the church as an organised commuity'.[127] The facilitative nature of church law is summed up in the idea that 'canon law is applied ecclesiology ... the life of the Church is given, as law, specific embodiment and is structured in its institutions and organisations as is thought pastorally appropriate to any particular moment of Christ's life, death and resurrection'.[128] Theology and law are intimately connected: having reflected on divine revelation, the church formulates theology, itself providing a definition of the purpose of the church and of Christian values, and the church implements these values in the form of law; theological reflection forms the data for the discipline of church law.[129]

Order   Church law is also used to effect order, as '[e]very society, ecclesial or secular, requires its own rules for the regulation of its affairs'.[130] It exists to 'prevent anything creeping into [the church's] life that may hinder it from performing its proper functions'.[131] As such: '[w]here a number of people are united in a community ... such as the Anglican Church ... the mutual rights, obligations and duties of the members of the community must be measured and determined by rules of some kind.'[132] In turn, church law seeks to establish a just order for the church, in its distribution, protection and enforcement of rights and duties:[133] it aims to effect a 'responsible autonomy of the individual against all eventual interference and abuse', 'to promote the growth of the community', and is 'a pastoral means of constantly fostering and preserving peace'.[134] Consequently, church law has an educative role: it 'spells out the expectations of members ... and the ideals of religious life ... to lead the people to a virtuous life, not simply an external compliance with rules'.[135] Indeed, facility and order are mutual: for Pope John Paul II, the law 'facilitates ... an orderly

---

[127]   29 January 1970, 15 *The Pope Speaks* (1970–1), 56.
[128]   R. Ombres, 'Why then the law?', *New Blackfriars* (1974), 296.
[129]   T. Urresti, 'Canon law and theology: two different sciences', 8 *Concilium* (1967), 10; see also N. Doe, 'Towards a critique of the role of theology in English ecclesiastical and canon law', 2 *ELJ* (1990–2), 328.
[130]   Const., Prefatory Note.
[131]   *The Canon Law of the Church of England*, Report of the Archbishops' Commission (London, 1947), 3.
[132]   *Re St Hilary, Cornwall* [1938] 4 All ER 147 at 152 *per* Stable, Deputy Dean of the Arches Court.
[133]   Coriden, *Introduction*, 5.
[134]   4 February 1977, 22 *The Pope Speaks* (1977), 177, 179; ibid., 15 (1970–1), 55.
[135]   Coriden, *Introduction*, 6.

development in the life of both the ecclesial society and of the individual persons who belong to it'.[136] On a practical level, the purpose of the domestic law of the Church in Wales is determined by the intent of its legislators, the Governing Body and other ecclesiastical authorities which exercise law-making power within the church, as they seek to regulate its governmental, ministerial, doctrinal, liturgical, proprietorial, and ecumenical life.

The Status and Enforceability of Church Law in Civil Law

The principal effect of secular ideas about the legal nature and position of the Church in Wales, as an unincorporated voluntary association, is that the domestic law of the church has the status in civil law of a contract entered into by the members of the church. Pre-1920 ecclesiastical law, whilst it ceases to exist as the law of the land, together with post-1920 modifications or alterations to it (duly made according to the constitution and regulations of the church), have the status of a statutory contract. Under the Welsh Church Act 1914, which presents the matter in quasi-contractual terms, these are 'binding on the members for the time being of the Church in Wales in the same manner as if they had mutually agreed to be so bound'.[137] Also, new post-1920 law of the church (not being modifications or alterations to the pre-1920 ecclesiastical law), in accordance with well-settled principles of civil law, has the status of the terms of a contract recognized as such at common law. An Anglican church, 'in places where there is no Church established by law, is in the same situation with any religious body – in no better, but in no worse position: and the members may adopt, as the members of any other communion may adopt, rules for enforcing discipline within their body which will be binding on those who expressly or by implication have assented to them.'[138]

Consequently, the domestic law of the Church in Wales, its canonical contract, is enforceable in the civil courts, in certain circumstances, as a matter of private law.[139] However, normally secular courts do not take

---

[136] *Sacrae Disclipinae Leges*, Apostolic Constitution (25 January 1983), promulgating the Code of Canon Law (1983).

[137] Welsh Church Act 1914, s. 3(2); see also *Welsh Church Commissioners v Representative Body of the Church in Wales and Tithe Redemption Commission* [1940] 3 All ER 1 at 6: with regard to a property matter, Greene MR speaks of the 'quasi-contractual obligation enforceable in the temporal courts'.

[138] *Long v Bishop of Cape Town* (1863) 1 Moo NS 411; see also *Davies v Presbyterian Church of Wales* [1986] 1 WLR 323 (*per* Lord Templeman): 'The church is thus an unincorporated body of persons who agree to bear witness to the same religious faith and to practise the same doctrinal principles by means of the organisation and in the manner set forth in the constitutional deed.'

[139] However, the Welsh Church (Burial Grounds) Act 1945 Rules, made by the Representative Body in pursuance of s. 4(2), of the 1945 Act, as State-approved

cognizance of domestic church law, and they are generally reluctant to intervene in ecclesiastical disputes. Under the Welsh Church Act 1914, pre-1920 ecclesiastical law and post-1920 modifications or alterations to it are 'capable of being enforced in the temporal courts in relation to any property . . . held on behalf of the . . . Church and its members'.[140] The same applies to new post-1920 domestic law of the church (not being modifications or alterations to the pre-1920 ecclesiastical law) dealing with property; at common law, it has been decided that '[t]he law imposes upon [a] church a duty to administer its property in accordance with the provisions of the book of rules' of that church.[141] Moreover, in non-property cases, the domestic law of a church may be enforced in the civil courts when breaches of it within the church result in the violation of a right or interest under civil law.[142] Similarly, if the application of the domestic law of a church results in breach of the civil law, the secular court may intervene; in a case concerning the Scottish Episcopal Church it was held that: 'A Court of Law will not intervene with the rules of a voluntary association unless to protect some civil right or interest which is said to be infringed by their operation.'[143] As a result, the domestic law of the Church in Wales is inferior to the law of the State: 'the Church in Wales remains bound by the secular law of England and Wales.'[144] However, were a court of the State to entertain a challenge to the domestic law of the church,[145] on the basis that it violates the civil law,[146] the court must have particular

secondary legislation, have status in the public law of the State and are enforceable as such.

[140] Welsh Church Act 1914, s. 3(2): the pre-1920 ecclesiastical law with modifications and alterations effected after the passing of the Act, duly made according to the constitution and regulations of the church, 'shall be capable of being enforced in the temporal courts in relation to any property which by virtue of this Act is held on behalf of the said Church or any members thereof, in the same manner and to the same extent as if such property had been expressly assured upon trust to be held on behalf of persons who should be so bound'.

[141] *Davies v Presbyterian Church of Wales* [1986] 1 WLR 323 at 329.

[142] See the Scottish case of *Rt Revd Dilworth v (First) Lovat Highland Estates and (Second) Trustees for St Benedict's Abbey, Fort Augustus* (1999), unreported: in addition, the courts may intervene when non-compliance with domestic church law results in loss of reputation or some other civil wrong; see also generally *Buckley v Cahal Daly* [1990] NIJB 8.

[143] *Forbes v Eden* (1867) LR 1 Sc & Div 568.

[144] Const., Prefatory Note: especially 'regarding such matters as the ownership and management of property, the solemnisation of marriage and rights of burial in its churchyards'.

[145] In *R v Dean and Chapter of St Paul's Cathedral and the Church in Wales, ex parte Williamson* (1998) 5 ELJ 129: a challenge, to the decision of the Church in Wales to ordain women as priests, was dismissed on the basis that the applicant, a vexatious litigant under the Supreme Court Act 1981, s. 42, lacked *locus standi*.

[146] For challenges to the domestic law of the church on the basis that such law is in conflict with the constitution of the Church in Wales, see below, Ch. 2.

regard to the importance of the right of freedom of religion.[147] In such a case, it would be unlawful for a State court, being a public authority, to fail to have regard to this right, or to act in a way which is otherwise incompatible with this or other European Convention rights.[148]

The Binding Effect of Domestic Law within the Church

The provincial law of the Church in Wales employs three devices which express and implement, within the church, the notion in civil law that the domestic law of the church binds its members as terms of a contract.

Particular Instruments   The constitution specifies the binding effect of particular instruments, thereby indicating the consensual requirement of compliance with them. The overriding principle is that: 'The Constitution shall be binding on all office-holders in the Church in Wales, all clerics and deaconesses in receipt of a pension from the Representative Body and all persons whose names are entered on the electoral roll of any parish in Wales.'[149] Accordingly, chapters, further chapters, canons and all rules and regulations made under the authority or with the consent of the Governing Body are binding on these ecclesiastical classes.[150] The constitution also provides specifically for the binding effect of the canons of the Church in Wales,[151] and the pre-1920 ecclesiastical law.[152] The same applies to other forms of law in the church, made under powers conferred by the constitution, such as resolutions of the Diocesan Conference, which are binding in the diocese.[153] Moreover, prescribed church bodies are obliged to comply with directions of superior ecclesiastical authorities.[154] The binding effect of ecclesiastical quasi-legislation is more problematic, however.[155] Sometimes church law provides for the binding effect of directions from ecclesiastical persons.[156]

---

[147]   Human Rights Act 1998, s. 13; see also P. Cumper, 'The protection of religious rights under section 13 of the Human Rights Act 1998', *Public Law* (2000), 254.
[148]   Human Rights Act 1998, s. 6.
[149]   Const. I.2.
[150]   Const. I.1(1).
[151]   Const. II.42(2): on promulgation canons are 'binding on all the members' of the church.
[152]   Const. XI.47: pre-1920 ecclesiastical law 'shall be binding on the members (including any body of members) of the Church in Wales'.
[153]   Const. IV.33.
[154]   See e.g. Const. VI.22(3)(c): a parochial church council must implement any provision made by the Diocesan Conference.
[155]   See above.
[156]   See e.g. Const. VI.21: 'Any dispute arising out of this section, or otherwise connected with the inventory, shall be referred to the Archdeacon, whose decision shall be final.'

Declarations   Compliance with the law of the church is effected by means
of declarations. Clergy must make a written 'declaration and undertaking',
'to be bound by the Constitution, and to accept, submit to and carry out
any sentence or judgment . . . [of] the Archbishop, a Diocesan Bishop or
any Court or the Tribunal of the Church in Wales'.[157] Clergy must also
make 'the declaration of canonical obedience to the Bishop', to obey lawful
and honest episcopal directions.[158] Churchwardens must agree to 'faithfully and diligently perform the duties of Churchwarden' and 'to accept and
obey any decision of the Bishop or of the Diocesan Chancellor as to [any]
right at any time to hold the office of Churchwarden'.[159] Those whose
names are entered on an electoral roll must make a declaration 'to accept
and be bound by the Constitution of the Church in Wales'.[160]

Enforcement and Sanctions   Within the church, compliance with its law
and with the directions of ecclesiastical authorities is effected by means of
arrangements for their enforcement. Mechanisms for enforcement depend
on the nature of the non-compliance and the status of the body or person to
whom the law or direction is addressed. The normal method to enforce
compliance by clergy and lay office-holders is through an executive order
of a bishop. Failure by clergy or lay office-holders to comply with the law
of the Church in Wales may result, in serious cases, in disciplinary or
judicial proceedings in the church; the same applies to clerical breaches of
the declaration of canonical obedience.[161]

The constitution prescribes a variety of sanctions in the event of non-
compliance with its provisions.[162] Most sanctions are administered as a
result of legal process within the church. Some are directed to the
individual: for example, every member of the Church in Wales must attend
and give evidence, when duly summoned, at any trial or investigation held
under the authority of the constitution; if any member wilfully and without
sufficient cause neglects or refuses to do so, any office held by that person
may be declared vacant.[163] Sanctions may also be directed to a group: for
instance, the Diocesan Board of Finance with the approval of the bishop is
empowered to place on a defaulters' list a parish which 'culpably neglects
to meet its financial obligations'.[164] Other sanctions may involve process in
civil law: an incumbent is responsible for the results of any negligence and

---

[157]   Const. VII.66; the effect of the declaration has been recognized in civil law: *R v
Provincial Court of the Church in Wales, ex parte Williams* (1999) 5 ELJ 217.
[158]   Const. VII.66: see below, Ch. 7.
[159]   Const. VI.18.
[160]   Const. VI.3.
[161]   See below Chs. 5, 6, 7, 8.
[162]   See N. Doe, 'A facilitative canon law', 69.
[163]   Const. XI.39(3).
[164]   Const. IV.18.

for wilful damage done to the parsonage and, if repairs are not carried out to the satisfaction of the Parsonage Board, the Representative Body may sue in debt.[165] Similar arrangements are employed in all Anglican churches.[166]

---

[165] Const. X.17, 20
[166] See Doe, *Canon Law*, Ch. 3.

PART II

THE INSTITUTIONAL ORGANIZATION
OF THE CHURCH

2

THE PROVINCE: GOVERNING BODY

It is often said that, in Anglican polity, the church is episcopally led and synodically governed. As such, constitutional arrangements in the Church in Wales, in common with other churches of the Anglican Communion,[1] are based on the principle of representative ecclesiastical government.[2] The institutional organization of the Church in Wales, operating implicitly a notion of subsidiarity, is shaped by its territorial units: the province itself, the six dioceses, and, within each of these, archdeaconries, rural deaneries and, at the most local level, the parish. Each ecclesiastical unit has its own assembly. For the whole province, the Governing Body acts as the highest law-making authority within the Church in Wales.[3] For the diocese, the Diocesan Conference, for the deanery, the Deanery Conference, and for the parish, the Parochial Church Council, all have administrative and deliberative functions. In addition, each institution is assisted by a host of committees, boards and councils. The constitution defines the membership of these institutions, assigns to them particular functions, confers powers, imposes limitations designed to control the exercise of those powers, and fixes the relationship of one institution to another. The constitution also protects, in the institutional organization of the church, the jurisdiction of the episcopacy, whilst at the same time enabling the participation of the laity in the governance of the church.[4] Generally, there is a high degree of unity between the Church in Wales and the institutional organization of other Anglican churches. The Representative Body, which has functions in respect of provincial administration and the property of the church, is treated in Chapter 13.

---

[1] See N. Doe, *Canon Law in the Anglican Communion* (Oxford, 1998), Ch. 2.
[2] LC 1920, Res. 14: 'every branch of the Anglican Communion should develop the constitutional government of the Church and should make a fuller use of the capacities of its members for service.'
[3] 'Wales' means 'the Province of Wales': Const. I.6(a).
[4] The other provincial institutions of government are dealt with elsewhere in this study.

COMPOSITION

The Governing Body,[5] sometimes informally described as 'the Parliament of the Church in Wales',[6] has been understood as 'the organ through which the common mind of the Church in Wales becomes articulate'.[7] Created in pursuance of a freedom recognized by the Welsh Church Act 1914,[8] the Governing Body first met on 8 January 1918, and is treated by the civil courts as an institution of private law.[9] Its equivalent, in national or regional churches of the Anglican Communion, is styled variously the General Synod, General Convention, or Synod,[10] and, in Anglican churches consisting of a single province, the Provincial Council or Synod.[11] The following describes in outline the constitutional law of the Church in Wales which regulates the Governing Body: its membership, officers, meetings, functions (powers and duties) and committees.

The Orders: Bishops, Clergy and Laity

The Governing Body consists of three Orders: the Bishops, the Clergy, and the Laity.[12] The Order of Bishops comprises the Archbishop of Wales and the

[5]   Const. II.76: the Governing Body is empowered 'at any time to change its name and title'.
[6]   W. Price, *The Governing Body of the Church in Wales*, St David's Papers (Penarth, 1990), 3: the title 'Governing Body' was employed as the archbishop and bishops of the Church in Wales constitute the ancient Provincial Synod: see below, Ch. 6.
[7]   C. A. H. Green, *The Setting of the Constitution of the Church in Wales* (London, 1937), 191f.: this describes the historical background to its creation; for the idea that the representative government is declaratory of Cans. 139 and 140 of the Canons Ecclesiastical 1603, see ibid., 196.
[8]   Welsh Church Act 1914, s. 13(1): 'Nothing in any Act, law, or custom shall prevent the bishops, clergy, and laity of the Church in Wales from holding synods or electing representatives thereto, or from framing, either by themselves or by their representatives elected in such manner as they think fit, constitutions and regulations for the general management and good government of the Church in Wales and the property and affairs thereof, whether as a whole or according to dioceses, and the future representation of members thereof in a general synod or in diocesan synods, or otherwise.'
[9]   See *R v Dean and Chapter of St Paul's Cathedral and the Church in Wales, ex parte Williamson* (1998) 5 *ELJ* (1998), 129.
[10]   In the Church of England, it is the General Synod: Synodical Government Measure 1969, s. 2; Ireland, Const. I (General Synod); Scotland, Can. 52 (General Synod); ECUSA has its supra-provincial General Convention: Const. Art. I.1; North India has its synod: Const. II.IV.
[11]   Southern Africa, Can. 1 and Central Africa, Can. 1 (Provincial Synod); Papua New Guinea, Const. Art. 1 (Provincial Council).
[12]   Const. II.1 (there are about 350 members in all); in most Anglican churches, the central assembly is composed of three 'Houses', though in some the institution is bi-cameral: in Ireland (Const. I.2), the General Synod consists of a House of Bishops and a House of Representatives; in ECUSA (Const. Art. I.2–4), the General Convention consists of the House of Bishops and the House of Deputies (composed of clerical and lay representatives).

five diocesan bishops. Together these sit and act 'as representing the ancient Provincial Synod',[13] and they have 'the right to meet apart for private debate and decision before voting as an Order'.[14] All other bishops, residing and assisting the archbishop or any diocesan bishop in Wales, must also be members of the Governing Body; they must vote with the Order of Clergy, but are required to retire with the Order of Bishops for private debate.[15] The Order of Clergy consists of four clerical classes:[16] all cathedral deans and archdeacons; *ex officio* clerical members holding positions in prescribed ecclesiastical bodies;[17] fifteen clerical members for each diocese, elected by the clerical members of each Diocesan Conference,[18] and co-opted clergy.

The Order of Laity consists of three lay classes: *ex officio* lay members holding positions in prescribed ecclesiastical bodies,[19] thirty lay members for each diocese elected by the lay members of each Diocesan Conference; and co-opted lay members.[20] For the election of clerical and lay members, each Diocesan Conference may form electoral districts from archdeacon-ries, area deaneries or groups of parishes. The Diocesan Conference may also apportion the number of diocesan representatives to be elected by the Conference for these districts, and arrange the manner and method of election.[21]

The Governing Body is obliged to co-opt members. It must co-opt fifteen clerics; of these at least six, one from each diocese, must be unbeneficed clerics in pensionable service in the Church in Wales at the time of their co-option.[22] It must also co-opt thirty lay persons of whom at least twelve must be under the age of thirty at the time of their co-option.[23]

[13] Unless the constitution provides otherwise, the Provincial Synod shall retain and exercise 'all the authority and powers of and belonging from of old to a Provincial Synod' (Const. II.2); for a discussion of possible interpretations of this provision, see P. Jones, *The Governance of the Church in Wales* (Cardiff, 2000), 77ff.; see also above n. 6 and below, Ch. 6.

[14] Const. II.2.

[15] Const. II.4; they are members until the age of seventy.

[16] Const. II.5.

[17] Const. II.7: unless they are already *ex officio* members of the Governing Body under some other provision of the constitution, these are (when they are clerics): the Warden of St Michael's College, Llandaff; the chairman and deputy chairman of the Representative Body; the respective chairmen of the Finance and Resources Committee, the Investment Subcommittee, the Staff and Services Subcommittee, the Property Subcommittee and the Maintenance of Ministry Subcommittee of the Representative Body; the chairman of the Widows, Orphans and Dependants Society of the Church in Wales; and the chair and deputy chair of the Council for Mission and Ministry.

[18] Const. II.5.

[19] These are, when they are lay people, those contained in the list appearing in Const. II.7: see above, n. 17.

[20] Const. II.6.

[21] Const. II.8.

[22] Const. II.9(a): an unbeneficed cleric, so co-opted, must continue membership of the Governing Body only while that person remains a cleric in the Church in Wales.

[23] Const. II.9(b). Interestingly, the terms of this provision are: 'The Governing Body

Eligibility for Membership

Rights of admission to membership of the Governing Body are governed by rules on eligibility, which vary as between the classes of member. Every cleric who holds or has held a dignity, cathedral preferment, benefice, or office within the Church in Wales, is eligible to be a member, as is any cleric who holds or has held a licence from a Welsh diocesan bishop. However, no cleric in full-time salaried employment of the Representative Body, a Diocesan Board of Finance, or any other such provincial or diocesan body within the Church in Wales, is eligible for membership of either the Governing Body itself or of any of its committees or sub-committees.[24] A lay person is eligible for membership provided that person is: a communicant;[25] over eighteen years of age; resident in, or has resided for a period of twelve months in, a parish in Wales, or is a person whose name appears on the electoral roll of a parish in Wales; and, a person 'who does not belong to any religious body which is not in communion with the Church in Wales'.[26] However, a salaried employee of the Representative Body, a Diocesan Board of Finance or any other such provincial or diocesan body within the Church in Wales, is not eligible for membership of either the Governing Body or of any of its committees or sub-committees.[27]

Elected or co-opted membership of the Governing Body ceases on attainment of the age of seventy-five.[28] A clerical member, elected for the diocese in which that member serves, continues as a member only whilst either serving or residing in that diocese.[29] A lay member, elected for the diocese in which that member resides, continues as a member only whilst residing in that diocese. However, if a lay member does not so reside, but holds diocesan office or appears on the electoral roll of a parish in that diocese,

---

shall co-opt as members': in short, co-option is cast here as a 'duty'; however, II.29 refers to the Governing Body's 'powers of co-option'.

[24] Const. II.10.

[25] That is: 'a person who has lawfully received Holy Communion in the Church in Wales or some Church in communion therewith and is entitled to receive Holy Communion in the Church in Wales' (Const. I.6(b)).

[26] Const. II.11(1); moreover, any member of the Governing Body who joins a religious body which is not in communion with the Church in Wales, and any *ex officio* member who ceases to hold the office giving rise to membership, ceases to be a member (Const. II.11(2)). For criticism of this as anti-ecumenical, see A. T. Lewis, 'The case for constitutional renewal in the Church in Wales', in N. Doe (ed.), *Essays in Canon Law* (Cardiff, 1992), 175 at 185. For 'communion' in the ecumenical context, see below, Ch. 12.

[27] Const. II.11(1).

[28] Const. II.12(1): however, if attainment of this age occurs during a meeting of the Governing Body or of its committees, membership continues until the termination of the meeting; II.12(2): where a person, in order to hold some office, is required to be 'qualified to be a member of the Governing Body', the fact that such a person is over seventy-five does not preclude that person from holding such office; II.12(3): the rule contained in II.12(1) does not apply to *ex officio* members of the Governing Body.

[29] Const. II.13(1).

that person may continue as a member.[30] Elected and co-opted members serve for a term of three years.[31] On 31 December each year, one-third of the members elected by each diocese, and one-third of co-opted members, must retire. In their place, like numbers of members must be elected by each diocese, and co-opted by the Governing Body, provided always that a cleric is to be elected or co-opted to succeed a cleric and a lay person to succeed a lay person.[32] If they are qualified, retiring members are eligible for re-admission on as many occasions as they wish.[33] Casual vacancies amongst elected and co-opted members are filled from candidates appearing on supplemental lists consisting of persons who stood for election but failed to be elected.[34] Every member of the Order of Laity, before taking their seat, must sign a declaration.[35]

Elections and Resignations

The Diocesan Conference is responsible for electing clerical and lay members to represent the diocese on the Governing Body. The conference must also make the supplemental lists of clerical and lay persons from which casual vacancies are filled.[36] Each election must be held, and each list made, in time to enable the newly elected members to take office immediately on the expiration of the term of office of the retiring members.[37] Immediately following the last ordinary meeting of the Governing Body (in each year), and before each election by the Diocesan Conference, the secretaries of the Governing Body must send to the secretaries of each Diocesan Conference a list of the attendances of diocesan representatives at Governing Body meetings since their election.[38] Within one week after the election, the secretaries of each conference must return to the secretaries of

---

[30] Const. II.13(2).

[31] Const. II.15(1): this rule applies subject to the provisions contained in II.9, 12(1) and 13 (for which see above).

[32] Const. II.15(2).

[33] Const. II.15(3).

[34] Const. II.16: the person holds office until the date at which the member, whom the appointee replaces, would have been due to retire; II.22: each Diocesan Conference must make the supplemental lists; see also II.27, 31.

[35] Const. II.14: the person must solemnly declare: 'that I am a communicant over eighteen years of age, and qualified to be a member of the Governing Body of the Church in Wales, and that I do not belong to any religious body which is not in communion with the Church in Wales'; the declaration is put in a register to be kept for this purpose by the Secretaries of the Governing Body.

[36] Const. II.22: the clerical and lay persons must appear according to the order in which they are placed on the list by the conference.

[37] Const. II.22: the Governing Body must make 'due provision' for the purposes of admission of new members.

[38] Const. II.23.

the Governing Body the names and addresses of both elected members and those on the supplemental list.[39]

Any elected member may, by written notice to the bishop of the diocese for which that member has been elected, resign their seat on the Governing Body.[40] Seats becoming vacant on the death, expulsion or disqualification of an elected member, are to be filled from the appropriate supplemental list of members of the diocese for which the member sat.[41] Failure by a diocese to elect or return clerical or lay members, or to make and forward supplemental lists, or the failure by the Governing Body to co-opt, does not prevent the Governing Body from transacting its business, nor does it invalidate its proceedings.[42] Co-opted members may, by written notice to the secretaries of the Governing Body, resign their seats; and any vacancy created by the resignation, expulsion, disqualification or death of a co-opted member, must be filled by the Governing Body by co-option.[43] Membership may also be lost as a result of a decision of the disciplinary tribunal and courts of the Church in Wales.[44]

OFFICERS AND MEETINGS

In most Anglican churches, the president of the provincial assembly is the metropolitan or archbishop.[45] Similarly, the President of the Governing Body is the Archbishop of Wales; in the case of a vacancy in the office of archbishop, the archbishop's incapacity or absence from the British Isles, or his refusal to act, the senior diocesan bishop acts as president, provided he is willing and capable of doing so.[46]

Convening Meetings   All meetings of the Governing Body must be convened in the name of, and by the authority of, the President. To this end, the President must deliver his mandate to the secretaries of the

---

[39] Const. II.24; see also II.25: if a person is elected for more than one diocese, the secretaries of the Governing Body must (within one week of receiving the names of the elected members) notify in writing that member, calling the member to choose (in writing) the diocese which they will serve; if the member fails to do so, the President must choose the diocese; the vacated seat is filled from the appropriate diocesan supplemental list.

[40] Const. II.26: on receipt by the bishop of a resignation, the seat in question becomes vacant and is filled from the appropriate diocesan supplemental list.

[41] Const. II.27; see also II.28: if there is any change in the representation of a diocese, the diocesan bishop must notify this to the secretaries of the Governing Body.

[42] Const. II.29.

[43] Const. II.30, 31.

[44] See e.g. Const. XI.39; see below, Ch. 5.

[45] See e.g. Uganda, Const. Art. 5; see generally, Doe, CLAC, 50f.

[46] Const. II.17: this applies provided the diocesan bishop is not himself then absent from the British Isles.

Governing Body to summon it by citation for meeting at a time and place fixed by the Governing Body, by its Standing Committee, or by the President himself, as the case may be. An ordinary or a special meeting of the Governing Body is known as a session.[47] Seven weeks before an ordinary meeting, the secretaries must send the President's citation in writing to all members to attend at the given time and place. An agenda-paper of the business to be brought before an ordinary meeting must be sent to each member fourteen days before the commencement of the meeting.[48] The Governing Body is empowered to appoint and pay secretaries;[49] any clerical secretary must be a cleric in the Church in Wales, and any lay secretary must be a communicant of the Church in Wales, or of a church in communion with it.[50]

Chair and Agenda   Ordinarily, the chairman is the President or, in his absence, the senior diocesan bishop next in order of precedence present and willing to act.[51] Alternatively, meetings may be chaired by a person chosen by the President (or in his absence the senior diocesan bishop), from a panel of chairmen approved by the Governing Body.[52] Whilst the constitution requires at least one ordinary meeting each year,[53] as a matter of ecclesiastical convention two annual meetings are held. The time and place are fixed by the Governing Body,[54] though its Standing Committee may alter these.[55] The secretaries of the Governing Body must attend every meeting, keep minutes of its proceedings, receive notices of proposed bills, motions and other business, and must prepare the agenda-paper for the meetings, according to the instructions of the President.[56] The President, with the advice of the Standing Committee, must decide the order of entering on the agenda-paper for any ordinary meeting business which he desires to bring before the Governing Body, or of which notice has been received from

---

[47] Const. II.18: at the opening of every session, the secretaries must certify the due execution of the mandate; II.82: any citation or notice directed to be sent or given may be sent or given through the post; proof of posting is *prima facie* evidence that such notice has been duly sent or given.

[48] Const. II.44(1) and (3).

[49] Const. II.79: the Governing Body may incur any reasonably necessary and incidental expenses for this purpose.

[50] Const. II.80; see also II.81: at any meeting, in the absence of the secretaries, the meeting must appoint a deputy secretary *pro tempore* who must render 'a full and faithful report to the Secretaries'.

[51] Const. II.19(a); precedence is determined according to the date of appointment as a diocesan bishop (see Const. II.3).

[52] Const. II.19(b).

[53] Const. II.20.

[54] Const. II.20.

[55] Const. II.21.

[56] Const. II.45.

members. The President may assign any such business to a particular day of the session.[57]

Standing Orders and Quorum   The Governing Body is empowered to make standing orders for the regulation of its procedures as it thinks fit, provided these are not inconsistent with the constitution. It may rescind, suspend or vary the standing orders.[58] A motion for the suspension of standing orders is not in order unless a majority of the members present rise in support.[59] Subject to the constitution and standing orders, the business and procedure at any meeting of the Governing Body must be regulated by the chairman who may appoint assessors for this purpose.[60] One hundred is the quorum. This must comprise not less than one diocesan bishop, thirty clerical and forty lay members. If any member draws attention to the fact that the meeting is not quorate, the chairman must count the Governing Body. If the chairman is satisfied that no quorum is present, he must either: adjourn the Governing Body to such time on the same or the next day as he thinks fit; or adjourn the Governing Body generally in order that the President may decide upon the future conduct of the meeting.[61] Any question relating only to standing orders or the conduct of business must be decided by a majority of the Governing Body.[62] At the conclusion of business, the proceedings and minutes must be authenticated by the signature of the chairman.[63]

Speeches and Questions   All meetings of the Governing Body must open with prayer.[64] Once the chairman has taken the chair, no member is to continue standing up, except when addressing the chair.[65] When two or more members rise simultaneously to address the chair, the chairman must decide which of them shall speak.[66] With the exception of speeches made by the mover and seconder of a resolution,[67] speeches must not exceed five

---

[57] Const. II.46.

[58] Const. II.47; GBSO, 16: the Revised Standing Orders (1996) do not apply to proceedings in committee.

[59] GBSO, 13.

[60] Const. II.48.

[61] Const. II.49: if adjourned, the President must subsequently determine that it stand adjourned either to a day (not less than seven weeks later) and place fixed by him, which must be notified to the members in accordance with II.44 (for which see above, n. 48), or without day, as he thinks fit.

[62] Const. II.50: the chairman of the meeting must decide whether any particular question falls within this section; II.51: any question within the meaning of II.50 may be brought forward by any member on notice of motion in writing, handed in during the meeting to the chairman.

[63] Const. II.69.

[64] Governing Body Standing Orders, GBSO, 1.

[65] GBSO, 2.

[66] GBSO, 3; under GBSO, 15, a member shall address the chair only from a position

minutes, or six minutes in the case of speeches requiring simultaneous translation throughout. Speeches made by the mover or seconder of a resolution must not exceed ten minutes, or twelve minutes in the case of speeches requiring simultaneous translation throughout.[68] The chairman may, with the leave of the meeting, extend the time for a speech.[69] No member is allowed to speak more than once on the same question, except in explanation, or to order; however, the mover of any resolution, not being an amendment, is allowed the liberty of reply.[70]

Whenever the chairman rises during a debate, any member speaking or offering to speak must sit down immediately.[71] If, during a debate, thirty members rise in their places and demand that a vote be then taken, the chairman must put that question to the meeting for a decision by show of hands.[72] If the meeting decides such question in the affirmative, a vote must thereupon be taken on the question before the meeting; but before the vote is taken, the mover of the resolution (not being an amendment) is at liberty to reply.[73] All motions and amendments must be in writing, signed by the mover.[74] No amendment on an amendment is permitted unless when an amendment shall have become a substantive motion.[75] Any member may move the previous business, and if this is carried, the next business must be immediately proceeded with.[76] Special provisions exist with regard to procedure for question time,[77] changes to Governing

which is within range of a microphone and must first give their name, office (if any), and the diocese from which they come.

[67] For resolutions, see below.

[68] GBSO, 4(1) and (2); an amendment is not a resolution within the meaning of this order (4(3)).

[69] GBSO, 5.

[70] GBSO, 6.

[71] GBSO, 7.

[72] GBSO, 8.

[73] GBSO, 9.

[74] GBSO, 10: unless given to the secretaries prior to the meeting, two copies of motions and amendments must be handed in by the mover, one to the chairman and the other to the secretaries. Under GBSO, 14, a motion which is set out in full on the agenda-paper, or its accompanying papers, need not be read before being put, unless either the chairman, or ten members (the latter signifying their intent by rising in their places), so require; all other motions or amendments shall be read immediately before the vote thereon is taken.

[75] GBSO, 11.

[76] GBSO, 12.

[77] Procedural Matters (1999), 2: questions are invited prior to the meeting, the information being enclosed with the archbishop's citation. Once the questions are received by the closing date, a list of questions received is circulated to members. The chairman invites the person most appropriate to answer, and refers to the questions by numbers rather than by reading them out in full since members will already have copies in front of them. Members may submit one question only and ask one supplementary question arising from the original one or make a brief comment on the answer given. Only the person who has asked the question (or his or her substitute) can ask a supplementary question

Body minutes,[78] and reporting back by members of the Governing Body to rural deaneries and parishes.[79]

Special Meetings   The Governing Body may be summoned by citation to a special meeting by the President at his own discretion. Moreover, the President must convene a special meeting at the written request either of any Welsh diocesan bishop or of not less than one-third of the clerical and lay members of the Governing Body.[80] The time and place of the special meeting is determined by the President.[81] The citation must state the business to be transacted at a special meeting, and it must be sent to all members at least seven days before the day fixed for the meeting.[82] No business may be transacted at a special meeting other than that stated in the notice convening it, but the powers and procedures of a special meeting are the same as those applicable to an ordinary meeting of the Governing Body.[83]

Validity and Access   No meeting is invalidated by any accidental omission to observe any of the regulations related to the summoning or holding of Governing Body meetings.[84] The Governing Body is free to decide for itself whether its proceedings are to be public or private; it would seem that the media have no right to attend ordinary or special meetings of the Governing Body, but may do so with its consent.[85]

LEGISLATIVE POWERS AND PROCESSES

In churches of the Anglican Communion, it is usually the formal constitution which deals with the jurisdiction of provincial assemblies.

or make a comment. The session is intended for questions and answers. It is not intended that there should be a general debate following replies to these questions.

[78] Procedural Matters (1999), 3: members of the Governing Body must give three working days' notice of any proposal to amend the minutes so that there is adequate time to consider the implications.

[79] Procedural Matters (1999), 4: members of the Governing Body are expected to report back frequently on the events of the Governing Body meetings to Deaneries and Parishes.

[80] Const. II.52: the President must deliver his mandate to the secretaries of the Governing Body to summon by citation a special meeting for any stated purpose.

[81] Const. II.53: it must be held on a day not earlier than the fourteenth day from the issue of the President's mandate.

[82] Const. II.54.

[83] Const. II.55.

[84] Const. II.81: nor do the absence or neglect of any of the secretaries of the Governing Body invalidate any secretarial act or meeting.

[85] The Public Bodies (Admission to Meetings) Act 1960 applies only to authorities listed in its Schedule: the Governing Body is not listed.

Jurisdictional laws are either positive, listing subjects over which the assembly has competence,[86] or negative, listing subjects over which it lacks competence.[87] These matters are normally dealt with under a separate title in the constitution.[88] The functions of the Governing Body of the Church in Wales are defined by the constitution primarily in terms of powers – but their lawful exercise is subject to a number of fundamental substantive and procedural limitations. The duty on the Governing Body to comply with the constitution of the church may be one of civil law.[89] The principal constitutional function of the Governing Body is to legislate, and to it is reserved the power to alter the constitution,[90] or to authorize its alteration.[91]

In accordance with a freedom recognized by the Welsh Church Act 1914,[92] the Governing Body has a basic power to make 'constitutions and regulations for the general management and good government of the Church' in Wales,[93] and it is empowered 'to add to, alter, amend or abrogate any of the provisions of the Constitution'.[94] It is also specifically empowered to make 'general regulations for the election of the Body', for

[86] See e.g. Uganda, Const. Art. 6: the Provincial Assembly has 'responsibility for the overall direction of the Church . . . to formulate broad, basic policies . . . and the right to require the Constituent Dioceses to ensure the smooth implementation of these policies'; it is competent to legislate e.g. on church courts and discipline, on ordination, on terms and conditions of clergy service, on the rites of the church, and on property matters.

[87] See e.g. West Indies, Const. Art. 3.4: the Provincial Synod may determine matters 'concerning the common life of the Church . . . save and except . . . such matters as lie within the jurisdiction of the Ecclesiastical Courts . . . such matters affecting the administration of the Province as, in the opinion of the President, the House of Bishops should debate and determine . . . and such matters as be within the rights and powers of a Diocesan Synod to determine for itself'.

[88] See generally, CLAC, 52.

[89] Welsh Church Act 1914, s. 3(2): this provides that pre-1920 ecclesiastical law continues to apply to the Church in Wales 'subject to such modification or alteration . . . as after the passing of this Act may be duly made therein, according to the constitution and regulations' of the Church in Wales. It has been argued 'that s.3(2) imposes a statutory duty on the Church in Wales to legislate in accordance with its Constitution', and, as such, 'that the Church's laws must be duly made arguably leaves open the possibility of an application for judicial review on the basis of procedural irregularity': see P. Jones, *Governance*, 54. For the duty in civil law for church bodies to comply with domestic law, particularly in matters relating to property, see above, Ch. 1.

[90] For the basic idea see P. Jones, *Governance*, 83: the Governing Body has 'a special position in that it is the only authority capable of altering the Constitution'.

[91] Under Const. I.1(1)(d), rules and regulations form part of the constitution, and these may be made 'under the authority or with the consent of the Governing Body'. Rules and regulations then, may be made by bodies other than the Governing Body, and still form part of the constitution, provided they are authorized or consented to by Governing Body.

[92] Welsh Church Act 1914, s.13(1): see above, n. 8.

[93] Const. II.33(1); this is declaratory of Welsh Church Act 1914, s. 13(1).

[94] Const. II.43.

the qualification of the electors, and for 'the property and affairs' of the church.[95] It may legislate for the church 'as a whole or according to dioceses, including regulations as to how and by whom appointments to diocesan bishoprics and to benefices shall be made'.[96] Moreover, the Governing Body may determine 'the manner and method in which such constitutions and regulations shall be created and carried out'.[97]

Amongst the most important substantive limitations, restricting the legislative competence of the Governing Body, are the following two principles, each designed to forbid the institution from intervention in functions reserved to the episcopacy. First, unless the constitution provides otherwise: 'no proceeding of the Governing Body shall interfere with the exercise by the Archbishop of the powers and functions inherent in the Office of Metropolitan, nor with the exercise by the Diocesan Bishops of the powers and functions inherent in the Episcopal Office'.[98] Secondly, the Governing Body cannot 'affect the rights at present existing in a Diocesan Bishop in respect of institution to any benefice or ecclesiastical office'; nor can it affect any right of the archbishop and bishops assembled as the Provincial Synod with regard to the confirmation of a bishop-elect; nor can it affect the right of the archbishop with regard to the consecration of a bishop-elect.[99]

Canons: Enactment and Promulgation

In common with other Anglican churches, which operate special procedures for changes in fundamental constitutional provisions,[100] the Governing Body of the Church in Wales is required to legislate in accordance with bill procedure, in relation to six prescribed subjects.[101] First, the Governing Body is empowered 'to make new articles, doctrinal statements, rites, ceremonies and formularies, and to alter those from time

---

[95]   Const. II.33(1); see also Welsh Church Act 1914, s. 3(2): laws of the Governing Body are 'capable of being enforced in the temporal courts in relation to any property which by virtue of this Act is held on behalf of the said Church or any members thereof'.
[96]   Const. II.33(1).
[97]   Const. II.33(1).
[98]   Const. II.32; for archiepiscopal and episcopal functions see below, Ch. 6.
[99]   Const. II.33(2); see below, Chs. 6 (for episcopal confirmation and consecration) and 7 (for institution).
[100]   See e.g.: Central Africa, Can. 33.1–2: the church's Fundamental Declarations may be altered by a two-thirds majority in the Provincial Synod only after approval by the diocesan synods and with subsequent endorsement by the Archbishop of Canterbury that the change will not affect the church's communion with the rest of the Anglican Communion; compare the absolute entrenchment of Fundamental Declarations in Australia (Const. XI.66). For the various legal models of constitutional change, see CLAC, 26ff.
[101]   For discussion of the possible use of referenda in the church, see T. G. Watkin, 'Consensus and the constitution', 3 ELJ (1994), 232.

to time existing'; in so doing, it must employ bill procedure backed and introduced by a majority of the Order of Bishops.[102] Secondly, any 'addition, alteration, amendment or abrogation . . . of any canon of the Church in Wales' must be effected by bill procedure.[103] Thirdly, 'any proposal concerning faith or discipline shall be introduced and enacted' by bill procedure.[104] Fourthly, bill procedure must be used to process any proposal to alter, amend or abrogate the constitutional provisions dealing with the passing of a motion.[105] Fifthly, it must be used for additions or alterations to, and amendment or repeal of, the rule which requires the enactment of canons by bill procedure for adding to, altering, amending or abrogating any provision of the constitution.[106] Finally, bill procedure is required for additions and alterations to, and amendment or repeal of, the rule which requires bill procedure for any proposal concerning faith or discipline.[107] There are four stages to bill procedure.[108]

The Preliminary Stage   A bill may be introduced by any two or more members of the Governing Body, or by a Diocesan Conference.[109] (However, in respect of new articles, doctrine, rites, ceremonies and formularies, the bill must be introduced and backed by a majority of the Order of Bishops.[110]) The Standing Committee must consider every proposed bill 'to satisfy itself that the bill is in order'. A copy of it, in English and in Welsh, with the names of the backers, must be forwarded to the secretaries of the Governing Body. This must be done not later than four weeks before the meeting of the Standing Committee at which the backers intend the proposed bill to be considered. In preparing the bill, and before forwarding it to the Standing Committee, those wishing to introduce a bill are entitled to obtain the advice and assistance of the Drafting Subcommittee of the Standing Committee. The Standing Committee must consider at its next meeting every proposed bill forwarded to it. If satisfied that the proposed bill is in order, the Standing Committee must so inform the backers and publish the bill forthwith by circulating a printed copy (in English and Welsh), with the names of its backers, to all members of the Governing

---

[102] Const. II.36; see below, Ch. 9.
[103] Const. II.43.
[104] Const. II.37.
[105] Const. II.37: that is, alteration or repeal of Const. II.34.
[106] Const. II.37 (see also II.43): that is, alteration or repeal of Const. II.43.
[107] Const. II.43: that is, alteration or repeal of Const. II.37.
[108] Bill procedure is also employed in the Church of Ireland, Const. I.25.
[109] Const. II.38(1). For general criticism of the legislative procedure, and an observation of the particular issue of introducing bills, see P. Jones, *Governance*, 85: 'There are apparently no constitutional means by which a member of the Church in Wales who is not a member of the Governing Body may propose a bill, other than by lobbying members of the Governing Body or a diocesan conference.'
[110] Const. 38(1); and II.36.

Body. The printed copy must be accompanied by a memorandum explaining the reason for the bill. If the Standing Committee is not satisfied that the bill is in order, it must inform the backers; and it may, with the consent of the backers or a majority of them, refer the proposed bill to its Drafting Subcommittee for further advice and assistance.[111]

The Deliberative Stage   On its publication, a Select Committee of Governing Body members must be appointed by the Standing Committee, to consider and collate any amendments which members of the Governing Body may wish to move to the bill. Any member of the Governing Body may move an amendment, provided written notice is given of every such amendment to the secretaries of the Governing Body. Written notice must be given within three months immediately following publication of the bill. On publication, the Standing Committee has a discretion to consult the dioceses regarding the bill,[112] in whatever manner it deems appropriate. The Select Committee must then submit a report to the Standing Committee, within six months of publication, but the Standing Committee may extend this period if it decides to consult the dioceses. In its report, the Select Committee must recommend on each amendment proposed. Moreover, it must recommend to the Standing Committee whether or not the bill should be deemed non-controversial. The report must indicate any significant difference of opinion within the Select Committee regarding its recommendations. The Select Committee itself may propose amendments to the bill.[113]

The Committee Stage   On receipt of the report, the Standing Committee must cause the report to be published to all members of the Governing Body. The bill must then be set down for consideration in committee at the next meeting of the Governing Body. Where the Standing Committee has accepted a recommendation of the Select Committee that a bill should be deemed non-controversial, the Standing Committee must so report to the members of the Governing Body. It must do so before the commencement of the meeting at which the committee stage of the bill is to be taken. Even if both the Select Committee and the Standing Committee deem the bill non-controversial, the bill must still proceed to the committee stage

---

[111] Const. II.38. See also the opinion of P. Jones, *Governance*, 86: 'the Standing Committee may not amend or reject [the proposed bill] unless it is badly drafted, in which case the Drafting sub-committee is required to assist. The Standing Committee may not reject a proposed bill because it disagrees with the content.'

[112] In many Anglican churches, the central legislative assembly has a duty to consult the dioceses: see e.g. Scotland, Can. 52.17–18; in others the consent of the diocesan synod is required to alter the constitution and canons: see e.g. Papua New Guinea, Const. Art. 19; Melanesia, Const. Art. 20; see generally CLAC, 30, 35f.

[113] Const. II.39.

provided one diocesan bishop or any ten members so request. In the event that no such request is made, the motion that the bill be passed must be voted on forthwith, without any further consideration or debate.[114]

For the purposes of the committee stage, the Governing Body must appoint one of its members to act as chairman of the Committee. At the committee stage, only those amendments received by the Select Committee must be moved. However, in addition, the following amendments may be moved at the committee stage: those proposed by the Select Committee; those arising out of other amendments made during the same session; and such other amendments as may be allowed with special leave of the chairman of the Committee and the meeting. After consideration in committee, the bill must be reported to the Governing Body, and the motion that the bill be passed must be set down for immediate debate. However, if the chairman of the Governing Body so decides, the bill must be set down for debate either on the next day or at the next meeting of the Governing Body. Where the motion that the bill be passed is not set down for immediate debate, it is permissible to refer the bill for further consideration both by the Select Committee and in committee at the Governing Body. If this occurs, only amendments proposed by the Select Committee, those arising out of other amendments made during the same session, or those allowed by leave of the chairman of the Committee and the meeting, may be moved. If the committee stage is not completed within three years of publication of a bill, the bill is deemed to have lapsed.[115]

Promulgation   On a motion that the bill be passed, no amendment is allowed. The votes of each order must be taken separately, but the Order of Bishops must not vote until after the declaration of the votes of the other two orders. On this declaration, the Order of Bishops may, as it thinks fit, retire for private debate and announce the result of its vote at such later time during that session of the Governing Body as the Order thinks fit.[116] If the bill is passed by a two-thirds majority of the members present and voting of each of the three orders, the President must promulgate it 'as a canon of the Church in Wales', from which time it is 'a law of the Church in Wales and binding on all the members' of the church. If a bill is rejected by two out of the three orders, it must not be introduced again for three years.[117]

---

[114] Const. II.40; the procedure in II.42 then applies; see below.
[115] Const. II.41.
[116] Const. II.42. A policy underlying these rules is suggested in P. Jones, *Governance*, 84: 'the requirement that the bishops must vote last suggests that they must at least be aware of the views of their clergy and laity before coming to a final view of their own. They are not obliged to take clerical and lay opinion into account when forming their view but they are not allowed to do so in ignorance of it.'
[117] Const. II.42. See also P. Jones, *Governance*, 84–5: 'The requirement of a two thirds

Other Instruments: Motions and Resolutions

In addition to canons, the Governing Body is also empowered to create further chapters, rules and regulations.[118] The Constitution of the Church in Wales is set forth in these forms of legislation – along with canons, they are part of the constitution.[119] Outside the six reserved cases of constitutional change (described in the previous section), for which bill procedure is obligatory (such as the enactment of canons), it would seem that the constitutional law contained in chapters, rules and regulations may be added to, abrogated or altered by simple majority without recourse to bill procedure.[120] Further chapters, rules and regulations may be made by the Governing Body, otherwise than by bill procedure, in pursuance of its general power 'to add to, alter, amend or abrogate any of the provisions of the Constitution',[121] as contained in existing chapters, rules, regulations,[122] when such constitutional change does not involve subjects requiring legislation by bill procedure. In this respect, the Church in Wales is rather different from most churches in the Anglican Communion in which special majority procedures must be followed to alter their formal constitutions.[123] However, remarkably, the constitution does not specify a procedure for the creation of further chapters, rules and regulations.[124] Nevertheless, other than bill procedure, the constitution does provide for the passing of motions and the making of resolutions. There are two sorts of motion: those not involving a change of the constitution, and those necessitating such a change.

Motions   Any member(s) wishing to propose a motion must, except by special leave of the Governing Body, give notice of this to the secretaries of the Governing Body not later than five weeks before the commencement of the Governing Body meeting.[125] To become effective, all motions before the

---

majority in all three orders presumably originates in the doctrine of reception, the view that a law must enjoy general acceptance in the community to be truly authoritative.'

[118] As a matter of practice, it also legislates by means of Schemes, though these do not appear in the formal list of constitutional sources contained in Const. I.1(1); see generally above, Ch. 1.

[119] Const. I.1(1); see generally above, Ch. 1.

[120] For a contrary view see P. Jones, *Governance*, 85: 'By s.43 the Governing Body has power to amend the Constitution itself but this power is also subject to the bill procedure and the requirement of a two thirds majority in all three Orders.'

[121] Const. II.43; in practice, canons and bill procedure are used to alter chapters. See also Green, *Setting*, 200.

[122] Const. I(1)(a), (b) and (d).

[123] See e.g. South East Asia, Const. Art. 19(12): a two-thirds majority is required; see generally CLAC, 28f.

[124] An example of its power to create rules and regulations is found in Const. II.66: it may make rules and regulations for its committees. See also above, Ch. 1.

[125] Const. II.44(2): the member must also give the name of a member who has agreed to second the motion.

Governing Body (except those introduced under bill procedure) must be passed by a majority of members present and voting. The majority may be ascertained by show of hands of the whole Governing Body: no vote by orders occurs. However, any one diocesan bishop or any ten members, rising in their places, may require a division or vote by orders (before or after the show of hands). When a division is required, a vote by orders must be taken: the motion is not passed unless it receives the assent of a majority in each of the three orders of Bishops, Clergy and Laity. A majority in any of the three orders could veto the motion. If such a motion obtains a majority in only two of the three orders, it may be introduced and moved at the next ordinary meeting of the Governing Body. If at that meeting it obtains the sanction of all the members of the Order of Bishops present and voting, as well as a two-thirds majority of either the Order of Clergy or the Order of Laity present and voting, it is deemed to be a *resolution* duly passed by the Governing Body.[126]

Motions and Constitutional Amendment   Special provisions apply to motions which necessitate amendment of the constitution. When passed, and in the absence of other direction, such a motion is deemed to include an instruction to the Drafting Subcommittee to prepare the appropriate amendment(s) to the constitution. However, when a motion of this type is stated to be made under this procedure, and without awaiting any amendment to the constitution which would otherwise be necessary, such a motion takes effect immediately – but at most only until the next ordinary meeting of the Governing Body. Such motions, effecting temporary constitutional amendment, are deemed to include an instruction to the Standing Committee to give effect to the appropriate amendment(s) to the constitution, once prepared by the Drafting Subcommittee, unless that subcommittee or the Standing Committee determine otherwise.[127]

ADMINISTRATIVE FUNCTIONS AND COMMITTEES

The Governing Body itself enjoys a range of administrative functions, including competence to issue administrative orders and directions, over other ecclesiastical authorities. For example, the Governing Body may issue directions: to the Representative Body which holds property, subject to statutory requirements, under the order and control of the Governing Body;[128] to the Diocesan Conference;[129] and to a parochial church

---

[126] Const. II.34; see also above for Governing Body Standing Orders applicable to resolutions and motions.
[127] Const. II.35.
[128] Const. III.21.
[129] Const. IV.29.

council.[130] Moreover, the consent of the Governing Body is required, for instance: for the transfer, union or division of dioceses;[131] for the alteration of the location of the Archbishop's Electoral College;[132] and for the entering of church-sharing agreements.[133] The Governing Body has power: to refer any question to a Diocesan Conference for discussion and report;[134] to provide houses, offices and other buildings or accommodation necessary for the purpose of its meetings;[135] to regulate the payment of expenses incurred by members in attendance at meetings and committees;[136] and to appoint and pay its secretaries.[137]

The Standing Committee   Like most Anglican provincial assemblies,[138] the Governing Body must appoint a Standing Committee of its members. The Standing Committee, appointed triennially, consists of five classes: the diocesan bishop and two members (one clerical and one lay) from each diocese;[139] the chairman and deputy chairman of the Representative Body; the chairman and deputy chairman of the Council for Mission and Ministry; not more than two members of the Governing Body as it decides to appoint on the nomination of the Standing Committee; and not more than two persons co-opted by the Standing Committee.[140] At its first meeting during each triennial period, and as necessary following any vacancy in either office, the committee must elect from its members a chairman and vice-chairman.[141] The Standing Committee must meet at least three times each year, but may also be convened and consulted by the President if and when he thinks fit. The secretaries of the Governing Body act as the secretaries, and they must attend and keep the minutes of every meeting of the Standing Committee; also, the secretary of the Representative Body must attend every meeting and may speak but not vote.[142]

The functions of the Standing Committee are as follows. It must advise

---

[130] Const. VI.22(3)(c): the council must implement any 'provision' made by the Governing Body.
[131] Const. II.61, 62.
[132] Const. IX.9.
[133] Sharing of Church Buildings Act 1969, Schedule.
[134] Const. II.58.
[135] Const. II.78.
[136] Const. II.78.
[137] Const. II.79.
[138] See e.g. Southern Africa, Can. 43(1)(b); see generally CLAC, 56.
[139] The two clerical and lay members must be nominated by the Standing Committee of the Diocesan Conference from among Governing Body members from that diocese (Const. II.64(2)(a)); any casual vacancy among these two members must be filled by the diocesan bishop (II.64(3)).
[140] Const. II.64(1) and (2).
[141] Const. II.64(4): in the event of absence of the chairman or vice-chairman from any meeting, the committee must appoint another member to preside.
[142] Const. II.64(5)–(7).

the Governing Body on matters of policy, including: long-term planning and the relationship of planning to resources; the establishment of priorities in the use of resources; and the approval of budgets.[143] The committee is empowered to regulate its own procedures, including the appointment of working groups and subcommittees of its members; it may co-opt any person(s) to serve on these. However, the committee is subject 'to the overall control of the Governing Body', and it must appoint the following bodies: a Business Subcommittee,[144] an Appointment Subcommittee, a Drafting Committee, and the chairman of a Legal Subcommittee.[145] Standing orders of the Governing Body do not apply to its proceedings in committee.[146]

The Standing Committee is responsible for recording the proceedings and minutes of the Governing Body.[147] The constitution (except canons amending the Book of Common Prayer or the chapters of the constitution) must be printed under the direction of the Standing Committee.[148] The Standing Committee is empowered to incur any expense reasonably necessary to carry out the duties entrusted to it, or imposed on it, under the constitution or any Governing Body regulation.[149]

Other Committees   The laws of many Anglican churches require the central assembly to establish commissions and committees on ministry, mission, doctrine, liturgy, ecumenism and canon law; each body has its own constitution for these purposes.[150] By way of contrast, the constitution

---

[143] Const. II.65(1): see below, Ch. 14.

[144] Const. II.65(3): for which see below, Ch. 14.

[145] Const. II.65(4): the chair of the Legal Subcommittee must appoint members to it in consultation with the chairman of the Standing Committee 'when occasion so requires'.

[146] GBSO, 16: 'These Standing Orders shall not apply to proceedings in committee.'

[147] Const. II.70: it must also cause such parts of these as shall be ordered, or which the committee thinks ought to be published, to be printed in English and Welsh for the general use of the church. Procedural Matters (1999), 3: members of the Governing Body must give three working days' notice of any proposal to amend the minutes so that there is adequate time to consider the implications. See also II.77.

[148] Const. II.71: when printed, three copies must be certified by the President as correct, and they must be filed in three books; II.72: one book is kept by the President, one deposited in the muniment room of the Governing Body, and one in the muniment room of the Representative Body; II.73: a copy of any part of the constitution certified by the secretaries of the Governing Body is *prima facie* evidence of such part of the constitution and as such may be received in evidence in all courts and the tribunal of the church; II.74: the Standing Committee may authorize the secretaries of the Governing Body to supply to any person a copy of any part of the English or Welsh versions of the constitution on such terms as it thinks fit.

[149] Const. II.75: the members of the committee must be indemnified by the Representative Body against any expense so incurred.

[150] See e.g. Korea, Const. Art. 41: the constitutions of the Canons Committee, Publications Board, Liturgical Commission, Evangelism Committee, and Church and Society Committee, are decided on by the National Executive Committee; see CLAC, 57. For equivalent Bench of Bishops' committees in Wales, see below, Ch. 6.

of the Church in Wales is generally rather more permissive in nature, conferring instead a discretion on the provincial assembly to set up such executive and advisory bodies. The Governing Body may appoint committees of its members, other than those prescribed, as it sees fit; and it may make rules and regulations for their powers and procedures. However, 'all acts and decisions of any committee, unless previously authorised, must be ratified and confirmed by the Governing Body before becoming valid'.[151]

Whilst the Governing Body receives and discusses reports made to it (including those of committees) for adoption, it is understood that, according to a ruling of the President, if any such act or decision of a committee imposes an obligation on any church member or body, or purports to change the constitution or ecclesiastical law, such ratification and confirmation requires a motion besides and in addition to the adoption of the committee report.[152] Any member of a committee ceasing to be a member of the Governing Body is deemed to have vacated their place on that committee.[153]

[151] Const. II.66; II.67: bill procedure does not apply to the appointment of any committee.
[152] Green, *Setting*, 199: no authority is given for this ruling.
[153] Const. II.68: the place must be filled by the Standing Committee and any member appointed acts until the next meeting of the Governing Body.

3

THE DIOCESE: UNITS AND ASSEMBLIES

The province of the Church in Wales is divided into six dioceses which, in turn, are composed of archdeaconries, deaneries and parishes. As the province is governed centrally by the Governing Body, so each diocese, under the oversight of the diocesan bishop, has its own assembly: the Diocesan Conference. Like the Governing Body, this too is an institution representative of both clergy and laity. Within each diocese there are archdeaconries. These do not have their own representative assembly as such, but function instead under the jurisdiction of an archdeacon. Furthermore, each archdeaconry is divided into deaneries, each having its own representative assembly, the Deanery Conference. Generally, whilst all deanery clergy are automatically members of the Deanery Conference, the parish elects lay representatives to the Deanery Conference; this then elects clerical and lay representatives to the Diocesan Conference, which in turn elects clerical and lay representatives to the Governing Body.[1] The purpose of this chapter is to describe the constitutional provisions regulating these institutions: their composition, functions, powers and duties. There would seem to be very little pre-1920 ecclesiastical law applicable to these subjects. Where appropriate, the chapter also compares arrangements in the Church in Wales with those operative in other Anglican churches having equivalent institutions and structures. The parish is considered in Chapter 4, and cathedrals in Chapter 7.

THE DIOCESAN CONFERENCE

A diocese is a legal division of a province and the circuit of a bishop's jurisdiction.[2] In the Church in Wales, the formation of a diocese is in the keeping of the Governing Body. The existing territorial arrangement of the

---

[1] For criticism of constitutional arrangements in the context of the system of representation, see P. Jones, *The Governance of the Church in Wales* (Cardiff, 2000), 41.
[2] See Co. Litt. 94a. For the origin of the word, see R. Phillimore, *Ecclesiastical Law* (2nd edn, London, 1895), I, 20; the diocese is sometimes treated in Anglican thought as the basic ecclesiastical unit: LC 1988, Res. 72. For definitions of 'diocese' in the laws of other Anglican churches, see below.

dioceses, under their respective diocesan bishops, and of the districts and parishes under the care of various ecclesiastical persons in charge of these, is to continue as at present except as expressly provided by the constitution.[3] Any diocesan bishop, with the consent of his Diocesan Conference, may make any change in the existing territorial arrangement of his diocese, as he thinks fit.[4] The Governing Body is empowered to make an order to transfer any part of a diocese to, and unite it with, any other diocese in the church, whether that diocese already exists or is one to be created. However, the order is not valid unless and until it is assented to by the Conference(s) of the diocese(s) affected. Such an order may not be carried out during the episcopate of the bishop(s) of such diocese(s) at the time the order was made, without the consent of the bishop(s) in question.[5] Moreover, the Governing Body may divide a diocese with the consent of the Conference of the affected diocese and, unless the see is vacant, with the consent of the diocesan bishop.[6] In the event of a division of a diocese during his episcopate, the bishop of the diocese in question is entitled to choose the see of which he will become bishop.[7] On the creation of a new diocese, the Governing Body must make provision, as it thinks expedient, for the purpose of securing the election of bishops.[8]

The Diocesan Conference, the assembly of the diocese, is governed by the provincial constitution of the Church in Wales; each conference is also regulated by its own particular constitution,[9] made internally by the conference itself as supplemental to the provincial constitution.[10]

---

[3]   Const. II.59.
[4]   Const. II.60.
[5]   Const. II.61.
[6]   Const. II.62.
[7]   Const. II.63: in this section, and in II.62, the word 'bishop' includes the archbishop.
[8]   Const. VIII.33: the provisions as to election must conform to 'the principles' contained in Const. VIII.
[9]   The provincial constitution does not, however, require each Conference to create for itself an internal constitution.
[10] See e.g. in the Diocese of Swansea and Brecon, 'The Constitution of the Diocesan Conference Supplemental to the Constitution of the Church in Wales' (DSAB, YB (2000), 12); see also e.g. DSA, YB (2000), 44. The draft Constitution and Regulations for the Llandaff Diocesan Conference (September 2001) deal with: powers of the Conference; membership; the secretaries and treasurer; meetings; the standing committee; elections to the Governing Body, the Electoral College, the Representative Body and the Diocesan Board of Patronage; and standing orders of the Conference.

Composition and Meetings

In pursuance of a freedom recognized under the Welsh Church Act 1914,[11] the constitution of the Church in Wales provides that in each diocese there must be a Diocesan Conference.[12]

Membership Under the provincial constitution, all members of the Conference must be communicants of the Church in Wales, and over the age of eighteen years.[13] The diocesan bishop, or in his absence a commissary specially authorized by him in writing, must be a member of and the President of all meetings of the Conference; the bishop, or his commissary, has a casting vote.[14] In the case of the death, resignation or incapacity of the bishop, or in his absence when no commissary has been appointed for the purpose, the President of the Governing Body must either act as President of the Diocesan Conference or appoint in writing a commissary to do so.[15] Without prejudice to the rights of the archbishop, the President so appointed possesses all the powers ordinarily exercised by the bishop of the diocese in the Conference.[16]

In addition to its President, the Diocesan Conference consists of elected, *ex officio*, nominated and co-opted members.[17] Each Conference must determine for itself the number and nature of the *ex officio*, co-opted and nominated members, provided that these together do not exceed one-sixth of the total number of members.[18] The Conference must determine the number of elected lay members. However, the clerical members must not exceed the number of lay members. Not fewer than three lay members must be elected for each deanery.[19] Subject to the rules contained in the constitution, the Diocesan Conference must determine for itself the necessary qualification for lay membership, as well as the time when and the manner in which members are to be elected. It must also decide whether election is to be by the Deanery Conference or by the Vestry Meetings. The clerical

---

[11] Welsh Church Act 1914, s. 13(1): this allows the church to make provision for representation of the bishops, clergy and laity 'in diocesan synods'.
[12] Const. IV.1.
[13] Const. IV.2.
[14] Const. IV.3.
[15] Const. IV.4; the Archbishop of Wales is the president of the Governing Body: for this rule, and exceptions to it, see Const. II.17.
[16] Const. IV.4: in the case of the death, resignation, incapacity or absence of the President of the Governing Body, the Welsh diocesan bishop next in order of precedence must act as President of the Diocesan Conference or appoint a commissary to do so.
[17] Const. IV.5.
[18] Const. IV.6. Ex officio members do not include clerical members under IV.9.
[19] Const. IV.7; IV.8: if, in the opinion of the bishop and the Diocesan Conference, a deanery has for any reason ceased to be effective, action may be taken (to change the territorial arrangement of the diocese), under II.60 (see above, n. 4).

members of the Diocesan Conference must be all stipendiary clerics and all other clerics holding a licence from the bishop of the diocese.[20]

At least seven days before the first meeting of each session of the Conference, the conference secretary must prepare and publish a list of its members. When signed by the bishop, the list provides conclusive evidence that those named in it, and no others, are the members of the Conference. A right of appeal, with respect to the list, lies to the Chancellor of the diocese, and the list may be amended as the Conference directs.[21] The failure of any district or area to return members does not prevent the Conference from proceeding to despatch its business.[22] The Diocesan Conference is empowered to deny admission to members elected to the Conference for a district or area, if such district or area fails to fulfil any engagement into which it has entered with the Conference; it may also deny admission if the district or area fails to make payment of any sum for which it has been assessed by the Conference, or which it has been called upon by the Conference to pay. In these circumstances, the qualified electors of the district or area in question are not allowed to return representatives to the Conference during the period of such default.[23] Every lay member of the Conference, before acting as such, must sign a declaration.[24] The Conference must appoint a secretary who holds office for four years at least.[25] The presence of the diocesan bishop, or his commissary, together with one-fourth of the clerical members and one-fifth of the lay members is required to constitute a meeting of the Conference.[26]

Meetings   The Diocesan Conference must be elected triennially and it must meet not less than once a year.[27] The diocesan bishop may, at his own discretion, instruct the secretary to convene a special meeting of the Conference; the bishop must do so at the written request (signed by not less than one-quarter) of the members of the Conference.[28] The secretary of the

---

[20] Const. IV.9: clerical membership ceases for a stipendiary cleric on retirement, and for licensed clerics on ceasing to hold appointment in the diocese, surrender or revocation of the licence, or reaching 70, whichever is first.

[21] Const. IV.10: this provision does not specify the precise grounds of appeal, nor does it identify those who enjoy the right of appeal.

[22] Const. IV.11.

[23] Const. IV.12.

[24] Const. IV13: 'I, J . . . S . . . of . . . do hereby solemnly declare that I am a communicant over eighteen years of age, and qualified to be a member of the . . . Diocesan Conference, and I do not belong to any religious body which is not in communion with the Church in Wales.'

[25] Const. IV.14.

[26] Const. IV.15: if the diocesan bishop or his commissary are absent, the President of the Governing Body, or the next senior Welsh bishop, or his commissary, must be present.

[27] Const. IV.24.

[28] Const. IV.25.

Conference must then convene a special meeting by notice in writing, stating the business to be transacted.[29] The notice must be sent to all members of the Conference, at least seven days before the day fixed for the special meeting.[30] No business may be transacted at the meeting other than that stated in the notice.[31] The supplemental constitutions of particular Diocesan Conferences also deal with both membership and meetings; for example, the supplemental constitution of the Diocesan Conference of Swansea and Brecon provides that the conduct of meetings of the Conference is to be governed by standing orders which cover opening and closing prayers, speeches, debates, questions and voting.[32]

Functions: Powers and Duties

The Diocesan Conference has administrative and some legislative functions. In performing these, the Conference is subject to a number of general duties and limitations. The Conference is obliged to 'conform to and carry out any order or direction of the Governing Body'.[33] Moreover, the Governing Body may, on a petition signed by not less than one-third of the members of the Diocesan Conference, repeal, alter or add to any of the rules contained in the provincial constitution relating to the Diocesan Conference.[34] As a matter of general principle, subject to the direction and control of the Governing Body, and the constitution, the Diocesan Conference is under a duty to manage its own affairs and its own property, if any, and any sums of money entrusted to it for distribution by the Representative Body. In discharging these duties, the Conference is always subject to any special trusts affecting the property and money, and to any regulations of the Representative Body.[35] The Diocesan Conference has no right to pass any resolution or to come to any decision upon any matter concerning discipline, faith, or ceremonial.[36]

Acts and Resolutions   The decisions of the Diocesan Conference can be effected by means of *acts* and *resolutions*.[37] Every *act* of the Conference

---

[29]   Const. IV.26.
[30]   Const. IV.27.
[31]   Const. IV.28.
[32]   See e.g. DSAB, YB (2000), 12.
[33]   Const. IV.29.
[34]   Const. IV.44; see also II.57, 58.
[35]   Const. IV.22.
[36]   Const. IV.45: the precise wording of this is: 'Nothing in this chapter shall be construed as giving' the Conference any right to make such resolutions or decisions. For the observation that this provision does not prohibit a conference from making doctrinal statements, and the practice of diocesan committees to treat doctrinal subjects, see P. Jones, *Governance*, 92–3. See generally below, Ch. 9.
[37]   The constitution refers to four forms of instrument capable of being made by the

binds both the Conference and all other members of the church in the diocese. This is so if the act is assented to by the President and by a majority of the clerics and laity present and voting conjointly, or, if so demanded by thirty members rising in their places, by a majority of the clerical and of the lay members present and voting by orders.[38] With respect to *resolutions* of the Diocesan Conference, the bishop may withhold his assent to a resolution. If he does so, any member may bring the resolution forward again at the next annual meeting of the Conference. If, at the next annual meeting, the resolution is passed by a two-thirds majority of the clerical members and of the lay members present and voting by orders, the resolution must be referred to the Synod of the province.[39] The decision of the Provincial Synod, in the matter, binds the Diocesan Conference and all other members of the church in the diocese.[40]

Acts of a Diocesan Conference are also subject to systems of review and appeal. First, '[a]ny *act* of a Diocesan Conference may be reviewed by the Governing Body', which has the power 'to control, alter, repeal, or supersede any regulation made by the Diocesan Conference'. The Governing Body may exercise this power 'so far as may be necessary . . . to provide against the admission of any principle inexpedient for the common interest of the Church in Wales'. The Governing Body is the final judge of such matters.[41] Secondly, in the case of property held under or administered by the Diocesan Conference, any person who considers himself aggrieved by 'an act of the Conference' has a right of appeal to the Provincial Court; the decision of the court in the matter is final.[42]

The Diocesan Conference itself has legislative power to control, alter, repeal, or supersede any regulation made by the Deanery Conference, the Vestry Meeting and the Parochial Church Council. The Diocesan Conference may exercise this power 'so far as may be necessary . . . to provide against the admission of any principle inexpedient for the common interest of the Church in Wales in the diocese'. The Diocesan Conference is the final judge in this regard.[43]

Diocesan Conference: acts (IV.32), resolutions (IV.33), regulations (II.57) and rules (IV.41); the conference is also involved in the making of diocesan decrees (IV.35). However, with the exception of Diocesan Decrees (for which see below), the constitution would not seem to be entirely clear as to the precise distinction between these instruments.

[38] Const. IV.32. The supplemental constitutions of particular conferences also deal with motions: see e.g. DSAB, YB (2000), 14.

[39] See below, Ch. 6.

[40] Const. IV.33.

[41] Const. II.57: the procedure by bill shall not apply to this section.

[42] Const. IV.23.

[43] Const. IV.43; for other powers over deaneries and the Deanery Conference (contained in Const. V.15, 16), see below.

Administrative Functions   The Diocesan Conference also has numerous specific administrative functions identified in various constitutional instruments of the church. It is responsible for making arrangements for elections of clerical and lay representatives to the Governing Body.[44] The Conference must appoint a Standing Committee.[45] It must appoint, or cause to be appointed, a Diocesan Board of Finance,[46] which in turn must appoint a Diocesan Parsonage Board.[47] The Conference must appoint clerical and lay members of the Patronage Board, and its supplemental members,[48] as well as episcopal electors,[49] and it is involved in elections to the Representative Body.[50] It must elect from its own members persons to serve on the Diocesan Churches and Pastoral Committee which must, amongst other things, keep under review the pastoral need for the church buildings in the diocese and advise the diocesan bishop and the Diocesan Conference accordingly.[51] In turn, the diocese may have a number of additional committees, boards and councils,[52] dealing with a wide range of specific diocesan matters, such as social responsibility, education, liturgy, ministry, resources and mission;[53] their terms of reference may be treated in the supplemental constitutions of particular Diocesan Conferences.[54] The Diocesan Conference is empowered to alter the number and method of appointment of churchwardens in a parish.[55] The Governing Body may refer any question to a Diocesan Conference for its discussion and report.[56] Finally, the Conference is directly involved in pastoral reorganization within the diocese; this is considered in the following section.

---

[44] Const. IV.30: it must 'from time to time duly elect the diocesan representatives to serve on the Governing Body and on the Representative Body, and the supplemental members of each'; see also Const. II.8 and 22, for which see above, Ch. 2.

[45] Const. IV.16. See e.g. DSA, YB (2000), 44: the standing committee consists of: the *ex officio* members of the conference (which includes the bishop, the dean and the archdeacons); and one clerical and one lay representative from each deanery conference (who are already members of the conference); and the secretary of the conference.

[46] Const. IV.16–19: see below, Ch. 14.

[47] Const. IV.19–21: see below, Ch. 13.

[48] Const. IV.31: this must be carried out in accordance with Const. VII.12, 15.

[49] Const. VIII.3, 4, 5.

[50] Const. III.3, 10, 13, 30: see below, Ch. 13.

[51] Constitution of Diocesan Churches and Pastoral Committees, 2(d) and 11(a); for the Diocesan Advisory Committee, see below, Chs. 5 and 13.

[52] These bodies are not known to the constitution. For critical comment about the 'profusion of diocesan committees . . . [as] too bureaucratic', see P. Jones, *Governance*, 198, 209–10.

[53] These are discussed, where appropriate, elsewhere in this volume. For example, the Diocese of Monmouth has a Council for Education, a Council for Social Responsibility, a Mission Forum, a Resources Centre and a Training for Ministry Committee.

[54] See e.g. DSAB, YB (2000), 13.

[55] Const. VI.17(1).

[56] Const. II.58.

Pastoral Reorganization and Diocesan Decrees

As a basic principle, unless and until it is otherwise altered, the Diocesan Conference has a duty to observe and maintain the division of the diocese into archdeaconries, deaneries and parishes existing at the date of the coming into force of the Welsh Church Act 1914.[57] Nevertheless, the diocesan bishop, with the consent of the Diocesan Conference, may make any change in the existing territorial arrangements of his diocese, as he thinks fit.[58] The territorial reorganization of the diocese, by the bishop with the consent of the Diocesan Conference, is governed by a complex body of rules dealing with a wide range of permissible reorganization schemes. Each scheme is intended to meet the pastoral needs of the units of the diocese.[59] Co-operation and consultation are the key elements in the process of territorial reorganization, a process effected by means of the issue by the bishop of a Diocesan Decree.

First, subject to the consent of the Diocesan Conference,[60] though the Conference must co-operate in this matter with the bishop,[61] the diocesan bishop is empowered to: (1) alter the boundaries of any parish; (2) disunite a united benefice or parish; (3) sever a portion(s) of any parish from it and incorporate it in an adjoining parish; (4) form a portion of a benefice or parish (or portions of two or more benefices or parishes), into a separate benefice or parish; (5) group any two or more benefices or parishes under one incumbent; (6) rearrange or dissolve groups of parishes grouped under one incumbent; (7) unite or merge permanently or temporarily two or more parishes into one parish; (8) group any church without a district with any benefice or parish (where the cleric in charge of each church desires it); or (9) assign any church without a district to a benefice or parish as a church or chapel of that benefice or parish. However, no alteration of the boundaries of existing parishes, nor any change in any grouping of parishes, may be carried out without the consent of the Representative Body; this rule applies if such alteration or change respectively involve additional expense.[62]

Secondly, any grouping, uniting or merging, disuniting, severing or alteration made under the powers described above, must be carried out by a Decree (called a Diocesan Decree) signed by the bishop and deposited in

---

[57] Const. IV.46.

[58] Const. II.60.

[59] For historical and introductory material on pastoral reorganization, see P. Jones, *Governance*, 213f.

[60] As required by Const. II.60.

[61] Const. IV.34: the duty to co-operate is 'subject to section 60 of chapter II', for which see above. The standing committee of the diocesan conference, if so empowered by the conference, must co-operate similarly.

[62] Const. IV.34: additional expense might include acquisition or disposal of land, construction work or the creation of new stipendiary offices.

the Diocesan Registry.[63] A Diocesan Decree, when relating to the grouping of parishes, or to the rearrangement or dissolution of a grouping, must make provision and contain directions as to which of the houses within the group must be the parsonage required to be occupied by the incumbent. In default of such provision and directions, the Decree is not valid.[64] In other cases of pastoral reorganization, a Diocesan Decree must make provision and contain directions as to: (1) the right of user of the parish church or churches and other churches in the area; (2) which shall be the parish church or churches in a parish formed by the uniting or merging of two or more parishes; (3) baptisms, marriages and burials; (4) the method by which the lay representatives, if any, for the Deanery Conference are to be elected; and (5) what is to be done with regard to the electoral roll, the Vestry and other meetings, churchwardens, sidesmen and the Parochial Church Council. If it fails to make these provisions and directions, the Decree is not valid.[65] No grouping, uniting or merging, disuniting, severing or alteration under these powers can take effect until the Diocesan Decree, signed by the bishop, has been deposited in the Diocesan Registry.[66]

Thirdly, the Diocesan Conference must also co-operate with the bishop,[67] who must obtain the consent of the Conference,[68] in forming any area (whether one or more parishes or portions of them) into a rectorial benefice.[69] The formation of a rectorial benefice must be carried out by a Diocesan Decree, but the Decree does not take effect until signed by the bishop and deposited in the Diocesan Registry.[70] The Diocesan Decree must make provision and contain directions as to: (1) the authority of and the offices, duties and services to be performed by a vicar, with or without any special duties or responsibilities; (2) meetings of the rector and vicar or vicars, in chapter or otherwise; (3) the rights of the rector and vicar or vicars with regard to Easter offerings and surplice and other fees; (4) if a rectorial benefice comprises more than one parish, matters including the right of user of the churches in the area, baptisms, marriages and burials;[71] and (5) such other matters as the bishop may consider necessary. Failure to make such provision and directions renders the Decree invalid.[72] The Diocesan Conference is empowered to make rules necessary for carrying

---

[63] Const. IV.35; see also VII.6.
[64] Const. IV.36: the parsonage must be occupied by the incumbent in accordance with Regulation 2 of the Supplementary Regulations to Const. X.
[65] Const. IV.37.
[66] Const. IV.38.
[67] Const. IV.39(1): or its standing committee if so empowered by the Conference.
[68] Const. IV.39(1) and II.60.
[69] For rectorial benefices, see below, Chs. 4 and 7.
[70] Const. IV.40(1).
[71] Namely, those matters listed in Const. IV.37, for which see above.
[72] Const. IV.40(2), and (3); see below, Ch. 4.

out any of these arrangements for pastoral reorganization.[73] Finally, the Standing Committee of the Diocesan Conference must co-operate with the bishop in the creation of conventional districts, and it must report to the Conference and to the Governing Body annually as to what conventional districts, if any, have been created.[74]

Dioceses and Diocesan Assemblies in Other Anglican Churches

It is useful to place these principles and provisions, operative in the Church in Wales, in their wider ecclesiastical context. In all Anglican churches, a diocese, a territory under the spiritual leadership and oversight of a bishop, is governed by a representative assembly. The laws of some churches treat the diocese itself as the primary unit of the church.[75] Moreover, according to the Lambeth Conference: '[i]n the organisation of Synodal order for the government of the Church, the Diocesan Synod appears to be the primary and simplest form of such organisation.'[76] These assemblies are styled, variously, the Diocesan Synod (the most usual title),[77] the Diocesan Convention,[78] or (rarely) the Diocesan Council.[79] The laws of churches deal in considerable detail with the creation, amalgamation, division, transfer, release and dissolution of dioceses. As with the Church in Wales, for the vast majority of Anglican churches, the formation of a new diocese, and the alteration of diocesan boundaries, is in the keeping of the national, regional or provincial assembly, which may act only with the consent of any diocese and diocesan bishop affected as a result.[80] In contrast, however, for some churches it is the central episcopal assembly which has the determinative voice.[81] The Lambeth Conference has set down a number of criteria to be satisfied in the formation and alteration of dioceses.[82]

[73] Const. IV.41.

[74] Const. IV.42.

[75] Australia, Const. III.1: 'A diocese shall in accordance with the historic custom of the One Holy Catholic and Apostolic Church continue to be the unit of organisation of this Church and shall be the see of a bishop.'

[76] LC 1867, Committee Report 'A', 58–60; LC 1988, Res. 59: 'care should be taken to make the diocese the centre of unity.'

[77] See e.g. England, Synodical Government Measure 1969, s. 5.

[78] ECUSA, Cans. 1.9.

[79] North India, Const. II.III.1.1.

[80] See e.g. West Indies, Can. 12.1: 'The Provincial Synod may, at the request of the Synod of a Diocese, or of its own initiative and with the concurrence of the Bishop or Bishops and the Synod or Synods of the Diocese or Dioceses concerned, form a new Diocese within the province, or re-arrange the boundaries of a Diocese or merge two or more Dioceses.'

[81] Southern Africa, Can. 21: the formation of dioceses is in the keeping of '[t]he Metropolitan and the Bishops of the Province in Synod'.

[82] LC 1978, Res. 17: for instance, when a new diocese is created, 'adequate financial support should be underwritten by the member Churches concerned'; and, proposals to form a new diocese should be referred to the Anglican Consultative Council.

As with the Church in Wales, for other Anglican churches, the diocesan assembly is composed of the diocesan bishop and representatives of the clergy and laity of the diocese. The president is, invariably, the diocesan bishop. The house or order of clergy consists of priests and deacons elected in accordance either with rules found in national, regional or provincial law, or in diocesan legislation. The same applies to the house or order of laity which is, similarly, composed of representatives of the laity of the diocese who are adult communicants.[83] There is less consistency, as between churches, with regard to the functions of diocesan assemblies, a subject very often left to be dealt with by diocesan law. One basic difference is that in most churches, the diocesan assembly enjoys legislative powers, whereas in others this is not the case. Two forms of diocesan law are commonplace: constitutions,[84] and canons,[85] or other forms of instrument (such as ordinances, regulations, resolutions, acts or decrees).[86] The power of the diocesan bishop in the Church in Wales to veto diocesan resolutions (subject to the limitations described earlier in this chapter) finds a parallel in a number of churches. In the province of Southern Africa, for instance, there is a right of appeal, against the bishop's veto of an act or resolution of a Diocesan Synod, to the Metropolitan and the diocesan bishops sitting in synod.[87]

Occasionally, the laws of Anglican churches require the bishop to consult with the diocesan assembly on matters of general concern and importance to the diocese,[88] but the assembly is expressly forbidden to make any declaration of the doctrine of the church.[89] The diocesan assembly has a general oversight of the lower ecclesiastical units within the diocese,[90] it must keep these informed of the policies and problems of the diocese, and it must consider any matter referred to it by the provincial assembly.[91] In some churches, the diocesan assembly is obliged to make an

---

[83] See e.g. Ireland, Const. II.2.–12; for composition see generally CLAC, 61f.
[84] See e.g. Uganda, Const. Art. 14: '[t]he Diocesan Synod shall make a Constitution for the government and administration of the Diocese, provided that a constitution of a Diocese shall be approved by the Provincial Assembly'; moreover: '[w]here there is a conflict between the Diocesan Constitution and the provisions of this Constitution, the Provincial Constitution shall prevail, at any rate to the extent of the inconsistency.'
[85] See e.g. New Zealand, Const. D, E and F.
[86] See e.g. Ireland, Const. II.I.28–33: every Diocesan Synod may make 'regulations as to the temporalities of the Church', 'not being repugnant to any law of the Church or to any regulation of the General Synod', or to any trusts, 'as the synod may deem necessary for the welfare of the Church in such diocese'; any such regulation may be varied, repealed or superseded by the General Synod.
[87] Southern Africa, Const. Art. VIII, IX, XI; Cans. 9, 10.
[88] See e.g. England, Synodical Government Measure 1969, s. 4(3).
[89] Ibid., s. 4(2).
[90] See e.g. North India, Const. II.III.III: 'The Diocesan Council shall have supervisory, legislative, and executive powers over Pastorates within its jurisdiction.'
[91] Papua New Guinea, Const. Art. 8.

annual report on the state of the church in the diocese to the provincial assembly or its standing committee.[92] It is the normal practice for each diocesan assembly to have, in addition to its standing committee, a wide variety of committees, boards, councils and commissions, of which bodies dealing with ministry, liturgy, finance and clergy residences are typical. These are accountable to and under the direct control of the diocesan assembly, whose lawful decisions they must obey.[93]

THE ARCHDEACONRY

Dioceses are usually divided into two or more archdeaconries,[94] territorial units designed primarily for administrative purposes. Whilst the existing territorial arrangements of archdeaconries, under the care of an arch-deacon, are to continue,[95] provision exists enabling the bishop, with the consent of the Diocesan Conference, to change the territorial boundaries of archdeaconries *within* the diocese.[96] Changes to the boundaries of archdeaconries resulting in the change of diocesan boundaries must be effected by the Governing Body.[97] However, it would seem that, as a matter of general principle, no single archdeaconry may extend beyond the territorial limits of one diocese.[98] For the purposes of elections to the Governing Body, the Diocesan Conference may make such arrangements as it thinks fit for treating archdeaconries as electoral districts, and for apportioning the number of diocesan representatives to be elected by the Conference for each district.[99] Above and beyond these provisions, there is very little law on the archdeaconry as such. The designated boundaries of the archdeaconry are employed principally in order to define the territorial limits of the jurisdiction of the archdeacon. By way of contrast, therefore, there is a considerable body of law applying to the office of archdeacon and this is

---

[92] See e.g. ECUSA, Cans. I.6.2.

[93] See generally, CLAC, 65.

[94] See e.g. DM, YB (2000), 4: two archdeaconries (Monmouth, Newport); DSAB, YB (2000), 6: two archdeaconries (Brecon, Gower); DSA, YB (2000), 44: three archdeaconries.

[95] Const. II.59.

[96] Const. II.60.

[97] Const. II.61–3; see also C. A. H. Green, *The Setting of the Constitution of the Church in Wales* (London, 1937), 136: 'The consent of the Diocesan Conference is requisite to any change in the existing territorial arrangement of a Diocese except Archdeaconries, changes in the boundaries of dioceses and archdeaconries being reserved to the Governing Body.'

[98] Archdeaconries and Rural Deaneries Act 1874, s. 1: this rule, presumably, still applies to the Church in Wales insofar as it is contained in a pre-1920 ecclesiastical law statute not listed as a repealed statute in Const. XI.47.

[99] Const. II.8: and the Conference may determine the manner and method of such election.

discussed in Chapter 7. An archdeaconry has no representative assembly, though there is an Archdeacon's Court.[100] Archdeaconries are rarely to be found in other Anglican churches.[101]

THE DEANERY CONFERENCE

Each diocese and archdeaconry of the Church in Wales is further divided into deaneries,[102] a territorial unit functioning under the general oversight of the area dean[103] and the Deanery Conference.[104] If, in the opinion of the bishop and the Diocesan Conference, a deanery has for any reason ceased to be effective, such action (if any) as the circumstances warrant, must be taken, by the bishop and with the consent of the Diocesan Conference, to make the appropriate change in the territorial arrangement of the diocese.[105] Whereas the functions of the Diocesan Conference are predominantly governmental, those of the Deanery Conference are both governmental and pastoral.[106]

Membership and Meetings

In each deanery there must be a Deanery Conference.[107] All members of the Conference must be communicants of the Church in Wales, and over the age of eighteen years.[108] The area dean, or failing him the vice-chairman,

---

[100] See below, Ch. 5.
[101] See e.g. Ireland, Const. II.39: the diocesan synod determines the boundaries of archdeaconries; Korea, Const. Ch. 4, Art. 62.
[102] As a general principle, every deanery must in its entirety be within an archdeaconry: Archdeaconries and Rural Deaneries Act 1874, s. 1: see above, n. 98.
[103] See below, Ch. 7.
[104] For comparisons with pre-disestablishment arrangements, for those currently operating in the Church of England, and for deanery chapters, see P. Jones, *Governance*, 38, 177, 216; see also Green, *Setting*, 129, for the origin of the deanery, which he suggests were so called from *decanus*, because they were groups of ten parishes.
[105] Const. IV.8.
[106] The law relating to deaneries has recently been the subject of review, the previous rural deaneries being replaced by deaneries, and rural deans by area deans (see *A Workbook for the Deaneries of the Church in Wales*, Governing Body Deaneries Working Group (2001)). The following references to Const. V are to provisions which are subject to final scrutiny by the Drafting Subcommittee of the Governing Body. The Report of the Standing Committee Working Group to Review Chapter V of the Constitution (June 2001) considered that the purpose of the deanery is: to provide fellowship for clergy through the deanery chapter; to provide contact and fellowship for clergy and laity; to provide a channel of communication; to provide effective adminsitration; to play a significant role in church government; and to enable mission (p. 6).
[107] Const. V.1; see also V.19: for the purposes of Chapter V of the constitution, the archbishop of the Church in Wales must be regarded as the bishop of the see over which he presides without prejudice to his rights as archbishop.
[108] Const. V.2.

must preside at all meetings of the Conference and has a second or casting vote.[109] In the event of the absence of the area dean and the vice-chairman, the Conference must appoint another member to preside at the meeting, who, whilst presiding, has a second or casting vote.[110] The Conference must appoint a secretary[111] and may appoint an Executive Committee.[112]

Membership The membership of the Deanery Conference consists of three classes. First, *ex officio* members comprise all clerics other than retired clerics, all deaconesses other than retired deaconesses, and all full-time stipendiary lay workers, officiating with the bishop's permission within the deanery, or so officiating elsewhere in the diocese but residing within the deanery. Secondly, elected members, being such number of lay qualified electors as representatives from each parish in the deanery as the Diocesan Conference of that diocese prescribes. Thirdly, co-opted members are drawn from the following: such number (if any) of licensed readers and licensed lay workers as the Diocesan Conference may prescribe for co-option in that deanery; and such number (if any) as the Deanery Conference may determine to co-opt of retired clerics and deaconesses officiating with the bishop's permission within the deanery, or so officiating elsewhere in the diocese but residing within the deanery. However, the number of clerical members must not exceed the number of lay members, and the number of co-opted members must not exceed the number of elected members.[113] In addition, if not already members of the Deanery Conference, deanery representatives on diocesan boards, members of the Governing Body residing in the deanery, and members of the Representative Body residing in the deanery, may at the invitation of the Conference attend any of its meetings and speak but not vote.[114]

The elected members of the Deanery Conference, and the supplemental lay representatives from the parish, are chosen for a period of three years by the Vestry Meetings.[115] In the event of any elected member being unable or unwilling to attend any meeting of the Conference, that member's place, for that meeting, must be taken by the first or next available lay representative from the parish, in the order of choice of such representatives by the Vestry Meeting.[116] Any casual vacancy among those elected, and the supplemental lay representatives from the parish,[117] must be filled up by the

---

[109] Const. V.3.
[110] Const. V.4.
[111] Const. V.10.
[112] Const. V.9.
[113] Const. V.5(1); co-opted members serve for three years.
[114] Const. V.5(2).
[115] Const. V.6(1). For the Vestry Meeting, see below, Ch. 4.
[116] Const. V.6(2).
[117] That is, any vacancy amongst those chosen under Const. V.6(1).

Parochial Church Council of the parish; the council must do so at a meeting held within three months of the vacancy.[118] The failure of any parish to elect or return members, or to choose supplemental lay representatives, does not prevent the Conference from proceeding to dispatch its business.[119]

The secretary of the Deanery Conference must, following the beginning of each three-year period, maintain a list of its members, and must update the list whenever a casual vacancy arises in the membership of the Conference.[120] Every lay member of the Conference, before acting as such, must sign a declaration in a book to be kept for that purpose by the secretary of the Conference; the same declaration must also be signed by any supplemental lay representatives before acting as a member of the Conference.[121]

Meetings There must be an annual meeting of the Deanery Conference held not later in the year than 30 June, and three other quarterly meetings, unless the Conference agrees from time to time to dispense with any quarterly meetings.[122] However, the area dean may at his own discretion summon further meetings of the Conference, and he must do so at the request of the bishop, or at a request in writing signed by not less than one-quarter of the members of the Conference.[123] Deanery Conferences in the same diocese may meet together (with the senior area dean normally presiding at the joint meeting).[124]

Functions: Powers and Responsibilities

As an overriding principle, in the exercise of its functions, the Deanery Conference is under a duty to conform to and carry out any order or direction of the Diocesan Conference.[125] Subject to the control of the Diocesan Conference, the Deanery Conference is under a duty to manage its own affairs.[126] The constitution provides that the work of the Conference *includes* eight specific functions,[127] which in turn may be grouped for the

---

[118] Const. V.7.
[119] Const. V.8.
[120] Const. V.11: under the provision which this replaces, such lists were subject to an appeal to the Rural Dean.
[121] Const. V.12: 'I, J . . . S . . . of . . . do hereby solemnly declare that I am a communicant over eighteen years of age, and qualified to be a member of the . . . Deanery Conference . . . and I do not belong to any religious body which is not in communion with the Church in Wales.'
[122] Const. V.13.
[123] Const. V.14.
[124] Const. V.18. In which case Const. V.4 applies: see above.
[125] Const. V.17.
[126] Const. V.15.
[127] Const V.15: whilst the word 'function' is employed in this provision, rather than 'duty', it may be presumed that these functions are responsibilities, obligatory rather than discretionary in nature.

sake of convenience into four basic clusters. The first cluster of functions relates to resources and finance: assessing the needs of the deanery in respect of finance, personnel and buildings,[128] and managing deanery finances.[129]

The second cluster of functions relates to pastoral care and liturgy. The Conference must promote the whole mission of the church, pastoral, evangelical, social and ecumenical.[130] It must also provide strategic planning for worship and pastoral care throughout the deanery.[131] The third cluster of functions concerns its deliberative and advisory roles. The Deanery Conference is to act on any communication from the Diocesan Conference or Parochial Church Council on such matters as the Conference deems appropriate.[132] The Conference is to discuss matters concerning the Church in Wales or otherwise of religious or public interest. However, this is subject to the rule that the discussion of any doctrinal matters by the Conference must not extend to any formulation or declaration of doctrine.[133] It must also advise on any matter properly referred to it.[134]

Finally, the Conference has a number of executive functions. It must elect a lay vice-chairman from among its members and, as necessary, following a vacancy in the office.[135] The Conference also has a special responsibility for elections to the Diocesan Conference. The Deanery Conference must elect to the Diocesan Conference, in a manner determined by the Diocesan Conference, such number of lay representatives as the Diocesan Conference prescribes for the deanery. However, it must do so subject to the rule that the lay members elect the lay representatives to the Diocesan Conference.[136] No election of representatives to the Diocesan Conference can be made at any joint meeting of Deanery Conferences.[137]

The Deanery in Other Anglican Churches

The practice of dividing dioceses into deaneries is employed only in a small number of Anglican churches.[138] In the Church of Ireland, for example, each archdeaconry may be divided into such number of deaneries as the diocesan synod determines.[139] By way of contrast, in some dioceses of ECUSA, the diocese must be divided into deaneries, '[t]o best promote its

---

[128] Const. V.15(b).
[129] Const. V.15(f).
[130] Const. V.15(a).
[131] Const. V.15(c).
[132] Const. V.15(e).
[133] Const. V.15(h).
[134] Const. V.15(d).
[135] Const. V.15(g).
[136] Const. V.16.
[137] Const. V.18; see above for joint meetings under V.18.
[138] The normal division is into parishes: see below, Ch. 4.
[139] Ireland, Const. II.21.

work'; the diocesan assembly may change the boundaries, names and number of deaneries, and each deanery must have its own council, composed of a dean, and elected clergy and laity; the deanery council must meet at least once a year, to consider, amongst other things, matters of common concern to the parishes and missions of the deanery.[140] Perhaps the fullest treatment of the functions of deanery assemblies in the Anglican Communion is that found in the law of the Church of England. There are several parallels with the Church in Wales.

In the Church of England, the deanery synod, a mandatory institution, is representative of both clergy and laity, and under the joint chairmanship of the rural dean and a member of the synod's house of laity. It has six basic functions. First, the deanery synod is to consider matters concerning the Church of England and to make provision for such matters in relation to the deanery, and to consider and express their opinion on any other matter of religious or public interest. Secondly, it is to bring together the views of the parishes of the deanery on common problems, to discuss and formulate common policies on those problems, to foster a sense of community and interdependence among those parishes, and generally to promote in the deanery the whole mission of the church, pastoral, evangelistic, social and ecumenical. Thirdly, the synod is to make known and so far as appropriate put into effect any provision made by the diocesan synod. Fourthly, it is to consider the business of the diocesan synod, particularly any matters referred to that synod by the General Synod, and to sound out parochial opinion whenever they are required or consider it appropriate to do so. Fifthly, it must raise such matters as the deanery synod considers appropriate with the diocesan synod. Finally, if the diocesan synod delegates to the deanery synod functions in relation to the parishes of the deanery, and in particular the determination of the parochial shares in quotas allocated to the deaneries, the deanery synod must exercise those functions.[141]

---

[140] ECUSA, Diocese of Western New York, Can. 9.
[141] England, Synodical Government Measure 1969, s. 5.

4

THE PARISH AND THE PAROCHIAL
CHURCH COUNCIL

To society at large, the parish church is the most visible sign of the existence of the Church in Wales. It is here that both the public and the members of the church experience the institutional organization and the sacramental ministry of the church, especially in public worship and in the administration of baptisms, marriages and funerals. Moreover, within the province of the Church in Wales, with its dioceses, archdeaconries and deaneries, the parish represents the most localized territorial unit and organ of government within the institutional framework of the church.[1] The purpose of this chapter is to examine the various categories of parish, their legal nature and governmental structure, and the electoral roll as the basis of representative church government. It concentrates particularly on the institutions of the parish: the Annual Vestry Meeting, the Parochial Church Council, the Congregational Meeting and the Church Committee, their composition, meetings, functions, as well as their authority and the limits of their legal competence. These subjects are regulated in the main by the provisions of the formal, provincial constitution of the church. They are also regulated, however, by certain elements of surviving pre-1920 ecclesiastical law, and by a growing volume of ecclesiastical quasi-legislation.[2]

THE PARISH AND THE ELECTORAL ROLL

In the vast majority of churches in the Anglican Communion, the law divides dioceses into parishes,[3] or equivalent local-level ecclesiastical units

---

[1] For cathedrals, see below, Ch. 7.
[2] The principal document of quasi-legislation is *Parochial Administration Handbook for Use in the Church in Wales* (2002 edn); hereafter the document is referred to by the abbreviation PA.
[3] See e.g. ECUSA, Cans. I.13: a parish is under the 'parochial Cure of the Member of the Clergy having charge thereof'.

such as pastorates,[4] incumbencies,[5] or other districts.[6] Anglican churches also operate registers of members, admission to which enables individuals to participate in the governance of the church.[7] So too in the Church in Wales,[8] which, following disestablishment,[9] retained the parish system as essential for the representative structures of ecclesiastical government.[10]

The Parish

Under the received ecclesiastical law of the Church in Wales,[11] a parish is a district committed to the charge of an ordained minister who has the cure of souls in that district.[12] According to ancient case-law, a parish is a unit created not for the benefit of the cleric but for the people in it.[13] Modern ecclesiastical quasi-legislation provides that: a parish is 'an area under the spiritual care of a cleric . . . to whose religious ministrations all its inhabitants are entitled . . . sometimes known as the "Cure of Souls"'.[14] This quasi-legislation enumerates a cluster of basic duties for the parish. Each parish is required to comply with the Constitution of the Church in Wales; it must keep an electoral roll; it must hold an Annual Vestry; it must appoint two churchwardens; it must appoint a Parochial Church Council

[4]   See e.g. South India, Const. VII.1: 'A pastorate is an organised congregation or group recognised as such by the Diocesan Council, under the superintendence of a presbyter, who may be in charge of more than one pastorate.'

[5]   See e.g. Scotland, Can. 36.1: an incumbency is a congregation, under the charge of an incumbent, with a church or suitable building provided for divine worship, and with a constitution approved by the bishop.

[6]   See e.g. Papua New Guinea, Const. Can. No. 5 of 1977: the diocese is divided into 'Ecclesiastical districts called respectively Parishes, Parochial Districts, and Missionary Districts as the Bishop-in-Council may from time to time determine'.

[7]   See e.g. New Zealand, Cans. B.V.4.3; see generally, CLAC, 162f.

[8]   For the origins of parishes, see R. Phillimore, *Ecclesiastical Law* (2nd edn, London, 1895), I, 217ff.

[9]   See also Welsh Church Act 1914, s. 9, and Welsh Church (Temporalities) Act 1919, s. 8, which made special provision for border parishes. With respect to a parish partly in Wales or Monmouthshire, the Welsh Commissioners were to determine (with reference to the general wishes of the parishioners) whether the parish was to be treated as wholly within or outside Wales or Monmouthshire, and the parish was to be so treated for the purposes of the statute. The Ecclesiastical Commissioners were to attach to an English diocese any parish which was situated in a Welsh diocese, but not in Wales or Monmouthshire. A parish which was wholly situated in Wales or Monmouthshire (or for the purposes of the statute was to be so treated), and which formed part of an English diocese, ceased at the date of disestablishment to form part of that English diocese, and was to be attached to such Welsh diocese as was determined in a manner provided by the constitution and regulations of the Church in Wales.

[10]   The retention of the parish system was the result of a positive decision made at the 1917 Convention: *Proceedings*, 22.

[11]   That is, the pre-1920 ecclesiastical law: see above, Ch. 1.

[12]   I Bl Com (14th edn), 110.

[13]   *Britton v Standish* (1704) Holt KB 141.

[14]   PA, 1, p. 5.

by election at the Annual Vestry; and it must appoint sidesmen (men or women). Subject to these requirements, each parish is responsible for its own affairs through its Vestry Meeting and Parochial Church Council.[15]

According to the constitution of the Church in Wales, there are in law five categories of parish in the church: an ecclesiastical parish (whether ancient or new); a rectorial benefice; a parish in a group; a united parish; or a parish into which another former parish (or part(s) of a parish or former parish) has been merged.[16] The existing territorial arrangement of parishes and districts, in each diocese, is to continue. However, the diocesan bishop may, with the consent of the Diocesan Conference, make any change to the existing arrangement as the bishop may think fit.[17] Subject to the consent of the Diocesan Conference, the diocesan bishop,[18] with whom the Diocesan Conference must co-operate, may by diocesan decree: alter any of the boundaries of a parish; group, unite, merge, disunite or sever benefices or parishes; rearrange or dissolve groups of parishes; group any church without a district with any benefice or parish (where the cleric in charge desires it); assign any church without a district to a benefice or parish as a church or chapel of it;[19] or form a rectorial benefice.[20] Also, the bishop may create a conventional district.[21]

Whilst the constitution does not define each of these categories of parish, ecclesiastical quasi-legislation seeks to elucidate more fully the meaning of each legal category. The traditional parish (i.e. the ecclesiastical parish) has a parish church and may have one or more daughter churches. Similarly, a rectorial benefice, formed from one or more parishes or portions of parishes, may have one or more churches, and one church is designated as a rectorial church.[22] Grouped parishes are those in which each parish in the group retains a separate entity, with the normal structure, but the parishes will share an incumbent.[23] A united parish consists of two or more parishes with a single incumbent, one Vestry Meeting and one Parochial Church Council.[24] A conventional district is an area placed under the care of a

---

[15] PA, 1, p. 8.
[16] Const. VI.1.
[17] Const. II.59, 60.
[18] For the purposes of Const. VI, dealing with parochial administration, the archbishop of Wales is to be regarded as the bishop of the see over which he presides without prejudice to his rights as archbishop (Const. VI.32).
[19] Const. IV.34–38; see above, Ch. 3.
[20] Const. IV.40.
[21] Const. IV.42: the standing committee of the Diocesan Conference must co-operate with the bishop in the creation of conventional districts; the standing committee must report annually to the Diocesan Conference and the Governing Body what conventional districts, if any, have been created.
[22] PA, 1, pp. 6, 7.
[23] PA, 1, p. 7.
[24] PA, 1, p. 6; one or more churches may be declared to be parish churches in 'the United Benefice'.

cleric-in-charge, licensed by the bishop, effected as a result of agreement between the bishop and the incumbent(s) of the parish(es) in which the district is situated. This arrangement requires renewal with every change of incumbency in the parish(es). Conventional districts are normally formed in anticipation of their subsequently becoming new parishes. However, in a conventional district, the parishioners remain parishioners of the original parish(es).[25] A parish may also be annexed to a cathedral.[26]

The Electoral Roll

In every parish in the Church in Wales, of whatever type, there must be an electoral roll.[27] The purpose of the roll is 'the determination of eligibility to exercise voting rights' in the church,[28] and to qualify parishioners to hold office in the Church in Wales.[29] In other words, entry of a person's name on the electoral roll generates an entitlement to participate in the governance of the church, by means of membership of its various assemblies. In other Anglican churches, the register of members is known variously as the electoral roll,[30] the parish roll or register,[31] or the roll of the congregation;[32] some churches have a communicants' roll,[33] and in others there is a roll of regular attendants at public worship.[34] The laws of most Anglican churches contain elaborate provisions dealing with admission, revision, removal, renewal and availability of such rolls, and with disputes arising with respect to these matters. So too the Church in Wales.

Admission   The law of the Church in Wales confers rights of admission to the electoral roll on specified classes of the laity. A lay person who is over sixteen years of age is entitled to have their name entered on the roll if four conditions are satisfied. First, the person must be both a communicant,[35] and someone who is not a member of any religious body which is not in communion with the Church in Wales. This latter requirement may be

---

[25] PA (1992 edn, 1995 reprint), 1.06.
[26] PA, 1, p. 7; for the concept of annexation, see Const. VI.15(2), 31; VII.5. For cathedrals, see below, Ch. 7.
[27] Const. VI.2(1).
[28] Const. VI.2(2); 2(3): the electoral roll must be put on display at every Vestry Meeting: see below.
[29] PA, 1, p. 9.
[30] England, Church Representation Rules, Pt. I.
[31] ECUSA, Cans. I.1.17.
[32] Scotland, Can. 41.1.
[33] Philippines, Cans. II.2.5.
[34] New Zealand, Cans. B.V.4.2.
[35] That is, 'a person who has lawfully received Holy Communion in the Church in Wales or some Church in communion therewith and is entitled to receive Holy Communion in the Church in Wales' (Const. I.6(b)); for excommunication, see below, Ch. 10.

relaxed through the written dispensation of the diocesan bishop.[36] Secondly, the person must be resident in the parish, or, if not so resident, the person must have habitually attended public worship in that parish during a period of six months prior to enrolment.[37] Thirdly, the person must have signed a form of application for enrolment.[38] Finally, the person must not have their name entered on the roll of another parish in Wales, save with the consent of the Parochial Church Councils of both parishes.[39] Admission to the electoral roll renders the individual a qualified elector in the Church in Wales.[40]

Revision   The Parochial Church Council is responsible for the management of the roll, and quasi-legislation recommends the establishment in the parish of a small Electoral Roll Committee or an Electoral Roll Officer to carry out revisions, and to report to the Parochial Church Council on its conclusions.[41] The electoral roll must be revised annually and renewed every five years.[42] According to the constitution, therefore, the maintenance of the electoral roll is under the direction of the Parochial Church Council, and it must be revised prior to each Annual Vestry Meeting. A copy of the roll, and notice of the intended revision of the roll, must be displayed near the principal door of the parish church for at least fourteen days before the commencement of the annual revision. The annual revision of the roll must be completed not less than fifteen days before the Annual Vestry Meeting. In parishes with more than one church, a copy of the roll, and of the notice, must be displayed at each church.[43]

Removal   The Parochial Church Council must remove the names of persons from the electoral roll in prescribed circumstances. The name must be removed if that person has died, or becomes a clerk in holy orders, or signifies in writing the desire that their name should be removed. It must also be removed if the person becomes, without the written permission of the diocesan bishop, a member of any religious body which is not in communion with the Church in Wales. The same applies if the person is a member of a religious body not in communion with the Church in Wales, having been admitted to the roll with the written dispensation of the diocesan bishop, and that dispensation has been withdrawn. The name

---

[36] Const. VI.2(4)(a)(i) and (ii).
[37] Const. VI.2(4)(b).
[38] Const. VI.2(4)(c).
[39] Const. VI.2(4)(d).
[40] Const. VI.1(c): a 'qualified elector' means a person whose name is entered on the electoral roll of a parish.
[41] PA, 1, p. 11.
[42] PA, 1, pp. 11, 12.
[43] Const. VI.2(5); PA, 1, p. 11 recommends display for at least 15 days prior to the Annual Vestry Meeting.

must be removed if the person ceases to reside in the parish, unless after ceasing to reside the person continues habitually to attend public worship in that parish. It must also be removed if the person is not resident in the parish and, unless prevented from doing so by illness or other sufficient cause, has not attended public worship in that parish during the previous six months. If at any time after the entry of their name on the roll, the person has their name entered on the roll of another parish, the original entry must be removed: this will not occur, however, if the Councils of both parishes consent. Finally, the name must be removed if the person was not entitled to have their name entered on the roll originally.[44]

Renewal   The rules governing preparation of a new electoral roll are as follows. By operation of the law of the church, the electoral roll lapsed immediately before the Annual Vestry Meeting in 1980, and the roll continues to lapse in every fifth year after that date, at which point a new roll must be prepared. Notice of the intention to prepare a new roll must be displayed near the principal door of every church in the parish for at least fifteen days before the commencement of the preparation of the new roll.[45] The new roll must be prepared under the direction of the Parochial Church Council. All persons wishing to have their names included on the roll must make an application to do so. A fresh application is required from those whose names appeared on the previous roll.[46] A copy of the new roll must be displayed near the principal door of the parish church for at least fifteen days before the Annual Vestry Meeting. The new roll comes into force at the commencement of that Annual Vestry Meeting. In parishes with more than one church a copy of the roll must be displayed at each church.[47] Any person may apply to the Parochial Church Council for their name to be entered on the electoral roll of the parish, provided that person signs a declaration agreeing 'to accept and be bound by the Constitution of the Church in Wales', and affirming that person's eligibility for admission to the roll.[48]

Availability   The electoral roll, when not otherwise required, must be kept in the safe of the parish church. In a parish with more than one church copies of the roll (or parts of it) may be kept in safe custody by each church.[49] The roll must be produced for inspection by any qualified elector in the vestry of the parish church at any reasonable time. Any dispute

---

[44] Const. VI.2(6).
[45] Const. VI.2(7).
[46] Const. VI.2(8).
[47] Const. VI.2(9).
[48] Const. VI.3; they are also bound by the constitution by virtue of Const. I.2.
[49] Const. VI.9.

arising in this regard must be settled by the archdeacon.[50] Moreover, a copy of the electoral roll must be produced by the incumbent to the bishop or the archdeacon on request.[51] A duty is placed on the archdeacon to take such steps as the archdeacon may think fit, to ensure in any parish due compliance with the relevant provisions of the constitution, described above, dealing with the existence of the roll, eligibility for admission, maintenance of the roll (by way of revision and renewal), removal of names from it, and its display.[52]

Disputes   Finally, the constitution deals with disputes arising from administration of the electoral roll. First, any person whose application, to have their name entered on the electoral roll, has been refused by the Parochial Church Council, or whose name has been expunged from the roll, may appeal in writing to the archdeacon. The archdeacon must then appoint one or more lay communicants as a court to consider and determine the appeal. The court so appointed is entitled to inspect all papers and to be furnished with all relevant information connected with the appeal. The decision of the court is final.[53] Secondly, any qualified elector of a particular parish may lodge with the Parochial Church Council an objection in writing, on grounds of lack of qualification, to the addition of a name or names to the electoral roll. Thirdly, a qualified elector may lodge an objection to the expunging of a name (or names) from the roll. In the latter two cases, the objection must be considered by the Council. Should the Council not allow the objection, the objector may appeal in writing to the archdeacon. The archdeacon must then appoint one or more lay communicants as a court to determine the appeal. The court may inspect all papers, and call for all relevant information, connected with the appeal, and its decision is final.[54] As a matter of principle, these processes should comply with the rules of natural justice,[55] though it is unlikely that judicial review would lie in the courts of the State in the event of their breach.[56]

---

[50] Const. VI.4.
[51] Const. VI.5.
[52] Const. VI.6.
[53] Const. VI.7.
[54] Const. VI.8.
[55] *Stuart v Haughley Parochial Church Council* [1936] Ch 32 (CA): this case involved an appeal against the decision of an electoral commission in the Church of England; the appeal, to reinstate a name on the electoral roll, was dismissed as it was held that the commission had not acted contrary to natural justice.
[56] *R v Imam of Bury Park Jame Masjid, ex p Sulaiman Ali* [1994] COD 142 (CA): the imam's decision that the applicants were not eligible to vote in the election of the executive committee of a mosque was held not to be subject to judicial review, as it lacked the requisite public element and involved matters intimate to a religious community.

THE ANNUAL VESTRY MEETING

Historically, as the parishioners originally met in the church vestry to transact the business of the parish, the word 'vestry' came to be applied both to the body of parishioners and to the meeting itself.[57] The Annual Vestry Meeting of parishioners is intended to deal with a wide range of matters above and beyond the basic administrative and financial affairs of the parish.[58] It is an institution commonly employed by other Anglican churches, particularly for the election of officers to the assembly of the most localized unit of the church.[59] The constitution of the Church in Wales deals with the composition and functions, powers and duties, of the Annual Vestry Meeting.

Meetings and Composition

In every parish there must be held, not later than 30 April in each year, the Annual Vestry Meeting for the whole parish.[60] Further Vestry Meetings may be called at any time, and, in particular, a further Vestry Meeting must be called at the request in writing of at least one-quarter or thirty of the qualified electors of that parish.[61] In parishes with more than one church, a Congregational Meeting may be held prior to any parish Vestry Meeting. Qualified electors, who belong to the church in question, and other prescribed classes of person, may attend the meeting.[62] Every Vestry Meeting must be called by the incumbent, or in his or her absence or incapacity by the churchwardens. It must be called by notice signed by the incumbent or churchwardens (as the case may be), setting out the agenda, and stating the place, day and hour of the meeting. The notice must be displayed near the principal door of the church or churches in the parish, and of every other building in the parish used for public worship and belonging to the Church in Wales. It must be so displayed for a period including the two Sundays immediately preceding the day of the meeting. Oral notice of the meeting must also be given at the principal services in the parish during such period.[63]

The incumbent, or in a vacancy or suspended incumbency the cleric-in-charge, where appointed, must take the chair at a Vestry Meeting, unless he

---

[57] *Wilson v McMath* (1819) 3 Phillim 67 at 82; in some parishes the powers of the general vestry were exercised by a select vestry existing by immemorial custom, by a local Act of Parliament or by adoption of the Vestries Act 1831.
[58] PA, 1, p. 15.
[59] It is used by Anglican churches in Papua New Guinea, Melanesia, Japan, Southern Africa, Ireland and England; see generally CLAC, 66.
[60] Const. VI.10(1).
[61] Const. VI.10(2).
[62] Const. VI.10(3); these persons are listed in VI.13(1)(a)–(f), for which see below.
[63] Const. VI.11.

or she wishes otherwise; in a rectorial benefice, a vicar designated by the rector may take the chair. In a vacancy or suspended incumbency, where no cleric-in-charge has been appointed, the chairman must be the area dean or the nominee of the area dean; in a vacancy in a rectorial benefice, the chairman must be a vicar of that benefice designated by the area dean. Where the office of area dean is vacant, the chairman must be the archdeacon or the nominee of the archdeacon. In any other circumstances, the chairman must be chosen by the meeting itself. The chairman has a second or casting vote. However, when the chairman is a cleric, this rule must not apply to the election of lay persons at the meeting.[64]

Seven classes of persons have the right to attend, speak and vote at Vestry Meetings: the incumbent; vicars in a rectorial benefice; assistant curates; deaconesses; full-time stipendiary lay workers; any other clerics with a licence or permission to officiate, who are resident in the parish and not beneficed in or licensed to any other parish; and qualified electors of that parish.[65] People falling outside these seven classes may join in the meeting only with special permission. First, with the approval of the Parochial Church Council, residents in the parish who are either communicants but not qualified electors of that parish, or are communicant members of churches in covenant with the Church in Wales, may attend and speak, but not vote.[66] Secondly, at the discretion of the chairman, other persons may attend, but neither speak nor vote.[67] In the case of a dispute as to the right of a person to attend, speak or vote at a Vestry Meeting, the chairman's ruling on the matter is, for that meeting, conclusive. However, any such person has the right to appeal to the area dean, provided always that where the incumbent is the area dean the appeal lies to the archdeacon.[68]

Functions

The functions of the Annual Vestry Meeting relate to three matters: the parish report;[69] other reports; and elections. First, the Annual Vestry Meeting must receive and discuss: a report and accounts for the previous year from the Parochial Church Council made in accordance with the

---

[64] Const. VI.12.
[65] Const. VI.13(1).
[66] Const. VI.13(2).
[67] Const. VI.13(3).
[68] Const. VI.14.
[69] Until recently, the meeting received a report for the previous year from the Parochial Church Council which had to deal with: the mission of the church in the parish, pastoral, evangelistic, social and ecumenical; the state of the electoral roll; all land held on trust for or used by the parish; the state and repair of any buildings in the parish, the contents of such buildings and the parochial insurances.

Church in Wales Accounting Regulations.[70] Secondly, it must receive and discuss reports on the proceedings of the Deanery and Diocesan Conferences each year, any other reports requested by the Council or allowed by the meeting, and, with the consent of the meeting, any other business of which notice has been given.[71] In a parish annexed to a cathedral, the meeting is not permitted to deal with property and accounts relating to the cathedral's Dean and Chapter, except with their consent.[72] It is considered good practice to make written reports widely available before the Annual Vestry Meeting, so that they may be studied by those who attend.[73]

Thirdly, the Annual Vestry Meeting must elect, in this order: a churchwarden; sub-wardens; the parochial church councillors; and the sidesmen, where required. In every third year, the Annual Vestry Meeting must elect the parochial representatives on the Diocesan Patronage Board. Again in every third year, it must elect the lay parochial representatives on the Deanery Conference and an equal number of supplemental lay representatives. Also, where appropriate, the Annual Vestry Meeting must elect the lay parochial representatives on the Diocesan Conference.[74] Needless to say, as an overriding principle, all those elected to hold office must be both communicant members of the church and qualified electors.[75] Furthermore, the Annual Vestry Meeting must, in accordance with the Charities Act 1993 (and with any regulations made under it), appoint an independent examiner or auditor, who must not be a member of the Parochial Church Council of the parish.[76] No person is eligible for election unless their consent to nomination has first been obtained.[77] Moreover, clerics are not permitted to vote in the election of a lay person.[78] It is considered good practice to include provision for early availability of nomination papers, and, at the vestry, for adequate numbers of voting papers; it is also considered good practice that all places are open for re-election, and not just specific vacancies.[79]

As soon as possible after the Vestry Meeting, the secretary (who must be appointed by the Parochial Church Council) must inform the appropriate persons concerning the election: the archdeacon, with the names and addresses of churchwardens; the area dean, concerning those elected to the

---

[70] See below, Ch. 14, n. 38.
[71] Const. VI.15(1).
[72] Const. VI.15(2).
[73] PA, 1, p. 17; reports should include information on meetings of the Governing and Representative Bodies.
[74] Const. VI.16(1); for the functions of, and the procedures to be employed in the appointment of churchwardens, subwardens and sidesmen, see below, Ch. 8.
[75] PA, 1, pp. 18, 19.
[76] Const. VI.16(2); see below, Ch. 14.
[77] Const. VI.16(3).
[78] Const. VI.16(4).
[79] PA, 1, p. 18.

Deanery Conference; the secretary of the Diocesan Conference (where appropriate), concerning those elected to that body; and the secretary of the Parsonage Board, with regard to those elected to that board.[80] Special rules apply if a number of prescribed matters, concerning the Vestry Meeting and its business, are brought to the notice of the bishop of the diocese: these are discussed in the following section, insofar as they may also involve the Parochial Church Council. The constitution sets out detailed provisions for the appointment of churchwardens, and these are described in Chapter 8.

THE PAROCHIAL CHURCH COUNCIL

In the Church in Wales, like the province itself, the diocese, and the deanery, so too is the parish governed by its own representative assembly: the Parochial Church Council. In every parish of the Church in Wales there must be one Parochial Church Council, and it must meet at least four times in every year.[81] The council must also make rules and regulations for its own procedure.[82] The Parochial Church Council is not, under the law of the State, a body corporate with juridic personality;[83] consequently, it has been suggested that its members may be personally liable, for example, for any debt arising under contractual obligations that they have agreed to.[84] Whilst rules, regulating a wide range of activities of the council in the life of the church, are dispersed amongst very many ecclesiastical instruments (and these are dealt with elsewhere in this book), the following sections describe the constitutional provisions relating to the composition and basic functions, rights and duties of the Parochial Church Council. Parish finance is considered in Chapter 14.

---

[80] Const. VI.28; see also PA, 1, p. 19.
[81] Const. VI.22(1).
[82] Const. VI.27(a).
[83] Welsh Church Act 1914, s. 2(1): this dissolved every ecclesiastical corporation aggregate; compare England, in which Parochial Church Councils enjoy corporate legal personality: Parochial Church Council (Powers) Measure 1956, s. 3.
[84] P. Jones, *The Governance of the Church in Wales* (Cardiff, 2000), 408; the author adds, however: 'There is nothing to stop Welsh PCCs from incorporating as limited companies and thus avoiding personal liability for debts' under the Companies Acts of the State. The author cites *Re St Peter, Roydon* [1969] 2 All ER 1233, a case decided by the Chelmsford Consistory Court in the Church of England, in which it was stated that a parish does not exist as a legal entity and can, as such, neither sue nor be sued. For Jones, then: 'The members of a PCC will therefore not escape personal liability for a debt on the ground that they incurred it on behalf of the parish, as officers of the parish.'

Composition and Officers

The membership of the Parochial Church Council consists of three classes: *ex officio*, elected and co-opted members. First, the *ex officio* members of the council are: the incumbent, vicars in a rectorial benefice, assistant curates, deaconesses, full-time stipendiary lay workers, the churchwardens and the sub-wardens. Secondly, the elected members are those lay persons elected by the Annual Vestry Meeting. The number on the council of elected lay persons must from time to time be fixed by the Annual Vestry Meeting; but the number must not exceed twenty-five. Thirdly, its co-opted members are: the secretary and treasurer, if not already *ex officio* or elected members; such number (not exceeding seven in total) of laymen or clerics as the council may determine; and such licensed readers (if any) as the council may determine. A retired cleric is not eligible to be co-opted.[85] The number of clerical members must in no case exceed the number of lay members.[86]

To be eligible for membership of the Parochial Church Council, every lay member must be a qualified elector of that parish, over eighteen years of age.[87] Before assuming office, each lay member of the Parochial Church Council must sign a declaration: that they are a communicant over eighteen years of age; that their name is properly entered on the electoral roll of the parish; that they will faithfully and diligently perform their duties as a parochial church councillor during their year of office; and that they agree to accept and be bound by the constitution of the Church in Wales. A book must be kept for this purpose by the secretary of the council.[88] Whilst elected members hold office for one year, membership of the council will terminate by loss of eligibility for inclusion on the electoral roll, by removal from the roll, and by decision of the disciplinary tribunal and courts of the Church in Wales.[89]

The constitution of the Church in Wales is silent as to the chairing of the meetings of the Parochial Church Council.[90] However, the Parochial Church Council must appoint a secretary of the council and of the Vestry

---

[85] Const. VI.24(1): whilst retired clergy are not eligible for co-option, there is no rule forbidding the council from enjoying a freedom to invite such clergy to be present at its meetings, particularly insofar as council decisions might involve retired clergy (authorized to serve in the parish), in the whole mission of the church, itself a subject which falls within the jurisdiction of the council: see below.

[86] Const. VI.24(2).

[87] Const. VI.25; for the concept of qualified electors, see above.

[88] Const. VI.26; they are also bound by the constitution by virtue of Const. I.2.

[89] See generally above, Ch. 1 and below, Chs. 5 and 8.

[90] See, however, P. Jones, *Governance*, 211: 'The incumbent is normally chairman of the PCC.' Needless to say, the council may provide for chairing, under its duty to make rules and regulations for its own procedure (Const. VI.27(a)). Compare the provision about the incumbent as the usual chair at the Vestry Meeting (Const. VI.12(1)).

Meetings. It is also entitled to appoint a deputy secretary, but in the event of both the secretary and the deputy secretary being absent from a meeting, the meeting itself must appoint someone as secretary of that meeting. The duties of the secretary are as follows: to attend and keep minutes of the meetings of both the council and the Vestry; to send to the archdeacon the names and addresses of the churchwardens; and to send to the area dean the names and addresses of the persons elected to the Deanery Conference. The secretary must send, where appropriate, to the secretary of the Diocesan Conference the names and addresses of the persons elected to the Diocesan Conference. Similarly, the secretary must also send to the secretary of the Diocesan Patronage Board the names and addresses of the persons elected to serve on the Patronage Board.[91] The council must also appoint a treasurer annually, and may appoint deputy treasurers, to administer the finances of the parish.[92]

Special rules apply if a number of prescribed matters are brought to the notice of the bishop of the diocese; namely, when: the Annual Vestry Meeting has not been held; churchwardens and parochial church councillors have not been elected or appointed; the parochial representatives on the Diocesan Conference (where appropriate), the Deanery Conference, or the Diocesan Patronage Board, have not been elected or appointed; or, meetings of the Parochial Church Council have not been held as provided by the constitution. In these circumstances, the bishop may appoint churchwardens, parochial church councillors or parochial representatives as the case may require. The bishop may also summon a meeting of the Parochial Church Council. However, the bishop must report any action taken by him, under these provisions, to the next meeting of the Diocesan Conference.[93]

Furthermore, special rules exist for a parish which is annexed to a cathedral. In this case, the constitutional provisions dealing with elections do not apply to the Vestry of such a parish. Nor do the constitutional provisions concerning the functions of churchwardens extend to any property owned by, or under the control of, the cathedral Dean and Chapter. Also, the secretary of the Parochial Church Council of such a parish is not required to send to the secretary of the Diocesan Parsonage Board details of those elected to serve on that board.[94]

The Basic Functions of the Parochial Church Council

The jurisdiction of the Parochial Church Council, its competence and the limits of its freedom are defined carefully by the constitution, which itself

---

[91] Const. VI.28.
[92] Const. VI.23(2); see also below, Ch. 14.
[93] Const. VI.30.
[94] Const. VI.31.

casts the functions of the council in terms of both rights and duties. These conciliar functions relate to a host of activities central to the life of the church in the parish, ranging from its governance, to its missionary, liturgical and proprietorial life. The council has, in the main, administrative functions, including strategic planning in the parish, though it also has modest rule-making tasks.

Consultation and Co-operation   The work of the Parochial Church Council is subject to two overriding principles, each appearing in quasi-legislation of the Church in Wales: the Parochial Church Council is accountable to the Annual Vestry Meeting;[95] and the affairs of the parish are the joint responsibility of clergy and laity in council, by which clergy are to work in 'consultation and collaboration with the laity'.[96] According to the constitution of the Church in Wales, it is 'the duty of the Incumbent and the Council to consult together and co-operate in all matters of concern and importance to the parish'.[97] This principle is well established in the canon law of the Anglican Communion,[98] and there is persuasive judicial authority that consultation and co-operation must not be a sham.[99]

The generality of these principles of consultation and collaboration is of profound significance for parochial governance. All ministry in the parish, ordained, lay and conciliar, must be characterized by meaningful collaboration. The constitutional imperative that the incumbent and council must consult and co-operate in all matters of concern and importance to the parish has two legal aspects. On the one hand, the principle requires the council to consult and co-operate with the incumbent over the exercise by the council of its functions, powers and duties, and over parish business generally. And, on the other hand, it requires the incumbent to consult and co-operate with the council in the exercise of his or her legal rights and

---

[95] PA, 1, p. 31.

[96] *Cure of Souls*, 4 (hereafter CS); see also PA, 1, p. 31.

[97] Const. VI.22(2).

[98] See e.g. Scotland, Can. 60.1: 'The Vestry shall co-operate with and generally assist the Rector or Priest-in-Charge in all matters relating to the spiritual welfare of the congregation and the mission of the whole Church, subject always to the canonical rights and duties of the clergy'; see also England, Parochial Church Councils (Powers) Measure 1956, s. 2(2); Australia, Diocese of Sydney, *The 7th Handbook*, 7.23.

[99] *Re St Peter, Roydon* [1969] 2 All ER 1233 (the decision of a consistory court of the Church of England); Chancellor Forbes remarked: 'In the true spirit of charity a clash between the incumbent and a council becomes unthinkable', but he emphasized that the requirement for co-operation between them must be genuine and informed, or else it is no more than a 'solemn farce'; he added, concerning the councillors: 'in carrying out any particular duty with which they are entrusted they must pay proper regard to the wishes and suggestions of the minister if the discharge of the duty impinges on church work in respect of which the minister has expressed a wish or suggestion, but having done that they must be free to differ from him if in their view the honest discharge of the particular duty requires them to so do.'

duties in the parish. The principle operates, in other words, in relation to the manner and form in which both the incumbent and the council exercise their functions, rights and duties. The final decision in the exercise of duties and rights, assigned or reserved to either the incumbent or the council, is of course a matter for the incumbent and council respectively.[100]

Council Functions   The functions of the Parochial Church Council may, for the sake of convenience, be understood as falling into five broad categories.[101] First, the council's functions include 'promotion of the whole mission of the Church, pastoral, evangelistic, social and ecumenical, in the parish'.[102] Secondly, its functions include 'consideration and discussion of matters concerning the Church in Wales or otherwise of religious or public interest'. However, 'the discussion of any doctrinal matters by the Council shall not extend to any formulation or declaration of doctrine'.[103] Thirdly, the council is responsible for the executive 'propagation and implementation of any provision made by the Governing Body, the Representative Body, the Diocesan or Deanery Conferences, but without prejudice to the powers of the Council on any particular matter'.[104]

Fourthly, it has three financial tasks, since, with the exception of special trusts (which provide otherwise), and the incumbent's discretionary fund, all parish finance is under the control of the Parochial Church Council.[105] The preparation of the parochial budget is assigned to the council, which must include the various church expenses, the parochial contributions to the diocesan quota and home and overseas missions, and any other branches of church work; preparation of the budget must be effected together with arrangements for raising the moneys required.[106] The council is responsible for effecting an annual review of the expenses for which the clergy should be reimbursed by the parish.[107] Its functions also include the discharge of the duties placed upon it by the Church Fabric Regulations, as well as the production of a report and accounts in accordance with the Charities Act 1993, any regulations made under it, and with the Church in

---

[100] See below, Ch. 7 for the rights and duties of incumbents and other parochial clergy. See also P. Jones, *Governance*, 203: 'The duty on the incumbent to consult the PCC means that, although he is not bound to defer to the PCCs opinions, he is obliged at least to consider them.'

[101] Const. VI.22(3): the constitution provides that the following list is inclusive, rather than exclusive, of the council's functions ('The functions of the Council shall include'); further functions are treated elsewhere in this volume; see also, in this regard, PA, 5.02: 'The Council's responsibilities are clearly not limited by the eight areas referred to' in VI.22(3).

[102] Const. VI.22(3)(a).

[103] Const. VI.22(3)(b); see also Ch. 9.

[104] Const. VI.22(3)(c).

[105] Const. VI.23(1). Parish finance is discussed more fully below, in Ch. 14.

[106] Const. VI.22(3)(d); it may appoint a Finance Committee (VI.27(b)).

[107] Const. VI.22(3)(g).

Wales Accounting Regulations (such report and accounts being signed by the chairman).[108] Finally, the council is charged with giving advice on any matter properly referred to it, and with communication with the Diocesan or Deanery Conferences on such matters as the council deems appropriate.[109]

The Exercise and Control of Council Functions   The exercise by the Parochial Church Council of these basic functions is subject to a number of constitutional provisions cast, once more, in terms of rights and duties. In the exercise of its functions, the council is under a duty to take into consideration any expression of opinion by any properly constituted church meeting.[110] Moreover, as a general principle, the council must be 'the normal channel of communication between the parishioners and the bishop of the diocese'.[111] Whilst spiritual care and public worship are primarily the responsibility of ordained and lay ministers in the parish,[112] and matters involving ornaments in churches are subject principally to the faculty jurisdiction,[113] the council is specifically entitled to process issues conerning these matters: it has 'the right to make representations to the Bishop concerning the affairs of the Church and the cure of souls in the parish, alterations in services, and ornaments'.[114] It has been suggested that this means that one of the council's functions is 'to scrutinize the ministry of the incumbent and assistant clergy within the parish, on behalf of the other parishioners'.[115]

The constitution and principles deduced from pre-1920 ecclesiastical law provide special mechanisms for the resolution of disputes relating to matters falling within the jurisdiction and competence of the Parochial Church Council. Such disputes may be dealt with not only by designated ecclesiastical persons, such as the archdeacon and bishop, but also by the courts of the church.[116] For instance, the Diocesan Court, presided over by the chancellor, has jurisdiction to hear and determine complaints against churchwardens and lay parochial church councillors, disputes concerning

---

[108] Const. VI.22(3)(h); see below, Part V.
[109] Const. VI.22(3)(e) and (f).
[110] Const. VI.22(4).
[111] Const. VI.22(5).
[112] See below, Part IV.
[113] See below, Part V.
[114] Const. VI.22(5).
[115] P. Jones, *Governance*, 211; however, the 'incumbent's chairmanship of the parochial church council ... and the *ex officio* membership of the PCC of all parish clergy arguably reduces the PCCs effectiveness as an instrument of scrutiny of the ministry of the clergy.' For related issues, see also below, Ch. 7, particularly for visitation as a vehicle for scrutiny.
[116] See below, Chs. 5 and 7.

their election, and any dispute between a member of the Church in Wales and the Vestry or Parochial Church Council, or between these bodies.[117]

To carry out its functions, the Parochial Church Council enjoys modest rule-making power. Subject to the provisions of the constitution, the council is under a duty to make rules and regulations for its own procedure.[118] The council has a right to appoint committees (including a Finance Committee) as necessary from amongst the members of the council, and it may make rules and regulations governing the powers and procedure of any such committee (including powers of co-option). However, all acts and decisions of any committee, unless previously authorized, must be ratified by the council.[119] When the council makes rules and regulations on any of these matters, they must be consistent with the terms of the constitution. Moreover, the Diocesan Conference is empowered to challenge and to overturn council rules and regulations: it may control, alter, repeal, or supersede any regulations made by the Parochial Church Council (and by the Annual Vestry Meeting) if this is necessary to provide against the admission of any principle inexpedient for the common interest of the church in the diocese; the Diocesan Conference is the final judge in this regard.[120]

Miscellaneous Matters   The functions of the Parochial Church Council include a number of specific administrative responsibilities, of which the following are examples. It must furnish the Annual Vestry Meeting with the parish and other reports.[121] If there is any vacancy among those chosen by the Annual Vestry Meeting for membership of the Deanery Conference, the vacancy must be filled by the Parochial Church Council of the parish in question at a meeting held within three months of the vacancy arising.[122] It has a right to be consulted on suspension of the incumbency.[123] The consent of the council is required for the establishment of a Local Ecumenical Project affecting the parish.[124] Under the data protection legislation of the State,[125] the council may be registered as an organization collecting, processing and using personal data.[126] The council is to receive the quinquennial report resulting from inspection of churches in the parish.[127] Amongst its many functions exercisable with regard to church

---

[117] Const. XI.6.
[118] Const. VI.27(a).
[119] Const. VI.27(b).
[120] Const. IV.43.
[121] Const. VI.15.
[122] Const. V.7.
[123] Const. VII.6; see below, Ch. 7.
[124] Can. 26–9–91, 1(c).
[125] Data Protection Act 1998, s. 2; see below, Ch. 8.
[126] See below, Ch. 8.
[127] Const. IV.17(d); see also below, Part V.

property, the council is responsible to the Representative Body for the proper care, maintenance and upkeep of all churchyards in the parish.[128] Moreover, the constitution provides that the conservation of churchyards is a concern and duty of the council.[129]

Local Church Assemblies in Other Anglican Churches

The Church in Wales shares the parochial system, and the principle of conciliar government within the parish, with many other Anglican churches. Usually, in common with the Church in Wales, these subjects are governed by national, regional or provincial canon law, though in some churches (particularly in Africa) by diocesan legislation.[130] Each local ecclesiastical unit,[131] has its own assembly representative of clergy and laity in that unit, styled the council, vestry or committee, composed of clergy and lay officers as *ex officio* members, and elected lay members for whom the core qualification is adult communicant membership of the church; sometimes, an added qualification for membership is evidence of regular contributions to the funds of the church.[132] The meetings of the assembly are under the presidency of the minister-in-charge,[133] and elaborate rules govern notice of meetings, quorum and decision-making, normally by a simple majority of members present.[134] Sometimes the minister has a casting vote.[135]

There is a high degree of legal consistency throughout the Anglican Communion as to the functions of these assemblies. First, the spiritual functions of the assembly are, as in the Church in Wales, to promote the whole mission of the church, pastoral, evangelistic, social and

---

[128] Regulations for the Administration of Churchyards, rr.1, 2. It would seem, however, that as a general principle the council is not bound to perform this duty if it has no funds for this purpose: *Northwaite v Bennett* (1834) 2 Cr & M 316 at 317; *Millar and Simes v Palmer and Killby* (1837) 1 Curt 540 at 554, 555.

[129] Regulations for the Administration of Churchyards, r.2; see below, Part V.

[130] See e.g. Central Africa, Can. 19: with respect to vestries and church councils: 'Dioceses shall legislate for their own needs'; West Africa, Diocese of Gambia and Guinea, Const. (1982), Art. 15(1): 'A parish is an area of [an] organised congregation or group of congregations' and 'shall be in the charge of a clergyman in priest's orders who shall be called a priest-in-charge'.

[131] See above, for the types of unit.

[132] See e.g. ECUSA, Cans. I.14: the number, mode of selection and term of office of members of the vestry is determined by State law or by diocesan law; Diocese of Western New York, Cans. 13: members must be at least 21, baptized, regular attendants at worship and contributors to the parish's expenses; New Zealand, Cans. B.V.3.1.1: the Vestry consists of up to ten parishioners being communicants of eighteen years or more.

[133] See e.g. Philippines, Cans. I.6.3.

[134] See e.g. Papua New Guinea, Can. No. 5 of 1977, 25–9: it must meet at least every two months; seven days' notice is required and the quorum is 20.

[135] Ireland, Const. III.20.

ecumenical.[136] In some churches, however, unlike the Church in Wales, the assembly has a special and explicit constitutional responsibility towards the Christian education of children in the local community.[137] A duty which commonly appears in church law is for the assembly to provide those items necessary for church services, and the assembly often has rights to be involved directly in the choice of services for public worship.[138] Secondly, the governmental functions of local assemblies include: submission of reports to the diocesan assembly or its standing committee, and of data on baptisms, confirmations, marriages, burials and numbers of church members;[139] the election of individuals to superior ecclesiastical assemblies;[140] the appointment of various officers in the parish, such as the treasurer;[141] and the implementation of matters referred to it by the diocesan bishop.[142] Thirdly, the assembly is responsible for the administration and maintenance of church property, the provision and preservation of ecclesiastical registers and records,[143] and for finance in the parish, including the expenses of clergy.[144]

THE CONGREGATIONAL MEETING AND CHURCH COMMITTEE

In the institutional organization of the Church in Wales, the principles of subsidiarity and representative government are taken by the constitution to the level, within a parish, of a particular church and its worshipping community. In parishes with more than one church a Congregational Meeting may be held prior to any parochial Vestry Meeting, ordinary or extraordinary. The congregational meeting must be 'open to qualified electors who normally attend the church in question'. It must also be open to the incumbent, vicars in a rectorial benefice, assistant curates, deaconesses, full-time stipendiary lay workers, and any other clerics licensed or permitted to officiate who are resident in the parish and not beneficed in or licensed to any other parish. Other qualified electors of the parish have no right to attend the congregational meeting.[145] In parishes

---

[136] See e.g. North India, Const. II.V; Brazil, Cans. I.11.
[137] See e.g. Korea, Const. Art. 92.6.
[138] See e.g. England, Can. B3; Ireland, Const. III.24.
[139] See e.g. ECUSA, Cans. I.6.1.
[140] See e.g. Korea, Const. Art. 92.5.
[141] See e.g. Ireland, Const. III.21.
[142] See e.g. Southern Africa, Can. 28.4(f).
[143] See e.g. Scotland, Can. 60.3.
[144] See e.g. Australia, Diocese of Sydney, *The 7th Handbook*, 7.23.
[145] Const. VI.10(3): this entitles to attend only those listed in VI.13(1)(a)–(f); qualified electors of the parish are listed as (g), and, therefore, have no right to attend the congregational meeting. Qualified electors are those on the electoral roll.

with more than one church, two qualified electors of that parish may be designated as sub-wardens for the church which they normally attend. One of these must be elected by the Annual Vestry Meeting after nomination by the congregational meeting, and the other must be appointed by the incumbent.[146]

In parishes with more than one church, the congregational meeting of a particular church is empowered to elect a Church Committee. The sub-wardens for that particular church, and any other members of the Parochial Church Council who normally attend that church, must be *ex officio* members of the Church Committee. The Church Committee has constitutional authority 'to deal with matters concerning that particular church'. The committee must be responsible to the Parochial Church Council,[147] and, presumably, it must comply with the lawful decisions of a Parochial Church Council, provided the council has authority to act. Moreover, the general principle of collaboration applies also to Church Committees: 'clergy will consult and co-operate with the other members and officers of the Church',[148] which would include the members and officers of the Church Committee, concerning the whole mission – liturgical, pastoral, evangelistic, social, and ecumenical – and governance of a particular church. There being no rule against it, it would seem that the Church Committee enjoys a legal freedom to frame its own constitution for the mission and governance of that particular church, provided that constitution is consistent with the law of the Church in Wales.[149]

Indeed, whilst the constitution of the Church in Wales does not elaborate the functions of the church committee beyond these provisions, it is understood that such committees improve the efficient running of a parish, though 'it must always be remembered that they cannot replace the authority vested in either the Parochial Church Council or the incumbent and churchwardens'.[150]

[146] Const. VI.20.
[147] Const. VI.29.
[148] CS, 5.
[149] Such constitutions are employed, e.g., in Scotland, Cans. 36 and 37.
[150] PA, 1, p. 34.

5

THE DISCIPLINARY TRIBUNAL AND COURTS OF THE CHURCH

The diversity of judicial bodies in the Church in Wales is a result not only of the wide range of matters which may be the subject of judicial determination, but also of hierarchical court structures existing prior to disestablishment. There are five categories of judicial body in the church, and they deal with discipline, disputes and property matters.[1] At the lowest level, the Archdeacon's Court handles, in the main, disputes relating to parochial elections. The Diocesan Courts deal primarily with property matters under their faculty jurisdiction, but also enjoy disciplinary powers over lay officers. The Disciplinary Tribunal exercises jurisdiction over both clergy and lay discipline. The Provincial Court entertains appeals from the Diocesan Courts and the Disciplinary Tribunal, and has an original jurisdiction over certain disputes. The Special Provincial Court treats cases concerning the discipline of bishops. The Supreme Court is the final court of appeal in the church.[2] Under civil law, which enables the church to establish a court system, their jurisdiction is consensual rather than coercive.[3] In addition to the courts and tribunal, the law of the church assigns extensive quasi-judicial functions:[4]

---

[1] Their subject-matter jurisdiction and hierarchical ordering are not dissimilar to arrangements in most Anglican churches: see N. Doe, *Canon Law in the Anglican Communion* (Oxford, 1998), Ch. 3.

[2] Const. XI.1(1); see also Const. XI.1(2)(a) and (b): for the purposes of the courts and disciplinary tribunal, 'a member of the Church in Wales is a person on whom the Constitution is binding' by virtue of Const. I.2; and a person is legally qualified if he or she has been a member of the Bar of England and Wales or a Solicitor of the Supreme Court of England and Wales.

[3] Welsh Church Act 1914, s. 3(3): the constitution of the Church in Wales may provide for 'the establishment for the Church in Wales of ecclesiastical courts . . . but no such courts shall exercise any coercive jurisdiction and no appeal shall lie from any such court to His Majesty in Council'.

[4] A quasi-judicial power is one designed to resolve, in a more informal manner, a particular dispute; it involves the authority in question ascertaining the facts at issue, interpreting provisions relevant or applicable to the dispute, and the resolution of the dispute by means of recourse to legal instruments: for the use of quasi-judicial powers in the Church of England, see e.g. N. Doe, *The Legal Framework of the Church of England* (Oxford, 1996), Ch. 5.

for example, to the archdeacon,[5] the bishop,[6] the archbishop,[7] the Provincial Synod of Bishops,[8] and arbitrators;[9] these are considered, where appropriate, elsewhere in this volume.[10] Members of the Church in Wales are under a duty to attend and give evidence at any trial or investigation held under the authority of the constitution,[11] and the Rule Committee is responsible for making rules regulating the administration of justice in the tribunal and courts of the church.[12]

THE ARCHDEACON'S COURT

In each archdeaconry there must be an Archdeacon's Court. It is presided over by the archdeacon or, where the constitution so permits, by one or more lay communicants of the Church in Wales appointed by the archdeacon. Unless the constitution provides otherwise, the Archdeacon's Court exercises the jurisdiction and powers to which an archdeacon was entitled on the date of disestablishment, according to the law and practice at that time prevailing. It also has such additional jurisdiction and powers as are expressly conferred upon it by the constitution.[13]

---

[5]   For Const. XI.17(3), and quasi-judicial aspects of the archdeacon's visitatorial jurisdiction, see below, Ch. 7.

[6]   See e.g. BCP (1984), vi: disputes concerning the provisions of the BCP must be referred to the bishop 'for his determination of the matter'; for Const. XI.16(2) (concerning dispensations) and XI.17(2) (concerning episcopal visitations) and the quasi-judicial nature of these, see below, Ch. 6.

[7]   See e.g. BCP (1984), vi: the bishop may refer any question of interpretation of the BCP to the archbishop; see also e.g. Const. II.50: any question relating to standing orders of the Governing Body, or to the conduct of its business, must be decided by a majority of the Governing Body; the chairman (who may be the archbishop), decides whether any particular questions falls within this rule; for Const. XI.16(1), (concerning dispensation), and XI.17(1), (concerning archiepiscopal visitations), and the quasi-judicial aspects of these, see below, Ch. 6.

[8]   See e.g. Const. IV.33: if the diocesan bishop withholds his consent to a resolution of the Diocesan Conference which, at its next annual meeting, overrides this in a vote by orders, the resolution must be referred to the Provincial Synod, the decision of which binds the Conference and the members of the church in the diocese.

[9]   See e.g. Const. X.22ff.; see below, Ch. 13.

[10]   For criticisms of the existing court system, and for proposals for reform, see T. G. Watkin, 'Welsh church courts and the rule of law', 5 ELJ (2000), 460.

[11]   Const. XI.39: witnesses must solemnly declare to speak the truth; wilful neglect or refusal to attend and give evidence, when duly summoned to do so, may result in the court or tribunal declaring vacant any office held by that person, who may also be deprived or suspended from the right to vote in the church.

[12]   Const. XI.41; see also XI.42: all fees payable in respect of cases heard by any court or the tribunal must be paid to and collected by its Registrar, who must account for the fee quarterly to the Representative Body.

[13]   Const. XI.2. For a proposal to give this court a 'higher profile', see Watkin, 'Welsh church courts', at 461.

The principal jurisdiction of the Archdeacon's Court is to hear and determine appeals arising from disputes concerning the electoral roll.[14] Any person whose application for inclusion on the roll has been refused by the Parochial Church Council, or whose name has been expunged from the roll by the council, may appeal in writing to the archdeacon. The archdeacon must then appoint one or more lay communicants to form the court to consider and determine the appeal. The court is entitled to inspect all papers and to be furnished with all relevant information. Its decision is final.[15] Similarly, a qualified elector may appeal to the court against the council's decision to disallow objections to the inclusion or exclusion of names on the electoral roll.[16] In such cases, the appellants must apply to the archdeacon's registrar for directions. The registrar must direct what steps are to be taken, and in particular what parties are to be served with a Notice of Appeal and what security (if any) must be given by the appellant for the costs of the appeal.[17] The Archdeacon's Court should comply with the principles of natural justice,[18] though there is authority for the proposition that election disputes within a voluntary religious organization are a matter of private law and, as such, public law judicial review does not lie.[19]

The archdeacon must, as occasion requires, appoint the Diocesan Registrar as registrar of the archdeaconry and of the Archdeacon's Court. Where on 20 September 2001, there is a registrar of the Archdeacon's Court who is not the Diocesan Registrar that registrar, not having previously resigned or been removed from office, must retire at seventy.[20] Also, if appointed after 20 September 2001, the Archdeacon's Registrar, not having previously resigned or been removed from office, must retire at the age of seventy.[21] A registrar, holding office on 20 September 2001 (not being the Diocesan Registrar) is entitled to a salary fixed and paid by the Representative Body, and cannot be removed from office except by order of the archdeacon.[22] There is a right of appeal, against the order of the archdeacon, to the Provincial Court. The right of appeal must be exercised

---

[14] See above, Ch. 4.

[15] Const. VI.7.

[16] Const. VI.8; the provisions of VI.7 also apply to this process.

[17] Rules of the Diocesan Court (hereafter RODC), Rules of the Archdeacon's Court, rr.1 and 2.

[18] *Stuart v Haughley Parochial Church Council* [1936] Ch 32 (CA): clear evidence of a breach of the principles of natural justice is needed before a State court may entertain intervention.

[19] *R v Imam of Bury Park Jame Masjid, ex parte Sulaiman Ali* (1994) COD 142: an imam's decision that persons were not eligible to vote at an election of the executive committee of a mosque was held not to be subject to judicial review.

[20] Const. XI.3(1) and (2).

[21] Const. XI.3(3).

[22] Const. XI.3(4).

within a period of six weeks after receipt by the registrar of notice of the making of the order of the archdeacon.[23]

THE DIOCESAN COURT

Until disestablishment in 1920, the court of the diocese was the Consistory Court, an ancient institution exercising jurisdiction over both clergy discipline and the property of the church.[24] At disestablishment, this was replaced in the Church in Wales by the Diocesan Court, the main function of which is to deal with matters relating to church property, by means of its faculty jurisdiction. The Diocesan Court also exercises a limited jurisdiction over suits concerning the discipline of lay officers, and disputes between members of the Church in Wales and prescribed authorities within it.[25]

Composition: Chancellors and Registrars

In each diocese there must be a Diocesan Court presided over by the chancellor.[26] The diocesan bishop must appoint a fit and proper person to be chancellor of the diocese; the person to be appointed must be a communicant, over the age of thirty years, legally qualified, and qualified to be a member of the Governing Body of the Church in Wales.[27] The diocesan bishop must also appoint a fit and proper person to be registrar of the diocese and of the Diocesan Court. The person so appointed must be, similarly, a communicant, over thirty years of age, legally qualified, and qualified to be a member of the Governing Body of the Church in Wales.[28] Moreover, the diocesan bishop has a discretion to appoint a fit and proper person to act as deputy chancellor or deputy registrar. These have all the powers and may perform all the duties of the chancellor or registrar for whom the deputy is appointed to act. Persons are eligible for appointment as deputy chancellor and deputy registrar provided they are communicants

---

[23] Const. XI.3(4). Until 20 September 2001, prior to the promulgation of a new canon, the office of Archdeacon's Registrar had been a separate office; the archdeacon had also been able to appoint a deputy registrar.

[24] See generally, R. Phillimore, *Ecclesiastical Law* (2nd edn, London, 1895), I, 912–33.

[25] At the time of writing, the Rules of the Diocesan Court (RODC) are being revised; references in this book are to the draft rules, to be finalized by the Rule Committee later in 2002. I understand it is unlikely that the draft rules will be altered before their final approval.

[26] Const. XI.6.

[27] Const. XI.8: the appointment must be made 'from time to time and as occasion may require'.

[28] Const. XI.9: the appointment must be made 'from time to time and as occasion may require'.

over the age of thirty, legally qualified and qualified to be members of the Governing Body.[29]

Every chancellor and deputy chancellor, unless they have previously resigned or been removed from office, must retire at seventy, but the bishop in his absolute discretion may postpone the retirement date for not more that two consecutive periods of twelve months. They may not be removed from office except by order of the bishop, confirmed by the Provincial Court.[30] Every diocesan registrar and deputy registrar, not having previously resigned or been removed from office, must (if holding office on 17 April 1980) retire at seventy-five; if appointed to office after that date, they must retire at seventy. They may not be removed from office except by order of the bishop, and they have a right of appeal to the Provincial Court within six weeks of receiving notice of the making of the order.[31] All the powers and duties of a chancellor or a registrar, as set out in their deed of appointment, continue to be exercisable regardless of whether there is a vacancy in the see.[32] Whereas the offices of chancellor and deputy chancellor are honorary, the registrar is entitled to a salary, to be fixed and paid by the Representative Body. The diocesan bishop, on the appointment of a deputy registrar, may indicate in writing to the Representative Body what proportion, if any, of the salary of the registrar is to be paid to the deputy. The Representative Body is then obliged to pay the registrar and the deputy in accordance with the proportion indicated by the bishop.[33] Before entering office, all four officials must make and sign a declaration, in the presence of the bishop.[34]

Jurisdiction over Complaints and Disputes: Suits

The Diocesan Court has jurisdiction over three classes of suit. First, it may hear and determine complaints against churchwardens and lay parochial church councillors, and disputes with regard to their election.[35] Secondly, it is to deal with all matters referred to it by the constitution:[36] for instance, the chancellor may hear appeals as to membership of the Diocesan Confer-

---

[29] Const. XI.10.
[30] Const. XI.11(1) and (3)(s. 11(1) comes into force on 20 September 2006). It has been suggested that '[t]his effectively preserves [chancellors'], independence from episcopal influence whilst preserving their accountability to their bishop': T. G. Watkin, 'Welsh church courts', at 461.
[31] Const. XI.11(2) and (4).
[32] Const. XI.11(5): there is no need for a further deed of appointment during a vacancy.
[33] Const. XI.12. For fees, see XI.14.
[34] Const. XI.13: that they are communicants, over thirty, legally qualified, qualified to be members of the Governing Body, and that they do not belong to a religious body not in communion with the Church in Wales.
[35] Const. XI.6(b).
[36] Const. XI.6(c).

ence.[37] Similarly, concerning arbitrations resulting from parsonage inspection reports, any person dissatisfied with the award of an arbitrator in respect of costs may appeal to the chancellor, whose decision is final.[38] Thirdly, the Diocesan Court may hear and determine any dispute between a member of the Church in Wales and a Diocesan Board of Finance, Diocesan Parsonage Board, Diocesan Board of Patronage, Deanery Conference or Chapter, Vestry or Parochial Church Council, or between any such bodies, the determination of which is not otherwise provided for by the constitution.[39] The diocesan chancellor also has jurisdiction with respect to marriage licences and the appointment of surrogates.[40] In the exercise of its jurisdiction, the Diocesan Court is not bound by any decision of the English courts in relation to matters of faith, discipline or ceremonial.[41]

The procedure applicable to suits deals, amongst other things, with: pleadings; documents; the hearing; witnesses; costs; and court practice.[42] Suits must be commenced by the petitioner lodging with the diocesan registrar a Statement of Claim, and such security for costs and expenses as may be determined by the diocesan chancellor.[43] The registrar must then serve on the parties a notice requiring their attendance at a fixed date in the Diocesan Court,[44] and at the same time must serve on the respondent a copy of the Statement of Claim. In turn, the respondents must lodge with the registrar an Answer to the Statement, and send a copy to the petitioner.[45] The petitioner and respondent must state their contentions in the Statement of Claim and the Answer, and no further pleadings may be allowed except by leave of the chancellor. On the application of any party, and after giving the other party opportunity to be heard, the chancellor

---

[37] Const. IV.10: the list of conference members, compiled by the conference secretary and signed by the bishop, is subject to an appeal to the diocesan chancellor; see above, Ch. 3.

[38] Const. X.25; see below, Part V.

[39] Const. XI.6(a).

[40] Const. XI.15; see below, Ch. 11.

[41] Const. XI.47.

[42] See Diocesan Court Suit Rules, draft RODC, Pt. II, r.1. The court must give effect to all rules and regulations made by or under the authority of the Diocesan Conference so far as these are not inconsistent with the Constitution of the Church in Wales. Save as otherwise provided by the RODC, the practice and procedure in the Registry must be in accordance with that obtaining at the date of the passing of the Welsh Church Act 1914.

[43] Draft RODC, Pt. II, r.2; the chancellor must fix the nature and amount of security within seven days of the registrar receiving the Statement of Claim; the registrar must notify the petitioner accordingly; if the petitioner does not give the required security within fourteen days of notification, the suit must not proceed. The Statement of Claim must follow Form 1 in the Schedule to Pt. II.

[44] The date must not be earlier than six weeks nor later than six months from the date of the Statement of Claim. The notice must follow Form 2 in the Schedule to RODC, Pt. II.

[45] The respondent must do so within fourteen days of being served with the Statement of Claim. The Answer must follow Form 3.

may strike out or amend a Statement of Claim or Answer as scandalous, or as tending to prejudice, embarrass or delay the fair trial of the cause. Any party may withdraw the suit or answer.[46]

Unless otherwise ordered by the chancellor, all contentious proceedings must be heard in open court. Each party may appear in person or be represented by a cleric, solicitor or counsel, or by such persons as the court permits.[47] The chancellor may postpone or adjourn a case or motion at any stage of the proceedings. Each party must submit a list of witnesses, whom the party desires to call at the hearing, to the registrar who must send the list to the chancellor. The registrar must then issue a summons to those named on the list to attend the hearing.[48] On the application of any party, the chancellor may allow evidence of any witness to be taken by deposition before an examiner.[49] If judgment is not delivered in open court, the registrar must send a copy of it to the parties concerned.[50] As an alternative to a hearing in open court, the parties may agree to set out the issue in the form of a Special Case, and may require the judgment of the chancellor on it without further proceedings.[51] All costs are in the discretion of the chancellor.[52] After giving opportunity to the parties to be heard, the chancellor may enlarge the prescribed times governing the proceedings.[53]

The Faculty Jurisdiction: Scope

The Diocesan Court is empowered to hear and determine all applications for faculties in the diocese.[54] In so doing the court is not bound by any

---

[46] The leave of the chancellor must be obtained, and withdrawal takes place on such terms as to costs as the chancellor determines. Notice of Withdrawal must follow Form 4 or 5 in the Schedule.

[47] On the application of a party (not less than fourteen days before the hearing), the registrar may order any party to make a list of documents material to the proceedings, and to produce these for inspection and copying at a time or place fixed by the registrar.

[48] This must be done at least fourteen days before the hearing; the list must include the names and addresses of the witnesses. The witnesses are to bring with them any books and documents in their possession or power relating to the cause. The summons must follow as far as possible Form 6.

[49] This is the case provided the chancellor is satisfied that there is reasonable ground for non-attendance; the depositions may be given in evidence at the trial.

[50] This must be done within three days of the registrar's receipt of the judgment.

[51] The Special Case must be signed by the parties, their counsel or solicitors.

[52] The chancellor may make the necessary orders or directions. All money lodged with the registrar must be paid into a bank account called the Diocesan Fees Fund, standing in the joint names of the registrar and the chairman of the Diocesan Board of Finance.

[53] The registrar must provide all books, documents and other necessaries at the cost of the Representative Body, and is not obliged to receive or deliver any document which is not in accordance with these rules or hear any application without prior payment of the appropriate fee. The registrar has custody of all documents, and must keep the records of the court in a minute book.

[54] Const. XI.6(a). See above, n. 25, for the draft faculty rules.

decision of the English courts in matters of faith, discipline or ceremonial,[55] though as a matter of practice, chancellors do have recourse to these from time to time.[56] The faculty jurisdiction represents, in practical terms, by far the greatest volume of the business of the court, and functions as an integral part of the ecclesiastical exemption operative under the law of the State.[57] A faculty is a special licence, privilege or dispensation authorizing something which otherwise could not lawfully be done; its grant is a matter of discretion for the Diocesan Court.[58] The faculty jurisdiction and procedure of the Diocesan Court covers both consecrated and unconsecrated property. First, it extends to consecrated churches and consecrated land vested in the Representative Body, in a Diocesan Board of Finance or in any other trustees who agree to be bound by the church's faculty rules.[59] Secondly, it extends to unconsecrated churches, churchyards and burial grounds, if: (1) they are listed under the appropriate State legislation as being of special architectural or historic interest;[60] or (2) they are situated in a conservation area; or (3) the diocesan bishop so decrees in writing,[61] a decree which the bishop may at any time revoke (by further written decree).[62] Cathedrals too will come within the faculty jurisdiction.[63] The grant or refusal of a faculty must be evidenced in writing signed by the diocesan chancellor (or deputy chancellor).[64]

Where faculty procedure applies, a faculty is required for the following: (1) any change of use of a church or land;[65] (2) any alteration, addition or

---

[55] Const. XI.47.

[56] See e.g. the decision of the St Asaph Diocesan Court in *Re All Saints, Gresford* (2000): the chancellor relied on the decision of the Court of Arches in *Re St Mary the Virgin, Sherbourne* [1996] 3 WLR 435.

[57] See below, Ch. 13.

[58] For pre-1920 sources conveying these ideas, and the idea that the exercise of the discretion is governed by distinct legal principles, see Halsbury, *Ecclesiastical Law* (4th edn, London, 1975), paras. 1273, n. 6, 1306, 1310. For adoption of the idea that the grant of a faculty is discretionary, see the decision of the Bangor Diocesan Court in *Roberts v PCC of Criccieth with Treflys* (1997): 'The fact that a Faculty has been granted in one case does not mean that it will be granted in another case, and the problem of how to differentiate between cases is the Chancellor's problem, and not anybody else's.'

[59] Const. XI.7(1)(a); Draft RODC, Pt. I, r.1(1)(a): the interest may be 'a freehold or lesser estate'; see also r.35: Part I of these, the Rules of the Diocesan Court, may be cited as the Faculty Procedure Rules. See above, n. 25.

[60] That is, the Planning (Listed Buildings and Conservation Areas) Act 1990.

[61] Const. XI.7(1)(b); Draft RODC, Pt. I, r.1(1)(b).

[62] Const. XI.7(2); the decree must be lodged in the diocesan registry, with a copy sent by the registrar to the Representative Body and to the secretary of the Parochial Church Council concerned (XI.7(3)); Draft RODC, Pt. I, r.1(2).

[63] This will require alteration of Const. XI.7(1)(b), which currently excludes cathedrals from the faculty jurisdiction; see Draft RODC, Pt. I, r.2.

[64] Const. XI.7(6).

[65] Const. XI.7(4)(a): this does not apply to a church or land used by another denomina-

repair to, decoration, redecoration or demolition of or removal from the fabric of a church or land;[66] (3) the introduction, removal, or alteration or repositioning of furniture, fittings, murals, monuments (including gravestones), plate and other precious objects, into, from or in, a church or land; (4) the repair of furniture, fittings, murals or objects (other than in the case of a loan to a museum or similar institution);[67] (5) the acquisition of a permanent or exclusive right of burial in any grave, grave space, vault or tomb; and (6) the removal of a corpse, or human or cremated remains, from an existing grave, vault or tomb.[68]

However, faculty procedure does not apply to cases (1), (2), (3) and (4) where approval has been granted for these matters under the Regulations for the Administration of Churchyards.[69] Nor does it apply when any work is urgently necessary in the interest of safety or health, or for the preservation of a building. Authorization for such work, without faculty, is limited to the minimum measures reasonably necessary to effect it. In this case, written notice must be given as soon as reasonably practicable to the following, provided any of them is not a party promoting the work: the Representative Body; the incumbent or cleric-in-charge; the churchwardens; the Parochial Church Council; and the diocesan registrar.[70] Finally, faculty procedure does not apply to such minor matters as the Rule Committee of the courts of the Church in Wales from time to time determines.[71]

Minor matters, which may be processed without a faculty, fall into five broad categories. First, maintenance does not require a faculty, provided this does not include replacements, redecoration or rewiring.[72] The same

---

tion under an agreement pursuant to the Sharing of Church Buildings Act 1969; see also Draft RODC, Pt. I, r.3(a): (building) and r.4(5) (for church sharing).

[66] Draft RODC, Pt. I, Faculty Procedure Rules, r.3(c), proposes adding 'any alteration or addition to land, including the construction of new buildings'.

[67] Draft RODC, Pt. I, 3(d) proposes faculties for 'the repair of any such furniture, fittings, murals, monuments, plate or objects' as well as 'the alteration or addition to an inscription on any monument or gravestone'; for museums, see r.4(6).

[68] Const. XI.7(4)(a)–(e); references in these provisions to a 'church' or 'land' include any part or parts of such church or land and any fixtures in or on them; see also Draft RODC, Pt. I, r.3(g): this adds 'plot'.

[69] Const. XI.7(4)(e)(i). For these Regulations, see below, Part V. See also Draft RODC, Pt. I, r.4(4).

[70] Const. XI.7(4)(e)(ii): the written notice must justify the work in detail; Draft RODC, Pt. I, r.4(1) proposes that the Rule Committee, and in the case of a cathedral, the dean or most senior member of Chapter available, and, in the case of a parish, the archdeacon (or in his absence area dean), or in the case of St Woolos, the dean, must be consulted; r.4(2): this proposes that in the case of cathedrals notice must be given to the Chapter clerk; it also proposes that as soon as reasonably practicable an application for a faculty must be made; r.4(3).

[71] Const. XI.7(4)(e)(iii).

[72] Draft RODC, Pt. I, Third Schedule, 1.

applies to work which[73] keeps the church, its contents and the churchyard clean and tidy, or which keeps electrical or mechanical items in good working order.[74] Secondly, a faculty is not required for the introduction to or movement within a church of two groups of movable items: for the first group, the agreement of the bishop is required;[75] for the second group, no such agreement is required.[76] Thirdly, a faculty is not required for the introduction to, movement within or removal from a church, of a listed group of movable items.[77] Fourthly, no faculty is required for the introduction, movement or removal, for a special occasion or other strictly limited period of time, of seating comprising unfixed pews or chairs.[78] Finally, a faculty is not required for the introduction to, removal from or movement within a churchyard of gravestones[79] and garden seats.[80]

Faculty Applications and Procedure

There are seven matters central to an application for a faculty: the petition; notification of petition; involvement of the Representative Body; citations; notice of opposition; hearings; and grant or refusal of the faculty.[81] The role of the Diocesan Advisory Committee is integral to faculty procedure; for the sake of convenience, the committee is dealt with at the end of this section.

---

[73] That is, work without effecting replacements (other than light bulbs and heating elements), or without involving redecoration or rewiring.

[74] Draft RODC, Pt. I, Third Schedule, 1: electrical and mechanical items include heating and lighting equipment, musical instruments, and bells.

[75] Draft RODC, Pt. I, Third Schedule, 2(a)(i); namely: processional crosses, sanctuary lamps and sanctuary bells, votive lamps, candlestands, statues, statuettes, icons, thuribles, incense boats, pyxes, tabernacles and monstrances.

[76] Draft RODC, Pt. I, Third Schedule, 2(a)(ii); namely: communion plate, cruets, wafer boxes, lavabos, aspergilla, ewers, alms dishes, and vases.

[77] Draft RODC, Pt. I, Third Schedule, 2(b); namely: decorative banners used for displays lasting no longer than three months, temporary structures of devotional or educational value (eg Christmas cribs, Easter gardens), altar linen (other than frontals and falls), vestments, albs, surplices, cassocks, choir robes, vergers' robes, bibles, prayer books, hymn books, psalters, musical scores and other printed material used in divine services, books of remembrance, literature approved by the incumbent or cleric-in-charge and churchwardens (in the case of cathedrals the Chapter must approve), fire extinguishers, hymn boards, collection plates, kneelers, hassocks, pew runners and cushions (other than complete or substantially complete sets), registers of births, baptisms, banns, marriages, deaths and burials.

[78] Draft RODC, Pt. I, Third Schedule, 2(c).

[79] Draft RODC, Pt. I, Third Schedule, 2(d): provided the gravestones comply with the Churchyards Regulations 15(1), or 15(2).

[80] Draft RODC, Pt. I, Third Schedule, 2(e): garden seats include any memorial inscription approved by the incumbent or, in the case of a cathedral by the Chapter.

[81] Draft RODC, r.27: procedure for which no provision is made in RODC, Pt. I, must be in accordance with RODC, Pt. II.

The Petition   Any of the following may apply for a faculty: persons wishing to erect, remove or alter monuments (including gravestones), or alter or add any inscription on any monument or gravestone; persons wishing to reserve grave spaces, remove a corpse or human or cremated remains; persons otherwise having an interest to promote; the Representative Body; the Dean and Chapter of a cathedral (or a person applying on their behalf); an incumbent, cleric-in-charge, or, where there is no incumbent or cleric-in-charge, an area dean; the churchwardens; and a member or members of a Parochial Church Council.[82] An application for a faculty must be by petition lodged with the diocesan registrar.[83]

Notice of intention to present a petition, giving reasonable details of the works envisaged, must be put, for a prescribed period,[84] on prominent public display: there are rules relating to cathedrals,[85] and to parishes.[86] In the case of listed buildings, or those in a conservation area, copies of the Notice must be sent, by the secretary of the Diocesan Advisory Committee, to CADW and to the local planning authority.[87] Where the work envisaged would change or affect the character of a building, a copy of the Notice must be published in a local newspaper, and, if the work involves demolition, sent to the national amenities societies,[88] and to the Royal Commission for Ancient and Historic Monuments Wales.[89] Every petition must be lodged with the diocesan registrar, with its relevant sections duly answered and completed,[90] together with prescribed documents.[91]

---

[82] Draft RODC, Pt. I, r.5(a)–(h).

[83] Draft RODC, Pt. I, r.6: the petition must, as far as possible, follow Form 3 in Sched. 1. See also r.34: the diocesan registrar is not obliged to receive or deliver any document which is not in accordance with these Rules, or to hear any application without prior payment of the appropriate fee.

[84] Draft RODC, Pt. I, r.7(1): the display must be for twenty-eight days prior to the presentation of the petition, and on or before the date of display a copy of the Notice must be sent to the Diocesan Registrar; the Notice must follow Form 4 in Sched. 1.

[85] Draft RODC, Pt. I, r.7(1)(a): the display must be in the cathedral concerned and in its vicinity; this includes St Woolos Cathedral.

[86] Draft RODC, r.7(1)(b): the display must be in the parish church and all other churches in the parish, and in the vicinity of each and every such church or churches.

[87] Draft RODC, r.7(2): that is, buildings under the Planning (Listed Buildings and Conservation Areas) Act 1990 of special architectural or historic interest; any other documents lodged by the petitioner with the diocesan registrar must also be sent to them.

[88] These are listed in Draft RODC, Sched. 2, para. 14, namely, any of the following: the Ancient Monuments Society, the Georgian Group, the Society for the Protection of Ancient Buildings, the Victorian Society, the Council for British Archaeology, the 20th Century Society, and any other body as may be designated by the Governing Body.

[89] Draft RODC, r.7(2)(a) and (b); see also r.7(3): in the case of a cathedral, including St Woolos (whether or not the building is within r.7(2)), copies must also be sent by the secretary of the Diocesan Advisory Committee to the Cathedrals and Churches Commission.

[90] Draft RODC, Pt. I, r.8(1).

[91] Draft RODC, Pt. I, r.8(2); namely: (a) a copy, certified by the Chapter clerk, or the

Notification of Faculty Petitions   Within seven days of receiving the petition and the other required documents,[92] and of any relevant representations made by that time in response to the Notice, the diocesan registrar must send copies of these to the Diocesan Advisory Committee and, where appropriate, to the Cathedrals and Churches Commission.[93] Within twenty-eight days of receiving these copies, the committee and commission must submit their advice to the diocesan registrar. The advice must be addressed to the diocesan chancellor as to the artistic, aesthetic or architectural merits of the works proposed in the petition. The archdeacon, in whose archdeaconry the property lies (if he sees fit or if requested by the chancellor before such submission), must add his separate written advice to the chancellor as to the theological merits of the works.[94]

The Representative Body   If the works proposed in the petition involve certain prescribed matters,[95] the diocesan registrar must send to the Representative Body copies of the petition, accompanying documents, and the advices of the Diocesan Advisory Committee and the Cathedrals and Churches Commission.[96] The Representative Body may require a further report, on any matter it wishes to raise on the petition, from the Diocesan Advisory Committee, the Cathedrals and Churches Commission, the archdeacon or other appointee of the bishop.[97] Within fifty-six days of

---

secretary of the Parochial Church Council, to be a true copy, of the resolution which the Chapter or council has adopted after consideration of the objects of the petition; (b) if the petitioners are those listed in r.5(a)–(d), (see above), a written statement signed by the Chapter clerk in the name of the chapter, or by the incumbent, or cleric-in-charge, or area dean and the churchwardens, indicating whether or not they are opposed to the object of the petition; and (c) if the case arises, certification by the Chapter clerk or secretary of the Parochial Church Council of compliance with r.7(1) and (2) (see above).

[92] Namely, those referred to in r.8, for which see above.

[93] Draft RODC, Pt. I, r.9; they must be sent to the commission in any case falling within r.18(a) of the Cathedrals and Churches Commission Rules.

[94] Draft RODC, Pt. I, r.10: if the archdeaconry is vacant, or if the archdeacon is unavailable or incapacitated, and in the case of all petitions relating to any cathedral (including St Woolos), the diocesan bishop must appoint a suitable person to act in place of the archdeacon; the appointment must follow Form 5 in Sched. 1.

[95] Draft RODC, Pt. I, r.11(2)(a)–(h); namely: the demolition of, material alterations or additions to, the fabric of a building; the construction of new buildings; the setting aside of areas for the interment of cremated remains; a proposal within the Regulations Relating to the Removal of Monuments and Gravestones; the disposal of any part of the fabric or contents of a building; works which could affect significantly the insurance of a building; works the execution of which would require the grant of an easement or wayleave; and, any change in use of a building or land.

[96] Draft RODC, Pt. I, r.11(1): this must be done within seven days of receipt of the written advice of the committee and commission, as the case may be, together with that (if furnished) of the archdeacon (or the episcopal appointee under r.10 (see above)).

[97] Draft RODC, Pt. I, r.13: notice must be addressed to the diocesan registrar, and within twenty-eight days of the notice, the committee, the commission and archdeacon

receipt of the copies or the further report, the Representative Body must return the papers to the diocesan registrar, accompanied either by written observations, representations or objections it wishes to raise, or by a written statement that it has none to offer.[98] Within seven days of receiving these from the Representative Body, the diocesan registrar must refer the petition, with accompanying documents and all other relevant papers, to the diocesan chancellor. Otherwise, the registrar must refer these papers to the chancellor within seven days of receiving them from the Diocesan Advisory Committee and the Cathedrals and Churches Commission, where applicable.[99] If the petition relates to a church other than a cathedral, at any time before the grant of a faculty, or the issue of the citation, the diocesan chancellor, the diocesan registrar, or the Diocesan Advisory Committee, may seek the advice of the Cathedrals and Churches Commission on the petition; in this case proceedings must be stayed.[100]

Citations   Within twenty-eight days of receiving the petition, documents and papers, the diocesan chancellor must either grant the faculty, or issue a citation addressed to the petitioner and all other interested persons.[101] The citation must be displayed by the chapter clerk or the churchwardens for fourteen days commencing within three days of receipt of the citation. The citation must be returned to the diocesan registrar within three days after expiry of the display period.[102] Within fourteen days of issuing the citation, the registrar must send a copy of it to any person, body or society who has made representations.[103] At any stage, the diocesan chancellor may order the issue of further citations.[104] When a citation has issued, no faculty can be granted or refused until after the period for lodging Notices of Opposition has expired.[105]

Notice of Opposition   A Notice of Opposition to a faculty must be lodged with the diocesan registrar within twenty-eight days of the date

(or other person appointed by the bishop under r.10) must submit the further report in writing to the registrar who must then send a copy to the Representative Body.

[98] Draft RODC, Pt. I, r.12.

[99] Draft RODC, Pt. I, r.14.

[100] Draft RODC, Pt. I, r.15: that is, the proceedings for citations (i.e. under r.16) must be stayed for no longer than twenty-eight days, during which the advice of the commission must be furnished and, if sought by the registrar or the committee, be made available by them to the chancellor.

[101] Draft RODC, Pt. I, r.16: these include the archdeacon (or episcopal appointee, under r.10) and the Representative Body; the citation must follow Sched. 1, Form 6.

[102] Draft RODC, Pt. I, r.17(1): the location for display is governed by r.7, for which see above; the citation must be endorsed with a certificate of due execution.

[103] Draft RODC, Pt. I, r.17(2): that is, representations in accordance with Sched. 1, Form 4.

[104] Draft RODC, Pt. I, r.18: the procedure in rr.16 and 17 must be followed in so doing.

[105] Draft RODC, Pt. I, r.19.

when the citation (or latest citation) was first displayed.[106] Every notice
must set out the grounds of opposition.[107]

Hearings   If by the relevant date no Notice of Opposition has been
lodged, the diocesan chancellor may grant or refuse the faculty without a
hearing, and must do so within seven days after the period for lodging
notices of opposition has expired. Otherwise, the chancellor must fix a date
for a hearing, not less than twenty-one nor more than forty-two days after
the expiry of the period. The diocesan registrar must inform the petitioner,
opponents and all other interested parties of the date of the hearing.[108]
Should he consider it appropriate, the chancellor may invite the parties to
accept judgment on the basis of written representations, rather than by way
of hearing. If all the parties agree in writing, the diocesan registrar must
require them to submit their representations to him within twenty-one days
of the expiry of the period for lodging notices of opposition.[109] After
receiving representations, the registrar must furnish each party with a copy
of the other party's representations and allow them twenty-one days to
reply in writing.[110] Opponents must lodge with the registrar as security for
costs such sum as the chancellor determines.[111] Neither the archdeacon, the
diocesan bishop, nor the Representative Body is liable in costs.[112] At the
hearing, the chancellor may give leave to be heard to any person, body or
society when, for good cause, they had not previously been a party to the
proceedings.[113]

---

[106] Draft RODC, Pt. I, r.20: the notice of Opposition must follow Sched. 1, Form 7.

[107] Draft RODC, Pt. I, r.21: the notice must be set out in paragraphs, numbered consec-
utively; the notice is deemed to be the answer to the petition. See also r.33: the chancellor
after giving an opportunity to the parties to make representations, may enlarge the time
appointed under the rules for doing any act or taking any proceedings upon such terms
as the circumstances require; any such enlargement may be ordered although the
application is not made until after the expiry of the time appointed.

[108] Draft RODC, Pt. I, r.22.

[109] Draft RODC, Pt. I, r.23(1): the chancellor may do so before fixing the date for a
hearing.

[110] Draft RODC, Pt. I, r.23(2).

[111] Draft RODC, Pt. I, r.24: this must be done within fourteen days of receiving notification of the hearing date, or after submission of written representations (under r.23);
the rule applies to any person, body or society who has given notification of opposition;
the opponents may, alternatively, execute a bond (following Form 8) for the same
purpose and sum, with any sureties required by the chancellor. Failing such lodgement or
bond, the chancellor may grant the faculty disregarding the Notices of Opposition.

[112] Draft RODC, Pt. I, r.25: the same applies to a person appointed by the bishop under
r.10: see above.

[113] Draft RODC, Pt. I, r.26: the leave may be given on such terms as the chancellor
determines.

Grant or Refusal of Faculties   Within twenty-eight days after the hearing,[114] the chancellor must either grant or refuse the faculty; in either case, the chancellor must give reasons for his decision.[115] The grant or refusal must be evidenced in writing.[116] A grant must be implemented within a period of five years from the date of its issue, otherwise the grant lapses.[117] The registrar must send the grant or notice of refusal to the petitioner, with copies to prescribed parties.[118] On completion of the works authorized by a faculty,[119] the petitioner must send to the registrar a certificate of execution, with copies to prescribed bodies,[120] to the effect that the works have been carried out in accordance with the terms of the faculty.[121]

The Diocesan Advisory Committee   In every diocese there must be established a Diocesan Advisory Committee.[122] The committee consists of the archdeacons of the diocese and not less than nine other members; when the subject before the committee relates to a cathedral church or churchyard, the dean must be an additional member of the committee.[123] The nine other members must be: (a) two persons appointed by the Diocesan Conference of the diocese from among its members; (b) not less than seven other persons appointed by the Diocesan Conference of the diocese, of whom one must be an archaeologist appointed after consultation with the Council for British Archaeology, one appointed after consultation with CADW, one appointed after consultation with the relevant associations of local authorities, and one appointed after consultation with the national amenity societies; and (c) such other persons as may be co-opted.[124] The

---

[114] Draft RODC, Pt. I, r.28: or within twenty-eight days of the last day allowed by the registrar for filing replies to any written representations.

[115] Draft RODC, Pt. I, r.28. See also the decision of the St Davids Diocesan Court in *Re St Katherine and St Peter, Milford Haven* (2000), in which the chancellor employed the balance of probabilities as the standard of proof in faculty cases.

[116] Draft RODC, Pt. I, r.29(1): the grant or notice of refusal, which must be signed by the chancellor (or deputy), must follow Sched. 1, Forms 1 and 2.

[117] Draft RODC, Pt. I, r.29(2).

[118] Draft RODC, Pt. I, r.30: namely, the Representative Body, the secretaries of the Diocesan Advisory Committee and the Cathedrals and Churches Commission (if the latter is involved), the Chapter clerk or the secretary of the Parochial Church Council, the archdeacon (or episcopal appointee, under r.10), and all others who may have made material representations.

[119] Draft RODC, Pt. I, r.31: or of such part of the works as, for the time being, has been carried out.

[120] Namely, the Representative Body, and the secretaries of the Diocesan Advisory Committee and the Cathedrals and Churches Commission (if the latter was involved). The certificate must follow Form 9.

[121] Draft RODC, Pt. I, r.31: the certificate must be countersigned by the architect, chartered building surveyor or other professional adviser (if one has been engaged).

[122] Draft RODC, Pt. I, r.32; see also Sched. 2, Pt. I.

[123] Draft RODC, Pt. I, Sched. 2, Pt. I, para. 2.

[124] Draft RODC, Pt. I, Sched. 2, Pt. I, para. 3; para. 11 deals with co-opted members:

chairman must be appointed from among the members by the diocesan bishop after consultation with the Diocesan Conference, the chancellor and the Council for the Care of Churches.[125]

In making its appointments, the Diocesan Conference must ensure that the persons appointed have, between them: knowledge of the history, development and use of church buildings; knowledge of Church in Wales liturgy and worship; expertise in architecture, archaeology, art and history; and experience of the care of historic buildings and their contents.[126] The term of office for all members (other than archdeacons) including subsequent members is six years. All members are eligible for reappointment without limit on the number of terms served.[127] A member of the committee who ceases to hold a necessary qualification ceases to be a member.[128] Where a casual vacancy occurs among the chairman and other non-coopted members, the bishop must appoint a person to fill the vacancy. If the person whose place is to be filled was a member of the committee by virtue of membership of the Diocesan Conference, the person appointed must also be a member of that conference.[129] Any person appointed to fill a casual vacancy holds office only for the unexpired portion of the term of office of the person in whose place he is appointed.[130] The diocesan bishop may appoint suitably qualified persons to act as consultants to the committee if it requests him to do so.[131] The committee secretary is appointed by the Representative Body consulting the diocesan bishop and committee chairman.[132]

The Diocesan Advisory Committee has five functions. First, acting as an advisory body on matters affecting places of worship in the diocese, it must give advice when requested by prescribed persons (see below) on matters relating to: the grant of faculties; the architecture, archaeology, art and history of places of worship; the use, care, planning, design and redundancy of places of worship; the use and care of the contents of such places; and the use and care of churchyards and burial grounds. Secondly, the committee is to review and assess the degree of risk to materials, or loss to archaeological or historic remains or records, arising from proposals

---

with the consent of the diocesan bishop, the committee may co-opt such persons (not exceeding one-third of the total number of other members), as it thinks fit, but co-opted persons cease to be members after six years; for national amenity societies, see above; 'relevant association of local authorities' means any association designated as such by the Governing Body.

[125] Ibid., para. 4.
[126] Ibid., para. 5.
[127] Ibid., para. 6.
[128] Ibid., para. 8.
[129] Ibid., para. 9.
[130] Ibid., para. 10.
[131] Ibid., para. 12.
[132] Ibid., para. 13.

relating to the conservation, repair or alteration of places of worship, churchyards and burial grounds and the contents of such places. Thirdly, the committee is to make recommendations as to the circumstances when the preparation of listed records should be made a condition of a faculty.[133] Fourthly, the committee is to encourage the care and appreciation of places of worship, churchyards and burial grounds, and their contents; for that purpose it is to publicize methods of conservation, repair, construction, adaptation and redevelopment. Finally, it is to perform such other functions as may be assigned to the committee by any resolution of the Governing Body or the Diocesan Conference, or as the committee may be requested to perform by the diocesan bishop or chancellor.[134]

The persons to whom the committee must give advice are: the diocesan bishop; the diocesan chancellor;[135] the archdeacons of the diocese; the Cathedrals and Churches Commission; the cathedral Chapter; the Parochial Church Councils in the diocese; intending petitioners for faculties in the diocese; persons engaged in the planning, design or building of new places of worship in the diocese, not being places within the jurisdiction of the Diocesan Court; such other persons as the committee may consider appropriate; and the Representative Body of the Church in Wales.[136]

THE DISCIPLINARY TRIBUNAL

As a result of recent debate in the Church in Wales,[137] the Disciplinary Tribunal has been established, by canon of the Governing Body,[138] to process complaints against clergy and other members of the church.[139]

---

[133] Namely: records relating to the conservation, repair and alteration of places of worship, churchyards and burial grounds and other material (including inspection reports, inventories, technical information and photographs) relating to the work of the committee.

[134] Ibid., Pt. II., para. 1.

[135] See the decision of the Llandaff Diocesan Court in *Re St Fagan's, Aberdare* (1999): as to whether a faculty should be granted, the chancellor held: 'The ultimate decision . . . is mine and not the Committee's, and so while I must have regard to their advice . . . I am not bound to follow it if I am satisfied there are contrary arguments which outweigh their advice.'

[136] Ibid., para. 2.

[137] The establishment of a new tribunal was recommended by *Cure of Souls* (1996); the tribunal takes over a disciplinary jurisdiction previously vested in the Provincial Court.

[138] Can. 21-9-2000, which effects the necessary amendments and additions to the constitution.

[139] Const. XI.18(1). See also Rules: the tribunal shall hear 'only such complaints . . . as are considered appropriate to be referred to the Tribunal by any Diocesan Bishop' (r. 1); every reference by a bishop must be made in writing to the diocesan registrar (r. 2); every reference must be accompanied by such letters, documents, statements or other material relied on by the bishop making the reference (r. 3).

Composition and Officers

The tribunal is composed of eighteen persons: six members appointed by the Bench of Bishops; six clerical members, one from each diocese, elected by the Order of Clergy of the Diocesean Conference of that diocese; two legally qualified members, being chancellors or persons eligible to be a chancellor, appointed by the Standing Committee of the Governing Body; two members, each being medically qualified or a trained counsellor, appointed by the Standing Committee of the Governing Body; and two lay persons appointed by the Standing Committee of the Governing Body. No member of the tribunal may also be a member of the Provincial Court. Five members of the tribunal form a quorum and their decision or the decision of a majority of them constitutes the decision of the tribunal.[140] The tribunal's Investigatory Committee comprises a minimum of five persons drawn from the membership of the tribunal.[141]

Members of the tribunal hold office for five years and are eligible for reappointment, but their membership ceases when they reach the age of seventy (except for the purposes of completing a hearing in which the member is already engaged).[142] A member may be removed from office only by order of the Bench of Bishops confirmed by separate majorities of the Orders of the Clergy and the Laity of the Governing Body.[143] Any vacancy among the membership must be filled by appointment in the same manner as the original appointment.[144] The tribunal may, if it thinks fit, summon for their assistance one or more persons of skill and experience in a matter to which proceedings relate to act as assessors.[145]

There must be a President of the tribunal appointed by the Standing Committee of the Governing Body from among the legally qualified members of the tribunal.[146] The tribunal must, from time to time as occasion may require, appoint fit and proper persons to be registrar and one or more deputy registrars. These must be over the age of thirty and legally qualified. They must be paid for their services such sums as the Representative Body thinks fit. They are to hold office for five years and are eligible for reappointment, but they must retire from office at the age of seventy-five.[147]

---

[140] Const. XI.19(1)–(3): the quorum must consist of two clerical members and at least one of these must have been drawn from the six (one from each diocese) elected by the Order of Clergy of the Diocesan Conference.

[141] Const. XI.19(4): two of these must be clerical members at least one of whom must have been elected by the Order of Clergy of a Diocesan Conference; Rules, r. 4.

[142] Const. XI.20.

[143] Const. XI.21.

[144] Const. XI.22.

[145] Const. XI.23.

[146] Const. XI.24.

[147] Const. XI.25.

Jurisdiction and Powers

The Disciplinary Tribunal is empowered 'to hear and determine a complaint against any member of the Church in Wales'. Its jurisdiction covers six forms of complaint:[148] teaching, preaching, publishing or professing doctrine or belief incompatible with that of the Church in Wales; neglect of the duties of office, or persistent carelessness or gross inefficiency in the discharge of such duties; conduct giving just cause for scandal or offence; wilful disobedience to or breach of any of the provisions of the constitution; wilful disobedience to or breach of any of the rules and regulations of the Diocesan Conference of the diocese in which such member holds office or resides; and disobedience to any judgment, sentence or order of the archbishop, a diocesan bishop, the tribunal or any court of the Church in Wales.[149] The exercise by the tribunal of its functions is subject to an overriding principle: '[i]n discharging its task of maintaining the highest standards of professional and personal conduct by members of the Church in Wales, the Tribunal shall have as one of its objectives the resolution of conflict, where appropriate through reconciliation.'[150]

The powers of the tribunal include:[151] the making of a judgment, sentence or order of absolute discharge, conditional discharge, rebuke, monition, inhibition, disqualification, deprivation or suspension of preferment, office, membership of a body or right to vote in the Church in Wales, and deposition from holy orders and expulsion from the office of cleric of the Church in Wales.[152] The tribunal also has power to suspend from any

---

[148] Const. XI.18(1)(a)–(f): neglect of duties (XI.18(1)(b)) would include breach of any duty found in pre-1920 ecclesiastical law (which continues to bind the church: see above, Ch. 1). For referral of complaints by the bishop, see above n. 139.

[149] See the decision of the Provincial Court, acting under its former jurisdiction, in *Re Petition Against Revd Clifford Williams* (1997): to determine the meaning of conduct giving just cause for scandal or offence, the court appealed to the Canons Ecclesiastical 1603, Can. 109, holding that such conduct would include adultery, uncleanliness or other wickedness of life. The court also relied on *Bishop of Ely v Close* [1913] P 184: 'all conduct of a dishonest, immoral and disorderly nature, whether or not it constitutes also a temporal offence' was actionable. The Provincial Court held that the judicial task of deciding whether conduct was scandalous or offensive was part theological, and part factual. The course of conduct must be: knowingly entered into; judged, in the eyes of the church, inherently wrong; and bring such discredit on the cleric and the church that a person of reasonably robust persuasion would describe it as scandalous or offensive.

[150] Const. XI.18(2). In *Hewitt* (2002) the tribunal held sexual harassment as actionable.

[151] According to general principles of ecclesiastical law: *rebuke* is a less severe censure; *monition* is a formal written warning, order or injunction; *inhibition* disqualifies a person from exercising certain functions; *suspension* is the temporary taking away of the right to perform acts and functions (usually for a specified period); *deprivation* is a permanent taking away of the right to perform acts and functions of a particular office or appointment. For these in other Anglican churches, see CLAC, 88f.: laws usually define the sanctions.

[152] Const. XI.26; see also XI.36(1): a judgment or order of the tribunal may include an order that a cleric be deposed from holy orders and expelled from the office of cleric in

preferment, office, membership of a body, and the right to vote in the Church in Wales any person against whom a complaint has been made and is under investigation by the tribunal until the hearing and determination of the complaint. The bishop of the diocese of such person may make arrangements for carrying out the duties of that person during such suspension.[153] Also, the diocesan bishop may suspend from office, until the hearing and determination of a case, any person holding office in the diocese against whom a charge is pending.[154]

Procedure

The Rule Committee of the tribunal has power to make and publish rules to carry into effect the provisions of the constitution and to regulate all matters relating to the administration and procedure of the tribunal. The committee consists of two legally qualified members of the tribunal, four other members of the tribunal nominated by a majority of the whole membership of the tribunal, and the President of the Provincial Court. The committee may alter or vary these rules. The Rules may be found in the Appendix on page 355.[155]

THE PROVINCIAL COURT

The Provincial Court acts both as an appellate court and as a first-instance court. Its appellate jurisdiction covers cases coming from the Diocesan Court and the Disciplinary Tribunal, and cases involving patronage. Its original jurisdiction covers disputes between church members and prescribed institutions, and matters referred to it under the constitution.

Composition: Judges and Officers

The Provincial Court consists of four ecclesiastical judges and six lay judges.[156] The judges are appointed by the Bench of Bishops, which must from time to time nominate one of the judges to be President. The ecclesias-

---

the Church in Wales; for deposition and expulsion, see below, Ch. 7; see also XI.36(5): the tribunal may order that a suspended cleric or deaconess shall not reside in the parsonage or retain possession of the glebe lands during suspension, and that they must deliver up all books, keys and other property held by them in virtue of office to such person(s), as the tribunal may appoint.

[153] Const. XI.27. The Investigatory Committee may also suspend: Rules, r. 9.

[154] Const. XI.46: and the bishop may make arrangements for carrying out the duties of that office during the suspension.

[155] Const. XI.28. The Investigatory Committee determines whether there is a case to answer for transmission to the Tribunal (see Rules 17–21).

[156] Const. XI.30(1).

tical judges must be bishops or clerics of not less than fifteen years' standing in holy orders; and the lay judges must be communicants over the age of thirty-five and legally qualified. The judges must be qualified to be members of the Governing Body of the Church in Wales or, which would appear to be a vestige of establishment, of the General Synod of the Church of England. Before entering office, they must make and sign a declaration in the presence of a diocesan bishop.[157]

Each judge holds office for seven years, or until resignation or removal from office, but is eligible for reappointment. No judge may be removed from office except by order of the Bench of Bishops, confirmed by separate majorities of the clerics and laity of the Governing Body. The Bench of Bishops must fill any vacancy in the judgeships of the court by appointing an ecclesiastical or a lay judge, as the case may be, in the same manner and on the same conditions as obtained in the original appointment.[158] A judge is not disqualified or prevented from hearing and determining a case by reason of being a member of a body in the Church in Wales which is a party to the proceedings. However, on the trial of a member of the Church in Wales, the bishop and the chancellor of any diocese in which that member either holds office or resides must not sit.[159] One ecclesiastical and two lay judges form a quorum; their judgment, or that of the majority, represents the judgment of the court.[160]

The Provincial Court must, from time to time as occasion may require, appoint a fit and proper person to be its registrar.[161] In the case of the illness or temporary incapacity of the registrar, the court may appoint a fit and proper person to act as deputy registrar during such illness or incapacity.[162] Both the registrar and deputy registrar must, before entering

---

[157] Const. XI.30(1)–(3): in it clerics declare that they have been ordained for more than fifteen years; lay persons declare that they are communicants over thirty-five years of age and legally qualified; both declare that they are qualified to be a member of the Governing Body or of the General Synod of the Church of England, and that they do not belong to any religious body not in communion with the Church in Wales.

[158] Const. XI.30(4)–(6).

[159] Const. XI.31.

[160] Const. XI.32.

[161] Const. XI.33: the appointee must be a communicant over thirty, legally qualified and qualified to be a member of the Governing Body; the registrar is entitled to a salary (fixed and paid by the Representative Body), is subject to retire at seventy and to any further terms or conditions laid down by the Provincial Court. The registrar may be removed by order of the president, and may appeal to a panel appointed by the Archbishop.

[162] Const. XI.34: the appointee must be a communicant over thirty, legally qualified, and qualified to be a member of the Governing Body; the deputy must retire at seventy-five, and is subject to any further terms and conditions laid down by the court; the deputy has all the powers and must perform all the duties of the registrar for whom they are appointed to act; the deputy must be paid for his or her services such sum as the Representative Body in its uncontrolled discretion thinks fit.

office, make and sign a declaration in the presence of a judge of the Provincial Court.[163]

Jurisdiction and Powers

The Provincial Court has both an appellate and an original jurisdiction. First, it may hear and determine: (1) appeals from a Diocesan Court; (2) appeals with reference to institutions, collations, nominations to cures, incapacity and rights of appointment relating to clerics and deaconesses;[164] and (3) appeals from the Disciplinary Tribunal.[165] Secondly, the court may hear and determine: (1) any dispute between a member of the Church in Wales and the Representative Body; (2) any dispute between a member of the Church in Wales and a Diocesan Conference; and (3) any matter referred or reported to the Provincial Court in accordance with the constitution.[166] The court is not bound by any decision of the English courts in relation to matters of faith, discipline or ceremonial.[167]

The Provincial Court may employ a number of sanctions over both clergy and laity involved in cases falling within its jurisdiction. As a general principle, subject to the provisions of the constitution, the power of the Provincial Court includes that of passing sentence of monition, suspension or expulsion from office in the Church in Wales.[168] A judgment, sentence or order of the Provincial Court may include an order that a cleric be deposed from holy orders and expelled from the office of cleric in the Church in Wales.[169] In the case of a suspended cleric or deaconess, the Provincial Court or the diocesan bishop may order them not to reside in the parsonage, not to retain possession of glebe lands during suspension, and to deliver up all books, keys and other property held by them in virtue of office to such person(s) as the court or bishop appoint to have custody for and on behalf of the Representative Body.[170] Finally, the court may suspend

---

[163] Const. XI.35: that they are communicants over thirty, legally qualified, qualified to be a member of Governing Body, and that they do not belong to any religious body not in communion with the Church in Wales.

[164] For Const. VII.58–60, 68, see below, Ch. 7. For fees, see XI.14.

[165] For the appellate jurisdiction of the Provincial Court, see Const. XI.29(a)–(c).

[166] Const. XI.29(d)–(f); for referrals see e.g. Const. IV.23 and VII.35, 46, 47, for which see below, Ch. 7.

[167] Const. XI.47.

[168] Const. XI.45.

[169] Const. XI.36(1): if such an order is made by the Disciplinary Tribunal and an appeal to the Provincial Court is dismissed, a right of appeal lies to the Provincial Synod: see below, Ch. 7.

[170] Const. XI.36(5); XI.36(6): the court on pronouncing judgment, and the bishop on making an order of deprivation or suspension, must give notice to the following: the secretaries of the Governing Body, the secretary of the Representative Body, the secretary of any body in the Church in Wales of which the party affected is a member, and the secretary of the Parochial Church Council of any parish in which the party either holds

any body of the Church in Wales (except the Governing Body or the Representative Body) for neglecting or refusing to obey any judgment, sentence or order of the archbishop, a diocesan bishop or any court or the tribunal of the Church in Wales. However, no order suspending a Diocesan Conference is valid without the consent of the diocesan bishop.[171]

Procedure

The procedure of the Provincial Court, to be followed in the exercise of its appellate and original jurisdiction, is contained in the rules of the Provincial Court.[172] Any matter for which the rules make no provision is to be referred to the president for determination, by means of application to the registrar.[173] A party making an application to the registrar must deposit such fee as the registrar deems proper.[174] Any time limits fixed by the rules may be enlarged by the registrar,[175] who may also strike out or amend pleadings as scandalous or vexatious, or as tending to prejudice, embarrass or delay the fair trial of the cause.[176] The registrar must make a record of all actions, pleadings, and judgments.[177] On neglect or refusal to obey an order of the registrar, the registrar may dismiss the proceedings or make such other order as he deems just.[178] An appeal lies to the president against any decision of the registrar;[179] the appeal may be opposed,[180] but no party may appear before the president on appeal, except by leave of the president.[181]

---

office or resides. See also XI.37: the bishop may, by writing under his hand, order that any stipend otherwise payable to a suspended cleric or deaconess (or any part of it), be sequestered for such period and subject to such conditions as the bishop thinks fit; the bishop must forward a copy of the order to the secretary of the Representative Body, who must then carry out its terms. See also XI.40.

[171] Const. XI.38.

[172] At the time of writing, these are the subject of review in the church.

[173] ROPC, I.1–6; see also I.2: however, the registrar may may decide interlocutory matters not amounting to an adjudication on the merits of the case, before or subsequent to a hearing.

[174] ROPC, I.7: until the fee is deposited no further steps shall be taken; the registrar may also make any order concerning the costs of an application.

[175] ROPC, I.8.

[176] ROPC, I.9.

[177] ROPC, I.10: the registrar has the custody of all documents in the registry.

[178] ROPC, I.11: the registrar must give every other party notice of such neglect or refusal.

[179] ROPC, I.12: in cases other than relating to the taxation of costs; the appeal must be made within fourteen days of the registrar's decision; the President's determination is final.

[180] ROPC, I.13.

[181] ROPC, I.14; I.15: the President, after considering the Notice and Grounds of Appeal, and the contentions (if any) and reaching a decision, must inform the registrar who, within seven days, must communicate the decision to each party.

Any party to a cause, after receiving notice of trial from the registrar, must lodge with the registrar a list of the names and addresses of the witnesses whom that party desires to call at the hearing.[182] The decision of the court may be founded on written or oral testimony. Wherever in the opinion of the court justice so requires, it may admit as evidence any statement or document which the court considers relevant.[183] The president, on the application of any party, may allow the evidence of any witness to be taken by deposition before an Examiner.[184] Subject to the provisions of the constitution, the awarding of costs and expenses is within the jurisdiction and at the discretion of the court,[185] though there are special provisions for poor persons.[186]

Any party has the right to call witnesses and to appear in person or be represented by a cleric, solicitor or counsel before the Provincial Court and before the registrar.[187] The registrar, after deciding that the pleadings are complete, must inform the president accordingly, who then must fix a time and a place for the hearing. Once notified of this, the registrar, by way of Notice of Trial, must inform the parties of the time and place fixed for the hearing.[188] Hearings must be in open court unless the president directs otherwise.[189] The judgment of the court must be in writing signed by the president.[190]

Special rules apply to the different classes of case falling within the jurisdiction of the Provincial Court. With regard to suits and proceedings, all proceedings must be commenced by the petitioner lodging with the

---

[182] ROPC, I.16: the registrar then issues a summons to such persons to attend at the hearing and to bring with them any books and documents in their possession or power relating to the cause; documents and service are governed by I.18–21.

[183] ROPC, I.22; see also I.23: copies of documents certified by the registrar as true copies must be received in evidence.

[184] ROPC, I.24: provided the president is satisfied that there is reasonable ground for the non-attendance of a witness at the hearing, any depositions may be given in evidence at the trial.

[185] ROPC, I.25; I.26: there can be no hearing until any party who is required to give security for costs or to enter into a bond has complied with this requirement; if a party fails to comply, the cause is dismissed; see also I.27–8, dealing with payment of costs by the Representative Body, and exceptions to this.

[186] ROPC, I.29–31.

[187] ROPC, I.32.

[188] ROPC, I.33: the court may adjourn as it deems fit; if before the date for the hearing a party applies to the registrar for postponement of the hearing, or if the president considers there should be either postponement or adjournment, the president may direct accordingly.

[189] ROPC, I.35.

[190] ROPC, I.36: the registrar must inform the parties of the judgment as soon as may be thereafter, and send them a copy if written; a member of the Church in Wales is entitled to a copy of any judgment on payment of such fees as the Registrar deems proper; but the archbishop, any diocesan bishop and any judge of the Provincial Court may have a copy without payment; judgments must be entered in the Judgment Book of the Church in Wales.

registrar a Statement of Claim,[191] accompanied by the relevant fee.[192] After receiving the Statement of Claim, the registrar must send a copy to the petitioner and the respondent,[193] who, if wishing to defend the case, must lodge an Answer with the registrar.[194] A copy of the Answer must then be sent to the petitioner and respondent.[195] Provision is made for admissions,[196] counterclaims of the respondent,[197] amendments,[198] security for costs,[199] and special cases.[200]

Any person wishing to appeal against the decision of a diocesan chancellor must, within six weeks of such decision, apply to the registrar for directions.[201] An appeal against the decision of a chancellor must be heard in open court, and will not be a rehearing of the evidence unless the court so directs in the light of circumstances then prevailing. Argument will be submitted to the court by the appellant and answered by the respondent.[202]

With regard to proceedings for the removal of incumbents and vicars in a rectorial benefice, any bishop wishing to obtain the opinion of the Provincial Court must submit a Case for the Opinion of the Court to the registrar.[203] The cleric may file an Answer,[204] but if no Answer is sent within the prescribed time, the court may hear the case in the absence of the cleric.[205] The court must sit to consider the case and formulate its opinion;

---

[191] ROPC, II.1; II.3: the Statement of Claim must set out the facts of the petitioner's case, and the petitioner's contentions, referring specifically to any provision of the constitution of the Church in Wales and other instruments upon which the petitioner relies.

[192] ROPC, II.2.

[193] ROPC, II.5.

[194] ROPC, II.6: the Answer must be lodged within fourteen days of receiving the Statement of Claim; II.7 and 8 relate to the form of the Answer.

[195] ROPC, II.10.

[196] ROPC, II.11–12.

[197] ROPC, II.13.

[198] ROPC, II.14–17.

[199] ROPC, II.18.

[200] ROPC, 19–25: a special case is one which may be processed when the facts are agreed.

[201] ROPC, IV.1: the registrar must direct what steps are to be taken, and in particular what parties are to be served with Notice of Appeal and what security (if any), is to be given by the appellant as to the costs; the appellant, if dissatisfied with the registrar's directions, may appeal to the president within fourteen days of being informed of such directions, and the decision of the president is final.

[202] ROPC, IV.2.

[203] ROPC, V.1: ie process under Const. VII.46(1)(b) and 47(1)(b); V.2: the Case must contain a short statement of the facts and matters on which the bishop desires the opinion of the court, together with the names and a short summary of the evidence of every witness; a copy of the Case must be served on the incumbent or vicar, accompanied by a Notice requiring them, within fourteen days of service, to submit an Answer.

[204] ROPC, V.3.

[205] ROPC, V.4.

at least ten days' written notice of the date and place of the sitting must be given by the registrar to the bishop and to the incumbent or vicar; if the Answer of the incumbent or vicar consists of a general admission, written notice to that effect must also be given by the registrar to the bishop.[206] The opinion of the court must be in writing, and this constitutes the judgment of the court.[207] Finally, if an appeal to the Supreme Court is allowed, the registrar of the Provincial Court must give all directions necessary as to the procedure to be followed.[208]

THE SPECIAL PROVINCIAL COURT

The Special Provincial Court consists of the archbishop, the remaining diocesan bishops and the judges of the Provincial Court. The archbishop, two diocesan bishops and four judges of the Provincial Court form a quorum.[209] The jurisdiction of the court relates to the disciplining of bishops. First, it has jurisdiction over disciplinary charges involving diocesan bishops.[210] Secondly, the court has jurisdiction over a bishop, concerning the same disciplinary charges, residing in the province and assisting the archbishop or any diocesan bishop.[211] The decision of the court, on the facts of a case, is final. However, a bishop must not be found guilty of any charge unless the archbishop and the majority of the diocesan bishops of the Church in Wales, assembled in the Provincial Synod, are of the opinion that the bishop is guilty of such offence. In this event the archbishop must pronounce sentence.[212] A bishop found guilty by the Special Provincial Court has a right of appeal to the Supreme Court.[213] Subject to the provisions of the constitution, the power of the Special Provincial Court includes that of passing sentence of monition, suspension or expulsion from office in the Church in Wales.[214] In exercising its jurisdiction, the court is not bound by any decision of the English courts in relation to matters of faith, discipline or ceremonial.[215]

---

[206] ROPC, V.5; V.6–7 deal with amendment of the Case and Answer.
[207] ROPC, V.7.
[208] ROPC, I.37.
[209] Const. XI.43(1).
[210] Const. XI.43(1): that is, any charge over which the Disciplinary Tribunal has jurisdiction under Const. XI.18(1), for which, see above.
[211] Const. XI.43(2).
[212] Const. XI.43(3).
[213] Const. XI.43(4); see, however, T. G. Watkin, 'Welsh church courts' at 463: 'Given that the Special Provincial Court's findings of fact are expressly stated to be final and that that court cannot find a bishop guilty of an offence unless the diocesans in Synod are of that opinion, it is not clear what an appeal from the Special Provincial Court as such involves.'
[214] Const. XI.45.
[215] Const. XI.47.

THE SUPREME COURT

The Supreme Court consists of the archbishops of Canterbury, York, Armagh, and Dublin, and the Primus of the Scottish Episcopal Church, sitting with four Assessors nominated by the President of the court. The Assessors, of whom at least two must be lay members of the Special Provincial Court, have no vote. Any of the archbishops or the Primus may nominate a diocesan bishop in communion with the Church in Wales to sit in his place. Four members of the court form a quorum, of whom at least one must be an archbishop or the Primus, and the President of the court must be an archbishop or the Primus.[216]

The Supreme Court has both original and an appellate jurisdiction. First, it carries out the trial of the archbishop.[217] Secondly, the court is responsible for the hearing of appeals from the Special Provincial Court. Thirdly, it hears appeals from the Provincial Court, provided that such appeal is allowed by the Provincial Court.[218] Subject to the provisions of the constitution, the power of the Supreme Court includes that of passing sentence of monition, suspension or expulsion from office in the Church in Wales.[219] In the exercise of its jurisdiction, the Supreme Court is not bound by any decision of the English courts in matters of faith, discipline or ceremonial.[220]

CHURCH COURTS AND THE COURTS OF THE STATE

The Welsh Church Act 1914 confers upon the Church in Wales the right to establish its own ecclesiastical courts, but these are forbidden to exercise coercive jurisdiction.[221] Submission to their jurisdiction is voluntary, and compliance with their decisions is effected by means of declarations made by prescribed ecclesiastical classes.[222] A number of principles of pre-1920 ecclesiastical law, derived from the decisions of the courts of the State, continue to apply to the courts and tribunal of the Church in Wales: they must be satisfied about their competence to determine a matter;[223] they must not exceed their jurisdiction;[224] they must not determine a matter in

---

[216] Const. XI.44(1).
[217] Const. XI.44(1) and (2)(a): that is, for those charges listed in XI.18(1), for which see above.
[218] Const. XI.44(2)(b) and (c).
[219] Const. XI.45.
[220] Const. XI.47.
[221] Welsh Church Act 1914, s. 3(3).
[222] See e.g., for clergy, Const. VII.66: clergy undertake 'to accept, submit to, and carry out any sentence of . . . any Court or the Tribunal of the Church in Wales'.
[223] *R v Twiss* (1869) LR 4 QB 407.
[224] *Blunt v Harwood* (1838) 8 Ad & El 610.

accordance with rules which are contrary to the common law;[225] they must not decline to exercise jurisdiction in a case in which they ought to do so;[226] but there is a presumption that they act within their jurisdiction.[227] In exercising their jurisdiction, however: 'the Courts of the Church in Wales shall not be bound by any decision of the English Courts in relation to matters of faith, discipline or ceremonial.'[228] Whether State courts exercise a supervisory jurisdiction over the tribunal and courts of the Church in Wales depends on the subject in issue.

Disciplinary Cases

The relationship between the courts of the Church in Wales and those of the State, in clergy discipline cases, has been the subject recently of judicial consideration by the High Court, in *R v The Provincial Court of the Church in Wales, ex parte Reverend Clifford Williams* (1998).[229] The case concerned an application for leave for judicial review, a public law process, to quash decisions of the Provincial Court, which found the applicant guilty of clerical indiscipline, recommended deposition, and refused to grant leave to the applicant to appeal to the Supreme Court of the Church in Wales. First, whilst the courts of the established Church of England were 'part of the fabric of the State', and judicial review generally lies in respect of their decisions,[230] the authority of the Church in Wales, as a voluntary association, was based on a consensual submission to its jurisdiction.[231] Consequently, the Provincial Court being a domestic (or private) body, the High Court lacked jurisdiction to review its decisions.[232]

---

[225] *Tey v Cox* (1613) 2 Brownl 35; *Veley v Burder* (1841) 12 Ad & El 265.
[226] *R v Archbishop of Canterbury* (1856) 6 E & B 546; *R v Arches Judge* (1857) 7 E & B 315.
[227] *Mackonochie v Lord Penzance* (1881) 6 App Cas 424 at 446.
[228] Const. XI.47: no definition of 'the English Courts' is given.
[229] (1998) CO/2880/98. At the time of the case, the Provincial Court had original jurisdiction over clergy discipline cases; this jurisdiction has now passed to the Disciplinary Tribunal, to which the High Court's decision would now apply.
[230] See M. Hill, 'Judicial review of ecclesiastical courts', in N. Doe, M. Hill and R. Ombres (eds), *English Canon Law* (Cardiff, 1998), 104.
[231] The Church in Wales was analogous to other non-established religious bodies; and, it was decided, the High Court 'has consistently declined to exercise jurisdiction over such bodies'; the court cited in support *R v Chief Rabbi of the United Hebrew Congregations of Great Britain and the Commonwealth, ex parte Wachmann* [1992] 1 WLR 1306 at 1042: as to whether 'someone is morally or religiously fit to carry out the spiritual and pastoral duties of his office ... [the] court must inevitably be wary of entering into so self-evidently sensitive an area, straying across the well-recognised divide between church and state'.
[232] The High Court did not consider that 'this Court has any jurisdiction to supervise the Provincial Court of the Church in Wales'. In short, unlike the courts of the Church of England, exercising coercive statutory and governmental functions, the Provincial Court

Secondly, it was held that, 'where there is no express provision to the contrary the appropriate standard of proof in domestic proceedings is the civil standard'.[233] Thirdly, whilst State courts may, in an appropriate case, interfere with a perverse sanction imposed by a body, it is likely 'to be very slow to interfere in a case such as this, where the judgment has been made within an area of religious faith and discipline by a body charged with the protection of that faith and ensuring discipline within a religious community'.[234] In short, whilst they are reluctant to intervene in disciplinary decisions of religious tribunals, the State courts will nevertheless do so, even if the tribunal is private or domestic rather than public, in serious cases (such as a breach of the principles of natural justice).[235]

Property Cases and Civil Rights Cases

The domestic law of the Church in Wales which regulates the property of the church is enforceable both in the courts of the church and in the courts of the State.[236] It is a general principle of secular law that for the due disposal and administration of property, the courts of the State will take cognizance of the rules of a voluntary religious organization entered into for the regulation of its own property affairs.[237] The rationale underlying

was a creature of private law – the necessary public element, essential for judicial review, was, therefore, lacking in the jurisdiction of the Provincial Court.

[233] The court adopted this general principle from *R v Hampshire County Council, ex parte Ellerton* [1985] 1 WLR 749 (CA).

[234] The High Court did not consider that the recommendation of the Provincial Court 'can be categorised as perverse or disproportionate'; in any event, the applicant had not exhausted the remedies available to him within the Church in Wales, that is, appeal to the Provincial Synod. The applicant subsequently lost the appeal to the Synod.

[235] See e.g. *R v Lord President of the Privy Council, ex parte Page* [1993] AC 682 (HL): whilst it was recognized that a university visitor had exclusive jurisdiction to determine what were the relevant rules applicable and their proper application, for Lord Browne-Wilkinson this exclusive jurisdiction extended 'so as to prohibit any subsequent review by the court of the correctness of a decision made by the visitor acting *within his jurisdiction and in accordance with the rules of natural justice*'. For persuasive authorities, see e.g. from Ireland, *State (Colquhoun) v D'Arcy* [1936] IR 641: church members 'bind themselves to conform to certain laws and principles, the obligation to such conformity and observances resting wholly in the mutual contract of the members, enforceable only as a matter of contract by the ordinary tribunals of the land when brought within their cognizance and not enforceable under any independent coercive jurisdiction'.

[236] Welsh Church Act 1914, s. 3(2): pre-1920 ecclesiastical law applicable to the Church in Wales 'shall be capable of being enforced in the temporal courts in relation to any property which by virtue of this Act is held on behalf of the said Church or any members thereof, in the same manner and to the same extent as if such property had been expressly assured upon trust to be held on behalf of persons who should be so bound'.

[237] *Forbes v Eden* (1867) LR 1 Sc & Div 568; for the Church in Wales, see e.g. *Powell v Representative Body of the Church in Wales* [1957] 1 All ER 400.

this principle is that 'where property is involved the consensual compact [of a religious organization] is given the same effect, in relation to property matters, as if it were a common law contract.'[238] Consequently, failure by a court of the Church in Wales to comply with the internal rules of the church governing property held on behalf of its members may, as a matter of general principle, be subject to the supervisory jurisdiction of the courts of the State.[239] Finally, the secular courts may upset a decision of a court or tribunal of the Church in Wales when that decision, in applying the internal rules of the church, is in breach of a civil right,[240] that is, rights found in the law of the State, such as rights arising under the principles of natural justice,[241] or rights to marriage and burial.[242]

---

[238] *Scandrett v Dowling* [1992] 27 NSWLR 483 (CA NSW): this applies even 'when spiritual matters become mixed with property matters' as 'an incident of the consensual compact or contract'; see also *Ex p Hay* (1897) 18 LR (NSW), 206; *McQueen v Frackelton* (1909), 8 CLR 673; *AG v Wylde* (1948) 48 SR 366 and *Gent v Robin* (1958) SASR 328.

[239] Indeed, it is arguable that the faculty jurisdiction of the Diocesan Court of the Church in Wales is subject to the supervisory jurisdiction of the secular courts by way of judicial review, insofar as this jurisdiction may be understood as containing a public element, being exercisable, under the ecclesiastical exemption, in place of that enjoyed by the planning authorities of the State. It is certainly a rule of pre-1920 ecclesiastical law that the courts of the State may supervise decisions about church property made under the faculty jurisdiction: see e.g. *R v Tristram* [1898] 2 QB 371; (1899) 80 LT 414; [1902] 1 KB 816.

[240] *Forbes v Eden* (1867) LR 1 Sc & Div 568: 'A Court of Law will not interfere with the rules of a voluntary association unless to protect some civil right or interest which is said to be infringed by their operation.'

[241] See e.g. *R v Lord President of the Privy Council, ex parte Page* [1993] AC 682 (HL): see above. In *R v The Provincial Court of the Church in Wales, ex parte Revd Clifford Williams* (1998) CO/2880/98, it was held that there was no breach of natural justice: the applicant claimed that the bishop acting as prosecutor and sentencer was a breach of natural justice and, as such, in contravention of the ECHR, Art. 6(1); the applicant cited the case of *Findlay v UK* 24 EHRR 221 in which it was held that a Court Martial was not an independent and impartial tribunal, as required by ECHR Art. 6(1); the High Court concluded: 'the applicant, by being ordained in and serving as a Minister of the Church in Wales, consented to the procedures set out in its Constitution, which were followed in this case. He cannot, in those circumstances, have, by reason of the procedures themselves, a legitimate sense of grievance. Further, there is, in my judgment, no real risk of bias. The Constitution makes it clear that the Bishop cannot play any part in the decision as to guilt; and as to sentence, he cannot impose any greater sanctions than those recommended by the Court. The decision of the European Court of Human Rights in *Findlay* is not in point. The jurisdiction of the Provincial Court does not involve the applicant's "civil rights and obligations" under Article 6 of the Convention, which is therefore not relevant to the present case.'

[242] See below, Part IV.

PART III

THE MINISTERS OF THE CHURCH

6

EPISCOPAL MINISTRY: THE OFFICE OF BISHOP

The Church in Wales is committed to the classical Anglican doctrine of the threefold historic and apostolic ministry of bishops, priests and deacons.[1] The office of bishop is central to the government, ministry and law of the Church in Wales. The law of the church contains a complicated set of legal arrangements designed both to facilitate and to order episcopal ministry. Episcopal ministry in the church consists of the ministries of the archbishop, the diocesan bishops and assistant bishops. The archbishop, who has metropolitical jurisdiction in the province, exercises a general episcopal ministry of oversight, particularly in relation to the other bishops. The diocesan bishops are involved directly or indirectly with wide-ranging aspects of ecclesiastical life in the diocese: pastoral, ministerial, doctrinal, liturgical, governmental, ecumenical and proprietorial. The ministry of assistant bishops is very much in the keeping of the diocesan bishop. The main body of the law regulating these ministries deals with the individual episcopal office, appointment to it and its functions, but some law also regulates the bishops acting corporately as the Bench of Bishops and Provincial Synod.

THE ARCHBISHOP

In common with all provincial churches in the Anglican Communion, the principal episcopal office in the Church in Wales is that of archbishop (or metropolitan).[2] A province has been defined as 'the circuit of an archbishop's jurisdiction', and, according to pre-1920 jurisprudence, an archbishop is 'that minister of the Word who within that province . . . has . . . supreme power, authority and jurisdiction in all causes and things

---

[1] See Can. 19-9-96: 'it is the intention of the Church in Wales to continue the ministry of the universal Church in its threefold order of Bishops, Priests and Deacons and to remain part of the One, Holy, Catholic, and Apostolic Church.'
[2] See N. Doe, *Canon Law in the Anglican Communion* (Oxford, 1998), 105.

ecclesiastical'.[3] In the Church in Wales, being a single province of the Anglican Communion: 'the title of the Archbishop of the Church in Wales shall be the *Archbishop of Wales*'.[4] There being no permanent metropolitical see in Wales,[5] the archbishop is also the bishop of the see over which he presides, without prejudice to his rights as archbishop.[6] The appointment of the archbishop is governed by the constitution of the Church in Wales, and archiepiscopal ministry and jurisdiction is governed both by the constitution and by a substantial body of pre-1920 ecclesiastical law.

Appointment

It is a general principle of Anglican canon law that the archbishop is appointed by means of election; sometimes election is by the central assembly of the church but more commonly it is by a special electoral college.[7] So too in the Church in Wales. The office of archbishop must be held by a diocesan bishop of the Church in Wales.[8] The election of the archbishop is carried out by an Archbishop's Electoral College. The college consists of the diocesan bishops,[9] and the first three clerical and the first three lay episcopal electors on the list of episcopal electors of each diocese in the Church in Wales.[10] The senior diocesan bishop is, if willing to act, the President of the college.[11] If any clerical or lay episcopal elector is unable or unwilling to act, that elector's place must be taken by the next member, lay or clerical, on the list of electors for his or her diocese.[12] There are four stages to the election process and appointment to office: summoning the college; the meeting and vote; acceptance by the candidate and the declaration; and enthronement.

First, within thirty days after a vacancy arises in the archbishopric, the

---

[3]   HLE (1910), paras. 719 and 720.

[4]   Const. IX.1; in Scotland, for example, the archbishop is styled 'Primus': Scotland, Can. 3.1: 'The Primus shall have no powers or prerogatives other than those expressly conferred by the Canons.'

[5]   Compare England, Ireland, Australia and Southern Africa: see CLAC, 105, n. 13.

[6]   Const. IV.47; V.20; VI.32; XI.16, 17.

[7]   For election by the central assembly, see e.g. Papua New Guinea, Const. Art. 9; for electoral colleges, see e.g. Melanesia, Const. Art. 8; Tanzania, Const. IV.8. The Church of England, where there is a system of royal appointment, is exceptional: see CLAC, 105f.

[8]   Const. IX.3.

[9]   Const. IX.4. In Chapter IX of the constitution (entitled 'The Election of the Archbishop'), the word 'bishops' means the diocesan bishops of the church (Const. IX.2).

[10]   Const. IX.5.

[11]   Const. IX.6: if the senior diocesan bishop is absent or unwilling to act, the diocesan bishop next in order of precedence, present and willing to act, must act as president; see also Const. II.3: precedence is determined according to the date of the person's first appointment as a diocesan bishop in Wales.

[12]   Const. IX.7.

senior diocesan bishop must summon by letter each member of the college to a meeting to elect a new archbishop. The meeting must be held not less than fourteen days (and not more than thirty days) after the posting of the letter of summons.[13] However, if a vacancy in any see exists or arises on the date on which the archbishopric becomes vacant, or any such vacancy arises within fourteen days after this, proceedings to fill the archbishopric must not be taken[14] until after the enthronement of a new bishop for that see. Once that enthronement takes place, the college is to be summoned in the ordinary way. The date of the latest enthronement is then substituted for the date on which the vacancy in the archbishopric arose.[15] Other than in these circumstances, it is not necessary that before the election of an archbishop takes place every see in Wales must be filled.[16] The college cannot delegate its power of electing an archbishop.[17]

Secondly, on the day and at the time and place appointed for the election,[18] and after celebration of the holy communion, the president must take the chair and declare the college to be assembled for the election of the archbishop. The meeting of the college must be in private.[19] The college must make its own regulations as to the method and manner of voting for, and electing, the archbishop. Any regulations made must be consistent with the constitutional provisions on archiepiscopal elections.[20] The voting must be by ballot,[21] there must be no vote by orders,[22] and the president does not have a second vote.[23] Any dispute as to a vote must be referred to the president, whose decision is final.[24] Failure to summon any member to a meeting, or the absence of any member, does not invalidate the meeting unless more than one diocese is entirely unrepresented at the meeting.[25] The meeting must not extend beyond three consecutive days.[26] If a person

---

[13] Const. IX.8(1): the letter must be sent by recorded delivery.

[14] If proceedings have been taken, they must be annulled.

[15] Const. IX8(2).

[16] Const. IX.8(3): that is, an election may take place when a see is vacated more than fourteen days after the archbishopric becomes vacant.

[17] Const. IX.21.

[18] Unless and until Governing Body determines otherwise, the meeting to elect the archbishop must be held in the Church of the Holy Trinity at Llandrindod; if that church is unavailable, it must be held at some other church selected by the Standing Committee of the Governing Body (Const. IX.9).

[19] Const. IX.10.

[20] Const. IX.11. This subject is currently under review: for this and draft regulations, see Report of the Review of Electoral College Procedure (February 2001), a review conducted for the Bench of Bishops and the Standing Committee of the Governing Body.

[21] Const. IX.12.

[22] Const. IX.13.

[23] Const. IX.14.

[24] Const. IX.15.

[25] Const. IX.16.

[26] Const. IX.17.

receives two-thirds of the votes of those present and voting, the diocesan bishops must declare that person to be archbishop-elect.[27] However, if at the close of the meeting no person has received two-thirds of the votes, the election must pass to the diocesan bishops and the person they elect is declared (by them) to be archbishop-elect.[28] The election also passes to the diocesan bishops if there is no election within three months of the day upon which it was first possible to have elected someone.[29]

Thirdly, the appointment must be accepted by the archbishop-elect. If the archbishop-elect refuses to accept the appointment, or does not within twenty-eight days accept it by writing addressed to the bishops, another election must be held in similar manner. However, for the purpose of this election, the vacancy of the archbishopric is deemed to have taken place on the date of the refusal, or on the twenty-eighth day after the election of the archbishop-elect, whichever happens first. If the archbishop-elect accepts the appointment, the diocesan bishops must declare that person to be archbishop. The diocesan bishops must then send written notification of the election and accession to the secretaries of the Governing Body.[30] At the next meeting of the Governing Body, held after the election and accession, the senior diocesan bishop present and willing to act takes the chair and calls on one of the secretaries to produce and read the document notifying the election and accession of the archbishop.[31] After the documents are read, the archbishop must take the chair and say prayers, including the Lord's Prayer and the Apostles' Creed.[32] At the conclusion of prayers the archbishop must proceed with the business of the Governing Body.[33] Finally, the enthronement of the archbishop must take place within three months of his election, or as soon after as may be, at a place in Wales to be appointed by him.[34]

The Jurisdiction and Functions of the Archbishop

With regard to the general jurisdiction and functions of the archbishop, the law of the Church in Wales is very similar to most provincial churches in the Anglican Communion in which the archbishop has, typically, 'authority, leadership and visitatorial power over the whole province', including presidency of the provincial assembly and its house of bishops.[35]

---

[27] Const. IX.19.
[28] Const. IX.17.
[29] Const. IX.18.
[30] Const. IX.20.
[31] Const. IX.22.
[32] Const. IX.23.
[33] Const. IX.24.
[34] Const. IX.25.
[35] See e.g. West Indies, Const. Art.2.2–3: the archbishop is 'the focus of Provincial

The archbishop of Wales is the metropolitan of the province, exercising metropolitical jurisdiction[36] and takes precedence of all diocesan bishops in the Church in Wales.[37] The functions of the archbishop are scattered throughout the law of the church.

Governing Body The archbishop plays a leading role in the work of the Governing Body, including its legislative processes. The archbishop is the president of the Governing Body, which is convened, summoned and, ordinarily, chaired by him.[38] It is the archbishop, with the advice of the Standing Committee, who decides the order of business at ordinary meetings of the Governing Body.[39] Any question relating to the standing orders of, or the conduct of business at, the Governing Body is decided by a majority of the Governing Body; however, the archbishop, when acting as chair, decides whether any particular question falls within this rule.[40] It is for the archbishop to choose which diocese a member of the Governing Body is to serve when that member has been elected for more than one diocese and the member in question fails to choose which diocese they are to serve.[41] The archbishop is empowered at his own discretion to summon an extraordinary meeting of the Governing Body; he must do so at the written request of any diocesan bishop or of not less than one-third of the clerical and lay members of the Governing Body.[42] The archbishop may also convene and consult the Standing Committee of the Governing Body if and when he thinks fit.[43] Responsibility for the promulgation of canons belongs to the archbishop.[44]

unity' and 'shall exercise Metropolitical authority as determined by the Constitution and Canons'; see generally CLAC, 107.

[36] ACC-4, 1979, Ontario, 6.B: the following is a rare attempt to define metropolitical authority: it is 'the focus of ultimate decision-making in a Province, and the process by which it is exercised'; it relates to the 'general welfare and growth of the whole Church in which it is exercised' to help the church grow within 'the general Anglican ethos'; it is 'expressed through canonical responsibilities laid upon bishops' and is exercised within 'synodical structures, but sometimes may still be exercised individually by the Metropolitan'; metropolitans exercise 'their authority synodically with the clergy and laity for the government and good ordering of the Church'; '[t]he degree to which Metropolitical Authority is exercised individually or corporately in association with the House of Bishops or the Provincial Synod, is determined by the Constitution and Canons of the particular Church'; it includes: the exercise of pastoral oversight, 'ensuring that both the Provincial constitution and canonical development are in accordance with general Anglican tradition and practice, and that the provisions of the Provincial Constitution and canons are adhered to'.

[37] Const. II.3.
[38] Const. II.17, 18, 19; see also II.44.
[39] Const. II.46.
[40] Const. II.50.
[41] Const. II.25.
[42] Const. II.52.
[43] Const. II.64(5).
[44] Const. II.42(2).

Policy and Committees The archbishop is involved in the formulation of church policy, and its implementation, through membership of several key provincial institutions. The archbishop is a member of the Order of Bishops of the Governing Body, the Provincial Synod,[45] the Standing Committee and Business Subcommittee appointed by the Standing Committee of the Governing Body,[46] and the Representative Body.[47] The archbishop is also the chairman of the Council for Mission and Ministry,[48] and acts as president of the Electoral College.[49]

Ministry The archbishop is directly involved in a number of administrative activities, particularly relating to ministry. The archbishop decides the procedure to be adopted by the Provincial Patronage Board,[50] and receives the resignations of diocesan bishops.[51] The archbishop has the right to consent to pluralism,[52] the duty to declare an assistant bishop-designate,[53] the right to collate to a vacant cure during the vacancy of a see,[54] and the right to consecrate bishops.[55] Indeed, the archbishop has, and may use, all the powers of granting licences, dispensations, faculties and other writings which the archbishop of Canterbury enjoyed in Wales at the date of disestablishment.[56]

Metropolitical Oversight and Discipline The archbishop has a number of powers relating to general oversight and discipline. The archbishop may hold archiepiscopal visitations and the law applicable to these is that which prevailed at the date of disestablishment.[57] The archbishop may visit and inspect the bishops and inferior clergy of his province, and, when so doing, it is usual for him to visit first his own cathedral and diocese, then in every other diocese to begin with the cathedral and proceed subsequently as he pleases to the other parts of the diocese.[58] Unless the constitution provides otherwise, the Governing Body must not interfere with the exercise by the

---

[45] Const. II.2.
[46] Const. II.65(3).
[47] Const. III.2(a): see below, Ch. 13 for other archiepiscopal functions related to property.
[48] See Composition of Committees (October 2001), 11 and 16 (hereafter referred to as COFC).
[49] Const. VIII.9.
[50] Const. VII.45.
[51] Const. VIII.28.
[52] Const. VII.37.
[53] Const. VII.73.
[54] Const. VIII.29.
[55] Const. II.33; VII.73.
[56] Const. XI.16(1): this rules applies 'insofar as such powers were lawfully transferable'.
[57] Const. XI.17(1).
[58] HLE (1910), para. 728.

archbishop of the powers and functions inherent to the office of metropol-itan.[59] The archbishop's rights concerning the consecration of a bishop-elect are also protected.[60] The archbishop has an implicit right to obedience to any judgment, sentence or order issued by him,[61] and is a member of the Special Provincial Court.[62] The archbishop is assisted, in the discharge of his functions, by the Archbishop's Registry.[63]

Termination of Archiepiscopal Ministry

In churches of the Anglican Communion, generally, archiepiscopal ministry terminates on death, resignation, completion of the term of office (commonly tenure is for a fixed period), the attainment of a prescribed age, ceasing to be a diocesan bishop, or removal.[64] In the Church in Wales, the law provides for termination on: retirement; resignation; pronouncement of incapacity through infirmity; or removal.

Retirement   The Archbishop of Wales may retire (as diocesan bishop) at any time between the ages of sixty-five and seventy.[65] He may also retire, before reaching the age of sixty-five, on grounds of permanent disability preventing the performance of his duties; permanent disability must be established by medical certificate and other evidence.[66]

Resignation   The archbishop may resign archiepiscopal office by written notice to the senior diocesan bishop – this may be done without the archbishop resigning his see (that is, his position as diocesan bishop).[67] Moreover, the archbishop may resign his see (that is, his position as diocesan bishop), by notice in writing to the next senior Welsh bishop. If this is done, the next senior bishop becomes President of the Electoral College. As President, the senior bishop must instruct the secretaries of the

---

[59] Const. II.32.
[60] Const. II.33(2).
[61] Const. XI.37: the Provincial Court may suspend any body of the church (except the Governing Body and the Representative Body) for neglecting or refusing to obey any judgment, sentence or order of the archbishop.
[62] Const. XI.43(1); see also XI.45: subject to the provisons of the constitution, the powers of the archbishop include that of passing sentence of monition, suspension of or expulsion from office in, the Church in Wales.
[63] See e.g. Const. XI.25; the registry administers the Electoral College and the Provincial Patronage Board (see COFC, 6).
[64] In e.g. South East Asia, Const. Art. 1(b), tenure is for four years and vacancy at fifty-five; in Uganda, Const. Art. 10(b), tenure is for ten years and retirement at sixty-five; see generally CLAC, 106.
[65] Const. XII.2(1). As diocesan bishop, he must retire at seventy.
[66] Const. XII.3: see below, Ch. 14 for pensions.
[67] Const. IX.26.

Governing Body to give notice of the resignation to each diocesan bishop, to the chairman of the Representative Body, and to each episcopal elector.[68]

Infirmity   When it appears to the Bench of Bishops, on such evidence as they deem sufficient, that the archbishop is incapacitated by infirmity, from the due performance of his duties as archbishop, the Bench may report the fact to the Supreme Court. On due inquiry and such evidence as the court deems sufficient, and after giving the archbishop an opportunity of being heard, the court may by judgment pronounce him to be incapacitated. The judgment has the same effect, and the same proceedings must be taken, as if the archbishop had resigned his office on the day the judgment was pronounced. The court must send a minute of the judgment to each diocesan bishop. However, before pronouncing judgment, the court must be satisfied that adequate maintenance has been, or will immediately be, secured for the archbishop by the Representative Body.[69]

Removal   Proceedings may be taken against the archbishop in the Supreme Court for breach of ecclesiastical discipline,[70] and provision for the removal of the archbishop as a diocesan bishop is the same as that applicable to diocesan bishops.[71]

Incapacity or Absence   When the archbishop is incapacitated or absent from the British Isles, the senior diocesan bishop must act as the guardian of the spiritualities of any vacant see in the province. The senior bishop does so if he is willing and able to act, and not himself absent from the British Isles. In these circumstances, the senior bishop must act as guardian as long as the archbishop remains incapacitated or absent from the British Isles. The guardian of spiritualities has and exercises all the other rights of the archbishop. If, during this period, the senior bishop dies or becomes incapable of acting, or is absent from the British Isles for more than three consecutive days, his place must be taken by the diocesan bishop next in order of precedence.[72]

Vacancy   When the office of archbishop falls vacant, the senior diocesan bishop (other than the retiring archbishop) becomes the guardian of the spiritualities of any vacant see in the province. The senior bishop must do so as long as the archbishopric is vacant, and provided the senior bishop is willing and able to act. As guardian of the spiritualities, the senior bishop

[68]   Const. IX.28, VIII.28 and 30. See also VIII.13.
[69]   Const. VIII.32.
[70]   Const. XI.33: see above, Ch. 5.
[71]   Const. VIII.31: see below.
[72]   Const. IX.27(2).

occupies the position of the archbishop, and has and exercises all the other rights of the archbishop. However, if, whilst acting as guardian of the spiritualities during the vacancy, the senior bishop dies, or becomes incapable of acting, or is absent from the British Isles (for more than three consecutive days), his place as guardian of spiritualities must be taken by the diocesan bishop next in order of precedence. This occurs provided the latter is willing to act, is capable of acting, and is not then absent from the British Isles. This arrangement lasts as long as the original bishop remains incapacitated or absent from the British Isles.[73]

DIOCESAN BISHOPS

Admission to the office of diocesan bishop in the Church in Wales is by means of election. The jurisdiction, powers and duties of the diocesan bishop touch on very many aspects of ecclesiastical life: governmental, ministerial, pastoral, liturgical, ecumenical and proprietorial.[74] The bishop is 'the chief minister and pastor' in the diocese,[75] and is commonly known in law as the ordinary.[76] The diocesan bishops are ranked in order of precedence, according to the date of their first appointment as a diocesan bishop in Wales,[77] and each should reside in his diocese.[78] Whilst the constitution seems to be silent on eligibility for episcopal ordination, according to pre-1920 instruments, a person must be thirty years of age.[79] In this respect the law of the Church in Wales is less detailed than that in other Anglican churches in which, typically, the law: prescribes minimum ages (usually from thirty to forty);[80] reserves episcopal ordination expressly

---

[73] Const. IX.27(1).

[74] Some episcopal functions are understood by the church to be inherent to the office of bishop, whilst others are conferred, and their exercise limited, by the law of the church: see below; the notion of inherent jurisdiction does not formally appear in the laws of other Anglican churches.

[75] BCP (1984), 714.

[76] See R. Phillimore, *Ecclesiastical Law* (2nd edn, London, 1895), II, 1420. See also John Godolphin, *Reportorium Canonicum* (3rd edn, London, 1687), 23, 74: 'The Ordinary, according to the acceptation of the Common Law with us, is usually taken for him that hath Ordinary Jurisdiction in Causes Ecclesiastical immediate to the King . . . In the civil law, from which the word is taken, *ordinarius* signifies any judge authorised to take cognisance of causes *proprio suo jure*, and not be way of deputation or delegation.' See also R. Burn, *Ecclesiastical Law* (5th edn, London, 1788), III, 22: the ordinary has the proper and regular jurisdiction. The bishop is not a corporation sole: Welsh Church Act 1914, s. 2(1).

[77] Const. II.3.

[78] *Barton v Wells* (1789) 1 Hag Con 21 at 28 *per* Lord Stowell.

[79] BCP 1662, for which see HLE (1910), para. 754(n).

[80] For thirty as the minimum age see e.g. England, Can. C2(3) and New Zealand, Cans. A.1; for thirty-five as the minimum age, see e.g. Philippines, Const. Art. V.3 and Brazil, Cans. III.16.

to priests who have been in holy orders for a fixed number of years;[81] requires candidates to be of 'competent learning', 'sound mind' and 'good morals'.[82] In several churches medical examination is mandatory to determine not only the physical but also the mental fitness of candidates,[83] and in some churches women are eligible for admission to episcopal orders.[84]

Appointment: Election and Consecration

In common with the vast majority of churches throughout the Anglican Communion,[85] the election of a diocesan bishop of the Church in Wales must be by an Electoral College.[86] The law of the church deals with: episcopal electors; membership of the Electoral College; summoning the college, the meeting and the vote; acceptance by the candidate and confirmation; and consecration (or ordination) and enthronement.[87]

Episcopal Electors   Each Diocesan Conference must, at its first meeting, appoint six clerics, who hold a licence from the bishop to officiate and reside in the diocese, and six lay persons to act as episcopal electors. The clerics are appointed by the clerical members and the laypersons by the lay members of the Diocesan Conference.[88] Also, a supplemental list of nine clerical and nine lay members must be made at the same time, and in a similar manner, from which casual vacancies in the number of episcopal electors are filled.[89] The order in which the names of the persons appointed appear on the lists of episcopal electors, and on the supplemental lists, must

---

[81] See e.g. Papua New Guinea, Const. Art. 14: the candidate, who must be at least thirty, must have been in priestly orders for six years (an archiepiscopal faculty may dispense with this requirement); and North India, Const. II.IV.VIII: experience of ten years as a presbyter is required and the candidate must be at least forty and not more than sixty years of age.

[82] See e.g. Southern Africa, Can. 7.2 and Nigeria, Can. XII.

[83] ECUSA, Cans. III.22.3.

[84] See e.g. Ireland, Const IX.22: 'Men and women alike may be ordained to the holy orders of deacons, of priests and of bishops, without any distinction or discrimination on grounds of sex, and men and women so ordained shall alike be referred to and known as deacons, priests or bishops.'

[85] For Anglican electoral systems and law, see CLAC, 109–13; England, in which episcopal appointment is by the monarch, is exceptional.

[86] Const. VIII.2; VIII.33: on the creation of a new diocese, the Governing Body must make provision as it thinks expedient for the purpose of securing the election of bishops in accordance with the principles of Const. VIII; see also above, Ch. 3. See also the Report of the Review of Electoral College Procedure (February, 2001).

[87] For historical material on this subject, see P. Jones, *The Governance of the Church in Wales* (Cardiff, 2000), 340ff.

[88] Const. VIII.3: it must also do so at each subsequent first meeting of any newly elected conference.

[89] Const. VIII.4.

be determined by a vote taken by ballot at the time of appointment. In the case of an equality of votes, the order must be determined by the diocesan bishop as President of the Conference.[90] If there is a vacancy in the number of episcopal electors, the first name on the supplemental list must be placed at the bottom of the list of episcopal electors, and that person becomes an episcopal elector.[91]

To qualify as an episcopal elector, a person must be under the age of seventy, and either a member of the Governing Body, or qualified to be a member of it.[92] An episcopal elector who at the time of appointment was a cleric, in the full-time stipendiary ministry of the Church in Wales, ceases to be an episcopal elector on ceasing to hold office in the full-time stipendiary ministry of the Church in Wales; but the person is eligible for reappointment as an episcopal elector. A cleric who is appointed an episcopal elector, continues to do so only whilst that cleric both holds a licence from the bishop to officiate and resides in the diocese. A lay person, appointed as an episcopal elector for the diocese of their residence, continues as an episcopal elector only whilst residing in that diocese. However, this rule does not apply to a lay person holding diocesan office, or whose name is on the electoral roll of a parish in the diocese in question.[93]

The Electoral College The Electoral College is composed of three classes: the archbishop and diocesan bishops; the six clerical and six lay episcopal electors from the diocese of which the see is vacant; and the first three clerical and the first three lay episcopal electors on the list of each of the other dioceses. The archbishop, or in his absence the diocesan bishop next in order of precedence and willing to act, is the President of the college.[94] If any elector is unable or unwilling to attend any meeting of the college, their place is taken for that meeting by the next member, lay or clerical, on the lists or supplemental lists.[95] A list of the episcopal electors for each diocese must be sent immediately after their appointment by the secretary of the Diocesan Conference to the archbishop and to each diocesan bishop and to the secretaries of the Governing Body.[96] An episcopal elector may resign from office by notice in writing, addressed to the secretary of their Diocesan Conference.[97]

---

[90] Const. VIII.5.
[91] Const. VIII.6.
[92] Const. VIII.7.
[93] Const. VIII.8.
[94] Const. VIII.9; the VIII.1: 'bishops' in Chapter VIII means the diocesan bishops.
[95] Const. VIII.10.
[96] Const. VIII.11: the secretary must also give a similar notice of any person subsequently becoming an episcopal elector.
[97] Const. VIII.12.

The Election   Where the bishop gives notice of his intention to resign, the President of the college must summon (within seven days of receiving the notice) each member to a meeting to elect a new bishop. The meeting must be held not more than thirty days after the date when the resignation is to take effect. When such a vacancy arises without prior notice given to the President, the President of the Electoral College must summon each member to a meeting to elect a bishop. The meeting must be held not less than fourteen days, nor more than thirty days, after posting the letter of summons.[98] The meeting must take place in the cathedral of the vacant see.[99]

On the day of the meeting, and after celebration of holy communion in the cathedral, the President takes the chair and declares the college to be assembled for the election of the bishop of the diocese. The meeting must be in private.[100] The college must make its own regulations as to the method and manner of voting,[101] but the voting must be by ballot; there must be no vote by Orders; the President does not have a second vote, and any dispute as to a vote must be referred to the President whose decision is final.[102] Failure to summon any member to a meeting, or the absence of any member, does not invalidate any election unless more than one diocese is entirely unrepresented at the meeting.[103]

If at the close of the meeting, which must not extend beyond three consecutive days, no person has received two-thirds of the votes of those present and voting, the right to fill the vacancy passes to the Bench of Bishops.[104] Moreover, if the college does not elect any person as bishop-elect within three months of the vacancy of the see, the vacancy must be filled by the Bench of Bishops.[105] When a person receives two-thirds of the votes of those present and voting that person must be declared by the President to be the bishop-elect.[106] The college is not entitled to delegate its power of electing a bishop.[107]

Acceptance and Confirmation   If the bishop-elect refuses to accept the appointment, or does not do so within twenty-eight days by writing addressed to the President, another election must be held in similar

---

[98] Const. VIII.13: the letters must be sent by recorded delivery.
[99] Const. VIII.14.
[100] Const. VIII.15.
[101] Const. VIII.16: the rules are subject to the provisions in Const. VIII.
[102] Const. VIII.17–20.
[103] Const. VIII.21.
[104] Const. VIII.22: this applies unless and until the Governing Body determines otherwise.
[105] Const. VIII.26: this applies unless and until the Governing Body determines otherwise.
[106] Const. VIII.23.
[107] Const. VIII.27.

manner.[108] When the bishop-elect accepts the appointment, the President must send his name to each member of the Bench of Bishops for confirmation of the election. The bench may refuse to confirm the election on the ground of unfitness of the bishop-elect. Provided the Bench of Bishops, or a majority of them assembled in Synod, are satisfied of his fitness, the President must take the necessary steps to give effect to the election. If the Bench of Bishops or a majority of them are not so satisfied, another election must be held in similar manner.[109]

Consecration and Enthronement The final part of the process is consecration (or ordination), when the person is not already in episcopal orders, and enthronement. At the ordination service: the candidate is presented to the archbishop; the mandate for the consecration is read; the archbishop presents the candidate to the people, reads the charge and administers the examination (during which the candidate makes a number of declarations).[110] Following the prayer of the people, the archbishop and the other bishops lay their right hands on the candidate invoking the Holy Spirit for the office and work of a bishop in the church. The archbishop then presents the Bible to the new bishop, places a ring on the candidate's finger, and presents the pastoral staff.[111] Subsequently, the bishop is enthroned.[112] These arrangements, election, confirmation and consecration, are typical of Anglican churches, though in some, objections prior to confirmation may be made to a special tribunal.[113] A rule appearing in several Anglican churches is that the metropolitan must take order for consecration of a bishop-elect and that consecration may take place by not less than three bishops, of whom the archbishop must be one.[114]

---

[108] Const. VIII.24: however, for the purpose of another election the vacancy of the see is deemed to have taken place on the date of the refusal, or on the twenty-eighth day after the election of such bishop-elect, whichever happens first.

[109] Const. VIII.25: however, for the purpose of another election the vacancy of the see is deemed to have taken place on the date of the Synod at which the Bench of Bishops or a majority of them were not satisfied of the fitness of the bishop-elect.

[110] See below for episcopal functions.

[111] BCP (1984), 710ff., The Ordination of Bishops.

[112] See C. A. H. Green, *The Setting of the Constitution of the Church in Wales* (London, 1937), 33, 35.

[113] See generally CLAC, 109–13; for challenges see e.g. Southern Africa, Can. 7: the Court of Confirmation determines objections based, for example, on procedural defects; lack of canonical age; and lack of competent learning, sound faith, or good morals.

[114] See e.g. West Indies, Can. 8.8; ECUSA, Const. II.2 and BCP (1979): the presiding bishop is 'chief consecrator' with at least two other bishops.

The Functions of a Diocesan Bishop

The Church in Wales, like all Anglican churches,[115] recognizes the centrality of the office of bishop in ecclesiastical life. Its canon law acknowledges that personal, collegial and communal oversight (*episcope*) is embodied and exercised in the church, and that 'the episcopal office is valued and maintained . . . as a visible sign expressing and serving the Church's unity and continuity in apostolic life, mission and ministry'.[116] The church teaches that 'the ministry of a bishop is to be the chief shepherd in the Church; to guard the Faith; to ordain and confirm; and to be the chief minister of the Word and Sacraments in his diocese'.[117] The authority of the bishop may be ordinary,[118] inherent,[119] and conferred by law.[120] The functions of a diocesan bishop, which legal instruments of the Church in Wales define in considerable detail, fall into three broad categories: teaching and pastoral; liturgical and ministerial; and governmental and disciplinary.[121] As an overriding principle, in the exercise of episcopal oversight, the diocesan bishop is bound by the law of the church.[122]

---

[115] Unlike most Anglican churches, however, the Church in Wales possesses no distinct and separate treatment of episcopal responsibilities; for functions of the diocesan bishop in canonical systems of the Communion, see generally CLAC, 113f.; e.g. Papua New Guinea, Const. Art. 14.1: a bishop is 'the servant of Christ and the servant of all', the 'chief shepherd of souls in his diocese and . . . the friend and guide of his clergy and people'; see also Korea, Const. Ch. 3, Art. 12.1: '[t]he duties of the diocesan bishop' include 'the representation and pastoral oversight of the diocese'.

[116] Can. 28–9–1995 (the Porvoo Canon).

[117] BCP (1984), 691 (Catechism).

[118] For ordinary jurisdiction, see above, n. 76. The bishop is not, however, the only ordinary in the diocese: see below, Ch. 7 for the archdeacon and the cathedral dean. In Scottish canon law 'No Bishop of one diocese, except as provided in these Canons, shall interfere with the concerns of another diocese' (Can. 6.4); this is a common provision: see CLAC, 115. For a discussion of the delegation of ordinary authority, see P. Jones, *Governance*, 220.

[119] Const. II.32: subject to the constitution, the Governing Body cannot interfere with the exercise by diocesan bishops of the powers and functions inherent in the episcopal office; see also II.33: the Governing Body may not exercise its powers so as to affect the rights at present existing in a diocesan bishop in respect of institution to any benefice or ecclesiastical office. See also RODC, Sched. of Fees: the Bench of Bishops is to prescribe fees for marriage licences under their 'inherent jurisdiction'.

[120] Commonly the law confers powers and imposes duties on the bishop. Even with regard to functions which are inherent to the episcopal office, the Governing Body may legislate on these, but it cannot interfere with them other than under the constitution, which it may alter; the prohibition against interference by the Governing Body is, after all, 'Subject to the Constitution' (Const. II.32).

[121] For the traditional classification of episcopal *munera* as teaching, sanctifying and governing, see P. Jones, *Governance*, 161ff.

[122] Const. I.2: as an office-holder the bishop is bound by the constitution; Const XI.36: the bishop is bound by pre-1920 ecclesiastical law.

Teacher and Pastor   With regard to his teaching role, at consecration the bishop is charged to be 'a teacher of the Faith', to proclaim the Gospel, and 'to guide the people of God in the way of eternal life'.[123] As such, the bishop is required to believe in holy scripture and the doctrines of the Christian faith as received by the Church in Wales, and promises to uphold these and to be a diligent minister of the Word of God, proclaiming the Gospel and teaching the Christian faith.[124] Secondly, with regard to his pastoral role, the bishop is charged at consecration 'to be a chief . . . pastor', 'the centre of unity'; he is to 'watch over the people committed to [his] charge', to know them and be known by them; and to feed and guide priests and deacons in his care.[125] As chief pastor, the bishop at consecration undertakes: to guard his people and nourish them out of the riches of God's grace; to devote himself to prayer and study; with his family, to order his life in accordance with the teachings of Christ, so that he is a wholesome example to his people; to be gentle and merciful to all, to show compassion to the poor and needy, and to defend those who have no helper.[126]

Liturgy and Ministry   With regard to his liturgical role, at consecration the bishop is charged 'to be faithful in ordaining and sending out new ministers', to be chief minister of the sacraments, and to confirm the baptized.[127] The bishop also undertakes to administer faithfully the sacraments to the glory of God and the sanctification of his people.[128] In the field of ministry, then, the diocesan bishop appoints people to a host of clerical and, in certain cases, lay offices in the diocese.[129] The bishop must consult the parish regarding patronage,[130] make arrangements for cover during the infirmity of a cleric,[131] may permit the absence of clergy, their non-residence, and pluralism,[132] countersign pension applications and postpone the retirement of clergy.[133]

Government and Discipline   With regard to his governmental role, the diocesan bishop is President of the Diocesan Conference and the Diocesan

---

[123] BCP (1984), 714.
[124] BCP (1984), 714–15.
[125] BCP (1984), 714.
[126] BCP (1984), 714–15.
[127] BCP (1984), 714.
[128] BCP (1984), 714–15.
[129] The bishop appoints the dean, canons, prebendaries, archdeacons, area deans, incumbents, vicars in rectorial benefices, assistant curates, deaconesses, readers, and lay workers: see Const. IV.39; VII.1, 2, 3, 52, 30.
[130] Const. VII.9.
[131] Const. VII.56.
[132] Const. VII.49, 48, 37.
[133] Const. XII.1.

Patronage Board,[134] and a member of the Governing Body, the Electoral College, the Provincial Patronage Board, the Representative Body and the Special Provincial Court.[135] The bishop is required to fill vacancies on the Standing Committee of the Governing Body,[136] and to notify changes in diocesan representation on the Governing Body.[137] The bishop is empowered to introduce bills in the Governing Body, to issue diocesan decrees, to change territorial arrangements in the diocese, to declare benefices vacant and parsonages redundant,[138] and to prevent certain sales by the Representative Body.[139] Episcopal duties include consultation with prescribed bodies in the exercise of functions relating to parsonages,[140] the creation of rectorial benefices,[141] and the suspension of incumbencies.[142] The bishop is empowered to grant licences, dispensations and faculties,[143] and is involved in decision-making relating to ecumenical matters.[144] The bishop may be assisted by a Bishop's Council.[145]

Finally, as chief minister, at consecration the bishop is charged to be 'a guardian of discipline in the Church'.[146] To this end, the bishop is empowered to hold an episcopal visitation of the diocese at such intervals and in such form as the bishop may decide.[147] In common with the purposes of the laws of the vast majority of Anglican churches (in which, in contrast, periodic visitation is often mandatory),[148] the object of the visitation in Wales is for the bishop to obtain a 'good knowledge of the state, sufficiency and ability of the Clergy, and other persons whom they are to visit',[149] concerning church government and discipline, and to enjoin any

---

[134] Const. IV.3; VII.14.
[135] Const. II.2; VII.10; VIII.9; VII.41; III.2; and XI.43.
[136] Const. II.64.
[137] Const. II.28.
[138] Const. II.36; IV.35f.; II.60; X.SR.2; VII.50, 51.
[139] Const. III.26.
[140] Const. X.SR.2 (the duty to consult the Parsonage Board); see below, Ch. 13.
[141] Const. IV.39.
[142] Const. VII.6.
[143] Const. XI.16: they have such powers as they enjoyed at the date of disestablishment.
[144] See below, Ch. 12.
[145] See e.g. Bangor Diocesan Handbook (2001), 61.
[146] BCP (1984), 714; see also *Combe v De la Bere* (1881) 6 DP 157: 'The duty of correcting and holding in check parochial clergy has from the earliest times of the Church devolved upon the bishops.'
[147] Const. XI.17.
[148] Laws stress the pastoral and liturgical dimensions of visitation: see e.g. ECUSA, Cans. III.24.4(a)–(b): 'Each Diocesan Bishop shall visit the Congregations within the Diocese at least once in three years. Interim visits may be delegated to another Bishop of this Church.' The bishop must preach the Word, examine the records of the congregation and 'examine the life and ministry of the Clergy and Congregation'; see also Scotland, Can. 6.1: the bishop must visit each congregation personally at least once every three years and 'formal visitations by the Bishop may from time to time be held.'
[149] Canon 137 of the Canons Ecclesiastical 1603.

necessary remedial action.[150] It is usual for the bishop first to visit the cathedral,[151] and afterwards the diocese in which persons, clerical and lay officers,[152] and places are visitable. Moreover, as guardian of church discipline, the bishop is empowered to remove incumbents and vicars in a rectorial benefice,[153] and, following due judicial process, to impose on clergy sentences of expulsion, monition, suspension and deprivation.[154] The bishop must also adjudicate on parsonage and liturgical disputes,[155] and, in the administration of justice, appoint a diocesan chancellor and registrar.[156]

Termination of Episcopal Ministry

It is a general principle of Anglican canon law that a diocese is vacated on the death, retirement, resignation, pronouncement of incapacity, or removal of the diocesan bishop.[157] So too in the Church in Wales. First, a diocesan bishop must retire at the age of seventy, may retire at any time between sixty-five and seventy, and may retire before sixty-five on grounds of permanent disability preventing the performance of his duties.[158] Secondly, a bishop may resign his see by written notice to the archbishop, who must in turn instruct the secretaries of the Governing Body to give written notice of the resignation to each diocesan bishop, to the chairman of the Representative Body, and to each episcopal elector.[159] During the vacancy of a see, the right to collate to a vacant cure, as well as the right to appoint to any vacant ecclesiastical office (which would have belonged to the diocesan bishop), must be exercised by the archbishop. However, if the archbishop has not exercised this right during the vacancy, it must pass to

---

[150] See generally *Philips v Bury* (1694) Skin 447; for elements of pre-1920 law, see also P. Smith, 'Points of law and practice concerning ecclesiastical visitation', 2 *ELJ* (1990–2), 810.

[151] See below, Ch. 7.

[152] HLE (1910), paras. 783–9; lay people, except churchwardens and sidesmen, are not visitable: *Anon.* (1607) Noy 123; hospitals are visitable: *Philips v Bury* (1694) Skin 447.

[153] See below, Ch. 7.

[154] See above, Ch. 5. For an implicit right in the bishop to have compliance with an episcopal judgment, sentence or order, see Const. XI.38. For canonical obedience, below, Ch. 7.

[155] Const. X.17, 22: see below, Ch. 7; BCP (1984), vi: see below, Ch. 9.

[156] See above, Ch. 5.

[157] See generally CLAC, 116f; for retirement at seventy-two see ECUSA, Const. Art. II.9 and Cans. III.28.2; at seventy years see Southern Africa, Can. 14.3; for the duty to retire at sixty-five see e.g. South East Asia, Const. Art. IV(b).

[158] Const. XII.1, 2, 3: the disability must be proved by medical certificate and other evidence.

[159] Const. VIII.28. See also VIII.13.

and be exercised by the new bishop.[160] When the bishop in question is also archbishop, he may resign by written notice to the next senior bishop.[161]

Thirdly, when it appears to the Bench of Bishops, on such evidence as they deem sufficient, that any bishop is incapacitated by infirmity from the due performance of his duties, the Bench may report the fact to the Special Provincial Court. On due inquiry and such evidence as the court deems sufficient, and after giving the bishop an opportunity of being heard, the court may pronounce him to be incapacitated. Before pronouncing judgment, the court must be satisfied that adequate maintenance is arranged for the bishop by the Representative Body. A minute of the judgment must be sent to each diocesan bishop.[162] Finally, the diocesan bishop may be removed as a result of proceedings in the Special Provincial Court for breaches of ecclesiastical discipline; the finding of the court must be approved by the Provincial Synod and the sentence is pronounced by the archbishop.[163]

ASSISTANT BISHOPS

Laws of churches throughout the Anglican Communion make detailed provision for a wide range of episcopal offices in addition to that of diocesan bishop.[164] The principal episcopal offices designed to provide assistance to the diocesan bishop are coadjutor (with a right of succession),[165] suffragan,[166] and auxiliary bishops (with no right of succession); often the

---

[160] Const. VIII.29: if it so passes, the vacancy in the cure or ecclesiastical office is deemed to have occurred on the day upon which the election of the new bishop was confirmed.

[161] Const. VIII.30: the next senior bishop then becomes President of the Electoral College and must instruct the secretaries of the Governing Body to give written notice of the resignation to the bishops, the chairman of the Representative Body and to each episcopal elector.

[162] Const. VIII.31: the judgment has the same effect, and the same proceedings are to be taken, as if the bishop had resigned his office on the day judgment was pronounced.

[163] Const. XI.43; see above, Ch. 5.

[164] LC 1968, Res. 40: 'This Conference affirms its opinion that all coadjutor, suffragan and full-time assistant bishops should exercise every kind of episcopal function and have their place as bishops in the councils of the Church.'

[165] See e.g. ECUSA, Cans. III.25: when the diocesan bishop is unable to perform the functions of office, by reason of permanent mental, psychological or psychiatric condition, or by reason of the extent of diocesan work, a coadjutor bishop may be elected in accordance with the rules governing the election of bishops; the coadjutor has a right of succession to the see.

[166] See e.g. Southern Africa, Cans. 8.3 and 10: the office must not be created in any diocese without the approval of the provincial Synod of bishops; the diocesan bishop may apply to the Synod only with the concurrence of the Diocesan Synod; some laws explicitly provide that a suffragan has no right of succession (see e.g. ECUSA, Const. Art. II.4).

law requires the agreement of the diocesan assembly before their appointment.[167] The Church in Wales operates a permissive system of assistant bishops.[168]

Assistant Bishops: Appointment and Functions

In the Church in Wales, any diocesan bishop may, if he so desires, have an assistant bishop or bishops to assist him in the diocese. An assistant bishop has no right of succession to any see.[169] The ministry of the assistant bishop is in the keeping of the diocesan bishop: an assistant bishop exercises only such powers and functions in the diocese as are from time to time committed to him by the bishop for the time being of the diocese by his commission under his episcopal seal.[170] Only priests are eligible to be an assistant bishop. If the diocesan bishop wishes to have for an assistant bishop a cleric in priest's orders, he must send the name of the cleric to the archbishop who must submit the name to each member of the Bench of Bishops. If the Bench of Bishops, or a majority of them, assembled in Synod are satisfied of the fitness of the nominated cleric, the archbishop must declare the person to be an assistant bishop-designate for the diocese. The archbishop must then take such steps as may be necessary to give effect to the appointment.[171] However, if the Bench of Bishops, or a majority of them, are not satisfied as to the fitness of the nominated cleric, the diocesan bishop may submit another name to the Bench. The diocesan may also submit another name if an assistant bishop-designate declines, or does not (within twenty-one days after receiving notification of the archiepiscopal declaration) accept the appointment by writing addressed to the archbishop.[172]

In the Church in Wales, the constitutional provisions governing assistant bishops do not prejudice or affect the exercise by the archbishop of the powers and functions inherent in the office of metropolitan. Nor do they prejudice or affect the exercise by the diocesan bishop of the powers and functions inherent in the episcopal office.[173] All assistant bishops, assisting the archbishop or a diocesan bishop in Wales, are members of the Governing Body until they reach the age of seventy; at the Governing Body

---

[167] See e.g. Papua New Guinea, Const. Art. 15: this requires the appointment to be made with the concurrence of the Diocesan Synod; there is no right of succession.

[168] See D. G. James, 'The office of assistant bishop and the canon law of the Church in Wales' (LL M dissertation, University of Wales, Cardiff, 1994).

[169] Const. VII.70, 71.

[170] Const. VII.72.

[171] Const. VII.73.

[172] Const. VII.74.

[173] Const. VII.75: in other words, it would seem that the authority of both the archbishop and a diocesan bishop is jurisdictional, inherent or flowing from law, and that of an assistant bishop commissioned.

assistant bishops must vote with the Order of Clergy, but must retire with the Order of Bishops for private debate.[174] These provisions, in the Church in Wales, are far less detailed than those operative in other Anglican churches.

For example, in the Province of Southern Africa, the suffragan bishop holds the commission of the diocesan bishop and, during a vacancy, of the archbishop. The suffragan bishop must reside in the diocese and minister there in conformity with the commission and the law of the church. The suffragan is subject to the authority of the diocesan bishop in all matters of policy, doctrine and discipline. If the suffragan bishop has any grievance against a decision of the diocesan bishop, he may appeal to the Provincial Synod of bishops. The commission may be withdrawn by a new, incoming diocesan bishop (after a hearing by the synod of bishops), and it may be altered for any good cause shown to the synod; and provision also exists for its revocation by the diocesan bishop.[175]

The Provincial Assistant Bishop

In 1996 the Bench of Bishops declared its willingness to recognize a continuing place in the Church in Wales for clergy and laity who are not in conscience able to accept the ordination of women to the priesthood.[176] As a result,[177] a provincial assistant bishop was appointed to provide a focus of pastoral and sacramental ministry for such clergy and laity, to assure them that their views would be represented in the life of the province at large. The assistant bishop is commissioned by all the diocesan bishops to act on their behalf where the need arises, and his sacramental ministry is available under the direction of the diocesan bishop.[178] The intent of the Bench of Bishops is that the assistant bishop is not to function as the leader of a semi-independent group (opponents to the priesthood of women), but

---

[174] Const. II.4.

[175] Southern Africa, Cans. 8.3 and 10.

[176] For historical material on this development, see P. Jones, *Governance*, 170ff.

[177] Whilst traditionally episcopal office is fundamentally a territorial jurisdiction, a recent development in some churches of the Anglican Communion has been an increase in posts enabling episcopal ministry to classes of individual dispersed across diocesan boundaries of a particular provincial, regional or national church. In Australia, for example, there is a bishop to the defence forces: Australia, Defence Force Ministry Canon 1985, Can. 19 of 1985; see CLAC, 124f.; in England the so-called 'flying bishops' provide episcopal ministry to those opposed to the ordination of women as priests: England, Act of Synod 1992.

[178] Guidelines for Use of the Provincial Assistant Bishop (1996): the assistant bishop plays a full part in the Governing Body, the Representative Body, and the Council for Ministry and Mission: his responsibilities are not restricted to one sector of the church. See above for law governing the appointment of assistant bishops. See also P. Jones, *Governance*, 219: 'the authority of assistant bishops in the diocese, including the Provincial Assistant Bishop, is dependent on the licence of the diocesan bishop.'

to maintain a healthy relationship between people of differing convictions in the church.[179]

Guidelines issued by the Bench of Bishops seek to define the position and ministry of the provincial assistant bishop. The fundamental principle is that 'the powers of jurisdiction remain solely in the hands of the diocesan bishops'. Two forms of ministry are contemplated in the guidelines – sacramental and pastoral. First, an application for the sacramental ministry of the provincial assistant bishop 'must be made' to the diocesan bishop. A parish should be made aware of any application made on its behalf and 'the feeling of the parish should be consulted'. An assurance should be given by the parish priest and the churchwardens that this process has taken place. In the case of disagreement on this matter, 'the bishop shall nominate a person to chair a meeting with members of the [Parochial Church Council] to seek resolution of the difficulty, and to report to the bishop'. If a parish desires the sacramental ministry of the provincial assistant bishop, in a case where the incumbent has not requested it, 'the bishop shall again nominate' a person to chair a meeting with the members of the Parochial Church Council on the matter. Secondly, and by way of contrast, the pastoral care of individuals, whether ordained or lay, does not require an application in accordance with this procedure. Instead, the provincial assistant bishop 'will be able to build up these personal links at his own discretion'.[180]

EPISCOPAL ASSEMBLIES: THE BENCH OF BISHOPS

The law of the Church in Wales commonly provides for the collective action of the bishops of the province. Collective action takes place, ordinarily, through three episcopal assemblies: the Order of Bishops, the Provincial Synod and the Bench of Bishops.[181] However, the constitution lacks a general and separate statement of the functions of these collegial episcopal assemblies: functions are dispersed through the provisions of the constitution dealing with discrete subjects. This may be compared with other churches in the Anglican Communion, the laws of which assign corporate episcopal responsibility to a single episcopal assembly styled variously, depending on the church in question, the College of Bishops, the

[179] Guidelines (1996): the assistant bishop is to animate and inspire mission and service in those congregations in which he ministers, so that their life can continue to enrich the life and mission of the whole province.

[180] Guidelines (1996), paras. 1–5; for mention of the office in the dioceses, see e.g. DSD, YB (2000–1), 6 and DSA, YB (1999–2000), 6. See below, Ch. 12 for the idea of an ecumenical bishop.

[181] The Order of Bishops is classified here as an assembly for the sake of convenience, insofar as in the Governing Body it congregates and functions in a manner similar to a House of Bishops in the central legislatures of other Anglican Churches (see above). The Welsh Church Act 1914, s. 13(1) recognizes the right of bishops to hold synods.

Synod of Bishops, the Council of Bishops, or, when it also constitutes a chamber of the central church assembly, the House of Bishops; laws define with a high degree of precision the jurisdiction and functions of such bodies.[182]

First, the Order of Bishops, one of the houses of the Governing Body, consists of the archbishop and the diocesan bishops of the Church in Wales. When the Order functions at the Governing Body, it sits and acts 'as representing the ancient Provincial Synod'. As such, the Order of Bishops, subject to the constitution, retains and exercises 'all the authority and powers of and belonging from of old to a Provincial Synod'. At the Governing Body, the Order of Bishops has the right to meet apart for private debate and decision before voting as an Order.[183] The Order of Bishops is under a duty to vote last during bill procedure at the Governing Body.[184] Its sanction is required, in certain circumstances, with regard to motions in the Governing Body,[185] and action taken by the Governing Body with regard to new articles, doctrinal statements, rites, ceremonies and formularies must be effected by bill procedure backed and introduced by a majority of the Order of Bishops.[186]

Secondly, the Provincial Synod has several specific powers and functions dispersed throughout the constitution. The Governing Body's power to make constitutions and regulations for the general management and good government of the church must not affect the present right of the Provincial Synod with regard to the confirmation of episcopal elections.[187] When the bishop withholds his assent to a resolution of the Diocesan Conference, any member may bring the resolution forward again at the next annual meeting of the conference; if passed by a two-thirds majority of the lay and clerical members of the conference voting by Orders, the resolution must be referred to the Provincial Synod. Its decision then binds the Diocesan Conference and all the members of the church in the diocese.[188] The Provincial Synod is also responsible for the determination of appeals against deposition from holy orders and expulsion from office.[189]

Thirdly, ordinarily the Bench of Bishops means the archbishop and the diocesan bishops.[190] The functions of the Bench of Bishops include: making

---

[182] See CLAC, 124ff.

[183] Const. II.2; all other bishops residing and assisting the archbishop or any diocesan bishop vote at the Governing Body with the Order of Clergy, but retire with the Order of Bishops for private debate (II.4). For bill procedure and voting by Order see above, Ch. 2.

[184] Const. II.42.

[185] Const. II.34: see above, Ch. 3.

[186] Const. II.36.

[187] Const. II.33: see above, Ch. 2.

[188] Const. IV.33; see also above, Ch. 3.

[189] Const. XI.36(2).

[190] See e.g. Const. VIII.1. See also P. Jones, *Governance*, 219: 'The Bench of Bishops (or

regulations for the administration of Local Ecumenical Projects;[191] the appointment and removal of ecclesiastical and lay judges of the Provincial Court, the nomination of the court's president, and filling vacancies in the court's membership;[192] the appointment of certain members of the Disciplinary Tribunal and removal of all members of the tribunal;[193] the removal of the archbishop or of any bishop;[194] nominations to vacant cures when the diocesan bishop fails to collate and when the Provincial Patronage Board does not exercise its right of nominating to a cure;[195] determining the fitness of candidates nominated for appointment to the offices of diocesan bishop and assistant bishop;[196] and the issuing of statements, policy documents or ecclesiastical quasi-legislation.[197] The Standing Liturgical Advisory Commission, the Provincial Selection Panel, the Council for Mission and Ministry, and the Bishops' Advisers on Child Protection are committees of the Bench of Bishops.[198]

Finally, the constitution sometimes requires collective episcopal action without providing that this is to be done through the Order, the Bench or the Provincial Synod. For example: the diocesan bishops are responsible for declaring an archbishop and an archbishop-elect;[199] they constitute, along with others, the Special Provincial Court for the trial of a bishop;[200] they are members of the Standing Committee of the Governing Body;[201] and the archbishop and diocesan bishops 'acting collectively' must signify nominated members of, and may fill casual vacancies among members nominated by them to, the Representative Body.[202]

Provincial Synod) exercises no ordinary or metropolitical authority over the province, except where this is conferred by the Constitution.'

[191] Can. 26–9–1991, 3.
[192] Const. XI.29.
[193] Const. XI.19(1) and 21.
[194] Const. VIII.32 and 31 respectively; see above.
[195] Const. VII.24, 25: see below, Ch. 7.
[196] Const. IX.25, 26; for assistant bishops, see VII.73, 74.
[197] See e.g. Marriage and Divorce, A Statement by the Bench of Bishops (1998); Guidelines for Initiating the Ministry of Lay Eucharistic Assistants (1991); Guidelines for the Use of the Provincial Assistant Bishop (1996); and Cure of Souls (1996). See also RODC, Sched. of Fees: the Bench of Bishops is to prescribe fees for marriage licences 'under their inherent jurisdiction'.
[198] COFC, 7–11; the functions of these bodies are considered where appropriate elsewhere in this volume.
[199] Const. IX.19, 20.
[200] Const. XI.43.
[201] Const. II.64(2).
[202] Const. III.5(b), 14.

7

THE MINISTRY OF PRIESTS AND DEACONS

The ordained ministries of priests and deacons complete the historic threefold ministry to which the Church in Wales is committed.[1] Theologically, ordained ministers are treated as called by God to serve the church and the community, but the church regulates the manner in which that service is fulfilled by means of law. Whilst in civil law clergy do not have the status of employees,[2] clerics of the Church in Wales exercise a canonical ministry, one in which ministerial life and work are facilitated and ordered by the law of the church. The rules of the church which define the work of its ordained ministers are scattered throughout many legal instruments dealing with specific subjects. The purpose of this chapter is to describe the core elements of the law as it relates to the various ecclesiastical offices and other positions in which ordained ministers serve. As well as laws on ordination, and rules common to all clergy, the following examines cathedral staff, archdeacons, area deans, incumbents, rectors and vicars in rectorial benefices, priests-in-charge, and assistant curates. The bodies of

---

[1] Can. 19-9-96: 'it is the intention of the Church in Wales to continue the ministry of the universal Church in its threefold order of Bishops, Priests and Deacons'; see also BCP (1984), v (the 'three orders of Ministers': 'It is the intention of the Church in Wales to maintain and continue these three orders'). See also the Welsh Church Act 1914, s. 38: for the purposes of this statute, 'ecclesiastical person' means 'a bishop and the holder of any ecclesiastical office who is in holy orders'; 'ecclesiastical office' means 'any bishopric, ecclesiastical dignity, or preferment' within the meaning of the Church Discipline Act 1840 (since repealed: Const. XI.47). In civil law, an office is a 'subsisting, permanent, substantive position which had existence independently of the person who filled it, which went on and was filled in succession by successive holders': *McMillan v Guest* [1942] AC 561 at 564 *per* Lord Atkin.

[2] According to classical civil law doctrine, clergy are not in law employees and, therefore, they have no right of recourse to the industrial tribunals of the State; the doctrine is based on the idea of incompatibility between the spiritual nature of their functions and the existence of a contract; however, the courts have accepted the possible existence of contracts, depending on the facts of the particular case; those in sector ministry (for example) may operate under contract: see below, Ch. 8; see generally N. Doe, *The Legal Framework of the Church of England* (Oxford, 1996), 198–9 and N. Doe, 'Ministers of religion and employment law in the United Kingdom: recent judicial developments', *Anuario de Derecho Eclesiastico del Estado*, 13 (1997), 349.

law involved deal with: appointment, functions, and termination of ministry. Clergy in hospitals, prisons and sector ministry are discussed in Chapter 8.

ORDINATION AND CANONICAL MINISTRY

In common with all churches of the Anglican Communion,[3] admission to holy orders in the Church in Wales is effected by ordination, initially as a deacon, and subsequently as a priest. The ordination process is in the keeping of the diocesan bishop. The church operates a system of law and a growing body of ecclesiastical quasi-legislation of general applicability to all clergy, deacons and priests, irrespective of the particular ecclesiastical posts they hold. The church acknowledges that its ordained ministries are 'given by God as instruments of his grace, and as possessing not only the inward call of the Spirit but also Christ's commission through his body, the Church'.[4]

Admission to Holy Orders: Ordination

No person is authorized to execute the office of priest or deacon in the Church in Wales unless evidence can be produced of ordination with the laying on of hands by bishops who are themselves duly qualified and authorized to confer holy orders.[5]

Eligibility To be eligible for admission to the diaconate, candidates must have attained the age of twenty-three.[6] Women may be ordained as deacons.[7] A candidate for ordination as a priest must have attained the age of twenty-four, but the archbishop may grant a faculty to a person over the age of twenty-three to be admitted as a priest in any diocese in the province and to preach and administer the sacraments.[8] Men and women may be ordained as priests.[9] Marriage following divorce during the lifetime of a

---

[3] CLAC, 128ff.; for the permanent diaconate, see e.g. Korea, Const. Art. 110.
[4] Can. 28-9-1995, First Schedule, (a)(iv) (Porvoo).
[5] BCP (1984), v–vi; the term 'holy orders' implies episcopal ordination: *St Albans (Bishop) v Fillingham* [1906] P 163. See also Canons Ecclesiastical 1603, Can. 48: 'No Curate or Minister shall be permitted to serve in any place without examination and admission of the Bishop of the diocese, or Ordinary of the place.'
[6] Canons Ecclesiastical 1603, Can. 34. 'Cleric' means clerk in holy orders: Const., I.3.
[7] Can. 16-4-1980: being a woman does not constitute a canonical impediment.
[8] Can. 19-4-1990: the canon repeals the Clergy Ordination Act 1804.
[9] Can. 19-9-1996: no bishop is obliged to bring proceedings in respect of a cleric or other member of the church who dissents in conscience to the ordination of women as priests. Being cast in terms of the absence of an episcopal obligation to do so, this provision seems to suggest that a bishop is empowered to bring such proceedings; para.

former spouse, and marriage to a divorced person during the lifetime of that person's former spouse, are recognized as canonical impediments, by reason of which a person must not be admitted to holy orders. However, the Bench of Bishops may grant dispensations from these impediments in individual cases. The bench must consult with a provincial panel of advisers on which each diocese must be represented.[10] Irregularity of birth is not a canonical impediment to ordination.[11] It is lawful throughout the province to ordain on such days as may from time to time be appointed for that purpose by the Bench of Bishops.[12] Holy orders are indelible.[13]

Suitability and Preliminaries Unlike other Anglican churches,[14] the modern law of the Church in Wales does not explicitly deal with the preliminaries to ordination, though diocesan quasi-legislation sometimes does so.[15] Legally, the matter is still governed, in its essentials, by principles of pre-1920 ecclesiastical law. Ordination is in the keeping of the bishop. Whilst the bishop has a wide discretion as to suitability,[16] the exercise of this discretion is limited. 'None should be admitted either Deacon or Priest', without first having been assigned a post from which to serve.[17] Candidates from another diocese must exhibit letters dimissory from the bishop of that diocese, and all candidates must exhibit letters testimonial of their good life and conversation.[18] The bishop must cause every candidate to be examined by those ministers who are to assist him at the ordination, at which, also, the bishop must diligently examine the candidates in the presence of those ministers.[19] The office of deacon is held ordinarily for one

3: any reference in the constitution, the BCP or any other form of service lawfully authorized for use in the church, to a priest is deemed to include women priests.

[10] Can. 13-9-1998: the panel is set up under the authority of the canon.

[11] Can. 28-9-1961: i.e. being born out of wedlock.

[12] Can. 15-9-1982: this canon repeals a canon of 27-9-1973, but nothing in the new canon is deemed to revive any earlier canon repealed by the 1973 canon; see Canons Ecclesiastical 1603, Can. 31.

[13] Canons Ecclesiastical 1603, Can. 76: see below for relinquishment of the exercise of orders.

[14] See e.g. ECUSA, Cans. III.4; see generally CLAC, 133f.

[15] See e.g. DSD, YB (2000–1), 132: candidates should write to the bishop who 'may require them to attend a Diocesan Selection Board and, if recommended, they must attend a Provincial Selection Board'; no candidates can be ordained deacon until attaining the age of twenty-three and candidates 'must be provided with a title to Ordination before the date of Ordination'; diaconal candidates must have followed an approved course and send the following to the diocesan registry: letters testimonial; for diaconal candidates, nomination to a curacy or other title, *si quis*; baptismal and birth certificates; and college testimonials.

[16] *R v Archbishop of Dublin* (1833) Alc & N 244: cited by HLE (1910), para. 1071: 'A bishop has an absolute discretion as to whether he will ordain a person or examine him for ordination, and need not assign any reason for refusing to do so.'

[17] Canons Ecclesiastical 1603, Can. 33.

[18] Canons Ecclesiastical 1603, Can. 34; see also Ministers (Ordination) Act 1571.

[19] Canons Ecclesiastical 1603, Can. 35.

year, and no bishop may make any person a deacon and a priest on one and the same day.[20] Prior to ordination to both the diaconate and priesthood, candidates must make the declaration of canonical obedience and the undertakings concerning the discipline of the church.[21] Ordinations may take place in a cathedral or a parish church.[22]

The Provincial Selection Panel is responsible to the Bench of Bishops for advising the diocesan bishops as to the suitability of candidates for training for ordination.[23] The Council for Mission and Ministry, also reponsible to the Bench of Bishops, assists the Bench in the promotion of ministry.[24] The Council's Ministry Team is to provide support for all forms of lay and ordained ministry and training in the church,[25] and the team carries on its work with its research group and five committees.[26]

Ordination and Functions   At the service of diaconal ordination, the person to be ordained deacon is presented, and if no lawful impediment is alleged, the bishop asks the people to declare their assent to ordination. The bishop then administers the charge, by which the deacon is called to work with the bishop and priests as a fellow servant. The tasks of the deacon are: to assist the priest in leading the worship of the people, especially at the eucharist; to help the priest in the ministration of baptism and in preaching; and to seek out and care for those in need. Candidates are charged to take Jesus Christ as the pattern of their calling, study his teaching, meditate upon it, and pray constantly that their life may be a

---

[20] Canons Ecclesiastical 1603, Can. 32: a deacon must function as such, before ordination as a priest, for one whole year so that there be 'some time of trial of their behaviour in the office of Deacon', unless the bishop finds 'good cause to the contrary'.

[21] For Const. VII.66, see below.

[22] See H. Cripps, *A Practical Treatise on the Law Relating to the Church and Clergy* (8th edn, London, 1937), 32.

[23] COFC, 9: it is composed of a chairman, two deputy chairs, nine clerical and nine lay members (each diocese represented by three members) appointed by the Bench.

[24] COFC, 11: the council works in six teams: Inter-Church; Church and Society; Communication; Ministry; Education; and Renewal. The council consists of the archbishop (chair), the diocesan bishops, provincial assistant bishop, clerics (one appointed from each diocese), lay persons (one appointed from each diocese), and a representative of the Representative Body. The council is: to exercise overall responsibility for its work; initiate and co-ordinate its work; monitor its work and determine its priorities; be responsible for its budget; and receive regular reports from its officers and prepare an annual report for the Bench.

[25] COFC, 16: the team consists of a bishop, two designated members of the council, one representative from each of its committees; there is a relationship between the Ministry Team and the Provincial Selection Panel, which is 'an independent panel answerable to the Bench of Bishops'.

[26] COFC, 16: namely: Ministry Research Working Group; Provincial Validating Board (which oversees and accredits training for ordained ministry); Resources for Training Committee (which administers the scheme of financial provision for training for ordained ministry); Continuing Ministerial Education Committee; Nurture and Selection Committee; and Provincial Readers Committee.

pattern of obedient service and so reveal the power of the kingdom of God. At the examination, candidates must affirm their commitment to holy scripture, the doctrines of the Christian faith, to prayer and study, to order their lives (with their families) according to the teachings of Christ, and to be wholesome examples to the people. Ordination is effected by laying on of hands by the bishop and the invocation of the Holy Spirit.[27]

At the service of priestly ordination, the person to be ordained priest is presented, and the place where that person is to serve is read. If no lawful impediment is alleged, the bishop asks the people to declare their assent to ordination. The bishop then administers the charge according to which the priest is called to work with the bishop and his fellow priests as servant and shepherd. The tasks of the priest are: to proclaim the gospel, to call sinners to repentance, and to declare God's forgiveness to them; to teach; to baptize; to preside at the eucharist; to perform the other ministrations entrusted to them; and to care for all alike, young and old, strong and weak, rich and poor. Candidates are charged to keep Jesus Christ as the pattern of their calling, study his teaching, meditate upon it,[28] and pray constantly that their life may be a pattern of obedience and holiness and so reveal the power of the kingdom of God. At the examination, candidates must affirm their commitment to holy scripture, the doctrines of the Christian faith, to be diligent ministers, to prayer and study, to order their lives (with their families) according to the teachings of Christ, and to be wholesome examples to the people. Ordination is effected by laying on of hands by the bishop and the invocation of the Holy Spirit.[29] Following ordination, letters of orders are issued by the bishop.[30]

Canonical Ministry and Canonical Obedience

The Church in Wales teaches that the ministry of a deacon is to help the priest both in the conduct of worship and in pastoral care,[31] and that of a priest is: to preach the Word of God; to teach; to baptize; to celebrate the eucharist; to pronounce absolution and blessing in God's name; and to care for the people entrusted by the bishop to their charge.[32] In the exercise of their ministry, all clergy are bound by the law of the church.[33] Before

[27] BCP (1984), 726ff.
[28] See also Canons Ecclesiastical 1603, Can. 75: clergy must 'at all times convenient . . . hear or read somewhat of the Holy Scriptures, or shall occupy themselves with some other honest study or exercise'.
[29] BCP (1984), 718ff.
[30] Canons Ecclesiastical 1603, Can. 137.
[31] BCP (1984), 691 (Catechism)
[32] BCP (1984), 691 (Catechism).
[33] See above, Ch. 1. See also Canons Ecclesiastical 1603, Can. 48: a bishop must not 'by any means' allow clergy to officiate in the diocese 'without testimony of the Bishop

ordination, institution, collation, licensing, or appointment to an ecclesiastical office, all persons must, in addition to the declaration of canonical obedience to the bishop, make a declaration and undertaking.[34] In these: they declare their belief in the faith of the church; they undertake to use in public prayer and the administration of the sacraments only the lawful services of the church;[35] and they undertake to be bound by the constitution, and to accept, submit to, and carry out any sentence or judgment passed upon them by the archbishop, a diocesan bishop, the disciplinary tribunal or any court of the church.[36]

Like the vast majority of Anglican churches,[37] in the Church in Wales the declaration of canonical obedience, taken before ordination and appointment to an office, requires clergy to declare that they will pay true and canonical obedience to the bishop and his successors in all things lawful and honest.[38] According to judicial dicta, 'the oath of canonical obedience does not mean that every clergyman will obey all the commands of the Bishop against which there is no law, but that he will obey all such commands as the Bishop by law is authorised to impose'.[39] Thus, clerical disobedience to an episcopal direction, when that direction is a representation of a provision or requirement appearing in the law of the church, is itself unlawful. Clerical disobedience of an episcopal direction which the bishop is by the law empowered (expressly or impliedly) to issue is unlawful. Equally, clerical disobedience of an episcopal direction which is contrary to the law of the church is lawful. When the law is silent as to the bishop's direction, according to the judicial statement referred to above, it

of the diocese . . . whence they came . . . of their honesty, ability and conformity' to the laws of the church.

[34] Const. VII.66: 'All persons admitted to Holy Orders of deacons or priests, or instituted or collated to the cure of souls, or licensed as Assistant Curates or Deaconesses, and all clerics appointed to any ecclesiastical office in the Church in Wales, shall, in addition to the declaration of canonical obedience to the Bishop, make and subscribe before such ordination, institution, collation, licence or appointment, in the presence of the Bishop or his Commissary appointed in writing', the declaration and undertaking 'and none other'.

[35] For the precise formulae used, see below, Ch. 9.

[36] Const. VII.66.

[37] CLAC, 150f.

[38] The declaration is required by Const. VII.66; for its terms, see *Cure of Souls*, 7 n.1: 'I, A.B. . . . declare that I will pay true and Canonical Obedience to the Lord Bishop of C . . . and his Successors, in all things lawful and honest, so help me God.' Whilst the duty to make the declaration is found in Const. VII.66, the *form* of the declaration does not appear in the constitution or the BCP (1984); it derives from pre-1920 ecclesiastical law.

[39] *Long v Bishop of Cape Town* (1863) 1 Moo PCCNS 411 at 465. See also *Re Petition Against Revd Clifford Williams* (1997), in which the Provincial Court of the Church in Wales held: 'We would understand "lawful" (in "lawful and honest"), to refer to the provisions of the Canon Law, the constitution of the Church in Wales, and such synodical resolutions (i.e. of the Governing Body), as may be in force for the time being; "honest" may be taken to refer to the constraints of natural justice. This is all a very proper defence of the clergy against the dictates of episcopal whim.'

would seem that clerical obedience is not required – it cannot be said, in such a case, that the law authorizes the bishop's direction.[40] In any event, failure to comply with an honest and lawful episcopal direction may result in disciplinary proceedings for neglect of duty.[41]

The Professional Standards of Priests and Deacons

Recent years have seen in the Church in Wales a growing awareness of the professional standards of clergy.[42] The promotion of professional standards is today the subject of provincial quasi-legislation.[43] Although ordained and 'set apart' for their office and work, priests and deacons remain members of the one body, the church. The ministry they exercise, on behalf of the church, is a representative ministry. Within the church clergy have 'a special professional role, defined in terms of special duties and relationships, calling for competence and care'.[44] By accepting 'the distinctive vocation of ordination', they embark 'not simply on a profession, but also on a representative ministry and an exemplary way of life'. Participation in the cure of souls involves clergy in: duties of office; responsibilities of professional and pastoral relationships; and standards of personal behaviour. Together these constitute 'a clergy ethic'.[45]

First, with regard to the duties of office, clergy exercise: *leadership and authority*, under which 'they owe a duty of obedience to their superiors in office', of collaboration with their colleagues, and 'of consultation and co-operation with the laity'; *liturgical responsibility*, to lead the people in public worship in accordance with the authorized forms of service; *preaching and teaching*, leading people to a deeper exploration and fuller understanding of the gospel and its challenges; *pastoral care*, caring for the people committed to their charge and sharing with them in the work of service and in a common witness to the world; *administrative responsibility*, 'to ensure that their administrative practices are both competent and courteous'; and *pastoral ministry* to the church and community, so that all people of the

---

[40] See Doe, *The Legal Framework*, 212–15.

[41] See *Cure of Souls* (1996), 7. According to pre-1920 ecclesiastical law, breach of canonical obedience is perhaps the most serious ecclesiastical offence: *Combe v De La Bere* (1881) 6 PD 157 at 172; *Rugg v Bishop of Winchester* (1868) LR 2 PC 223 at 235: disobedience to episcopal directions went 'beyond . . . neglect of duty'; see also the Statement of the Provincial Synod, 27 January 1999: the seriousness of an offence of causing scandal (under Const. XI.18), may be 'compounded by a refusal to comply with legitimate demands of the bishop to whom [a cleric] had promised canonical obedience'.

[42] For periodic clergy reviews, see e.g. DSAB, YB, 26: the process is voluntary.

[43] *Cure of Souls* (1996): the statements in this document are often re-presentations of legal provisions discussed elsewhere in this volume; clergy standards are enforceable in the Disciplinary Tribunal: see above, Ch. 5.

[44] *Cure of Souls* (1996), 1–3. See also Canons Ecclesiastical 1603, Can. 76: no cleric shall 'use himself in the course of his life as a layman'.

[45] *Cure of Souls* (1996), 4.

parish, and congregation members, are given special oversight, particularly fostering ecumenical relations.[46]

Secondly, with regard to responsibilities of professional and pastoral relationships, clergy are under a general duty of confidentiality, both 'inside and outside the confessional', and their '[e]motional detachment appropriate to a pastoral and professional relationship must at all times be maintained'; 'all persons, of whatever age, race, creed or ability, must be treated with the care and respect that lie at the heart of all human community and with the wisdom and love that lie at the heart of all Christian ministry'.[47] Thirdly, since their ministry is representative, and their behaviour expected to be exemplary, clergy should seek to fashion their own lives according to the manner and pattern of the life and teaching of Jesus Christ. They should always have in mind that they represent to others the gospel of Christ and the authenticity of the church, and in all they say and do they should show honesty and integrity, temperance and self-restraint.[48]

CATHEDRALS

There are six cathedrals in the Church in Wales.[49] Each cathedral is regulated by the general provincial constitution, the ecclesiastical law received and enacted by the Governing Body,[50] by particular provincial law found in the six Cathedral Schemes,[51] and by its own domestic law,[52] found in its constitution, statutes, ordinances, customs, orders, regulations and

---

[46] *Cure of Souls* (1996), 4–5; see also 7–11. For clerical apparel, designed to enable clergy to be 'known to the people', see Canons Ecclesiastical 1603, Can. 74.

[47] *Cure of Souls* (1996), 5; see also 12–14; see below, Ch. 8 for responsibilities towards children.

[48] *Cure of Souls* (1996), 6; see also 15–16; these echo aspects of the ordination charge: see above. See also Canons Ecclesiastical 1603, Can. 75: clergy 'ought to excel all others in purity of life and should be examples to the people to live well and christianly'.

[49] A cathedral is 'a centre of worship and mission and . . . the seat of a bishop': Cathedrals and Churches Commission Rules, r.1. Parishes may be annexed to cathedrals: where this is the case, fund-raising (for example) for staff and for the maintenance and improvement of its fabric and contents, is mostly undertaken by the parish, but the cathedral makes the final decision under the Schemes; see also CSM, III: the church of St Woolos, Newport is both the cathedral church of the diocese of Monmouth and the parish church of St Woolos.

[50] See e.g. CSSD, II.1.

[51] Other provincial law applicable to cathedrals includes the Cathedrals and Churches Commission Rules, for which see below, Ch. 13.

[52] Some domestic law may be very ancient: see e.g. J. Barrow (ed.), *St Davids Episcopal Acta: 1085–1280* (Cardiff, 1998), 104f: this deals with the statutes of Bishop Iorwerth agreed with the Chapter in 1224.

by-laws; domestic cathedral law must be consistent with the Cathedral Scheme.[53]

The Appointment of Cathedral Staff

The governing body in each cathedral is the Cathedral Chapter (more commonly called the Dean and Chapter),[54] composed of the dean, canons and, in some, prebendaries, ranked in order. Appointment of the dean, canon or prebendary vests, unless otherwise ordered by the Governing Body, in the diocesan bishop. To be appointed as dean a person must have been at least six years in priest's orders, and to be appointed as canon or prebendary the person must be a cleric. The diocesan bishop is also entitled to appoint honorary canons, though not more than three for any cathedral, but they are not members of the Chapter.[55] The Chapter must appoint the clerical and lay officials of the cathedral and, when a parish is annexed to a cathedral, the dean acts as incumbent.[56]

On admission, each Chapter member must undertake to observe the domestic law of the cathedral and to perform their duties.[57] Every canon or prebendary, holding an incumbency or other office in the diocese, must resign the prebend or canonry when they cease to hold that incumbency or other office, unless the bishop determines otherwise. When conferring a prebend or canonry on a cleric who holds an office outside the cathedral (other than a parochial benefice), the bishop may provide in the letters of collation that the individual receiving collation must vacate the prebend or canonry when they cease to hold that office. If at any time an additional emolument is assigned to any prebendary or canon, the bishop may, with the consent of the Chapter, assign to that prebendary or canon such additional duty within the cathedral, under the direction of the dean, as the bishop thinks reasonable.[58]

[53] St Asaph, Bangor, St Davids, and Llandaff are regulated by their own constitution, statutes, ordinances and customs, and Brecon and St Woolos solely by custom; these domestic laws, operative on 1 January 1974, have been confirmed and continued by the Governing Body's Cathedral Schemes, unless they are contrary to or inconsistent with those Schemes: CSSA, I.1 and 2; CSBG, I.1 and 2; CSSD, I.1 and 2; CSL, I.1 and 2 (revised, 2001). However: CSM, I.1 and 2, and CSB, I.1 and 2: only customs are confirmed and continued. See below for orders, regulations and by-laws.
[54] The Dean and Chapter is not in civil law a corporation aggregate: Welsh Church Act 1914, s. 2(1).
[55] Const. VII.1 and 2. Deans, prebendaries and canons must retire at 70 (XII.1).
[56] Const. VII.4 and 5.
[57] See e.g. CSSA, II.3: the declaration is 'faithfully to observe the Constitution, Statutes, Ordinances and Customs of the cathedral'. The declaration is made after collation and on presentation of the bishop's mandate; the member is then installed by the dean and admitted to the Chapter.
[58] CSSA, II; CSBG, II; CSSD, II; CSL, II; CSM, II; CSB, II: an additional emolument includes remission or reduction of house rent received in virtue of the prebend or

Functions of Cathedral Staff

The Cathedral Schemes define in general terms the functions, rights and duties of cathedral clergy, as well as those of the diocesan bishop in relation to the cathedral. The St Asaph Cathedral Scheme may be used to illustrate these rights; the terms of the Scheme are basically the same as those of the other Schemes, though there are some differences in detail.[59]

The Bishop In the St Asaph Scheme, the diocesan bishop enjoys a number of governmental and liturgical rights in the cathedral.[60] As an overriding principle, the existing powers of the bishop as visitor of the cathedral, and his ordinary jurisdiction over the cathedral and Chapter, are to continue 'as in times past'.[61] The bishop may hold ordinations, confirmations, synods and visitations in the cathedral at such times and in such manner as the bishop determines; the bishop may also hold other special services in the cathedral, after consultation with the dean.[62] The bishop has the right to take such part in divine service and to preach at such times in the cathedral as he thinks reasonable, after consultation with the dean. It is the duty of the Dean and Chapter to assist the bishop, if he so requires, at all services or administrations in the cathedral at which the bishop is the principal officiant.[63]

The bishop may, as occasion arises, summon the Chapter to meetings with him in the Chapter house over which the bishop must preside, but he may retire while the Chapter determines its response to his proposals or questions.[64] It is the duty of every member of the Chapter to attend such meetings. The bishop may, with the consent of the Chapter, abrogate, alter, abridge, enlarge, interpret, or add to the constitution, statutes or ordinances of the cathedral, or abolish any cathedral custom, but this power does not

canonry; a copy of the letter assigning the emolument must be deposited in the chapter archives.

[59] Key differences between the St Asaph Scheme and the other Schemes are indicated, where appropriate, in the following footnotes.

[60] CSSA, III; see also CSBG, III; CSSD, III; CSL, III; CSM, IV; CSB, III; when the bishop comes to be enthroned (for which see above, Ch. 6), the dean must summon every member of the Chapter to be present and take part.

[61] Compare CSM, IV.1: the bishop is visitor of the cathedral and Chapter; no mention is made of the bishop's ordinary jurisdiction.

[62] Compare CSL, III.3 and CSB, III.3: the bishop may hold special services only with the consent of the dean 'but not so as to interfere with the ordinary services of the cathedral'; see also CSM, IV.3: the bishop must simply give notice to the dean and there must be 'no undue interference with ordinary services'. See also Welsh Church Act 1914, s. 38: 'synod' includes 'any assembly or convention'.

[63] CSM, IV.6 adds that at such cathedral or diocesan services, members of the cathedral staff must, if so desired by the bishop, be present and ready to take part.

[64] Neither CSM, III nor CSB, III make provision for venue or retirement; in CSSD, IV.1 the dean is styled the 'Official Head of the Chapter'.

extend to anything contained in the Cathedral Scheme.[65] The bishop also has the right to hold a consistory court in the cathedral.[66]

The Dean   In the St Asaph scheme,[67] the dean, the principal member of the Chapter,[68] must keep residence for at least eight months each year; he must live and sleep in the official deanery house,[69] and attend divine service in the cathedral regularly.[70] The dean must preside at all Chapter meetings, and in cases of equal voting has a second or casting vote.[71] The dean is responsible for the due performance of their respective duties by the dignitaries, prebendaries, canons, vicars choral or chaplains, and officials of the Chapter. The dean must ensure that the regulations concerning their duties are made known to them, and must instruct, advise, and admonish them if need be, for the proper discharge of their duties; but the dean must not take further proceedings without the consent of the Chapter.[72] The Chapter must from time to time nominate one or more of its members to act in place of the dean whenever the latter is out of residence, or incapacitated by sickness or other urgent cause.[73] In a vacancy in the office of dean, the bishop may nominate a member or members of the Chapter to act in

---

[65] CSSA, III; CSM deals only with interpretation of the Scheme (there is no episcopal power to abolish customs): 'Any question or doubt arising as to the interpretation of this Scheme, including the relation of the parish church of St Woolos to the cathedral, shall be referred to the Bishop, whose decision shall be binding on all concerned'; CSB, III makes no mention of the subject.

[66] See also CSL, III.6. This is not the case with the other cathedrals.

[67] CSSA, IV.

[68] The dean is similarly styled in CSM, IV.1; CSBG, IV.1: the dean as principal member of the Chapter must be someone other than the bishop; CSL, IV.1: the dean is the principal member of the Chapter and 'is technically styled its Numeral Head', being the first in the number of chapter members; CSB, IV.1: the dean is styled 'Official Head' of the Chapter.

[69] CSBG, IV.2 and 4: the dean must live and sleep in the official house attached to the deanery, 'or such other place as the Chapter may . . . determine'.

[70] The same provision is found in CSSD, IV.2, CSL, IV.2 and CSB, IV.2; compare CSBG, IV.4: the dean must attend regularly at cathedral services on Sundays and weekdays.

[71] See also CSSD, IV.4; CSBG, IV.5; CSL, IV.4; CSB, IV.4.

[72] CSBG, IV.6: the dean must instruct, advise or admonish any of the dignitaries, canons, minor canons, organists, servants or employees of the Chapter, 'in order that they may the better discharge their respective duties, but shall not take any further proceedings without the consent of the Chapter'; in CSSD, IV.5 the same formula is used though there is no reference to organists (and the dean is responsible to the Chapter for seeing that their regulations 'are made known to all parties concerned and are duly observed by them': IV.6); in CSL, IV.5 the same duties apply to dignitaries, prebendaries or canons, chaplains, servants or employees of the Chapter (further proceedings cannot be taken without the consent of the Chapter); IV 5: the dean is responsible to the Chapter to see that their regulations are made known to all parties concerned and are performed by them; see also CSB, IV.5: the same provision applies to canons, minor canons and lay officials of the Chapter.

[73] CSBG, IV.7; CSSD, IV.7; CSL, IV.7; CSM, V.2; CSB, IV.6.

place of the dean.[74] In other Cathedral Schemes, the dean's liturgical duties are more fully prescribed.[75]

Dignitaries, Prebendaries and Canons   In the St Asaph Scheme, the Chapter, with the concurrence of the bishop, must adopt one of three systems relating to the residence and duties of dignitaries, prebendaries and canons. First, the prebendaries and canons may be required to reside for such period every year, and in such rotation, as the Chapter determines.[76] Secondly, residence at the cathedral may not be required of any of the prebendaries and canons, but provision is to be made as to their attendance and participation in cathedral services.[77] Thirdly, the Chapter may adopt a system under which there must be one full-time residentiary canon, who holds office for a period or periods not exceeding twelve years in all.[78] In any event, Chapter members must attend all of its meetings, and take due part in its business.[79] Similar arrangements may be adopted by the Chapters of the other cathedrals.[80]

The Chapter   In the St Asaph Scheme,[81] there must be two ordinary meetings of the Chapter each year, on dates approved by the Chapter; but

---

[74]   CSBG, IV.8; CSSD, IV.8; CSL, IV.8; CSM, V.3; CSB, IV.7.

[75]   CSBG, IV.3, CSSD, IV.3, CSL, IV.3, CSM, IV.3: during the period of residence the dean must officiate at such services and preach on such occasions in the cathedral as the Chapter may arrange with him.

[76]   Residence means: living and sleeping in the place the Chapter requires, attending divine service in the cathedral regularly throughout the period of residence, and preaching as often in the cathedral as the Chapter prescribes, but the prebendary or canon in residence may preach additional sermons in the cathedral at the request or with the permission of the dean.

[77]   One prebendary or canon, nominated by the Chapter must be present at the cathedral services on every Sunday, and must take such part in services as the dean may direct, in accordance with the regulations of the Chapter. The prebendary or canon present in the cathedral must preach as often on that Sunday as the Chapter prescribes, but may preach additional sermons at the request or with the permission of the dean. The Chapter must endeavour to ensure that at least one of their number is present at Morning and Evening Prayer in the cathedral, daily throughout the year.

[78]   Each residentiary canon must live and sleep in such place and for such period or periods in each year as the bishop may determine. The residentiary canon must undertake such work in the diocese and in the cathedral as the bishop, after consultation with the dean, may determine.

[79]   CSSA, V and Schedule: the chapter with the consent of the bishop may adopt the third system described in this paragraph, in addition to one of the other two systems; if the Chapter adopts the first and second systems, the non-requirement of residence contained in the second system does not extend to the residentiary canons for whom provison is made if the second system is adopted.

[80]   CSBG, V; CSSD, V; CSL, V; CSM, VI; CSB, V.

[81]   CSSA, VI. For criticism of Chapters see P. Jones, *The Governance of the Church in Wales* (Cardiff, 2000), 423ff.

the dates may be altered for adequate reason at the discretion of the dean.[82] Special Chapter meetings may be summoned at any other times when, in the opinion of the dean, the business of the cathedral so requires; they may also be required on the written requisition of any four members of the Chapter.[83] The Chapter is a college or society, and the decision of the majority of its members must be accepted as the decision of the whole Chapter and it binds all the members. Five members of the Chapter constitute a quorum, but they cannot conclude any business for which the consent of a majority of the Chapter is required.[84] Any resolution receiving the consent of eight members of the Chapter present and voting constitutes an Act of the Chapter.[85]

The Chapter must make such orders, regulations and by-laws as may be necessary to give effect to the Cathedral Scheme. It may revise, annul or add to these, provided notice of the proposal to do so is given to each Chapter member at least fourteen days before the meeting.[86] The Chapter must appoint a Chapter clerk who must: attend all Chapter meetings; take minutes of proceedings; perform any duties under the Chapter's orders, regulations or by-laws; keep in safe custody all books, deeds and papers belonging to the Chapter, unless and until the Chapter otherwise orders.[87] Stipendiary vicars choral or chaplains may also be appointed by the

---

[82] CSBG, VI.1 and CSB, VI.1; compare CSSD, VI.1: this provides for an annual meeting; CSL, VI.1 provides for four annual meetings the dates of which may, for adequate reason, be altered at the discretion of the dean; CSM contains no special provision on the Chapter.

[83] CSL, VI.2 contains the same rule; CSBG, VI.1: in addition to the two ordinary annual Chapter meetings, other meetings may be summoned at the discretion of the dean or by written request of four or more Chapter members; CSSD, VI.1: this provides for meetings other than the annual meeting which may be held at the discretion of the dean or on the written request of any four members of the Chapter; CSB, VI.1: besides the two ordinary annual meetings, the dean may summon other meetings as he deems necessary.

[84] CSBG, VI.2 and CSSD, VI.2: eight members constitutes a quorum; CSL, VI.3 and CSB, VI.2: five members constitute a quorum.

[85] CSBG, VI.2 and CSSD, VI.3: the decision of the majority binds all and constitutes an Act of the Chapter; CSL, VI.4 and 5: decision is by majority and every resolution receiving the consent of the members constitutes an Act of the Chapter.

[86] CSBG, VI.3, CSSD, VI.4, CSL, VI.6: the Chapter may make orders, regulations and by-laws to give effect to the Scheme and may revise, annul or add to these; CSB, VI.3: the Chapter may make orders, regulations and by-laws, and revise, annul or add to these, subject to the constitution of the Church in Wales and any regulations made by the Governing Body.

[87] These must be done in person or by deputy approved by the chapter. CSSD, VI.5: this makes provision only for the appointment of a Chapter clerk; the Chapter must also appoint a Master of the Fabric (see below, Ch. 13); CSL, VI.7 provides for the appointment of a Chapter clerk (and deputy), and 8 that the chancellor is responsible for the safe custody of all the books, deeds and papers within the cathedral and belonging to the Chapter, except those entrusted to the Chapter clerk (such as minutes of Chapter meetings).

Chapter to do such work in the cathedral church as the dean directs in accordance with Chapter regulations. One of the vicars choral or chaplains may be succentor. Finally, the Chapter may, if it thinks fit, appoint two honorary vicars choral to perform such duties as the Chapter determines.[88]

THE ARCHDEACONRY AND THE DEANERY

Unlike most Anglican churches,[89] each diocese of the Church in Wales is divided into archdeaconries,[90] composed, in turn, of deaneries. An archdeaconry is assigned to the charge of an archdeacon, and a deanery to an area dean. This section examines their appointment and ministry.

The Office of Archdeacon

Appointment to the office of archdeacon, unless otherwise ordered by the Governing Body, vests in the diocesan bishop. To be eligible for appointment, a person must have been at least six years in priest's orders.[91] It is commonly understood that the archdeacon ranks in the diocese next to the bishop,[92] and has ordinary jurisdiction in the archdeaconry.[93] Under pre-1920 ecclesiastical law, the archdeacon is styled *oculus episcopi*, the eye of

---

[88] See also CSBG, VII.1 and 2: the minor canons must attend and take part in services regularly on Sundays and weekdays, and preach, as the dean appoints, and they must perform such other duties as the dean directs; CSSD, VII: priest vicars must do such work and attend such services in the cathedral as the dean prescribes, with the consent of the Chapter; CSL, VII: the minor canons do such work, within or without the cathedral, as the dean directs, subject to any regulations made by the Chapter; CSB, VII: the minor canons must attend services regularly on Sundays and weekdays, and take part in them, and carry out such other duties in connection with the cathedral as the dean directs in accordance with Chapter regulations.

[89] The office of archdeacon is known only in some Anglican churches, e.g. England, Can. C22; Ireland, Const. II.38–42; see generally CLAC, 148ff.

[90] Bangor, Swansea and Brecon, and Monmouth each have two archdeaconries; Llandaff, St Asaph and St Davids have three each.

[91] Const. VII.1(1) and (2); see also VI.1(b): for the purposes of Const. VI (on parochial administration) 'archdeacon' means the archdeacon of the archdeaconry in which a parish is situated.

[92] See Godolphin, *Reportorium Canonicum*, 60; the principle had statutory recognition in the Ecclesiastical Commissioners Act 1840, preamble and s. 19, but this statute was repealed by the Church in Wales (see Const. XI.47).

[93] According to Halsbury, 'It is doubtful whether an archdeacon as such has a cure of souls' (*Ecclesiastical Law* (4th edn, London, 1975), para. 496), but for Phillimore, archdeacons share, for part of the diocese, with bishops in their spiritual cure of the whole diocese (*Ecclesiastical Law* (1895), I, 382); see also Canons Ecclesiastical 1603, Can. 119: the archdeacon has 'ecclesiastical jurisdiction'. There is a difference of opinion as to whether an archdeacon is inferior in rank to a dean, but it would appear to be clear that an archdeacon is inferior in rank to the diocesan chancellor, the latter treated as representing the person of the bishop: see HLE (1910), para. 860.

the bishop, having the charge of parochial churches.[94] Before admission to office, the archdeacon must make a declaration of canonical obedience and the other declarations concerning ecclesiastical discipline required of those appointed to ecclesiastical office in the church.[95] The archdeacon, who must retire as such at seventy,[96] exercises within the archdeaconry administrative, judicial and quasi-judicial functions.

Administration   As to administrative responsibilities, an archdeacon is a member *inter alia* of the Governing Body, the Diocesan Advisory Committee, the Diocesan Parsonage Board,[97] and, as a matter of ecclesiastical practice, various diocesan bodies.[98] Entitled to production of an electoral roll on request,[99] the archdeacon must ensure that a parish complies with the law governing administration of the roll.[100] In a vacancy or suspended incumbency, with no cleric-in-charge, the archdeacon chairs the Vestry Meeting when the office of area dean is vacant.[101] Declarations on admission as churchwarden may be made in the presence of the archdeacon or his appointee.[102] The archdeacon has functions with regard to the parish inventory,[103] certain powers over the parsonage, and is entitled to a copy of the quinquennial church inspection report,[104] and the names and addresses of churchwardens.[105] When an incapacitated incumbent is also the archdeacon, the bishop must be notified and arrange for his duties to be carried out.[106]

---

[94] Godolphin, *Reportorium Canonicum*, 61; before 1920, it was debated whether the archdeacon has a cure of souls: see HLE (1910), para. 856.

[95] Const. VII.66; see above, and below, Ch. 9.

[96] Const. XII.1(1).

[97] Const. VII.10, 11, 21; II.5; RODC, Pt. I, Sched. 2, Pt. 1, para. 2.

[98] See e.g. DSA, YB, 44, 46, 49: the three archdeacons are *ex officio* members of the Diocesan Conference, the Diocesan Board of Finance and the Diocesan Advisory Committee on the Care of Churches.

[99] Const. VI.5.

[100] Const. VI.6: see above, Ch. 4.

[101] Const. VI.12(3): also, in a vacancy in a rectorial benefice, the chairman is the vicar of that benefice designated by the area dean, and, if the office of area dean is vacant, the chair is the archdeacon.

[102] Const. VI.18.

[103] Const. VI.21: the archdeacon: may issue written directions concerning the control of it; must inspect it and the accompanying report submitted to him by churchwardens in a vacancy in an incumbency; must deliver the inventory and report to the new incumbent; and is entitled to receive any parish inventory when he requests it. Any dispute or question concerning the inventories must be referred to the archdeacon; see below, Ch. 13.

[104] Const. X.17 and IV.17: see below, Ch. 13.

[105] Const. VI.28(2)(b).

[106] Can. 21-4-82, First Schedule, paras. 2(2), and 5(1).

Adjudication   As to judicial and quasi-judicial functions, the archdeacon is president, ordinarily, of the Archdeacon's Court,[107] and empowered to appoint a registrar to both the court and archdeaconry.[108] If any dispute arises as to the right of a person to attend, speak or vote at a Vestry Meeting, whilst the chairman's ruling for that meeting is conclusive, that person may appeal to the archdeacon when the incumbent is also the area dean.[109] Any dispute arising out of the rule that the electoral roll must be produced for inspection by a qualified elector must be settled by the archdeacon.[110] If any difficulty is foreseen concerning compliance with the rule that churchwardens are ineligible for re-election or reappointment after six years in office, the archdeacon may dispense with the application of this rule, and must report the matter to the bishop.[111]

Visitation   The archdeacon's visitatorial powers represent a mixture of administrative and quasi-judicial functions. The archdeacon must conduct regular visitations of all parishes in the archdeaconry and, subject to any direction of the Governing Body, the form of the visitation must be determined by the archdeacon.[112] Whilst the form of the visitation under the modern law of the church is a matter solely for the archdeacon, several principles of pre-1920 ecclesiastical law offer guidance on the conduct of the visitation. The purpose of the visitation is that the archdeacon 'may get some good knowledge of the state, sufficiency, and ability of the Clergy, and other persons whom they are to visit'.[113] If hindered from carrying out the visitation, the archdeacon may appoint a commissary.[114] The archdeacon supplies articles of inquiry and on these the churchwardens make presentments on the state of the parish.[115] It seems the archdeacon is expected to deliver an address at the visitation (called a charge);[116] he may require clergy to preach a visitation sermon,[117] and may cite the clergy, churchwardens and perhaps sidesmen to attend, but not the laity generally.[118] Letters of orders, institution and induction, dispensations,

---

[107] Const. XI.2; see above, Ch. 5.
[108] Const. XI.3, 4; see above, Ch. 5.
[109] Const. VI.14: normally appeal is to the area dean.
[110] Const. VI.4: see above, Ch. 4.
[111] Const. VI.17(8): see below, Ch. 8.
[112] Const. XI.17.
[113] Canons Ecclesiastical 1603, Can. 137.
[114] HLE (1910), para. 861.
[115] Canons Ecclesiastical, Can. 119: a convenient time must be given for the churchwardens to prepare their presentments; Cans. 113–20 make full provision for the conduct of visitation.
[116] HLE (1910), para. 861.
[117] See *Huntley's Case* (1626) 4; see also R. Burn, *Ecclesiastical Law* (5th edn, London, 1788), 27.
[118] *Anon* (1608) Noy 123.

licences and faculties must be produced by clergy if required.[119] The archdeacon customarily admits churchwardens to office at the visitation.[120] A visitation may be held by grouping parishes.[121] During an episcopal visitation, the archdeacon is inhibited from the exercise of his jurisdiction and his ministerial duties are suspended, power being vested in the bishop alone.[122]

The Office of Area Dean

Appointment to the office of area dean (formerly known as rural dean) vests in the diocesan bishop. To be eligible for admission the candidate must be a beneficed or licensed cleric. On a vacancy arising in the office of area dean, the clerics of the deanery, who are beneficed or licensed by the bishop to officiate, must select three of their number for nomination to the diocesan bishop. The bishop must appoint one of those so nominated to the vacant office.[123] Before admission to office, the area dean must make a declaration of canonical obedience and the other declarations concerning ecclesiastical discipline required of those appointed to ecclesiastical office in the church.[124] The area dean is not a permanent officer, but may, it seems, be removed from that office at the will of his superior whose minister he is.[125] The law of the church contains no discrete treatment of the functions of the area dean,[126] though under pre-1920 ecclesiastical law their general function was confined to inspection and report to the bishop on matters related to the deanery.[127] Today, the area dean summons and presides at the Deanery Conference, in which he has a second or casting vote,[128] hears appeals about the right to attend, speak or vote at a Vestry Meeting,[129] and receives names and addresses of the persons elected to the

---

[119] Canons Ecclesiastical 1603, Can. 137.

[120] PA, 1, p. 24.

[121] *Shepherd v Payne* (1862) 12 CB (NS), 414, 434, 435.

[122] *R v Sowter* [1901] 1 KB 396.

[123] Const. VII.3: the meeting must be specially held for this purpose, and the three nominees must be serving in the parochial ministry of the Church in Wales; seven clear days' notice of the meeting must be given by the archdeacon of the archdeaconry in which the deanery is situated.

[124] Const. VII.66; see above, and below, Ch. 9.

[125] Godolphin, *Reportorium Canonicum*, Appendix, 6.

[126] Whilst the rural dean was an important officer in medieval canon law, the office fell into disuse after the Reformation but was revived in 1836: see HLE (1910), para. 862.

[127] Phillimore, *Ecclesiastical Law*, I, 213: the function of reporting would seem to imply a right to be consulted by parishes in cases of difficulty, and, in conjunction with the expectation on parish clergy to collaborate with fellow clergy in the deanery, a right to give pastoral advice and direction in cases of difficulty: see *Cure of Souls* (1996), 7.

[128] Const. V.3: see above, Ch. 3.

[129] Const. VI.14.

Deanery Conference.[130] Other functions of the area dean relate to vacant incumbencies.

In a vacancy or suspended incumbency, with no cleric-in-charge, the area dean must act as chairman at the Vestry Meeting.[131] During a vacancy in an incumbency, or where a parsonage in a suspended incumbency is vacant, the area dean (together with the churchwardens) is the custodian for the parsonage and is responsible for its care.[132] The area dean must be notified when an incumbent is incapacitated.[133] When an incumbent is incapacitated, the area dean must arrange for the maintenance of ministry in the affected benefice; when the incapacitated incumbent is the area dean, the archdeacon must be notified and must arrange for the area dean's duties to be carried out.[134] If an incumbent is incapacitated, or in a vacancy or suspended incumbency, the appointment of a churchwarden may be made by the area dean.[135] During vacancies the churchwardens should exercise their functions in consultation with the area dean who is also understood, by custom, to be responsible for arranging services.[136] Indeed, parochial clergy are expected to work collaboratively with the area dean.[137]

PARISH CLERGY: INCUMBENTS

Clergy at the most local level of the Church in Wales fall into two general categories: beneficed clergy (that is, incumbents and rectors); and unbeneficed clergy (that is, vicars in rectorial benefices, priests-in-charge, and assistant curates).[138] The following deals with incumbents.[139] The law of patronage governs their appointment,[140] a process which has two broad stages: collation or nomination;[141] and institution (and induction). The law

---

[130] Const. VI.28(c).

[131] Const. VI.12(3): or, the dean's nominee may act; also, in a vacancy in a rectorial benefice, the chairman is the vicar of that benefice designated by the area dean.

[132] Const. X.39: the area dean is responsible for care other than for such purposes as are the responsibility of the Diocesan Parsonage Board: see below, Ch. 13.

[133] Can. 21–4–82, First Schedule, para. 2(1): this does not apply to parishes annexed to cathedrals.

[134] Can. 21–4–82, First Schedule, paras. 2(2), and 5(1).

[135] Const. VI.17(4): this applies if there is no cleric-in-charge.

[136] PA, 1, p. 27.

[137] *Cure of Souls* (1996), 7: and: 'Failure to collaborate with fellow clergy and ministers is a breach of duty.'

[138] For the concept of beneficed and unbeneficed clergy, and for models of appointment generally, in the Anglican Communion, see CLAC, 137ff.

[139] For the various categories of parish, see above, Ch. 4.

[140] Welsh Church Act 1914, s. 38: for the purposes of this statute, 'right of patronage' includes 'any advowson, right of presentation, or right of nomination to an ecclesiastical office'.

[141] Collation is when the bishop nominates.

also provides for the suspension of incumbencies. For the sake of convenience, rectors, who are incumbents of rectorial benefices, are dealt with in the next section.

Appointment: Collation and Nomination of Incumbents

The Right of Patronage   The right to collate or nominate a priest belongs to: the diocesan bishop; the Diocesan Patronage Board; the Provincial Patronage Board; or an individual endowing a benefice.[142] The right to collate or nominate to vacant benefices is exercised in turns. It vests in the bishop once in four vacancies, in the Diocesan Patronage Board twice in four vacancies, and in the Provincial Patronage Board on the remaining occasion. The order or cycle of turns is as follows: bishop; the Diocesan Patronage Board; the Provincial Patronage Board; and the Diocesan Patronage Board; and so on in succession.[143] Special provisions apply: when two or more parishes are grouped or united together under one incumbent; when the suspension of an incumbency is terminated, other than upon a grouping; when a new parish is created;[144] and when a grouped parish becomes a separate parish.[145]

The law also provides for private patronage. A person endowing a benefice may, by permission of the Representative Body, exercise the right of nominating a cleric in priest's orders to a newly created cure. The person may also nominate, if the cure is not newly created, to the first vacancy after endowment. The written permission of the Representative Body must have been obtained before the right can be exercised.[146] The bishop, the Provincial Patronage Board, and the private patron cannot exercise any right of collation or nomination until the names of the persons proposed

---

[142] Const. VII.6. Whilst parish representatives are to represent the wishes of the parish, these have no right to veto a nomination: for comment, see P. Jones, *Governance*, 320.

[143] Const. VII.7(1)–(2); lots are drawn for each benefice to determine at which of the four turns the cycle begins, and the other turns follow in sequence (VII.7(3)).

[144] Const. VII.7(4): in these cases, the turn of patronage is that of the bishop, as the first of a new cycle of four turns for the benefice concerned, and the order of the remaining turns follows successively in the manner described above.

[145] Const. VII.7(5): the order of turns is as follows: (a) if the parish was grouped before 1 June 1969, the order is the same as on the creation of a new parish; (b) if the parish was grouped after this date, the order is the same as previously pertained to the parish before it became grouped, and the turns must be exercised as if no such grouping had taken place; for the purposes of this subsection a parish includes two or more parishes grouped together; VII.7(6): when a person endowing a benefice is allowed to exercise the right to nominate, or when an exchange of the benefice is made by the incumbent with the consent of the bishop and the Patronage Board, these do not count as one of the vacancies covered in Const. VII.7.

[146] Const. VII.8: the permission must specify the time within which the nomination must be made; the person endowing a benefice is the private patron, and must send the bishop within the time full particulars of the person nominated.

have been submitted. Full opportunity to make their views known must have been afforded to those persons who, if the right to nominate had been vested in the Patronage Board, would have been the representatives of the parish on that Board.[147]

The Diocesan Patronage Board The composition of the Diocesan Patronage Board varies depending on the vacancy in question. First, for a vacancy in a single parish incumbency, the Diocesan Patronage Board consists of: the diocesan bishop; the archdeacon of the archdeaconry in which the cure is vacant; two clerics and three lay persons, who are members of the Diocesan Conference;[148] and two lay communicants representing the parish in which the cure is vacant.[149] Secondly, for a vacancy in an incumbency which comprises two or more grouped parishes, the Diocesan Patronage Board consists of: the diocesan bishop; the archdeacon of the archdeaconry in which the cure is vacant; one cleric (in respect of each parish in the group) and three lay persons who are members of the Diocesan Conference;[150] and one lay communicant, representing each parish in which the cure is vacant.[151] When in any diocese there is more than one archdeacon, every archdeacon must be summoned to attend, advise and assist the Diocesan Patronage Board.[152]

At the first meeting of a newly elected Diocesan Conference, its clerical members must elect twelve clerical members, and its lay members must elect nine lay members, whose names are placed on a list in the order in which they are to act on the Diocesan Patronage Board. The two or more persons whose names appear at the head of the clerical list, and the three persons whose names appear at the head of the lay list, become members of the board. The place of a board member who dies is taken by the person next on the clerical or lay list. Any board member unable or unwilling to attend must notify the board secretary, who then summons the person next on the list able and willing to attend; the person becomes a board member for that meeting.[153]

---

[147] Const. VII.9.
[148] The clerics must be elected triennially by the clerical members of the Conference; the three lay persons must also be elected triennially by the lay members of the Conference.
[149] These must be elected triennially by the Vestry Meeting.
[150] Such clerics must be elected triennially by the clerical members of the Conference; the three lay persons must be elected triennially by the lay members of the Diocesan Conference.
[151] Const. VII.10: the lay person must be elected triennially by the Vestry Meeting.
[152] Const. VII.11: this must be done in accordance with VII.41: see below. However, no archdeacon, unless a member of the board at that meeting, is entitled to a vote except for the purpose of electing the lay representative, and supplemental representatives, to the Provincial Patronage Board.
[153] Const. VII.12.

The Vestry Meeting, at which the representatives of the parish on the Diocesan Patronage Board are elected, must elect six lay communicants and place their names on a list in the order in which it is desired they are to act on the board. The parish must be represented on the board by the person whose name appears at the head of the list. Where two representatives are required, the parish must be represented on the board by the two persons whose names appear at the head of the list. If unable or unwilling to attend any Diocesan Patronage Board meeting, they must notify the board secretary, who then summons the person next on the list able and willing to attend.[154]

The bishop (or his commissary appointed in writing) presides at the Diocesan Patronage Board and has a casting vote. If the bishop (or commissary) is absent, the board must elect a chairman from among its members, who has a casting vote.[155] The Diocesan Conference must settle for itself the manner of electing the members of the board.[156] Moreover, the bishop may summon a meeting of the archdeacons, and the clerical and lay members of the Diocesan Patronage Board elected by the Diocesan Conference, to confer with him on the general policy of patronage in the diocese.[157] Intermediate meetings may be convened by the bishop, and must be convened by him on the written request of two members of the board.[158]

The Provincial Patronage Board This consists of: the diocesan bishops; the chairman of the Representative Body (if a layman) or his lay nominee;[159] and the lay person representing the diocese in which the cure is vacant.[160] A

---

[154] Const. VII.13(1): the person becomes a board member for that meeting; VII.13(2): a copy of the list (with full names and addresses) must be sent as soon as possible after election by the secretary of the Parochial Church Council to the secretary of the Diocesan Patronage Board. If one or either of these persons have their name removed from the electoral roll, their place must taken by the person next on the list.

[155] Const. VI.14; VII.21: in a vacancy in a see, the senior archdeacon presides; see also VII.17: no consideration of a vacancy or prospective vacancy can be entertained, and no nomination made, unless fourteen days' notice of the time and place of the meeting, of the vacancies to be filled, and of the intent to nominate has been given to all members of the board (as constituted under VII.10); subject to VII.20, the board must meet four times a year; VII.19: the secretary of the Diocesan Conference is the secretary of the board and must attend all its meetings; VII.20: if one week before the quarterly meeting there is no vacancy to be filled, the secretary (unless the bishop directs otherwise) must notify the members that the meeting is cancelled.

[156] Const. VII.15: the settlement must be subject to the rules of Const. VII; VII.22: subject to the control of the Governing Body and of the Diocesan Conference, the Board must manage its own affairs and regulate its own procedure.

[157] Const. VII.16.

[158] Const. VII.18.

[159] Const. VII.41(1): if the chairman is not a lay person, then a lay person.

[160] The diocesan lay representative is appointed by the Diocesan Patronage Board: VII.41(2).

quorum consists of three persons: the archbishop;[161] the bishop of the diocese in which the vacancy has occurred; and a lay chairman of the Representative Body (or his nominee) or the diocesan lay representative.[162] The secretary of a Diocesan Patronage Board must within seven days of hearing of a vacancy (to which the Provincial Patronage Board is entitled to nominate), notify the archbishop's registrar.[163] The archbishop must decide and inform the registrar of the procedure to be adopted by the Provincial Patronage Board for making the nomination to the vacancy; and the registrar must give notice of this to the other members of the board.[164]

Failure to Collate or Nominate   When the Diocesan Patronage Board does not nominate to a vacancy within four months, or the private patron within the time specified in the permission granted by the Representative Body, the appointment passes to the bishop.[165] If the bishop does not collate within four months of the vacancy, or fails to collate within four months of a right of collation devolving on him, the right to nominate passes to the Bench of Bishops.[166] Similarly, if the Provincial Patronage Board does not nominate within four months, nomination passes to the Bench of Bishops.[167]

Acceptance of the Nomination   The secretary of the Diocesan Patronage Board must send the bishop, within seven days, full particulars of all nominations made at its meeting.[168] The secretary must also send, within seven days, notice of nomination to the cleric nominated; a private patron must likewise notify their nominee.[169] If the cleric does not accept the nomination by letter to the bishop within four weeks, the nomination is null and void. The same applies if the cleric accepts, but through his own

---

[161] Or, if absent, the next senior diocesan bishop willing to act other than the bishop of the diocese in which the vacancy occurs.

[162] Const. VII.42: if the vacancy occurs in the diocese of which the archbishop is the diocesan bishop entitled to nominate, the quorum must include the next senior diocesan bishop willing to act.

[163] Const. VII.43; VII.44; the notice must state: the reason for the vacancy (e.g. death or resignation); the date of the late incumbent's appointment; the number of curates (if any) and the number of services in Welsh (if any); the scheduled stipend of the benefice; whether there is a parsonage or an allowance (and if so, how much); the archbishop's registrar must within three days of receiving the notice send a copy to each member of the Provincial Patronage Board.

[164] Const. VII.45: the nomination decision must be by a majority of the board.

[165] Const. VII.23.

[166] Const. VII.24: the nomination is deemed to have been made by the bishop or the Provincial Patronage Board as from the date on which it is made.

[167] Const. VII.25: the nomination is deemed to have been made by the bishop or the board as from the date on which it is made.

[168] Const. VII.26.

[169] Const. VII.27: notice must be by recorded-delivery letter to the cleric's last known address.

fault, fails to be instituted within the time fixed by the bishop.[170] When a nomination becomes null and void, notice must be given to the secretary of the Diocesan Patronage Board or the private patron. If a nomination by the board becomes null and void, the secretary must convene a special meeting to make another nomination.[171] If a nomination by a private patron becomes null and void, the patron has until one month from his receipt of the notice from the bishop to nominate.[172] The secretary of the Diocesan Patronage Board, on receipt of the letter of acceptance of a cure from the cleric, must notify this to the bishop.[173]

The Provincial Court may determine all questions arising with respect to nomination, at the request of the diocesan bishop, or on the petition or suit of the cleric, any two members of the relevant Diocesan Patronage Board or the private patron.[174] If it considers that the nomination has been improperly made, the court must declare the cure vacant as from the date of its judgment, and make such further order as may seem just under the circumstances.[175]

Suspension of Patronage Rights First, if a vacancy occurs in an incumbency the bishop may, with the consent of the Diocesan Patronage Board,[176] suspend that incumbency by decree, signed and deposited in the Diocesan Registry. The bishop may do so only after giving full opportunity to the Parochial Church Council to state the case for the parish. At the termination of suspension the incumbency revives.[177] Secondly, if a vacancy occurs in an incumbency of a parish previously placed on a defaulters' list,[178] the bishop (with the consent of the Diocesan Patronage Board)[179] may either (1) collate a priest as incumbent; or (2) suspend the incumbency following the above procedure. The bishop may do either of these for a

[170] Const. VII.28: this runs from the date on which the recorded-delivery letter might have reached his address; the four-week period and the time fixed for institution may be extended by the bishop.

[171] Const. VII.29: the bishop must cause notice to be given; in this case the time of four months allowed to the board to make the nomination extends until a date one month after the notice convening the meeting.

[172] Const. VII.29.

[173] Const. VII.30.

[174] The petition or suit is subject to the rules and regulations of the court, but no petition or suit can be brought after a period of one month from the date of institution.

[175] Const. VII.58–60. See above, Ch. 5.

[176] The board must be constituted in accordance with Const. VII.16 (i.e. the archdeacons, and the clerical and lay members of the Diocesan Patronage Board elected by the Diocesan Conference).

[177] Const. VII.6(2); however, the bishop may block revival under the provisions of Const. IV.34–40, that is, by means of pastoral reorganization effected by diocesan decree: see above, Ch. 4.

[178] Const. IV.18: parishes may be placed on a defaulters' list for, *inter alia*, failure to meet financial obligations: see Chs. 4 and 14.

[179] The board must be constituted in accordance with Const. VII.16; see above, n. 157.

period he determines, and may make other provision for the spiritual needs of the parish as he thinks fit. When the collated incumbent vacates the benefice, the normal right to nominate is resumed. At the end of the period of suspension of an incumbency of a defaulters' list parish, the incumbency must be revived. Then, the person or board who had the right to nominate at the date of the suspension resumes the right; it must be exercised within four months from the end of the suspension.[180]

Institution of Incumbents

Institution is in the keeping of the bishop.[181] No cleric can be instituted while a petition or suit concerning his nomination is pending,[182] nor, if the person is coming from another diocese, without testimonials.[183] If the bishop institutes a cleric nominated by a board or private patron, he must notify this to the board's secretary or the patron. The Diocesan Registrar must inform the secretary of the Representative Body of all collations and institutions.[184] If the bishop refuses to institute a cleric nominated by a Patronage Board or a private patron, he must send written notice of the refusal, together with the reasons for it, to the cleric, and (as the case may be) to the private patron or board secretary, who must then convene a special meeting of the board.[185]

There is a right of appeal to the Provincial Court in the case of a refusal by the bishop to institute. The right may be exercised by the cleric whom the bishop refuses to institute, or, with the cleric's consent, either the Provincial Patronage Board or the Diocesan Patronage Board, or the private patron.[186] If the court decides that the cleric nominated is a fit and proper person to be instituted, the bishop must institute that cleric.[187] If the

---

[180] Const. VII.6(3): the end of the suspension period is (for the purposes of the sections following VII.6) deemed to be the date of the vacancy.

[181] Under pre-1920 ecclesiastical law, a bishop may refuse to institute because of, for instance: poor character (*Marriner v Bishop of Bath and Wells* [1893] P 137); insufficiency of learning (*Willis v Bishop of Oxford* (1877) 2 PD 192); lack of orthodoxy (*Heywood v Bishop of Manchester* (1883) 12 QBD 404); and lack of fitness (*Walsh v Bishop of Lincoln* (1875) LR 10 CP 518). In the Church of England, for example, grounds for refusing to institute are spelt out in the formal law: see Can. C10.

[182] Const. VII.31. See also the Simony Act 1588, s. 5 for corrupt institutions.

[183] Canons Ecclesiastical 1603, Can. 39: 'No Bishop shall institute any to a Benefice, who hath been ordained by any other Bishop, except he first show him his Letters of Orders, and bring him sufficient testimony of his former good life and behaviour, if the Bishop shall require it; and lastly, shall appear, on the examination, to be worthy of his ministry.'

[184] Const. VII.32; VII.33: the stipend of a cleric runs from the date of institution or from any earlier date determined by the Representative Body in any particular case.

[185] Const. VII.34.

[186] Const. VII.35: the appeal must be made within one month of refusal.

[187] Or his commissary appointed in writing.

court decides that the cleric is not a fit and proper person, the right of nomination must be exercised, within one month of the court's decision, by the board or patron whose first nomination has been rejected. If the bishop again refuses to institute, and the court on appeal decided that the cleric nominated is not a fit and proper person, the appointment passes to the bishop.[188]

Whenever a cleric nominated is already an incumbent of another cure in Wales, the institution of the cleric to the new cure operates as a resignation of the cure previously held, unless the bishop with the consent of the archbishop agrees to the cures being held together.[189] Special rules apply to a cleric who holds office outside Wales. If the diocesan bishop considers the office held outside Wales is inconsistent with the Welsh appointment, or that it is undesirable for the cleric to hold that office with a Welsh cure, the institution must be postponed until the cleric resigns that office and has produced evidence satisfying the bishop of the cleric's resignation of that office.[190] If such evidence is not produced within two months of the nomination, the nomination becomes null and void. Then the Patronage Board or private patron must nominate some other cleric as if a vacancy had taken place on the day after the expiration of the period of two months.[191] Whenever a cleric holding an ecclesiastical office or cure in Wales accepts an ecclesiastical office or cure outside Wales, this operates as a resignation of his ecclesiastical office or cure in Wales, unless the bishop decides to the contrary, and the office becomes vacant accordingly.[192] Induction into possession of the church and the temporalities of the benefice normally takes place at the same time as institution.[193]

Rights and Duties of Incumbents

In addition to rights and duties applicable to all clergy in the Church in Wales (see above), the law assigns to incumbents, having the cure of souls within a parish,[194] a number of specific rights and duties. First, every

---

[188] Const. VII.36.

[189] Const. VII.37.

[190] Const. VII.38

[191] Const. VII.39.

[192] Const. VII.40.

[193] See generally Halsbury, *Ecclesiastical Law* (4th edn, London, 1975), paras. 849–51. See also *Re Petition Against Revd Clifford Williams* (1997), in which the Provincial Court of the Church in Wales stated: 'According to the formula of institution or collation, this cure is committed to the Parish Priest by the Bishop as "my cure and thine", an ancient formula reflecting the collegiality which exists between the Bishop and his priests, and in particular with the priest to whom a particular parish is committed as the primary sphere of his ministry.'

[194] Whilst the bishop has the general cure of souls throughout the diocese (*Duke of Portland v Bingham* (1792) I Hag Con 157), the incumbent has the cure of souls in the

incumbent must reside within the limits of the parish, unless the bishop, on sufficient cause, has granted a licence of non-residence. No incumbent may be absent from the benefice without providing a fit and proper substitute, unless with special leave in writing from the bishop. If absent from the benefice for a period of two consecutive months without episcopal permission, the bishop may call on the incumbent to return; if at the expiration of one month he is still absent, the bishop may declare the benefice vacant. If an incumbent, without episcopal permission, is absent for non-consecutive periods amounting to eight weeks in any six months, the bishop may call on him to reside more regularly, and in the case of disobedience may declare the benefice vacant.[195]

Secondly, the incumbent must: summon and chair Vestry Meetings; be a member of and consult and co-operate with the Parochial Church Council; appoint churchwardens; keep inventories, report gifts and carry liability for the parsonage.[196] Their pastoral, liturgical, ecumenical and proprietorial functions are discussed elsewhere in this volume.[197] Failure to discharge their legal duties may result in proceedings in the Disciplinary Tribunal.[198] Incumbents may seek from the bishop the appointment of assistant curates and deaconesses;[199] they are entitled to provision for housing, maintenance and a pension,[200] and may appoint all such parochial officers as their predecessor in the benefice would have been entitled to appoint before the passing of the Welsh Church Act 1914.[201] Rights and duties such as these are scattered throughout the laws of the church. In contrast to many other Anglican churches, the Church in Wales lacks a systematic statement of the functions of an incumbent.[202]

Termination of the Ministry of Incumbents

The ministry of an incumbent is terminated by death, retirement, resignation, removal or exchange of benefices. As a general rule, incumbents must retire at the age of seventy.[203] Special provisions exist for the maintenance of incapacitated incumbents.[204]

---

parish, and no other cleric (except the bishop), has any right publicly to officiate or perform clerical ministrations without the incumbent's consent (see e.g. *Nesbitt v Wallace* [1901] P 354. See also above, n. 193.

[195] Const. VII.48–51.
[196] See Chs. 4, 8, 13 and 14.
[197] See below, Part III.
[198] See above, Ch. 5.
[199] Const. VII.52: see below.
[200] For Const. X see below, Ch. 13.
[201] Const. VII.54.
[202] See CLAC, 146ff.
[203] Const. XII.1(3): see below, Ch. 14.
[204] Can. 21–4–82: see below, Ch. 14.

Resignation   An incumbent may, with episcopal leave, resign the benefice by giving written notice to the bishop. The notice must fix a definite time, not earlier than two months nor later than six months, at which the resignation will take effect. A bishop may, within one month of receiving the notice, allow it to be withdrawn. If it is not withdrawn within this period, and the bishop accepts the resignation, the benefice becomes vacant at the time specified in the notice. However, at the incumbent's request, the bishop may in special circumstances (of which the bishop is sole judge) allow the cleric to resign the benefice immediately, or else at a date earlier than two months from the date of the request. The resignation must be effected by a deed duly executed and the benefice becomes vacant at the date specified in the deed as the date upon which the resignation takes effect.[205] When the cure is vacant, the bishop may appoint to it a priest-in-charge.[206]

Removal of Incumbents   A cleric duly instituted to a cure is deemed the incumbent of the benefice, and must not be removed without his consent. However, an incumbent may be removed on four grounds. First, an incumbent may be removed by the bishop to another benefice or other ecclesiastical office in the church in those cases where, in the opinion of the bishop, such a change is necessary; the bishop may remove the cleric only after consultation with, and with the consent of, the Diocesan Patronage Board.[207] Secondly, the bishop may remove an incumbent for any reason which, in the judgment of the Provincial Court, renders his continuance in office grievously prejudicial to the welfare of the church.[208] Thirdly, the bishop may require an incumbent to retire from full-time service in the ministry of the church in any case in which in the opinion of the bishop such retirement is necessary.[209] Finally, an incumbent may be removed by an exercise of the inherent jurisdiction of the bishop in cases where the incumbent has been absent from the benefice.[210] The powers conferred on the bishop in the first three cases described above are exercisable only if he gives not less than six months' previous written notice to the incumbent. However, the incumbent has a right of appeal to the Provincial Court within a period of six weeks after receiving the notice.[211]

---

[205] Const. VII.55. See also the Simony Act 1588, s. 7: this prohibits corrupt resignations in which there is a giving or receiving of unlawful benefits.
[206] See below.
[207] Const. VII.46(1)(a): the board must be constituted as under VII.10; on a change such augmentation may be made to the stipend of the benefice or other ecclesiastical office to which the incumbent is removed as may be decided by the Diocesan Board of Finance in consultation with the bishop.
[208] Const. VII.46(1)(b): failing other employment, the cleric must receive such maintenance, if any, as the court recommends to the Representative Body.
[209] Const. VII.46(1)(c): on such retirement the incumbent is entitled to a pension.
[210] Const. VII.46(1)(d): see VII.50 and 51. For residence and absence, see above.
[211] Const. VII.46(2). These provisions are far less detailed than those operative in other

Exchange of Benefices When two incumbents wish to exchange their benefices, each of them must apply in writing to their own diocesan bishop for permission. The bishop, or, in the case of two parishes in different dioceses, either bishop, may refuse permission. If permission is granted, the bishop(s) must convene the Patronage Board(s) of the diocese(s).[212] If the Diocesan Patronage Board(s) consents, the exchange takes effect accordingly. The bishop(s) must fix a day on which the cure in each parish is to become vacant, and must then institute the clerics to their respective cures. These provisions do not apply when an incumbent of a parish or district outside Wales wishes to exchange a benefice for a benefice in Wales.[213]

PARISH CLERGY: RECTORS, VICARS AND CURATES

This section deals with the law of the church applicable to: clergy in rectorial benefices, the rector (who is beneficed) and vicars (who are not beneficed); priests-in-charge of vacant incumbencies; and assistant curates serving in benefices in the charge of an incumbent.

Clergy of a Rectorial Benefice

A rectorial benefice is an area consisting of one or more parishes, or portions of them.[214] The incumbent of a rectorial benefice, with the title of rector, has the cure of souls and responsibility for 'the control and co-ordinating of the work of the ministry throughout the benefice'. The rector is entitled to the assistance of one or more other clerics, who must be licensed by the diocesan bishop, with the title of vicar; a rectorial benefice may also have one or more assistant curates.[215] The appointment of rectors is governed by the rules described earlier in this section applicable to the appointment of incumbents.[216] A vicar in a rectorial benefice must be

Anglican churches; for the Church of England, in which the Incumbents (Vacation of Benefices) Measure 1977 deals with vacation on a serious breakdown of pastoral relations, see Doe, *Legal Framework*, 419ff.

[212] This must be done within one month after the application. The Patronage Board consists of the bishop, the archdeacons of the archdeaconries in which the parishes are situated, the members of the board elected by the Diocesan Conference, and the parish representatives from each parish.

[213] Const. VII.61–5: in this case the bishop of the diocese into which the incumbent wishes to exchange must decide 'what shall be done in the matter'.

[214] Const. IV.39(1). For formation of a rectorial benefice, see Ch. 3.

[215] Const. IV.39(2): the vicar has a right, unless in non-stipendiary ministry, to a stipend not less than the minimum stipend laid down for incumbents of ordinary parishes, and a house or house allowance: see below, Chs. 13 and 14.

[216] Const. IV.39(3): i.e., in accordance with the provisions of Const. VII, for which see above. However, under IV.39(4), on the formation of a rectorial benefice, the first turn of patronage (which includes appointment of the previous incumbent as rector of the

appointed by the bishop by licence under seal after consultation with the rector. Prior to the appointment, the bishop, or the archdeacon on his behalf, must consult with the other vicar (or vicars), if any, in the rectorial benefice, as well as with the two parochial representatives who serve on the Diocesan Patronage Board.[217] Any vicar appointed may be publicly admitted in a church in the rectorial benefice.[218] Vicars must reside in the rectorial benefice unless the bishop, on sufficient cause, has granted a licence of non-residence.[219]

Vicars cannot be removed without their consent, nor can their appointment be terminated without their consent, except on three grounds. First, the vicar may be removed by the bishop to another rectorial benefice, or to a benefice or other ecclesiastical office in the church, when in the opinion of the bishop such a change is necessary.[220] Secondly, the bishop may remove for any reason which, in the judgment of the Provincial Court, renders the continuance of the vicar in office grievously prejudicial to the welfare of the church.[221] Thirdly, the bishop may require a vicar to retire from full-time service in the ministry of the church if the bishop considers retirement is necessary.[222] The powers are exercisable by the bishop only on his giving not less than six months' previous written notice to the vicar. The vicar may appeal to the Provincial Court within six weeks after receipt of the notice.[223]

An incumbent or vicar in a rectorial benefice may, with episcopal leave, resign the benefice or appointment by giving written notice to the bishop. The notice must fix a definite time, not earlier than two months nor later than six months, at which the resignation will take effect. A bishop may within one month from receiving the notice allow it to be withdrawn; but, if it is not withdrawn within this period, and the bishop accepts the resignation, the benefice becomes vacant or the appointment terminates at the time specified in the notice. However, at the request of the incumbent or vicar the bishop may in special circumstances (of which the bishop is sole judge) allow the cleric to resign the benefice or appointment immediately or at a date earlier than two months from the date of the request.[224]

---

new rectorial benefice) vests in the bishop, though further appointments are effected in turns (see above).

[217] Const. IV.39(5).

[218] Const. IV.39(6).

[219] Const. VII.48. Clerics in extra-parochial office have the status of vicar: VII.76.

[220] Const. VII.47(1)(a).

[221] Const. VII.47(1)(b): failing other employment, the vicar must receive such maintenance, if any, as the court recommends to the Representative Body.

[222] Const. VII.47(1)(c): the vicar is entitled to a pension.

[223] Const. VII.47(2).

[224] Const. VII.55: the resignation must be by a deed duly executed and the benefice becomes vacant or the appointment terminates at the date specified in the deed as the date on which the resignation takes effect.

Ministry in Vacant Cures: Priests-in-Charge

During a vacancy, the bishop is entitled to appoint a cleric in priest's orders to discharge the duties of the cure, or to appoint a cleric, reader or deaconess to take services. The bishop must determine the salary, if any, of a cleric discharging the duties of the cure, and the salary must be paid out of the income attached to the cure. Whenever a cleric is suspended from office, or absent without licence, the diocesan bishop may appoint a cleric in priest's orders to discharge the duties of the cure or office, at such salary, if any, as to the bishop seems fit; the salary must be paid out of the income, if any, attached to the cure or office.[225] The churchwardens or trustees of any church in the cure must allow the free use of the church to any cleric so appointed by the bishop to officiate in the cure.[226] A priest-in-charge has, whilst in charge, the rights and duties of the incumbent with reference to the services in the church and the cure of souls of the parish.[227]

Assistant Curates

When circumstances require it and, in the judgement of the bishop, sufficient maintenance can be guaranteed, the incumbent of a benefice is entitled to nominate to the bishop for his approval a cleric (to act as licensed assistant curate) or a deaconess. The assistant curate or deaconess cannot be removed from office without their consent unless upon the decision of the bishop or the avoidance of the benefice.[228] The bishop may, during the period of four years from the ordaining of a deacon, prescribe the benefice in which the deacon is to serve as a licensed assistant curate.[229] The bishop, before licensing, must be satisfied of the fitness of the candidate.[230] Prior to appointment candidates must make the declaration of canonical obedience and undertake to be bound by the law and discipline of the church.[231]

Every licensed assistant curate and deaconess must reside within the

---

[225] Const. VII.56.

[226] Const. VII.57.

[227] *Pinder v Burr* (1854) 4 E&B 105.

[228] Const. VII.52; compare the detailed provisions governing removal contained in other Anglican systems of canon law: CLAC, 154ff.: see e.g. England, Can. C12: this deals with the procedure for revocation of licences (including a right to be heard) and rights of appeal to the archbishop; for revocation under pre-1920 ecclesiastical law, see e.g. *Re Sinyanki* (1864) 12 WR 825.

[229] Const. VII.53.

[230] Canons Ecclesiastical 1603, Can. 48; see also Const. VII.32, 33: the diocesan registrar must inform the secretary of the Representative Body of all licences granted to assistant curates. Unlike in the case of institution of incumbents, there is no formal right of appeal against a bishop's refusal to license.

[231] Const. VII.66.

limits of the parish, unless the bishop, on sufficient cause, has granted a licence of non-residence.[232] As an unbeneficed cleric, in order to minister, an assistant curate requires, in addition to authorization from the bishop, the consent of the incumbent of the parish.[233] The assistant curate must act under the direction of the incumbent, who is responsible for what is done by the curate under his directions or with his consent. An assistant curate may be temporarily in charge of a parish during a short absence of the incumbent, but in that case acts as the representative of the incumbent and under his directions.[234]

Finally, any appointment to an office in the Church in Wales not especially provided for by the constitution, may be made by those entitled to make it at the date of the passing of the Welsh Church Act 1914, or, if there has been any change, their official successors. However, the Governing Body may at any time make regulations as to how and by whom such appointments are to be filled up. Any dispute as to the person or persons entitled to make such an appointment must be decided by the Provincial Court.[235]

HOLY ORDERS: RELINQUISHMENT AND DEPOSITION

Whilst holy orders are indelible,[236] a cleric of the Church in Wales may voluntarily relinquish holy orders, or be deposed from them as a result of disciplinary process in the church. Arrangements in the Church in Wales find a direct parallel in the canonical systems of the vast majority of Anglican churches.[237]

Relinquishment of Holy Orders

Any person admitted to the office of cleric in the Church in Wales may, after having resigned that office, execute a Deed of Relinquishment.[238] Once the deed has been enrolled and recorded,[239] the following conse-

---

[232] Const. VII.48

[233] Canons Ecclesiastical 1603, Cans. 48–50; see also *Carr v Marsh* (1814) 2 Phillim 198 and *Kitson v Drury* (1865) 11 Jur (NS), 272.

[234] *Martyn v Hind* (1785) Rothery's Precedents, No. 178, 89; *Parnell v Roughton* (1874) LR 6 PC 46, 53.

[235] Const. VII.67–8. VII.69 deals with archiepiscopal rights.

[236] *Barnes v Shore* (1846) 8 QB 640 at 671; see also Statement of the Provincial Synod, 27 January 1999.

[237] See CLAC, 88ff. and 156ff.

[238] Can. 19-4-1990 (the canon may be cited as the Clerical Disabilities Canon 1990): the form of the deed is set out in the schedule to the canon; this canon repeals the Clerical Disabilities Act 1870 (Const. XI.47).

[239] Can. 19-4-1990, para. 2(2): within twenty-eight days of executing the deed, the

quences ensue. First, the person is incapable of officiating or acting in any manner as a cleric of the Church in Wales, and of taking or holding any preferment in the church. Secondly, the person ceases to enjoy all rights, privileges, advantages and exemptions attached to the office of cleric in the Church in Wales. Thirdly, every licence, office and place held by that person[240] is determined and void. Fourthly, the person is discharged from all disabilities, disqualifications, restraints and prohibitions to which, under the law of the church or any other law, that cleric has been subject as a cleric in the Church in Wales.[241] However, relinquishment does not relieve a person from any liability in respect of dilapidations or from any debt or other pecuniary liability incurred or accrued before or after execution of a Deed of Relinquishment.[242]

The law also provides for the vacation of a Deed of Relinquishment. Any person who has relinquished the office of cleric in the Church in Wales,[243] may at any time after the Deed of Relinquishment has been recorded, present to the archbishop of the province, in which the diocese of record is situated, a written petition verified by a statutory declaration.[244] After consultation with the bishop of the diocese in which the deed was recorded, and any other enquiry and consultation as he deems necessary, the archbishop must communicate his decision to the petitioner. The archbishop may, if he thinks fit, request the vacation of the enrolment of

cleric must: cause it to be enrolled in the archbishop's registry; deliver an office copy of enrolment to the bishop of the diocese in which the cleric held preferment or, if the cleric has not held any preferment, to the bishop of the diocese in which the cleric is then residing (stating, in either case, their then place of residence); on delivery of an office copy to the bishop of the diocese, give notice of delivery to the archbishop of the province within which the diocese is situated: if these are not done, the deed is void. At the expiration of six months after an office copy is delivered to a bishop, the bishop must on the written application of the cleric involved cause the deed to be recorded in the diocesan registry.

[240] For which it is by law an indispensable qualification that the holder be a cleric of the Church in Wales.

[241] Can. 19-4-1990, para. 2(3): the person is also free from all jurisdiction, penalties, censures and proceedings to which, if the canon allowing relinquishment had not been passed, the cleric would or might, under the law of the church or any other law, have been subject, and of any act or thing done or omitted by the person after admission as a cleric. However, if no written application has been received at the expiration of nine months after enrolment, the deed is deemed void and the original endorsed accordingly; para. 2(4) deals with service; para. 2(7): a copy of the record in the diocesan registry is evidence of due execution, enrolment and recording of the deed.

[242] Can. 19–4–1990, para. 2(6): these may be enforced or recovered as if the canon or the Clerical Disabilities Act 1870 had not been passed.

[243] That is, the rights, privileges, advantages and exemptions of the office of cleric in the Church in Wales.

[244] The declaration must set out: the circumstances and reasons underlying execution of the deed; the nature of the work or employment in which the person has been engaged; the place(s) of residence subsequent to executing the deed; and the circumstances and reasons in and for which the person wishes to resume the position of an officiating cleric.

the deed executed by the petitioner.[245] On production of the request the enrolment must be vacated. After vacation of enrolment, the bishop of the diocese (in the registry of which the deed is recorded) must cause the vacation of the enrolment to be recorded in that diocesan registry. Finally, the consequences of relinquishment cease to have effect.[246]

Deposition from Holy Orders

The Disciplinary Tribunal and the Provincial Court are empowered to pass a sentence of deposition from holy orders and expulsion from the office of cleric of the Church in Wales.[247] Deposition is 'a penalty which prohibits a cleric from any exercise of the ministry committed to him or her in ordination'.[248] A cleric against whom an order of deposition and expulsion has been made by the Disciplinary Tribunal, and whose appeal to the Provincial Court has been dismissed, may on written notice appeal to the Provincial Synod, the decision of which is final.[249] On expiry of the period for giving notice of appeal, or on the dismissal of the appeal by the Provincial Synod, the bishop of the diocese in which the cleric holds office or resides must execute a Deed of Deposition, and cause the deed to be enrolled in the registry of the Archbishop of Wales. The archbishop's

---

[245] This must be done under his hand and archiepiscopal seal.

[246] Can. 19-4-1990, para. 3. However, the cleric is for two years after recording vacation, incapable of holding any benefice or other preferment, including the office of licensed curate, but may subject to such conditions as the bishop of any diocese may determine, officiate as a cleric in the diocese under the permission of that bishop. After the two years, the cleric is capable of holding any benefice or other preferment which he is entitled to hold under the constitution or canon law of the Church in Wales, in any diocese; this may be done subject to the consent of the bishop of that diocese being first obtained: episcopal consent may be either a general consent or consent given in respect of some particular benefice or preferment.

[247] Const. XI.26, 36(1). Subject to the constitution, the archbishop, a diocesan bishop, the Provincial Court, the Special Provincial Court and the Supreme Court may pass a sentence of expulsion from office in the Church in Wales (as well as of monition and suspension (see XI.45); see also above, Ch. 5.

[248] Statement of the Provincial Synod, 27 January 1999: deposition is not 'in conflict with the doctrine that Holy Orders once conferred are indelible'; its purpose is not only to express the church's judgement upon certain kinds of behaviour, but also 'to protect the Church as a whole from the destructive effects of a ministry exercised by someone whose conduct has been shown to result in such a degree of scandal and hurt to individuals and the Church community as to make any future exercise of that ministry unacceptable'; it is 'an appropriate penalty where it is established that there has been significant and repeated betrayal or abuse of pastoral trust, especially if there has been no indication of repentance or of a recognition of the seriousness of the offence. Such cases would include the sexual exploitation or harassment of those for whom a cleric has particular responsibilities, and where a consistent pattern of reprehensible behaviour had been established.'

[249] Const. XI.36(2): written notice of the appeal must be delivered to the archbishop's registrar within twenty-eight days of the dismissal of the appeal by the Provincial Court.

registrar must then deliver an office copy of the enrolment to the diocesan bishop and to the cleric, and give notice to the archbishop of having done so. On receipt of the office copy of the enrolment of the deed, the diocesan bishop must cause the deed to be recorded in the Diocesan Registry. The same consequences then ensue as if that person had executed, enrolled and recorded a Deed of Relinquishment.[250] A Deed of Deposition may be vacated in the same manner, and to the same effect, as a Deed of Relinquishment.[251]

---

[250] Const. XI.36(3), (4).
[251] Can. 19-4-1990, para. 5; for the reversibility of deposition in other Anglican churches, see CLAC, 91f., 157, n. 134.

8

THE LAITY AND LAY OFFICERS

The repeated recommendations of Lambeth Conferences, that the role of the laity in ecclesiastical life be enhanced, are based on the theology of clergy and laity together as comprising the whole people of God; the church is a body built up through the interdependent activities of its members, each exercising their individual vocations.[1] This chapter explores how legal and other structures within the Church in Wales give juridic expression to this ecclesiological emphasis on the ministry of the laity within the institutional church. Along with a description of the classes of church member and the common ministry of the laity, their basic rights and duties, the following examines the ways in which the church, and the State, seek to meet in church and in society at large the special needs of children, and those in hospitals and prisons. This chapter also deals with the lay officers of the church, their appointment, functions, and termination of their ministries.

CHURCH MEMBERSHIP

The concept of the membership of the Church in Wales appears in both civil law and the domestic law of the church. That the Church in Wales has a membership is recognized in the law of the State, both by parliamentary statute[2] and by the common law, under which the Church in Wales itself is understood as organized 'as a matter of agreement between those persons

---

[1] LC 1908, Res. 46: 'The ministry of the laity requires to be more widely recognized, side by side with the ministry of the clergy, in the work, administration, and the discipline of the Church'; LC 1958, Res. 58: 'The Conference calls on every Church member, clergy and laity, to take an active part in the mission of the Church'; LC 1958, Res. 94: 'The Conference, believing that the laity, as baptized members of the Body of Christ, share in the priestly ministry of the Church and in the responsibility for its work, calls upon Anglican men and women throughout the world to realise their Christian vocation both by taking their full part in the Church's life and by Christian witness and dedication in seeking to serve God's purpose in the world'; LC 1988, Res. 45: the Conference acknowledges 'that God through the Holy Spirit is bringing about a revolution in terms of the total ministry of all the baptized'.

[2] See e.g. Welsh Church Act 1914, s. 3(3): pre-1920 ecclesiastical law is 'binding on the

who are members of that body'.[3] However, whilst membership of the Church in Wales has been recognized in civil law, it has not been defined. Nevertheless, a member of the Church of England has, for the purposes of trusts law, been defined as a person who is baptized, confirmed and a regular communicant,[4] and as a baptized and confirmed person who attends church regularly and who conforms to the church's discipline.[5] This definition may by analogy apply to the Church in Wales. The 'laity of the Church in Wales' is also an entity recognized by parliamentary statute.[6]

The internal law of the Church in Wales also employs the notion of membership. According to the constitution, pre-1920 ecclesiastical law binds 'the members . . . of the Church in Wales'; certain decisions of the Provincial Synod bind a Diocesan Conference 'and all the other members of the Church in the diocese'; the tribunal and courts of the church have jurisdiction over proceedings against and disputes concerning members of the church; and members are obliged to attend any trial or investigation held under the authority of the constitution.[7] The only definition of the term in the constitution of the church, however, is that, for the purposes of its tribunal and courts, 'a member of the Church in Wales is a person on whom the Constitution is binding';[8] that is, with regard to the laity, all office-holders and all persons whose names are entered on the electoral roll of any parish in Wales.[9] In addition, the law of the church identifies different classes of person associated with the church: parishioners;[10] residents in a parish;[11] habitual worshippers;[12] communicants;[13] qualified electors;[14] members of ecclesiastical bodies;[15] and persons holding office in

members for the time being of the Church in Wales'; see too s. 13. See also Prison Act 1952, s. 10 (see below).

[3] *Re Clergy Orphan Corporation Trusts* [1933] 1 Ch 267.

[4] *Re Perry Almshouses* [1898] 1 Ch 391 at 400; see also *Schoales v Schoales* [1930] 2 Ch 76.

[5] *Re Allen, Faith v Allen* [1953] 1 Ch 810; see also *Re Barnes, Simpson v Barnes* [1930] 2 Ch 40.

[6] Welsh Church Act 1914, s. 13(1): nothing in law prevents 'the bishops, clergy, and laity of the Church in Wales' from holding assemblies.

[7] See respectively: Const. XI.47; IV.33; XI.6, 18 and 39.

[8] Const. XI.1(2)(a). For the idea of collective faith as defining membership, see P. Jones, *The Governance of the Church in Wales* (Cardiff, 2000), 47f, 149ff.

[9] Const. I.2.

[10] Const. VI.17(2); for pre-1920 definitions, see HLE (1910), para. 931. Parishioners (if they are not also members of the church), as such, are not bound by the domestic law of the Church in Wales: see Jones, *Governance*, 73.

[11] Const. VI.13(2).

[12] Const. VI.2(6)(e).

[13] Const. I.6(b): a communicant is 'a person who has lawfully received Holy Communion in the Church in Wales or some Church in communion therewith and is entitled to receive Holy Communion in the Church in Wales'.

[14] Const. VI.4.

[15] Const. XI.39(3).

the church who are not members of religious bodies not in full communion with the Church in Wales.[16] The law of the church also commonly uses the generic terms 'laity' (being persons not in holy orders),[17] 'lay person',[18] and 'lay members of ecclesiastical bodies'.[19] Baptism confers membership of the church universal rather than membership of the institutional Church in Wales.[20]

For many Anglican churches the need for a legal definition of 'member' is stimulated in part by the law of the State in which they exist: for some it is essential to determine membership to ascertain benefits under a gift to the church;[21] and for others only church members have *locus standi* to enforce internal church law in the secular courts.[22] Consequently, and by way of contrast to the Church in Wales, the laws of the vast majority of Anglican churches define membership carefully; but definitions are not uniform. In a minority, baptism effects both incorporation into the church universal and membership of the institutional church in question.[23] In other churches baptism and confirmation generate membership of the institutional church, though often to these is added reception of holy communion.[24] For some churches, the law provides: '"Member of this Church" means a baptized person who attends the public worship of this Church and who declares that he is a member of this Church and of no Church which is not in Communion with this Church.'[25] In many churches, membership is further divided into classes,[26] such as that of 'received member' (that is, an adult who, after appropriate instruction, and having made a mature public affirmation of their faith, has been received by a bishop into the church).[27]

---

[16] Const. II.14.
[17] Const. VI.17(2): for the laity as those not in holy orders, see *Bishop of St Albans v Fillingham* [1906] P 163 at 177; and *Walsh v Lord Advocate* [1936] 3 All ER 129 at 139. For the purposes of the Welsh Church Act 1914, an 'ecclesiastical person' means a bishop and the holder of any ecclesiastical office who is in holy orders (s. 38).
[18] For 'lay person', see e.g. Const. II.6.
[19] Const. II.13.
[20] See below, Ch. 10; see this also for loss of communicant status by excommunication.
[21] See e.g. England: *Re Allen, Faith v Allen* [1953] 1 Ch 810.
[22] See e.g. Nigeria: *Chief Dr Irene Thomas et al v The Most Revd Timothy Omotayo Olufosoye* [1986] 1 All NLR 215 (Supreme Ct): communicant members had insufficient interest to challenge an episcopal election; South Africa: *Mtshali v Mtambo and Another* [1962(3)] SALR 469: 'a member of a church has *locus standi in judicio* to bring proceedings to protect his rights without joining other members of such church as applicants.'
[23] See e.g. ECUSA, Can. I.17(a): 'All persons who have received the Sacrament of Holy Baptism ... whether in this Church or in another Christian Church, and whose Baptisms have been duly recorded in this Church, are members thereof.'
[24] See e.g. Tanzania, Const. 12: 'member' means 'a person baptized and confirmed who has received Holy Communion not less than three times in the past twelve months unless prevented or forbidden from so doing'.
[25] Australia, Const. XII.74.1.
[26] Usually for the purposes of eligibility for admission to individual lay offices in the church: see CLAC, 162f.
[27] See e.g. England, Can. B28.

THE COMMON MINISTRY OF THE LAITY

An obvious gap in the laws of many Anglican churches is a systematic treatment of the common ministry of the laity, their rights and duties. So too in the Church in Wales. First, with respect to *rights*, Anglican churches fall into two broad groups. On the one hand, there are churches with a system of fundamental rights, and anti-discrimination laws.[28] On the other hand, more commonly, there are churches with no distinct compendium of the rights of lay people. In these, rights are scattered amongst laws on discrete subjects, such as rights, reserved to people whose names are on the church roll, to participate in church government, or to be considered for admission to office.[29] The Church in Wales follows the pattern of the latter group. Though occasionally the notion of specific rights or entitlements surfaces in its formal law, such as the right to vote or the entitlement to holy communion,[30] lay rights are the by-product of clerical duties, such as the right of parishioners to infant baptism, marriage and burial.[31]

Secondly, it is rare for Anglican churches, in their laws,[32] to spell out the *duties* of the laity, though some implement a Lambeth Conference resolution, from 1948,[33] on this subject.[34] Most church legal systems do

---

[28] See e.g. ECUSA, Cans. I.17.5: 'No one shall be denied rights, status, or access to an equal place in the life, worship, and government of this Church because of race, color, ethnic origin, national origin, marital status, sex, sexual orientation, disabilities or age, except as otherwise specified by Canon'; Uganda, Const. Art. 3: the church 'shall not allow discrimination in the membership and government of the Church solely on grounds of colour, sex, tribe or region.'

[29] See CLAC, 164ff.

[30] See e.g. Const. VI.2(2): 'The purpose of the [electoral] roll shall be the determination of eligibility to exercise voting rights'; see also e.g. Const. I.6(b): a communicant is a person who has received holy communion in a church in communion with the Church in Wales 'and is entitled to receive Holy Communion in the Church in Wales'.

[31] See below, Chs. 10 and 11. For parishioners' rights to the ministrations of the church, see *St Davids (Bishop of) v Baron de Rutzen* (1861) 7 Jur NS 884. For rights in prisons of those 'belonging' to the Church in Wales, see below.

[32] Chile, Can. A.2: both in their personal lives and in the common ecclesial life, church members are required: to model their daily lives by the example of Christ; to maintain the practice of daily devotion; to participate in the eucharist and other services; to use and develop their talents for the edification of the church and for the community; and to assist the church financially for the work of God.

[33] LC 1948, Res. 37: all Church people should 'look upon their membership of Christ in the Church as the central fact in their lives'. Moreover, '[t]hey should regard themselves as individually sharing responsibility for the corporate life and witness of the Church in the places where they live.' This is to be realized by: 'the regularity of their attendance at public worship and especially at Holy Communion'; the 'practice of private prayer, Bible reading, and self-discipline'; 'bringing the teaching and example of Christ into their everyday lives'; 'the holiness of their spoken witness to their faith in Christ'; 'personal service to Church and community'; and 'the offering of money, according to their means, for the support of the work of the Church, at home and overseas'; see also LC 1958, Res. 125.

[34] See e.g. England, *Acts of Convocation* (1953–4), 173; see also Korea, Cans. 42–5: the

not contain general statements of the duties of church members.[35] In common with the majority, for the Church in Wales, the duties of church members are normally communicated in catechetical and liturgical norms, and only occasionally in the formal law. The mission of the church is carried out through 'the ministry of all its members', who are: 'to represent Christ and the Church; to bear witness to him wherever they may be; according to the gifts given to them, to carry out Christ's work of reconciliation in the world and to play their part in the worship and life of the Church'.[36] Every confirmed person should communicate regularly.[37] It is the duty of a Christian to contribute to the maintenance of worship and the proclamation of the gospel,[38] to bring their children to baptism, and to see that they are instructed in the catechism and confirmed.[39] Members of the church must attend any investigation or trial authorized by the constitution,[40] and those who attend public worship must comply with the law of the State on public order at divine service.[41] Indeed, as in other Anglican churches,[42] insofar as church members are bound by the constitution,[43] bishops may exercise discipline over lay members of the church,[44] and proceedings may be instituted in the Disciplinary Tribunal against any member of the Church in Wales.[45]

Thirdly, many Anglican churches have authorities charged with a special canonical responsibility to develop the ministry of the laity; these bodies function at both provincial and diocesan levels.[46] In the Church in Wales,

---

four basic 'duties of the laity' are to 'attend the eucharist every Sunday and Holy Day of obligation'; to 'observe the Church's laws of fasting'; to 'be responsible for the expenses of evangelism and the livelihood of clergy'; and to 'strive to live according to Christ's teachings, to preach the gospel and to realise God's justice in society'.

[35] See e.g. South India, Const. VI.1: '[i]t is the duty and privilege of every member of the Church to share in the Church's ministry.'

[36] BCP (1984), 691; for the duties of 'Christian obedience' (the 'duty to God' and the duty to neighbour), see 693ff.; for duties generated by baptism and confirmation, see below, Part IV.

[37] BCP (1984), 3 (general rubric 1): see below, Ch. 10.

[38] BCP (1984), 3 (general rubric 2): see below, Ch. 14.

[39] BCP (1984), 654: see below, Ch. 10.

[40] Const. XI.39.

[41] See below, Ch. 9.

[42] See above, Ch. 5 and CLAC, Ch. 3.

[43] See Const. I.2 and XI.1(2)(a); see also above, Ch. 1.

[44] As 'guardian of discipline in the Church': see BCP (1984), 714. For the exercise of episcopal discipline with regard to holy communion and, over parishioners, with regard to marriage, see below, Part IV.

[45] See above, Ch. 5.

[46] See e.g. ECUSA, Cans. III.2–3: each diocese must provide for 'the development and affirmation of the ministry' of 'all baptized persons in the Church and in the world'; each diocese must have a Commission on Ministry: its canonical functions include recruiting lay persons for ordination; providing guidance and pastoral care for clergy and laity; promoting continuing education for clergy and lay professionals employed in

this is achieved by quasi-legislation rather than by formal law.[47] At provincial level, of the six teams of the Council for Mission and Ministry of the Church in Wales,[48] itself accountable to the Bench of Bishops,[49] the Ministry Team is to provide support for all forms of lay ministry and training in the church.[50] At the diocesan level, there is a general absence of structures devoted to the development of the common ministry of the laity.[51] Unlike a small number of other Anglican churches, the Church in Wales possesses no canon law facilitating life in religious communities.[52]

Finally, computerized or paper-based files containing information on members of the Church in Wales, or others, are subject to the law of the State on data protection.[53] In general, any church person or organization which processes or handles personal data (the data controller),[54] being information about an identifiable living person (the data subject), is required to notify the Information Commissioner for registration.[55] However, ecclesiastical bodies and persons (as non-profit-making bodies) keeping records solely for the purposes of staff administration or to maintain membership or support for

the church; and supporting the development, training, utilization and affirmation of the ministry of the laity in the world.

[47] Const. II.65 has a passing reference to the Board of Mission.

[48] The functions of the former Board of Ministry (replaced by the council in 2001), were to: assist the Bench of Bishops to promote a renewed vision of the whole people of God within the church; recognize that ordained ministry and the common ministry of the laity are interdependent; and be alert to developments in ministerial formation within the Anglican Communion and other Christian traditions.

[49] COFC, 11; see above, Ch. 7.

[50] COFC, 16.

[51] However, see e.g. DSD, YB (2000–1), 129: the Diocesan Youth Committee exists 'to encourage fellowship, recreation, and spirituality among the youth of our churches and the community at large. To this end, the Committee arranges Summer Camps and day events whereby the Christian faith and commitment to it are made relevant.'

[52] LC 1930, Res. 74: this recommended 'the establishment, by canon or other means, of closer co-operation between the episcopate and the communities'; the subject is regulated by canon in e.g. ECUSA, Cans. III.30.1, and by quasi-legislation in England, *A Directory of Religious Life* (1990), issued by the Advisory Council on the Relations of Bishops and Religious Communities: see CLAC, 171–2.

[53] The Data Protection Act 1998 came into force on 1 March 2000; the main rules dealing with paper-based files came into force on 24 October 2001, and other rules on this subject will not come into force until 2007. The statute replaces the Data Protection Act 1984, and implements EU Data Protection Directive 95/46/EC.

[54] It is understood that (e.g.) Parochial Church Councils, incumbents, bishops, archdeacons, Diocesan Boards of Finance, diocesan registrars need to be registered. In the Church of England (e.g.) the Archbishops' Council, the Central Board of Finance, and the Pensions Board are all registered.

[55] Notification is application for registration as a data controller. Those already registered under the 1984 Act need not notify, but will be sent a renewal form when their existing registration expires: Sched. 14. Data Protection Act 1998, s. 36: there is an exemption where data are processed only for the purpose of their personal, family, household or recreational affairs.

the organization, need not register.[56] Eight principles apply to everyone, whether registered or not, who holds records containing personal data.[57] Ecclesiastical bodies or persons must normally obtain the consent of the data subject to keep and process records relating to that data subject.[58] Sensitive personal data, including data about a person's religious belief, are subject to special rules, and it cannot be passed on to a third party without the data subject's consent.[59] Members of the public have a right to know who has information about them, what information is held, the purposes for which it is held, and to whom the information is to be disclosed.[60]

SPECIAL NEEDS OF THE LAITY:
CHILDREN, HOSPITALS AND PRISONS

Needless to say, the common ministry of the laity is carried out both within the institutional church and within society at large. When practising the faith in the context of civil society,[61] along with other denominations and faiths, members of the Church in Wales enjoy the civil law right of freedom of religion.[62] This section explores three areas in which both the State and the Church in Wales address the special needs of particular classes of the

---

[56] That is, where the organization provides or administers activities for its members or those who have regular contact with it. See Data Protection (Notification and Notification Fees) Regulations 2000, Sched., para. 2 (staff administration exemption), para. 4 (accounts and records exemption) and para. 5 (non-profit-making organizations exemption).

[57] Personal data must be processed fairly and lawfully, and only if certain conditions are met; data must only be obtained or processed for the purposes for which the data controller (i.e. the data user) has registered; they should be adequate, relevant and not excessive in relation to the purposes for which they are processed; they should be accurate and, where necessary, kept up to date; they should not be kept longer than necessary for the purpose for which the data were obtained; data should be processed in accordance with the rights of data subjects; measures should be taken to prevent unauthorized or unlawful processing, and against accidental loss or damage; data must not be transferred to any country outside Europe which does not have adequate data protection.

[58] Data Protection Act 1998, Sched. 2, para. 1.

[59] Data Protection Act 1998, s. 2; for additional requirements, see Sched. 1, para. 1 and Sched. 3.

[60] For rights of access, see Data Protection Act 1998, s. 7; see ss. 40, 42 for compliance and enforcement with the Information Commissioner. But: a person has no access rights with regard to references for education or employment or appointments to any office (see Sched. 7, para. 1).

[61] For freedom of religion in civil law (in e.g. employment, education and charity work), see e.g. A. Bradney, *Religions, Rights and Laws* (Leicester, 1993), S. Poulter, *Ethnicity, Law and Human Rights* (Oxford, 1998), and C. Hamilton, *Family, Law and Religion* (London, 1995). Rights to religious instruction and education are dealt with below, in Ch. 9.

[62] For the Human Rights Act 1998 and the European Convention on Human Rights, see above, Ch. 1.

faithful: child protection in the church; spiritual care in hospitals; and special provision in State law for those in prisons who belong to the Church in Wales.

Child Protection and the Church

The Church in Wales's provincial system of quasi-legislation sets out 'the actions expected of each diocese and parish . . . to implement and monitor [the] policy of the Bench of Bishops on the care and protection of children'.[63] Implemention of the policy is 'the duty of each Diocese and Parish'. Its aim is to uphold five basic principles: (1) the unique status of children: they are owed both respect as persons in their own right and special protection due to their vulnerability; (2) the principle of the Children Act 1989: the welfare of the child is paramount in all circumstances; (3) the church and its workers, ordained and lay, paid and voluntary, must act towards children responsibly and with integrity: their position of trust must be safeguarded, with no advantage taken of those in their care; (4) no exploitation of trust for the purposes of self-gratification will be tolerated: the highest standards of care must be maintained in all circumstances (such as pastoral care, counselling, worship, education and recreation); and (5) any allegation of abuse or of risk of harm to children will be treated seriously.[64]

Child Protection Authorities in the Church The functions of the Advisory Panel on Child Protection,[65] a provincial body, are: to advise the Bench of Bishops on issues relating to the development of policy and procedures on child protection; to advise on the implementaton of policy; and to give advice in specific cases with child protection concerns.[66] Whilst

---

[63] *The Care and Protection of Children: Statement of Policy and Guidance for Implementation*, produced by the Panel of Bishops' Representatives on behalf of the Bench of Bishops of the Church in Wales (1997) (hereafter, CPC); CPC, I (p. 2): the authority for the policy is based on: scripture (Matt. 18: 2–10, 19: 14; Mark 9: 36–42; and Luke 18: 16); the UN convention on the Rights of the Child; and the Children Act 1989; see also DB, YB (2000), 103.

[64] CPC, II, p. 2; p. 3 contains a summary of recommendations; see also A. McFarlane, 'Child protection: the Church of England and the law' (LL M dissertation, University of Wales, Cardiff, 1998): Ch. 7 of this carries a study of child protection in the Church in Wales.

[65] CPC, III (p. 4): the panel, otherwise known as the Bishop's Representatives, is composed of clerical and lay members bringing a range of expertise and experience in the work of parish ministry, child care, education, paediatrics, police, probation, voluntary organizations and residential education; p. 5: there is one appointee from each diocese.

[66] CPC, III (p. 4): its aims are: to raise awareness within the church of child protection issues; to ensure liaison with statutory and voluntary agencies; to help people in the church to identify their training needs; to ensure the provision of advice and guidance, as

the Bench of Bishops 'carries ultimate responsibility' for all child protection matters in the church, each diocesan bishop has 'the duty to ensure that the policy is implemented throughout the diocese'. Each diocese must: give information to parishes about agreed policy and actions expected; monitor the progress of parishes in ensuring 'a child-safe organisation'; and provide help and advice on child protection matters when needed.[67] Each diocesan bishop should appoint a diocesan child protection officer,[68] to convene a Diocesan Child Protection Group.[69] Each parish must provide a safe environment for children, by ensuring: that anyone working with children, or with access to children, is known to be suitable to do so;[70] that all work with children is conducted in a manner which minimizes risk for both children and adults; and that any disclosure, discovery or suspicion of abuse is dealt with in an appropriate way.[71]

Good Practice and Procedure   Provincial guidelines prescribe the norms of good practice in relation to child protection.[72] The overriding principle is that the protection of the child can be done only by the statutory agencies. There is no role for church members in investigation or ongoing direct management.[73] First, in dealing with concern about a child, evidence or suggestions of physical abuse, neglect, emotional or sexual abuse in a child should never be ignored.[74] Every individual involved has a responsi-

---

appropriate, on the management of child protection concerns (including the approval process for those working with children) to children, their families and all church members (clerical and lay); and to ensure that appropriate documentation and record-keeping systems are in place in relation to child protection issues.

[67] CPC, IV (p. 5).

[68] CPC, IV (p. 6): the person must have skills and experience relevant to child protection (e.g. social work, police, education); the officer is to ensure the dissemination, implementation and monitoring of the policy throughout the diocese.

[69] CPC, IV (p. 6): the group should reflect a balance of clergy, laity and gender; it should include at least some of the key diocesan officers, such as diocesan children's officer, education officer, youth officer, and the officer for social responsibility: see below; an archdeacon should also be in the group.

[70] By using the declaration form (CPP/1): see *Cure of Souls* (1996), 31–2: the declaration requires disclosure of criminal convictions, probation and conditional and absolute discharges with regard to relevant offences (such as crimes of violence, including physical abuse against children or young people, sexual offences, drug-related offences, drunkenness, careless driving, neglect of children, and offences of dishonesty). It is lawful to inquire about past convictions for criminal offences of anyone applying for work with children since this work is exempt from the provisions of the Rehabilitation of Offenders Act 1974, s. 4(2), by virtue of the Rehabilitation of Offenders Act 1974 (Exceptions) Order 1975: see *Cure of Souls* (1996), 19.

[71] CPC, IV (p. 5).

[72] CPC, V (pp. 7–9). For Sunday schools, see the Guidelines in *The Essential Sunday School Teachers Manual*, prepared by the Children's Sector of the Church in Wales (1999).

[73] Pastoral roles should be kept entirely separate.

[74] This may include evidence, for example, of bruises, challenging behaviour, sexualized

bility to report immediate, serious concerns about the care of a child urgently to the proper secular authorities (usually Social Services or the NSPCC). Individuals may wish to take advice or discuss the problem initially with the diocesan child protection officer. In all cases of serious and urgent concern, there should be no delay in acting or in seeking advice. Written records should be made at the time and kept safe.[75]

Secondly, a cleric or lay church worker who hears a child disclose that they have been physically or sexually assaulted, must promptly discuss this with Social Services or the NSPCC. The cleric or lay worker is not to question the child about the allegation, but write down verbatim what the child says. When a child, young person, parent, carer, family member or friend makes direct or indirect allegations (including to a third party) about abuse by a cleric or lay church worker, and the child is a minor (or was at the time of the alleged act), this must be treated in the same way as a direct disclosure by the child. It must be referred to Social Services or the NSPCC without delay.[76] Any rumours concerning child protection issues must be dealt with promptly: rumours may be repeated only to the diocesan bishop, parish priest or diocesan child protection officer, along with information about its source, with a view to reporting it to Social Services, as appropriate.[77]

Thirdly, whenever there is a child protection concern, the grounds for it, any factual information, and any discussions with others should be written down at the time, with copies sent to the diocesan bishop.[78] Each parish must be able to demonstrate that it has appropriate mechanisms in place to reduce risk to a minimum. This will include the use of supervision, avoidance of high-risk situations (such as one-to-one isolation), and a clear system by which children may talk with an independent person where appropriate.[79] Each parish must discuss the policy and guidelines of the church and should formulate an action plan for their implementation.[80] Special provisions of secular law regulate day care schemes operated by the church.[81]

---

behaviour, constant hunger, inadequate clothing or supervision, or involvement in child pornography.

[75] CPC, V.1.

[76] CPC, V.2 and 3.

[77] CPC, V.4: anyone heard promulgating the rumour must be asked to deal with it in the same way; rumour and gossip must be distinguished from allegations; this process must bypass anyone named in the rumour.

[78] CPC, V.5: the record should be kept in a safe place.

[79] CPC, V.6: such as in residential care settings.

[80] CPC, V.7: this must include a plan to meet training needs; assistance in this is available from the diocesan child protection officer or group; CPC, V.9: 'Matters of conflicting loyalty or responsibility (such as the seal of the confessional) should be clarified, in discussion with the Bishop if necessary'; see also below, Ch. 11.

[81] Children Act 1989, ss. 71–8, 80(1)(i); DHSS: The Children Act Guidance and Regulations, vol. 2, and CDC, V.8: these apply only for care given to children under

Monitoring the System   The Advisory Panel on Child Protection must provide a rolling programme to monitor the provincial system on behalf of the Bench of Bishops. In the diocese, monitoring is the duty of the bishop, who may involve the diocesan child protection officer. Information from parishes on child protection structures may be gathered from parishes as part of the archdeacon's visitation.[82] Each parish should develop a system which demonstrates that routine documentation is being handled adequately, and forms giving information on past convictions, consent for police checks and references must be kept safely.[83]

In the parish, declarations and consents to police checks must be repeated every five years, and at a move of post (for both clergy and lay workers). Those who must complete the declaration form and consent to police checks are: all clergy (stipendiary, non-stipendiary and retired);[84] licensed readers; church workers; all positions in the parish likely to involve working with children; and any other individuals who may work with or come into contact with children.[85] It is for the bishop and the Advisory Panel on Child Protection to decide what action should be taken in respect of a person accused, who, pending the outcome of inquiries, should be removed from work with children. Whether the person is suspended, or has leave of absence, is a matter for the joint decision of the bishop, the panel and the diocesan registrar. In the case of clergy, if there is a conviction, the offender must not be allowed to return to the work of the ordained ministry.[86]

Child Protection in Other Anglican Churches   Provisions in the Church in Wales on child care and protection are not dissimilar, in their essentials, to arrangements in other Anglican churches.[87] In Canada, the Diocese of Toronto has very detailed guidance (1991) on the subject, formulated in part at least as a response to developments in secular law. The policy that 'sexual abuse or harassment of any kind by any staff, person or volunteer will not be tolerated' is placed within a theological context in which abuse

---

eight years of age away from their parent on non-domestic premises for over two hours per day; local authorities must be approached for approval and registration.

[82] See above, Ch. 7.

[83] CPC, VI: this also contains the monitoring criteria.

[84] See also *Cure of Souls* (1996): candidates for ordination and licensed lay ministry are to be asked to make the declaration and consent to police checks.

[85] CPC, VI: these include: children and youth officers; organists and choir leaders; Sunday school or crèche leaders and helpers; confirmation class leaders; and foundation governors of church schools. See also the Protection of Children Act 1999 which requires employees to make a declaration and forbids employers from employing people with prescribed convictions.

[86] *Cure of Souls* (1996), 22: see ibid. and above, Ch. 5 for possible proceedings in the Disciplinary Tribunal.

[87] See CLAC, 169.

is 'to deny Christian identity'. First, the document sets out guiding principles: the protection of children is of fundamental concern; allegations must be taken seriously; an accused person will be presumed innocent until proven otherwise; the protection of the complainant and their family is of paramount concern; and nothing should be done which might impede a secular criminal investigation. Secondly, the mechanisms for response include: a diocesan sexual abuse resource person who must work with the bishop to determine the truth of allegations and to recommend action; a Crisis Response Team to visit the parish, consult and recommend action to the bishop; and the use by the bishop of ecclesiastical disciplinary processes. Thirdly, complaints of suspected child abuse must be reported immediately to a secular Children's Aid Society (which is required by the Ontario Child and Family Services Act 1985). If the complaint against a minister is substantiated, the bishop may caution, reprimand, censure, inhibit or suspend that minister. Fourthly, the policy provides for pastoral care of the victim of the abuse, and disciplinary action is presented as 'a pastoral and caring act, providing for the common good of the church and also offering the possibility for restoration and healing'.[88]

Spiritual Care in Hospitals

In contrast to several States in the European Union, in which the subject is regulated by law,[89] spiritual care in British hospitals is based on extra-legal instruments of the State. There is no right under civil law to the meeting of spiritual needs in hospitals. Nevertheless, whereas the entitlement under the Patients' Charter, to respect for religious beliefs, is not a legal right, failure to meet charter rights generally falls within the investigative powers of the health service ombudsman.[90] The governing regime, which the National Assembly for Wales inherits,[91] is found in health service guidelines: these recommend the National Health Service to make 'every effort' to provide for the spiritual needs of patients and staff, Christian and non-Christian.[92]

---

[88] See *Journal of the Church Law Association of Canada*, 1(3) (1994), 325.

[89] For France, Denmark, Italy and Spain, see G. Robbers (ed.), *State and Church in the European Union* (Baden-Baden, 1996).

[90] See generally, J. Montgomery, *Health Care Law* (Oxford, 1997), 60f., and *Airedale NHS Trust*, Case E 867/93–4 HC 545, 172–80; see also D. Longley, *Health Care Constitutions* (London, 1996), 166.

[91] The Transfer of Functions Order contains several statutes dealing with health care; see also Government of Wales Act 1998, s. 27: the Assembly may by order make provision for the transfer to the Assembly of any or all the functions of a Welsh health authority.

[92] HSG (92)2; see also PN (86)15 and PM (84)10; for recent historical antecedents to these guidelines, see J. Jacob (ed.), *Speller's Law Relating to Hospitals* (6th edn, London, 1978), 140–1.

Appointment of Staff   The guidelines suggest a number of optional schemes for the appointment of staff to provide spiritual care: employing suitably qualified persons to meet the spiritual needs of all patients and staff; contracting with religious organizations to provide services on a sessional or other basis; and facilitating visits to patients by religious leaders or spiritual advisers on a voluntary basis. Chaplains from the main Christian denominations ought to be appointed in consultation with the appropriate church authorities. Anglican appointments should be made in consultation with the diocesan bishop. Hospitals may seek the advice of national or local religious organizations on the appropriate services to be provided by staff, and the qualifications for, and restrictions on, carrying out rites or ceremonies. Hospital management may also appoint other staff if they consider that local needs warrant this.[93]

Staff Pay and Conditions of Service   No part-time hospital chaplain should be required to work more than five sessions. Where more than five sessions are required, another part-time chaplain should be appointed. Health authorities should determine the chaplaincy services needed, but there is no authority to make payments direct to churches. Nevertheless, if a church wishes a part-time chaplain to undertake additional hospital work, the health authority should agree only on the understanding that the additional duties are paid for by the church.[94] Staff, other than hospital chaplains, covered by agreements of the Whitley Council, may be appointed on such terms and conditions of employment as the employer considers appropriate in local circumstances.[95] As a general principle, in addition to any contract of employment, Church in Wales clergy are licensed to minister in hospitals.[96]

Facilities   The guidelines provide that patients and staff should have reasonable facilities for religious observance: a chapel or rooms and accessories required for worship or for storing items provided by religious organizations.[97] In deciding on facilities for each religious group, hospitals should consider: the numbers of patients in that group; the nature of spiritual support and services appropriate to the belief of that group; and

---

[93] Advisory notes on the criteria for appointment of hospital chaplains may be obtained from the Joint Committee for Hospital Chaplaincies of the Church of England. See also the committee's *Code of Best Practice: Hospital Chaplains* (1994).

[94] DHSS, PM (85)15: if a health authority wishes a part-time chaplain to work more than five sessions, employing authorities should approach the DHSS for permission to create part-time chaplaincy posts in excess of five sessions, and for the authority to pay the appropriate salary rate.

[95] HSG (92)2. Clerics in extra-parochial office have the status of vicar: VII.76.

[96] For licensing, see above, Ch. 7.

[97] See also DHSS, PM (86)15: in some hospitals, the chapel may be consecrated (rather than dedicated), in which case secular use is not generally permitted.

local administrative and management arrangements.[98] Where possible, a room should be set aside for use by chaplains for private meetings, and secretarial facilities should also be provided.[99]

Records and Review Hospitals should record a patient's religious persuasion when the patient is willing to declare this. The hospital must ensure that this information is not passed to any religious organization or its members outside the hospital without the consent of the patient.[100] The provision by hospitals to parish clergy of names of patients admitted, without the patients' consent, is a breach of confidentiality, but 'this should not detract from the right of any patients to be visited by their own parish priest or minister if they so wish'.[101] Finally, health authorities should regularly review their chaplaincy needs, and should make an assessment of the proportion of patients in each religious persuasion in consultation with local church authorities.[102]

Spiritual Care in Prisons

In contrast to those in hospitals, people in prison have a legal right to the services of a chaplain. Every prison in Wales must have a chaplain and, if large enough, may also have an assistant chaplain. Both the chaplain and, if there is one, the assistant chaplain must by civil law be a cleric of the Church in Wales.[103] Appointment belongs to the secretary of state.[104] Prior to appointment, notice of the nomination of a chaplain or assistant chaplain must be given to the diocesan bishop within a month of nomination. The chaplain or assistant may officiate only under the authority of a licence from the bishop.[105] In cases of absence, a person approved by the secretary of state may act for the chaplain.[106]

---

[98] HSG (92)2.

[99] DHSS, PM (86)15.

[100] HSG (92)2; see also the Data Protection Act 1998, s. 2: 'sensitive personal data' includes the religious beliefs of a data subject; Sched. 3, para. 4: sensitive data may be processed, *inter alia*, when the processing is carried out in the course of its legitimate activities by any body or association which is not established or conducted for profit but exists for religious purposes.

[101] DHSS, PM (86)15.

[102] DHSS, PM(85), 15.

[103] Prison Act 1952, s. 7(1), (3) and (4); s. 53(4): references in the statute to the Church of England must be construed as including references to the Church in Wales; this is a further vestige of establishment (see Ch. 1).

[104] Prison Act 1952, s. 7(5). For their church status, see Const. VII.76.

[105] Prison Act 1952, s. 9(2): a chaplain may serve in two prisons only if they are within convenient distance of each other and together are designed to receive not more than 100 prisoners: s. 9(1).

[106] See generally Prison Rules 1999, SI 1999/728. Prison Act 1952, s. 10: the secretary of state may appoint a minister of a denomination other than the Church in Wales if the number of prisoners belonging to that denomination requires such an appointment.

When a prisoner is received into prison, the governor must record the religious denomination to which the prisoner declares himself to belong.[107] The prisoner must then be treated as being of that denomination, though the governor may amend the record in a proper case and after due inquiry.[108] The chaplain must interview every prisoner belonging to the Church in Wales soon after the prisoner's reception in the prison and shortly before his release.[109] The chaplain must regularly visit prisoners belonging to the Church in Wales.[110] The chaplain must visit daily all prisoners belonging to the Church in Wales who are sick, under restraint or undergoing cellular confinement.[111]

Special rights to the ministry of Church in Wales chaplains are enjoyed by prisoners who are not members of the Church in Wales. Every prisoner not belonging to the Church in Wales must be allowed, in accordance with the arrangements in force in the prison, to attend chapel or be visited by the Church in Wales chaplain.[112] If the prisoner is willing, the chaplain must visit any such prisoner who is sick, under restraint or undergoing cellular confinement and is not regularly visited by a minister of his own denomination.[113]

The prison chaplain must conduct divine service for prisoners belonging to the Church in Wales at least once every Sunday, Christmas Day and Good Friday, and such celebrations of holy communion and weekday services as may be arranged.[114] Arrangements must be made in the prison so as not to require prisoners of the Christian religion to do any unnecessary work on Sunday, Christmas Day or Good Friday.[115] The prison must make available, so far as is reasonably practicable, for the personal use of every prisoner, such religious books recognized by his denomination as are approved by the secretary of state.[116] Prisoners are entitled to a diet that

---

[107] Prison Act 1952, s. 10(5).

[108] Prison Rules 1999, r.13; see also Prison Act 1952, s. 10(4): any other ministers appointed to the prison, or permitted to visit prisoners, must be given by the governor a list of prisoners declaring themselves to belong to his denomination; the minister may visit only those prisoners.

[109] Prison Rules 1999, r.14(1).

[110] Prison Rules 1999, r.15(1); prison ministers of other denominations must also do so as they reasonably can: r.15(2); where a prisoner belongs to a denomination for which no prison minister has been appointed, the governor must do what he reasonably can, if requested by the prisoner, to arrange for regular visits by a minister of that prisoner's denomination: r.15(3).

[111] Prison Rules 1999, r.14(2): a prison minister must also do so, so far as he reasonably can, for prisoners of his own denomination.

[112] Prison Act 1952, s. 10(4).

[113] Prison Rules 1999, r.14(3).

[114] Prison Rules 1999, r.16(1).

[115] Prison Rules 1999, r.18: the same applies to prisoners of other religions on their recognized days of religious observance.

[116] Prison Rules 1999, r.19.

accords with the demands of their religion.[117] If other arrangements have not been made, the chaplain must also read the burial service at the funeral of any member of the Church in Wales who dies in the prison.[118] Similar provisions exist for Detention Centres.[119]

LAY OFFICERS IN THE CHURCH

One of the achievements of canon law throughout the Anglican Communion is the provision of a multiplicity of ecclesiastical offices open to the laity at all levels of the church.[120] The Church in Wales is no exception.[121] The following describes key offices available to the laity at the most local level of the church, the parish: churchwarden, sidesman, lay worker and lay reader. Other parochial, provincial and diocesan positions, and lay employees of cathedrals, are discussed elsewhere in this volume.[122] This section also deals with employees in the parish.

Churchwardens

The ancient position of churchwarden, existing in post-Reformation canon law,[123] still constitutes the principal administrative office open to lay people in the parish. The office is governed by the constitution and by pre-1920 ecclesiastical law.[124]

---

[117] Prison Services Standing Order 7A: the demands must be as agreed between the religious body and the Prison Services Headquarters. For a general discussion of racial discrimination amongst prisoners, see *Alexander v Home Office* [1988] 1 WLR 968 (CA).

[118] Prison Rules 1999, r.14.

[119] Detention Centre Rules 1952, SI 1952 No. 1432; rr.50 and 53(2): the chaplain has duties to conduct worship and instruction, but his duty to visit is limited to sick trainees. For chaplains in the armed forces, see D. Bailey, 'Legal regulation of the appointment, ministry and episcopal oversight of army chaplains' (LL M dissertation, University of Wales, Cardiff, 1999).

[120] For the very many provincial, diocesan, parochial, administrative, liturgical and pastoral offices, see CLAC, 173–84.

[121] For the purposes of the Welsh Church Act 1914, 'ecclesiastical office' includes 'any lay office' in connection with the Church Discipline Act 1840 (since repealed: Const. XI.47): see s. 38.

[122] For parochial church councillors, and members of Church Committees, see above, Ch. 4; for lay eucharistic assistants, see below, Ch. 10; for lay members of provincial, diocesan and deanery assemblies, boards and committees, and ecclesiastical judges, registrars and assessors, see above, Chs. 2, 3 and 5.

[123] A churchwarden is not a corporation sole (such corporations were dissolved under the Welsh Church Act 1914, s. 2(1)); compare England: M. Hill, *Ecclesiastical Law* (2nd edn, London, 2001), 3.46: Hill also treats the new Churchwardens Measure 2001.

[124] The office is open to men and women: *Gordon v Hayward* (1905) 21 TLR 298. The Welsh Church Act 1914 transferred the 'powers, duties and liabilities' of churchwardens,

Appointment   In every parish there must be two churchwardens. To be eligible for office, a person must be a qualified elector of that parish and over the age of eighteen.[125] One churchwarden must be elected by the Annual Vestry Meeting.[126] A person is not eligible for election by the Vestry unless their consent to the nomination has first been obtained; no cleric can vote in the election.[127] The other must be appointed at that meeting by the incumbent. However, where in a parish it was customary, before the passing of the Welsh Church Act 1914, to have more than two churchwardens, the number must remain unchanged. Moreover, the method of appointing them must continue in force until the Diocesan Conference orders otherwise.[128]

The secretary of the Parochial Church Council must send the names and addresses of churchwardens to the archdeacon.[129] If it is brought to the notice of the diocesan bishop that the churchwardens have not been elected or appointed, the bishop may appoint the churchwardens. Any action taken by him must be reported to the next meeting of the Diocesan Conference.[130] In any vacancy or suspended incumbency, where a cleric-in-charge has been appointed, the appointment of one churchwarden is made by the cleric-in-charge. If in a vacant or suspended incumbency, where a cleric-in-charge has not been appointed, or if the incumbent is incapacitated, one churchwarden may be appointed by the area dean.[131] These provisions are typical of those Anglican churches having the office of churchwarden.[132]

Admission, Tenure and Resignation   Churchwardens are elected or appointed annually and generally hold office until their successors are admitted.[133] Before being admitted to office, every churchwarden must

other than those relating to the affairs of the church and to charitable trusts, to local authorities (s. 25).

[125] Const. VI.17(1): for qualified electors see above, Ch. 4; under pre-1920 ecclesiastical law, Jews are not eligible for office: *Anthony v Seger* (1789) 1 Hag Con 9.

[126] Const. VI.17(1).

[127] Const. VI.16(1)(a), (3) and (4); see also *R v Hagbourne (Vicar)* (1886) 51 JP 276: before proceeding to election, the meeting may inquire as to the character of the candidate proposed and, if the person has held office before, may investigate correspondence as to the candidate's conduct.

[128] Const. VI.17(1).

[129] Const. VI.28(2)(b).

[130] Const. VI.30.

[131] Const. VI.17(3) and (4).

[132] See CLAC, 178.

[133] Const. VI.17(5). Admission may take place in a liturgical setting: see A Form of Affirmation for Churchwardens and Members of the Parochial Church Council (1997): all who hold office should attend the service, a public act of worship which should be held after the visitation of the bishop or archdeacon; normally the churchwardens should make the declarations and responses together.

make and sign a declaration in the presence of either the bishop, the diocesan chancellor, the archdeacon or a person appointed for that purpose by the archdeacon. In it the person undertakes faithfully and diligently to perform the duties of their office, and agrees to accept and obey any decision of the bishop or the diocesan chancellor as to any right at any time to hold the office of churchwarden.[134] It would seem that the act of admission by the ordinary is administrative and not judicial. Therefore, the ordinary has no discretion to judge the fitness of the candidate, though they may be justified in refusing to admit an unqualified candidate.[135]

A churchwarden may resign the office by written notice to the bishop. The office becomes vacant on receipt of the notice by the bishop. The bishop must immediately acknowledge the resignation, and notify the incumbent, cleric-in-charge or area dean (as the case may be), and the other churchwarden(s) of the vacancy. A casual vacancy among the churchwardens may be filled at any time by election or appointment (as the case may be) effected at a Vestry Meeting called for this purpose.[136] Churchwardens are not eligible for re-election or reappointment in the year following the completion of six consecutive terms of office.[137] However, if difficulty is foreseen in complying with this rule, the archdeacon, on a petition from a Vestry Meeting, or on his own initiative, may issue a dispensation from the rule; the archdeacon must report the matter to the bishop.[138] Churchwardens are not eligible for re-election or reappointment on reaching the age at which membership of the Governing Body ceases, namely seventy-five.[139] Once more, these provisions are typical of Anglican churches having the office of churchwarden.[140]

Functions and Discipline When admitted, the churchwardens are officers of the bishop,[141] and they must discharge such duties as are by custom assigned to them. They must be foremost in representing the laity and in consulting and co-operating with the incumbent. Churchwardens must use their best endeavours 'to promote peace and unity amongst the parishioners, and by example and precept to encourage the parishioners in

[134] Const. VI.18; see also *R v Sowter* [1901] 1 KB 396 (CA): in years where an episcopal visitation takes place, admission is conducted by the bishop or the chancellor, but in other years by the archdeacon, generally during his visitation.

[135] *R v Rice* (1697) 5 Mod Rep 325; *R v Bishop of Sarum* [1916] 1 KB 466.

[136] Const. VI.17(6).

[137] Const. VI.17(7).

[138] Const. VI.17(8).

[139] Const. VI.17(9); for II.12(1), and membership of the Governing Body, see above, Ch. 2.

[140] CLAC, 179.

[141] Const. VI.17(2); for the duty of churchwardens to report to the bishop, as officer of the bishop, see *Ritchings v Cordingley* (1868) LR 3 A&E 113 at 121: the office of churchwarden is one of 'observation and complaint but not of control'.

the practice of true religion'. They must also maintain order and decency in the church and churchyard, especially during the time of public worship, and must discharge the duties placed on them by the Church Fabric Regulations.[142] Also, in the exercise of their functions, they are bound by the constitution of the church and by pre-1920 ecclesiastical law.[143] As a general rule, churchwardens must concur in doing any official act.[144]

Other duties and rights of churchwardens, discussed elsewhere in this volume, include: allowing the free use of any church to any cleric appointed by the bishop during the vacancy of a cure or during the suspension or absence of the incumbent;[145] administration of the inventory;[146] custodianship and care of the parsonage during vacant or suspended incumbencies;[147] summoning a Vestry Meeting during the incapacity or absence of the incumbent;[148] membership of the Parochial Church Council,[149] and participation in a visitation.[150]

The Diocesan Court has a specific jurisdiction to hear and determine any complaints against churchwardens, as well as disputes with regard to their election.[151] Disciplinary proceedings may also be brought against them in the Disciplinary Tribunal of the Church in Wales.[152] Any diocesan decree effecting parish reorganization must make provision as to what is to be done with regard to churchwardens.[153] Again, these provisions are typical of Anglican churches having the office of churchwarden,[154] and in several secular states, the office has been the subject of both legislation and judicial consideration.[155]

Sub-wardens and Sidesmen   In parishes with more than one church, two qualified electors of that parish may be designated as sub-wardens for the church which they normally attend. One sub-warden must be elected by the

---

[142] Const. VI.17(2): see also Canons Ecclesiatical 1603, Cans. 18, 19, 85, 88, 90, 111 and below, Ch. 13.
[143] As office-holders they are bound by the constitution (Const. I.2) and as members by pre-1920 ecclesiastical law (Const. XI.47).
[144] *Ritchings v Cordingley* (1868) LR 3 A&E 113.
[145] Const. VII.57.
[146] Const. VI.21; see below, Ch. 13.
[147] Const. X.39. Along with the area dean.
[148] Const. VI.11.
[149] Const. VI.24.
[150] See above, Ch. 7.
[151] Const. XI.6(b).
[152] See above, Ch. 5.
[153] Const. IV.37(e); see also IV.40(d).
[154] CLAC, 180.
[155] See e.g. Bermuda, Church of England in Bermuda Act 1978, s. 6: this recognizes the right of the Synod to regulate the office of churchwarden; Canada, *Johnson v Glen* (1879) 26 Gr 162 (Ch): Anglican canons requiring consultation by the bishop with churchwardens prior to the appointment of a rector were enforced as a matter of contract law.

Annual Vestry Meeting of the parish after nomination by the Congregational Meeting of the particular church. The other must be appointed by the incumbent.[156] The sub-wardens for the particular church in question are *ex officio* members of its Church Committee,[157] and they are *ex officio* members of the Parochial Church Council.[158] No person is eligible for election by the Annual Vestry Meeting as sub-warden unless their consent to nomination has first been obtained.[159] Where required, sidesmen must also be elected by the Annual Vestry Meeting,[160] to assist the churchwardens in the performance of their duties,[161] particularly in keeping order in the church and churchyard, especially at the time of divine worship.[162] Any diocesan decree effecting parish reorganization must make provision as to what is to be done with regard to sidesmen.[163]

Lay Workers and Readers

Resolutions of the Lambeth Conference have consistently encouraged the development of structures enabling qualified lay people to serve in liturgical and pastoral capacities.[164] Law throughout the Anglican Communion is today well developed, in terms of regulation of eligibility, appointment, functions and discipline. Churches either employ distinct canons of general applicability to all liturgical and pastoral lay offices,[165] or particular law on specialized lay ministries,[166] or a mixture of these approaches.[167] Many churches have the offices of pastoral leader, lay preacher, lay catechist, lay worker, lay reader, lay eucharistic minister[168] and pastoral assistant.[169] Local lay ministry teams have been the subject of recent discussion in the

---

[156] Const. VI.20.

[157] Const. VI.29.

[158] Const. VI.24(1)(a).

[159] Const. VI.16(1)(b): clergy cannot vote in the election of a person to the office of sub-warden.

[160] Const. VI.16(1)(d): a person is eligible if their consent is obtained prior to nomination (VI.16(3)), and no cleric may vote on the election (VI.16(4)).

[161] Const. VI.19(1); each sidesman must be a qualified elector of that parish over eighteen years of age (VI.19(2)); diocesan decrees must make provision for them (Const. IV.37 and 30).

[162] Canons Ecclesiastical 1603, Cans. 19, 88, 90, 111; see also *Palmer v Tijou* (1824) 2 Add 196 at 200, 201.

[163] Const. IV.37(e); see also IV.40(d). For the ancient office of parish clerk, see Canons Ecclesiastical, 1603, Can. 91: they were appointed by the incumbent and received their 'ancient wages' from the parish.

[164] LC 1930, Res. 65; LC 1958, Ress. 90, 91; CLAC, 159.

[165] See e.g. Australia, the Authorised Lay Ministry Canon 1992; see CLAC, 181.

[166] See e.g. England, Cans. E4–6.

[167] See e.g. Philippines, Cans. III.2, 3.

[168] All these offices are available in ECUSA, Cans. III.3.

[169] For England, see N. Doe, *The Legal Framework of the Church of England* (Oxford, 1996), 249.

Church in Wales,[170] though, as yet, the law provides for very few specialist lay ministries at the level of the parish.

Lay Workers   A lay worker, in the Church in Wales, is a lay person who officiates in accordance with a licence from the bishop or with the permission of the bishop.[171] A full-time stipendiary lay worker, officiating with the bishop's permission within a deanery, or officiating elsewhere in the diocese but residing within the deanery, is an *ex officio* member of the Deanery Conference.[172] Full-time lay workers are also *ex officio* members of the Parochial Church Council,[173] and may attend, speak and vote at Vestry Meetings.[174] Lay workers are also subject to the jurisdiction of the Disciplinary Tribunal.[175]

The law of the Church in Wales on lay workers is silent on a number of matters normally dealt with in the laws of other Anglican churches. In the Church of England, for example, the bishop admits lay workers by certificate. Admission cannot be repeated if the person moves to another diocese. An episcopal licence is required to serve, no licence may be issued unless the bishop is satisfied that, in relation to stipendiary lay workers, adequate provision has been made for a salary, insurance and a pension. Every lay worker must make declarations concerning the doctrine of the church and a declaration of canonical obedience to the bishop. Revocation of licences of lay workers is subject to explicit procedural safeguards and rights of appeal.[176] Lay workers may preach, bury the dead, lead morning and evening prayer, distribute the sacrament, and publish banns of marriage.[177] Lay workers may also function under a contract of employment.[178]

Readers   In the Church in Wales, the office of reader is governed by provisions dispersed throughout the law, as well as by provincial and diocesan quasi-legislation.[179] According to the latter, a reader engages in 'a

---

[170] Discussion of the matter has been stimulated, in part at least, by such theological works as: R. Greenwood, *Practising Community: The Task of the Local Church* (London, 1996).

[171] Const. I.6(c).

[172] Const. V.5(1)(a); see also V.5(1)(c): 'lay licensed workers' may also be co-opted to the Conference in such numbers as the Diocesan Conference may prescribe for co-option in that deanery.

[173] Const. VI.24(1)(a).

[174] Const. VI.13(1)(e).

[175] Const. XI.18: see above, Ch. 5.

[176] England, Can. E8.

[177] England, Can. E7.

[178] *Legal Opinions Concerning the Church of England*, Legal Advisory Commission, 125.

[179] *Martyn v Hund* (1779) 2 Cowp 437 at 444 *per* Lord Mansfield: 'The term reader is made use of by the canon law: but a reader known to the canon law is always put in opposition to a clergyman. It is one of the five orders of the Romish Church inferior to

ministry which is normally voluntary, nationally accredited [and] episcopally licensed'.[180] It is lawful for a reader: 'to visit the sick, to read and pray
with them, to teach in Sunday School and elsewhere, and generally to
undertake such pastoral and educational work and to give such assistance
to any minister as the Bishop may direct'. Readers are permitted: '[d]uring
the time of divine service [to] take Morning and Evening Prayer (save for
the Absolution), to preach, to publish banns of marriage (in accordance
with the requirements of the law), to read the Word of God'. They are also
permitted 'to preach at the service of Holy Communion, to catechise the
children, and to receive and to present the offerings of the people'.[181] As a
matter of provincial policy, clergy are expected to work collaboratively
with readers who should be encouraged to play their appropriate parts in
public worship.[182]

Under the constitution, licensed readers may be co-opted to the Deanery
Conference in such numbers (if any) as the Diocesan Conference may
prescribe for co-option in that deanery.[183] Licensed readers may be co-
opted to the Parochial Church Council as the council may determine,[184]
and are treated in the law of the church dealing with local ecumenical
projects.[185] Readers are subject both to the constitution,[186] and to the
jurisdiction of the Disciplinary Tribunal.[187] The tribunals of the State are
tending to the view that a stipendiary reader is an employee with a right of
recourse to the industrial tribunals of the State in cases of unlawful and
unfair dismissal.[188]

Before admission to the office, some dioceses provide that candidates are
usually recommended by their incumbent to the Parochial Church Council
and then to the bishop, and should go through a diocesan selection
procedure and training scheme.[189] The Provincial Readers' Committee, a

---

the deacon; they are always considered laymen in the idea of the canon law . . . I have
been informed that in the Welsh dioceses, where there is no endowment worth the while
of a clergyman to accept (and in Chester there are many such), many persons officiate as
readers in opposition to clergymen.'
[180] DSAB, YB (1999–2000), 110. The scope of their ministry depends on the terms of
the licence.
[181] DSAB, YB (1999–2000), 110.
[182] *Cure of Souls* (1996), 8.
[183] Const. V.5(1)(c).
[184] Const. VI.24(1)(c)(iii).
[185] See below, Ch. 12.
[186] Const. I.2.
[187] See above, Ch. 5.
[188] *Barthope v Exeter Diocesan Board of Finance* [1979] ICR 900: the Employment
Appeal Tribunal, reversing the decision of an industrial tribunal, decided that a stipendiary reader of the Church of England was employed, and remitted the case to the
tribunal to identify the employer; the case was settled before the tribunal gave judgment
on the matter.
[189] DSAB, YB (1999–2000), 110. There is a form of service for the admission and
licensing of readers.

body responsible to the Council for Mission and Ministry, co-ordinates the work of the Diocesan Readers' Committees in all matters concerning readership, especially training and continuing education.[190] They are entitled to be reimbursed for any expenses incurred in officiating at services, but do not receive fees.[191] Some dioceses operate systems of parish assistants and worship leaders.[192]

The law of the Church in Wales is rather less well developed with regard to readers than that of other Anglican churches. In English canon law, candidates for the office of reader must be baptized, confirmed and regular communicants. They are nominated to the bishop by the minister. To be admitted, candidates must have 'a sufficient knowledge' of holy scripture and the doctrine and worship of the church. They owe obedience to the bishop and must comply with the directions of their ordained ministers. It is lawful for a reader: to visit the sick, to undertake such pastoral and educational work and to assist any minister as the bishop may direct; to assist in divine service by reading, preaching and receiving and presenting the offerings of the people; to distribute the holy communion; and to conduct funerals. The bishop must keep a register of readers in the diocese. Episcopal licences may be revoked summarily, when appeal lies to the archbishop, or by notice.[193] Scottish canon law is similar: it requires communicant status, nomination, testimony of character and fitness, a declaration of compliance with the directions of the bishop and the cleric in charge; and the latter may apply for termination of the licence which 'may be cancelled at any time at the discretion of the Bishop'.[194]

Employees in the Parish

Laws of Anglican churches are in the main silent on the subject of employees of the church. The applicability of secular employment law in this area has led some churches to develop quasi-legislation prescribing good practices for churches towards their employees, as well as the need for contracts to regulate appointment, functions, grievance procedures and dismissal. In the Australian Diocese of Sydney, when a lay person is employed, there should be an exchange of letters between that person and the churchwardens of the principal church. These should outline the terms and conditions of employment and include: a broad description of the

---

[190] COFC, 14: the chair is appointed by the Bench of Bishops, and the diocesan wardens of readers and secretaries of Readers' Committees are *ex officio* members.
[191] PA, 2, p. 15.
[192] See e.g. DSA, YB (1999–2000), 101: this governs commissioning. For organists, see HLE (1910), para. 928; see also R. Phillimore, *Ecclesiastical Law* (2nd edn, London, 1895), II, 1519–21.
[193] England, Can. E4–6.
[194] Scotland, Can. 20 and Resolution 1.

hours, days of work and duties to be carried out; the amounts or benefits to be paid; sick leave; provision for housing; an undertaking to apply for any necessary authority from the bishop where relevant; superannuation; annual leave; long-service leave and workers' compensation.[195] In Melanesia, all church bodies must structure their personnel contractual arrangements so that they require, as a professional condition of employment, 'compliance with the Christian moral code'.[196]

Parishes (and persons or organizations within them) in the Church in Wales commonly employ people (including lay members of the church), on a part-time or full-time basis, to assist in the work of the parish.[197] An employee is a person who has entered or works under a contract of employment, which itself may be express or implied, oral or written.[198] The subject is governed by the employment law of the State which forbids both discrimination on grounds of sex,[199] race[200] and disability,[201] and the employment of those who are not entitled to live or work in the United Kingdom.[202] Special provisions instituted by the church apply to the employment of persons working with children.[203] During the course of their employment, employees enjoy a number of rights contained in the State legislation.

First, an employee is entitled to pay statements,[204] and to a statement

---

[195] Australia, Diocese of Sydney, *The 7th Handbook*, 10; for England, see Opinions of the Legal Advisory Commission, 120–6.

[196] Melanesia, Standing Resolution 27, 1989; see generally CLAC, 184f.

[197] The following rules also apply to employees of other church organizations. See P. W. Edge, 'The employment of religious adherents by religious organisations', in P. W. Edge and G. Harvey (eds), *Law and Religion in Contemporary Society* (Aldershot, 2000), 151.

[198] Employment Protection (Consolidation) Act 1978, s. 153; Employment Rights Act 1996, s. 230. The relationship of employee–employer is constituted by evidence of: control (by the employer over selection, work and dismissal): *Short v Henderson Ltd* (1946) TLR 427; integration (the employee must be part and parcel of the employer's organization): *Beloff v Pressdram Ltd* [1973] 1 All ER 241; and economic provision (remuneration): *Ready Mixed Concrete (SE) Ltd v Minister of Pensions* [1988] 2 QB 497.

[199] Discrimination on grounds of homosexuality is not sexual discrimination under the Sex Discrimination Act 1975: *Smith v Gardner Merchant Ltd* [1996] 1 IRLR 342; but such discrimination may be in breach of the European Equal Treatment Directive 76/207/EEC: see *R v Secretary of State for Defence, ex parte Perkins* [1997] IRLR 297 and *Grant v South West Trains* (1998) Times 23/2/98.

[200] Race Relations Act 1976: Sikhs and Jews are regarded as a racial as well as a religious grouping: see *Mandla v Dowell Lee* [1983] 2 AC 548 and *Seide v Gillette Industries* [1980] IRLR 427.

[201] Disability Discrimination Act 1995, s. 7: this applies, however, where the employer has twenty or more employees.

[202] Asylum and Immigration Act 1996, s. 8.

[203] See above.

[204] Employment Rights Act 1996, s. 8; as amended by the Employment Relations Act 1999; see also the Employment Relations (Dispute Resolution) Act 1998.

setting out the main terms of their employment.[205] When the number of employees is below twenty, this statement should contain the name of a person to whom the employee may turn in cases of grievance.[206] Secondly, in addition to sick pay,[207] employees have a right to time off for ante-natal care,[208] to maternity leave,[209] and to return to work following the birth of children.[210] Failure by the employer to allow the employee to return after childbirth constitutes unfair dismissal, but this does not apply if the employer has five or fewer employees.[211] Finally, in cases of termination of employment, the employee is entitled: to a minimum period of notice;[212] to a written statement explaining any dismissal;[213] not to be dismissed unfairly;[214] to payment of damages for unfair dismissal, and to a payment if they are made redundant.[215]

In a recent case, the State industrial tribunal held that the applicant, a verger, was an employee for the purposes of civil law. The tribunal decided that she had been unfairly dismissed, but her complaint of sex discrimination was dismissed. The tribunal concluded that the church authority in question had failed to undertake any consultation in relation to the reorganization of its staffing, and there were no objective criteria used to select the applicant for redundancy. The tribunal was also critical of 'an almost complete lack of proper disciplinary rules and procedures' in the church institution concerned.[216]

---

[205] Ibid., s. 1.
[206] Ibid., s. 3(3): if twenty or more are employed, the statement should provide details of disciplinary and grievance procedures.
[207] Statutory Sick Pay Act 1994.
[208] Employment Rights Act 1996, s. 55.
[209] Ibid., s. 71; see also Employment Relations Act 1999, s. 7.
[210] Ibid., s. 79.
[211] Ibid., s. 96.
[212] Ibid., ss. 86, 87: an employee who has been employed for one month or more, but for less than two years, must be given at least one week's notice; after two years' employment, a right exists to one week's notice for each year of continuous employment up to a maximum of twelve weeks' notice.
[213] Ibid., s. 92.
[214] Ibid., s. 94; see also Employment Relations Act 1999, ss. 10, 11: this deals with disciplinary and grievance hearings (including the right to be accompanied) and with the employer's failure to comply with the statutory provisions governing these.
[215] Ibid., s. 135.
[216] *Ivory v Dean and Chapter of St Paul's Cathedral* (1995) 6/11/95 (unreported), Stratford Industrial Tribunal, 10316/93/S; for rudimentary rights of employees in Welsh cathedrals, under the church's Cathedrals Schemes, see above, Ch. 7.

PART IV

The Doctrine, Liturgy and Rites of the Church

9

FAITH, DOCTRINE AND LITURGY

Faith, doctrine and liturgy are central to the identity of the Church in Wales, not least as a member of the Anglican Communion. The Christian faith is represented formally in the doctrine (or teaching) of the church. In turn, faith and doctrine are expressed in the liturgy, or public worship, of the church. As such, the doctrinal law of the Church in Wales plays a key role in the proclamation, protection and development of the faith as it is communicated to contemporary society. The law of the State too promotes the Christian faith, particularly in its regulation of religious education and worship in State schools.[1] Moreover, the law of the State recognizes and protects the freedom of the Church in Wales to administer its own schools in a Christian ethos. Today, many administrative functions over both religious education and worship in State schools, and the running of church schools, are in the keeping of the National Assembly for Wales. Similarly, the liturgical law of the Church in Wales regulates: the making, development and authorization of liturgy; the performance of public worship and liturgical acts within it; and the maintenance of liturgical discipline.

FAITH, DOCTRINE AND MISSION

The Lambeth Conference has, from time to time, enunciated the theological principle that the church exists to proclaim the word of God as revealed in Christ.[2] This principle is fundamental to the organization of the law of the

---

[1] Such arrangements bring into question judicial attitudes of the type expressed in *R v Disciplinary Committee of the Jockey Club, ex p Aga Khan* [1993] 1 WLR 909, 932 *per* Hoffman J: 'The attitude of the English legislator to racing is much more akin to his attitude to religion . . . it is something to be encouraged but not the business of government.' See also: N. Doe and A. Jeremy, 'Justifications for religious autonomy', in R. O'Dair and A. Lewis (eds), *Law and Religion*, Current Legal Issues, 4 (Oxford, 2000), 421.

[2] See e.g. LC 1930, Res. 1: 'the Christian Church is the repository and trustee of a revelation of God, given by himself, which all members of the Church are bound to transmit to others'; for the 'teaching office' of the church, see e.g. LC 1930, Ress. 6, 70, 71 and LC 1978, Res. 3.

Church in Wales. Rules exist to ensure that the church acts as a trustee of the faith; their aim is to facilitate its proclamation, to protect and enable the development of doctrine, and to manage and effect a degree of doctrinal discipline. Under civil law, the members of the Church in Wales have a right to freedom both to hold and to profess their religious beliefs.[3]

The Proclamation of the Faith

Proclamation of the faith, as one of the fundamental tasks of the institutional church, is usually prescribed in the constitutions or canons of Anglican churches.[4] Formal laws are either purely descriptive,[5] or they cast a duty to proclaim the faith,[6] or else they present proclamation as both a right and a duty.[7] The ecumenical law of the Church in Wales recognizes proclamation of the faith as fundamental to the work of the church.[8] Ecumenical law also acknowledges the church's share in 'the common confession of the apostolic faith' and that in the church 'the Word of God is authentically preached'.[9] Moreover, the teaching of the Church in Wales provides that '[t]he mission of the Church is to be the instrument of God in restoring all people to unity with God and each other in Christ'. The church 'carries out its mission as it prays and worships, proclaims the Gospel and serves God's will in promoting justice, peace and life in all the world'.[10]

Teaching Authority   In the Church in Wales, a primary magisterial duty is placed on the bishop, who is charged at consecration to be 'a teacher of the

---

[3]   European Convention on Human Rights, Art. 9(1): a person's right to freedom of thought and religion includes freedom 'to manifest [their], religion or belief, in. . .teaching'; under the Human Rights Act 1998, it is unlawful for public authorities to violate this right: for the right, and for limitations on its exercise, see above, Ch. 1.
[4]   See e.g. Rwanda, Const., Art. 1: 'The mission of the Province is . . . the proclamation of the Gospel of Jesus Christ.'
[5]   See e.g. Southern Cone, Const. Art. 1: the church 'professes the historic faith'; Burundi, Const. Art. 3: the church 'accepts and teaches the faith of Jesus Christ'.
[6]   New Zealand, Const. Pt. I, Ch. 1, 3: 'This Church will ever obey the commands of Christ [and], teach His doctrine'; South India, Const. II.3: the church 'purposes to be ever mindful of its missionary calling . . . and also take its share in the preaching of the Gospel and the building up of Christ's Church'.
[7]   Kenya, Const. 1979, Art. II(e): the church has a 'right and duty to discover the truth as it is in Jesus, and to express that truth in life and in liturgy'; North India, Const. I.I.VI.1: spreading the gospel is both 'duty and privilege'.
[8]   See e.g. Can. 1–5–1974 (a canon for covenanting between the Church in Wales and other churches for Unity in Wales), First Schedule (the Covenant), 1(b): 'We intend so to act, speak, and serve together in obedience to the gospel that we may learn more of its fulness and make it known more to others in contemporary terms and by credible witness.'
[9]   Can. 28–9–1995 (Porvoo), First Schedule (a)(ii), and (iii).
[10]   BCP (1984), 691 (Catechism).

Faith'.[11] The Bench of Bishops too exercises a teaching function.[12] Similarly, at ordination, priests are charged both 'to proclaim the Gospel of Jesus Christ to all men' and to teach.[13] Deacons are charged to assist the priest 'in preaching the Word of God'.[14] Priests have a special responsibility to teach the people in the centrality of the eucharist, to instruct them in the use of private confession,[15] and there are special provisions on the instruction of candidates for baptism and confirmation.[16] According to provincial quasi-legislation, it is the duty of clergy to instruct the people in the faith: they are to lead the people to 'a deeper exploration and fuller understanding of the gospel and its challenge to life in the contemporary world'; clergy 'must take their stand within the tradition of faith'. At the same time, 'they must be prepared to bring new insights and new knowledge to its interpretation and application, not in order to reflect the spirit of the age, but so that the gospel can be proclaimed to this age as the good news that it has been to past ages'.[17] In common with other Anglican churches,[18] lay persons in the Church in Wales are under no specific legal duties to proclaim the faith, but the ministry of all members is 'to represent Christ and his Church' and 'to bear witness to him wherever they may be'.[19]

Preaching   An incumbent is required to preach in the cure, 'soberly and sincerely', one sermon on every Sunday of the year, 'to the glory of God, and to the best edification of the people'.[20] The law requires the pulpit to be kept 'for the preaching of God's Word'.[21] Rights to use the pulpit must not be abused.[22] Its use must be in line with the general duty of clergy to be 'examples to the people to live well and christianly'.[23] Consequently, according to ecclesiastical quasi-legislation, '[n]eglect of preaching is a breach

---

[11] BCP (1984), 714.
[12] See e.g. A Statement of the Bench of Bishops (1988): this explains that, basing its teaching on scripture, Christian tradition and the example of Jesus, the church identifies as sinful promiscuity, fornication, adultery and homosexual acts; moreover: '[i]f any serious moral or spiritual charge can be substantiated, an ordination candidate will not be accepted for ordination and a cleric will not be allowed to remain in office. Such moral failings would include unrepentant promiscuity, fornication, adultery and homosexual practice.'
[13] BCP (1984), 722; see also 723: candidates undertake to be 'a diligent minister of the Word of God, proclaiming the Gospel and teaching the Christian Faith'.
[14] BCP (1984), 729.
[15] BCP (1984), 3 (General Rubrics).
[16] See below, Ch. 10.
[17] Cure of Souls (1996), 5.
[18] See generally CLAC, 188.
[19] BCP (1984), 691 (Catechism).
[20] Canons Ecclesiastical 1603, Can. 45.
[21] Canons Ecclesiastical 1603, Can. 83.
[22] Burder v Hale (1849) 6 Notes of Cases 611.
[23] Canons Ecclesiastical 1603, Can. 75.

of duty, especially in the Eucharist'; however, at morning and evening prayer, preaching is discretionary.[24] It is not necessary that the priest should undertake alone the duty of preaching: when others in the parish are licensed to preach (such as lay readers), the priest 'should ensure that they have the opportunity from time to time to share in this ministry'.[25] No minister, churchwarden or other officer of the church is to allow any person to preach unless they are authorized to do so by the bishop.[26] Special provisions apply to preaching in an ecumenical context.[27]

These provisions are not dissimilar in their essentials to those of other Anglican churches. In English canon law, for example, a sermon must be preached in every parish church at least once each Sunday, except for some reasonable cause approved by the bishop. Ordinarily it is preached by the minister, a reader or lay worker. However, at the invitation of the minister having the cure of souls: 'another person may preach with the permission [given occasionally or generally] of the bishop.' In the sermon the preacher must endeavour 'with care and sincerity to minister the word of truth, to the glory of God and to the edification of the people'.[28] Rarely do laws of Anglican churches prescribe in detail the content of sermons, though in Southern Africa the incumbent must preach, or cause to be preached, 'a sermon expounding and applying Holy Scripture' at least once each Sunday. In the Church of Ireland, the preacher must 'minister the word of truth according to holy scripture', agreeable to the Thirty-Nine Articles and the Book of Common Prayer, and 'to the glory of God and edification of the people'.[29]

Catechism and Instruction   The modern law of the Church in Wales is rather less well developed than that of other Anglican churches with regard to catechetical formation and instruction.[30] In Irish canon law, every minister must take care that 'the children and young persons within his cure are

---

[24] *Cure of Souls* (1996), 8; BCP (1984), 7: at the eucharist 'The Sermon follows the reading of the Gospel'; BCP (1984), 400 and 409: at morning and evening prayer: 'A sermon may be preached after the second lesson, before the intercessions or at the end of the service.'

[25] *Cure of Souls* (1996), 8; for lay readers see above, Ch. 8.

[26] Canons Ecclesiastical 1603, Can. 50; Can. 71 prohibits, other than in cases of necessity, preaching in private homes.

[27] See below, Ch. 12.

[28] England, Can. B18, C24(3), BCP (1662), 241.

[29] Southern Africa, Can. 24(4)(a); and Ireland, Const. IX.7.

[30] The modern law places no obvious duty on the clergy to instruct or catechize; with regard to the Catechism, BCP (1984), 685 merely states: 'The purpose of setting out this Outline of the Faith as a Catechism is to present it in a form suitable for teaching.' See, however, Canons Ecclesiastical 1603, Can. 59: this requires clergy to catechize every Sunday. For guidelines on the administration of Sunday schools, see *The Essential Sunday School Teachers Manual*, prepared by the Children's Sector of the Church in Wales (1999).

instructed in the doctrine, sacraments and discipline of Christ, as the Lord has commanded and as they are set forth in the holy scriptures, in the Book of Common Prayer and in the Church Catechism'. To this end, the minister, or 'some godly and competent person' appointed by him, must on Sundays or other convenient times 'instruct and teach them in the same'.[31] According to Philippine canon law: the minister must be 'diligent in instructing the children and youth in the Catechisms, and from time to time examine them in the same publicly before the Congregation'; ministers must also inform the youth on the holy scriptures and 'the Doctrine, Polity, History and Liturgy of the Church'; and they must instruct 'all persons in their Parishes and Cures concerning the missionary work of the Church at home and abroad'.[32] Finally, in Scottish canon law clergy must 'set apart a due portion of time on Sundays and other convenient days for publicly examining and instructing the younger members of their congregations in the Catechism contained in the authorized Service Books'; any other catechism or manual of instruction may be used if sanctioned by the diocesan bishop.[33]

The Council for Mission and Ministry The provincial Council for Mission and Ministry of the Church in Wales is regulated by ecclesiastical quasi-legislation rather than by constitutional or canon law. The Council is responsible to the Bench of Bishops and works in six teams.[34] The six teams are, in turn, responsible to the council, and each one consists of a bishop, two designated members of the council appointed on its recommendation, and others appointed as appropriate. Each team: is responsible for the work assigned to it by the council; is empowered to initiate work and annually present a written report of its progress to the council; and, after consultation with the principal officer of the council, must establish such working groups necessary to undertake defined and specific tasks, the groups being responsible to the appropriate team to which they must report as and when determined by the team.[35]

The Inter-Church Team is to enable those working with inter-church and inter-faith concerns to meet and co-ordinate their work; it is also to encourage and assist the Church in Wales at every level to benefit from and enrich its international catholicity.[36] The Church and Society Team is to provide an effective Christian witness in contemporary society.[37] The

---

[31] Ireland, Const. IX.27.
[32] Philippines, Cans. III.16.3.
[33] Scotland, Can. 28.
[34] In 2000, the work of the former Board of Mission and the Board of Ministry was reviewed and a new provincial Council for Mission and Ministry was formed in their stead, coming into being on 1 April 2001. See above, Ch. 7, for the council's basic responsibilities and composition.
[35] COFC, 12.
[36] COFC, 13: see also below, Ch. 12.
[37] COFC: as well as a bishop and two council appointees, its other members include the

Communication Team is to maintain 'the highest standards in communication within the Christian community and beyond', and utilize 'the most appropriate resources for Christian apologetics and communication of the Gospel'.[38] One of the functions of the Education Team is to co-ordinate, encourage and assist the dioceses in the work of mission among children, families and young people.[39] The Renewal Team is to support local witness to the Christian faith and the strengthening of the life of the church.[40] The Ministry Team is dealt with elsewhere in this volume.[41] The dioceses have institutions working in the area of mission.[42]

In contrast to the Church in Wales, for most other Anglican churches, bodies working in the fields of mission and evangelism are regulated by canon law.[43] The Boards of Mission in Australia and New Zealand have very proactive roles, rights and duties, binding as a matter of law. The principal function of the Australian Board is 'to lead, encourage and serve the Church in Christ's mission'. It is to: educate and stimulate the church in the responsibility of mission; recruit, train and support persons to serve in the churches of the Anglican Communion; raise, invest and administer funds and act as trustee of funds committed to it; and review and monitor missionary policy. The membership of the board includes the primate, a national director, five bishops, and representatives from the diocesan clergy, laity and youth. The

church and society officer, and 'various members involved in Church and Society concerns in the dioceses'.

[38] COFC, 15: its additional members are: communication officer; creative resources officer; translation/bilingual officer; the members of the Communication Technology Group and Editors Group; and various other members drawn from the diocesan communication officers and the diocesan language officers. The communication officer also acts as the public relations officer for the archbishop and the province.

[39] COFC, 17: see below for its other functions.

[40] COFC, 18: it is to work closely with its Renewal Strategy Group and various diocesan officials; its additional members are: the renewal officer; and one representative from each of the following groups: Renewal Strategy Group; diocesan missioners; diocesan ecumenism officers; diocesan evangelists; diocesan stewardship officers.

[41] See above, Chs. 7 and 8.

[42] See e.g. DSAB, YB (1999–2000), 30: the Diocesan Council for Mission; DM, YB (2001), 11: the Mission Forum is the co-ordinating body for various individuals and groups with a diocesan responsibility for some aspect of God's mission; DSD, YB (2000–1), 135: this lists missionary societies supported by the diocese. The Diocese of Bangor is about to introduce *A Language Scheme*, containing its Mission Statement; it states 'The diocese of Bangor is not a public body as defined by the Welsh Language Act 1993 and does not have a statutory obligation to have a Language Scheme. However, a decision was taken to develop a language scheme as a commitment to the principle of the equality of the Welsh and English languages within the diocese'; the scheme contains provisions on: delivery of the diocese's mission; standards on delivery in Welsh; Welsh in diocesan administration; dealing with the public; advertising and publicity; recruitment of staff; implementing and monitoring the scheme; and complaints procedures.

[43] ECUSA, Cans. I.1.2 and 11: General Convention has three Standing Commissions: on Evangelism; on World Mission; and on mission in metropolitical areas; the church also operates missionary dioceses.

board may operate within the provinces and dioceses, by appointing staff to them, but its powers operate in no way to limit the authority or rights of the diocesan bishop.[44]

The New Zealand board acts as an agent of the church 'in setting forward the mission of the Church in overseas areas'. The board must: 'assist and encourage the church at diocesan and local levels to arouse support among parishioners for the objects of the Board'; fix an annual budget and make annual reports and a statement of accounts to the Standing Committee of General Synod and, biennially, to the General Synod itself. The composition of the board includes, *inter alios*, diocesan bishops, representatives of diocesan synods, youth representatives, and Anglican women. The primate is the President. The Board must hold an annual meeting and may make by-laws, produce literature, appropriate funds for expenses, and borrow money and receive money.[45] Anglican churches also have canonical institutions working at the level of dioceses.[46]

Doctrine and its Development

Anglican churches are not confessional denominations with formal legal statements of their beliefs. Instead, their laws simply point to doctrinal documents, extrinsic to the law, accepted as normative of the faith. It is only in this oblique sense that law is used to define doctrine. Three broad approaches are used. First, legal approval is given to doctrine located in the trilogy of documents of the post-Reformation Church of England: the Thirty-Nine Articles 1571, the Book of Common Prayer 1662, and the Ordinal.[47] Secondly, canonical approval is given to doctrine located in holy scripture, the Creeds and pronouncements of the early councils.[48] Thirdly, the most common approach is the principle of reception: canon law approves doctrinal sources which have been received by the church; these may include the canonical scriptures (being the ultimate rule and standard of faith in the church), the faith of Christ as preached by the apostles, and the doctrine, sacraments and discipline set forth in the 1662 Prayer Book.[49]

---

[44] Australia, Can. 8 1995.
[45] New Zealand, Cans. B.IX.
[46] CLAC, 193f.
[47] See e.g. England, Cans. A2–5.
[48] See e.g. South India, Const. II.5.
[49] See e.g. Kenya, Const. Art. II: the church 'receives all the Canonical Scriptures of the Old and New Testaments, given by inspiration of God, as containing all things necessary for salvation and as being the ultimate rule and standard of the faith and life of the Church'. The church holds 'the faith of Christ as preached by the Apostles, summed up in the Apostles' Creed, and confirmed by the first Four General Councils of the Holy Catholic Church'; and it declares 'its acceptance of the Doctrine, Sacraments and Discipline of the Church' as set forth in the Prayer Book of 1662 and the Ordinal.

It is the first model which seems to be employed in relation to the Church in Wales. Parliament through the Welsh Church Act 1914 initially defined the doctrine of the Church in Wales, but it empowered the church to alter that doctrine. The articles and doctrines of the Church of England existing at the date of disestablishment are binding on the members of the Church in Wales in the same manner as if they had mutually agreed to be so bound. However, these articles and doctrines bind, subject to such modifications or alterations as after the passing of the Act may be duly made according to the constitution and regulations of the Church in Wales.[50] The constitution of the Church in Wales indicates the following as the formal sources of the church's approved doctrine: the faith revealed in the holy scriptures and set forth in the Catholic Creeds; and the historic formularies (which bear witness to scripture and the Creeds), that is, the Thirty-Nine Articles of Religion, the Book of Common Prayer and Ordinal of 1662.[51] Indeed, pre-1920 ecclesiastical law treats the Thirty-Nine Articles as 'the standard of doctrine . . . to be considered, and, in the first instance, appealed to . . . to ascertain the doctrine of the Church'.[52]

While the Welsh Church Act 1914 provides that pre-disestablishment doctrine forms part of the church's statutory contract, the exercise of the power to alter and develop this doctrine is now governed by the constitution of the Church in Wales.[53] The development of doctrine is in the keeping of the Governing Body, which has 'power to make new articles, doctrinal statements . . . and formularies, and to alter those from time to time existing'. However, no such action may be taken except by bill procedure backed and introduced in the Governing Body by a majority of the Order of Bishops.[54] The exercise of the Governing Body's power seems to be limited legally by the fundamental principle that 'it is not lawful for the Church to ordain any thing that is contrary to God's Word written'.[55]

The Church in Wales no longer has a provincial Doctrinal Commission.[56] The Diocesan Conference has no right to pass any resolution or to come to

---

[50] Welsh Church Act 1914, s. 3(2).
[51] Const. VII.66; see also Const., Prefatory Note; BCP (1984), 696 (Catechism): 'The Bible is the record of God's revelation of himself to mankind.'
[52] *Gorham v Bishop of Exeter* (1849) 2 Rob Ecc 1 at 55 *per* Sir Jenner Fust (Arches Court of Canterbury).
[53] Welsh Church Act 1914, s. 3(2): see above. Indeed, if the Church in Wales is understood legally to be a church established by the statutory contract contained in the Welsh Church Act (see above, Ch. 1), the principle in *General Assembly of the Free Church of Scotland v Lord Overtoun* [1904] AC 515 at 648 may apply: 'where the state has by legislative acts established a church identified by certain doctrines, that church cannot . . . exercise any power of altering those doctrines without the legislative sanction of the state'; this sanction was given by the State in the Welsh Church Act 1914, s. 3(2).
[54] Const. II.36; for the entrenched nature of this provision, see above, Ch. 2.
[55] Thirty-Nine Articles, Art. 20.
[56] The former Doctrinal Commission offered advice to the Bench of Bishops on any matters of doctrine referred to it: see COFC (2000), 8.

any decision on any matter concerning faith.[57] The 'discussion of any doctrinal matters' by the Deanery Conference must 'not extend to any formulation or declaration of doctrine'.[58] The same rule applies to the Parochial Church Council.[59]

Similarly, in other Anglican churches the authority to develop doctrine vests in national or provincial assemblies, but not in institutions at lower levels of the church.[60] In some churches the law enables doctrinal development, but special majority procedures must be complied with.[61] A small number of laws employ a reserved right for the church to adopt doctrinal alterations accepted by the Church of England.[62] Others prohibit doctrinal change but reserve a right to accept certain doctrinal adjustments if consistent with standards prevailing in the Anglican Communion generally.[63] Sometimes there is a right to adopt doctrinal change if permitted, at some time in the future, by a supra-provincial assembly of the Anglican Communion.[64] A minority of churches operate an absolute bar to change those doctrines recognized in their Fundamental Declarations.[65] Others recognize their authority simply 'to explain the meaning of the norms of faith' or to issue statements 'agreeable to Holy Scripture'.[66] Finally, several churches have a permanent, canonical Doctrine Commission to assist in the process of doctrinal development.[67]

Subscription and Doctrinal Discipline

Churches of the Anglican Communion generally employ two devices to effect doctrinal discipline amongst clergy and lay office-holders: rules which require acceptance of the faith; and rules which enable oversight or enforcement of doctrinal standards by means of executive action or judicial proceedings.[68] Very seldom do formal laws require the laity generally to assent intellectually

---

[57] Const. IV.45: at least, 'Nothing in this chapter shall be construed as giving' such a right.
[58] Const. V.15(h).
[59] Const. VI.22(3)(b).
[60] See generally CLAC, 200ff.
[61] See e.g. Kenya, Const. Art. II.
[62] See e.g. Indian Ocean, Const. Art. 2(iv).
[63] See e.g. Burundi, Const. Art. 3.3.
[64] See e.g. West Indies, Declaration of Fundamental Principles, (d)–(e).
[65] See e.g. Australia, Const. XI.66.
[66] See e.g. Zaire, Const. Art. 3.3.
[67] See e.g. Melanesia, Cans. E.11; New Zealand, Cans. B.XVII.
[68] LC 1968, Res. 43: this suggests that 'assent to the Thirty-Nine Articles be no longer required of ordinands' but that 'when subscription is required to the Articles or other elements in the Anglican tradition, it should be required, and given, only in the context of a statement which gives the full range of our inheritance of faith and sets the Articles in their historical context'.

to church doctrine:[69] in most churches the laity have a right of assent,[70] but in some they have a duty of assent;[71] in others church employees must sign a doctrinal statement.[72] Lay officers must in the vast majority of churches make a subscription to the doctrine of the church.[73] Provisions for subscription by candidates for ordination and admission to episcopal and clerical offices vary from church to church: some require 'assent', others 'belief',[74] and modes of subscription are variously by affirmation, declaration, promise or oath.[75]

In the Church in Wales, subscription applies to all persons admitted to the holy orders of priests and deacons, instituted or collated to the cure of souls, or licensed as assistant curates or deaconesses, and to all clerics appointed to any ecclesiastical office in the Church in Wales. These must before ordination or appointment, make and subscribe in the presence of the bishop or his commissary (appointed in writing), a declaration and undertaking. In it, they must declare their 'belief in the Faith which is revealed in the Holy Scriptures and set forth in the Catholic Creeds and to which the historic formularies, namely: the Thirty-Nine Articles of Religion, the Book of Common Prayer and the Ordering of Bishops, Priests and Deacons, as published in 1662, bear witness'.[76] At ordination, candidates for the priesthood and diaconate must declare: their belief that holy scriptures contain all things necessary to eternal salvation through faith in Jesus Christ; and their belief in 'the doctrines of the Christian Faith as the Church in Wales has received them', and to uphold these doctrines.[77]

According to provincial quasi-legislation, proclamation of the gospel by clergy 'must be in accordance' with the legally approved doctrines of the church. Consequently, '[t]he teaching of private and esoteric doctrine, and all

---

[69] Thirty-Nine Articles, Art. 20: the church 'ought not to enforce any thing to be believed for necessity of salvation'.

[70] See e.g. England, Cans. A1 and A2: the Thirty-Nine Articles 'may be assented to with a good conscience by all memebers of the Church of England' as agreeable to the Word of God; as to the canonical statement that the church belongs to the true and apostolic Church of Christ, no member 'shall be at liberty to maintain or hold the contrary'.

[71] See e.g. New Zealand, Const. C.14: 'No doctrines which are repugnant to the Doctrines and Sacraments of Christ as held and maintained by this Church shall be advocated or inculcated by any person acknowledging the authority of General Synod.'

[72] See e.g. Melanesia, Standing Resolution 28, 1989: all employees of the church must sign 'a doctrinal statement' that they are 'of the Christian faith'.

[73] See CLAC, 205.

[74] See e.g. England, Can. C15: priests and deacons must 'affirm' loyalty to the inheritance of faith, and to 'declare [their], belief in the faith'.

[75] See generally CLAC, 206f.

[76] Const. VII.66. Whilst the BCP (1984) is the authoritative text of collective worship, the 1662 Prayer Book is the authoritative statement of collective belief: for this and criticism of the declaration as out-of-date, see P. Jones, *The Governance of the Church in Wales* (Cardiff, 2000), 110, 156ff.

[77] BCP (1984), 723, 730.

interpretation of the Faith that is in clear contradiction of the formularies of the Church, is both an act of disloyalty and a breach of duty.'[78] Executive doctrinal discipline may in the first instance be carried out by the bishop as teacher of the faith, and 'guardian of discipline in the Church'. Indeed, at their consecration, bishops undertake to uphold the doctrines of the Christian faith as the Church in Wales has received them.[79] Disciplinary proceedings may be taken against any member (clerical or lay) of the Church in Wales for 'teaching, preaching, publishing or professing, doctrine or belief incompatible with that of the Church in Wales'.[80]

The notion of a formal legal right to doctrinal dissent is not well developed in the Church in Wales.[81] Indeed, under pre-1920 ecclesiastical law, maintaining opinions contrary to the Christian religion, depraving the Book of Common Prayer, holding doctrines contrary to the Thirty-Nine Articles, and heresy, are all classified and actionable as doctrinal offences.[82] However, the courts of the Church in Wales are not bound by any decision of the English courts in relation to matters of faith or discipline.[83] There is also a general reluctance on the part of the courts of the State to become involved in doctrinal disputes,[84] but everyone has the right in civil law to change their religion or belief.[85]

Several Anglican churches have laws which allow complaints about doctrinal standards to be processed either by the bishop,[86] or by the arch-

---

[78] Cure of Souls (1996), 8.

[79] BCP (1984), 714, 715; Thirty-Nine Articles, Art. 20: 'The Church hath . . . authority in Controversies of Faith.'

[80] Const. XI.18(1)(a); for proceedings in the Disciplinary Tribunal, see above, Ch. 5.

[81] For an exceptional provision, see Can. 19–9–1996: 'No bishop shall be obliged to bring proceedings . . . in respect of a cleric or other member of the Church in Wales who dissents in conscience' from the principle that women may be ordained as priests. Rather than being a conscience clause and a right to dissent, this simply relieves a bishop from the duty to bring disciplinary proceedings.

[82] Gathercole v Miall (1846) 15 M&W 319; Williams v Bishop of Salisbury (1864) 2 Moore PCCNS 375; Kelly v Sherlock (1866) LR 1 QB 686; Botterill v Whytehead (1874) 41 LT 588; Magrath v Finn (1877) IR II CL 152.

[83] Const. XI.47.

[84] See e.g. R v Ecclesiastical Committee of Both Houses of Parliament, ex parte Willamson (1993) Times 4/11/93 per Simon Brown LJ: 'I would certainly deprecate any attempt on either side to put before the court essentially theological or doctrinal disputes'; Varsani and Others v Jesani and Others [1998] 3 All ER 372 (CA). See generally, M. Hill, 'Judicial approaches to religious disputes', in O'Dair and Lewis (eds), Law and Religion, 409.

[85] European Convention on Human Rights, Art. 9(1). This freedom includes the right to leave a religious organization.

[86] Scotland, Can. 16.2: the bishop is obliged to 'uphold sound and wholesome doctrine, and to banish and drive away all erroneous and strange opinions'; see also Ireland, Const. IX.29: every minister 'having within his cure persons holding any erroneous and strange doctrines, contrary to the Word of God, shall endeavour to reclaim them from their errors'.

deacon.[87] Judicial proceedings too are available in cases of public statements in conflict with the doctrine of the church.[88] Indeed, in some churches private withholding of assent is actionable.[89] Finally, the laws of a number of churches provide for the external referral of a doctrinal disagreement to an institution of the Anglican Communion for consultation and advice,[90] or sometimes for determination,[91] whilst in other churches doctrinal disputes are resolved within the church by means of a special tribunal.[92]

CHRISTIAN EDUCATION IN SECULAR SOCIETY

Both the Church in Wales and the State have a direct interest in Christian education in secular society. The church runs its own schools and has a number of advisory bodies concerned with education, and the State has its own laws on religious education and worship in schools.[93] Under civil law, the State must respect the right of parents to ensure education of their children in conformity with their own religious convictions.[94]

[87] Southern Africa, Can. 29.7: a duty is placed on churchwardens to complain to the bishop or the archdeacon 'if there should be anything plainly amiss or reprehensible in the life or doctrine of the Incumbent'.

[88] See e.g. Canada, Can. XVIII.8(g): proceedings may be taken against clergy and lay officers for 'teaching or advocating doctrines contrary to' those of the church.

[89] ECUSA, Cans. IV.1.1: it is an offence to hold or teach publicly or privately any doctrine contrary to that of the church.

[90] South East Asia, Fundamental Declarations, 4: the Provincial Synod may consult with the archbishop of Canterbury or the primates of the Anglican Communion; Kenya, Const. Art. II(e), (g), (h): referral is to the Anglican Consultative Council.

[91] Central Africa, Const. Art. V: the matter is determined by the archbishop of Canterbury and two other bishops.

[92] New Zealand, Cans. C.V. the special tribunal on doctrine acts 'for the purposes of deciding all questions of doctrine duly referred to it'.

[93] What follows in the text is only an outline of the law: specialist works must be consulted for a more detailed exposition. There is also a body of State law dealing with religious instruction and observance in children's homes: when a child is accommodated by a local authority, or by or on behalf of a voluntary organization, in making decisions about the welfare of the child, these must give consideration 'to the child's religious persuasion' (Children Act 1989, ss. 20, 61); for community homes, voluntary homes and registered children's homes, regulations may be made to 'impose requirements as to the facilities which are to be provided for giving religious instruction to children' in them (Children Act 1989, ss. 53, 60, 63; see also e.g. Children's Homes Regulations 1991, SI 1991/1506, r. 11). See also Residential Homes Act 1984 (as amended 1991), s. 16: regulations may be made for those under eighteen 'to receive a religious upbringing appropriate to the religious persuasion to which they belong'.

[94] European Convention on Human Rights, Protocol 1, Art. 2.

Provincial and Diocesan Education Bodies

The Education Team of the Council for Mission and Ministry is: to co-ordinate, encourage and assist the dioceses in the work of mission among children, families and young people; to support and encourage the continued contribution of the Church in Wales to education in Wales; and to support ecumenical chaplaincies in higher and further education. The team is to work closely with groups representing the various levels of educational activity within the church. The team consists of a bishop, and two designated members of the council appointed on the recommendation of the council. Its additional members are the education officer, and one representative from each of the following groups: the Diocesan Directors of Education Group; the Higher/Further Education Group; the Children and Families Group; and the Youth Group. The Diocesan Directors of Education Group includes representatives of the Roman Catholic Church.[95] In turn, each diocese has a board or council for education.[96]

The provincial Education Team and diocesan boards or councils of education are not creatures of the provincial law of the Church in Wales.[97] By way of contrast, many Anglican churches have canonical advisory bodies responsible for education in both state and church schools. Some are national or provincial bodies and it is common for dioceses to have a local equivalent.[98] For example, in the Church of Ireland, the Board of Education must 'define the policy of the Church in education both religious and secular', promote this policy, and co-ordinate activities in all fields of education affecting the interests of the church. The board must maintain close contact with secular government, diocesan boards of education and schools, and it is 'to study any legislation or proposed legislation likely to affect the educational interests of the Church of Ireland and to act as necessary'. The board must report annually to the General Synod.[99] In contrast to these other Anglican churches, then, education authorities within the Church in Wales are not regulated, nor are their functions defined, by the law of the church.

---

[95] COFC, 17.
[96] DM, YB (2001), 11: the Council for Education is '[t]o promote within the Diocese, the policy of the Church in Wales in regard to all aspects of education, both voluntary and statutory'; DSAB, YB (1999–2000), 27: the Diocesan Council for Education.
[97] The constitution makes no mention of them; they are creatures of practice and policy.
[98] See CLAC, 194; e.g. Melanesia, Cans. E.16: Education Board; Australia, Can. 9 1962, Can. 5 1969; Can. 2 1973: General Board of Religious Education.
[99] Ireland, Const. approved by the General Synod 1965–94: there are two boards, one for the Republic of Ireland and the other for Northern Ireland.

Religious Education and Worship in State Schools

Schools fall into various legal categories.[100] As a basic principle, civil law requires all state schools to provide for non-denominational religious education as part of the basic curriculum.[101] The syllabus must 'reflect the fact that the religious traditions in Great Britain are in the main Christian whilst taking account of the teaching and practices of the other principal religions represented in Great Britain'.[102] The syllabus must be agreed locally by a conference, the Standing Advisory Council on Religious Education (SACRE). The conference is appointed by the local education authority, and consists of representatives of the principal Christian denominations and other religious traditions as, in the opinion of the authority, reflect the principal religious traditions in the area. The agreed syllabus, which may be different for different schools, classes or pupils, must be reviewed every five years.[103] It is difficult for parents to challenge an agreed syllabus.[104] Community, foundation and voluntary schools (not of a religious character) must adopt the agreed syllabus for religious education. They cannot teach by means of a catechism or formulary distinctive of a particular religious denomination, though studying these is not prohibited.[105] Parents may withdraw their children from religious education.[106]

Civil law requires state schools to provide a daily act of collective worship. It need not be at the beginning of the day and separate acts of worship may be provided for pupils in different age or school groups.[107] The act of worship must be wholly or mainly of a broadly Christian character without being distinctive of any particular Christian denomination.[108] The local SACRE

---

[100] Schools are either: independent (i.e. self-governing and receiving no direct financial aid from the State); controlled (i.e. entirely maintained by the local education authority, with the majority of governors appointed by that authority); aided (i.e. not wholly maintained by the local education authority, and with a majority of governors chosen in accordance with the school's constitution, the foundation governors); and foundation schools (with a minority of foundation governors). Controlled and aided schools are also voluntary schools.

[101] Education Reform Act 1988, s. 2(1); Education Act 1996, s. 352(1).

[102] Education Reform Act 1988, s. 8(2), and (3); see also Education Act 1996, s. 375(3).

[103] Education Reform Act 1988, s. 11: unlike the Chuch of England, the Church in Wales has no special right to representation on the SACRE; see also Education Act 1996, ss. 387, 390, 391, 396.

[104] D. Harte, 'Religious education and worship in state schools', in N. Doe, M. Hill, and R. Ombres (eds), *English Canon Law* (Cardiff, 1998), 115 at 119: see *R v Secretary of State for Education, ex parte Ruscoe and Dando*, CO/2209/92, 26/2/1993.

[105] School Standards and Framework Act 1998, s. 69.

[106] Education Reform Act 1988, s. 9(3); Education Act 1996, s. 389.

[107] Education Reform Act 1988, s. 6; Education Act 1996, ss. 385, 386.

[108] Education Reform Act 1988, s. 7; see also *R v Secretary of State for Education, ex parte Ruscoe and Dando* [1994] ELR 495: this concerned the failure to provide collective worship contrary to ss. 6 and 7.

may disapply the requirement in a school, or for a particular class or description of pupils, that daily worship should be mainly Christian.[109] Parents have a right to withdraw their children from collective acts of worship, and no reason has to be given.[110] As a general rule, no person is to be disqualified from being a teacher by virtue of religious opinions.[111] Whilst the National Assembly for Wales has no competence to alter these statutory duties and rights, it is empowered to regulate their administration and exercise,[112] by defining their scope and meaning, in regulations and other instruments.[113]

Church Schools

Schools may be designated as schools of a religious character,[114] and these fall into a number of legal categories.[115] Church in Wales schools are not, under the domestic law of the church, constitutionally linked to the institutional Church in Wales.[116] Each school is regulated by State law, its own trust deed and governing body.[117] Religious education in schools of a religious character may be in accordance either with the local education authority's agreed syllabus or, where parents request it, with the trust deed, or, if the trust deed is silent, with the tenets of the religion concerned.[118] Church schools

[109] Education Reform Act 1988, s. 12

[110] Education Reform Act 1988, s. 9(3); Education Act 1996, s. 389; School Standards and Framework Act 1998, ss. 70, 71; teachers too may opt out: Education Act 1996, s. 146; Education Act 1996, s. 444(3)(c): this entitles pupils to be absent from school on any day set apart for religious observance by the religious body to which the parents belong.

[111] Education Act 1944, s. 30: nor by reason of attending or refusing to attend religious worship; see below for church schools.

[112] Under the Government of Wales Act 1998, and the Transfer of Functions Order, responsibility for ministerial functions under most of the key education statutes passes to the Assembly.

[113] See e.g. School Standards and Framework Act 1998, s. 71(7): regulations must secure that, so far as practicable, every pupil in a community or foundation school receives religious education and attends worship or is withdrawn from these in accordance with parental wishes.

[114] School Standards and Framework Act 1998, s. 69.

[115] Church schools may be controlled, aided, foundation or independent: see above, n. 100.

[116] The constitution makes no mention of church schools. It has been observed that 'Church in Wales schools are constitutionally separate from the rest of the Church', but they are 'part of the Church if they collectively profess the Church's faith': P. Jones, *Governance*, 196.

[117] See generally Duncan and Lankshear, *Church Schools: A Guide for Governors* (1996); and Harris, *The Law Relating to Schools* (2nd edn, 1995). Officers and authorities within the church may, under the trust deed and school constitution, function as trustees, governors or visitors. See also R. Charles, 'Church schools and the law' (LLM dissertation, University of Wales, Cardiff, 1997).

[118] School Standards and Framework Act 1998, s. 69, Sched. 19, para. 3; for religious worship see s. 70, Sched. 20, para. 4; see also Education Reform Act 1988, ss. 27, 28; Education Act 1993, ss. 138–41.

may give priority to children whose parents genuinely desire a Christian ethos.[119] Moreover, religion may lawfully be used as a criterion in the employment and dismissal of school staff.[120] However, it is possible that a church school is a public authority for the purposes of the Human Rights Act 1998: whilst church schools maintain a distinctive religious ethos under the terms of their trust deeds, they are also underpinned by 'a specific statutory regime designed to secure their special position outside local education authority control but within the State framework for most purposes'.[121]

The National Assembly for Wales discharges certain functions in relation to church schools. For example, the Assembly is involved: in approving education development plans affecting church schools;[122] in the appointment in a voluntary aided school of additional governors, when it must consult, in the case of Church in Wales schools, the appropriate diocesan authority;[123] and in the modification of the trust deeds of a church school.[124] Designation of a school as one having a religious character is for the Assembly, which must have in place regulations governing procedure for designation.[125] Any promoter proposing to establish a new church school, must, in the case of the Church in Wales, obtain approval from the appropriate diocesan authority; the constitution of the proposed school must be consistent with the proposal; and there are requirements about representation of the church in the school's governing body, about the use of property for religious charitable purposes if

---

[119] Department of Education and Employment, *Excellence in Schools*, 1997, Cm. 3681, p. 71.

[120] See e.g. *Board of Governors of St Matthias Church of England School v Gizzle* (EAT 409/90): the tribunal found that a denominational school was justified in insisting that the head be a communicant Christian in order to preserve the religious character of the school; see also *Lal v Board of Governors, Sacred Heart Comprehensive School, Dagenham* (unreported, 7/11/1990), and *Ahmad v ILEA* [1975] 1 All ER 574 and *Ahmad v UK* (1982) 4 EHRR 126. See generally P. W. Edge, 'The employment of religious adherents by religious organisations', in P. W. Edge and G. Harvey (eds), *Law and Religion in Contemporary Society* (Aldershot, 2000), 151.

[121] See I. Leigh, 'Towards a Christian approach to religious liberty', in P. R. Beaumont (ed.), *Christian Perspectives on Human Rights and Legal Philosophy* (Carlisle, 1998), 31 at 67; in parliamentary debate on the matter, the Lord Chancellor preferred to leave the question as to whether a church school was a public authority to the courts: HL Debs. 24/11/1997, cols. 796–7 and 800; however, the Home Secretary considered that where the church stood in the place of the State (for example, in education), it was right that the ECHR should apply: HC Debs. 20/5/1998, col. 1015; see also *National Union of Teachers and Others v Governing Body of St Mary's Church of England Junior School* [1997] 3 Common Market Law Reports 630: the Court of Appeal decided that a Church of England school was an emanation of the State and therefore bound by the direct effect of a European Union directive.

[122] School Standards and Framework Act 1996, s. 11.

[123] School Standards and Framework Act 1998, s. 18.

[124] School Standards and Framework Act 1998, s. 82.

[125] School Standards and Framework Act 1998, s. 69(3): a foundation or voluntary school has a religious character if it is designated as such by an order of the secretary of state: this function passes to the Assembly.

the school is discontinued, and about religious education in the school.[126] Within the Church in Wales, diocesan bodies have special responsibilities towards church schools.[127]

LITURGICAL LAW: PUBLIC WORSHIP

The Church in Wales teaches that worship is the response of an individual to the love of God: first, 'by joining with others in the Church's corporate offering of prayer, celebration of the Sacraments and reading of his holy Word'; and secondly, 'by acknowledging him as the Lord', and by the individual working for his honour and glory.[128] The relationship between liturgical action and law is often problematic. Worship is an occasion of spiritual intimacy between the individual and God. Yet the public nature of worship, the desire for order, and the organization of corporate worship as liturgy, necessitate the existence of some regulation. As in other Anglican churches,[129] in the Church in Wales, this is effected by means of law,[130] liturgical rubrics,[131] directions[132] and quasi-legislation. A considerable body of pre-1920 ecclesiastical law also regulates this subject; under it, liturgical custom too enjoys an authoritative place. A fundamental principle is that clergy and laity must consult and co-operate meaningfully in the liturgical life of the church. The members of the Church in Wales enjoy in civil law the right to freedom, either alone or in community with others, and in public or private, to manifest their religion in worship.[133]

[126] Religious Character of Schools (Designation Procedure) Regulations 1998, SI 1998/2535.
[127] See e.g. DM, YB (2001), 9: the Diocesan Trust is responsible for the financial administration of all church schools within the diocese, and for funding.
[128] BCP (1984), 695 (Catechism); compare e.g. Southern Africa, Prayer Book 1989, 9: 'liturgy is the public worship of the Church of God, a living tradition'; Ireland, Alternative Prayer Book 1984, 8: 'liturgy becomes worship when the people of God make the prayers their own prayer, and turn in faith, to God.'
[129] See generally CLAC, 215ff.
[130] BCP (1984), v: 'The law of worship of the Church in Wales is contained in the Book of Common Prayer', but not exclusively.
[131] Liturgical Commission, 1949 and 1951: 'rubrics' are 'directions on order, ceremonial, and other matters'; 'Rubrics: there is a need for the excision of absolute rubrics; for the provision of new ones to recognise a number of practices which have become customary but of whose strict legality there is doubt; and for the expression of certain rubrics. . .so as to make clear what they allow or do not allow': see E. Lewis, *Prayer Book Revision in the Church in Wales* (Penarth, 1958), 3; for rubrics treated like binding statutory rules, see *Martin v Mackonochie* (1882) 7 PD 94; in the Church of England, today, the general view is that rubrics must not be interpreted like statutes: see *Bishopwearmouth (Rector and Churchwardens) v Adey* [1958] 3 All ER 441.
[132] See e.g. BCP (1984), 22.
[133] European Convention on Human Rights, Art. 9(1). For the Human Rights Act 1998, which forbids public authorities to violate this right, and the limits on its exercise (under Art. 9(2)), see above, Ch. 1.

The Making and Authorization of Liturgy

The Welsh Church Act 1914 incorporated at disestablishment the liturgical rites of the Church of England in the statutory contract of the Church in Wales. But Parliament empowered the church to alter that liturgy.[134] The Governing Body may make new rites and ceremonies, and alter existing ones, provided these are done in accordance with bill procedure backed and introduced in the Governing Body by a majority of the Order of Bishops.[135] The Standing Liturgical Advisory Commission acts as an advisory body in this regard,[136] and is responsible directly to the Bench of Bishops. Its functions are: to monitor liturgical developments and serve as a reference point for all liturgical matters arising in the province; and, at the request of the Bench, to prepare new draft services from time to time.[137] Between the Book of Common Prayer (1984), and the Alternative Orders, there are forms of service for the eucharist, morning and evening prayer, compline, public and private baptism of infants and adults, baptism with confirmation, thanksgiving for the birth or adoption of a child, confirmation, ordination, holy matrimony, blessing a civil marriage, the ministry of healing, and burial of the dead. According to the law of the church, the Book of Common Prayer 1984 'contains nothing contrary to Holy Scripture or to sound doctrine'.[138]

The canon law of the Church in Wales also facilitates the experimental use of proposed forms of service. Before a bill for the revision of a part (or parts) of the Book of Common Prayer is submitted by the Bench of Bishops for the consideration of the Governing Body, the proposed revision may be used experimentally in parishes for a defined period. A diocesan bishop may authorize for experimental use in the churches within his diocese any proposed revisions of a part or parts of the Book of Common Prayer which have been provisionally approved by the Bench. However, authorization must be for a limited period not exceeding ten years, and the prior assent of

---

[134] Welsh Church Act 1914, s. 3(2): as from the date of disestablishment 'the then existing . . . rites . . . of the Church of England shall, with and subject to such modification or alteration, if any, as after the passing of this Act may be duly made thereto, according to the constitution and regulations . . . of the Church in Wales, be binding on the members . . . of the Church in Wales . . . as if they had mutually agreed to be so bound'.

[135] Const. II.36; see above, Ch. 2 for the alteration of this principle.

[136] In 1950 the Governing Body requested the Archbishop of Wales to appoint the Standing Liturgical Commission 'whose duty should be to submit from time to time recommendations to the Bench of Bishops concerning such amendments as might be necessary or desirable in the Church's law of worship': Can. 29-9-1955, preamble. For prayer book revision, see P. Jones, *Governance*, 108ff.

[137] COFC, 8: its officers and members are appointed by the Bench.

[138] BCP (1984), v; AO (1991), Public Baptism of Infants and Baptism with Confirmation; AO (1994), The Holy Eucharist; AO (1992), Morning and Evening Prayer. Crown permission was obtained to reproduce material in the BCP (1984), from the 1662 Book of Common Prayer: for background see P. Jones, *Governance*, 111.

the Governing Body to the experimental use of the proposed revision (without alteration) must be obtained. Moreover, a diocesan bishop must not authorize such experimental use until after the next meeting of the Governing Body following the circulation to the members of the Governing Body of printed copies of the proposed revision.[139]

The canon law of the Church in Wales preserves in limited circumstances, as an available liturgical text, the Book of Common Prayer 1662. It is not unlawful to continue the use of the service of holy communion contained in the 1662 Prayer Book, and the Welsh version of this, with such variations permitted by the ordinary as have been customary in the Church in Wales.[140] Whilst it is sometimes asserted that the *jus liturgicum* of the bishop is inherent in the episcopal office,[141] it is unlikely that a bishop may legally authorize a collection of services for use in the diocese to be employed instead of those services which have been authorized by canon.[142] The perception that canonical authority was needed to authorize the services contained in the 1984 Prayer Book, those authorized for experimental use, and the 1662 Prayer Book service for holy communion, suggests that this view represents the common understanding in the Church in Wales today. The confinement of permanent liturgical creation to the central church assembly and the use of experimental liturgies authorized episcopally, are standard features of laws throughout the Anglican Communion.[143]

The Administration of Public Worship

There are two principles fundamental to the administration of public worship: the principle of uniformity, which provides for a single liturgical use in all dioceses; and the principle of conformity, which requires clergy to use only the lawful forms of service. The law of worship of the Church in Wales states that it is 'the intention of the Church in Wales that there be one Use in this Province, and ... that the language of public worship be clearly understood by the people'. Moreover, it is 'an important and constant principle that the whole range of biblical teaching drawn from every part of the Scriptures should be read in the Services of the Church'.[144] This principle

---

[139] Can. 29-9-1955.

[140] Can. 17-9-1981.

[141] C. A. H. Green, *The Setting of the Constitution of the Church in Wales* (London, 1937), 14, 113: it is defined here as 'the right to determine the form and manner of public worship'; see also P. Jones, *Governance*, 115f.

[142] See J. Gainer, 'The *jus liturgicum* of the bishop and the Church in Wales', in N. Doe (ed), *Essays in Canon Law* (Cardiff, 1992), 111.

[143] See generally CLAC, 223ff; England, Can. B1 lists the many authorized services and alternatives.

[144] BCP (1984), v: 'By this regular and systematic reading of Holy Scripture and meditation upon it both clergy and people are encouraged to grow in the knowledge and love of God.'

of uniformity, providing a single provincial liturgical use, is employed in a very small number of other Anglican churches.[145] The laws of the vast majority operate a system under which a multiplicity of forms of service may be used in the public worship of the church.[146]

The duty of conformity applies to all persons admitted to holy orders of deacons or priests, or instituted or collated to the cure of souls, or licensed as assistant curates or deaconesses, and all clerics appointed to any ecclesiastical office in the Church in Wales. Before ordination or appointment, these clerical classes must, in the presence of the bishop or his commissary (appointed in writing), subscribe by declaration and undertaking, that they 'will use only the forms of service which are allowed by lawful authority, and none other'.[147] In other words, clergy may use only those forms of service contained in the Book of Common Prayer or a revised service authorized for experimental use in the diocese by the diocesan bishop.[148] Unlike in most Anglican churches,[149] deviations from the authorized liturgies, and variations within them,[150] are not expressly covered by the formal law of the Church in Wales.[151]

According to provincial quasi-legislation, the conduct of public worship is 'an especial responsibility of the parish priest',[152] who must lead their people in praise and thanksgiving to God, and 'ensure a reverent, regular and careful ordering of divine service'. Whilst appropriate patterns of service will vary from time to time and from place to place, within the duty of conformity, clergy 'should use their own sensitivity and discretion in the conduct of public prayer, so that the people may participate with sincerity and under-standing'.[153] However, clerical responsibility for the conduct of public worship does not mean that clergy must undertake everything themselves: their duty is one of oversight. Since clergy are expected to work collaboratively with others, those licensed to share in the performance of public duties, should

---

[145] See e.g. Burundi, Const. Art. 5: '[t]he aim and desire of the Church of this Province is to have, as far as possible, one single liturgical model for the whole Province.'
[146] See generally CLAC, 228ff.
[147] Const. VII.66.
[148] See above.
[149] See e.g. England, Can. B5: the minister may in his discretion make and use variations which are not of substantial importance in any authorized form of service; variations must be reverent, seemly, and consistent with the doctrine of the church; questions arising may be referred to the bishop for his pastoral guidance, advice or direction.
[150] Canons Ecclesiastical 1603, Can. 14: 'All Ministers . . . shall observe the Orders, Rites, and Ceremonies prescribed in the [1662] Book of Common Prayer, as well as in reading the holy Scriptures, and the saying of Prayers, as in administration of the sacraments, without either diminishing in regard of preaching, or in any other respect, or adding any thing in the matter or form thereof'; for the idea in the Church of England that this is subject to the *de minimis* rule, see R. D. H. Bursell, *Liturgy, Order and the Law* (Oxford, 1996), 45.
[151] The norm is for forms of service to indicate choices or discretions to deviate or vary.
[152] *Cure of Souls* (1996), 8.
[153] *Cure of Souls* (1996), 4.

also be encouraged to play their appropriate parts in worship.[154] Whilst special rules apply to specific rites of the church and to ecumenical liturgical action,[155] it is 'the duty of the clergy, unless they are prevented by sickness or other weighty cause, to say Morning and Evening Prayer daily, preferably in church after tolling the bell'.[156]

The Control and Conduct of Public Worship

The control of public worship in the parish is regulated in the main by pre-1920 ecclesiastical law.[157] A fundamental principle is that clergy carry out their ministry collaboratively, in consultation and co-operation with fellow clergy and with the laity, particularly lay officers.[158] The incumbent and Parochial Church Council must consult together and co-operate in all matters of concern and importance to the parish, including liturgical matters, these being within the council's function of promoting the whole mission of the church.[159] Specifically, the council may make representations to the bishop concerning alterations in services and ornaments.[160] During a vacancy, it is understood that the area dean is, by custom, responsible for arranging services,[161] though the bishop may appoint a cleric, reader or deaconess to take services.[162] Churchwardens must allow the free use of the church to any cleric appointed by the bishop.[163]

An incumbent is bound to observe the legal requirements and restrictions with regard to the performance of divine worship in the parish,[164] and is subject to the rights of the bishop as chief pastor of all the parishes in the diocese.[165] A priest-in-charge has, whilst in charge, the rights and duties of

[154] *Cure of Souls* (1996), 8.
[155] See below, Chs. 10, 11 and 12.
[156] BCP (1984), 400, 409; see also Can. 17-4-1980: this substituted new forms of service relating to morning and evening prayer for those previously contained in the Book of Common Prayer, together with new forms of service in Welsh.
[157] For cathedrals, see above, Ch. 8.
[158] *Cure of Souls* (1996), 4; in civil law, 'consultation' imposes the duty to reveal proposals, to give reasons for them, to allow reasonable opportunity for the expression of views and objections, and to take these into account: see e.g. *R v Secretary of State for Health, ex parte USTII* [1992] 1 QB 353.
[159] Const. VI.22(2), and (3); in parishes with more than one church, the duty to collaborate with lay officers would include consultation and co-operation with a Church Committee, which has constitutional authority 'to deal with matters concerning that particular church' (Const. VI.29); see also above, Ch. 4.
[160] Const. VI.22(5).
[161] PA, 1, p. 27.
[162] Const. VII.56(1); see also VII.6(3), for episcopal provision of spiritual need when a parish is placed on a defaulters' list.
[163] Const. VII.57.
[164] *Parnell v Roughton* (1874) LR 6 PC 46 at 53.
[165] *Down (Bishop) v Miller* (1861) 11 I Ch R Appendix p. i; see HLE (1910), para. 865, n. (a).

the incumbent with regard to divine service.[166] The incumbent enjoys a general authority and control over the performance of public worship throughout the parish. Assistant curates and other clergy (including visiting clergy) may perform divine service (in whole or in part) in the parish only with the consent of the incumbent.[167] When an incumbent consents to a cleric being licensed by the bishop to minister at a particular place of worship within the parish, the incumbent cannot afterwards withdraw the consent, but his consent does not bind succeeding incumbents.[168]

The incumbent has the right to conduct divine service in all churches in a parish.[169] If a parish has more than one place of worship, the incumbent is required to conduct divine service, or provide for its being conducted, in each place of worship.[170] It is neglect of duty if he fails to do so,[171] or if he closes one of them and disobeys the bishop's direction to perform a duty in it.[172] In contrast to, for example, English canon law,[173] the law of the Church in Wales seems to be silent as to who enjoys the right to choose which of the authorized forms of service is to be used for a particular service.[174]

When the incumbent has consented to a cleric officiating, the right to control directly the ordering of liturgical acts and music at a particular service of public worship belongs to the officiating minister.[175] The right does not belong to the incumbent.[176] Whether a particular part of the service is to be

---

[166] *Pender v Burr* (1854) 4 E&B 105.

[167] *Richards v Fincher* (1874) LR 4 A&E 255; *Wood v Burial Board of Headingley-cum-Burley* [1892] 1 QB 713.

[168] *Richards v Fincher* (1873) LR 4 A&E 107.

[169] *Moysey v Hillcoat* (1828) 2 Hag Ecc 30.

[170] See e.g. *Rugg v Bishop of Winchester* (1868) LR 2 PC 223; this applies unless a place of worship is exempt by law from the incumbent's control (i.e. extra-parochial places, such as prison chapels).

[171] *Carr v Marsh* (1814) 2 Phillim 198; *Farnworth v Bishop of Chester* (1825) 4 B&C 555 at 568–70; *Hodgson v Dillon* (1840) 2 Curt 388 at 392, 393; *Jones v Jelf* (1863) 8 LT 399.

[172] *Rugg v Bishop of Winchester* (1868) LR 2 PC 223 at 235–7; *Llandaff (Bishop of), v Belcher* (1687) Rothery's Precedents, No. 91.

[173] England, Can. B3: decisions as to choice of service must be taken jointly by the minister and the Parochial Church Council.

[174] As the general control of public worship in the parish belongs to the incumbent, it may be presumed that the incumbent has the right to choose whether a Prayer Book service, a service authorized for experimental use, or, in the case of holy communion, the 1662 service, is to be used. The right should be exercised in accordance with duties to collaborate, consult and co-operate: see above.

[175] H. Cripps, *A Practical Treatise on the Law Relating to the Church and Clergy* (8th edn, London, 1937), 514: 'The manner in which the services are to be performed is at the direction and discretion of the officiating minister, subject to any directions from the ordinary.'

[176] Phillimore, *Ecclesiastical Law* (1895), I, 765: 'the minister has the right of directing all parts of the service, even those which he does not perform himself, as, for instance, those performed by the organist or the choir'; see also Cripps, *A Practical Treatise*, 515: 'Where it is directed that a particular part of the service is to be said or sung, it is for the

said or sung, therefore, is a matter for the discretion of the officiating minister, whether this is the incumbent or any other minister to whom consent to officiate has been given.[177] Once consent has been given to a minister to officiate, it is for that minister to direct the service at his discretion, but within the terms of the authorized service itself.[178] However, the officiating minister cannot arbitrarily forbid the performance of music: a right of appeal to the Ordinary exists in cases of arbitrary prohibitions; but, until the Ordinary directs in the matter, the directions of the minister must be complied with provisionally.[179] Moreover, whilst forms of services commonly provide discretions about singing,[180] 'to sing with plain congregational music is a practice fully authorised', and the minister should consult the wishes of the congregation in this regard.[181]

Ministerial decisions about the conduct of divine service are also limited by the effect of long-standing established liturgical practices. According to pre-1920 ecclesiastical law, '[u]sage, for a long series of years . . . is entitled to

minister, at his discretion, to choose which alternative should be adopted, according to what he might think best adapted to his congregation.' This is also the current position in the Church of England: see Can. B20: where there is an organist, choirmaster or director of music, 'the minister shall pay due heed to his advice and assistance in the choosing of chants, hymns, anthems, and other settings and in the ordering of the music of the Church, but at all times the final responsibility and decision in these matters rests with the minister.'

[177] *Hutchins v Denziloe and Loveland* (1792) 2 Hag Con 170: this case concerned directions of the 'officiating and licensed curate'; *Wood v Headingley-cum-Burley Burial Board* [1892] 1 QB 729; and *Wyndham v Cole* (1875) 1 PD 130; according to HLE (1910) para. 1320, 'an incumbent has the control of the performance of divine worship, including the singing, throughout his benefice' (the same view is proposed by Green, *Setting*, 163); a reading of the three cases cited in this footnote does not support this view; the position (that direction of music is for the officiating minister, not the incumbent), is correctly described, and these cases correctly cited by them, in Cripps (515, n. (d)), and Phillimore (I, 765, n. (p)) (see above).

[178] Whilst an incumbent can recommend to the minister a way of conducting a particular service, legally that recommendation cannot fetter the officiating minister's legal right to direct; the incumbent though, in extreme cases, may exercise his authority to withdraw consent to officiate, provided there are lawful grounds for so doing.

[179] *Wyndham v Cole* (1875) 1 PD 130 (Arches Court), *per* Sir Robert Phillimore: 'If the minister did arbitrarily forbid the defendant to play on the organ, I think the defendant might have appealed to the ordinary, but, in any event, he should have obeyed the directions of the minister provisionally, and until the ordinary directed the right course for the minister to follow.'

[180] See e.g. BCP (1984), 23: in the eucharist, 'appropriate parts of the service may be either said or sung'.

[181] *Hutchins v Denziloe and Loveland* (1792) 2 Hag Con 170 at 180: as to adverse remarks about the minister's views concerning the suitability of singing portions of the service, the court explained: 'The Court would not therefore advise the minister to introduce what may be liable to such remarks, against the inclination of the parishioners, and the approbation of the Bishop. But this is matter of expediency and discretion, which the Court must leave to the consideration of others.'

the greatest respect; it has every presumption in its favour.'[182] A long-standing liturgical practice generates legal duties on those engaged in the conduct of divine worship: they must respect and comply with that practice,[183] provided the practice is otherwise lawful.[184] Finally, wherever in the Book of Common Prayer, or in a revised service authorized for experimental use, a portion of scripture is set out or appointed to be read or sung, a diocesan bishop may, within his diocese, authorize that the corresponding portion contained in any version of the Bible, or part of the Bible for the time being approved for that purpose by the Bench of Bishops, may be used at the discretion of the minister, in place of that set out or appointed in the Book of Common Prayer or in a revised experimental service.[185]

Public Order at Divine Service

Public order at divine service is protected by the criminal law of the State. First, it is a criminal offence[186] to commit riotous, violent or indecent behaviour,[187] whether during the celebration of divine service or at any other time, in any certified place of worship or in any churchyard or burial ground.[188] Secondly, it is a criminal offence to molest, let, disturb, vex or

---

[182] *Ridsdale v Clifton* (1877) 2 PD 276 at 331; the authority of liturgical custom is expressly recognized in the Church in Wales: see Can. 17-9-1981.

[183] *Howell v Holdroyd* [1897] P 198: 'if on entering office, he finds a practice . . . established, and to which no legal objection can be taken, his duty is to continue it, and if he considers it objectionable or inconvenient it is no part of his duty to take the law into his own hands and of his own mere motion to alter it, but he should refer the matter to the bishop'; the case concerned a churchwarden who 'in deviating from the prevailing practice . . . without the bishop's order . . . committed an offence against the laws ecclesiastical'; the principle has been understood to apply also to clergy (Bursell, *Liturgy, Order and the Law*, 4, nn. 28 and 108), by virtue of the general authority of ecclesiastical custom: *Read v Bishop of Lincoln* [1892] AC 644.

[184] See generally R. D. H. Bursell, 'What is the place of custom in English canon law?', 1 *ELJ* (1989), 16.

[185] Can. 2-5-1974: in this canon Book of Common Prayer means the Book of Common Prayer for the time being in use in the Church in Wales.

[186] For the Ecclesiastical Courts Jurisdiction Act 1860, see generally Bursell, *Liturgy, Order and the Law*, 247, n. 87: the penalty is a fine or imprisonment not exceeding two months.

[187] The object of the statute is to preserve the sacredness of the place and controversial matters cannot be dealt with by interruptions in church without violating it: *Jones v Catterall* (1902) 18 TLR 367: 'Idolatory' called out during the service was held to be indecent; *Girt v Fillingham* [1901] P 176: 'indecent' has no sexual connotations; *Matthews v King* [1934] 1 KB 505: organized loud singing to make the minister's voice inaudible may constitute an offence; see also *Abrahams v Cavey* [1968] 1 QB 479.

[188] Ecclesiastical Courts Jurisdiction Act 1860, s. 2: this applies to any cathedral church, parish or district church or chapel of the Church of England or any place of worship duly certified under the Places of Worship Registration Act 1855. Peter Tatchell was convicted under this statute for disturbing a service in Canterbury Cathedral on Easter Day 1998.

trouble, or by any other unlawful means disquiet or misuse, any preacher duly authorized to preach, or any person in holy orders ministering or celebrating any sacrament or divine service, rite or office.[189] Thirdly, it is a criminal offence for a cleric to act in an indecent or violent way in his own church or churchyard.[190] Fourthly, it is a criminal offence to obstruct,[191] by threats or force, any cleric in or from celebrating divine service or otherwise officiating in a place of worship. Finally, it is a crime to strike, or offer any violence,[192] to any cleric engaged in any of these rites or duties.[193] It has been suggested that a delicate balance needs to be struck now that the right to freedom of expression under the European Convention on Human Rights has a place in civil law.[194]

Churchwardens have special duties, under the domestic law of the church, with regard to the maintenance of order at public worship. First, they must maintain order and decency in the church and churchyard, especially during the time of public worship.[195] They may be assisted in so doing by sidesmen.[196] Secondly, if the minister introduces any impropriety or irregularity into the service, the churchwardens have no authority to interfere, but they have a duty to complain to the Ordinary about the conduct. However, in cases of 'instant and overbearing necessity', if the minister acts in a 'grossly offensive' manner, and when 'private and decent application' to the minister fails, the churchwardens, 'and even private persons', 'may repress, and ought to repress, all indecent interruptions of the service by others'.[197] Thirdly, to prevent disturbances, churchwardens may remove any person from the church.[198] Fourthly, it is arguable that churchwardens are protected from charges of assault in the discharge of their duties provided they use reason-

---

[189] Ecclesiastical Courts Jurisdiction Act 1860, s. 2; a clergyman in holy orders normally excludes a minister not episcopally ordained: *Glasgow College v AG* (1848) 1 HL Cas 800.

[190] *Vallancey v Fletcher* [1897] 1 QB 265.

[191] Or attempt to obstruct.

[192] This also applies if the cleric is, in the offender's knowledge, about to engage in any of these rites, or going to or returning from their performance.

[193] Offences Against the Person Act 1861, s. 36; Criminal Law Act 1967, s. 1.

[194] M. Hill, *Ecclesiastical Law* (2nd edn, Oxford, 2001), para. 3.50; see Human Rights Act 1998, Sched. 1, Art. 10. As Hill notes, however: 'the inter-relationship with freedom of . . . religion in art. 9, the importance of the exercise of the right of which by any religious organisation must be given particular regard by the courts: ibid. s. 13(1).'

[195] Const. VI.17(2).

[196] Const. VI.19.

[197] *Hutchins v Denziloe and Loveland* (1792) 1 Hag Con 170 at 173–4 *per* Sir William Scott.

[198] *Reynolds v Monkton* (1841) 2 Mood & R 384; indeed, at common law, anyone has a right to remove a person disturbing a service: *Glover v Hynde* (1673) 1 Mod Rep 16 and *Burton v Henson* (1842) 10 M&W 108, but the primary duty is on the churchwardens: *Cox v Goodday* (1811) 2 Hag Con 138.

able force.[199] Any person may use such force as is reasonable in the circumstances in the prevention of crime.[200]

Liturgical Disputes and Discipline

Like all other Anglican churches, the Church in Wales operates a system of liturgical discipline.[201] At ordination to the priesthood, candidates undertake to minister diligently the Word of God and faithfully to minister the sacraments.[202] As all clergy must use only forms of service authorized lawfully,[203] according to provincial policy, '[t]he use of other forms of service, without the permission of the diocesan bishop, is a breach of duty'.[204] Failure to collaborate and consult in liturgical matters, particularly with fellow clergy and ministers, may also be a breach of duty.[205] The church provides a number of procedures for the resolution of liturgical disputes and indiscipline. Being the normal channel of communication between the parishioners and the bishop, the Parochial Church Council has a specific 'right to make representations to the bishop concerning . . . alterations in services',[206] and the churchwardens a duty to complain about liturgical irregularity.[207]

The primary governance of liturgical discipline belongs to the diocesan bishop as chief minister and guardian of discipline in the church.[208] If any doubt or dispute arises concerning any of the provisions of the Book of Common Prayer 1984, reference must in every case be made to the bishop of the diocese for his determination of the matter. The bishop is under a duty

---

[199] See e.g. *Palmer v Tijou* (1824) 2 Add 196 at 200, 201; *Burton v Henson* (1842) 10 M&W 105 at 108; see also P. Barber, 'Outrageous behaviour', 4 *ELJ* (1996), 584. For the right of churchwardens to arrest, see Ecclesiastical Courts Jurisdiction Act 1860, s. 3 (as amended by the Police and Criminal Evidence Act 1984, ss. 26(1), 119(2), Sched. 7, Pt.I).

[200] Criminal Law Act 1967, s. 3(1): this applies when the offence is being committed or is about to be committed; a person may be removed for disturbing the congregation at any time of divine service even though no part of that service is actually proceeding at the time: *Williams v Glenister* (1824) 2 B&C 699.

[201] See generally, CLAC, 237ff.

[202] BCP (1984), 723.

[203] See above for Const. VII.66.

[204] *Cure of Souls* (1996), 8.

[205] *Cure of Souls* (1996), 7.

[206] Const. VI.22(5): there would appear to be no rule forbidding, in cases of liturgical dispute generally, recourse to the area dean or archdeacon; whilst there is no express provision on the subject, liturgical disputes in a particular church in a parish with more than one church may be an issue for the church committee, as this has a general constitutional authority to deal with matters concerning that particular church (Const. VI.29), clergy and lay officers being under a general duty to collaborate and consult (*Cure of Souls* (1996), 4).

[207] See above for *Hutchins v Denziloe and Loveland* (1792); see also *Bishop of St Albans v Fillingham* [1906] P 163.

[208] BCP (1984), 714.

not to allow any practice which conflicts with the provisions of the Prayer Book.[209] By virtue of canonical obedience, clergy must obey the lawful and honest directions of their bishop with regard to liturgical disputes.[210] In cases of doubt the bishop may refer any question of interpretation to the archbishop.[211] In appropriate cases, disciplinary proceedings may be instituted against ministers and lay officers for neglect of liturgical duties, wilful disobedience to the law of the church, and disobedience of orders of ecclesiastical authorities concerning liturgy.[212] The courts of the Church in Wales are not bound by any decision of the English courts in relation to matters of ceremonial or discipline.[213] State courts are reluctant to become involved in liturgical disputes,[214] and it may be the case that the Human Rights Act 1998 does not apply to the regulation of divine worship within the Church in Wales.[215]

---

[209] BCP (1984), vi.

[210] For canonical obedience, see above, Ch. 8; one function of the bishop is to apply the law relating to liturgy, and the bishop cannot allow practices in conflict with the Prayer Book (BCP (1984), vi): for episcopal duties generally, see above, Ch. 7.

[211] BCP (1984), vi: this does not deal with the effect of the decision of the archbishop.

[212] See above, Ch. 5. Holding services without lawful authority was one of the charges entertained by the Provincial Court of the Church in Wales in *Re Petition Against the Revd Clifford Williams* (1997): the Provincial Court held that officiating contrary to the direction of the bishop is unlawful, but the bishop must in so directing act in accordance with natural justice.

[213] Const. XI.47.

[214] See e.g. *Gill v Davies and Others* (1998) 5 ELJ 131 *per* Smith J: 'for my part I would be reluctant to interfere with the right of any person's wish to go through a form of Service in accordance with his or her own religious beliefs.' Nevertheless, Smith J granted an *ex parte* injunction of very limited duration to prevent an ordination service in the Church of England which was not authorized by the acting bishop, in order that the matter could be resolved when the newly appointed bishop took up office.

[215] HC Debs, 20/5/1998, col. 1015 by the Home Secretary: 'the regulation of divine worship, the administration of the sacrament, admission to church membership or to the priesthood and decisions of parochial church councils about the running of the parish church are, in our judgment, all private matters.'

10

BAPTISM, CONFIRMATION
AND THE HOLY EUCHARIST

According to classical Anglican tradition, Christian initiation is effected by participation in the ritual sequence of baptism, confirmation and holy communion.[1] The Church in Wales regulates the administration of these rites by means of provisions on celebration, preparation, admission and exclusion.[2] This schematic arrangement is common to all churches of the Anglican Communion. Whilst historically church law on initiation has enjoyed a high degree of stability, recent theological debate has resulted in the juridical readjustment of the sequential pattern: admission of the unconfirmed to holy communion is the most notable instance where Anglican canonical systems differ. In the Church in Wales, baptism, confirmation and the eucharist are rarely treated in the constitution and canons of the church. Instead, they are regulated by liturgical rubrics and directions, by ecclesiastical quasi-legislation and by a substantial body of pre-1920 ecclesiastical law. Generally, the law of the State on these subjects is silent.

BAPTISM

For the Church in Wales, a sacrament is 'the use of material things as signs and pledges of God's grace'. It is a 'means by which we receive [God's] gifts', and consists of 'the outward and visible sign and the inward and spiritual grace'.[3] The traditional doctrine of the Church in Wales, as contained in the Thirty-Nine Articles, treats baptism as a dominical sacrament, 'a sign of

[1] See e.g. P. J. Jagger, *Christian Initiation: 1552–1969* (London, 1970); D. K. Holeton, 'Initiation', in S. Sykes and J. Booty (eds), *The Study of Anglicanism* (London, 1988), 261.
[2] Special legal provision does not exist in the church for the mentally handicapped: see J. A. Griffiths, 'Cognitive faith and the problem of mental handicap in canon law', in N. Doe (ed.), *Essays in Canon Law* (Cardiff, 1992), 89.
[3] BCP (1984), 696 (Catechism): 'Christ in the Gospel has appointed two sacraments for his Church, as needed by all for fulness of life: Baptism and the Holy Eucharist.' See also AO (1990), Baptism with Confirmation, 10: 'Baptism is the universal sign of admission to the Church of Christ.'

Regeneration or new Birth', by which 'they that receive baptism rightly are grafted into the Church'. By baptism 'the promises of forgiveness of sin, and of our adoption to be the sons of God by the Holy Ghost, are visibly signed and sealed; Faith is confirmed, and Grace increased by virtue of prayer unto God.'[4] The Church in Wales also teaches that baptism, 'where it may be had, is necessary for salvation'.[5] The ecumenical canon law of the Church in Wales acknowledges that in the church the sacrament of baptism is duly administered.[6] It also recognizes that all its members are 'members of Christ in virtue of their . . . baptism'.[7] That baptism is a sacrament ordained by Christ, effecting membership of the church universal, is a principle commonly appearing in the formal laws of Anglican churches.[8]

In the Church in Wales, there are three forms for the liturgical celebration of baptism: the public baptism of infants (commonly called christening); the private baptism of infants; and the baptism of adults.[9] In common with all other Anglican churches,[10] to be valid baptism must be administered with water in the name of the Father, and of the Son, and of the Holy Spirit.[11] This has been held judicially to be the essence of baptism.[12] Whereas amongst Anglican churches a variety of approaches to the administration of the water is permitted,[13] in the Church in Wales, having blessed the water, 'the Priest

---

[4]   Thirty-Nine Articles, Arts. 25, 27; see also BCP (1984), 660: in baptism the candidate is made 'a member of Christ'.
[5]   BCP (1984), 654; 660: 'No one can enter into the kingdom of God unless he is born again of water and of the Holy Spirit'; see also 697 (Catechism): 'Baptism is the sacrament in which, through the action of the Holy Spirit, we are made Christ's or "christened"'; and Alternative Order for the Public Baptism of Infants (1990), 1, 1.
[6]   Can. 28-9-1995, First Schedule, (a)(ii).
[7]   See e.g. Can. 1-5-1974, First Schedule, 4(a).
[8]   See generally CLAC, 242; see e.g. Korea, Const. Fundamental Declaration: 'this Church administers the sacraments of Baptism and the Holy Eucharist which Christ instituted for the salvation of all and, through his words and ordinance commanded to be continued in his Church'; and Can. 7: 'In order . . . to become a Christian one must . . . be baptized'; England, Can. B21: the newly baptized is received 'into Christ's Church'.
[9]   BCP (1984), 653. If administration is in accordance with the Book of Common Prayer 1662, different rules would seem to apply: e.g. the minister may dispense with the requirement of confirmation for godparents; and the minister may delay for the purpose of instructing the parents or godparents; and there is a right of appeal to the bishop in cases of refusal.
[10]   See CLAC, 243.
[11]   BCP (1984), 661: 'N, I baptize you in the Name of the Father, and of the Son, and of the Holy Spirit. Amen'; see also BCP (1984), 66: these are described as 'the essential parts of Baptism'; see also 697 (Catechism): 'the outward or visible sign in baptism is water and the requisite words; the inward and spiritual gift is union with Christ in his death and resurrection, the forgiveness of sins, and a new birth into God's family the Church.'
[12]   *Kemp v Wickes* (1809) 3 Phillim 264: 'the use of water with the invocation of the name of the Father, of the Son, and of the Holy Ghost, [is] held to be the essence of baptism.'
[13]   Pouring, sprinkling, immersion and submersion are all lawful: see CLAC, 243; see

pours water three times on [the candidate] or dips him three times in the water'.[14] The priest makes the sign of the cross on the forehead of the baptized person,[15] though in law this does not add to the substance of the sacrament.[16] Any doubt or dispute about the provisions of the Book of Common Prayer regarding the administration of baptism must be referred to the bishop for determination, who in cases of doubt may refer any question of interpretation to the archbishop.[17] Baptism is indelible and cannot be repeated.[18] No fee may be charged for the administration of a baptism.[19]

The Public Baptism of Infants

The Church in Wales recognizes that it is 'the duty of Christians to bring their children to Holy Baptism'.[20] According to liturgical provisions, when infants are to be baptized, due notice must be given to the parish priest with the names of at least two sponsors, one godfather and one godmother. There may, however, be three sponsors: parents may be sponsors for their own child, provided there is at least one other sponsor. To be eligible to become a sponsor, a person must be a baptized Christian. Moreover, it is desirable, but not obligatory, that they should be regular communicants of the Church in Wales or of a church in communion with it.[21]

The Right to Baptism   There is a right to infant baptism in the Church in Wales.[22] The right is generated by a ministerial duty to baptize: 'No Minister shall refuse or delay to christen any child, according to the form of the Book of Common Prayer, that is brought to the Church to him upon Sundays or Holy-Days to be christened', 'convenient warning' having been given beforehand.[23]

---

e.g. Papua New Guinea, *Anglican Prayer Book* 1991, 108: '[i]n baptism water shall be poured on the head of the candidate three times, or he may be dipped in the water three times.'

[14] BCP (1984), 661 (infants), 677 (adults).

[15] BCP (1984), 662 (infants), 678 (adults): this is done as a token of the individual's commitment to the faith.

[16] Canons Ecclesiastical 1603, Can. 30; see also England, Can. B25: 'The Church of England has ever held and taught, and holds and teaches still', that signing is 'no part of the substance of the sacrament'.

[17] BCP (1984), vi.

[18] *Kemp v Wickes* (1809) 3 Phillim 264.

[19] Baptismal Fees Abolition Act 1872.

[20] BCP (1984), 654, 2; AO (1990), 1, 2; see also *Cure of Souls* (1996), 8: 'The parish priest is specifically charged with bringing new members into the Church by baptism.'

[21] BCP (1984), 654, 1 and 2 (this replaces Canons Ecclesiastical 1603, Can. 29); AO (1990), The Public Baptism of Infants, 1, 2; see also LC 1948, Res. 106: this recommends that no unbaptized person act as a sponsor and that at least one 'should be a practising communicant'.

[22] It is not clear whether this (correlative) right is vested in the infant or in the parent(s) or guardian(s).

[23] Canons Ecclesiastical 1603, Can. 68; this rule, arising under the statutory contract of

Best pastoral practice calls for 'the preparation of candidates, parents and godparents, as appropriate, for the responsibilities to which baptism commits them'.[24] Provincial policy states that '[t]o refuse to baptize is *prima facie* a breach of duty'. Similarly, baptizing a person from another parish without the permission of the cleric licensed to administer in that parish is a breach of the duty to collaborate.[25] Under received ecclesiastical law, in the event of a refusal to baptize, the bishop may suspend the minister for three months.[26] Furthermore, in cases of refusal, under the modern law of the Church in Wales disciplinary proceedings may be instituted for neglect of duty.[27]

Parental Consent Special consideration has been given recently, in the Church of England, to baptism of children when one parent objects or withholds consent.[28] The matter raises issues of civil law of equal applicability to the Church in Wales. In civil law, 'parent' is understood as referring to a person having parental responsibility for the child in question.[29] Even though the law of the State permits one parent (or guardian) to act without the authority of the other,[30] if the other parent (or guardian) does not agree to baptism, or refuses to be prepared or instructed, the minister should apply to the bishop for guidance and direction.[31] If the minister learns that a civil court order to prohibit baptism has been issued, or is being sought, the minister is advised to refuse baptism until the matter has been resolved by the court. In the meantime the minister should inform the bishop as to the reason

the Church in Wales (see above, Ch.1), may be understood as an expression of the quasi-established position of the church. See also for the 1662 rite, above n. 9.

[24] *Cure of Souls* (1996), 8. The formal law of the church is silent on this subject.

[25] *Cure of Souls* (1996), 8; no legal authority is given for this proposition. However, see LC 1988, Res. 107: 'The Conference recommends that a minister, baptising the child of parents not resident in his parish or on his Membership Roll, should consult the minister of the parish in which the parents of the child reside, in order that the child and family concerned may be the more surely linked up with the life of the congregation.' The current position in the Church of England is that the host minister should seek 'the good will' of the minister of the parish in which the parents reside: Can. B22(5).

[26] Canons Ecclesiastical 1603, Can. 68: 'if he shall refuse to christen ... he shall be suspended by the Bishop of the diocese from his ministry by the space of three months.'

[27] For neglect of duty see above, Ch. 5.

[28] *Legal Opinions Concerning the Church of England*, Legal Advisory Commission, 16a.

[29] Children Act 1989: where a child's father and mother are married to one another at the time of the birth each parent has parental responsibility (s. 2(1)); if they are not married at the time the natural father can only gain parental responsibility under the provisions of the Act (ss. 4 and 12); this must be by order of a civil court or by a parental responsibility agreement. An adoption order gives parental responsibility to the adopters, and the rights, powers and obligations of the natural parents or any guardian are extinguished (Adoption Act 1976, ss. 12(1), 39 and 41). A guardian may be appointed either by the civil courts, by a person having parental responsibility, or by a guardian (Children Act 1989, s. 5).

[30] Children Act 1989, s. 2(7).

[31] *Legal Opinions Concerning the Church of England*, 16c; in the context of the Church in Wales, this would seem the course by virtue of BCP (1984), vi (referral to the bishop in cases of doubt and dispute).

for the refusal.[32] Indeed, the paramount welfare of the child has actually been invoked by State courts to justify injunctive relief against infant baptism,[33] as it has to justify prohibition of other ritual acts claimed to have been carried out in pursuance of the right to freedom of religion under the Human Rights Act 1998.[34]

Administration   As far as possible, the baptism of infants must be administered on Sundays or on other holy days in the presence of the congregation.[35] Special provisions apply to baptisms at morning or evening prayer,[36] at the holy eucharist,[37] and at other times.[38] When a priest cannot be present, it is lawful for a deacon to baptize.[39] If no priest or deacon is available, it is lawful for any lay person to baptize in the form prescribed for the private baptism of infants (see below).[40] The priest must make certain that children brought for baptism have not already been baptized.[41] Sufficient water must be poured into the font immediately before the service.[42] In the service, the minister may preach a sermon (after the Gospel) or give such instruction as he considers desirable.[43]

At the baptismal service, prior to the baptism, the parents and godparents undertake: to see that the baptized person is brought to worship with the church, taught the Creed, the Lord's Prayer, and the Ten Commandments, and instructed in the Catechism; to take care that the baptized person is

---

[32] Ibid., 16c: 'If told of the existence of an order of the courts forbidding the baptism, a minister who nevertheless administered baptism would be in danger of having to answer to the civil court.'

[33] See Canon Law Society *Newsletter*, No. 96 (1993), 17, 'Exercise of parental role of a Muslim father over Christian baptism of daughter', extract from the *Independent*, 24 July 1993 (the action was under the Children Act 1989).

[34] See J. Nicholson, 'Male circumcision', in Centre for Law and Religion, *Newsletter*, 1(2), (2000), 4: in *Re J (A Minor)* (1999) (unreported), the CA held that a boy should not be circumcised in accordance with the wishes of his Muslim father in the face of opposition from the boy's mother.

[35] BCP (1984), 654, 3; AO (1990), The Public Baptism of Infants, 1, 3.

[36] BCP (1984), 654, 3: when administered at morning or evening prayer, the baptism must follow the Apostles' Creed, and after the baptism the minister must say the three collects of morning and evening prayer; see also AO (1990), The Public Baptism of Infants, 1, 3.

[37] BCP (1984), 654, 3: when baptism is administered at the holy eucharist, it must begin after the Nicene Creed, and then the eucharist must continue with the intercession or the offertory; see also AO (1990), 1, 3: it takes place after the sermon.

[38] BCP (1984), 654, 3: 'When baptism is administered other than at the Holy Eucharist or Morning or Evening Prayer, the Minister shall first use the Ministry of the Word set out herein.'

[39] BCP (1984), 654, 4; deacons must help the priest in the administration of baptism (BCP (1984), 729); AO (1990), The Public Baptism of Infants, 1, 4.

[40] BCP (1984), 654, 4; AO (1990), The Public Baptism of Infants, 1, 4; see also *Kemp v Wickes* (1809) 3 Phillim 264.

[41] BCP (1984), 654, 5; AO (1990), The Public Baptism of Infants, 1, 5.

[42] BCP (1984), 654, 6; AO (1990), The Public Baptism of Infants, 1, 6.

[43] BCP (1984), 658.

brought to the bishop to be confirmed; and to pray with and help the baptized person to keep the promises made on the child's behalf.[44] In the case of infants, the priest may place a white vesture on the child and give a lighted candle to one of the godparents.[45] A register of baptisms must be kept in every parish church,[46] and immediately after the service the priest must enter the customary record in the baptismal register of the parish.[47] The Church in Wales also makes provision for a service of thanksgiving for the birth or adoption of a child,[48] and for family baptism.[49]

The Private Baptism of Infants

Children must not be baptized privately, except in an emergency.[50] When any minister is duly informed of the weakness and danger of death of any unbaptized infant in his parish, that minister must not wilfully refuse to baptize the child. Nor shall the minister, purposely or by reason of gross negligence, defer the baptism when the minister might otherwise conveniently go to the place where the child is to baptize that child.[51] In an emergency, if no priest or deacon is available, it is lawful for any lay person to baptize.[52]

---

[44] BCP (1984), 660; 661: the priest asks the parents and godparents questions, concerning their belief and obedience to the will of God, which they answer on behalf of the infant; see also 697 (Catechism): 'It is required [of us at baptism], that we should turn from sin, believe the Christian faith, and give ourselves to Christ to be his servants.' See also AO (1990), The Public Baptism of Infants, 2–9.

[45] BCP (1984), 662, 678.

[46] Canons Ecclesiastical 1603, Can. 70; for registers see below, Ch. 13; see also HLE (1910), para. 1358.

[47] BCP (1984), 663.

[48] BCP (1984), 681: the order is intended for use in church either during a public service or as a separate service; it may be used, where necessary, at home or in hospital; it is fitting that both parents and other members of the family be present.

[49] AO (1990), Baptism with Confirmation, 10: this Order assumes that baptism with confirmation takes place in the context of the eucharist. It also provides for children who are not old enough to answer for themselves to be baptized at the same time as their parents, when it is fitting that the children are baptized immediately after their own parents. When candidates for confirmation are presented at the same time as candidates for both baptism and confirmation, the detailed ordering of the service shall be determined by consultation between the bishop and the parish priest.

[50] BCP (1984), 664.

[51] Canons Ecclesiastical 1603, Can. 69: 'If any Minister, being duly, without any manner of collusion, informed of the weakness and danger of death of any infant unbaptized in his parish, and thereupon desired to go or come to the place where the said infant remaineth, to baptize the same, shall either wilfully refuse so to do, or of purpose, or of gross negligence, shall so defer the time, as, when he might conveniently have resorted to the place, and have baptized the said infant, it dieth, through such his default, unbaptized; the said Minister shall be suspended for three months; and before his restitution shall acknowledge his fault, and promise before his Ordinary, that he will not wilfully incur the like again.'

[52] BCP (1984), 654, 4: it is lawful for lay persons to baptize in the form prescribed for the private baptism of infants.

Liturgical provisions prescribe the manner of administration in cases of private baptism of infants.[53] If no ordained minister is available, one of those present must name and pour water upon the child reciting the words necessary for a valid baptism.[54] None is to doubt that the child is truly baptized and is not to be baptized again.[55] Any person, who ministers baptism privately, must notify the parish priest without delay, and the customary record must be entered in the baptismal register.[56] In view of the teaching that baptism is necessary for salvation only where it may be had, it may no longer be argued that baptism ought to be administered against the wishes or beliefs of the child's parents on the ground that the salvation of the child must be of paramount concern.[57]

In the event that the child lives, the child must be brought to the church, so that the people may be certified that the child has been baptized, and so that the promises may be made on his behalf.[58] The duty to bring to church a child who has been privately baptized, as soon as may be convenient, falls on the parents and godparents.[59] A special form of service exists in such cases.[60] When a child has been baptized by some other person, the parish priest must satisfy himself that all has been done in due order concerning the baptism of the child. The priest must, if necessary, question those who bring the child to the church.[61] If the parish priest himself baptized the child, or is satisfied by the answers of those who bring the child that all things were done in due order, the priest must not christen the child again. Rather, having asked the godparents the name of the child, the priest shall certify that the child has been truly baptized.[62] If those who bring the child to the church make such uncertain answers to the priest's questions, that it is doubtful whether the child was baptized with water and the recitation of the requisite words, the priest administers a conditional baptism of the child in the form appointed

---

[53] BCP (1984), 664: the parish priest (or in his absence any other ordained minister of the church), with those present, must call upon God and say as many of the prayers appointed to be said in the form of Public Baptism of Infants as the emergency allows; then, the child being named by someone present, the minister pours water three times upon the child reciting the prescribed words necessary for a valid baptism.

[54] BCP (1984), 665 (i.e. 'N. I baptize you in the Name of the Father, and of the Son, and of the Holy Spirit'): then they all may say the Lord's Prayer and the Grace.

[55] BCP (1984), 665.

[56] BCP (1984), 665.

[57] *Legal Opinions Concerning the Church of England*, 16d: that is, in view of the Children Act 1989.

[58] BCP (1984), 665.

[59] BCP (1984), 665: 'Children who have been privately baptized shall be brought to the church by the parents and godparents as soon as may be convenient.'

[60] BCP (1984), 665.

[61] BCP (1984), 666: the questions are: By whom was this child baptized? Who was present when this child was baptized? Was this child baptized with water? Was this child baptized in the Name of the Father, and of the Son, and of the Holy Spirit?

[62] BCP (1984), 666.

for the public baptism of infants.[63] Undertakings are made by the parents and godparents in the same manner as in the public baptism of infants.[64]

The Baptism of Adults

The law of the Church in Wales on the baptism of adults applies to persons who are of sufficient age to make the baptismal promises for themselves.[65] When they have been instructed in the Christian religion, and are ready for baptism, the parish priest must exhort them to prepare themselves by prayer and repentance to receive the sacrament of baptism. Each candidate must have two baptized Christians as sponsors, to present the candidate at the font, who should be regular communicants of the Church in Wales or of a church in communion with it.[66] Whereas there is a right to the baptism of infants, an adult, it would seem, has no right to baptism.[67]

As far as possible, baptism of adults must be administered on Sundays or other holy days in the presence of the congregation.[68] Special provisions apply to baptism at morning or evening prayer,[69] at the holy eucharist (when also confirmation may be administered),[70] and at other times.[71] When a priest cannot be present, it is lawful for a deacon to baptize.[72] If no priest or deacon is available, it is lawful for any lay person to baptize in the form prescribed for the private baptism of infants (see above).[73] The priest must make certain that adults brought for baptism have not already been baptized.[74] The provisions applicable to public baptism of infants also apply to the administration of the sacrament for adults, though the baptismal promises are undertaken by the candidate rather than by the sponsors.[75] If the priest and the adult baptized so desire, the priest may put a white vesture

---

[63] BCP (1984), 666: 'If you are not already baptized, N. I baptize you in the Name of the Father, and of the Son, and of the Holy Spirit.'

[64] BCP (1984), 667f.; for signing with the cross, see above.

[65] BCP (1984), 670, 1: 'person of age' is not defined.

[66] BCP (1984), 670, 1 and 2.

[67] See above for infants: the Canons Ecclesiastical 1603 impose no duty on ministers to administer adult baptism (Can. 68 deals only with infants).

[68] BCP (1984), 670, 3.

[69] BCP (1984), 670, 3: when administered at morning or evening prayer, the baptism must follow the Apostles' Creed, and after the baptism the minister must say the three collects of morning and evening prayer.

[70] BCP (1984), 670, 3: when baptism is administered at the holy eucharist, it must begin after the Nicene Creed, and then the eucharist must continue with the intercession or the offertory, unless Confirmation is to follow immediately.

[71] BCP (1984), 670, 3: 'When baptism is administered other than at the Holy Eucharist or Morning or Evening Prayer, the Minister shall first use the Ministry of the Word set out herein.'

[72] BCP (1984), 670, 4.

[73] BCP (1984), 670, 4.

[74] BCP (1984), 670, 5.

[75] BCP (1984), 677.

on the person, and may give a lighted candle.[76] Immediately after the service the priest must enter the customary record in the baptismal register of the parish.[77]

Baptismal Law in Other Anglican Churches

These arrangements in the Church in Wales, whilst much the same in essentials, are in their details quite different from those operative in other Anglican churches. Elsewhere, rules on baptism are more often found in canon law, rather than in liturgical rubrics.

Minister For most churches baptism may be administered by both ordained and, in cases of emergency, lay people: the duty on the latter to report such baptisms to the priest is common, and is usually followed by reception, on recovery, into the church at a public service.[78] Public baptism is the norm throughout the communion.[79] Some churches prescribe that 'if possible' it is to be administered in certain seasons, usually at Easter and at Pentecost, and many prefer its celebration at holy communion.[80] Private baptism, consequently, is permitted as the exception: and sometimes rules prescribe that at such baptisms the congregation must be represented.[81]

Sponsors The number of sponsors (or godparents) for infants varies between Anglican churches. Some churches require one or more, some two and some at least three; similar provisions exist with respect to sponsors for adult candidates.[82] Many churches prescribe that two sponsors shall be the same sex as the candidate and at least one of the opposite sex.[83] Most churches permit parents or guardians to function as sponsors, and occasionally it is recommended that one of the sponsors be a parent.[84] Whilst eligibility rules vary,[85] rules about the functions of sponsors are consistent: they are responsible for helping candidates to grow in the knowledge and

---

[76] BCP (1984), 678.
[77] BCP (1984), 679.
[78] See generally CLAC, 245ff.
[79] Laws incorporate LC 1948, Res. 105.
[80] See e.g. Korea, Can. 11.
[81] See e.g. Scotland, Can. 27.3.
[82] See e.g. Scotland, Can. 27.2: in cases of necessity, one sponsor 'shall be deemed sufficient'; Melanesia, Cans. A.1.B–K (two); Australia, Can. P5 1992 ('usually' three).
[83] See e.g. England, Can. B23(1).
[84] See CLAC, 248.
[85] See e.g. Chile, Can. Fl.c.12: they must be confirmed persons; Ireland, Const. IX.26(4): they must be members of the Church of Ireland; England, Can. B23(4): the person must be baptized and confirmed but the minister may dispense with the requirement of confirmation if need so requires.

love of God and in the fellowship of the church, and to support the candidates by prayer and example of Christian living.[86]

Preparation   The Church in Wales differs from other Anglican churches with regard to preparation for baptism. In most churches the subject is dealt with by canon law. Typically, in the case of infants, the minister has a duty 'before baptizing infants or children to prepare the sponsors by instructing both the parents and godparents concerned'.[87] With adult candidates, '[t]he minister shall instruct and prepare or cause to be instructed or prepared . . . any person able to answer for himself or herself before baptizing that person'.[88] Very occasionally, responsibility for preparation and instruction rests with the bishop who may delegate this function to priests, deacons and lay ministers.[89] Provisions vary considerably as to the content of instruction. Some laws require adults to be instructed simply in the 'Christian faith' or 'the principles of the Christian religion',[90] but others require 'extensive instruction' in the faith of Christ and biblical doctrine.[91] In some laws the minister must simply instruct sponsors for children in their responsibilities for the spiritual nurture of the candidate.[92] Very few laws expressly require instruction in the meaning or 'the significance of baptism'.[93]

Admission and Exclusion   The vast majority of Anglican churches regulate admission to and exclusion from baptism. Some prescribe a period of notice for both infant and adult baptism.[94] Generally, Anglican churches operate a right to infant baptism: in Australia '[n]o minister may refuse or, except for the purpose of preparing or instructing the parents or guardians or godparents, delay baptizing a child who has a sponsoring parent, guardian or godparent *who professes to be a Christian*.'[95] Several churches prohibit absolutely ministers to delay baptism in emergencies, but others qualify this.[96] As to adults, rules are stricter: sometimes the consent of the bishop must be obtained before baptism,[97] and occasionally laws forbid baptism

[86]   See e.g. Southern Africa, Can. 35.4.
[87]   West Indies, Can. 28.2.
[88]   Australia, Can. P5 1992.
[89]   Southern Africa, Prayer Book 1989, 417.
[90]   See e.g. Spain, Cans. I.10.
[91]   Chile, Can. Fl.c.12.
[92]   Ireland, Alternative Prayer Book 1984, 755: they must instruct that 'the same responsibilities rest on [parents and guardians], as are in the service of Holy Baptism required of godparents'.
[93]   See e.g. Philippines, Cans. III.16.3(b).
[94]   See e.g. Australia, Can. P5 1992 (a week's notice).
[95]   Australia, Can. P25 1992, 6; see also England, Can. B22(4): no minister 'shall refuse or . . . delay to baptize any infant within his cure that is brought to the church to be baptized'.
[96]   England, Can. B22(6).
[97]   Papua New Guinea, Anglican Prayer Book 1991, 193.

until the person has received instruction approved by the bishop.[98] In cases of refusal, few churches explicitly allow recourse short of full judicial proceedings; the Church of Ireland is untypical: '[i]f the Minister shall refuse or unduly delay to baptize any such child, the parents or guardians may apply to the bishop who shall, after consultation with the minister, give such directions as he shall think fit.'[99] Finally, the vast majority of churches operates a system of conditional baptism.[100]

CONFIRMATION

In the doctrine of the Church in Wales, confirmation is 'not to be counted for [a sacrament] of the Gospel', for it has 'not any visible sign or ceremony ordained of God'.[101] The church teaches that confirmation is 'the rite by which we make a mature expression of the commitment to Christ made at Baptism, and receive the strength of the Holy Spirit through prayer and the laying on of hands by a bishop'.[102] Confirmation seals baptism, and is known as *Bedydd Esgob*, the bishop's baptism,[103] a sacramental rite.[104] Canonically, confirmation is effected by the bishop laying hands on the baptized, praying over them, and blessing them.[105] Other Anglican churches stress different aspects of confirmation.[106]

As to eligibility for confirmation, there seems to be a mild dissonance in Church in Wales provisions. On the one hand, according to the catechism, to be confirmed '[i]t is required' that a person be: baptized; sufficiently instructed in the Christian faith; penitent for their sins; and ready to confess Jesus Christ as Saviour and to obey him as Lord.[107] On the other hand, according to liturgical provisions, to be confirmed, a person must: have been baptized; have worshipped regularly with the church; have been instructed in the Catechism; and, be able to say the Creed, the Lord's Prayer, and the Ten

---

[98] Southern Africa, Cans. 35.1–3.
[99] Ireland, Const. IX.26.2.
[100] See generally CLAC, 254f.
[101] Thirty-Nine Articles, Art. 25.
[102] BCP (1984), 698 (Catechism).
[103] See J. Gainer, 'The *jus liturgicum* of the bishop and the Church in Wales', in Doe (ed.), *Essays in Canon Law*, 129.
[104] BCP (1984), 698 (Catechism).
[105] Canons Ecclesiastical 1603, Can. 60.
[106] For example: as a profession of the faith and a mature expression of the commitment to Christ made at baptism; as a reaffirmation of baptismal promises; and most state that in it, through the bishop's laying on of hands, the power of the Holy Spirit strengthens the candidate in the Christian life. See generally CLAC, 256; in Southern Africa, Can. 25.7 it is treated as a sacrament.
[107] BCP (1984), 699 (Catechism).

Commandments.[108] Every person confirmed must have a witness to their confirmation.[109]

The parish priest must make certain that those whom he presents for confirmation have been baptized. If there is a doubt about the baptism of any candidate the priest must baptize the person conditionally.[110] No minister may present for confirmation candidates who have not been instructed in his own parish, unless certified in writing by their own parish priest that they have been baptized and properly instructed.[111] Parents and godparents have a special responsibility to bring children for confirmation.[112] Moreover, ministers must use their best endeavours to procure as many as they can to be brought to the bishop for confirmation.[113]

In the Church in Wales, as for other Anglican churches,[114] confirmation is reserved to the bishop,[115] who may for good reason add to or alter the christian name of the person confirmed.[116] Special provision exists where the only candidates present for confirmation are those to be confirmed immediately following baptism,[117] and where confirmation is administered at the holy eucharist.[118] Except with episcopal permission, no person may receive holy communion until they are confirmed, or ready and desirous to be confirmed.[119] At the service, the candidates must declare publicly that they are bound to believe in the faith and do all things to which baptism has pledged them. Confirmation is effected by the bishop's laying on of hands and the invocation of the Holy Spirit.[120] Any doubt or dispute about provisions of the Book of Common Prayer on confirmation must be referred

[108] BCP (1984), 704, 1: the requirement of regular worship is also found in Papua New Guinea, Anglican Prayer Book 1991, 203.

[109] BCP (1984), 704, 1.

[110] BCP (1984), 704, 2: for conditional baptism see above.

[111] BCP (1984), 704, 3.

[112] BCP (1984), 660; AO (1990), The Public Baptism of Infants, 1, 2.

[113] Canons Ecclesiastical 1603, Can. 61.

[114] See e.g. Scotland, Can. 30.1: it must be administered by the bishop at least once every three years in each ecclesiastical unit in the diocese, and more frequently as the circumstances require; it may be administered by the bishop personally or by his commissary; for a similar provision, see also Ireland, Const. IX.28(2), (3).

[115] BCP (1984), 714: at episcopal ordination, the bishop is charged 'to confirm the baptised'; see also Canons Ecclesiastical 1603, Can. 60.

[116] Co. Litt. 3a; HLE (1910), para. 1363, n. (m).

[117] BCP (1984), 704, 4: the service must begin at 'Our help is in the Name of the Lord'; for the single rite of baptism and confirmation, see e.g. Korea, Can. 10: 'Baptism and Confirmation shall normally be administered as a single rite.'

[118] BCP (1984), 704, 5: a sermon may be preached after the Gospel or after the laying on of hands; at the eucharist, the confirmation begins before or after the Nicene Creed and ends with the laying on of hands and the blessing of the newly confirmed, after which the eucharist must continue, but the intercessions may be omitted.

[119] BCP (1984), 74, 6; see below.

[120] BCP (1984), 705–7: on presentation of the candidates, the minister must assure the bishop that the candidates have all been baptized and properly instructed: see above.

to the bishop, who must not allow any practice in conflict with its provisions; in cases of doubt, the bishop may refer any question of interpretation to the archbishop.[121]

Confirmation may also be regulated by diocesan quasi-legislation.[122] For example, in the diocese of Bangor: if a record of baptism cannot be found, or there is any doubt or uncertainty, conditional baptism should be administered. Preparation should begin at least four months before confirmation, and special care given to worship and devotion as well as instruction. It is desirable that there be a sponsor or witness for a child at confirmation who may or may not be one of the baptismal sponsors. A cleric intending to present candidates in a parish other than his own should inform the incumbent of that parish well in advance. The bishop should be informed, well in advance, of the number of candidates, a short note about them, the language in which they are to be confirmed, and the time of the service. Churchwardens and Parochial Church Council members should be present at the service. English- and Welsh-speaking candidates should be allowed to make their promises and receive laying on of hands in their own language.[123]

In other Anglican churches, the duty to bring candidates for confirmation is placed on the baptismal sponsors and sometimes, in addition, on the parents. Occasionally, a special duty either to seek out or to encourage candidates is imposed on ordained ministers.[124] Unlike the Church in Wales, some churches fix an appropriate age for confirmation, which varies as between churches, or they require the candidate to have attained the age of discretion.[125] Witnesses are required in some churches, as are certificates of confirmation.[126] The Church in Wales is rather different from other Anglican churches with respect to preparation and instruction. For example, in Melanesia, candidates 'must normally receive teaching' for two years; the priest 'must try to be sure of their faith and repentance and their wanting to try to live the Christian life'; and the priest must give candidates the chance to make their confession before confirmation.[127]

---

[121] BCP (1984), vi.

[122] This is designed to supplement and re-present the formal liturgical provisions of the Church in Wales.

[123] DB, YB (2001), 72: Notes for Confirmation; with some variations, these provisions are repeated in DSAB, YB (1999–2000), 43 and DSD, YB(2000–1), 103: Confirmation Instructions.

[124] See e.g. West Indies, Can. 30.2: every minister with cure of souls 'shall diligently seek out persons whom he thinks meet to be confirmed'; for the duty to encourage confirmation, see e.g. Ireland, Const. IX.28(1).

[125] See e.g. Melanesia, Can. A.3.A–D: normally the candidate must be at least twelve, but the bishop has a discretion to confirm at a younger age; Australia, Diocese of Sydney, *The 7th Handbook*, 8.4: fourteen years; for those who have come to the years of discretion, see e.g. England, Can. B27(3).

[126] See e.g. Scotland, Can. 30.5: the certificate is signed by the bishop.

[127] Melanesia, Cans. A.3.A–D: this includes the Lord's Prayer, the Creed, the Ten Commandments and the Catechism.

THE HOLY EUCHARIST

According to the doctrine of the Church in Wales, the holy communion (the eucharist or the Lord's Supper)[128] is a sacrament instituted by Christ.[129] Most Anglican churches treat the eucharistic celebration as 'the central act of worship'; some present it as an act of 'the whole church' or of the 'whole people of God'.[130] The Church in Wales teaches that the holy eucharist is the sacrament commanded by Christ for the continual remembrance of his life, death and resurrection, until his coming again.[131] According to its ecumenical canon law, the Church in Wales acknowledges that in the church the sacrament of the eucharist is duly administered.[132] Communicant status is required for eligibility for ordination and a wide range of lay offices in the church.[133] Any doubt or dispute which arises about the provisions of the Book of Common Prayer as to the eucharist, must in every case be referred to the bishop for his determination of the matter, who must not allow any practice which conflicts with those provisions; and in cases of doubt the bishop may refer any question of interpretation to the archbishop.[134]

Celebration

According to liturgical rubrics of the Church in Wales, the holy eucharist is 'the principal act of Christian worship', the sacrament of fellowship in the Body of Christ. Every confirmed person should communicate regularly and frequently after careful preparation, which should include self-examination leading to repentance and reconciliation.[135] It is the responsibility of the

---

[128] The Church in Wales recognizes these various styles: BCP (1984), 697 (Cathechism): 'The Holy Eucharist is called the Lord's Supper, the Breaking of Bread, and Holy Communion; it is also known as the Liturgy, and the Mass.'

[129] Thirty-Nine Articles, Arts. 25, 28.

[130] See generally CLAC, 259.

[131] BCP (1984), 697 (Catechism): see this also for the inward and outward grace given in the eucharist and the benefits received; 'It is required that, having a living faith in God's mercy, we should examine our lives, repent of our sins, and be in love and charity with all people': these are required when individuals come to the eucharist.

[132] Can. 28–9–1995, First Sched. (a)(ii).

[133] Const. I.6(b): 'communicant' means 'a person who has lawfully received Holy Communion in the Church in Wales or some Church in communion therewith and is entitled to receive Holy Communion in the Church in Wales'; for the offices open to communicants, see above, Chs. 2, 3, 4, 5, 7, 8. For a Form of Commitment to Christian Service, see AO (1990), Public Baptism of Infants, 20: this may be used when a baptized and confirmed person wishes to make or renew a commitment to Christ, either in general terms or on undertaking some new responsibility in the church.

[134] BCP (1984), vi.

[135] BCP (1984), 3, 1; see also Canons Ecclesiastical 1603, Can. 21: 'parishioners may communicate at least thrice in the year (whereof the feast of Easter to be one)'; see also Can. 22: 'every lay person is bound to receive the holy Communion thrice every year.'

priest to teach and help the people in these matters.[136] Public notice of the eucharistic celebration must be given by the minister.[137] The Book of Common Prayer order for the celebration of the holy eucharist consists of: the preparation; the ministry of the word; the intercession; and the ministry of the sacrament (the offertory, the great thanksgiving; the communion, the post-communion, and the dismissal).[138] In other Anglican churches, frequent and regular participation in holy communion is often treated as a duty of the faithful.[139] Other than for the sick, holy communion must as a general rule be administered in church.[140] It is not unusual for church rules to prescribe that a given number of people must be present for the celebration of the eucharist.[141]

In the Church in Wales, the celebration of the holy eucharist is governed, in the main, by liturgical directions. The holy table must be covered with a clean white cloth.[142] The churchwardens must, with the advice and direction of the minister,[143] and at the expense of the parish, provide the bread and the wine; the bread must be wheat bread, leavened or unleavened, and the wine pure grape wine to which a little water may be added.[144] If present, it is the right of the bishop to be the celebrant of the eucharist and to preach. If he is not the celebrant, the bishop pronounces the absolution and gives the blessing.[145] As far as possible, the celebrant should be seen to preside over the whole of the eucharist to emphasize the unity of the service. When present, a deacon should read the Gospel and assist in the administration of the

---

[136] BCP (1984), 3, 1 and 3: the priest should also instruct them in the use of private confession: see below, Ch. 11.

[137] Canons Ecclesiastical 1603, Can. 22: 'we do require every Minister to give warning to his parishioners publicly in the Church at Morning Prayer, the Sunday before every time of his administering that holy Sacrament, for their better preparation of themselves.'

[138] BCP (1984), 4–17; see also AO (1994), The Holy Eucharist; pre-1920 ecclesiastical law prohibits celebration without at least three communicants in addition to the priest: *Parnell v Roughton* (1874) LR 6 PC 46, and *Clifton v Ridsdale* (1876) 1 PD 316 (based on the BCP 1662 rubric).

[139] See e.g. England, Can. B15(1): '[i]t is the duty of all who have been confirmed to receive the Holy Communion regularly, and especially at the festivals of Christmas, Easter and Whitsun or Pentecost.'

[140] See e.g. Korea, Can. 19: the bishop may dispense from this requirement.

[141] See e.g. Ireland, Alternative Prayer Book 1984, 19: 'Holy Communion shall not be celebrated unless there is at least one person present to communicate together with the priest.'

[142] BCP (1984), 22, General Directions, 1; for the directions described in this paragraph, see also AO (1994), The Holy Eucharist, 3; at 39 there is also an Outline Order for the Holy Eucharist.

[143] Canons Ecclesiastical 1603, Can. 20.

[144] BCP (1984), 22, General Directions, 2.

[145] BCP (1984), 22, General Directions, 3; see also AO (1994), The Holy Eucharist, 3: 'It is the bishop's right to preside' at celebrations of the eucharist, and to preach.

sacrament, and may, if necessary, lead the post-communion. A deacon may administer holy communion from the reserved sacrament.[146]

A deacon or reader may say such parts of the service to the end of the intercession (omitting the absolution) as may be required; lay persons may assist in the administration of the sacrament (see below). At the discretion of the parish priest, lay persons may read the Old Testament lesson and epistle and lead the intercession. The directions to stand, kneel or sit indicate the postures which are appropriate for the people at various stages of the service. Appropriate parts of the service may be either said or sung.[147] The use of silence is commended as a means of recollection, especially before the general confession and immediately after the communion of the people.[148]

The minister administering the eucharist must receive the sacrament first. The bread and wine newly brought must be used, but first the words of institution must be rehearsed when the elements are presented on the communion table. The minister must deliver both the bread and wine to every communicant severally.[149] Special provisions apply in the event that additional consecration is needed, if the consecrated bread proves insufficient, and where it is necessary to consecrate in both kinds.[150] There are also arrangements for posture of communicants, their passing around the elements amongst themselves, naming, and consumption of excess elements.[151] In the wider context of the Anglican Communion, these provisions are standard.[152]

---

[146] BCP (1984), 22, General Directions, 4, 5; see also AO (1994), The Holy Eucharist, 3: 'It is the duty of the deacon to proclaim the Gospel, to prepare the elements of bread and wine, and to administer the holy communion and to dismiss the people.' In other Anglican churches reservation is the subject of specific rules: see e.g. West Indies, Can. 31.4: '[i]t is the right and duty of a Priest with a cure of souls, if he considers it desirable for the spiritual well-being of his people, to reserve the Blessed Sacrament permanently in his Church, subject to such Regulations as the Bishop from time to time shall make.'

[147] The right to direct saying or singing parts of the servce belongs to the officiating minister: see above, Ch. 9.

[148] BCP (1984), 22–3, General Directions, 3–7, 10–12; when the ministry of the sacrament is not to follow the ministry of the word, the service must end with the Lord's Prayer and the Grace (8); on weekdays which are not holy days, the psalm and either the Old Testament Lesson or the Epistle may be omitted (9). See also AO (1994), The Holy Eucharist, 3.

[149] Canons Ecclesiastical 1603, Can. 21.

[150] BCP (1984), 21.

[151] AO (1994), Outline Order for the Holy Eucharist, 41 (Notes): 'At the priest's discretion, the consecrated bread and wine may be shared by being passed around by the communicants (standing); if so, care needs to be taken that the elements may be passed around simply and reverently. The Christian name of each communicant may be used at the administration. Consecrated bread and wine not required for communion is consumed after the Sharing or immediately after to service.'

[152] See generally CLAC, 260f. See also: 'Are Anglican women priests being bullied or harassed', A Survey by MSF Clergy and Church Workers (February 1998): this includes information on problems faced by women priests in the Church of England, including those associated with their celebration of the eucharist.

Lay Eucharistic Assistants

In common with other Anglican churches,[153] in the Church in Wales a lay person may assist in the administration of holy communion, subject to the church's regulations.[154] According to these regulations, the bishop may permit a lay person to assist the incumbent or other priest in the administration of the elements of the holy eucharist in a particular parish. Three conditions must be satisfied. First, after consulting with the bishop, the incumbent must apply to the bishop in writing, naming the person for whom permission is requested, and giving the reason for the application. Secondly, the application must be accompanied by a certified copy of the resolution of the Parochial Church Council supporting the request. Thirdly, the permission must be given for one year or a lesser period, and may be renewed at the discretion of the bishop.[155] The subject is also governed by guidelines issued by the Bench of Bishops.[156]

Lay Eucharistic Ministries   There are two categories of lay eucharistic ministry. The first is that of *lay eucharistic assistants*. These are authorized to assist the cleric with the distribution of the elements during a celebration of the eucharist in church. Appointment must be in accordance with the regulation described above. The guidelines provide that it is important for clergy to understand that nominations should be sparing and arise out of a genuine need. Renewal is not automatic and must be applied for on the same basis as the original application, with the support of the Parochial Church Council.[157]

The second category is that of *lay pastoral eucharistic assistant*. These are authorized to administer the sacrament to the elderly and house-bound under the direction of the incumbent. The appointment is authorized, after consultation with the bishop, for parishes where 'a real need has been established and where the incumbent cannot cope without such assistance'. Once the need is recognized, nomination is on the same basis as that for lay eucharistic assistants. There are to be regular reviews, and renewal may be granted up to a maximum of three years from the issuing of the licence.[158]

Candidacy and Training   Candidates should be 'faithful communicants showing a genuine humility, and a consistency in faith and action which is

---

[153] See e.g. Australia, Can. 17 1992.

[154] BCP (1984), 22, General Directions, 7; see also AO (1994), The Holy Eucharist, 3.

[155] Const., Regulation for the administration by a lay person of the elements of the holy eucharist: this regulation is designed to permit lay assistance not only at a eucharist in church but to administer the sacrament outside church for those unable to attend church.

[156] Guidelines for Initiating the Ministry of Lay Eucharistic Assistants (1991).

[157] Guidelines, p. 2.

[158] Guidelines, p. 2: this is due to '[t]he sensitive nature of this ministry'.

allied with a willingness to grow in Christian discipline'. They must also have: a capacity to listen and keep confidential information; a capacity to display empathy and compassion; an ability to know when to ask for help; and a willingness to accept all types of people and situations. Candidates are expected to participate in a diocesan preparation course designed: to instruct on administration of the elements; to deepen their understanding of the eucharist; and to encourage ways of developing their devotional life.

Pastoral eucharistic assistants should receive additional training in: use of the communion rite for the sick; awareness of the healing ministry and the need to alert the parish priest to the particular sacramental needs of those to whom they minister; understanding the special needs of the elderly, the sick and the dying; creating a prayerful environment; and the special skill of ministering to an individual at home or to a larger group in a residential establishment. Each lay minister should be committed to continuing training and should regularly meet for support with the parish cleric and other lay ministers.[159]

Initiation   The initiation of a lay eucharistic ministry requires proper preparation by the local church. Once the bishop issues a licence, an act of commissioning should take place in the context of a parish eucharist.[160] The ministry is designed to supplement, not to replace, the pastoral ministry of parish clergy; these must continue regularly to visit and retain responsibility for confessions, absolution, laying on of hands and/or anointing. From time to time, parish clergy themselves should administer the eucharist to those normally receiving communion from lay assistants. Clerics must also be involved in the training and supervision of lay assistants.[161]

Admission and Exclusion

In the Church in Wales, holy communion is open to those who have been confirmed or are ready and desirous to be confirmed.[162] The Sacrament Act 1547 states: the 'minister shall not without a lawful cause deny the [holy communion] to any person that will devoutly and humbly desire it, any law, statute, ordinance or custom contrary thereto in any way notwithstanding.' The person seeking communion must 'try and examine his own conscience before he shall receive the same'.[163] As such, for the courts of the State, there is 'an

---

[159] Guidelines, pp. 3–4.

[160] This is to demonstrate that the ministry is supported by the church in the parish. Commissioning should also take place on renewal of a licence. A special form of service is appended to the guidelines.

[161] Guidelines, pp. 4–5.

[162] BCP (1984), 704, 6: 'Except with the permission of the Bishop, no one shall receive Holy Communion until he is confirmed, or is ready and desirous to be confirmed.' See below, Ch. 12 for admission of members of other churches.

[163] Sacrament Act 1547, s. 8; being received ecclesiastical law, this legislation forms part

absolute right to receive [holy communion] in the absence of lawful cause'.[164] Not only does this right form part of the statutory contract of the Church in Wales: the provincial constitution too recognizes a right to holy communion.[165] The right is enjoyed by all qualified persons,[166] and members of the Church in Wales may enforce it within the church: breach of the ministerial duty to admit may result in disciplinary process.[167]

A person may be excluded from holy communion only if there is a lawful cause.[168] The power to excommunicate is reserved to the bishop: a priest cannot exclude a person unilaterally. The procedure is as follows. First, the priest is under a duty to 'warn any communicants who by their public conduct bring the Church into disrepute that they ought not to receive the Holy Mysteries until they amend their way of life'. Secondly, '[i]f they do not heed the warning, the Priest shall report the matter to the Bishop and proceed as he directs.'[169] In other words, the authority of the priest is only to warn, to report, and to implement the direction of the bishop.[170] The bishop may

of the statutory contract (under the Welsh Church Act 1914) of the Church in Wales: see above, Ch. 1.

[164] *R v Dibdin* [1910] P 57 at 120 (CA), *per* Fletcher Moulton LJ: '[t]he particular rights which we have here to consider are the rights of the members of the Established Church to receive Holy Communion in the church of their own parish. That they have an absolute right so to receive it in the absence of lawful cause to the contrary is not denied. It is a right expressly given by statute.' This *dictum* applied, of course, to the Church of England, prior to its disestablishment. Disestablishment destroyed the status of the right as one of the law of the land, but the Welsh Church Act 1914 preserved the right on the footing of a statutory contract: see generally above, Ch. 1.

[165] See Const. I.6(b): a communicant is, *inter alia*, one who 'is entitled to receive Holy Communion in the Church in Wales'.

[166] That is: those who are not excluded for lawful cause; those (and this may include any person, resident in a parish, or not), who are confirmed or ready and desirous to be confirmed (BCP (1984), 704, 6; see above); and members (see above, n. 164), of the Church in Wales who are confirmed or ready and desirous to be confirmed. For 'membership' see above, Ch. 8.

[167] See above, Ch. 5; see also e.g. *Jenkins v Cook* (1876) 1 PD 80.

[168] Sacrament Act 1547, s. 8: see above.

[169] BCP (1984), 3, General Rubrics, 3. Different procedures apply if the administration of holy communion is in accordance with the Book of Common Prayer 1662: if a person is in 'malicious and open contention with his neighbours, or other grave and open sin without repentance', the minister must give an account to the Ordinary and obey his order and direction; the minister is not to refuse admission until such directions are given. However, in cases of grave and immediate scandal to the congregation, the minister must not admit, and must also give an account to the Ordinary within seven days, and then obey the Ordinary's direction; the Ordinary must afford the excluded person an opportunity for interview (BCP 1662, 236).

[170] Under the Canons Ecclesiastical 1603, when there was lawful cause, the *minister* was under a *duty* to exclude. This arrangement has been replaced by the provisions in BCP (1984), 3; Canons Ecclesiastical 1603, Can. 26: 'No Minister shall in any wise admit to the receiving of the holy Communion, any of his cure or flock, which be openly known to live in sin notorious, without repentance; nor any who have maliciously and openly contended with their neighbours, until they shall be reconciled.' For consideration of the 1603 regime, see *R v Dibdin* [1910] P 57 at 123, 137: 'It is both the duty and

exclude when the conduct in question brings the church into disrepute: but this is not defined.[171] In cases of doubt, the bishop may refer any question of interpretation to the archbishop.[172]

In respect of the established Church of England, the right to holy communion may be enforced in State courts, insofar as it is one of public law.[173] By way of contrast, in respect of the Church in Wales, the right to holy communion is not a matter of public law: it is a right under the domestic law of a private body.[174] Generally, such rights are not enforceable in State courts. A Canadian court has declined jurisdiction over exclusion by an Anglican priest.[175] In New Zealand, a court decided that the matter, concerning the Anglican church, was most appropriately dealt with by the church tribunals.[176] By way of contrast, in the USA and South Africa, cases on exclusion from religious rites broadly establish that the matter may be justiciable: internal procedures must be complied with.[177] In any event, it has been understood that the Human Rights Act 1998 will not affect the administration of the sacrament, as this lacks a sufficient public dimension.[178]

Finally, the Church in Wales's approach to exclusion from holy communion is rather more minimalistic than that of other Anglican churches. First, as to grounds for exclusion, churches use: 'living in grievous sin', which is 'open' and 'without repentance';[179] 'malice and hatred', without reconciliation and repentance;[180] being in 'malicious and open contention' without forgiveness or reconciliation;[181] and causing 'scandal to the

---

the privilege of the priest to administer the sacrament; it can never be his privilege, though it may in some cases be his duty, to refuse to administer it, for privilege is that which he claims for himself, duty is that which he owes to others.' See also Canons Ecclesiastical 1603, Can. 27: this deals with exclusion of schismatics.

[171] Under pre-1920 ecclesiastical law, for the purposes of the Canons Ecclesiastical 1603 (see above), 'open sin' has been classified as a course of life (as opposed to some particular action or isolated act), which is in conflict with 'Christian morality and causes offence to the public conscience'; the sin is not open if known only to the minister; it has also been held that persons cohabiting under a void marriage live in open sin; but, for example, marriage of a man to his deceased wife's sister is not open sin as such a marriage is valid under civil law: see *R v Dibdin* [1910] P 57 at 123, 137. Under the Sacrament Act 1547, s. 8, the person must also 'devoutly and humbly' desire communion: presumably the bishop may exclude if this is not satisfied.

[172] BCP (1984), vi.

[173] See N. Doe, *The Legal Framework of the Church of England* (Oxford, 1996), 343.

[174] For the legal position of the church, see above, Ch. 1.

[175] *Dunnet v Forneri* (1877) 25 Gr 199.

[176] *Baldwin v Pascoe* (1889) 7 NZLR 759.

[177] See e.g. *Servatlus v Pickee* 34 Wis 292: the excommunication must be *bona fide*; see generally CLAC, 270, nn. 159 and 160.

[178] HC Debs., 20 May 1998, col. 1015: the Home Secretary explained that 'the regulation of . . . the administration of the sacrament' and other ecclesiastical transactions are 'all private matters'.

[179] See e.g. England, Can. B16(1).

[180] See e.g. Australia, Can. P4 1992.

[181] See e.g. Southern Africa, Can. 35.9.

congregation'.[182] Secondly, church laws vary as to the administrator of exclusion: some reserve all decisions of excommunication to the bishop;[183] some impose a duty on the minister to exclude if the grounds are made out, whilst others confer a discretion.[184] Thirdly, procedures vary: normally there is a warning, report to the bishop, investigation by the bishop, which may include an interview with the parties, and the decision.[185] Occasionally, laws allow a minister to exclude summarily, particularly when there is an immediate likelihood of scandal,[186] and most churches confer a right of appeal against the bishop's direction either to a court or to an assembly of bishops.[187] Lastly, Anglican churches sometimes have provisions for restoration.[188]

Holy Communion and the Unconfirmed

The Church in Wales is very different from many other Anglican churches in that its regulation of admission of the unconfirmed to holy communion is minimal. In the Church in Wales: 'Except with the permission of the Bishop, no one shall receive Holy Communion until he is confirmed, or is ready and desirous to be confirmed.'[189]

However, recent guidelines of the Bench of Bishops authorize parishes 'to admit baptised children to Holy Communion, provided that the proposal has received appropriate support from the clergy, [the Parochial Church Council], and parishioners'. Parish clergy and the council, and those engaged in ministry with children, 'should actively be involved in the introduction and implementation of this new practice in the parish'. Before a scheme is introduced, it is desirable that as many parishioners as possible understand the reasons for the new practice; the admission of children to communion should be seen as part of the parish's 'whole programme for nurture in the Christian faith'. An appropriate period of preparation for children and parents or sponsors should precede it. The parish should ensure that the children admitted have the active support of parents or sponsors and other members of the congregation. Infants are baptised and children admitted to holy communion in the expectation that they will wish to seek confirmation in due course. When a child communicant moves home, the clergy of the new parish should be informed of the child's communicant status; the child 'should be received as a communicant in the new parish and communicant

---

[182] See e.g. England, Can. B16.
[183] See e.g. Spain, Can. 1.7.
[184] See e.g. Ireland, Const. IX.16: if they do not repent or they neglect pastoral advice, the minister 'shall not admit'; for discretion see e.g. Australia, Can. P4 1992, 6.
[185] See e.g. Southern Africa, Can. 35.8.
[186] See e.g. England, Can. B16.
[187] Scotland, Can. 26: appeal is to the College of Bishops.
[188] See generally CLAC, 268.
[189] BCP (1984), 704, 6.

status should not be withdrawn'. Children should normally be admitted to communion for the first time at a Sunday celebration, and the emphasis should be celebratory rather than interrogatory. A record of names of those admitted to holy communion should be kept with the parish registers. When appointing clergy to parishes authorized to admit children to Holy Communion, full account should be taken of the existence of the practice.[190]

In all churches of the Anglican Communion, to qualify for holy communion, the individual must be baptized and, normally, confirmed. Yet, in several churches both a confirmed person, and a person who is unconfirmed but ready and desirous to be confirmed, have a right to holy communion.[191] Other churches use a variety of different approaches: the following represent three contrasting models.

In Scotland, '[t]he normal rule of the Church is that none shall be admitted to the Holy Communion until confirmed or be ready and desirous to be confirmed'. However, 'a Bishop may, at the request of a Rector or Priest-in-Charge, and in accordance with the directions of the College of Bishops, admit to the Holy Communion such as are excluded by the normal rule'. In its directions permitting departures from the normal rule, the College of Bishops must make reasonable inquiry, as it thinks right, to satisfy itself that 'the causes are good and sufficient and not unacceptable to this Church generally'.[192]

In New Zealand, it is permitted as alternative practice for baptized children to be admitted to holy communion prior to confirmation after instruction approved by the bishop. The General Synod may approve guidelines to be followed in administering the alternative practice: '[b]aptism provides the ground for admission to the holy communion'; '[a]ll may therefore receive communion from the time of their Baptism irrespective of age.'[193]

In Australia, dioceses may adopt the principle that: 'A child who has been baptized but who has not been confirmed, is eligible to be admitted to the Holy Communion if the minister is satisfied that the child has been adequately instructed, gives evidence of appropriate understanding of the

---

[190] Children and Holy Communion: Guidelines and Resources for Parishes, p. 5, Guidelines of the Bench of Bishops (2001).
[191] See generally CLAC, 263–6. See e.g. England, Can. B15A: '[t]here shall be admitted to the Holy Communion . . . members of the Church . . . who have been confirmed . . . or are ready and desirous to be so confirmed'; for quasi-legislation which seeks to regulate this right, see N. Doe, 'Ecclesiastical quasi-legislation', in N. Doe, M. Hill and R. Ombres (eds), English Canon Law (Cardiff, 1998), 92 at 101.
[192] Scotland, Can. 25.
[193] New Zealand, Cans. G.VIII.1–3; GS Standing Resolution, 1990: the unconfirmed may receive holy communion 'when judged pastorally appropriate by priest and family, or at a special service after more formal instruction, or after receiving laying on of hands for confirmation'.

nature and meaning of the Holy Communion and has fulfilled the conditions of repentance and faith.' The diocesan bishop may make regulations concerning the practice and procedure to be followed and the diocesan synod may by ordinance regulate the practice and procedure.[194]

---

[194] Australia, Can. 6 1985: the child is also eligible if, with the sponsorship of his parents or other confirmed members of the congregation, he seeks admission while awaiting confirmation.

11

MARRIAGE, CONFESSION AND BURIAL

Solemnization of holy matrimony according to the rites of the Church in Wales is regulated by a complex web of both civil and church law. The right to marry in the parish church is regarded as a vestige of establishment, the ecclesiastical law relating to it having survived, as the law of the land, disestablishment of the Church of England in Wales. This chapter explores the terms of the right to marry, requirements for a valid marriage, procedural rules governing solemnization, and ecclesiastical quasi-legislation on the remarriage of divorced persons (including the civil law context within which this operates). It also examines confession, its administration, and the seal of the confessional. Like marriage, the law of burial is another vestige of establishment. It embraces a substantial body of rules on funerals and the administration and maintenance of burial grounds.

THE LAW OF MARRIAGE

In keeping with traditional Anglican doctrine,[1] the Church in Wales teaches that holy matrimony is 'a life-long union, instituted by God, into which a man and a woman enter',[2] and it is dissolved only by the death of one of the parties.[3] Liturgical provisions present marriage as a gift of God, a vocation, compared in holy scripture with the union of Christ with his church. Marriage exists: for the mutual love of the parties, that their love be made holy; for the procreation of children, that the parties may bring up their children to grow in grace and learn to love God; and for the mutual society of the parties, that they may honour, help and comfort one another in prosperity

---

[1] Thirty-Nine Articles, Art. 25: marriage is 'an honourable estate, instituted of God in the time of man's innocency, signifying unto us the mystical union that is betwixt Christ and his Church'; it is a state in which the parties are 'joined together by God', and, as such, is treated as more than a contract, but it springs from a contract, from the free exchange of consents (see below). These ideas are represented in BCP (1984), 738.
[2] BCP (1984), 699 (Catechism): 'Christians make their vows before God and the Church, and receive the grace and blessing of God to help them fulfil their vows.'
[3] BCP (1984), 736 (Holy Matrimony): 'The Church teaches that marriage is the lifelong union of one man and one woman, and is dissolved only by the death of either party.'

and in adversity.[4] The concept of the divine institution of marriage surfaces in church laws throughout the Anglican Communion: marriage is affirmed as 'according to the teaching of Christ',[5] and occasionally it is described as a sacrament.[6] The laws of Anglican churches deal with the permanence of marriage: in line with Lambeth Conference resolutions,[7] most laws provide that marriage *is* a lifelong union, lasting until the death of one partner,[8] but others present marriage as *intended* to be a permanent union.[9] The purpose of marriage is summed up in Lambeth Conference resolutions, often reflected in the laws of churches: it exists for the procreation and nurture of children, to direct the natural instincts and affections of the parties, and for their mutual society, help and comfort.[10]

The Right to Marry

The law of the State provides that nothing in the Welsh Church Act 1914 or the Welsh Church (Temporalities) Act 1919 affects 'the law with respect to marriages in Wales and Monmouthshire' or 'the right of bishops of the Church in Wales to license churches for the solemnization of marriages'.[11] As a result, pre-1920 ecclesiastical law on marriage continues to apply to the Church in Wales as the law of the land,[12] as does the current general marriage law of the State.[13] Marriage is treated by the State as a human right.[14]

---

[4]   BCP (1984), 738.

[5]   See e.g. England, Can. B30(1).

[6]   This idea is rare: see e.g. Papua New Guinea, Can. No. 2 of 1995, Arts. 1–5: 'marriage is the sacrament endorsed by Christ himself.'

[7]   LC 1958, Res. 119; for incorporation of these ideas in Anglican canon laws, see CLAC, 273f.

[8]   See e.g. England, Can. B30(1): 'marriage is in its nature a union permanent and lifelong.'

[9]   See e.g. New Zealand, Prayer Book (1989), 779: '[m]arriage is intended by God to be a . . . life-long covenant'; see also West Indies, Can. 29.1: this treats 'the ideal of Christian marriage as a lifelong union'.

[10]   LC 1958, Res. 113.

[11]   Welsh Church (Temporalities) Act 1919, s. 6. The Welsh Church Act 1914, s. 23, had provided that '[t]he law relating to marriages in churches of the Church of England (including any law conferring any right to be married in such a church) shall cease to be in force in Wales and Monmouthshire'; this section was repealed by the Welsh Church (Temporalities) Act 1919, s. 6.

[12]   For the idea that this is one of the vestiges of establishment, see T. G. Watkin, 'Disestablishment, self-determination and the constitutional development of the Church in Wales', in N. Doe (ed.), *Essays in Canon Law* (Cardiff, 1992), 25 at 33ff.

[13]   Marriage Act 1949, s. 78(2): 'Any reference in this Act to the Church of England shall, unless the context otherwise requires, be construed as including a reference to the Church in Wales.'

[14]   Human Rights Act 1998 and ECHR, Art. 12: men and women of marriageable age have a right to marry according to the national laws governing the exercise of this right; the right is exercisable only when the prospective parties are members of the opposite sex; Art. 12 does not allow same-sex marriages; see also *Corbett v Corbett (Otherwise*

Under State law, in Wales 'every resident of a parish is entitled to marry in his/her parish church.'[15] Consequently, '[t]he incumbent or priest-in-charge has a duty to solemnize the marriage of parishioners on request (or to provide an assistant curate to do so), and is guilty of neglect of duty if he/she refuses (for which disciplinary proceedings may be taken in the ecclesiastical courts).'[16] The right to marry in the parish church has been recognized by Parliament,[17] by the secular courts,[18] and by pre-1920 decisions of the ecclesiastical courts.[19] Whilst the source or origin of the right to marry in the parish church is difficult to ascertain, the right may be conceived in nature as a powerful legal fiction.[20]

Special legal protection under State law is given to clergy in three cases. The ministerial duty to solemnize the marriages of parishioners does not apply: where one of the parties is divorced and has a surviving former spouse;[21] where there is a relationship of affinity between the parties;[22] or where the superintendent registrar's certificate procedure has been used instead of a grant of a licence or publication of banns. In these cases, the incumbent or priest-in-charge cannot be compelled to solemnize the marriage nor to make the church available for its solemnization.[23]

No special protection is given by State law to clergy with regard to marriage of the unbaptized. Yet, according to liturgical provisions of the Church in Wales, a Christian marriage is 'a marriage between two baptized persons'. If one of the parties is unbaptized, 'the Minister shall act in

---

Ashley) [1971] P 83: in domestic law a marriage between persons of the same sex is prohibited, and a person cannot change their sex by means of a medical operation which effects a 'sex change' for the purposes of marriage.

[15] *Anglican Marriage in England and Wales: A Guide to the Law for Clergy* (hereafter AMEW), issued by the Faculty Office of the Archbishop of Canterbury (1999), 6.1: moreover, 'The right has been extended to those on the electoral roll of a parish' (ibid.).

[16] AMEW, para. 6.1. For neglect of duty and the Disciplinary Tribunal, see above, Ch. 5.

[17] See e.g. Matrimonial Causes Act 1965, s. 8: here the proposition 'No clergyman of . . . the Church in Wales shall be compelled' to solemnize the marriages of divorced persons (see below) is an exception to what is otherwise assumed to be a ministerial duty.

[18] *Davis v Black* (1841) 1 QB 900; *R v James* (1850) 3 Car & Kir 167; *R v Dibdin* [1910] P 57 (CA), at 129 *per* Fletcher Moulton LJ: 'One of the duties of the clergyman within this realm is to perform the ceremony of marriage, and parishioners have the right to have that ceremony performed in their parish church.'

[19] *Argar v Holdsworth* (1758) 2 Lee 515; see also generally *Tuckniss v Alexander* (1863) 32 Ch 794.

[20] For the development of the fiction subsequent to Lord Hardwicke's Marriage Act 1753, see N. Doe, *The Legal Framework of the Church of England* (Oxford, 1996), 357–62: the position is the same for the Church of England.

[21] See below for the Matrimonial Causes Act 1965, s. 8.

[22] The marriage being authorized by the Deceased Wife's Sister's Marriage Act 1907, the Deceased Brother's Widow's Marriage Act 1921, or the Marriage (Prohibited Degrees of Relationship) Acts 1931 and 1986.

[23] AMEW, para. 6.2.

accordance with the Bishop's direction.'[24] Furthermore, it is fitting that the newly married persons should receive holy communion at the time of their marriage, or at the first opportunity after their marriage.[25] However, by virtue of the right to marry under the law of the land, and the absence from State law of special provision on the unbaptized, the duty to solemnize also applies to unbaptized persons resident in a parish; if these are legally qualified to marry, they too enjoy the right.[26] Baptism is generally considered not to be a precondition to marriage.[27] In contrast, the laws of the vast majority of churches in the Anglican Communion contain no explicit reference to a right to marry in church; instead, they emphasize the discretionary rights of the minister, [28] and baptism is commonly a precondition to ecclesiastical marriage.[29]

Preliminaries to Marriage

Marriage in the Church in Wales may be solemnized as a result of: publication of banns; the grant of a common licence; the grant of a special licence; or on the issue of a superintendent registrar's certificate. Ministers must not proceed to the solemnization of marriage unless one or other of these preliminaries has been satisfied.[30]

Marriage after Banns   Marriage according to the rites of the Church in Wales normally takes place after banns have been published on three Sundays at the service at which the greatest number of people is usually present.[31] If

---

[24] BCP (1984), 736.

[25] BCP (1984), 736.

[26] As such, it is submitted, the only direction a bishop is legally capable of making (under BCP (1984), 736), is that the marriage must be solemnized. However, although the duty to solemnize is one of public law, it is unlikely that judicial review would lie for a refusal to solemnize, as marriage by ecclesiastical licence or civil marriage are available as alternative remedies. For the possibility of enforcement within the church, see T. Watkin, 'Disestablishment', 25 at 36: neglect of the duty to solemnize being an ecclesiastical offence under the statutory contract of the church (based on pre-1920 ecclesiastical law), only parties to that contract could proceed.

[27] HLE (1910), para. 1375; see also *Jenkins v Barrett* (1827) 1 Hag Ecc 12, *per* Sir John Nicholls (Arches Court): 'As to the question whether a clergyman is bound to marry a dissenter, baptized or unbaptized', 'to the merits of this question . . . I shall not avert in any way.'

[28] See e.g. ECUSA, Can. I.18.4: '[i]t shall be within the discretion of any Member of the Clergy of this Church to decline to solemnize any marriage'; see also West Indies, Can. 29.6: 'It shall be within the discretion of any Clergyman to decline to solemnize any marriage on grounds of conscience only.'

[29] See generally CLAC, 275ff.

[30] BCP (1984), 737, 3.

[31] BCP (1984), 736, 1; the officiating minister must publish them in the prescribed form: 'I publish the Banns of Marriage between N of . . . and N of . . . If any of you knows cause or just impediment why these two persons should not be joined together in

the persons to be married reside in the same parish, banns must be published in the parish church of that parish.[32] When the parties live in different parishes, the banns must be called in both parishes. The minister of one parish must not solemnize the marriage without the production of a certificate of the publication of banns from the minister of the other parish. The certificate must state that no impediment has been alleged. If the name of either of the persons to be married is on the electoral roll of a parish in which neither lives, the marriage may take place in that parish, provided the banns have been published in that parish and in the parish or parishes in which they live.[33]

A minister is not obliged to publish banns of matrimony unless the persons to be married deliver to him, at least seven days before the intended first publication, a written notice stating the christian name and surname and the place of residence of each of them and the period during which each has resided there.[34] For the purposes of banns, residence is understood as 'a physical presence and occupation of premises as a home', which 'need not be a permanent arrangement, but it must subsist at the relevant time'.[35] Banns must be published by the officiating minister at the service,[36] in an audible manner.[37] All banns must be published from a register provided by the Parochial Church Council, and after each publication the relevant entry must be signed by the person publishing the banns or by someone under his direction.[38] Ordinarily, banns must be published at a Sunday morning service, but may be published at an evening service if there is no morning service.[39] If a marriage is not solemnized within three months after completion of publication of banns, the publication is void. No cleric may solemnize the marriage on the authority of those banns, and the whole process must be repeated.[40] Solemnization without due publication of banns, unless the marriage was solemnized under a licence or certificate, is a crime.[41]

For minors, banns are published in the same manner as for adults.

Holy Matrimony, you are to declare it. This is the first (second or third) time of asking'; see also Marriage Act 1949, s. 7: they do not have to be successive Sundays.
[32] Marriage Act 1949, s. 6(1)(a).
[33] BCP (1984), 736, 1; see also Marriage Act 1949, ss. 6(1)(b), 11.
[34] Marriage Act 1949, s. 8.
[35] AMEW, para. 5.5: this is the view of the Faculty Office.
[36] BCP (1984), 736.
[37] Marriage Act 1949, s. 7(2). A person's true name must be stated, along with that of the parish. A true name need not be a person's baptismal name, but simply that which he customarily uses. The inclusion of a wrong name in the banns will not invalidate the marriage in the absence of a wilful concealment: *Chipchase v Chipchase* [1939] 3 All ER 895.
[38] Marriage Act 1949, s. 7(3).
[39] Marriage Act 1949, s. 7(1).
[40] Marriage Act 1949, s. 12(2). Special provisions exist concerning publication of banns outside Wales and England: see Marriage Act 1949, s. 13.
[41] Marriage Act 1949, s. 75(4).

Parental consent is not required when a minor applies for publication of banns.[42] However, at publication of banns, the right to object to the marriage is vested in: either parent of the minor (if the parents are living together); the parent with custody (if the parents are separated by agreement or court order); both parents if they have alternate custody; the deserted parent (in a case of desertion); a surviving parent (if the other is dead); a guardian appointed by a deceased parent; a person appointed by a court to have custody or guardianship of the minor (if both parties are dead or deprived of custody).[43] The objector must openly and publicly cause their dissent to be declared at the time of publication of banns; the publication then becomes void.[44]

Common Licences   Marriage according to the rites of the Church in Wales, without banns, may follow the grant of a licence by a diocesan bishop, a diocesan chancellor or surrogate,[45] provided all civil and ecclesiastical conditions are satisfied.[46] Marriage by licences is an extraordinary process. There is a legal right to publication of banns, but no right to an ecclesiastical marriage licence; the grant is discretionary, 'a matter of favour, and not of right'.[47] However, the grant of a licence generates a duty to solemnize the

---

[42] AMEW, para. 7.7. See below for the age of capacity in relation to the marriage of minors.

[43] See AMEW, para. 7.8. Special arrangements also apply as a result of the Children Act 1989: orders for custody are no longer made; where parents are divorced or separated by court order, they will both automatically have parental responsibility, unless the order directs otherwise; a parent with parental responsibility may object to the marriage whether or not the child is living with that parent. The natural father of an illegitimate child is not as such entitled to object, but will be entitled if a court order for custody or parental responsibility had been made in his favour.

[44] Marriage Act 1949, s. 3(3); having satisfied themselves of the objector's standing, the objection should be noted in the banns register by the cleric.

[45] Welsh Church (Temporalities) Act 1919, s. 6(b): this provides that nothing in the Welsh Church Act 1914 or the Welsh Church Temporalities Act 1919 affects 'the right of bishops of the Church in Wales to grant licences to marry'; Marriage Act 1949, s. 5: the power is one of dispensation (to dispense with the requirement for banns). See also Const. XI.16(2): this recognizes in diocesan bishops 'the powers of granting licences' which existed at the date of disestablishment; and Const. XI.15: subject to the constitution, each chancellor, with respect to the granting of marriage licences and the appointment of surrogates, has that jurisdiction (except as to fees), which existed at the date of disestablishment in addition to any jurisdiction conferred by the constitution; the chancellor must 'exercise such jurisdiction and powers according to the law and practice at that time prevailing'; for surrogates, see BCP (1984), 737. The power to grant licences is ancient: see the Ecclesiastical Licences Act 1533.

[46] BCP (1984), 737, 2; see also Marriage Act 1949, s. 16(4). For fees, see RODC, Sched. of Fees: fees for a licence are as prescribed by the Bench of Bishops. For customary marriage fees, see *St Davids (Bishop of) v Lucy* (1699) Carth 484.

[47] *Prince Capua v Count de Ludolf* (1836) 30 LJPM & A 71n; granting a licence is conceived as a dispensation from the normal rule (i.e. marriage by banns): see AMEW, para. 9.6.

marriage: the minister of the parish (if satisfied that all civil and ecclesiastical conditions have been observed) 'is bound to proceed to the solemnization of matrimony upon the production to him of . . . a common licence'.[48]

Before a common licence may be granted, one of the parties must make a sworn declaration: that there is no impediment to the marriage; that for at least fifteen days prior to its grant one of the parties has been resident in the parish of the church in which the marriage is to be solemnized; and that, if either party is a minor, the law relating to consent has been complied with.[49] A false declaration, provided it is made wilfully and knowingly, is a criminal offence.[50] The licence is granted or refused there and then.[51] The grant of a licence may be opposed by the entering of a caveat stating the objection, and no licence may be granted until either the caveat is withdrawn or the authority which is to issue the licence has certified that the matter has been examined and that it 'ought not to obstruct the grant of the licence'.[52] A caveat entered in one diocese does not prevent the grant of a licence in another.[53]

Common licences may also be available, as a matter of discretion, in the case of marriage of the unbaptized and the divorced,[54] and special guidance exists regarding common licences for marriages of foreign nationals.[55] If the marriage is not solemnized within three months of the grant of the licence, the licence becomes void; no cleric may solemnize the marriage on its authority.[56]

Special Licences   In exceptional circumstances, the Archbishop of Canterbury may grant a special licence for the solemnization without banns, at any convenient time or place, of a marriage according to the rites of the Church in Wales. If satisfied that all civil and ecclesiastical conditions have been observed, the minister of the parish is bound to solemnize the marriage on

---

[48] BCP (1984), 737, 2; failure to solemnize may be a breach of canonical obedience: see *Tuckniss v Alexander* (1863) 32 Ch 794. See also Marriage Act 1949, s. 15: the licence may be granted for the parish church of the parish in which one of the parties has their usual place of residence for fifteen days immediately before grant of the licence.

[49] Marriage Act 1949, s. 16(1), as amended by the Marriage (Prohibited Degrees of Relationship) Act 1986, s. 1(4), Sched. 1, para. 4.

[50] Perjury Act 1911, s. 5(1).

[51] Provision for appeal to the Lord Chancellor may be found in the Ecclesiastical Licences Act 1533, s. 11. Also, given the public nature of the licensing function, whilst judicial review would presumably lie in cases of unreasonable refusal (e.g. in a case of discrimination), it is unlikely that the civil courts would compel the grant of a licence (in virtue of its discretionary nature), but an order to reconsider the application would be possible.

[52] Marriage Act 1949, s. 16(2).

[53] AMEW, para. 9.8.

[54] AMEW, para. 9.4; see below (n. 118) for divorced persons.

[55] See AMEW, para. 9.3.

[56] Marriage Act 1949, s. 16(3).

production to him of the special licence.[57] The power of the archbishop is regulated by civil law,[58] and by English ecclesiastical and canon law.[59] The grant of a special licence is discretionary, and the usual reason is for the parties to marry in a building not normally authorized for ecclesiastical marriage.

No procedure, it would seem, is to be found in formal law. However, according to guidance, the parties should first approach the cleric who they think may wish to officiate, and then those clergy who control the proposed venue. The proposed officiant should make the clergy of the parish(es) where the parties live or worship aware of the intended marriage, and ascertain whether they have any objection to its solemnization in the chosen location. The parties should also seek the goodwill of close relatives. The parties must swear an affidavit giving details and about impediments.[60] There is a right of appeal against a refusal by the Archbishop of Canterbury to grant a special licence.[61]

This archiepiscopal jurisdiction 'is sparingly exercised, and good cause must always be shown why a more normal preliminary to Anglican marriage cannot be used'.[62] The archbishop is not limited as to the timing or venue of the marriage in granting the licence.[63] Generally, solemnization for the housebound or detained persons may take place where they are living, receiving treatment or detained.[64] The current policy is that, if one of the parties is unbaptized or divorced, the licence is not to be granted, and fees are chargeable.[65]

Certificates of the Superintendent Registrar   Marriage in and according to the rites of the Church in Wales may follow the issue of a certificate by the State's superintendent registrar. There is no right to marriage in church on the

---

[57] BCP (1984), 737, 2.
[58] Marriage Act 1949, s. 79(6).
[59] Ecclesiastical Licences Act 1533 and Cans. B34 and C17.
[60] AMEW, paras. 10.1–10.6: the officiant may administer the oath.
[61] Ecclesiastical Licences Act 1533, ss. 11, 12: a writ would issue from the Chancery requiring the archbishop to show cause why he refused; the Lord Chancellor then may allow the cause; if the archbishop refuses, the Lord Chancellor may commission two other bishops to grant the licence.
[62] AMEW, para. 10.1.
[63] The licence may omit the normal time for solemnizations (ie between 8 a.m. and 6 p.m.): Marriage Act 1949, s. 4. In theory, the archbishop may authorize marriage in buildings belonging to other denominations, in the open air, or anywhere. However, it is the archbishop's 'usual policy only to permit marriage in buildings customarily used for Anglican worship'; otherwise, some medical need normally has to be established. If the marriage is to take place, e.g. in a private house, with a chapel, the archbishop's policy is that some 'real connection' must exist between the parties and the case: AMEW, para. 10.
[64] Marriage Act 1949, ss. 17, 26.
[65] AMEW, paras. 10.3, 10.6.

issue of a certificate.[66] A minister may consent to solemnize a marriage upon the production to him of a certificate in place of banns issued by the superintendent registrar of marriages in accordance with the law governing the issue of certificates in Wales. However, the minister may consent to solemnization 'if he so desires and is satisfied that there is no ground on which the law of the Church forbids it'.[67] Notice of the marriage must be given to the superintendent registrar of the civil registration district in which both parties reside; the party giving it must sign a declaration as to residence, parental consent if required, and absence of impediments.[68] The registrar enters the details in a marriage notice book open for public inspection.[69] If at the end of twenty-one days no impediments are shown, the parties apply for the issue of the certificate.[70] Such a marriage must be solemnized within twelve months from the entry in the marriage notice book.[71] Special provision exists for the use of certificates by persons who are housebound, detained, or in danger of death.[72]

Validity and Solemnization

Validity and solemnization of marriage are governed by both civil law and church law. Each element of the law of the Church in Wales finds a parallel in canon law throughout the Anglican Communion, though in many churches arrangements concerning preparation and instruction are rather more rigorous than those operative in the Church in Wales.[73]

Validity   As is the case with most Anglican churches,[74] the Church in Wales generally follows the law of the State with regard to capacity to marry. Each

---

[66] This is one of the exceptions to the general rule: see above. Also the civil registrar-general may issue a marriage licence, but this cannot be used for Anglican marriages: AMEW, para. 11.

[67] BCP (1984), 737, 3.

[68] Marriage Act 1949, s. 28: one of the parties must have resided for seven days within the civil district and the ecclesiastical parish in which the marriage is to occur, or else the church must be the usual place of worship of one or both of the parties.

[69] Marriage Act 1949, s. 27(4); these must be displayed at the register office for twenty-one days (s. 31(1)).

[70] Marriage Act 1949, s. 31(2); the periods of notice will be reduced to fifteen days in cases under the Asylum Act 1999: both parties must give notice.

[71] Marriage Act 1949, s. 33.

[72] This is a result of the amendment of the Marriage Act 1949 by the Marriage Act 1983: AMEW, para. 8.4.

[73] See e.g. Southern Africa, Can. 35.6: this forbids marriage of persons 'until they have received such instruction on Christian Marriage as has been approved by the Bishop of the Diocese'; West Africa, Can. 7.4(b): this forbids a minister to solemnize unless '[h]e shall have ascertained that both parties understand' the nature and purpose of holy matrimony; see generally CLAC, 278f.

[74] See generally CLAC, 280ff.

party must be at least sixteen years of age,[75] and they must not fall within the prohibited degrees of kindred and affinity.[76] If the parties lacked capacity, or the formalities were not satisfied, the marriage is void *ab initio* (it is treated as never having existed).[77] A marriage may also be voidable (it is taken to have existed unless and until declared void by a competent court) and may be annulled subsequently on several grounds.[78] Lack of residence will not invalidate.[79] When there is doubt about the validity of a marriage, there is a presumption that it is valid until the contrary is established.[80] In the Church in Wales, a table of kindred and affinity lists the prohibited relationships: 'No person shall marry within the degrees expressed in this Table.'[81]

Venue   Ordinarily,[82] marriage according to the rites of the Church in Wales must be solemnized in a parish church or in a chapel licensed for marriages by the bishop.[83] The right of Welsh bishops to license buildings for marriage is protected by State law.[84] Provision is made for marriage in shared church buildings in accordance with the rites of the participating churches.[85]

---

[75] Marriage Act 1949, s. 2. If either party (not being a widow or widower) is under the age of eighteen, an appropriate form of consent is required: see Marriage Act 1949, ss. 3(1), (3), 78(1) ('child'); Family Law Reform Act 1969, ss. 2(1)(c), 33(1), Sched. 2, paras. 9, 10.

[76] Marriage Act 1949, s. 1(1), Sched. 1, Pt. I (amended by the Children Act 1975, s. 108(1)(a), Sched. 3, para. 8; and the Marriage (Prohibited Degrees of Relationship) Act 1986, s. 1(6), Sched. 1, para. 8.

[77] Matrimonial Causes Act 1973, s. 11: the parties lack capacity if within the prohibited degrees, if under the age of sixteen, if either party is already lawfully married at the time, or if they are not male and female respectively.

[78] Matrimonial Causes Act 1973, s. 12: namely: if it is unconsummated (through inability or refusal); if there was a lack of consent (through unsoundness of mind, duress, fraud or mistake); if at the time of the marriage either party was suffering from mental disorder; if at the time the respondent was suffering from venereal disease in a communicable form; or, if at the time the respondent wife was pregnant by someone other than the petitioner; see s. 13 for bars to relief.

[79] *Pouget v Tomkins* (1812) 2 Hag Con 142.

[80] *Re Bradshaw* [1938] 4 All ER 143.

[81] BCP (1984), 733–4: in this table 'brother' includes a brother of the half-blood, and 'sister' includes a sister of the half-blood.

[82] See below for marriage by licence.

[83] Marriage Act 1949, ss. 6, 20, 21; cathedrals (unless it is a parish church), must be licensed by the bishop (s. 21); for military chapels licensed for marriage, see s. 69; buildings which are not parish churches but are licensed for public worship by the bishop may also be licensed by the bishop for marriage of persons living in a stated district (AMEW, para. 3.1).

[84] Nothing in the Welsh Church Act 1914 or the Welsh Church (Temporalities) Act 1919 affects 'the right of bishops of the Church in Wales to license churches for the solemnization of marriages': Welsh Church (Temporalities) Act 1919, s. 6(b).

[85] Sharing of Church Buildings Act 1969, s. 6: a church building shared by the Church in Wales under a sharing agreement may be registered for non-Anglican marriages, and it may be used for the publication of banns and the solemnization of Anglican marriages. A church-sharing agreement does not confer any status on a building used for

Marriage of persons who are housebound or detained may take place where those persons live, receive treatment or are detained.[86]

Solemnization Solemnization must be effected by a clerk in holy orders in the presence of at least two other witnesses,[87] but if there is only one additional witness, this will not invalidate.[88] A marriage may be solemnized at any time between the hours of eight in the morning and six in the afternoon (unless another time is permitted by a special licence). It is a criminal offence to solemnize outside these hours.[89] Marriage is probably constituted as soon as there has been a reciprocal agreement of both parties to take each other as husband and wife, at the joining together of their hands, and the minister's pronouncement that they are man and wife.[90] The precise language of the marriage service is not a criterion of validity, nor need the words of the ceremony be spoken by the parties: consent may be communicated otherwise.[91] The opening address, the statement by the parties that there is no lawful impediment, the placing of rings, and the benediction are not essential for validity; they are merely symbolic.[92]

It is the ancient tradition of the church that marriages should not take place in Lent.[93] All those who wish to be married according to the rites of the Church in Wales 'are to receive due instruction from the Minister of the parish in which the marriage is to take place'.[94] The minister must solemnize the marriage according to the prescribed forms of service.[95] Choice of liturgy and music rests, in law, with the officiating minister.[96] Special provision exists for marriages conducted in an ecumenical setting.[97]

---

worship as a place for marriage, but a shared building (unless already a parish church) may be licensed for marriages by the bishop; the same building may also, at the same time, be registered as a place of worship of some other denomination and thereby qualify to be registered for Nonconformist marriages (i.e., under the Marriage Act 1949, s. 41).

[86] Marriage Act 1949, ss. 17, 26 (as amended by the Marriage Act 1983).

[87] Marriage Act 1949, ss. 22, 25, 78; impersonation of a clerk is a criminal offence (s. 75(1)(d)); the cleric must be a person other than one of the parties to the marriage: *Beamish v Beamish* (1861) 9 HL Cas 274; solemnization by a deacon is lawful: Can. 22-4-1987; see also: *R v Millis* (1844) 10 Cl & Fin 534 at 656.

[88] *Wing v Taylor* (1861) 2 Sw & Tr 278.

[89] Marriage Act 1949, ss. 4 and 75.

[90] *Quick v Quick* [1953] VLR 224.

[91] *Harrod v Harrod* (1854) 1 K & J 4; see also Registration of Marriages (Welsh Language) Regulations 1986, SI 1986/1445.

[92] *Beamish v Beamish* (1861) 9 HL Cas 274: the joining of hands is not required for civil purposes.

[93] BCP (1984), 736.

[94] BCP (1984), 736.

[95] BCP (1984), 737, 5: if the parties desire it, the BCP 1662 rite may be used.

[96] See above, Ch. 9; see Can. 15-9-1982 for solemnization in Welsh.

[97] See below, Ch. 12.

Allegations of Impediment   If any person alleges an impediment which is recognized by the law of God or the laws of the land, that person must give an indemnity against any pecuniary loss, in the event of the allegation failing, which his action brings upon the parties. If such an allegation is made and an indemnity given, the marriage must be deferred until the truth has been established.[98]

Registration   The marriage must be registered by the cleric by whom it was solemnized; this must be done immediately in duplicate books supplied for this purpose.[99] When the marriage takes place in a building with its own register books, those books must be used.[100] Marriages of the housebound or detained must be registered in the books of a church or chapel where the marriage is solemnized, or, if they have no books, in an adjoining parish.[101] The entries in the books must contain all the details required by the printed form, and must be signed by the couple, the officiating minister and the two witnesses.[102] The entry is completed when signed by the minister. If an error is discovered subsequently, corrections may be made (by a marginal note without obliterating the original entry) within one month of the entry in question. The minister who made the entry must make and sign the correction (in both register books) in the presence of the married couple, and all three must sign it. If the couple cannot attend when the correction is made, the churchwardens of the parish may act in their place.[103] Fees and maintenance of the register books are discussed elsewhere.[104]

Divorce and Remarriage

In civil law, a marriage is terminated by death, dissolution or annulment: a marriage is null (invalid) when a declaration of nullity has been made by a

---

[98] BCP (1984), 739.

[99] Marriage Act 1949, ss. 53–5: the civil registrar-general must supply register books to the minister in charge of every church or chapel authorised for marriages. See also BCP (1984), 737, 4: immediately afterwards, the two witnesses must, with the newly married persons and officiating minister, sign the marriage registers.

[100] The only exception is when a building is closed temporarily and the marriage takes place elsewhere; then the register books of the closed building must be used: Marriage Act 1949, s. 18(3); if a church has no books, the register of the parish church (or nearest one), should be used.

[101] Marriage Act 1949, s. 55(4).

[102] Marriage Act 1949, ss. 55–6: the entry should indicate whether the marriage was 'after banns', 'by superintendent registrar's certificate', 'by common licence' or 'by special licence': AMEW, para. 17.3.

[103] Marriage Act 1949, s. 61.

[104] See below, Chs. 13 and 14. It might be noted here, however, that there would seem to be no express provision in the formal law of the Church in Wales dealing with, nor indeed specifically authorizing, the levying and distribution of fees for marriage: compare the law on burial fees (for which see below).

competent court in the United Kingdom; a marriage (otherwise valid) is dissolved by a decree absolute when it is established that there has been an irretrievable breakdown.[105] Unlike several Anglican churches, though like the Church of England, the Church in Wales does not operate a nullity system.[106] Those whose marriages have been annulled enjoy the same legal right to marry in the parish church as any parishioner.[107] Whilst the Church in Wales teaches that a marriage 'is dissolved only by the death of either party',[108] the remarriage of divorced persons, whose former marriages have been civilly dissolved, is the subject of regulation by parliamentary statute and by ecclesiastical quasi-legislation.[109] In making provision for the remarriage of divorced persons, the policy of the Church in Wales is now in line with that of the vast majority of Anglican churches. Seldom do Anglican churches operate a blanket rule forbidding clergy to solemnize such marriages; three models are used: laws confer a ministerial right to refuse,[110] sometimes based on an explicit right of conscientious objection;[111] laws allow remarriage with prior episcopal consent;[112] and some laws confer a ministerial discretion but impose a duty to consult with the bishop.[113]

Clerical Discretion and Conscientious Objection   The law of the State provides that 'No clergyman . . . of the Church in Wales shall be compelled (a) to solemnize the marriage of any person whose former marriage has been dissolved and whose former spouse is still living; or (b) to permit the marriage of such a person to be solemnized in the church or chapel of which he is the minister.'[114] This provision has been understood as meaning that civil law allows clerics 'to refuse to solemnize such remarriages and to refuse to allow the churches of which they are the ministers to be used for such a purpose'. The decision whether or not divorcees are to be remarried is that of the

---

[105] See Matrimonial Causes Act 1973, s. 1: this is evidenced by proof of: adultery; unreasonable behaviour; desertion; two years' separation; or five years' separation.
[106] See generally CLAC, 284ff.
[107] See above and AMEW, para. 12.3; decrees of nullity in the Roman Catholic Church are not recognized by State law.
[108] BCP (1984), 736.
[109] The statute and quasi-legislation are discussed below; see also *Marriage and Divorce*, A Statement by the Bench of Bishops of the Church in Wales (1998).
[110] See e.g. New Zealand, Can. G.III.4.1–2: '[a]ny Bishop or Priest shall be entitled to refuse to solemnize the marriage of a divorced person.'
[111] Scotland, College of Bishops Guidelines (1981), 4: no priest can 'be required to officiate at a marriage contrary to his conscience'.
[112] See e.g. Southern Africa, Can 34: this is given by means of a licence and the grounds for processing, granting or refusing a licence are carefully prescribed: see CLAC 288f.
[113] See e.g. Ireland, Const. IX.31–3–6: the minister must not solemnize 'unless he has first sought from the bishop his opinion as to the advisability of solemnizing the marriage'; the minister 'shall consider and take into account the opinion of the bishop in exercising the discretion, vested in him by law, as to whether or not he should solemnize the marriage'.
[114] Matrimonial Causes Act 1965, s. 8(2).

individual cleric concerned, whose decision (being based on a personal statutory right or discretion) should not be restricted by episcopal prohibition.[115] In short, the right to marry in the parish church does not apply to divorced persons (and a cleric is not required to solemnize such a marriage), provided the cleric has a conscientious objection to it.[116]

Recommended Practice   Under guidelines issued by the Bench of Bishops, when approached by divorced persons seeking marriage in church, clergy are recommended to talk to the parties in the first place without a commitment to solemnize the marriage. This is so that the appropriateness of their proposed marriage might be explored in the light of the church's teaching that 'marriage is intended to be a life-long union'. When a cleric decides to proceed, in the process of thorough preparation it may be appropriate, in some cases, to offer an opportunity for private expression of repentance or sorrow with respect to a former marriage. Clergy should also be alert to issues which may arise over the care of children from a former marriage. A cleric should make every effort to consult with and inform any other clergy who may have been pastorally involved with either party. The bishop's advice might be sought: where the collapse of a previous marriage has been a matter of public scandal; where it is known that the proposed partner was directly involved in the failure of the first marriage; where there is a continuing problem over children of a former marriage; or where a third or subsequent marriage is in view.[117]

Clergy are to exercise their discretion in each and every case, and must see the decree(s) absolute in every case. But clergy have no discretion about the calling of banns or issuing certificates.[118] It is recommended that clergy should inform their Parochial Church Councils of 'the general principles by which they intend to exercise this discretion, for this will be a matter of concern and importance within the parish'. However, this recommendation

---

[115] *Marriage and Divorce* (1998), paras. 5.1, 5.2; see also Marriage and Divorce: Guidelines (issued by the Bench of Bishops: undated), para. 3.13: 'clergy who themselves have conscientious objections may allow the church(es), of which they are the minister to be used for the solemnization of such a marriage by another cleric.'

[116] Section 8(2) lifts what would otherwise be a duty to marry; similar provisions in associated matrimonial statutes have been understood by the courts of the State to confer on clergy a right of conscientious objection: see e.g. *R v Dibdin* [1910] P 57; it is submitted that if the cleric has no objection in conscience, the ordinary duty to marry operates.

[117] Marriage and Divorce: Guidelines, para. 2.

[118] Marriage and Divorce: Guidelines, para. 3.1 and 3.2; para. 3.3: clergy must call banns as 'divorced parishioners who give the required notice and details are entitled to have their banns called on the next three Sundays, and to receive a certificate of banns'; para. 3.4: in the calling of banns, there is no need to announce the marital status of either party; 'Alternatively, a general licence may be obtained in the usual way'; para. 3.7: in the marriage registers, the normal entry for the marital status is 'Previous marriage dissolved'.

must not be taken to imply that the council has 'any power to direct clerics in this matter', nor should the council seek to do so.[119] If a marriage has been arranged by the previous incumbent, 'the new incumbent should, as a matter of courtesy and pastoral common sense, accept the former incumbent's decision, at least to the extent of guaranteeing that the marriage takes place at the date and place agreed', even if the new incumbent does not feel able personally to conduct the service.[120] If clergy, or the couple, have problems of conscience about the use of the form of service for holy matrimony, use may be made of the blessing following a civil marriage.[121] Finally, the Bench of Bishops recognizes that 'the legal discretion afforded to the clergy may leave them in an uncomfortably exposed position'; the bishops 'will support the decisions of individual clergy, and are ready to offer any practical assistance or advice possible'; 'no cleric can be compelled to act against his or her conscience in this matter.'[122]

THE LAW OF CONFESSION

In contrast with other Anglican churches, regulation in the Church in Wales of confession is minimal. The ministry of absolution is exercised only by priests; absolution can be given generally, as in the public services of the church,[123] or individually and privately.[124] The Church in Wales teaches that in the ministry of absolution, those who are truly sorry for their sins and determined to renounce them for the future, having confessed their sins to God freely and fully in the presence of a priest, receive through the ministry of the priest the forgiveness of God.[125] With regard to their responsibilities towards the people, priests 'should instruct them in the use of private confession'. Private confession 'is available for all those who cannot otherwise find

[119] Marriage and Divorce: Guidelines, para. 3.10.
[120] Marriage and Divorce: Guidelines, para. 3.11.
[121] Marriage and Divorce: Guidelines, para. 3.12; see BCP (1984), 751: when two persons have contracted a civil marriage and wish to receive the blessing of the church upon their union, the priest must ask them to produce the certificate of the civil marriage. If the priest is satisfied that the union is not contrary to the laws of the Church in Wales, the form prescribed is to be followed, the Blessing of a Civil Marriage.
[122] Marriage and Divorce: Guidelines, para. 3.13.
[123] For general confession, see BCP (1984), 5–6 (holy eucharist), 392 (morning prayer), and 404 (evening prayer); see also 756 for the Ministry of Healing, which affords private confession. See also AO (1994), The Holy Eucharist, 3; AO (1992), Morning and Evening Prayer, 2: in the place of absolution, provision is made for a prayer to be said by a deacon or lay minister.
[124] BCP (1984), 23. See also Order for Holy Communion outside the Eucharist (2000), 2: this contains a form of prayer for divine forgiveness to be used by deacons or lay ministers.
[125] BCP (1984), 699 (Catechism); see also 23: 'Our Lord Jesus Christ gave power to his Church to forgive sins in his Name.'

the assurance of God's forgiveness',[126] provided those persons are penitent.[127] Confession is also 'the opportunity to ask for informed counsel when in doubt or difficulty'.[128] If the penitent has not confessed privately before, that person should be told how to prepare himself.[129] In other Anglican churches, private confession is the subject of more extensive regulation, by canon law: confession is rarely treated as a sacrament;[130] absolution may be exercised only by bishops and priests;[131] some laws confer a right to confession;[132] giving spiritual advice is discretionary;[133] absolution may be either discretionary or obligatory;[134] and some churches operate a system of public penance.[135]

Many Anglican churches impose an absolute prohibition against disclosure by a priest of information given at confession,[136] and occasionally this also applies to the penitent.[137] In some churches the prohibition continues beyond the death of the penitent,[138] but in others the law allows disclosure with the consent of the penitent.[139] In the Church in Wales, liturgical provisions state that the practice of confession operates 'under the seal of secrecy'.[140] According to pre-1920 ecclesiastical law, which continues to apply to the church as part of its statutory contract: 'if any confess his secret and hidden sins to the Minister, for the unburdening of his conscience, and to receive spiritual consolation and ease of mind from him; we do not any way bind the said Minister by this our Constitution, but do straitly charge and admonish him, that he do not at any time reveal and make known to any person whatsoever any crime or offence so committed to his trust and secrecy (except they be such crimes as by the laws of this realm his own life may be

---

[126] BCP (1984), 3, General Rubric 1.
[127] BCP (1984), 23: 'Those who fail by themselves to find peace of mind can, if penitent, be assured of God's forgiveness through the exercise of this ministry.'
[128] BCP (1984), 23.
[129] The priest may first bless the penitent who then makes his confession using the prescribed or a similar form; the priest may then give counsel, if required, and ask the penitent to use an appropriate devotion; the priest absolves with the prescribed words: BCP (1984), 24.
[130] Melanesia, Cans. A.6.A.1–5.
[131] See e.g. England, Can. B29(1).
[132] See e.g. Scotland, Can. 29.1.
[133] See e.g. Southern Africa, Prayer Book 1989, 449; compare Melanesia, where there is a duty to advise.
[134] Compare Scotland, Can. 17.3 (clergy 'shall provide opportunity . . . for absolution'), with England, Can. B29(3) (the minister 'may' exercise the ministry).
[135] See CLAC, 293.
[136] ECUSA, Cans. IV.14.23: 'the secrecy of a confession is morally absolute for the confessor, and must under no circumstances be broken'; see CLAC, 294.
[137] Melanesia, Cans. A.6.A.6.
[138] Scotland, Can. 29.2.
[139] Australia, Can. 10 1992, 2; see also New Zealand, Prayer Book 1989, 750: the disclosure may occur only if the penitent requests it.
[140] BCP (1984), 23.

called into question for concealing the same), under pain of irregularity.'[141] This would seem to suggest that, in the Church in Wales, the prohibition against disclosure is not absolute.

There is doubt as to whether State courts would consider priest–penitent communications to be privileged, though the weight of opinion tends to the view that they are not.[142] The effect of this is that a priest has no legal right in a State court to refuse to answer questions relating to confession.[143] However, in criminal cases, the courts have a discretion to exclude evidence of a confession made to a priest.[144] It is possible that a penitent may seek in civil proceedings an injunction to prevent a priest from disclosing confidential information received by way of confession, or any other information given in confidence.[145] Individuals also have a right to privacy under the Human Rights Act 1998.[146] According to provincial policy in the Church in Wales, when confidential information is received by clergy in virtue of their role as such, its improper disclosure is a breach of duty.[147] Provision also exists for the ministry of deliverance (or exorcism).[148]

---

[141] Canons Ecclesiastical 1603, Can. 113.

[142] See e.g. R. Bursell, 'The seal of the confessional', 2 *ELJ* (1990), 84; and D. W. Elliott, 'An evidential privilege for priest-penitent communications', 3 *ELJ* (1995), 272.

[143] The Criminal Law Revision Committee decided not to recommend that confessional communications be privileged: 11 Report (1972), paras. 273–4.

[144] Police and Criminal Evidence Act 1984, ss. 76, 78 and 82. The effect on this of the Human Rights Act 1998 remains to be seen: see generally above, Ch. 1.

[145] For the relevant judicial decisions see Doe, *The Legal Framework*, 353–5.

[146] ECHR, Art. 8.

[147] *Cure of Souls* (1996), 13. For disciplinary proceedings, see above, Ch. 5.

[148] BCP (1984), 770: with this 'the priest should exercise great care to ensure that he acts only with the knowledge and authority of the diocesan bishop and, whenever possible, with the co-operation of the medical profession'; afterwards, the priest may, where appropriate, celebrate the eucharist and administer, as necessary, the confession and absolution, the laying on of hands and anointing; the ministry of deliverance and healing should be followed by pastoral after-care, the responsibility not only of the priest but of the whole congregation. See also The Ministry of Deliverance: General Guidelines for Clergy and Parishes (2002), issued by the Council for Mission and Ministry; this endorses the appointment of diocesan teams to assist the bishop and adviser; the ministry should be exercised: in collaboration with the resources of medicine; in the context of prayer and sacrament; with minimum publicity; by experienced persons authorized by the bishop; and followed up by pastoral care. Records should be kept (confidentially) and clergy and laity trained and supervised. See also Canons Ecclesiastical 1603, Can. 72. There is currently a bill before Parliament on this subject. The Exorcism of Children (Prohibition) Bill proposes to criminalize exorcism on young persons under sixteen. Exorcism is defined as 'any rite or ceremony the purpose of which is, or purports to be, to rid an individual of a menacing or oppressive condition or thing'.

THE LAW OF BURIAL

In contrast with very many Anglican churches,[149] the law of burial applicable to the Church in Wales is complicated: it is found in both church-made and State-made law. According to pre-1920 ecclesiastical law: 'No Minister shall refuse or delay . . . to bury any corpse that is brought to the Church or Churchyard, convenient warning being given thereof before, in such manner and form as is prescribed' by the rites of the church.[150] Only parishioners are entitled, as of right, to be buried in the parish burial ground. Parishioners are defined for this purpose as: persons normally residing in the parish; persons dying in the parish; ex-parishioners and non-parishioners for whom family graves or vaults are desired to be opened and whose close relatives have been buried in the churchyard; and persons on the electoral roll at the date of death.[151]

Except so far as rights are preserved by the Welsh Church (Burial Grounds) Act 1945, no discrimination may be made between the burial of a member of the Church in Wales and that of other persons.[152] The right of parishioners to burial in the parish burial ground,[153] provided the burial ground has not been closed by Order in Council,[154] has been understood as a vestige of disestablishment.[155] The Welsh Church (Burial Grounds) Act 1945 provided for the transfer and maintenance of burial grounds to the Representative Body of the Church in Wales, which may make rules relating to burial provided they have been approved by the National Assembly.[156]

---

[149] See CLAC, 297f.

[150] Canons Ecclesiastical 1603, Can. 68; see also *Cure of Souls* (1996), 9: 'Failure to observe this canonical requirement within the parish . . . is a breach of duty'; moreover, 'Burying the dead from another parish without the permission of the cleric licensed to administer in that parish is a breach of the duty to collaborate.' But see below, n. 160.

[151] Burial Grounds Rules (hereafter BGR), Second Schedule, Notes; however, Canons Ecclesiastical 1603, Can. 68 excludes persons who have been excommunicated 'for some grievous and notorious crime, and no man able to testify of his repentance'; it is also understood that burial in consecrated ground according to the rites of the church must not take place with regard to the unbaptized or those who have committed suicide; see HLE (1910), para. 1412; see also Burial Laws (Amendment) Act 1880, s. 13; in England, in such cases, the minister must use a form of service approved by the bishop: Can. B38.

[152] BGR, Second Schedule, Notes; strictly, in law, the right is that of the personal representatives, as it is they (rather than the deceased), who would seek to enforce it; Welsh Church (Burial Grounds) Act 1945, s. 4: there must be no discrimination except as may be necessary to comply with any trust or condition affecting any part of a burial ground which is a private benefaction within the meaning of the Welsh Church Act 1914 (see also s. 24 of the 1914 Act).

[153] For relevant cases, see Doe, *The Legal Framework*, 386ff.

[154] A churchyard is closed if it has been closed for burials by an Order in Council under the Burial Acts; whether closure prohibits disposal of cremated remains depends on the terms of the Order: see generally *Re Kerr* [1894] P 284.

[155] See T. G. Watkin, 'Disestablishment', at 36ff.

[156] Welsh Church (Burial Grounds) Act 1945, s. 4, as to notice, fees and services.

Funerals and Interments: Notice and Fees

Notice   Notice of an interment must be delivered to the incumbent,[157] of the parish in which the burial ground is situated, at least forty-eight hours prior to interment in an unbricked grave, and at least sixty hours prior to interment in a bricked grave. Notice must not be delivered on Sunday, Good Friday, Christmas Day or other bank or public holiday unless for sufficient reason to the satisfaction of the incumbent.[158] Shorter periods of notice may be allowed by the incumbent if he thinks fit, and he must allow a shorter period, in case of emergency, if certified by a medical practitioner.[159] Notice must be given in the prescribed form, which may be obtained from the incumbent.[160]

The Funeral Service   The time for a funeral must be arranged with the incumbent. No funeral is to take place in a burial ground which adjoins a church at a time when a service is ordinarily held in the church.[161] Interments must not take place on Sunday, Good Friday or Christmas Day, except in cases of emergency certified as such by a coroner or by a registered medical practitioner.[162] A certificate of the registration of the death or, in cases of an inquest, the coroner's order, must be delivered to the incumbent or his representative before a burial.[163] Notice of the proposed burial of a still-born child must be accompanied either by a certificate given by the registrar or, if there has been an inquest, an order of the coroner.[164] The burial must be recorded in the register of burials.[165]

For a funeral, the minister must use the authorized forms of burial service.[166] Prayers may be said in a house 'where this is the local custom'.[167]

---

[157]   BGR, r.1: for the purpose of these rules, incumbent means and includes a rector or the vicar of a parish or the rector of a rectorial benefice or, during a vacancy in or suspension of the incumbency, or during the incapacity of the incumbent, the area dean or such other cleric appointed by the bishop to be in charge of the parish or rectorial benefice.

[158]   BGR, r.2: notice must be delivered between 10 a.m. and 1 p.m. or 2.30 and 4.00 p.m. on Mondays to Fridays, and from 10 a.m. until 12 noon on Saturdays.

[159]   BGR, r.3.

[160]   BGR, r.4; see the First Schedule (Note: where the service is in accordance with Church in Wales rites, 'the Incumbent of the parish will officiate unless other arrangements are made by him or with his consent'). See also Welsh Church (Burial Grounds) Act 1945, s. 4(2).

[161]   BGR, r.5.

[162]   BGR, r.6.

[163]   Regulations for the Administration of Churchyards (hereafter CYR), r.11.

[164]   As required by the Births and Deaths Registration Act 1926, s. 5.

[165]   CYR, r.12; see also Burial Act 1857, s. 25.

[166]   BCP (1984), 774 (The Order for Burial of the Dead); 792 (The Order for the Burial of a Child); unordained persons may conduct funerals: Burial Laws (Amendment), Act 1880, s. 6. See also above, n. 160.

[167]   BCP (1984), 778.

Liturgical provision also exists for those who are sick,[168] for the laying on of hands and anointing as part of the ministry of healing.[169] Unordained persons may conduct funeral services.[170] If the ground in which the burial is to take place is not consecrated, a priest says, immediately before the committal, the prayer provided for the blessing of the grave.[171] A faculty is required both for the acquisition of permanent or exclusive rights to burial in any grave, grave space, vault or tomb, and for the removal of a corpse or human remains from an existing grave, vault or tomb.[172] If the reburial is not to be in consecrated ground, a Home Office licence is also required for the exhumation of human remains.[173] To dig up a corpse unlawfully is a criminal offence.[174] The Diocesan Courts are developing a body of jurisprudence in faculty cases on exhumation.[175]

Fees   Any right of burial, in a burial ground vested in the Representative Body, is subject to such conditions as to fees as may be prescribed in the rules of the Church in Wales.[176] Fees for interment are legally prescribed, and no other fees may be charged. Where the burial service is solemnized in accordance with the rites of the Church in Wales all fees must be paid to the incumbent. Where the burial service is not so solemnized, the fee for services rendered by the officiating minister must be paid to that minister and all other fees to the incumbent. Fees payable to the incumbent must be paid at the time of giving notice of the interment, and fees payable to any other minister must be paid to that minister either before or immediately after the interment. The person having charge of the funeral must make all necessary arrangements with the officiating minister.[177] No monument or gravestone

---

[168] See also *Bibliography on Dying, Death and Bereavement*, issued by the Churches Group on Funeral Services at Cemeteries and Crematoria and circulated to clergy of the Church in Wales by the Bench of Bishops (1994).

[169] BCP (1984), 756–73.

[170] Burial Laws (Amendment) Act 1880, s. 6; also, under s. 6, the minister is bound to permit the burial to be conducted by anyone whom the relatives wish, provided this is done in a seemly and Christian fashion; notice in writing must be given. Deacons and lay ministers may also conduct the service: see above, Chs. 7, 8.

[171] BCP (1984), 789.

[172] Const. XI.7(4).

[173] Burial Act 1857, s. 25.

[174] *Re Sharpe* (1857) Dears & B 160.

[175] See e.g. *Re Webber* (1995), Llandaff Diocesan Court: '[T]o permit exhumation of remains from consecrated ground must always be regarded as something only to be done for cogent reasons, particularly when it is opposed by a surviving near relative of the deceased.' See also the English case *Re Christ Church, Alsager* [1999] 1 All ER 117 (York Chancery Court): once a body or ashes has been interred in consecrated ground, there should be no disturbance save for good and proper reason (e.g. for mistakes made in the burial); a change of mind on the part of relatives of the deceased will not normally suffice. See also R. Bursell, 'Digging up exhumation', 5 *ELJ* (1998), 18.

[176] Welsh Church (Burial Grounds) Act 1945, s. 4(2): the rules must have the approval of the National Assembly.

[177] BGR, r.7; see Schedule 2: fees are payable: for services rendered by the incumbent or

may be erected unless the appropriate fee has previously been paid to the incumbent.[178]

The Maintenance of Churchyards: Cremated Remains, Monuments and Gravestones

The Parochial Church Council is responsible to the Representative Body for the proper care, maintenance and upkeep of all churchyards in the parish.[179] The archdeacon must send to the Representative Body, when so requested by it, a report on any churchyard in his archdeaconry. The report must specify the condition of the churchyard and it must state whether it (or any portion of it) is in disuse.[180] The Parochial Church Council must establish a Churchyard Maintenance Fund. When required to do so, the council must render an account to the Representative Body of all receipts and payments into the fund.[181] The fund consists of prescribed fees.[182] Subject to the basic duty of the council, the incumbent is responsible for the general supervision of all church-yards in the parish and for the allocation of grave spaces.[183] No grave or vault

other minister officiating at an interment; for registration of burial; and for Churchyard Maintenance Fund in respect of burial in a grave or vault. No fee is payable in respect of the burial of a still-born infant, the service or for registration of that burial. For digging a grave, and if necessary for walling, the actual and necessary cost is payable, provided that no separate fee is payable to the person who does the work, then such fee shall be payable as in the opinion of the incumbent is reasonable having regard to the local costs of labour. See also below, nn. 181, 182 for fees under CYR, rr. 4, 5, and n. 194 for cremated remains under r.13.

[178] BGR, r.8.

[179] CYR, r.1: this includes the walls, gates, fences, paths, grass and trees and for the repair of any damage to these however caused. The council must effect suitable and adequate insurance cover with the designated insurers of the Church in Wales; CYR, r.2: the conservation of churchyards in all respects is a concern and duty of Parochial Church Councils. The procedure for transferring responsibility for closed churchyards from the council to local authorities has in recent years been simplified: Local Government Act 1972, s. 215(2), (3); a churchyard may become an open space with the agreement of the incumbent and parochial church council and the local authority, even if it remains consecrated ground: Open Spaces Act 1906, ss. 1, 6, 9, 10, 11. See also below n. 216.

[180] CYR, r.3: or else the archdeacon must cause the report to be sent to the Representative Body. For discussion of the background to these rules, see *Re St Leian, Gorslas* (2000), St Davids Diocesan Court.

[181] CYR, r.4: excluded from the Churchyard Maintenance Fund are those fees treated in BGR, Second Schedule (fees in respect of burials, and fees for the right to erect monuments and gravestones), which are retained by the incumbent.

[182] CYR, r.5: all fees received for services rendered by the incumbent and for registration of burial must be retained by the incumbent, unless the incumbent is also a dean of a cathedral or an archdeacon, when the fees must be paid to the council; all fees received for burial in a grave or vault must be paid into the fund; of the fees received for the right to erect monuments and gravestones, including those relating to cremated remains, one-half must be paid into the fund and one-half shall be retained by the incumbent.

[183] CYR, r.6.

can be made or opened without the consent of the incumbent; the cost and expense is borne by the person at whose request the work is done.[184] No permanent or exclusive right of burial in any grave or vault can be acquired except by faculty.[185] No burial shall take place within twelve feet of the fabric of a church except in an existing vault.[186] The top of a coffin buried in a grave must not be less than three feet below ordinary ground level.[187]

Cremated Remains   The ashes of cremated remains should be buried in consecrated ground. No cleric of the Church in Wales may take part in the scattering of ashes, nor may they permit ashes to be scattered in any churchyard under their control.[188] The incumbent may permit cremated remains to be deposited in a churchyard.[189] When cremated remains are to be buried in consecrated ground, cremation may take place without any formal service.[190] Subject to the grant of a faculty, the Parochial Church Council, with the consent of the incumbent, may set aside an area(s) of the churchyard exclusively for the interment of cremated remains.[191] Also,[192] subject to a faculty and the consent of the incumbent, the council may set aside an area(s) of a churchyard exclusively for the interment in individual plots of cremated remains.[193] The names of individuals whose cremated remains have been interred and other relevant details must be entered in the register of burials,

---

[184] CYR, r.7.

[185] CYR, r.8; see above, Ch. 5.

[186] CYR, r.9.

[187] CYR, r.10.

[188] BCP (1984), 797: when ashes are to be buried and the committal has been used at the crematorium, the minister may first use the service in church, with any of the prayers. For the prohibition against scattering, see also CYR, r.13(1).

[189] CYR, r.13(1). For the possibility that this rule is in conflict with the common law right to burial, see P. Jones, *The Governance of the Church of Wales* (Cardiff, 2000), 386. For the right to burial as attaching also to cremated remains, see *Re Kerr* [1894] P 284. The Church of England has formally recognized that the common law right of burial extends to cremated remains: Church of England (Miscellaneous Provisions) Measure 1992, s. 3(1).

[190] BCP (1984), 797: in this case, the form of committal must be used at the burial of the cremated remains.

[191] CYR, r.13(2): the remains may be deposited either without containers or in containers quickly perishable, and in any such area only a single monument may be erected for all the remains so deposited.

[192] This may be done additionally or alternatively.

[193] CYR, r.13(3): the remains may be deposited without containers, or in containers either quickly perishable or made of wood, and the individual plots may only be marked by simple flat slabs set below ordinary ground level, or with the archdeacon's approval, by ledger stones; r.13(4): otherwise cremated remains may be deposited only in a grave or vault; in no circumstances can containers made wholly or partly of plastic be admitted to a churchyard; rr.14 and 15 (see below), apply to flat slabs.

or otherwise in the parish records.[194] A faculty is required for the removal of cremated remains from an existing grave, vault or tomb.[195]

Erection of Monuments and Gravestones   All applications for permission to erect or modify a monument or gravestone, or to alter or add to an inscription, must be made to the incumbent in the form prescribed by the Representative Body.[196] Prescribed gravestones may be admitted to a churchyard on the written approval of the incumbent.[197] Other prescribed gravestones may be admitted on the written approval of the archdeacon.[198] An application for the replacement or renewal of a monument or gravestone must be dealt with similarly.[199] The removal of a monument or gravestone from its place in a churchyard to a different place in that churchyard, or to

---

[194] CYR, r.13: fees for services rendered by the incumbent or other minister officiating and for registration must be the same as the corresponding fees chargeable for burials. The fee chargeable for the deposit of cremated remains must be one-half of the fee chargeable for a burial; however, where the cremated remains are deposited in a new full-size grave or vault, the fee must be the same as that for a burial.

[195] Const. XI.7(4). For a restrictive approach to the grant of a faculty, see e.g. *Re Holy Trinity, Newcastle Emlyn* (1999), in which the St Davids Diocesan Court relied on *Re Christ Church, Alsager* [1999] 1 All ER 117: for which see above n. 175.

[196] CYR, r.14: the form must contain the wording of the proposed inscription and the proposed style of lettering; unless otherwise ordered by a court of the Church in Wales, all costs incurred in connection with the application must be borne by the applicant. For the application of these rules, see: *Re St Ilid and St Curig, Llanilid* (2000), Llandaff Diocesan Court; and *Roberts v PCC of Criccieth with Treflys* (1997), Bangor Diocesan Court. See also RODC, Sched. of Fees for fees on the grant of a faculty for a memorial, monument or tablet in a church as the Diocesan Court deems proper.

[197] CYR, r.15(1): namely, a gravestone which: consists of either an appropriate headstone or cross (neither more than four feet high), or a simple flat slab (set below ordinary ground level); is not made wholly or partly of reconstructed stone, metal or ceramics; and bears one or more or all of the following: a simple cross; a simple and appropriate inscription; an appropriate motif.

[198] CYR, r.15(2): namely: a gravestone within the above description (found in n. 197 above), but which the incumbent has declined to approve; a gravestone not complying with r.15(1), but nevertheless consisting only of a headstone, cross or flat slab, with suitable inscription and not made either wholly or partly of reconstructed stone, metal or ceramics; a gravestone incorporating a simple and appropriate engraving or photograph of the deceased; a ledger stone to mark an individual plot in which cremated remains have been deposited; r.15(3): otherwise no monument or gravestone can be admitted to a churchyard without a faculty; r.15(4): in a case where the approval of the archdeacon is sought for a gravestone, the archdeacon must, within twenty-eight days, signify approval or otherwise, in writing, to the person seeking approval and to the incumbent; r.15(5): no part of any concrete foundation can be above ordinary ground level.

[199] CYR, r.16(1): i.e. it must be dealt with under rr.14 and 15.

any other churchyard, must be the subject of a fresh application to erect or modify.[200] Special provisions apply to flowers, photographs[201] and trees.[202]

The Removal of Monuments and Gravestones   Any Parochial Church Council which proposes, by removing or altering the position of gravestones or other monuments, to tidy a churchyard or burial ground for which they are responsible must consult the Diocesan Advisory Committee before committing themselves to a particular project.[203] They should submit to the Diocesan Registrar a brief description of their proposals, together with a simple plan.[204] Parochial Church Councils and Diocesan Advisory Committees should have regard to the following five principles.

First, tidying churchyards and burial grounds should be done, where circumstances permit, without removing monuments or gravestones.[205] Secondly, where some removal is thought essential, the most careful consideration should be given to the question of removing any particular monument or gravestone.[206] Thirdly, if removal or repositioning of a monument or gravestone, or flattening a chest tomb, will enable the council to maintain the churchyard to a fair standard, then, in principle, such a course may be permitted, but a faculty is unlikely to be granted for total clearance.[207] Fourthly, no reordering should be allowed which deals only with the more ancient monuments or gravestones.[208] Fifthly, careful consideration should

---

[200] CYR., r.16(2): i.e. it must be dealt with under rr.14 and 15.

[201] CYR, r.17: other than for Remembrance Day poppies, no artificial wreaths or flowers, chippings, or ornaments, may be placed on any grave in a churchyard; no photograph or other likeness of the deceased may be placed on or attached to a monument or gravestone; no shrubs, permanent flower vases or containers may be placed in a churchyard without the consent of the incumbent

[202] CYR, r.18: trees must not be planted in a churchyard without the written consent of the archdeacon; r.19: the Parochial Church Council may, with the consent of the incumbent, apply to the archdeacon for permission to cut down trees in a churchyard who, without prejudice to the rights of the Representative Body and subject to any Tree Preservation Order, may grant such permission; any proceeds from a sale of such timber must be credited to the appropriate parochial fund. For the meaning of 'parish', 'churchyard', and 'kerb', see r.20.

[203] Preamble to the Regulations Relating to the Removal of Monuments and Gravestones (hereafter PRRMG); that is, the council must comply with RODC (see above, Ch. 5).

[204] This will prevent councils incurring the effort and expense of advertising, contacting the deceased's relatives and compiling detailed plans, only to find that a faculty is unlikely to be granted.

[205] PRRMG, Principle (a).

[206] PRRMG, Principle (b).

[207] PRRMG, Principle (c).

[208] PRRMG, Principle (d): consideration should also be given, where appropriate, to the removal of more recent monuments, gravestones, kerbs, railings, chains and posts; the fifty-year rule should not be regarded as automatically giving approval or authority for the removal of monuments or gravestones prior to that period.

be given to what is to be done with monuments and gravestones which are to be removed.[209]

If the Parochial Church Council and the Committee are unable to agree on a scheme, the council has the right to be heard in the Diocesan Court.[210] Before lodging a petition for a faculty to remove or reposition monuments or gravestones,[211] the council must submit the proposal for consideration by the committee.[212] When a faculty is sought, the diocesan registrar must furnish to the secretary of the Representative Body a certificate by the registrar.[213] Where a certificate is not furnished by the Diocesan Registrar to the Representative Body, that body, or the appropriate committee of it, must make representation in writing to the Chancellor that the petition is not to be granted.[214] When the archdeacon deems such a course necessary for purposes of safety, he may authorize, in writing, the removal of listed items.[215] Whilst the Representative Body owns churchyards, and has a statutory duty to maintain them in decent order,[216] ownership of a monument in a churchyard vests in the person by whom it was set up during his life, and after his death the monument becomes the property of the heir of the deceased in whose honour it was erected.[217]

---

[209] PRRMG, Principle (e): monuments and gravestones which are irreparably damaged, or the inscriptions on which are illegible, may be buried or removed altogether and destroyed, provided they have no aesthetic, historical or genealogical value: otherwise no stones should be destroyed. Gravestones should not be piled up as rubble. Gravestones which have been removed but which are to be kept may be repositioned, laid flat or, if suitable, used for paving: they should not be placed in serried ranks in a churchyard or around its boundaries, or against the wall of the church where they look ugly and collect weeds and brambles. Discarded kerbs may be used for the edging of paths.

[210] PRRMG: when a registrar receives a proposal from a Parochial Church Council, he should inquire whether or not there is an intention to redevelop any ground which will be cleared. If there is, he should direct the attention of the council to the provisions of the Disused Burial Grounds Acts 1884 and 1981.

[211] The petition as far as possible must embody the five principles.

[212] Regulations Relating to the Removal of Monuments and Gravestones (hereafter RRMG), r.1: the council must submit a brief description of the proposals together with a simple plan, for consideration by the Diocesan Advisory Committee. Not later than fifty-six days after submission of the description and plan, the Diocesan Advisory Committee must inform the council, through the registrar, whether or not the Committee is prepared, in principle, to recommend that the proposals be carried out.

[213] RRMG, r.2: this rule lists in detail matters which must be covered in the certificate; the registrar must also send a copy of the petition and any accompanying exhibits.

[214] RRMG, r.3.

[215] RRMG, r.4: namely: chains, posts and uninscribed kerbs, and the laying of a gravestone flat on a grave but set below ordinary ground level.

[216] Welsh Church (Burial Grounds) Act 1945, s. 3.

[217] R. Burn, *Ecclesiastical Law* (5th edn, London, 1788, I, 250.

12

ECUMENICAL RELATIONS

The relationship between Anglican and other Christian churches is increasingly becoming the subject of juridical regulation.[1] From the Anglican perspective, successive Lambeth Conferences have stressed the desirability of and need for ecumenical development.[2] However, scope for ecumenical advance is conditioned in a fundamental way by the terms of the canonical and other regulatory systems of churches themselves.[3] For the Church in Wales, ecumenism is promoted through its provincial Inter-Church Team,[4] and its ecumenical relations with other Christian churches are regulated by a growing body of canon law. Whilst rules on discrete subjects impact directly on members of other churches,[5] this canon law deals with four basic subjects: the establishment of intercommunion or of full communion with other churches; covenanting between the Church in Wales and other churches in Wales; local ecumenical projects; and the implementation of multipartite

---

[1] This is in part the result not only of the will for ecumenical dialogue shared as between churches, but also of the ecumenical will within particular churches. For example, in the Roman Catholic Church, see e.g. the Vatican II decree on ecumenism, *Unitatis Redintegratio* (1964), and Pope John Paul II's encyclical *Ut Unum Sint* (1996).
[2] The Conference has laid down a number of ground rules intended to guide Anglican churches in promoting and effecting ecumenism: see e.g. LC 1968, Res. 47; see generally CLAC, 355.
[3] Often a variety of ecumenical duties is incorporated in the laws of Anglican churches, for example: to seek unity (Southern Africa, Res. 1973); to maintain fellowship (South India, Const. II.2); to restore unity (Korea, Const., Fundamental Declaration).
[4] COFC, 13: the Inter-Church Team, of the Council for Mission and Ministry, exists: to enable those working in the inter-church and inter-faith concerns to meet and co-ordinate their work; and to co-ordinate, encourage and assist the Church in Wales at every level to benefit from and enrich its international catholicity; the Team is responsible to the Council and consists of a bishop, two designated members of the Council on the recommendation of the Council, the World Mission Officer, the Inter-Church Officer, and various members of ecumenical bodies and world mission agencies, including: Cytun (Churches Together in Wales: its constitution is to be found in *Cytun: Directory* (2000), 40–53), Enfys (Covenanted Churches in Wales), and the World Council of Churches: see COFC, 13; see also COFC, 17: the Education Team is to support ecumenical chaplaincies in higher and further education.
[5] See Part II for rules forbidding admission to office in the church to those belonging to religious bodies not in communion with the Church in Wales (see e.g. Const. II.14, with regard to membership of the Governing Body).

international ecumenical agreements.[6] State law governs agreements between the Church in Wales and another church for the sharing of church buildings. This chapter also deals with the associated matter of the relationship between the Church in Wales and the institutions and churches of the Anglican Communion.

THE ESTABLISHMENT OF COMMUNION

The Governing Body of the Church in Wales is competent to establish communion between the Church in Wales and other Christian churches by means of canon promulgated as a result of bill procedure.[7] Communion may take one of two forms: intercommunion,[8] which allows members of each church to receive the sacraments of the other, but does not allow interchange of ministers; or full communion,[9] which allows both sacramental and ministerial interchange.[10]

Intercommunion

Intercommunion has been established between the Church in Wales and four other churches: the Old Catholics, the Philippine Independent Church, the Spanish Reformed Episcopal Church,[11] and the Lusitanian Church.[12] Under its own canon law, the Church in Wales agrees to the establishment of intercommunion between the Church in Wales and the Old Catholics on the following terms: that each communion recognizes the catholicity and

[6] For the proposal to have in Wales an ecumenical bishop, see G. Abraham-Williams (ed.), *Towards the Making of an Ecumenical Bishop in Wales* (Penarth, 1997); those involved are the Church in Wales, the Methodist Church, the United Reformed Church and the Covenanted Baptist Churches of the Baptist Union of Great Britain. A bill is to be presented, in September 2002, to the Governing Body of the Church in Wales to deal with this subject. See also *The Ecumenical Face of the Province*, produced by the Division for Ecumenism, and published by the Board of Mission of the Church in Wales (1999).

[7] For bill procedure, see above Ch. 2.

[8] LC 1959, LC 1958, Res. 14: with intercommunion 'varying degrees of relation other than "full communion" are established by agreement between' two churches.

[9] LC 1958, Res. 14: full communion is 'unrestricted *communio in sacris*', which includes 'mutual recognition and acceptance of ministries'.

[10] For this understanding see T. G. Watkin, 'Disestablishment, self determination and constitutional development in the Church in Wales', in N. Doe (ed), *Essays in Canon Law* (Cardiff, 1992), 25 at 43, n. 20: 'This, it is submitted, is the correct distinction, although regrettably the terms "full communion" and "intercommunion" have become confused even within the canons themselves.'

[11] Spanish Reformed Church, Const. IV: the church is 'integrated in the Anglican Communion and is a member of full right in the same'.

[12] The Lusitanian Church was admitted as a full member of the Anglican Communion in 1980.

independence of the other, that each maintains its own catholicity and independence; and that each communion agrees to admit members of the other communion to participate in the sacraments. Intercommunion does not require from either communion the acceptance of all doctrinal opinion, sacramental devotion, or liturgical practice characteristic of the other, but implies that each believes the other to hold all the essentials of the Christian faith.[13] The same scheme and terms are employed with regard to the Philippine Independent Church,[14] the Spanish Reformed Episcopal Church,[15] and the Lusitanian Church,[16] though the basis of intercommunion is a mutual acceptance of a concordat, the terms of which are incorporated and spelt out in the canon law of the Church in Wales.[17]

Full Communion

The canon law of the Church in Wales provides for full communion with a number of prescribed churches.[18] The provisions of the canon effecting full communion with the United Church of South India are typical.[19] Communicant members of the Church of South India may be admitted to holy communion in the Church in Wales, and communicant members of the Church in Wales may receive holy communion in the Church of South India. Subject to the oversight of the Welsh diocesan bishop,[20] bishops, presbyters and deacons of the Church of South India may, when visiting the Province of Wales, exercise their ministry in the liturgy of the Church in Wales. Further, subject to the Constitution of the Church of South India,[21] bishops, priests and deacons of the Church in Wales may, when visiting South India, exercise their ministry in the liturgy of that church.[22] Whilst not so detailed, full communion between the Church in Wales and the Mar Thoma Syrian

[13] Can. 30-9-1937; the canon is based on resolutions of the Convocation of Canterbury 1932, approving the statements agreed between the representatives of the Old Catholic Churches and the Churches of the Anglican Communion at a conference held at Bonn on 2 July 1931.

[14] Can. 29-9-1966.

[15] Can. 29-9-1966.

[16] Can. 29-9-1966.

[17] Confusingly, the title of each of the three canons refers to intercommunion, but the enacted part to full communion: see above n. 10.

[18] See Can. 27-9-1973 (the Church of North India); Can. 27-9-1973 (the Church of Pakistan); Can. 23-9-1976 (the Church of Bangladesh). For communion with other Anglican churches, see below.

[19] Can. 26-4-1973: this canon states that Church of South India is under 'the jurisdiction of Bishops in the historic succession', and that 'all ordinations in [it] are episcopal and all ministers are in communion with their bishop'. The United Church of South India is a member of the Anglican Communion.

[20] See above Ch. 10.

[21] United Church of South India, Const. II(6): '[i]n every communion the true celebrant is Christ alone.'

[22] Can. 26-4-1973.

Church enables sacramental communion, though the church is not itself a member of the Anglican Communion.[23]

THE ECUMENICAL COVENANT FOR UNION IN WALES

The canon law of the Church in Wales implements, for the purposes of the Church in Wales,[24] a covenant entered between the Church in Wales and other churches for union in Wales,[25] namely: the Calvinistic Methodist Church of Wales or the Presbyterian Church of Wales, the Methodist Church, the United Reformed Church of England and Wales (Congregational and Presbyterian), the Union of Welsh Independents,[26] and certain churches belonging to the Baptist Union of Great Britain and Ireland.[27] Under its canon law, the Church in Wales solemnly covenants with these churches,[28] but nothing in the covenant or its canon law affects or is deemed to affect the faith, discipline, articles, doctrinal statements, rites, ceremonies or formularies of the Church in Wales.[29]

Canonical Commitments of the Church in Wales

The covenant places seven commitments on the churches.[30] First, the churches recognize in one another the same faith in the gospel of Jesus Christ

[23] Can. 24-9-1975: however, full communion does not require from either church the acceptance of all doctrinal opinion, sacramental devotion, or liturgical practice characteristic of the other, but it implies that each believes the other to hold all the essentials of the Christian Faith. The Mar Thoma church is in communion with some Anglican churches: see e.g. Scotland, Can. 15.1, Schedule.
[24] For full constitutional union in the Anglican Communion, between Anglican churches and other churches, see CLAC, 358–60: e.g. the United Church of South India (inaugurated in 1947) includes Anglican, Methodist, Congregational and Presbyterian churches.
[25] Can. 1-5-1974: certain churches in Wales, which are members of the Council of Churches for Wales, set up a Joint Committee; the covenant prepared by this joint committee forms the basis of the canon. See below (n. 29) for Enfys (The Commission of Covenanted Churches in Wales).
[26] Can. 1-5-1974, Sched. 2.
[27] Can. 21-9-1977: and with such other churches which may join the Baptist Union.
[28] The Church in Wales also covenants with those churches which shall enter into a like covenant with the Church in Wales. The covenant acknowledges that each church does not yet know the form union will take, but that the task will be approached with openness to the Spirit, believing that God will guide the church into ways of truth and peace, correcting, strengthening and renewing it in accordance with the mind of Christ.
[29] Can. 1-5-1974. For Enfys (Commission of Covenanted Churches in Wales), see *The Ecumenical Face of the Province*, produced by the Division for Ecumenism, and published by the Board of Mission of the Church in Wales (1999), 9: the Church in Wales has six representatives, appointed by the Governing Body, who sit on the Commission.
[30] Needless to say, insofar as the covenant is incorporated in the canon law of the

found in holy scripture, which the creeds of the ancient church and other historic confessions are intended to safeguard. As such, they intend to act, speak and serve together in obedience to the gospel, to learn more of its fullness, and to make it known to others in contemporary terms and by credible witness.[31] Secondly, the covenanted churches recognize in one another the same awareness of God's calling to serve his gracious purpose for all mankind, with particular responsibility for this land and people. As such, they intend to work together for justice and peace at home and abroad, and for the spiritual and material well-being and personal freedom of all people.[32]

Thirdly, the covenanted churches recognize one another as within the one church of Jesus Christ, pledged to serve his kingdom, and sharing in the unity of the Spirit. As such, they intend by the help of the Spirit to overcome the divisions which impair their witness, impede God's mission, and obscure the gospel of salvation, and to manifest that unity which is in accordance with Christ's will.[33] Fourthly, the churches recognize the members of all the covenanting churches as members of Christ in virtue of their common baptism and common calling to participate in the ministry of the whole Church. As such, they intend to seek that form of common life which will enable each member to use the gifts bestowed upon him in the service of Christ's kingdom.[34] Fifthly, the churches recognize their respective ordained ministries as true ministries of the word and sacraments. As such, they intend to seek an agreed pattern of ordained ministry which will serve the gospel in unity, manifest its continuity throughout the ages, and be accepted as far as may be by the church throughout the world.[35]

Sixthly, the churches recognize in one another patterns of worship and sacramental life, marks of holiness and zeal, which are manifestly gifts of Christ. As such, they intend to listen to one another and to study together the witness and practice of their various traditions, so that the riches entrusted to them in separation may be preserved for the united church which they seek.[36]

Church in Wales, the covenant commitments are, therefore, canonical commitments for the Church in Wales.

[31] Can. 1-5-1974, Sched 1, para. 1: the churches recognize in one another the same desire to hold this faith in its fullness.

[32] Can. 1-5-1974, Sched. 1, para. 2.

[33] Can. 1-5-1974, Sched. 1, para. 3.

[34] Can. 1-5-1974, Sched. 1, para. 4.

[35] Can. 1-5-1974, Sched. 1, para. 5: through these ministries, God's love is proclaimed, his grace mediated, and his Fatherly care exercised.

[36] Can. 1-5-1974, Sched. 1, para. 6. Enfys (Commission of Covenanted Churches in Wales) has produced: a Service of Holy Communion (1981, with a supplement issued in 1993); a Service of Baptism (1990: in 1991 the Governing Body of the Church in Wales resolved: 'That the Rite of Baptism prepared by the Commission . . . be commended for use in future, where: a candidate for baptism is, or the parents of a candidate are, particularly responsive to the aims of the Covenant; where the parents of a child presented for baptism do not come from a common denominational background; or where its occasional experimental use in place of the Church in Wales Rite is appropriate in the

Finally, the churches recognize in one another the same concern for the good government of the church for the fulfilment of its mission. As such, they intend to seek a mode of church government which will preserve the positive values for which each has stood. This is so that the common mind of the church may be formed and carried into action through constitutional organs of corporate decision at every level of responsibility.[37]

The Covenant and Solemnization of Marriage

The covenant urges all members of each church to accept one another in the Holy Spirit as Jesus Christ accepts them, and to avail themselves of every opportunity to grow together through common prayer and worship in mutual understanding and love so that in every place they may be renewed together for mission.[38] In part-furtherance of this exhortation, special canonical provision now exists in the Church in Wales, to promote ecumenical relations, permitting its clerics to officiate at marriage services in prescribed places of worship belonging to the other covenanted churches.[39] Five conditions must be satisfied before clerics of the Church in Wales may so officiate: (1) they must hold a licence from their diocesan bishop permitting them to officiate at such services in the parish in which the registered building is situated; (2) the form of service to be used must have been approved by their diocesan bishop; (3) the trustees or governing body of the registered building must consent to the cleric officiating; (4) the cleric must be a person authorized to officiate in the registered building;[40] and (5) there must be no impediment to the marriage of the couple according to the canon law of the Church in Wales.[41] A licence permitting a cleric to officiate may be revoked in writing by the diocesan bishop at any time.[42]

---

context of local circumstances'; and a Service of Affirmation and/or Reaffirmation of the Faith for those already baptized (1996): see *The Ecumenical Face of the Province* (1999), 9.

[37] Can. 1-5-1974, Sched. 1, para. 7: see above n. 6 for the proposal to establish an ecumenical bishop.

[38] Can. 1-5-1974.

[39] Can. 19-9-1985: it is lawful within and throughout the Province of Wales for a cleric of the Church in Wales to officiate at a marriage service in a place of religious worship which has been registered as a registered building for the solemnization of marriages in accordance with the Marriage Act 1949 or any statute amending or re-enacting this.

[40] That is, under the Marriage Act 1949 (or any statute amending or re-enacting this), or else solemnize the marriage in the presence of a registrar of the registration district in which the registered building is situated.

[41] Can. 19-9-1985, 1.

[42] Can. 19-9-1985, 2; 3: nothing in this canon may be held or interpreted as permitting a marriage to be solemnized in a registered building following the publication of banns or according to the rites of either the Church in Wales or the Church of England.

LOCAL ECUMENICAL PROJECTS

In common with a small number of other churches in the Anglican Communion,[43] the canon law of the Church in Wales deals with the role of the church in local ecumenical projects.[44] These are entered, under the licence of the diocesan bishop, 'to promote greater unity among all Christians in Wales'.[45]

Establishment, Administration and Termination

After reaching agreement with the appropriate authorities of each partici- pating church, it is lawful for a diocesan bishop of the Church in Wales to authorize (by written declaration) the establishment of a local ecumenical project in a parish or parishes within his diocese.[46] However, no such project can be established unless the consent of the following is obtained: the Bench of Bishops of the Church in Wales; the Diocesan Conference of the diocese in which the project is to be established; the Parochial Church Council(s) of the parish(es) in which the project is to be established;[47] and the incumbent(s) of the parish(es) in which the project is to be established.[48] Special provision exists for including extra-parochial ministry in the Church in Wales to be included in a local ecumenical project.[49]

After consultation with the appropriate authorities of each participating church, the Bench of Bishops of the Church in Wales may, from time to time, make regulations relating to the administration of a local ecumenical project. Similarly, after consultation with the appropriate authorities of each partici-

---

[43] See e.g. England, Cans. B43 and B44; New Zealand, Cans. B.V.2.8: it is lawful for a Diocesan Synod to authorize its standing committee to enter agreements for co-operative ventures with other Christian churches and such agreements shall be based on 'guidelines' approved by the General Synod.

[44] Can. 26-9-1991, Preamble (Local Ecumenical Projects Canon, 1991): this is the result of the Church in Wales having entered into 'a covenant with other Churches to work and pray for union in Wales'; for the covenant and its incorporation in the canon law of the Church in Wales, see above. For an explanation of these projects, see *The Ecumenical Face of the Province* (1999), 8.

[45] Can. 26-9-1991, Preamble.

[46] The project may also be established in a part or parts of a parish or parishes.

[47] If wishing to agree to the project, the council(s) must do so by resolution; the resolu- tion must then be communicated in writing to the diocesan bishop.

[48] Can. 26-9-1991, s. 1.

[49] Can. 26-9-1991, s. 10: this applies to a cleric, deaconess, licensed reader or other member of the Church in Wales, who has been appointed by a diocesan bishop by licence to an extra-parochial office within the ministry of the Church in Wales; in such a case, after reaching agreement with the appropriate authorities of each participating church, the diocesan bishop may (by written declaration) authorize within the diocese the establishment of a local ecumenical project including such extra-parochial ministry; paras. (a), and (b), of the proviso to s. 1, and ss. 2 to 9 apply to these projects, but para. (f), to the proviso of s. 7 and s. 8 do not.

pating church, a local ecumenical project may be ended at any time by the decision of the diocesan bishop. The decision of the bishop to terminate the project must be communicated to each and every person authorized to officiate within the project, and to each and every person or body whose consent was required for the establishment of the project.[50]

Authorization for Ministry: Episcopal Licence or Permission

A diocesan bishop of the Church in Wales may authorize the following to officiate in a local ecumenical project: clerics, deaconesses, licensed readers and other members of the Church in Wales;[51] and duly accredited ministers or other members of a church, other than the Church in Wales or a church in communion with the Church in Wales, if the church in question holds the Trinitarian Faith and administers the sacraments of baptism and holy communion.[52]

Clerics, deaconesses, licensed readers and members of the Church in Wales, who are to officiate *regularly* within a local ecumenical project, must hold an episcopal licence.[53] Clerics, deaconesses, licensed readers and members of the Church in Wales, or of churches in communion with the Church in Wales, who are to officiate *occasionally* in a project require the written permission of the diocesan bishop to do so; they must use only such forms of service as have been approved by the diocesan bishop.[54] Duly accredited ministers and members of other participating churches, who are to officiate regularly in a project, must be authorized in writing by the diocesan bishop of the Church in Wales.[55]

Services in Non-Church in Wales Places of Worship

Under a local ecumenical project, a cleric, deaconess, licensed reader or other member of the Church in Wales may officiate at any one or more of the services of holy communion, holy baptism, confirmation (or reception), morning service, evening service, ministry of healing, or burial of the dead.[56] They may do so at such place(s) of religious worship, not belonging to the Church in Wales, as may be permitted by licence of the diocesan bishop. However, certain conditions must first be satisfied. The cleric, deaconess, licensed reader or other member of the Church in Wales must hold a licence from the diocesan bishop permitting them to officiate at such services in the

---

[50] Can. 26-9-1991, ss. 3 and 4.
[51] Can. 26-9-1991, s. 2(1)(i): in accordance with s. 5 of the canon (see below).
[52] Can. 26-9-1991, s. 2(1)(ii): in accordance wth s. 7 of the canon (see below).
[53] Can. 26-9-1991, s. 2(2): in accordance with s. 5 of the canon (see below).
[54] Can. 26-9-1991, s. 2(3).
[55] Can. 26-9-1991, s. 2(4).
[56] Can. 26-9-1991, s. 5: the services are listed in Schedule 1.

parish(es) in which the place(s) of religious worship named in the licence is situated.[57] Any form of service to be used must have been approved by the diocesan bishop.[58]

A cleric, deaconess, licensed reader or other member of the Church in Wales may officiate only with the consent of the trustees or governing body of the relevant place of religious worship.[59] Moreover, in the place of worship belonging to a participating church, the cleric, deaconess, licensed reader or other member of the Church in Wales may only perform a duty similar to one which they are authorized to perform within the Church in Wales.[60]

Services in the Church in Wales

A duly accredited minister or other member of another church[61] may officiate in the Church in Wales at one or more of the following services: holy communion (according to the order of holy communion prepared by the Commission of the Covenanted Churches); holy baptism; morning prayer; evening prayer; the litany; communion of the sick; and burial of the dead.[62] They may so officate in any parish indicated by written authorization of the bishop of the diocese in which the parish is situated.[63] The conduct of services in the Church in Wales by persons from other churches is subject to a number of conditions.

First, the person must have written authorization from the diocesan bishop to officiate at such services in the parish(es) named in that authorization.[64] Secondly, the forms of service to be used, with the exception of holy communion, must be those contained in the Book of Common Prayer of the Church in Wales, or otherwise permitted by lawful authority or approved by the diocesan bishop.[65] Thirdly, celebrations of holy communion must be presided over by a duly accredited minister.[66] Fourthly, the bishop must ensure that a service of holy communion, according to the rites of the Church in Wales, is celebrated on Christmas Day, Easter Day, Ascension Day and

---

[57] Can. 26-9-1991, s. 5(a).
[58] Can. 26-9-1991, s. 5(b).
[59] Can. 26-9-1991, s. 5(c).
[60] Can. 26-9-1991, s. 5(d).
[61] Can. 26-9-1991, s. 7: namely: a church other than the Church in Wales or a church in communion with the Church in Wales, which holds the Trinitarian Faith and administers the sacraments of baptism and holy communion.
[62] Can. 26-9-1991, s. 7: the services are listed in Sched. 2. See above, n. 36 for Enfys services.
[63] Can. 26-9-1991, s. 7: the authorization may indicate more than one parish.
[64] Can. 26-9-1991, s. 7(a).
[65] Can. 26-9-1991, s. 7(b). For the authorized forms of service, see above, Ch. 9.
[66] Can. 26-9-1991, s. 7(c). And the form of service must be the order for the holy communion prepared by the Commission of the Covenanted Churches: see above.

Pentecost within the parish(es) concerned, where this is requested by communicants within the project.[67]

Fifthly, the authorities of the officiating person's own church must have consented in writing to that person being permitted to officiate in the Church in Wales.[68] Sixthly, the Parochial Church Council(s) of the parish(es) in which the person is to officiate must by resolution have agreed to accept their ministry; the resolution must also be communicated in writing to the diocesan bishop.[69] Seventhly, the person from the other church may only perform a duty within the Church in Wales similar to one which he or she is authorized to perform within his or her own church.[70] Finally, the person must also have agreed in writing to be bound by the directions of the diocesan bishop and such other lawful authorities as the Bench of Bishops of the Church in Wales may deem expedient with regard to their activities under the written authorization.[71]

Governance and Discipline

The Church in Wales allows its ministers to be involved in the governance of participating churches: a cleric, deaconess, licensed reader or any member of the Church in Wales (officiating in a local ecumenical project) may be permitted by the diocesan bishop to attend, speak and vote at meetings of the church(es) concerned to which they are invited by virtue of their ministry.[72] Similarly, the Bench of Bishops of the Church in Wales may make regulations relating to the administration of a parish (or parishes) in which a duly accredited minister or member of another church officiates,[73] where that parish is not part of a local ecumenical project. The regulations may provide for: (1) that person's right to attend, speak and vote at meetings of the Vestry Meeting, Parochial Church Council, Deanery Conference, Deanery Chapter and other such bodies; (2) the nomination of the warden to be appointed by the incumbent; (3) duties of residence within the parsonage and the maintenance of it; (4) the application of the rules and regulations relating to burials and burial grounds within the parish; and (5) such other matters relating to the administration of the parish as the Bench of Bishops may, from time to time, deem to be expedient. The regulations are valid only when approved by the Governing Body of the Church in Wales.[74]

---

[67] Can. 26-9-1991, s. 7(d).
[68] Can. 26-9-1991, s. 7(e).
[69] Can. 26-9-1991, s. 7(f).
[70] Can. 26-9-1991, s. 7(g).
[71] Can. 26-9-1991, s. 7(h).
[72] Can. 26-9-1991, s. 6.
[73] That is, a church other than the Church in Wales or a church in communion with it.
[74] Can. 26-9-1991, s. 8: Const. II.37 and 43 do not apply to the procedure for such approval.

The canon law of the Church in Wales also deals with questions of discipline. A licence issued to enable ministers of the Church in Wales to officiate under a local ecumenical project, and written authorization given to those of other churches to do so, may be revoked in writing by the diocesan bishop at any time.[75] Nothing contained in the canon regulating local ecumenical projects is taken to affect or be deemed to affect: the declaration of canonical obedience made by a cleric of the Church in Wales; the declaration made and subscribed by a cleric of the Church in Wales;[76] or the faith, discipline, articles, doctrinal statements, rites, ceremonies or formularies of the Church in Wales.[77]

INTERNATIONAL MULTIPARTITE ECUMENICAL AGREEMENTS

As well as its arrangements for ecumenism at both the national and the local levels, the Church in Wales provides for ecumenical relations with other Christian churches by means of incorporating the terms of multipartite international ecumenical agreements into its canon law. To date, canonical arrangements of this sort operate only in the context of Europe.[78]

The Porvoo Declaration

The Anglican churches of Britain and Ireland and the Lutheran churches of the Nordic and Baltic countries have reached a common understanding of the nature and purpose of the church, a fundamental agreement in faith, and an agreement on episcopacy in the service of the apostolicity of the church. The Church in Wales joined with the following churches in making the Porvoo Declaration: the Church of Denmark, the Church of England, the Estonian Evangelical-Lutheran Church, the Evangelical-Lutheran Church of Finland, the Evangelical-Lutheran Church of Iceland, the Church of Ireland, the Evangelical-Lutheran Church of Latvia, the Evangelical-Lutheran Church of Lithuania, the Church of Norway, the Scottish Episcopal Church, and the Church of Sweden.[79]

These churches recognize one another as churches belonging to the One, Holy, Catholic and Apostolic Church of Jesus Christ, and as truly partici-

---

[75] Can. 26-9-1991, s. 9.
[76] That is, under Const. VII.66.
[77] Can. 26-9-1991, s. 11: the provisions of Const. I.4 do not apply to this canon.
[78] For the Porvoo Communion, the Meissen Communion, the Conference of European Churches (founded 1959; this is composed of Anglican, Orthodox, Old Catholic and Protestant Churches of Europe and is governed by an Assembly), and the World Council of Churches, see *The Ecumenical Face of the Province* (1999), 11.
[79] Can. 28-9-1995 and Sched. 1; the churches are listed in Sched. 2.

pating in the apostolic mission of the whole people of God. They acknowledge that, in each of them, the Word of God is authentically preached, and the sacraments of baptism and the eucharist are duly administered. Each church shares in the common confession of the apostolic faith. In all the churches, ordained ministries are given by God as instruments of his grace: as such, these ministries possess not only the inward call of the Spirit, but also Christ's commission through his body, the church. The churches acknowledge that personal, collegial and communal oversight (*episcope*) is embodied and exercised in each other in a variety of forms, and in continuity of apostolic life, mission and ministry. Indeed, they acknowledge that the episcopal office is valued and maintained in one another as a visible sign which expresses and serves church unity and continuity in apostolic life, mission and ministry.[80]

The canonical commitments of the Church in Wales are:[81] (1) to share a common life in mission and service, to pray for and with the other churches, and to share resources; (2) to welcome members of the other churches to receive sacramental and other pastoral ministrations in the Church in Wales; (3) to regard baptized members of the other churches as members of the Church in Wales; (4) to welcome *diaspora* congregations into the life of the indigenous churches; (5) to welcome persons episcopally ordained in all the churches to the office of bishop, priest or deacon to serve in that ministry in the Church in Wales without reordination;[82] (6) to invite bishops normally to participate in the laying on of hands at the ordination of bishops in the Church in Wales;[83] (7) to work towards a common understanding of diaconal ministry; (8) to establish appropriate forms of collegial and conciliar consultation on significant matters of faith and order, life and work; (9) to encourage consultations of representatives of each church, and to facilitate learning and exchange of ideas and information in theological and pastoral matters; and (10) to establish a contact group to nurture growth in communion and to co-ordinate the implementation of the agreement.[84]

The Reuilly Agreement

The canon law which implements the Reuilly Agreement governs relations between the Church in Wales, the Church of the Augsburg Confession of Alsace and Lorraine, the Evangelical-Lutheran Church of France, the Reformed Church of Alsace and Lorraine, the Reformed Church of France, the Church of England, the Church of Ireland and the Scottish Episcopal

[80] Can. 28-9-1995, Sched. 1(a).
[81] Each of the other churches has the same commitments under the agreement.
[82] They may serve by invitation and in accordance with any regulations in force in the host church.
[83] That is, as a sign of the unity and continuity of the church.
[84] Can. 28-9-1995, Sched. 1(b).

Church. The acknowledgements contained in the agreement are largely the same as those appearing in the Porvoo declaration.[85]

The Church in Wales (by its canon law) and the participating churches (under the agreement) are committed to share a common life and mission, and will take steps to closer fellowship in as many areas of Christian life and witness as possible. As the next steps, the churches agree: (1) to seek appropriate ways to share a common life in mission and service, to pray for and with one another, and to work towards sharing spiritual and human resources; (2) to welcome their respective members to worship and to receive pastoral ministrations in each of the churches; (3) to welcome their members into the congregational life of each church; (4) to encourage shared worship; (5) to welcome ordained ministers of each church to serve in each other's churches, in accordance with the discipline of the respective churches, to the extent made possible by the agreement; (6) to continue theological discussions on the outstanding issues which hinder fuller communion, whether bilaterally or in a wider European, ecumenical framework; (7) to work towards closer relations in diaspora situations; (8) to encourage ecumenical visits, twinning and exchanges; and to establish a contact group.[86] Special provision is made for the celebration of the eucharist: whilst eucharistic hospitality is possible, as yet reciprocal arrangements do not include the interchangeability of ministers; and any eucharistic rite used should be that of the church to which the presiding minister belongs.[87]

CHURCH-SHARING AGREEMENTS

The Sharing of Church Buildings Act 1969 provides for the sharing of buildings between the Church in Wales and a prescribed number of other

---

[85] Can. 27-4-2000. See, however, Sched. (a)(iv)–(vi) of the Reuilly canon: the churches acknowledge that: their ordained ministries are given by God as instruments of grace for the mission and unity of the church and for the proclamation of the word and the celebration of the sacraments; their ordained ministries possess not only the inward call of the Spirit but also Christ's commission through the church, and they look forward to when their fuller visible unity makes possible the interchangeability of ministers; and, that personal, collegial and communal oversight (*episcope*) is embodied and exercised in them all in a variety of forms, as a visible sign expressing and serving the church's unity and continuity in apostolic life, mission and ministry.

[86] Schedule, (b), (i)–(iv), (vi)–(ix).

[87] Schedule, (iv): when eucharistic worship is judged to be appropriate, it may move beyond eucharistic hospitality for individuals; the participation of ordained ministers would reflect the presence of two or more churches expressing their closer unity in faith and baptism and demonstrate that 'we are still striving towards making more visible the unity of the One, Holy, Catholic and Apostolic Church'; nevertheless, such participation still falls short of the full interchangeability of ministers; the rite should be that of the church to which the presiding minister belongs, and that minister should say the eucharistic prayer.

churches.[88] Nothing in the statute affects any practice of the Church in Wales of lending church buildings temporarily for particular occasions to other religious bodies.[89] The statute applies to church buildings used, or proposed to be used, as a place of worship. It also applies to buildings to be used as a church hall or centre, as a youth club, centre or hostel, or as a residence for ordained ministers or lay workers.[90] The Church in Wales and any other church to which the statute applies may make agreements for the sharing of such buildings and for the carrying into effect their agreements. The agreement may apply to a single building or to two or more buildings in the same locality.[91] Provision is made to safeguard the purposes of a sharing agreement by way of trusts and to ensure that such purposes are exclusively charitable.[92]

Establishment and Termination The parties to a sharing agreement may provide that the ownership of the shared building(s) be vested solely or jointly in all or any of them.[93] The parties must be such persons as may be determined by the appropriate authority of the church in question, and those parties must obtain such consents as are required by the appropriate authority. In relation to the Church in Wales, the appropriate authority is the Governing Body.[94] The agreement is in the form of a covenant; it must be under seal and registered by the Governing Body, and is binding on the parties and their successors.[95] The person in whom ownership of the building is vested,[96] and any managing trustees, must also be parties to the agreement.[97] The agreement must make provision for its own termination, and it may provide for the withdrawal of a church if that church is not the sole or previous owner of the building.[98] The agreement may be amended

---

[88] The statute applies to the Church in Wales, the Church of England, the Roman Catholic Church, the Methodist and United Reformed Churches, any church of the Baptist denomination, any congregation of the Association of Churches of Christ in Great Britain and Ireland (s. 11(1), and Sched. 2); in addition, any church represented on the General Council of the British Council of Churches or the governing body of the Evangelical Alliance or the British Evangelical Council may give notice that the statute should apply to that church (s. 11(3)).

[89] S. 13.

[90] S. 12(1): schools are expressly excluded.

[91] S. 1(1),(2): locality is not defined.

[92] S. 2.

[93] S. 1(2).

[94] S. 1(3), (4), and Sched. 2.

[95] S. 1(8)–(10).

[96] In the Church in Wales this will be, ordinarily, the Representative Body: see *post* Ch. 13.

[97] S. 9.

[98] S. 9: where the agreement relates to two or more buildings, it must make provision for terminating the sharing of each building, so that the sharing of one may continue regardless of termination of the agreement concerning the other.

only with the agreement of the parties to it and with the same consents as were required for its creation.[99]

Management of the Shared Building   The statute requires the agreement to deal with the finances and other obligations of the parties for the provision, improvement and management of the shared building. Generally, the primary responsibility for these matters rests with the church which owns the building; if the shared building is jointly owned, the responsibility rests with the managing trustees. Nothing in the statute prevents the continuation of any legal powers which persons or bodies have in respect of the application of money for the provision, improvement or management of church buildings. Moreover, the duties of the church which owns the shared building, or those of the managing trustees, may be discharged in accordance with the the terms of the agreement, including any arrangements in the agreement for consultation with any sharing church. Management of a shared building includes the repair and furnishing of the building.[100] Special provisions, under the domestic law of the Church in Wales, apply to the operation of the faculty jurisdiction with regard to church buildings under a sharing agreement.[101]

Worship   When a shared building is used as a place of worship, the sharing agreement must make provision for determining the extent to which the building is available for worship in accordance with the forms of service and practice of the sharing churches respectively. The agreement may provide for the holding of joint services on such occasions as may be approved by those churches.[102] Notwithstanding any statutory or other legal provision, a minister, reader or lay preacher of one of the churches sharing a building under a sharing agreement may, by invitation of a minister, reader or lay preacher of another such church, take part in conducting worship in that building. This must be done in accordance with the forms of service and practice of that other church. However, the rights given here must be exercised in accordance with any rules or directions given by either church, and to any limitation imposed by or under the sharing agreement. As a general principle, therefore, the participation of the communities of the sharing churches in each other's worship must be governed by the practices and disciplines of those churches in like manner as if they worshipped in separate buildings.[103]

A church building to which a sharing agreement relates may be certified under the Places of Worship Registration Act 1855 as a place of religious

---

[99]   S. 9.
[100]   S. 3.
[101]   See above, Ch. 5.
[102]   Sharing of Church Buildings Act 1969, s. 4(1).
[103]   S. 4; see above for the law of the Church in Wales on local ecumenical projects.

worship of any church sharing the building.[104] The provisions of the Marriage Act 1949 relating to publication of banns and solemnization of marriages according to the rites of the Church in Wales apply to a church building shared by the Church in Wales under a sharing agreement.[105]

Residences   Where a sharing agreement is made with respect to a church building proposed to be used under the agreement as a residence(s) for ministers or lay workers, the purpose of the agreement must be to provide residential accommodation. This may be in the form of separate residences, or otherwise, and it must be available for occupation by the ministers or lay workers of the sharing churches in accordance with arrangements under the agreement.[106]

THE ANGLICAN COMMUNION: INTER-ANGLICAN RELATIONS

The Church in Wales functions both in the juridical order of its own binding legal system, and in the moral order of the worldwide Anglican Communion.[107] There is no formal, written Anglican canon law globally applicable to and binding upon member churches of the Communion.[108] No central institution exists with competence to create such a body of law.[109] Instead, member churches (including the Church in Wales), and the communion itself, are bound morally by a body of powerful but non-legal ecclesiastical conventions.[110]

Communion and the Instruments of Anglicanism   The Anglican Communion is a community of *sui juris* or self-governing churches in communion with the See of Canterbury and with each other: it is 'a fellowship, within the One Holy Catholic and Apostolic Church, of those duly

---

[104] The provisions of the Marriage Act 1949 relating to registration of buildings then apply to the registration so certified.

[105] Sharing of Church Buildings Act 1969, s. 6; s. 6(5) applies this section expressly to the Church in Wales.

[106] S. 7.

[107] For the links between these two orders, the (local) juridical and the (global) moral, see N. Doe, 'Canon law and communion', 30(3), *The Anglican* (2001), 5.

[108] However, for the unwritten *ius commune* of the Anglican Communion, see above, Ch. 1.

[109] LC 1930, Ress. 48, 49: churches are bound together 'not by a central legislative and executive authority, but by a mutual loyalty sustained through the common counsel of the bishops in conference'; see also Handbook, 1994, 19: 'Since the Anglican Communion does not have a central body with canonical authority, the list [of Anglican churches] is authorised by the Archbishop of Canterbury and the Anglican Primates.'

[110] Many of these conventional principles have been enunciated by the Lambeth Conference, the assembly of worldwide Anglican bishops: see below and CLAC, 345ff.

constituted dioceses, provinces and regional Churches in communion with the See of Canterbury'.[111] The principle of communion embraces a range of relationships. Anglican churches are assembled under the moral authority of the instruments of Anglicanism. First, there is the moral authority of the instruments of faith: holy scripture, tradition and reason; churches are held together by loyalty to scripture, the sacraments of baptism and eucharist, the historic episcopate, and common patterns of worship.[112] Secondly, there is the moral authority of the institutional instruments. At the global level, the Archbishop of Canterbury,[113] the Primates' Meeting, the Lambeth Conference,[114] and the Anglican Consultative Council,[115] exercise no legal authority over individual churches: their authority and leadership are moral, and their decisions do not bind particular churches as a matter of law.[116] Thirdly, the principle of autonomy provides that each church is free to govern itself: 'the true constitution of the Catholic Church involves the principle of autonomy of particular Churches based upon a common faith and order.'[117] Anglican churches 'promote [in] their territories a national expression of Christian faith, life and worship'.[118]

---

[111] LC 1930, Res. 49; see generally CLAC, 340. See also BCP (1984), 692 (Catechism): 'The Anglican Communion is a family of Churches within the Catholic Church of Christ, maintaining apostolic doctrine and order and in full communion with one another and with the See of Canterbury.'

[112] LC 1998, Res. III.8; see also LC 1998, Res. III.1.

[113] The Archbishop of Canterbury has no general metropolitical jurisdiction in the Church in Wales (see, however, above, Ch. 5 for the archbishop's role in the higher courts of the church, and above, Ch. 11 for the archbishop's power to issue special marriage licences). In other churches in the Communion, the Archbishop of Canterbury possesses metropolitical jurisdiction: see e.g. the Lusitanian Church (CLAC, 344).

[114] The Lambeth Conference, which first met in 1867, is an assembly of worldwide Anglican bishops and meets roughly every ten years at the invitation of the Archbishop of Canterbury. The Conference has no formal constitution, but successive decisons have defined its sphere of competence: counsel and encouragement. Its decisions, usually in the form of resolutions, cover all aspects of ecclesiastical life and are understood to have only persuasive or moral, and no binding legal, authority; as such they do not directly bind any church in the communion, including the Church in Wales: CLAC, 346.

[115] The council, regulated by a formal constitution, meets every two or three years and its standing committee administers its affairs between sessions. The council acts as 'an instrument of common action' and its functions include the following: to advise on inter-Anglican relations, including the formation of new provinces and church constitutions; to develop as far as possible agreed Anglican policies in the world mission of the church; to encourage churches to collaborate and to share resources; to promote ecumenical development; and to advise on proposed unions between Anglican and other churches: CLAC, 349.

[116] They bind only if incorporated into the legal system of the particular church.

[117] LC 1930, Res. 48. The concept of autonomy is sometimes linked to the principle of subsidiarity: see *The Virginia Report*, The Report of the Inter-Anglican Theological and Doctrinal Commission, in *The Official Report of the Lambeth Conference 1998* (Harrisburg, Pennsylvania, 1999), 15 at 43ff.

[118] LC 1930, Ress. 48, 49.

Inter-Anglican Relations   The Lambeth Conference has enunciated several principles to promote and regulate communion and autonomy, freedom and self-restraint,[119] in inter-Anglican relations.[120] Each church should respect the autonomy of each other church.[121] In the exercise of their autonomy, churches should take no unilateral action in matters of concern to the whole of the Anglican Communion.[122] Two bishops may not exercise jurisdiction in the same place.[123] No bishop or cleric should exercise their ministries in another diocese without the consent of the bishop of the host diocese, and no priest or deacon may minister in another diocese without letters testimonial from their own bishop.[124] Each church should inform member churches, and the Archbishop of Canterbury, of all new metropolitical and episcopal appointments.[125] Member churches should co-operate to further the mission of the whole church.[126] Dioceses should develop companion dioceses.[127] The life, polity and liturgy of churches should exemplify an understanding of community and common life.[128]

Several Anglican churches have expressly incorporated these principles into their own constitutional and canonical systems.[129] Nevertheless, in common with most, the Church in Wales has not developed a body of distinctly communion law on inter-Anglican relations.[130] By way of contrast, in some churches the law (for example): identifies the church with the See of Canterbury and deals with its membership of the Anglican Communion;[131]

---

[119] LC Report 1988, 298: 'in the Communion as a whole, the instruments of Communion or the organs of consultation provide appropriate checks and balances for each other . . . [we] seem to have a view of dispersed authority which relates not only to the sources of authority but also to its exercise.'

[120] LC 1998, Res. III.2: the Lambeth Conference 'is committed to maintaining the overall unity of the Anglican Communion, including the unity of each diocese under the jurisdiction of the diocesan bishop'.

[121] LC 1978, Recommendation 1: this is one of 'the principles of church order'; see also LC 1878, committee report.

[122] LC 1978, Res. 11: 'The Conference advises member Churches not to take action regarding issues which are of concern to the whole Anglican Communion without consultation with a Lambeth Conference or with the episcopate through the Primates Committee.'

[123] LC 1897, Res. 24; LC 1968, Res. 63.

[124] LC 1878, Recommendation 1.

[125] LC 1867, Res. 1.

[126] LC 1930, Res. 47.

[127] LC 1998, Res. II.3.

[128] LC 1998, Res. III.22.

[129] See CLAC, 351ff.

[130] For centripetal laws, neutral laws, and centrifugal laws in churches of the Anglican Communion, and for a proposal to develop the potential of canon law on this subject in light of the unwritten *ius commune*, see Doe, 'Canon law', 5.

[131] See e.g. ECUSA, Const. Preamble: the church is presented 'as a constituent member of the Anglican Communion . . . in communion with the See of Canterbury'; see also New Zealand, Cans. G.XIII.6: the church is in communion with 'the Church of England and all other churches of the Anglican Communion'.

requires bishops to 'respect and maintain the spiritual rights and privileges of all Churches in the Anglican Communion';[132] allows candidates 'from any church in full communion' to be elected as a bishop;[133] or else it requires the church in legislative, doctrinal and liturgical developments to have regard to the effect of these on the Anglican Communion.[134] Similarly, unlike the Church in Wales,[135] some Anglican churches employ *general law* applicable to non-Anglican churches with respect to: recognition and sharing of ministries,[136] admission and reception into church membership,[137] and admission to holy communion.[138]

[132] West Indies, Cans. 8.

[133] Southern Africa, Can. 4(1).

[134] Rwanda, Const. Art. 6.

[135] These matters are dealt with in the Church in Wales, not by general law, but by specific laws operative (in relation to prescribed churches) under the auspices of a covenant, concordat or local ecumenical project: see above.

[136] See e.g. ECUSA, Cans. I.16.2; III.10, 11; see CLAC, 364.

[137] See e.g. Australia, Cans. 1 1985 and 14 1995; England, Can. B28.

[138] See e.g. England, Can. B15A: any baptized member of a another Trinitarian church, in good standing in that church, has a right to holy communion in the Church of England. This is the result of resolutions of the Lambeth Conference: see e.g. LC 1968, Ress. 45, 46: to meet special pastoral needs, and under the direction of the bishop, baptized members of other churches may receive holy communion in Anglican churches; and Anglicans may receive communion in other churches 'as conscience dicates' and if welcomed in that church.

PART V

THE PROPERTY AND FINANCES OF THE CHURCH

13

THE LAW OF CHURCH PROPERTY

The interaction between the law of the Church in Wales and the law of the State is perhaps most evident in relation to church property.[1] The Welsh Church Act 1914 empowers the Church in Wales to frame constitutions and regulations for the property of the church.[2] The Governing Body may legislate on church property.[3] Moreover, the domestic law of the church in relation to any property,[4] held on behalf of the church or its members, is enforceable in the courts of the State.[5] This chapter examines the ownership and administration of real and personal property in the Church in Wales. Since the Church in Wales is an unincorporated association, it lacks capacity under civil law to hold property. As a result property is generally held on behalf of the church, and for its benefit, by the Representative Body, acting as provincial trustee. However, the administration of church property is the responsibility of a host of ecclesiastical authorities, bodies and persons. What follows describes their functions, powers and duties, with regard to the many forms of property: parsonages, parochial church buildings, cathedrals, their fabric and contents, and other ecclesiastical items. The doctrine of Christian stewardship, developed in part by resolutions of the Lambeth Conference,[6] provides a key concept within which rules about the administration of church property may be understood.

THE REPRESENTATIVE BODY

The Welsh Church Act 1914 enables the bishops, clergy and laity of the Church in Wales to appoint persons to represent them and 'hold property for

---

[1] For this interaction concerning the faculty jurisdiction, the use of places for public worship, marriage, and the care and maintenance of churchyards and burial grounds see, respectively, above, Chs. 5, 9, 10, 11.
[2] Welsh Church Act 1914, s. 13(1).
[3] Const. II.33(1).
[4] Welsh Church Act 1914, s. 38(1): '"property" includes all property, real and personal, including things in action and rights of action.'
[5] Welsh Church Act 1914, s. 3(2): this includes pre-1920 ecclesiastical law.
[6] See generally CLAC, Ch. 11.

any of their uses and purposes', and the Crown by charter to incorporate such persons, as a Representative Body.[7] Incorporated by royal charter at disestablishment, the Representative Body is a charitable trust corporation, and holds the legal title to churches, parsonages, and other forms of property,[8] on behalf of the members of the Church in Wales. The Representative Body is subject to such alterations in the numbers of its members, in the rules and regulations laid down for their qualification, election or retirement, or in its powers and duties, as may from time to time be adopted by the Governing Body. This is the case provided always that such rules, regulations and alterations in them do not conflict with the statutory authority, powers and duties of the Representative Body.[9] Like the Church in Wales, many Anglican churches have a centralized system of ownership with property vested in provincial trustees;[10] in some, property is held by diocesan trustees accountable to the diocesan synod,[11] and in others, at the most local level of the church.[12]

Composition and Officers

The Representative Body consists of four classes of member: *ex officio*, elected, co-opted and nominated.[13] The *ex officio* members are: the archbishop and diocesan bishops; the chairman of the Diocesan Board of Finance of each diocese; and the chairman of the Standing Committee of the Governing Body.[14] The elected members are six from each diocese, elected by the Diocesan Conference, four in each case being lay persons and two clerics.[15] The co-opted members, limited to ten, are co-opted by the *ex officio* and elected members of the Representative Body without any regard for dioceses.[16] The nominated members are: six archdeacons, one from each

---

[7] Welsh Church Act 1914, s. 13.

[8] For Welsh Church Act 1914, ss. 4 and 8 and Const. III.20, see below. For the disendowment of the Church of England in Wales, property acquired from the Welsh Commissioners, and legal arrangements for the distribution of property, see R. Brown, 'The disestablishment of the Church in Wales', 5 *ELJ* (1999), 252.

[9] Const. III.39; see COFC, 38 for the Representative Body Committees Casual Vacancy Regulations (1992).

[10] See e.g. Southern Africa, Const. Arts. XVI–XX and Can. 42; see also Ireland, Irish Church Act 1869 and Const. XI.11.

[11] See e.g. New Zealand, Cans. F.I.1, F.III and F.VIII.1. In the Church in Wales, the Diocesan Conference may also manage its own property: Const. IV.22.

[12] In England, as well as property owned at the national level, representative trustees include archbishops, bishops, archdeacons, and incumbents (as corporations sole), and parochial church councils (as corporations aggregate), and churchwardens: see generally, L. Leeder, *Ecclesiastical Law Handbook* (London, 1997), Ch. 8.

[13] Const. III.1; it has seventy-five members.

[14] Const. III.2.

[15] Const. III.3.

[16] Const. III.4.

diocese, nominated by the diocesan bishop after consultation within the diocese; and no more than ten persons nominated by the archbishop and diocesan bishops, acting collectively, without any regard to dioceses.[17] Eligibility for membership depends on whether the person is clerical,[18] or lay.[19]

Elected, co-opted or nominated members cease to be members when they reach the age of seventy-five.[20] Every lay person, before taking their seat, must sign a declaration (in the prescribed form) in a register to be kept for that purpose by the secretary of the Representative Body.[21] Each year, one-third of the members elected by each diocese must retire in rotation. In their place two members must be elected by each diocese to hold office for three years. A cleric must be elected to succeed a cleric and a lay person to succeed a lay person.[22] Co-opted members hold office for a period (not exceeding three years) determined by the Representative Body at the time of their co-option.[23] All members nominated by the archbishop and diocesan bishops hold office for a period (not exceeding three years) determined by the archbishop and bishops at the time of their nomination.[24]

Each Diocesan Conference must make supplemental lists of clerics and lay persons. From these, casual vacancies amongst elected members are filled according to the order in which they appear on the lists.[25] The archbishop and diocesan bishops may fill up a casual vacancy among those members nominated by them. The Representative Body may fill up a casual vacancy

---

[17] Const. III.5.
[18] Const. III.6: every cleric who holds (or has held) a dignity, cathedral preferment, benefice or office within the Church in Wales, or a licence from a Welsh diocesan bishop, is qualified to be a member of the Representative Body. However, no cleric in the full-time salaried employment of the Representative Body, a Diocesan Board of Finance or any other provincial or diocesan body in the church, is eligible to be a member of the Representative Body or any of its committees or subcommittees.
[19] Const. III.7: every lay communicant, over eighteen, is eligible if they either reside (or have resided) at any time for a period of twelve months in a parish which is in Wales, or have been a contributor to the funds of the Church in Wales (within the twelve months preceding the day of his nomination). They are not eligible if they belong to any religious body which is not in communion with the Church in Wales. However, no salaried employee of the Representative Body, a Diocesan Board of Finance or any other provincial or diocesan body within the Church in Wales is eligible to be a member of the Representative Body or any of its committees or subcommittees.
[20] Const. III.8: but if they reach this age during the currency of a meeting of the Representative Body, or any of its committees, membership continues until the termination of the meeting; a meeting adjourned beyond the next day is deemed to be terminated for the purposes of this section.
[21] Const. III.9: they declare their qualification for membership.
[22] Const. III.10: this occurs on 31 December each year.
[23] Const. III.11.
[24] Const. III.12.
[25] Const. III.13: the lists must be made at each annual election.

among those members co-opted by it.[26] Subject to the rules on retirement,[27] a person appointed to fill a casual vacancy holds office until the date when the member whom he replaces would have been due to retire.[28] On retirement, a member is eligible for continued membership, if otherwise duly qualified.[29]

Any member of the Representative Body may be removed for sufficient reason by the Governing Body.[30] A member may also resign from office.[31] The Representative Body must elect triennially from amongst its members a chairman and it may elect a deputy chairman.[32] The Representative Body may appoint and pay a secretary, and such other officers and servants as it deems necessary. Officers and servants may be removed when the Representative Body thinks it proper to do so.[33] Subject to the provisions of the Welsh Church Act 1914, and the charter of incorporation, the Governing Body may alter both the number of members of the Representative Body and the rules relating to their qualifications, election and retirement.[34]

Functions: Powers and Duties

The constitution of the Church in Wales provides a basic framework of functions for the Representative Body: it possesses and exercises any power conferred on it by the Governing Body,[35] and the latter may alter the powers and duties of the Representative Body.[36] The Representative Body holds all property, which becomes vested in it, 'in trust for the uses and purposes of the Archbishop, Bishops, Clergy, and Laity of the Church in Wales', and for other special trusts, pursuant to the provisions of the Welsh Church Act 1914.[37] All property vested in it is held by the Representative Body on these

---

[26] Const. III.14: it must also fill up a casual vacancy among the elected members from the supplemental lists; in the latter case, it must appoint a cleric to succeed a cleric and a lay person to succeed a lay person.

[27] That is, the rule in Const. III.8.

[28] Const. III.15.

[29] Const. III.16.

[30] Const. III.17: the Governing Body is final judge of what is a sufficient reason; see also Const. II.56(1) and (2).

[31] Const. III.18: by written notice addressed to the secretary of the Representative Body.

[32] Const. III.19: in the chairman's absence, the deputy chairman must preside at meetings of the Representative Body; if neither the chairman nor the deputy chairman is present at the meeting, the Representative Body must elect some other member to preside at that meeting.

[33] Const. III.34: the secretary must be a communicant of the Church in Wales or of any church in communion with it.

[34] Const. II.56(1).

[35] Const. III.29. Many of the following constitutional rules are taken from the royal charter of incorporation.

[36] Const. II.56(1): but this is subject to the Welsh Church Act 1914 and the charter of incorporation.

[37] Const. III.20; the following vest in the Representative Body: churches, ecclesiastical residences, and chattels held with them, funds, endowments allocated to work on the

trusts 'subject to its statutory authority, powers, and duties under the order and control of the Governing Body'.[38] The Representative Body is also subject to the jurisdiction of the courts of the State,[39] though it may bring, defend, or compromise any action, and may take any step or engage any legal or other assistance necessary for such purpose.[40]

Investments   All monies held by the Representative Body in trust for the Church in Wales, or for any purpose connected with it, may be invested in prescribed items.[41] On a sale of any land vested in the Representative Body,[42] the net proceeds of sale[43] must be held and invested or reinvested as capital. The net proceeds cannot be expended as income, unless this is authorized by a canon enacted in accordance with bill procedure.[44] The Representative Body may lend money on the security of any property.[45] It may also retain, temporarily or permanently, any investments by gift or legacy vested in it in

fabric of these, and private benefactions (these were all transferred to the Body by the Welsh Commissioners: Welsh Church Act 1914, s. 8(1)(a)); all plate, furniture and other movable chattels belonging to the churches in Wales, or used in connection with the celebration of divine worship, and not belonging to private individuals, were vested directly in the Body (Welsh Church Act 1914, s. 4(2)).

[38]   Const. III.21.

[39]   See *Welsh Church Commissioners v Representative Body of the Church in Wales* [1940] 3 All ER 1(CA); *Representative Body of the Church in Wales v Tithe Redemption Commission* [1944] AC 228 and [1944] 1 All ER 710 (HL); *Powell v Representative Body of the Church in Wales* [1957] 1 All ER 400. Whether the Representative Body is a public authority for the purposes of the Human Rights Act 1998 is a matter which has not been treated by the courts of the State.

[40]   Const. III.35; III.36: the Representative Body must have a Common Seal, and must execute documents by affixing the seal to them in the presence of the secretary (see below), or assistant secretary of the Representative Body, or the Legal Assistant to the secretary of the Representative Body and one member of the Body; the Body must provide for the safe custody of the seal which may be used only by the authority of the Body.

[41]   Const. III.23(1): namely, the purchase (or upon the security) of: freehold land in England or Wales; a perpetual rent charge(s) issuing out of land in England or Wales; the whole (or part) of any annuity or other sum payable to any holder (or former holder) of any ecclesiastical office whose interest was commuted under the Welsh Church Act 1914; stocks, funds, securities or other property on which trustees are authorized by law to invest trust monies (other than Irish investments); and any other stocks, funds, securities or property whatsoever. However, under III.23(2), no money can be invested in any stocks, funds, securities or other investment in bearer form or transferable by delivery with or without endorsement, with the exception of American and other overseas investments.

[42]   Being and representing glebe land or repurchased glebe land transferred to the Representative Body pursuant to the Welsh Church Act 1914.

[43]   And the property from time to time representing this. See below, Ch. 14 for the Church Fabric and Churchyard Maintenance Fund.

[44]   Const. III.22(1): this provision can be altered, amended or abrogated only by bill procedure (III.22(2)).

[45]   Const. III.23(3): it can properly lend up to the full value of the property, and may contract that such money must not be called in during any period of years.

trust for the Church in Wales, or any purpose connected with it.[46] Subject to any directions to the contrary given by the Governing Body, the Representative Body may raise money on mortgage, or otherwise, on the security of any property vested in it.[47] No member of the Representative Body is liable for any loss occasioned by the depreciation or failure of any investment, or otherwise, unless this is caused by the wilful default of the member.[48] The Investment Subcommittee of the Finance and Resources Committee of the Representative Body manages all investments of the Church in Wales.[49]

Sales, Exchanges, Leases and Management   The Representative Body may sell, exchange, lease and manage all real and personal property vested in it. However, in certain cases, the powers of sale or exchange cannot be exercised unless authorized by a resolution of a majority of the Representative Body, present and voting, and assented to (in writing) by the bishop of the diocese in which the property is situated.[50] The Representative Body cannot sell or exchange, lease or dispose of other prescribed classes of property unless authorized by a resolution of three-quarters of the members of the Finance and Resources Committee of the Representative Body, present and voting, and assented to in writing by the bishop of the diocese in which the property is situated.[51] All other powers of the Representative Body, to lease and manage, must be exercised only in the manner determined, and in accordance with rules and regulations made, by the Governing Body.[52]

---

[46] Const. III.23(4): this may be done notwithstanding that the same are not investments for the time being authorized under the constitution; the Representative Body may similarly retain all or any investments made or purporting to be made under or by virtue of its power of investment.

[47] Const. III.24: it cannot do so, however, with regard to: churches and sites for churches; funds and endowments specially allocated to the repair, restoration or improvement of any church; and plate, furniture or other moveable chattels belonging to any church. It may also apply money so raised to any purposes to which money under its control might for the time being be applied.

[48] Const. III.25.

[49] COFC, 28: church buildings are excluded.

[50] Const. III.26(a): namely, in relation to plate, furniture or other movable chattel (for exceptions see below) belonging to, or used in connection with the celebration of divine worship in any church, episcopal or capitular lands, glebes or sites for churches (see below), episcopal or glebe houses, ecclesiastical residences or any movable chattel held or enjoyed with or incident to the occupation of any such residence, or any school house or any land occupied with these.

[51] Const. III.26(b): namely, any consecrated site, or any church or building erected on it; this also applies to the disposal of ornaments, vessels or instruments used in connection with any of the sacraments.

[52] Const. III.26(c); III.26(d): any person or body of persons in the diocese where such property is situated may make representation to the Representative Body requesting it to take action under these provisions.

Miscellaneous Powers   The Representative Body may at any time appoint (at its expense) an architect or surveyor to obtain a report on any property vested in it. The architect or surveyor is entitled to inspect any such property on giving reasonable notice to its occupier.[53] The Representative Body may provide for premises in order to carry out its functions.[54] The Governing Body has a similar power.[55] Moreover, the Representative Body may reduce any stipend or grant payable by it on giving three months' previous notice, if at any time adverse circumstances affecting the revenue of the Representative Body make that reduction necessary.[56]

Proceedings and Committees

There must be at least one ordinary meeting of the Representative Body in every year, its place and date appointed by the Representative Body.[57] The chairman may call a special meeting on giving not less than fourteen days' previous written notice to the members.[58] The Representative Body may determine how many members present form a quorum, and it may make rules to regulate its procedure.[59]

The Finance and Resources Committee of the Representative Body is to: carry out the executive functions of the Representative Body; review resources and their deployment in consultation with the Standing Committee of the Governing Body;[60] formulate an annual provincial budget;[61] and prepare and submit the annual accounts of the Representative Body.[62] Subject to the

---

[53] Const. III.27.
[54] Const. III.28: namely, such houses, offices and other buildings or accommodation necessary for the purpose of: its meetings; a residence for its officers and servants; a safe place of custody for its securities, books, accounts, or other documents; it may also pay rent, insurance, and all other expenses caused by its providing such houses or offices, or which may otherwise be necessary.
[55] Const. II.78.
[56] Const. III.33; see below, Ch. 14.
[57] Const. III.37.
[58] Const. III.38: if there is no chairman, or the chairman is incapacitated or absent from the British Isles, the special meeting may be called by the deputy chairman.
[59] Const. III.30; III.31: if any diocese fails to elect or return members (clerical or lay), or to make and return supplemental lists, or if the Representative Body fails to exercise its powers to co-opt or fill vacancies, these do not prevent the Representative Body from dispatching business nor do they invalidate its proceedings; the same applies if the archbishop and diocesan bishops acting collectively fail to exercise their powers to nominate or fill vacancies.
[60] This is to effect the purposes of the archbishop, bishops, clergy and laity of the Church in Wales.
[61] This is for presentation to the Standing Committee of the Governing Body for approval; the budget must relate the total available financial resources to the policy and priorities decided upon by the Standing Committee.
[62] Const. III.32(1): the committee is mandatory; its membership consists of Representative Body members.

overall control of the Representative Body, the Finance and Resources Committee has a number of powers to transact its business.[63] The Representative Body may appoint such subcommittees of the Finance and Resources Committee as it deems fit.[64] When it appoints the Finance and Resources Committee, when this committee delegates executive functions to working groups and subcommittees, and when the Representative Body appoints subcommittees of the Finance and Resources Committee, the Representative Body must consult the Standing Committee of the Governing Body.[65]

The Representative Body may appoint further committees of its members, and make rules and regulations for their powers and procedures. However, all acts and decisions of any committee, unless previously specifically authorized, must be ratified and confirmed by the Representative Body to become valid.[66] In addition to the Audit Group,[67] the Finance and Resources Committee is responsible to the Representative Body for seven subcommittees on: maintenance of ministry,[68] property,[69] churches, investment, bishops' residences and expenses, staff and services, and cathedrals and churches.[70]

PARSONAGES

Few churches in the Anglican Communion possess formal law on clergy residences; those that do sometimes contain a right to housing,[71] and usually a duty to maintain the residence is placed on the occupying cleric.[72] In the Church in Wales,[73] a parsonage is any dwelling house held by the Represen-

---

[63] Const. III.32(2): it is empowered: to regulate its own procedures; to appoint working groups and subcommittees of its members; to co-opt, from time to time as it deems fit, any person or persons to serve on these working groups or subcommittees; and to delegate executive functions to these working groups and subcommittees.

[64] Const. III.32(3).

[65] Const. III.32(4).

[66] Const. III.32(5).

[67] COFC, 27: this reviews, in advance of meetings, budgets and plans, management accounts, financial accounts and annual audit letter together with long-term financial projections.

[68] See below, Ch. 14; this has a Provincial Housing Fund Group which deals with such matters as clergy loans.

[69] This is responsible for the Isla Johnston Trust which may award grants to eligible applicants under the terms of the trust.

[70] See COFC, 26–37 for the composition and functions of these subcommittees.

[71] See e.g. Ireland, Const. IV.51.5: the incumbent, vicar or curate's assistant is 'entitled to the enjoyment of a free residence'.

[72] See e.g. England, Parsonages Measure 1938 and Repair of Benefice Buildings Measure 1972: the 'proper care of the parsonage house, being a duty equivalent to that of a tenant, [is] to use the premises in a tenant-like manner'; Diocesan Parsonage Boards must organize quinquennial inspections; see generally CLAC, 316.

[73] Dioceses commonly produce guidance for clergy on parsonages: see e.g. DM, YB (2000), 30–1 (e.g. the fabric is insured by the Representative Body, but insurance does

tative Body which is required to be occupied by any dean, canon, incumbent, curate, or any holder of an ecclesiastical office in the Church in Wales.[74] When a house is no longer required to be occupied by these, it ceases to be a parsonage and the Parsonage Board's responsibility for its maintenance terminates.[75] Special provisions apply to the designation by the bishop of a house as the parsonage in the case of a grouping of parishes under one incumbent.[76]

The Diocesan Parsonage Board

The Finance Board of the diocese must appoint a Diocesan Parsonage Board which is: to have the general oversight of parsonages in the diocese and of any buildings or land annexed to them;[77] and to see that any repairs or work duly authorized to be done concerning parsonages, buildings or land are properly carried out.[78] The Diocesan Parsonage Board must conform to the directions and be under the control of the Representative Body.[79] The latter must give from time to time to each Parsonage Board such directions as appear to it to be necessary for the due maintenance and repair of any parsonage situated in the diocese for which that Board is responsible.[80] The Provincial Court may determine any dispute between a member of the Church in Wales and a Diocesan Parsonage Board.[81]

The Parsonage Board consists of not less than six members, with an equal number of clergy and laity,[82] and must meet as often as necessary and when

---

not cover goods, chattels or other private property, nor the public liability of individuals).

[74] Const. X.1(d): it includes deaneries, canons' houses, rectories, vicarages, minor canonries and curates' houses, together with any buildings adjudged to be within the curtilage of these and not excluded by a determination of the Diocesan Parsonage Board with the approval of the Representative Body.

[75] Const. X, Supplementary Regulations (hereafter, SR), r.1 (see below for exceptions).

[76] Const. X, SR, r.2: the bishop must do so after consultation with the Diocesan Parsonage Board. The diocesan registrar must immediately inform the Parsonage Board and the Representative Body of the bishop's decision. The bishop must also decide, after consultation with the Diocesan Parsonage Board, whether a house within the group is required to be occupied by an assistant curate or by any holder of an ecclesiastical office in the Church in Wales. Should the bishop decide that a house is to be so occupied, the Diocesan Registrar must inform the Diocesan Parsonage Board and the Representative Body of the bishop's decision.

[77] Const. IV.19(a): its oversight of the parsonage, buildings or land (other than farm buildings and land), includes their sanitary conditions and surroundings.

[78] Const. IV.19(b).

[79] Const. IV.21.

[80] Const. X.13.

[81] Const. XI.6(d): it may also determine a dispute between the board and the bodies listed in this subsection.

[82] Const. IV.20: these must be qualified to be, but need not be, members of the Diocesan Conference; the board holds office for three years from the date of its appointment.

required by the Representative Body.[83] The board must elect a chairman who summons its meetings.[84] The chairman, or in the chairman's absence, a member of the board elected by the meeting, presides and has a second or casting vote.[85] The necessary and reasonable cost of administration of the board, including salaries if necessary, must be paid out of the Diocesan Parsonage Board Account.[86] The board must, subject to the approval of the Diocesan Board of Finance,[87] appoint a secretary who must, on the instructions of the chairman, convene and send out the agenda for meetings.[88] The secretary, or in his absence a member of the board, must keep a minute of the proceedings.[89] Subject to the approval of the Representative Body, the board must settle its own procedure, and it may act by committee and decide the number of members for a quorum.[90] It must make a yearly written report to the Representative Body,[91] and the latter must keep for each diocese a separate Parsonage Board Account.[92]

Diocesan Inspectors and Parsonage Inspection

On the recommendation of the Diocesan Parsonage Board, the Representative Body must appoint one or more diocesan inspectors.[93] These are servants of the Representative Body which must fix their tenure of office, duties and remuneration.[94] Inspectors must send the Representative Body copies of all reports made by them (during the previous quarter) to the board.[95] The inspector must make a survey of each parsonage (including its interior decorations) when necessary, but at least quinquennially, and imme-

---

[83] Const. X.2; the Property Subcommittee of the Finance and Resources Committee of the Representative Body deals with parsonages.
[84] Const. X.3.
[85] Const. X.4.
[86] Const. X.5: the Diocesan Parsonage Board account is the fund held by the Representative Body for the benefit of the diocese concerned under X.12 (X.1(e)).
[87] See below, Ch. 14.
[88] Const. X.6.
[89] Const. X.7.
[90] Const. X.8.
[91] Const. X.9.
[92] Const. X.12: the Diocesan Board of Finance and the Representative Body must each contribute to the account such amount as the body may from time to time determine by regulation under the Maintenance of Ministry Scheme for the time being in force; see below, Ch. 14 for the Maintenance of Ministry Scheme.
[93] Const. X.10; each inspector is appointed for the diocese in which the parsonage is situated or, if more than one is appointed, the diocesan inspector is the inspector directed by the Representative Body to act for that part of the diocese in which the parsonage concerned is situated (X.1(b)).
[94] Const. X.10; see also X.41: the appointment ceases when the inspector reaches sixty-five, unless the board then recommends an extension of engagement for a period not exceeding five years.
[95] Const. X.11: this must be done 'on the usual quarter days'.

diately on the occurrence of a vacancy. The inspector must send a copy of the report to the incumbent.[96] A special survey may be ordered by the Representative Body at any time. The inspector must send his report direct to the Representative Body, and may at any time report direct to that body. A copy of the report must also be sent to the Diocesan Parsonage Board.[97] The board may appoint any one or more of its members to accompany the inspector on any survey.[98]

The Maintenance of the Parsonage

Unless granted a licence of non-residence by the bishop, the incumbent must reside in the parsonage.[99] The parsonage is held by the incumbent on a number of conditions.[100] The incumbent must pay all rates, charges, taxes and outgoings in respect of the parsonage.[101] The incumbent cannot let or part with possession of the parsonage (nor any part of it), except with the written consent of the Representative Body. The incumbent is responsible for the interior decoration and must keep and maintain the interior in good decorative condition to the satisfaction of the Parsonage Board.[102] The incumbent is responsible for the results of any negligence and wilful damage done to the parsonage.[103] The incumbent must keep parsonage hedges in good order,[104] must not cut down any tree without the written consent of the archdeacon or inspector, and must not make any structural alteration or addition to the parsonage or its permanent fittings without the consent of the board.[105]

The Parsonage Board may order structural work to be done as it deems

---

[96] Const. X.14.

[97] Const. X.15.

[98] Const. X.16.

[99] Const. X.17. This duty to reside generates a corresponding right to possession of the parsonage. XI.17: the duty does not apply if the incumbent is in non-stipendiary ministry.

[100] Const. X.17(a) to (g). 'Incumbent' means: a dean, canon, incumbent, curate, or any holder of an ecclesiastical office in the church; in a vacancy due to the preferment or retirement of the incumbent, it also means the former or outgoing incumbent; in a vacancy on the death of the incumbent, it means his or her personal representatives.

[101] But not fire insurance premiums, private street improvements, and other extraordinary expenses.

[102] In assessing the extent of the responsibility, the board must take into account the age and size of the parsonage. Interior decoration means: painting, papering, colouring and whitewashing, and includes the painting of all interior woodwork usually so treated. On the institution of a new incumbent, the inspector must make a general record of the interior decoration of the parsonage for purposes of future reference. The inspector must send a copy of the record to the incoming incumbent.

[103] This is the case if the negligence is by him, his household, family or tenants; liability is for wilful damage done or allowed to be done by him to any part (including the garden) of the parsonage. See below for proceedings.

[104] That is, those which form part of or belong to the parsonage. The board may make a grant towards the cost of this out of the Diocesan Parsonage Board Account.

[105] The incumbent must permit the Representative Body, the board and their authorized

necessary.[106] The board must from time to time specify the maximum sum which an incumbent may incur on urgent necessary repairs carried out by him.[107] During a vacancy in an incumbency (or where a parsonage in a suspended incumbency is vacant), the area dean and churchwardens of the parish are the custodians for the parsonage. They are responsible for the care of the parsonage, but not for those matters in the responsibility of the Parsonage Board.[108] The custodians are not responsible for making good the results of any failure by the former incumbent to comply with responsibilities for interior decoration, nor for the results of any negligence or wilful damage by the former incumbent, his household or family.[109]

Proceedings for Neglect and Wilful Damage

The results of neglect or wilful damage to the parsonage by the incumbent, his household, family or tenants, must be set out in the inspector's report. The inspector must send a copy of the report to the incumbent.[110] When, within a fortnight of receiving the report, the incumbent gives written notice to the Parsonage Board that he objects to it, and desires to appear before the board, the incumbent may attend the meeting of the board at which the report is discussed.[111] If he gives no notice of objection, the incumbent is deemed to have accepted the report. When in possession of the parsonage, the incumbent

inspectors, contractors, servants, agents or workmen, to enter the parsonage, at any time after reasonable notice, to view the general condition of the parsonage and to make estimates for and carry out repairs.

[106] Const. X.27: it may also order sanitary and other improvements and additions as is in accordance with the practice of good estate management; the cost must be defrayed out of the Diocesan Parsonage Board Account, but the board must not be the agents of, or entitled to pledge the credit of, the Representative Body.

[107] Const. X.28: the cost of this (not exceeding the specified sum) must be repaid to the incumbent by the Representative Body (on certificate of the inspector) and be charged to the Diocesan Parsonage Board Account; the incumbent must notify the inspector of such repairs within one month of their execution.

[108] Const. X.39: to discharge their reponsibilities, the custodians may defray the reasonable costs at an average rate of expenditure for the period of the vacancy, not exceeding such weekly rate as the Diocesan Board of Finance may determine. The amount expended must be refunded by the Representative Body on production of a statement of account with receipts for payment made by the custodians. The amount refunded must be charged against the Maintenance of Ministry Fund for the diocese concerned.

[109] Const. X.39: the custodians must: take precautions for the prevention of trespass; they must ensure that: the water, gas and electric services are cut off at the main; in frosty weather the water is drained from cisterns and pipes; gutters and drain-pipes are kept clear; from time to time the house is aired; and, if necessary, fires are lighted; and do what is practicable to prevent the garden from becoming a wilderness; if the parsonage is damaged by storms or other causes, the custodians must notify the diocesan inspector immediately.

[110] Const. X.18: the report must include an estimate of the amount required to rectify it.

[111] Const. X.19: notice must be given to the board's secretary; the incumbent must be

must carry out to the satisfaction of the board the repairs specified in the report within three months of the report. If he fails to do so, the board may order the work to be done.[112] In all other cases the board may order the work to be done as the board thinks fit.[113]

If the incumbent gives notice of objection but fails to attend the meeting, the notice is null and void, unless the board determines otherwise.[114] When the incumbent gives notice of objection and meets the board, but fails to reach agreement, the dispute must be referred to an arbitrator appointed by the bishop.[115] The arbitrator must give the parties an opportunity to state their case and appear before him if they so wish; subject to this, the arbitrator must settle the method and procedure to determine the dispute.[116] The award of the arbitrator is final and conclusive. The arbitrator may decide how and by whom the costs of the arbitration and award are to be paid.[117] Anyone dissatisfied with the award as to costs may appeal to the diocesan chancellor whose decision is final.[118] Any sum the incumbent agrees or is adjudged liable to pay, is a debt due by him to the Representative Body.[119]

Termination of Possession of the Parsonage

The incumbent must deliver up possession of the parsonage to the Representative Body on: (i) the determination of the incumbency; (ii) the expiration of a two months' notice to quit at any time served on him by the Representative Body; or (iii) the expiration of fourteen days' notice served on him by the Representative Body if the incumbent has failed or neglected to fulfil any of the conditions on which he holds the parsonage.[120] Any dispute between the Representative Body and the incumbent in the case of (iii) must be referred to the diocesan bishop. The decision of the bishop is final. The bishop may extend the time for delivering up possession provided that the

---

given notice of the meeting; the attention of the incumbent should be called to this rule when the copy of the report is sent to him.
[112] Const. X.20(1): the cost of the work is a debt due by the incumbent to the Representative Body and may be set off against any sum due or to become due by it to the incumbent.
[113] Const. X.20(2): the cost must be charged against the Parsonage Board Account. The cost is a debt due by the incumbent to the Representative Body. It may be set off against any sum due or to become due by it to the incumbent. The amount so recovered must be credited to the Parsonage Board Account.
[114] Const. X.21.
[115] Const. X.22.
[116] Const. X.23.
[117] Const. X.24.
[118] Const. X.25.
[119] Const. X.26: it may be set off against any sum due or to become due by it to the incumbent. The Provincial Housing Subcommittee has a fund to provide loans for clerics who wish to purchase property in which to live following retirement.
[120] Const. X.17(h): in (iii), the notice must state that it is given on that ground.

date for doing so is not later than three months after the service of the notice to quit.[121] If the incumbent fails to deliver up possession, the Representative Body may resume possession of the parsonage and remove from it any property belonging to the incumbent.[122]

If an incumbent dies during occupation of the parsonage, the personal representatives must be permitted to allow the incumbent's widow or widower, parent, sister or children to remain in the parsonage for two months from the death.[123] However, the personal representatives may apply to the bishop for an extension of the period. The bishop may grant an extension of not more than one month. Any dispute between the Representative Body and a personal representative, concerning occupation, must be settled by the diocesan bishop whose decision is final. If the personal representatives do not allow the relatives to continue in occupation, the bishop (or archdeacon if authorized by the bishop) may allow them to remain for a period not exceeding two months from the death. However, if the relatives apply, the bishop may grant an extension of not more than one month.[124] Disputes as to fixtures must be settled by an arbitrator agreed on by the parties (including the Representative Body); if they cannot agree, the arbitrator is to be appointed by the bishop.[125]

The Purchase, Sale and Leasing of Parsonages

Purchase and Sale   Subject to the control of the Diocesan Board of Finance and the Representative Body, it is the duty of the Parsonage Board to carry out preliminary negotiations in connection with: the sale of a parsonage or a site reserved for a parsonage; the gift or purchase of a parsonage or a site for a parsonage; and the building of a new parsonage.[126] On recommendations of the Parsonage Board and the Diocesan Board of Finance, the Representative Body may make grants for the purchase of a parsonage or parsonage site, or the building or rebuilding of a parsonage. Grants may be made in one sum or annually from the Diocesan Parsonage Board Account or the Diocesan Parsonage Improvement Fund.[127] Also, if a parish contributes towards the installation of central heating in a parsonage, the Diocesan Board of Finance may recommend a refund.[128]

---

[121] Const. X.17(i).
[122] Const. X.17(j).
[123] Const. X.17(k): this is subject to the performance and observance by the personal representatives of the conditions to which the incumbent would have been subject if then living: see above.
[124] Const. X.17(k): the same applies if a person (not a relation) resides there at the time of the death.
[125] Const. X.17(l): ss. 23–5 then apply to the arbitrator.
[126] Const. X.29; see also III.26: the decision to sell belongs to the Representative Body.
[127] Const. X.30.
[128] Const. X.38: the board may do so if: the parsonage is declared redundant and sold within five years of installation; and the proceeds of sale are to be credited to the Diocesan

No building of a parsonage may be commenced without the written con-sent of the Parsonage Board.[129] During construction, the Diocesan Inspector (or representative) may enter the premises to ascertain whether the work is being carried out in accordance with the plans and specifications approved by the board.[130] When a new parsonage is acquired and the former parsonage has not previously been sold or let, the incumbent and churchwardens are the custodians of the former parsonage.[131] If a house in a group of parishes is not required for the incumbent, assistant curate or any other office-holder, it is deemed to be redundant. The Diocesan Board of Finance must then recom-mend whether it be sold or let.[132] Pending the sale or letting of a redundant house, the incumbent of the group and the churchwardens of the parish in which it is situated, are the custodians.[133] When a parsonage is vacated by an incumbent on a notice to quit,[134] and it is decided that the house be sold or demolished, the house ceases to be a parsonage. The Diocesan Parsonage Board ceases to be responsible for its maintenance.[135] Sales by auction of par-sonage furniture are not permitted.[136]

Parsonage Improvement Fund. The maximum amount of the refund shall be the parochial contribution reduced by 20 per cent for each complete year since installation.

[129] Const. X.32: XI.31: plans and specifications of new parsonages, and any subsequent alterations to the plans, must be submitted to the Parsonage Board for approval.

[130] Const. X.33; X.34: subject to the approval of the Representative Body, the board may determine that any farm building, cottage or parcel of land within the curtilage shall cease to be a part of the parsonage; X.35: the board may order the demolition of such buildings it deems to be unnecessary or the conversion of such buildings or a part of them for other purposes; X.36: the cost of necessary repairs to a boundary wall or fence between the parsonage and land belonging to the Representative Body, must be shared equally between the board and the Representative Body.

[131] Const. X, Supplementary Regulations (hereafter, SR), r.6: they must perform the duties prescribed in r.4; in the event of damage by storms they must notify the secretary of the Representative Body immediately; they are entitled to be refunded the reasonable costs (at an average rate not exceeding a weekly rate determined by the Diocesan Board of Finance for the period up to the date when the former parsonage is either sold or let). The Representative Body may recover the amount so refunded out of the proceeds of sale or letting.

[132] Const. X, SR, 3: the recommendation must be approved by the Representative Body or its appropriate committee.

[133] Const. X, SR, 4; Const. X.37: the proceeds of a sale or letting of a parsonage which has become redundant as a result of a grouping of parishes, must be placed to the credit of the Diocesan Parsonage Improvement Fund; if, as a consequence of any rearrange-ment in regard to a group of parishes, it becomes necessary to provide a new parsonage in place of one that had been sold, an appropriate part of the cost must be deemed to be a charge upon the available resources of the Diocesan Parsonage Improvement Fund.

[134] Under Const. X.17(h).

[135] Const. X, SR, r.7: the decision to sell or demolish is made on the recommendation of the Diocesan Parsonage Board and the Diocesan Board of Finance. However, if notice to quit is given to enable major works of reconstruction, the responsibilities of the Parsonage Board continue; during the period when the house is not available for occupa-tion, the contributions of the Diocesan Board of Finance and the Representative Body continue.

[136] Const. X.17(m).

Leasing[137] With the consent of the Representative Body, the Parsonage Board may divide a parsonage into two or more dwelling houses.[138] Where such a house is let to a person who does not hold an ecclesiastical office in the Church in Wales, the rent must be fixed by the Representative Body.[139] Where it is required that such a house be occupied by the holder of an ecclesiastical office, no rent can be charged.[140] If the occupier is an assistant curate of the parish, the Representative Body may make a reasonable deduction from the grant assigned by it in respect of the curacy.[141] Any other matter in connection with the division of a parsonage not specifically provided for by the constitution, must be determined by the Representative Body.[142] When the parsonage is let by the Representative Body due to a lengthy vacancy in the incumbency, and under the lease the tenant is not responsible for exterior repairs, the Parsonage Board continues to be responsible for it.[143]

CHURCH BUILDINGS IN THE PARISH

In addition to oversight of stewardship through visitation and the faculty jurisdiction,[144] the law of the Church in Wales provides a complex regime for the care of parochial church buildings. In this respect it is very like other Anglican churches.[145] Under the law of the State, an ecclesiastical building which is used for ecclesiastical purposes is exempt from the need for listed building consent.[146] The ecclesiastical exemption applies to buildings of the

---

[137] See above for leasing by the incumbent (under Const. 17(b)), and by the Representative Body (under Const. III.26).

[138] Const. X.40(1): the cost of division (or a part of it) may, if the Diocesan Board of Finance also concurs, be charged against the Diocesan Parsonage Improvement Fund; see also Const. X.1(g): this is a fund set aside by the Representative Body for the benefit of a diocese, from which grants may be made towards the cost of new parsonages or for improvments to existing parsonages in the diocese concerned.

[139] Const. X.40(2): the proceeds of letting must be credited to the Diocesan Parsonage Improvement Fund; but, where the major portion of the cost of division comes from sources other than the Diocesan Parsonage Improvement Fund, the Representative Body may make other arrangements as to proceeds of letting.

[140] Const. X.40(3): and the provisions of Const. X apply.

[141] Const. X.40(3).

[142] Const. X.40(4).

[143] Const. X, SR, r.5: in this case it is let on the recommendation of the Parsonage Board; the appropriate contributions to the Parsonage Board Account continue to be paid; the net proceeds of the letting must be credited to the Diocesan Parsonage Improvement Fund.

[144] For visitation see above, Ch. 8 and for faculties above, Ch. 5.

[145] Whilst ownership vests in a variety of ecclesiastical trustees, responsibility for the day-to-day care and maintenance is assigned to parishes (or their equivalents), their clergy and councils: see CLAC, 308ff.

[146] Planning (Listed Buildings and Conservation Areas) Act 1990, s. 60(1). Although 'ecclesiastical building' is not defined, clergy residences are expressly excluded (s. 60(3)). Ecclesiastical purposes have been understood as denoting use for corporate worship and

Church in Wales vested in the Representative Body,[147] and its continued enjoyment depends on the church having in place a satisfactory internal system of control.[148]

The Diocesan Churches and Pastoral Committee

In each diocese there must be a Diocesan Churches and Pastoral Committee.[149] It consists of: the archdeacons of the diocese; the chairman or vice-chairman (if any) of the Diocesan Board of Finance; the chairman of the Diocesan Advisory Committee or another member nominated by him; three members elected by the Diocesan Conference from its own membership; and three members appointed by the diocesan bishop.[150] The committee may appoint suitably qualified persons to act as consultants.[151] The chairman must be appointed from its members by the diocesan bishop.[152] The committee may appoint subcommittees, must meet at least twice a year, and must decide its own procedure. It must also appoint a secretary who shall not be a member of the committee.[153]

The duties of the committee are: (1) to keep under review the pastoral need

---

this may extend to any purpose which church authorities consider likely to foster Christian fellowship: *AG ex rel Bedfordshire County Council v Howard United Reformed Church Trustees, Bedford* [1975] 2 All ER 337 (HL). Listed building consent is not required for the alteration or extension of a listed ecclesiastical building used for ecclesiastical purposes.

[147] Ecclesiastical Exemption (Listed Buildings and Conservation Areas) Order 1994, SI 1994/1771, arts. 4, 5: namely, any church building; any object or structure within a church building; any object or structure fixed to the exterior of a church building; or any object or structure within the curtilage of a church building which, although not fixed to that building, forms part of the land. (The curtilage is in effect an integral part of the church: it is such part of the churchyard which physically adjoins the church as is required to form some necessary or useful purpose of the church building: see Halsbury, para. 1308, n. 3.)

[148] The system must be approved by the State which may restrict or exclude particular buildings or categories from the exemption: Planning (Listed Buildings and Conservation Areas) Act 1990, s. 60(5).

[149] Constitution of Diocesan Churches and Pastoral Committees (hereafter CDCPC), s. 1.

[150] CDCPC, s. 2; s. 3: the members elected by the conference and those appointed by the bishop must hold office for six years and are eligible for re-election without limit on the number of terms served; the membership of a cleric ceases at the age of seventy and that of a lay member at seventy-five; s. 4: when a casual vacancy occurs the diocesan bishop must, after consultation with the Standing Committee of the conference, appoint a member of the Diocesan Conference to fill the vacancy; the appointee holds office only for the unexpired period of the term of office of the person whom they replace.

[151] CDCPC, s. 5.

[152] CDCPC, s. 6: the chairman holds office for three years, and is eligible for reappointment without limit on the number of terms served; in his absence the other members present must elect a chairman for the meeting.

[153] CDCPC, ss. 6–10: quorum for the committee and subcommittees is one-half of the number of its members.

for the church buildings in the diocese, and advise the bishop and the Diocesan Conference accordingly; (2) to administer the scheme for quin-quennial inspection of churches (see below); (3) to carry out its functions under the Redundant Churches Regulations (see below); (4) to advise the Diocesan Board of Finance (and any other body or person having disposable funds) on the disbursement of grants and loans for any purpose connected with church buildings, their curtilages and contents; (5) to give effect to any other provisions relating to the care of churches as may from time to time be prescribed;[154] (6) to consider matters referred to it by the Diocesan Advisory Committee, and seek its advice when appropriate; and (7) to carry out such other duties as may properly be required of it by the Diocesan Conference.[155]

The Fabric and Contents of the Church Building

Consecration   A building does not in law become a church until conse-crated.[156] Consecration is a discretion which vests in the bishop.[157] By the act or sentence of consecration, signed by the bishop,[158] buildings and land are dedicated to God in *sacros usus*, separated for ever from the common uses of humankind,[159] or until the decree is set aside, or its effects extinguished, by a competent authority.[160] Legal title to the ground on which a church is to be erected must have been secured,[161] and when consecrated the property ceas-es to be that of the donor.[162] While there are limits on permitting property for secular uses, nothing may be done which is inconsistent with the sanctity of the place.[163] Consecration brings property and its contents within the faculty jurisdiction.[164]

---

[154] That is, as prescribed in a schedule to CDCPC.

[155] CDCPC, s. 11. The Cathedrals and Churches Commission also plays an advisory role with regard to parochial churches (see below).

[156] 3 Co Inst 203; there is no necessity for the consecration of a churchyard: see Halsbury, para. 1068.

[157] *Segwick v Bourne* [1920] 2 KB 267: consecration is an exercise of spiritual office, and its validity cannot be questioned in State courts; see also *R v Tiverton Burial Board* (1858) 6 WR 662.

[158] Consecration of Churches Act 1867 and the Consecration of Churchyards Act 1867: additional ground adjacent to a churchyard may also be consecrated.

[159] *Wright v Ingle* (1885) 16 QBD 379 at 399 (CA).

[160] See Halsbury, para. 1069.

[161] *St Mary, Bishopstoke* (1909) 26 TLR 86.

[162] *Hilcoat v Archbishops of Canterbury and York* (1850) 10 CB 327 at 347.

[163] *Wood v Headingley-cum-Burley Burial Board* [1892] 1 QB 713, 725. The Church in Wales seem to have no formal law on this; compare e.g. England, Can. F16, concerning permissions for public performances.

[164] See above, Ch. 5. See also *Vicar of St John the Baptist, Cardiff v Parishioners of St John the Baptist, Cardiff* [1898] P 155: a faculty for a footpath (for the use of parish-ioners and the public), across the closed churchyard was granted subject to closure of the path one day a year to show it still remained integral to the churchyard.

Necessities for Divine Service   It is the duty of the churchwardens, at the expense of the parish, to provide the necessary requisites for divine service, including: a prayer book and bible,[165] a cloth for the communion table,[166] communion wine and bread,[167] a font,[168] a decent pulpit,[169] and books for the registration of baptisms and burials.[170] The keys of the church are under the control of the incumbent.[171] Every parishioner has a right to enter and remain in the parish church to participate in divine worship if there is accommodation available.[172] Certification and registration of a church, as a place of meeting for religious worship,[173] exempts the church from registration under the Charities Acts and from local council tax or rates.[174] Exemption from rates also applies to church halls and offices.[175] An action for common law nuisance and statutory liability may arise for bell-ringing if this constitutes unlawful interference with a person's use and enjoyment of their property, or for noise which is prejudicial to health or a nuisance.[176]

Maintenance   As with maintenance of the churchyard,[177] the Parochial Church Council must keep all churches in the parish in repair, and is responsible to the Representative Body for the proper care, maintenance and upkeep of churches and their contents. The Parochial Church Council must co-operate with the Diocesan Board of Finance and the Diocesan Churches and Pastoral Committee in quinquennial inspections and must effect all repairs

---

[165] Canons Ecclesiastical 1603, Can. 80.

[166] Canons Ecclesiastical 1603, Can. 82.

[167] BCP (1984), 22, 2.

[168] Canons Ecclesiastical 1603, Can. 81.

[169] Canons Ecclesiastical 1603, Can. 83.

[170] Canons Ecclesiastical 1603, Can. 70; see also above, Chs. 10 and 11.

[171] *Ritchings v Cordingley* (1868) LR 3 A&E 113.

[172] *Taylor v Timson* (1888) 20 QBD 671: churchwardens are entrusted with seating, but they have no right to prevent a parishioner from entering the church for divine service on the ground of insufficiency of convenient accommodation or from standing during the service if the parishioner cannot get a seat.

[173] Places of Worship Registration Act 1855: the building may be certified and registered as such by the registrar-general for England and Wales.

[174] General Rates Act 1967, s. 39: there is a large body of case-law on this subject: see Halsbury, *Laws of England*, vol. 39, para. 60.

[175] The same applies to church halls or similar buildings: Local Government Finance Act 1988, s. 51, Sched. 5, para. 11; Local Government Finance Act 1992, s. 117(2), Sched. 10, para. 3: 'office purposes' include administration, clerical work and handling money; and 'clerical work' includes writing, book-keeping, sorting papers or information, filing, typing, duplication, calculating (by whatever means), drawing and the editorial preparation of matter for publication.

[176] Environmental Protection Act 1990, s. 76(1)(g): what constitutes nuisance is a matter of fact and degree; see generally T. G. Watkin, 'Clocks, bells and cockerels', 3 *ELJ* (1995), 393.

[177] See above, Ch. 11. The council may seek the advice of the Cathedrals and Churches Commission as to maintenance: see below.

reasonably advised.[178] It must also observe the faculty rules applicable to churches and their contents, as well as those applicable to unconsecrated churches not subject to faculty procedure.[179] The churchwardens must report in writing annually to both the Parochial Church Council and the archdeacon on: the state of repair of all churches in the parish and their contents; any outstanding work they consider necessary to maintain them in good repair and condition; and the extent of the insurance which covers the churches and their contents together with any advice and communications received from the insurer.[180]

Insurance   The Representative Body must insure in such manner and for such amounts as it thinks fit: all churches in its ownership; all buildings within the curtilage of such churches; the contents of such churches and buildings; and against employer's liability and liability to third parties.[181] Insurance of churches within a parish not in the ownership of the Representative Body rests with the Parochial Church Council.[182]

Inventory   The incumbent and churchwardens must ensure that particulars of all church plate and other valuable articles belonging to the church, or used in the worship of any church or mission room in the parish, are entered in the inventory of the church or mission room.[183] They must also enter in it immediately particulars of any gift to the church of such items, stating the

---

[178] Church Fabric Regulations (hereafter CFR), r.1; these regulations apply to churches other than cathedral churches (see below); see also Const. VI.22(3)(h): the council must discharge duties placed on it by the CFR. Compensation received by the Representative Body with regard to some parishes is held in separate accounts, and income from the fund is available for the maintenance and insurance of chancels in certain parishes; for the applicable rules, see Regulations Relating to Chancel Repairs Funds Regarding Stock Issued to the Representative Body under s. 31 of the Tithe Act 1936, rr.4ff.; see also Halsbury, para. 326.

[179] CFR, rr.2, 3; see above, Ch. 5.

[180] CFR, r.4: they must complete the form prescribed by the Representative Body. See also Const. VI.15.

[181] CFR, r.5: the cost of insurance must be reclaimed *pro rata* from the Diocesan Boards of Finance; however, the Representative Body may, if it thinks fit, act as its own insurer in part or in whole. See also above, n. 180.

[182] CFR, r.6: the same applies to buildings in the curtilage of a church; the council must ensure that: all such churches in the parish (including all buildings within their curtilages), and their contents are insured in accordance with the advice of the insurer; however, other terms may be agreed with the insurer if the archdeacon so approves, and the Representative Body may require the insurance to be on such terms and amounts as it thinks fit; insurance must also be effected against employer's liability and against liability to third parties on such terms and amounts as the Representative Body may from time to time require.

[183] Const. VI.21(1); VI.21(2): unless the archdeacon in writing directs otherwise, each inventory is under the control of the incumbent and churchwardens, and it must be kept in a church safe.

name of the donor (if known), recording where each article is kept when not in use, and giving particulars of any insurance. The incumbent must report the gift to the next meeting of the Parochial Church Council and Vestry Meeting. The incumbent and churchwardens must send a copy of the entry of the gift to the bishop and the secretary of the Representative Body.[184] If requested, they must send any inventory to the bishop or the archdeacon. Any dispute arising out of these provisions, or otherwise connected with an inventory, must be referred to the archdeacon, whose decision is final.[185]

On a vacancy in any incumbency, the churchwardens must inspect the church plate and other valuable articles (belonging to the church or used in the worship of any church or mission room in the parish), checking them against the inventories. Within one month of the vacancy occurring, they must make a written report of their inspection to the secretary of the Representative Body, who must bring it before the Body's next meeting. The churchwardens must then send a copy of the report, with the inventories, to the archdeacon, who must inspect the inventories and deliver them in due course to the new incumbent.[186]

Log Book and Terrier   The incumbent and churchwardens of every parish must complete a log book and terrier relating to each church and every other building in the parish used for public worship and belonging to the Church in Wales.[187]

Quinquennial Inspection   The Diocesan Board of Finance must provide a scheme by which every church in the diocese must be inspected at least once every five years. The scheme must provide for: the establishment of a fund by means of contributions from parochial, diocesan or other sources; the payment (out of the fund or otherwise) of the cost of the inspection; the appointment of architects or chartered surveyors competent to inspect the churches in the diocese; and the architect or chartered surveyor to make a report to the Diocesan Board of Finance in the case of every church inspected.[188]

---

[184] Const. VI.21(3)–(6): the secretary must report the gift to the body's next meeting.
[185] Const. VI.21(9)–(10).
[186] Const. VI.21(7)–(8).
[187] Const. VI.21A: they must also complete an inventory of the contents of these buildings, and of any other articles belonging to the church and used in connection with the church in any place in the parish. These documents must be completed in such form and at such times as may from time to time be prescribed by the Representative Body, or its appropriate committee.
[188] Const. IV.17: copies of the report must be sent to the archdeacon of the archdeaconry and to the Parochial Church Council of the parish in which the church is situated. The scheme may also provide for any other detail not inconsistent with these provisions as the board deems fit.

Redundant Churches

The right to declare a church redundant belongs to the diocesan bishop. The procedure is composed of two stages: consultation and the declaration.[189]

Consultation   Before declaring a church building to be redundant, the bishop must seek and consider the advice of the Diocesan Churches Committee and the archdeacon.[190] In turn, prior to advising the bishop, the Diocesan Churches Committee must seek and consider the advice of: the Parochial Church Council; the incumbent and churchwardens; the Representative Body; and the Diocesan Advisory Committee.[191]

Within twenty-one days of being required to do so by the Diocesan Churches Committee: (1) the Parochial Church Council, the incumbent and churchwardens, and the Representative Body, must each submit to the Committee their advice and comments on the proposal to declare the church redundant; (2) the incumbent and churchwardens must send the committee and the Representative Body an inventory of all the contents of the church; and (3) the Representative Body must submit to the committee a report on the legal title to the church. Within fifty-six days of being required to do so by the Diocesan Churches Committee, the Diocesan Advisory Committee must submit to the Diocesan Churches Committee and to the Representative Body a report on the architectural, archeological, artistic and historical merit of the church and its contents.[192]

Within twenty-eight days of receiving the advice of the Diocesan Advisory Committee, the Parochial Church Council, the incumbent and churchwardens, and the Representative Body, the Diocesan Churches Committee must submit to the bishop its advice for the future of the church building and its contents.[193]

Declaration   Within twenty-eight days of receiving the advice of the Diocesan Churches Committee, the bishop must in writing either declare the church building to be redundant, or give notice that he does not propose to make such a declaration.[194] Before making a declaration of redundancy, the

---

[189] Redundant Churches Regulations (hereafter RCR): these regulations do not apply to churches which are closed but have not been declared to be redundant. When a church is closed for public worship, the churchwardens and the Parochial Church Council continue to be responsible for maintaining the building, the contents and the necessary insurance, and must take all reasonable steps to safeguard the building and its contents, and to secure the doors and windows (RCR, Explanatory Note).

[190] RCR, r.1.

[191] RCR, r.2(1).

[192] RCR, r.2(2); r.2(3): before advising the bishop, the Diocesan Churches Committee may also seek and consider the advice of the Cathedrals and Churches Commission.

[193] RCR, r.3.

[194] RCR, r.4: in either case the bishop must send copies to the Diocesan Churches

bishop may require further information or advice from the Diocesan Churches Committee. In turn, before advising the bishop, the Diocesan Churches Committee may seek further information or advice from the Parochial Church Council, the incumbent and churchwardens, the Diocesan Advisory Committee or the Representative Body.[195]

When a declaration of redundancy comes into effect, the management and insurance of the former church building and its contents cease to be the responsibility of the incumbent, the churchwardens and the Parochial Church Council. They become the responsibility of the Representative Body. The Diocesan Churches Committee must advise the Representative Body upon the use or disposal of the contents.[196] Special rules apply to the application of proceeds of sale of churches, church sites and churchyards.[197]

THE CARE OF CATHEDRALS

Unlike most other Anglican churches,[198] the Church in Wales provides extensively for the care and maintenance of cathedrals. As a general principle: 'Any body on which functions of care and conservation are conferred by [the Cathedrals and Churches Commission Rules] shall in exercising those functions have due regard to the fact that a church is a centre of worship and mission and that a Cathedral is also the seat of a bishop.'[199]

The Cathedrals and Churches Commission

Commission Membership   The Cathedrals and Churches Commission is a subcommittee of the Finance and Resources Committee of the Representative Body.[200] The commission consists of a chairman, vice-chairman, twenty-one

Committee, the Diocesan Advisory Committee, the incumbent and churchwardens, the Parochial Church Council and the Representative Body.

[195] RCR, r.5: the time periods in rr.2, 3 and 4 apply; r.6: when the legal title of a church is subject to a right of reverter, the bishop must consult the Representative Body before making a declaration of redundancy.

[196] RCR, r.7; r.8: the cost of managing and insuring a former church building is a charge on the Provincial Redundant Churches Fund.

[197] See below, Ch. 14.

[198] See CLAC, 76n., 190; the Church of England, though, has a great deal of law on the subject: see M. Hill, *Ecclesiastical Law* (2nd edn, Oxford, 2001), Ch. 8.

[199] Cathedrals and Churches Commission Rules (hereafter CACCR), r.1; r.38: the Governing Body (or its Standing Committee) may make such further provision as it considers necessary or desirable to give effect to these rules; r.39: nothing in these rules dispenses with any of the provisions of the constitution relating to the acquisition or disposal of property or any consent or approval required by or under a Cathedral Scheme (for which see above, Ch. 8); see also COFC, 36.

[200] CACCR, r.2: but the commission is not subject to the direction or control of the Representative Body or any committee or other subcommittee of the Representative Body in the exercise of its powers and duties under these rules.

other members, and not more than five co-opted members.[201] The chairman must be a lay person qualified to be a member of the Governing Body.[202] The vice-chairman must be qualified and appointed similarly after consultation with the Representative Body and the deans of the cathedrals.[203] Twelve members of the commission must be appointed by the Bench of Bishops,[204] and three by the Finance and Resources Committee of the Representative Body.[205] The members of the Churches Subcommittee of the Finance and Resources Committee of the Representative Body are also members of the commission.[206] These members collectively may co-opt not more than five additional members.[207]

The chairman and vice-chairman hold office for five years, and may be eligible for reappointment for one further term of five years.[208] Other members hold office similarly.[209] Provision is made for the filling of casual vacancies.[210] The Representative Body must appoint a secretary or secretaries

[201] CACCR, r.3.

[202] CACCR, r.4(1): the archbishop appoints the chair after consulting the Secretary of State for Wales.

[203] CACCR, r.4(2): no person who is a member of the Chapter or Cathedral Fabric Advisory Committee of any cathedral, or who is a member or officer of a relevant committee of any designated organization, is eligible for appointment as chairman or vice-chairman (r.4(3)); the Bench of Bishops may designate organizations as 'designated organisations' and may specify the committees of those organizations which are 'relevant committees'.

[204] CACCR, r.5: that is: the dean of a cathedral (appointed after consultation with the deans); a cathedral architect (appointed after consultation with the President of the Royal Institute of British Architects); two members, being either architects, chartered building surveyors or chartered engineers (with experience of the care of historic buildings), appointed after consultation with the President of the Royal Institute of British Architects, the President of the Institute of Chartered Surveyors, or the President of the Institute of Structural Engineers, as appropriate; an artist or sculptor (with experience of work for cathedrals or other churches), appointed after consultation with the Welsh Arts Council; and seven members being persons who between them have special knowledge of archaeology, architecture, archives, art, the care of books and manuscripts, history (including the history of art and architecture) and liturgy (including church music): of these seven, one must be appointed after consultation with the secretary of state for Wales, one after consultation with CADW, one after consultation with the chairman of the United Kingdom Institute of Conservation, two after consultation with the president of the Council for British Archaeology, two persons must be distinguished for their knowledge and experience of church worship, and one appointed after consultation with the director of the Royal School of Church Music.

[205] CACCR, r.6: these are appointed for their knowledge of the functions of cathedrals and their part in the work of the Church in Wales (of these, two must be members of the cathedral chapters, but not deans).

[206] CACCR, r.7.

[207] CACCR, r.8.

[208] CACCR, r.9(1).

[209] CACCR, r.9(2): however, the Bench of Bishops may direct that a member who became a member by virtue of reappointment is eligible for reappointment for a futher term or terms.

[210] CACCR, r.10: when a casual vacancy occurs among the members appointed by the

of the commission.[211] The commission may appoint committees, and persons who are not members of the commission may be appointed to any such committee.[212] Persons who are not members of the commission have no right to vote.[213] The quorum of the commission is eleven members, one of whom must be either the chairman or the vice-chairman.[214] The commission may delegate to one or more of its members the power to give advice on its behalf with regard to a particular specialism in a particular case.[215] The commission must regulate its own procedure.[216]

Commission Duties   The commission has four basic duties: (1) to advise a diocesan chancellor on any petition for a faculty relating to a cathedral when the proposal involves prescribed work;[217] (2) when required by a diocesan chancellor, registrar or Diocesan Advisory Committee, to advise on a petition for a faculty relating to a church other than a cathedral;[218] (3) if requested, and if the commission thinks fit, to advise any member or body of members within the Church in Wales on the care, conservation, maintenance, repair and development of a cathedral or other church;[219] and (4) in the absence of a Cathedral Fabric Advisory Committee, to designate objects to be included in the inventory compiled and maintained for the cathedral,[220] which it considers to be of outstanding architectural, archaeological, artistic or historic interest.[221]

Bench of Bishops, the bench after appropriate consultation may appoint a person to fill the vacancy; when a casual vacancy occurs among persons appointed by the Finance and Resources Committee of the Representative Body, that committee may fill the vacancy; persons appointed hold office for the unexpired portion of the term of office of the person in whose place they are appointed.

[211] CACCR, r.11.

[212] CACCR, r.12: but the number of such persons appointed to a committee must be fewer than half of the total number of members of that committee.

[213] CACCR, r.13.

[214] CACCR, r.14; r.15: subject to r.14, the commission may act notwithstanding any vacancy in its membership.

[215] CACCR, r.16.

[216] CACCR, r.17.

[217] CACCR, r.18(a): namely: to preserve, alter or add to the building or its contents which would materially affect the architectural, archaeological, artistic or historic character of the cathedral; or the sale, loan or other disposal of any object for the time being designated as being of outstanding architectural, archaeological, artistic or historic interest; it may be designated as such under r.18(d), or r.21(b); r.40(2): for the purposes of these rules, any object or structure permanently situated in a cathedral or in any building within the cathedral precincts, is treated as part of that cathedral or building as the case may be. For cathedrals and the faculty jurisdiction, see above, Ch. 5.

[218] CACCR, r.18(b).

[219] CACCR, r.18(c).

[220] Under CACCR, r.36(c).

[221] CACCR, r.18(d).

Commission Powers   The commission has six basic powers: (1) to promote co-operation between itself and organizations concerned with the care and study of buildings of architectural, archaeological, artistic or historic interest in Wales; (2) to assist the Representative Body, a cathedral chapter, and any other member or body of members of the Church in Wales, by participating in educational and research projects which in its view will promote the care, conservation, maintenance, repair and development of ecclesiastical buildings; (3) to maintain a library of books, plans, drawings, photographs and other material relating to churches and their contents; (4) to advise on the appointment of architects, archaeologists, surveyors and other experts; (5) to advise on the acquisition and use of grants for cathedrals and other churches; and (6) to promote conferences or other meetings for those concerned with the care, conservation, maintenance, repair and development of cathedrals and other churches.[222]

Cathedral Fabric Advisory Committees

Membership   Each Chapter may establish for the cathedral a Cathedral Fabric Advisory Committee. The committee consists of the dean, three (or four) others appointed by the Chapter, and three (or four) others appointed by the Cathedrals and Churches Commission.[223] After consultation with the Chapter and the commission, the committee must appoint a lay member to be chairman of the committee.[224] No person who holds paid office in the commission is eligible for membership of the committee.[225] Members hold office for five years and are eligible for reappointment for a further term(s).[226] Any expenses properly incurred by a member of the committee for its purposes must be reimbursed by the Chapter.[227] Where a casual vacancy occurs, the appropriate body may appoint a person to fill it; the appointee holds office for the unexpired portion of the term of office of the person replaced.[228] The committee must appoint a secretary.[229]

---

[222] CACCR, r.19. Under the Church of England's Care of Cathedrals Measure 1990, s. 11(1), that church's Cathedrals Fabric Commission may advise in relation to any cathedral church in Wales.

[223] CACCR, r.22: of the Chapter's appointees, at least one must be a member of the Chapter and at least one a lay person; the commission's appointees, who must be appointed after consultation with the Chapter, are to be persons having knowledge of the care and maintenance of buildings of outstanding architectural or historic interest.

[224] CACCR, r.23: the person must be qualified to be a member of the Governing Body.

[225] CACCR, r.24.

[226] CACCR, r.25.

[227] CACCR, r.26.

[228] CACCR, r.27.

[229] CACCR, r.28: the person appointed need not be a member of the committee.

Meetings   Quorum for committee meetings must be not less than half the number of members and must include at least two members appointed by the commission.[230] Subject to this rule, the committee may act notwithstanding any vacancy in its membership.[231] The cathedral architect and the archaeological consultant must attend all meetings of the committee, unless excused by the chairman if the latter deems it reasonable to do so.[232] The committee must hold at least two meetings each year. If by notice to the secretary three or more members so request, a special meeting must be held within four weeks of the receipt of the notice.[233] The secretary must place on the agenda for the next meeting any matter requested by a member.[234] Subject to these rules, the committee may regulate its own procedure.[235] Not later than seven days before each meeting, the secretary must send to the Chapter, the commission and the Representative Body, a copy of the agenda for that meeting. Within fourteen days after the meeting, the secretary must send them a copy of the minutes of the meeting.[236]

Functions   When required by the Representative Body or the cathedral Chapter, the committee must advise on the care, conservation, maintenance, repair and development of the cathedral. After consultation with the Cathedrals and Churches Commission, it must designate as such those objects in the cathedral inventory which it considers to be of outstanding architectural, archaeological, artistic or historic interest.[237]

The Cathedral Chapter

The Chapter has four basic duties with regard to the care and maintenance of the cathedral.[238] First, it must appoint a cathedral architect,[239] following consultation with the Cathedrals and Churches Commission, and an archaeological consultant to the cathedral,[240] after consultation with the Commission and Cadw. Secondly, the Chapter must complete in relation to

---

[230] CACCR, r.29.
[231] CACCR, r.31.
[232] CACCR, r.30.
[233] CACCR, r.32.
[234] CACCR, r.33.
[235] CACCR, r.34.
[236] CACCR, r.35.
[237] CACCR, r.21.
[238] CACCR, r.36; see also Const. VI.21A: in the case of a cathedral, the responsibility for completing the log book, terrier and inventory is that of the dean and chapter.
[239] CACCR, r.40: 'architect' means a person registered under the Architects Registration Acts 1931–69; 'cathedral architect', in relation to a cathedral, means the architect appointed, however designated.
[240] This means 'a person who possesses such qualifications and expertise in archaeological matters as the Commission may require'.

the cathedral a log book and terrier, a plan of the precincts,[241] and an inventory of its contents and any other articles belonging to and used in connection with it.

Thirdly, the Chapter must arrange every five years for the cathedral architect (in consultation with the archaeological consultant) to make an inspection on works which he considers need to be carried out as soon as practicable in relation to the cathedral. The report must specify the order in which they should be carried out. The architect must submit the inspection report in writing to the Chapter. The cathedral architect must send a copy of every such report to the commission, the Representative Body, the Diocesan Advisory Committee and the Cathedral Fabric Advisory Committee, if there is one. Finally, the Chapter must keep a record of all works carried out in relation to the cathedral or in its precincts.

When the Chapter proposes to make an application for listed building consent, conservation area consent,[242] or scheduled monument consent,[243] with regard to any building or monument within the cathedral precincts, the Chapter clerk must send to the commission, the Cathedral Fabric Advisory Committee (if any) and the Representative Body a written notice stating that representations (concerning the proposed application) may be sent to him before the end of a period of prescribed days from the date of service of the notice.[244]

HEALTH, SAFETY AND DISABILITY LAW

The laws of the State dealing with health and safety apply equally to premises owned and occupied by the Church in Wales. Premises should display the statutory health and safety notice,[245] and church authorities (such as a Parochial Church Council) should assess the risks to the health and safety of employees and others using the property.[246] If there are five or more employees, the church body should have a written safety statement,[247] and it should discuss with all employees matters affecting their health and safety before making any decisions on this subject.[248] The church body should

---

[241] CACCR, r.40: 'precincts' means 'the precincts indicated on the plan required for that Cathedral' under r.36(c).

[242] Under the Planning (Listed Building and Conservation Areas) Act 1990, ss. 8 and 74.

[243] Under the Ancient Monuments and Archaeological Areas Act 1979, s. 2.

[244] CACCR, r.37.

[245] Health and Safety Information for Employees Regulations 1989.

[246] If there are five or more employees, the council must write down the important findings from its risk assessment: Management of Health and Safety at Work Regulations 1992.

[247] Health and Safety at Work Act 1974, s. 2(3).

[248] See Health and Safety Consultation with Employees Regulations 1996.

ensure that employees using the premises receive prescribed information on health and safety risks.[249] Most employers must register with the local authority under the Offices, Shops and Railways Act 1963 before taking on employees.[250] State law on fire safety also applies to property owned and occupied by the church.[251]

State law on food safety applies to the making and sale of food on church premises, to small restaurants and cafés run by churches, and to food sales at church fund-raising events, whether or not the food is sold for profit. It is an offence to sell any food which fails to meet safety standards.[252] The law provides for registration with the local authority of premises used by the church, charitable and voluntary organizations, for the sale or supply of food (whether or not for profit) on five or more days within a period of five weeks.[253] Even if a church is not registered, it should comply with the basic hygiene principles set out in State regulations,[254] and with rules designed to prevent contamination.[255] When alcohol is to be sold at a church function, the body responsible should obtain an occasional permission from the licensing justices.[256] If it is intended to sell alcohol on more than four

[249] Employees who are exposed to risks should be instructed on how to protect themselves and how to prevent accidents; employees and others using the building should know emergency and evacuation procedures; a record of injuries and first aid treatment should be kept; and serious accidents and illnesses, and other dangerous events, should be reported to the local authority: see Reporting of Injuries, Diseases and Dangerous Occurrences Regulations 1995.

[250] Offices, Shops and Railways Premises Act 1963, s. 1: the definition of 'premises' would not seem to include a church.

[251] See e.g. Fire Precautions (Workplace) Regulations 1997 as amended by the Fire Precautions (Workplace) (Amendment) Regulations 1999: these apply to employers and those with control over premises in which employees work, including places of worship, offices or other buildings; a fire risk assessment of the workplace must be carried out; the findings of the assessment and those who might be especially at risk must be identified (if five or more persons are employed); fire precautions must be provided and maintained as are necessary to safeguard those using the workplace; and information, instruction and training of employees must be provided; if the fire safety rules do not apply to particular premises, nevertheless other legal requirements must be met.

[252] The Food Safety Act 1990 does not apply to food prepared at home for domestic use.

[253] Food Premises (Registration) Regulations 1991; failure to register may constitute a criminal offence; premises are subject to inspection by the local environmental health officers.

[254] Food Safety (General Food Hygiene) Regulations 1995.

[255] See e.g. Food Safety (Temperature Control) Regulations 1995: it is a criminal offence to serve or to sell food which is harmful or unfit to eat, though there is a defence if it is established that those concerned took all reasonable precautions and exercised all due diligence.

[256] Licensing (Occasional Permissions) Act 1983: the application should be made at least fifteen days before the meeting of the licensing justices, and four such applications may be made each year.

occasions in a year, an application must be made for a full on-licence.[257] No licence is required if no charge is made for the alcohol.[258]

The Disability Discrimination Act 1995 makes it unlawful for service providers to discriminate against disabled people in certain circumstances.[259] The Church in Wales is not exempt from the Act.[260] According to guidance, church bodies should review their practices, policies and procedures to see what changes could and should be made to ensure that disabled persons are not treated unfavourably.[261] The exact applicability of the Act to activities carried out in the Church in Wales remains to be seen.[262] A Disability Strategy for the Church in Wales, which contains a statement of policy, has recently been recommended for adoption by the Governing Body.[263]

[257] Licensing Act 1964: it is a criminal offence to sell alcohol without a licence.

[258] *Doak v Bedford* [1964] 2 QB 587: if a charge is made for a meal, and alcohol is supplied with the meal, this is treated as selling alcohol, even though no separate charge is made for the alcohol.

[259] Disability Discrimination Act 1995, s. 19: it is unlawful for a service provider to discriminate against a disabled person: (a) in refusing to provide, or deliberately not providing, to the disabled person any service which he provides, or is prepared to provide, to members of the public; (b) in failing to provide duties imposed under the statute in circumstances in which the effect of that failure is to make it impossible or unreasonably difficult for the disabled person to make use of any such service; (c) in the standard of service which he provides to the disabled person or the manner in which he provides it to him; or (d) in the terms on which he provides a service to the disabled person.

[260] *Re Cathedral Church of SS Peter and Paul, Llandaff* (2000), Llandaff Diocesan Court: 'The provisions of this Act have been creeping up on the Church slowly and silently . . . The sensible advice that has been given has been that all churches (and this includes cathedrals) should make an audit of the provisions made for the disabled.'

[261] See e.g. Churches Main Committee Circular No. 1999/4; see also Disability Discrimination Act 1995, s. 19: services to which the Act applies include access and use of any place which members of the public are permitted to enter.

[262] See *Disability Discrimination Act 1995*, Consultation Draft, Council for the Care of Churches (2001).

[263] See Report of the Standing Committee (April 2002), Appendix III.

14

CHURCH FINANCE

The basic framework for the management and control of finance in the Church in Wales resembles that applicable to real and personal property. Rules govern the administration of church funds, the accountability of their holders, and the regulation of income and expenditure. The diocesan quota system operates to enable the church to meet the cost of its ministrations and other services. In turn, rules regulate the cost of training people for ordained ministry, the payment of stipends to clergy during ministry, care for ministers in periods of incapacity, and the maintenance of clergy and their dependants on retirement. The application of proceeds from the sale of churches, church sites and churchyards is governed by provincial regulations. Legal structures in this field are in part an expression of principles of financial independence and stewardship enunciated from time to time by the Lambeth Conference.[1] In contrast with other Anglican churches, the Church in Wales possesses no formal law containing general principles for financial management applicable to all ecclesiastical bodies.[2] The law of the State also affects church finance.

DIOCESAN AND PAROCHIAL FINANCE

In most Anglican churches, control over finance belongs ultimately to the national or provincial assembly: oversight is effected by rules requiring submission of annual budgets and financial reports from church bodies accountable to the assembly.[3] Similarly, funds held at diocesan level are under the control of the diocesan assembly,[4] and those of the most local ecclesiastical unit, by its assembly.[5] So too in the Church in Wales: in addition to those

---

[1] See LC 1897, Res. 18: the 'principle of financial independence'; see also LC 1958, Res. 64: 'The Conference urges that the Church in every field be encouraged to become self-supporting'; LC 1920, Res. 34: local church units should be entrusted with 'a real share in the financial control and direction' of the church.
[2] See e.g. Australia, Financial Provisions Canon 1995, Can. 16 1995: this is designed 'to assist in the responsible financial management of the Church and its associated organisations'; for this and other such schemes, see CLAC, 320ff.
[3] See e.g. Ireland, Const. X.17.
[4] See generally CLAC, 322f.
[5] See e.g. Ireland, Const. III.24: the select vestry has control and charge of 'all

of the Governing Body and the Representative Body,[6] both the diocese and the parish have functions regarding finance. In the latter, the Parochial Church Council is responsible for: the control of finance; the parochial budget; parish audit and accounts; annual review of clergy expenses, and insurance.[7] The incumbent, churchwardens and council may also be responsible for the administration of charitable trusts.

Diocesan Finance and the Diocesan Board of Finance

Subject to the direction and control of the Governing Body, and to the constitution, the Diocesan Conference must manage its own property (if any) and such sums of money as may be entrusted to it for distribution by the Representative Body. Moreover, the Conference is subject to any special trusts affecting these, and to the regulations of the Representative Body.[8] Those who consider themselves aggrieved by an act of the Conference may, in the case of property held under or administered by the Conference, appeal to the Provincial Court. The decision of the court is final.[9] As a matter of church practice, not law, dioceses have bodies or persons to advise on matters of stewardship.[10]

The provincial law of the Church in Wales requires each Diocesan Conference to appoint, or cause to be appointed, a Board of Finance.[11] But the law is silent as to the general functions and composition of the board. These matters are dealt with at diocesan level. In the diocese of St Asaph, for example, the Diocesan Board of Finance, incorporated under the civil Companies Acts, is authorized as a trust corporation to hold property and funds for the diocese, acting in accordance with its Memorandum and Articles of Association. The board must promote the work and purposes of the Church in Wales and of the diocese of St Asaph in particular. It may raise, expend and accumulate funds and income for these purposes. The Board is composed of *ex officio* members (the bishop, dean and archdeacons), elected members (one clerical and two lay persons representing each archdeaconry

---

parochial charity and church funds not excluded from the operation of this clause by the trusts on which the same are held'.

[6] See above, Chs. 2 and 13.

[7] For insurance, see above, Ch. 13; for burial fees, see above, Ch. 11.

[8] Const. IV.22.

[9] Const. IV.23; any failure by the court to apply the law of the Church in Wales in relation to property, may result in the enforcement of that law by the courts of the State: see Welsh Church Act 1914, s. 3(2).

[10] See e.g. DSA, YB (1999–2000), 53: the Bishop's Advisory Committee on Christian Stewardship exists to promote an understanding of the Christian use of resources and to assist parishes in the practical application of that understanding; DSD, YB (2000–1), 134: the Diocesan Stewardship Committee. See also COFC, 18: the Renewal Team of the Council for Mission and Ministry has representatives from amongst diocesan stewardship officers.

[11] Const. IV.16.

and elected by the Diocesan Conference), and co-opted members. Its procedure is governed by standing orders.[12]

By way of contrast, the provincial law of the Church in Wales specifies a small number of particular functions for the board. The Diocesan Board of Finance must: appoint a Diocesan Parsonages Board;[13] contribute to the Parsonage Board account;[14] and provide parochial inspection schemes.[15] It also has functions with respect to financial maintenance for clergy,[16] and the sale, purchase, gift, building and division of parsonages.[17] The Diocesan Court may hear and determine any dispute between a member of the Church in Wales or prescribed church bodies and the Diocesan Board of Finance.[18] The functions of the Deanery Conference include assessing the needs of the deanery in respect of finance and managing deanery finances.[19]

The piecemeal character of the formal law of the Church in Wales, on diocesan finance, may be contrasted with the laws of other churches in the Anglican Communion. In the United Church of North India, for example, the law denies to the bishop any unilateral controlling power over finance within the diocese: the Diocesan Council is the controlling authority.[20] The administration of diocesan funds is carried out by the financial executive of the Diocesan Council, the executive being under the direction and control of the council.[21] The financial executive must scrutinize the annual budget before submission to the Diocesan Council for approval. Accounts of diocesan bodies must be audited annually and a report with the audited accounts must be submitted to the Diocesan Council. The allocation of all funds under the control of the diocesan council is determined by that body. Investigation of complaints of financial mismanagement in the diocese is carried out by a Finance Committee and an appeal lies to the central church assembly.[22]

---

[12] DSA, YB (1999–2000), 46.
[13] Const. IV.19: see above, Ch. 13.
[14] Const. X.12.
[15] Const. IV.17: see above, Ch. 13.
[16] See e.g. Const. VII.46(1); see generally below.
[17] Const. X.29, 30, 40: see above, Ch. 13.
[18] Const. XI.6(d).
[19] Const. V.15(b), (f).
[20] North India, Const. II.III.IX.13: 'The Diocesan Council shall be the ultimate financial authority of the Church in the Diocese in all matters concerning its internal administration.'
[21] See also England, Diocesan Boards of Finance Measure 1925.
[22] North India, Const. II.III.IX.

Parish Finance and Accounts

In several Anglican churches, offerings and alms are the subject of canonical regulation.[23] The Church in Wales exhorts contributions from the faithful.[24] In common with several other Anglican churches,[25] in the Church in Wales, all parish finance is under the control of the Parochial Church Council.[26] The council must appoint a treasurer, and may appoint deputy treasurers, to administer the finances of the parish.[27] A function of the council is the preparation of the parochial budget, which must include: the various church expenses, the parochial contributions to the diocesan quota and to home and overseas mission, and any other branches of church work, together with arrangements for raising the monies required.[28] The council must ensure that churches (and buildings within their curtilage) in the parish, which are not in the ownership of the Representative Body, and their contents, are insured.[29] The council's functions also include an annual review of the expenses for which clergy might be reimbursed by the parish;[30] parochial expenses of clergy and their reimbursement are treated in provincial guidance.[31] It is the

---

[23] See e.g. Philippines, Cans. III.16.3(a): ministers must instruct 'all persons in their Parishes and Cures concerning the missionary work of the Church at home and abroad, and give suitable opportunities for offerings to maintain that work'.

[24] BCP (1984), 3, 2: 'It is the duty of a Christian to contribute gladly and liberally to the maintenance of the worship of God and the proclamation of the Gospel.'

[25] See e.g. England, Parochial Church Councils (Powers) Measure 1956, s. 7; Portugal, Can. IX, Art. 4.4.

[26] Const. VI.23(1): special trusts (which provide otherwise), and the incumbent's discretionary fund are not under the control of the council; for trusts, see below.

[27] Const. VI.23(2); see also Const. VI.24(1); see also PA, 2, p. 9: this recommends that the council appoints a small Finance Committee: see n. 28 below.

[28] Const. VI.22(3)(d). It may appoint a Finance Committee (VI.27(b)). See below, and above, Ch. 11 for the Church Fabric and Churchyard Maintenance Fund.

[29] Church Fabric Regulations, r.6; see above, Ch. 13.

[30] Const. VI.22(3)(g). 'The functions of the Council shall include. . .an annual review of the expenses for which the clergy should be reimbursed by the parish'; the use of the word 'should', as opposed to 'shall', would seem to suggest that the parish does not have a legal duty to reimburse arising from this provision, and, therefore, that a cleric has no legal right to reimbursement. Indeed, this would seem to be the understanding in provincial guidance on this subject: 'it is our earnest hope that all parishes will make every effort to reimburse the expenses incurred by clerics in the course of their duties . . . It is stressed that these are advisory guidelines only but we trust that wherever possible clerics will be fairly reimbursed in the proper way': A Guide to the Reimbursement of Parochial Expenses of Clerics in the Church in Wales (1997), 1.

[31] Ibid., 4–7: 'Parochial expenses may be defined as all expenses wholly, exclusively and necessarily incurred in the performance of duty as a cleric. The duty of a cleric cannot be precisely defined but is reasonably interpreted by the Inland Revenue' as covering '1. any duties required to be performed by the cleric by law or by ecclesiastical superiors; and 2. other duties arising directly from obligations to his or her parishioners'. The guidance treats the following as parochial expenses: secretarial assistance; office equipment; parsonage water, sewerage and environmental charges; visiting officiants; postage and stationery; maintenance of robes; parsonage telephone; travel; heating, lighting and cleaning; hospitality; redecoration and repair or replacement of furnishings of study and

responsibility of the churchwardens, with the assistance of a sidesperson if required, to collect alms.[32] The incumbent has a right to Easter offerings.[33]

The Parochial Church Council must cause a copy of the audited accounts[34] to be displayed near the principal door of the church or churches, and of every other building in the parish used for public worship and belonging to the Church in Wales, for a period including the two Sundays immediately preceding the day of the Annual Vestry Meeting.[35] The Annual Vestry Meeting must receive and discuss a report and accounts for the previous year from the council made in accordance with the church's accounting regulations.[36] As such, the Parochial Church Council must produce, for the Annual Vestry Meeting, a written report together with parochial accounts for the year ending on the previous 31 December. A copy must be sent to the archdeacon.[37] The report must contain prescribed information, above all a report on the financial activities of the council, including the ways in which parish activities have been funded and the funding proposals for the future.[38] Save that the requirements of the Church in Wales on independent examination or audit apply to all councils irrespective of income, the report and accounts must comply with the requirements of the Charities Act 1993.[39]

---

other rooms used for parochial purposes; books; and in-service training and retreats; 8: all clerics of the Church in Wales are classified as 'higher paid' employees for the purposes of income tax; in some dioceses, reimbursement of expenses is organized at deanery level.

[32] *Cope v Barber* (1872) LR 7 CP 393.

[33] *Cooper v Blakiston* [1907] 2 KB 688 at 700 (CA); [1909] AC 104 (HL).

[34] Namely, the balance sheet as at the previous 31 December and the statement of income and expenditure to that date: Const. VI.23(3).

[35] Const. VI.23(3): the council may also cause copies to be so displayed at other buildings in the parish.

[36] Const. VI.15(1); VI.16(2): the meeting must also appoint an auditor (who must not be a member of the Parochial Church Council of the parish in question).

[37] Church in Wales Accounting Regulations (hereafter CWAR), r.1.

[38] CWAR, r.2 and Schedule: the report must include: (a) the full name of the Parish, the dedications and locations of its churches, and the name of its deanery and diocese; (b) the names and addresses of the incumbent, the auditors or independent examiners, the bankers, and any other such professional advisers as solicitors, church architect or surveyor; (c) the names of all the members of the council who have served during the year, and any parochial offices held; (d) a statement that it is the responsibility of the incumbent and the council to consult and to co-operate in all matters of concern and importance to the parish for the promotion of the whole mission of the church, pastoral, evangelistic, social and ecumenical in the parish; (e) a brief description of the structures through which the council functions in order to carry out its aims; (f) the number of persons on the electoral roll for the year and the average number of usual attenders at church in the year; (g) a report on the proceedings of the council and the activities in the parish, including any significant developments and achievements during the year, and any plans for the coming year; and (h) a report on the financial activities of the council, including the ways in which the activities of the parish have been funded and the funding proposals for the future.

[39] CWAR, r.3. See also the Charities (Accounts and Reports) Regulations 1995.

The report and accounts must be dated and signed by the chairman of the council.[40]

The parochial accounts must be in one of three forms, depending on whether the gross income of the Parochial Church Council is not more than £100,000,[41] more than £100,000 but less than £250,000,[42] or more than £250,000.[43] The Standing Committee of the Governing Body may from time to time alter these financial limits, provided the limits comply with the Charities Act 1993.[44] The council must observe the provisions of the Act and the guidelines set out from time to time in the Church in Wales with regard to the appointment of an independent examiner or auditor and the requirements of independent examination or audit.[45] The independent examiner or auditor must state in his report that the examination or audit has been carried out and the statement of accounts complies with the Act and with the Accounting Regulations of the Church in Wales.[46] If the archdeacon considers that the report and accounts do not comply with either the Charities Act or the Accounting Regulations, he must draw this to the attention of the council and the independent examiner or auditor.[47]

The Diocesan Quota

It is a general practice in the Anglican Communion that each diocese contributes a sum of money to a central authority, in the individual church, to fund schemes organized nationally or provincially: the sum is commonly known as the provincial or national quota. In turn, to fund this quota, local church units contribute to the diocese by means of the diocesan quota or

---

[40] CWAR, r.4: all parochial church councillors are deemed to have agreed the report and accounts unless the contrary is stated in the report.

[41] CWAR, r.5(a): a Parochial Church Council which has received a gross income from all sources of not more than £100, 000 in the year must produce either (a) a receipts and payments account together with a statement of assets and liabilities which have been examined by an independent examiner or (b) a statement of financial activities and a balance sheet prepared on an accruals basis which have been examined by an independent examiner.

[42] CWAR, r.5(b): a parochial church council which has received a gross income from all sources of more than £100,000 but not more than £250,000 in the year must produce a statement of financial activities and a balance sheet prepared on an accruals basis which have been examined either by an independent examiner or by a regulated auditor.

[43] CWAR, r.5(c): a parochial church council which has in any of the three years ending on the previous 31 December received a gross income from all sources or incurred total expenditure of more than £250,000 must produce a statement of financial activities and a balance sheet prepared on an accruals basis which have been examined by a regulated auditor.

[44] CWAR, r.9.

[45] CWAR, r.6: the guidelines are as set out in the Parochial Administration Handbook (i.e. PA, Section 2: this also deals with VAT, Gift Aid and bank accounts).

[46] CWAR, r.7.

[47] CWAR, r.8.

parish share.[48] This assessment is often formally listed amongst the permitted sources of diocesan income.[49] An apportionment is made as between the parishes, and various methods are used to determine the assessment: the assessment may be fixed by law,[50] or calculation is left to the diocesan assembly,[51] to be exercised in accordance with general notions of fairness and equity;[52] and parishes must be notified of the assessment.[53] Anglican laws uniformly treat its payment as a constitutional or canonical obligation.[54] In a number of churches, the law confers a right of appeal against the assessment to a designated authority in the diocese.[55] The laws of several churches also prescribe the consequences of non-payment, in the form of sanctions or remedial action.[56]

By way of contrast, the formal, provincial law of the Church in Wales contains very little on the diocesan quota.[57] The parochial budget, prepared by the Parochial Church Council, must include the parochial contributions to the diocesan quota.[58] The council is under a duty to implement any provision made by the Diocesan Conference and the Deanery Conference.[59] Presumably this could include allocation of the diocesan quota, though there is no express provision for this in the constitution.[60] The Diocesan Board of Finance, with the approval of the bishop, may place on a defaulters' list 'a parish which culpably neglects to meet its financial obligations'. Before taking action, the Board of Finance must give to the Parochial Church

---

[48] CLAC, 325ff.

[49] See e.g. North India, Const. II.III.IX.17.

[50] Papua New Guinea, Diocese of Port Moresby, Can. 12.

[51] Ireland, Diocese of Connor, Diocesan Regulations 1990, 17.

[52] ECUSA, Diocese of Western New York, Cans. 7.1–6.

[53] ECUSA, Cans. 1.4.6.

[54] See e.g. Scotland, Digest of Resolutions, 39: it is a 'duty' of every congregation (after paying the stipend) 'to contribute, either directly or through such general levy or Quota as the Diocesan Synod may require, to the Diocese and to the general funds of the General Synod'.

[55] See e.g. Papua New Guinea, Diocese of Port Moresby, Can. 12.

[56] See e.g. Ireland, Const. IV.13: if a parish fails to pay for two successive years, the assessment for stipends, expenses of office, allowances, locomotory allowances, and a free residence, or has failed to satisfy state requirements concerning social security, no nomination is to be made on a vacancy until arrears are paid and satisfactory provision has been made for these.

[57] Unlike other Anglican churches (see above), there is no explicit law: casting payment of the diocesan quota as a duty on the parish; setting out criteria for its assessment; or allowing appeals against assessment.

[58] Const. VI.22(3)(d).

[59] Const. VI.22(3)(c).

[60] Prior to recent reform, one of the functions of the former Ruridecanal Conference was to arrange 'the allocation of the diocesan quota between the parishes', but this is not now listed as one of the functions of the Deanery Conference (it does not appear in Const. V.15). However, the functions of the Conference do include assessing the needs of the deanery in respect of finance, managing deanery finances, and acting on any communication from the Diocesan Conference.

Council of the parish concerned 'full opportunity of stating the case for the parish'.[61] When a vacancy occurs in the incumbency of a parish entered on a defaulters' list, the incumbency may be suspended or a new incumbent appointed.[62]

Administration of the quota in the Church in Wales is regulated by means of diocesan provisions.[63] The method of assessment varies as between the dioceses. Apportionment is made on the basis of average attenders at Sunday worship,[64] on the basis of the average number of communicants,[65] or on the basis of average attendance figures and the size of population in the parish.[66] Similarly, in the absence of formal provision in provincial law, challenges to quota assessments are dealt with by diocesan arrangements. In the Diocese of

---

[61] Const. IV.18.

[62] Const. IV.18: the appointment is made under the procedure in Const. VII.6: see above, Ch. 8.

[63] A.W. Jeremy, 'The framework, assessment and juridical basis of the parish quota in the Anglican Communion', in J. Fox (ed.), *Render unto Caesar: Church Property in Roman Catholic and Anglican Canon Law* (Rome, 2000), 113 at 116. The following diocesan arrangements are taken from this study.

[64] The Diocese of Monmouth establishes the amount and apportions to each parish on the basis of the number of average attenders at church, Sunday to Sunday, having regard only to persons aged eighteen or over. This is accompanied by a request from the diocese that each parish undertakes a self-assessment into one of four categories (A to D), each category paying 10 per cent more than the next. Parishes then utilize broad criteria directed towards establishing whether they are well placed to undertake a Category A or Category B assessment; if less well placed they need to assess themselves in Category C or D.

[65] In the Diocese of Swansea and Brecon, 95 per cent opf the quota is based on the average number of communicants in each church, and only 5 per cent allocated with regard to the nature of the parish population. The method of calculating the average number of communicants involves taking the number of communicants at Easter, Christmas and Pentecost over three years, halving the Easter and Christmas numbers and calculating the average. The result is that the annual quota *per* communicant is roughly the same throughout the diocese and it is judged to be fair because the rural population is far less than the urban population.

[66] The Diocese of Llandaff uses attendance figures, but takes into account the size of the population in the parish on the broad principle that it is reasonable to expect larger congregations from larger populations. It then weighs the relative affluence of the parish and uses data relating to attendance, actual and potential, together with allowances for socio-economic conditions by reference to fifteen variables such as: the economic dimension (male and female employment, qualified persons, managers and professional persons, unskilled workers); the type and quality of housing; the dependency ratio related to the level of employment, and the number of deprived, owner-occupied, council-rented or overcrowded households. The Diocesan Board of Finance applies a cluster analysis by calculating the measure of similarity between every parish by taking parishes in pairs and measuring differences between them by reference to the fifteen factors. The smaller the resulting number, the greater is the degree of similarity between the parishes. The result is a group of seven clusters with cluster one having the most favourable socio-economic conditions, cluster seven the poorest. A cluster multiplier is then applied to the calculation so that the assessment is calculated by taking the quota for the whole diocese dividing it by the attendance figures potential and actual and applying the parish attendance figures modified by the cluster factor.

Llandaff, a parish may submit an application for review to the secretary of the Diocesan Board of Finance. The application must be made within twenty-one days of the parish receiving from the Diocesan Board of Finance notification of the amount allocated to the parish by the diocese. The application must be in writing, indicating the grounds on which it is made. It is considered by a committee of not more than four persons, appointed by the bishop, excluding members of the Diocesan Board of Finance. The committee submits its conclusions to the bishop for final determination.[67] Under regulations in the Diocese of Bangor, disagreements may be referred to an Appeal Committee the decision of which is 'final and conclusive'. The regulations do not contain criteria for determining the appeal.[68]

Proceeds from the Sale of Churches and Churchyards

Subject to any special trusts affecting the property, the net proceeds from the sale of any interest in a churchyard or burial ground (or any part thereof) in a parish, must be invested by the Representative Body in a Church Fabric and Churchyard Maintenance Fund. The income from the latter must be used for the repair or maintenance of any place of worship, churchyard, burial ground or church hall in that parish.[69]

Subject to any special trusts affecting the property, the following rules operate where in a parish a church or church site (or any part of it) vested in the Representative Body has been declared redundant and sold.[70] The

[67] Jeremy, 'The framework' at 118–19.

[68] DB, Handbook (2001), 79: Quota Appeal Regulations: These deal with differences between the diocese and a Deanery Conference over the contribution to diocesan funds required from the deanery, and with disagreements between a Deanery Conference and the parish concerning the deanery contribution which each parish ought to make. In both cases, the disagreement may be referred to an Appeal Committee. The referral must be in writing and made within fourteen days of the Deanery Conference. Two representatives nominated by the appellant may appear before the Appeal Committee, the decision of which is 'final and conclusive'. In both cases the Appeal Committee consists of: the archdeacon of the archdeaconry other than that in which the deanery is situated (the archdeacon acts as chairman); two lay members of the Diocesan Board of Finance (not being resident in the deanery in question), selected by the board; two clerical members of the Standing Committee (being neither members of the board nor serving in the deanery concerned), selected by the Standing Committee; and two lay members of the Standing Committee (being neither members of the board nor resident in the deanery concerned), selected by the Standing Committee.

[69] Regulations Governing the Application of the Proceeds of Sale of Churches, Church Sites and Churchyards (hereafter CSR), r.1(1): see above, Ch. 11 for the Churchyard Maintenance Fund; r.1(2): if the net proceeds of sale exceed £5,000 (or such other figure as the Representative Body may decide), the Representative Body may deal with the excess, or any part of it, as if it were the proceeds from the sale of a church or church site, in accordance with r.2 (see below). See also r.6: these regulations do not apply to the proceeds of any insurance claim in respect of the total loss of a church building; r.7: in these regulations, 'sale' includes disposal by way of the grant of a lease at a premium.

[70] CSR, r.2(1); r.5: where funds are to be applied under r.2, a copy of the most recent

proceeds of sale of the church (and its contents), or of the church site (or any part of it), must be applied for listed objects in an order of priority, namely: (1) the repayment of any loan made by the Diocesan Board of Finance in respect of that church or church site;[71] (2) defraying any costs incurred by the Representative Body in maintaining, making safe, insuring, demolishing and reinstating the site of the former church prior to its sale; (3) towards the cost of relocating items removed from the redundant church to other churches;[72] (4) towards the cost of providing or adapting another place of worship vested or to be vested in the Representative Body;[73] or (5) towards the cost of facilitating the sharing of church buildings with other denominations.[74] There are special rules to apportion any balance remaining after application of the proceeds.[75]

In any case where money is applied towards the cost of providing or adapting another place of worship in a parish, the application must be made within eighteen months from the date on which the parish and the bishop are notified of the receipt of the funds by the Representative Body.[76] Where the income from a licence, lease or other agreement in respect of a parish approved by the Representative Body does not exceed £5,000,[77] this sum must be paid to the parish for the maintenance of a place of worship in the parish. Where the income exceeds this sum, the Representative Body must determine how such excess is to be applied in consultation with the parish.[78]

audited accounts of the parish must be provided to the Representative Body. See above, Ch. 13 for declarations of redundancy.

[71] This includes the repayment of all interest on the loan.

[72] This is subject to the approval of the Representative Body with the advice of the Diocesan Advisory Committee and the Diocesan Churches and Pastoral Committee.

[73] The other place of worship must be in the same parish, or group of parishes of which such parish forms part; the proceeds may be applied thus if in the bishop's judgment this is required.

[74] That is, under the Sharing of Church Buildings Act 1969, for which see above, Ch. 13.

[75] CSR, r.2(2): one half, after consultation with the Diocesan Churches and Pastoral Committee, for either or both of: (i) the cost prior to redundancy of closing, insuring and making safe churches in the dioceses vested in the Representative Body; or (ii) subject to the approval of the bishop, towards the cost of providing or adapting another place of worship in the diocese (also vested or to be vested in the Representative Body); and the other half to the Provincial Redundant Churches Fund for maintaining, making safe, insuring, reinstating and demolishing redundant churches in the province. See also r.5: where funds are to be applied under r.2, a copy of the most recent audited accounts of the parish must be provided to the Representative Body.

[76] CSR, r.3.

[77] CSR, r.4: or such other sum as the Representative Body may from time to time decide; see also r.5: where funds are to be applied under r.4, a copy of the most recent audited accounts of the parish must be provided to the Representative Body.

[78] CSR, r.4. The distribution of the income may also be subject to the terms of a trust: see below.

Charitable Trusts

The law of the Church in Wales commonly makes special provision to ensure compliance with the terms of any trusts established for it.[79] This protection is designed in part to satisfy the civil law of trusts, which embraces charitable trusts for religious objects.[80] In civil law, a trust for the advancement of religion enjoys charitable status provided its purposes are for the public benefit.[81] The benefit to the public must be tangible,[82] and for an appreciably important part of society.[83] The advancement of religion includes pastoral or missionary promotion of spiritual teaching, and the maintenance of doctrine, observances, structures and property necessary for its promotion.[84] An 'ecclesiastical charity' is an endowment held for any lawful spiritual purpose, for the benefit of a spiritual person or ecclesiastical office, or for use by a church of a building as a church, chapel, mission room, Sunday school or otherwise. It also includes property held for the maintenance, repair, or improvement of any such building, the maintenance of divine service in it, or otherwise for the benefit of any particular church or denomination or any of its members.[85]

Charitable status is enjoyed by a wide range of objects,[86] if the gift is, for example: to increase clergy stipends, to preach commemorative sermons, to

[79] See e.g. Const. II.20: the Representative Body holds property 'in trust' for the uses and purposes of the archbishop, bishops, clergy and laity of the church; IV.22: the competence of the Diocesan Conference is subject to special trusts; VI.23(1): unless they provide otherwise, special trusts are under the control of the Parochial Church Council; VI.21: gifts must be entered in the inventory; CSR, rr.1, 2: sales of churches may be subject to special trusts.
[80] The subject is a large one, and the basic principles only are treated here; for more detailed studies, see e.g. G. Moffat and M. Chesterman, *Trusts Law* (London, 1988); N. Doe, *The Legal Framework of the Church of England* (Oxford, 1996), 439–445. See also P. W. Edge and J. M. Loughrey, 'Religious charities and the jurisdiction of the Charity Commission', 21 *Legal Studies* (2001), 36.
[81] *Commissioners of Income Tax v Pemsel* [1891] AC 531. See also F. Quint and T. Spring, 'Religion, charity law and human rights', 5 *The Charity Law and Practice Review* (1999), 153.
[82] *Gilmour v Coates* [1949] AC 426: a gift to a cloistered community engaged in private religious services of intercessory prayer is not charitable; see also *Re Warre's Will Trusts, Wort v Salisbury Diocesan Board of Finance* [1953] 2 All ER 99: a gift to establish a retreat house for 'religious contemplation and the cleansing of the soul' of members of the Church of England did not have a sufficient public element.
[83] *Verge v Somerville* [1924] AC 496; see also H. Picarda, 'Religious observance and the element of public benefit', 2 *The Charity Law and Practice Review* (1993), 155.
[84] *United Grand Lodge of Ancient, Free and Accepted Masons of England v Holborn Borough Council* [1957] 1 WLR 1080; *Keren Kayemouth Le Jisroel Ltd v IRC* [1931] 2 KB 465 at 477 (CA).
[85] Local Government Act 1894, s. 75(2); Charities Act 1993, s. 96.
[86] Gifts to 'the Church of England' and 'the Church of Rome' have been held to be charitable: see *Re Barnes* [1930] 2 Ch 80 and *Re Schoales* [1930] 2 Ch 75.

pay the expenses of clergy societies;[87] for clergy education,[88] Sunday school prizes,[89] the benefit of the work of a cathedral,[90] the relief of sick and aged clergy in a particular diocese; or to a parish church for such objects connected with it as the minister thinks fit, to provide an organist or choristers,[91] to provide, maintain or decorate a place of worship, or to maintain churchyards, burial grounds and parsonages.[92] However, a gift for 'parish work' may not be for the advancement of religion,[93] nor will a trust for superstitious purposes,[94] nor one which is subversive to morality,[95] though gifts associated with veneration of relics or the saints or miracles may enjoy charitable status, but not if public benefit cannot be established.[96] When a gift is made to a named holder of a particular ecclesiastical office, it must be established that the property is not to be used as a gift only to the person currently holding the office, but is to be held by that person and his successors in office as trustees.[97]

The fundamental duty of trustees is to give effect to the settlor's intentions as set out in the terms of the trust instrument. Trustees must discharge their duties in an honest and efficient manner. The Charity Commissioners exercise a supervisory jurisdiction with regard to charitable trusts.[98] For a person to enforce the terms of the trust, they must have *locus standi* as a beneficiary under it. Failure by the trustees to fulfil their duties may result in a breach of trust and various sanctions under civil law.[99] If the original purpose of a trust can no longer by carried out, an application may be made to the Charity Commissioners or the High Court for a *cy pres* scheme, provided it is established that the settlor had an overriding charitable intent. A new purpose may

---

[87]   See e.g. *Pennington v Buckley* (1848) 6 Hare 451; *Gibson v Representative Church Body* (1881) 9 LR Ir 1; *Re Parker's Charity* (1863) 32 Beav 654; *Re Charlesworth, Robinson v Archdeacon of Cleveland* (1910) 101 LT 908.

[88]   *Re Randell* (1888) 38 Ch D 213.

[89]   *Re Strickland* [1936] 3 All ER 1027.

[90]   *Re Martley* (1931) 47 TLR 392.

[91]   See e.g. *Re Williams* [1927] 2 Ch 283; *Re Forster* [1939] Ch 22; *Re Bain* [1930] 1 Ch 224; *Re Eastes* [1948] Ch 257; *Re Scowcroft* [1898] 2 Ch 638; *Re Royce* [1940] 2 All ER 291.

[92]   See e.g. *Re Robertson* [1930] 2 Ch 71; *Re Church Estate Charity* (1871) 6 Ch App 296; *Re Barker* (1909) 25 TLR 753; *Re Vaughan* (1886) 33 Ch D 187; *Bangor (Bishop of) v Parry* (1891) 2 QB 277: this concerned leasing of charity property.

[93]   *Re Stratton* [1931] 1 Ch 197.

[94]   *Thornton v Howe* (1862) 31 Beav 14.

[95]   *Bourne v Keane* [1919] AC 815.

[96]   See *Bourne v Keane* [1919] AC 815 at 855 and *Gilmour v Coates* [1949] AC 426.

[97]   *Re Flinn* [1948] Ch 241. Gifts to 'the incumbent for the time being', 'the churchwardens and their successors', or to a bishop 'for such purposes as he sees fit' are charitable.

[98]   Charities Act 1993, ss. 6–12.

[99]   Charities Act 1993, s. 72. Provided the trustee is a member of the Church in Wales, it may also lead to proceedings for neglect of duty in the Disciplinary Tribunal of the Church in Wales: see above, Ch. 5.

then be substituted, as close to the original purpose as possible, for the trust to be fulfilled.[100]

FUNDS FOR MINISTRY

This section deals with the law of the Church in Wales which regulates expenditure of funds allocated to the cost of training people for the ordained ministry, the payment of stipends to clergy during ministry, and care for ministers in periods of incapacity.[101]

Training for the Ordained Ministry

Provincial law of the Church in Wales provides for the establishment and administration of a fund to train candidates for the ordained ministry.[102] The Representative Body, or its appropriate committee, possesses the fund.[103] The fund consists of: a sum paid by the Representative Body;[104] contributions from Diocesan Boards of Finance; unexpended balances of awards which are withdrawn or otherwise not taken up; and such other sums, if any, as may from time to time be authorized or directed to be credited to the fund.[105] The following must be charged against the fund: awards made by the Bench of Bishops (or by those persons or bodies of persons nominated by the Bench) to provide for the training of candidates for the ordained ministry of the Church in Wales; and such other expenditure as may from time to time be incurred in the furtherance of the purposes of the fund.[106]

The Representative Body from its general income must allocate to the fund an annual sum determined by the Standing Committee and reported to the Governing Body. This sum must be placed to the credit of the fund.[107] The Board of Finance, of the diocese in which it is intended that a candidate's ministry is to commence, must contribute towards the cost of an award to that candidate. The contribution must be such fraction (if any) of the award,

---

[100] See e.g. *Re Lysaght* [1966] Ch 191.
[101] For expenditure on the maintenance of church property, including insurance, see above, Ch. 13.
[102] Regulations to Provide Resources for Training for the Ordained Ministry of the Church in Wales (hereafter RTOM), r.1: these regulations deal with the Fund to Provide Resources for Training for the Ordained Ministry of the Church in Wales. Ordained ministry includes the order of deaconesses. A candidate is a person who has been provisionally accepted for training for the ordained ministry of the Church in Wales by the bishop of the diocese in which it is intended that the person's ministry is to commence.
[103] RTOM, r.2.
[104] Namely, the sum paid under r.5, for which see below.
[105] RTOM, r.3: and these must be placed to its credit.
[106] RTOM, r.4.
[107] RTOM, r.5.

not exceeding one-quarter, as the Bench of Bishops must from time to time determine. The contribution must be paid to the Representative Body to the credit of the fund.[108] The provincial Resources for Training Committee administers the scheme of financial provision for training for ordained ministry.[109]

Clergy Stipends and Allowances

In some Anglican churches the responsibility for stipends falls on the congregation.[110] In the Church in Wales this is not the case.[111] The law of the Church in Wales on clergy stipends is found in the Maintenance of Ministry Scheme: this consists of regulations prescribed by the Representative Body.[112] The Representative Body may modify the Scheme as it thinks fit, but any modifications must be reported to the Governing Body.[113] The Maintenance of Ministry Subcommittee must keep the working of the scheme under review and it must report as necessary, and at least once in each triennial period, to the Representative Body. The Subcommittee is empowered to decide any question of interpretation for the purpose of the Scheme.[114]

The Maintenance of Ministry Fund   Under the Maintenance of Ministry Scheme, the amount of any sum, grant, fee, allowance, stipend or gratuity referred to in the scheme, must be determined by the Representative Body (or its appropriate committee).[115] The Representative Body must provide an annual sum of money for all dioceses, which represents the Maintenance of Ministry Fund, towards the cost of the maintenance of ministry. This sum must be apportioned quarterly to dioceses in accordance with the number of

---

[108] RTOM, r.6: the determination may be made by persons or a body of persons nominated by the Bench.

[109] COFC, 16: the committee (which has representation on the Ministry Team of the Council for Mission and Ministry), receives reports on candidates' progress, it liaises with diocesan bodies, and those engaged in providing theological education, as to funding. For the Ministry Team and the Council, see above, Ch. 8.

[110] See e.g. Scotland, Digest of Resolutions, 20–22, 39.

[111] For taxation of clergy, see the Churches Main Committee's *The Taxation of Ministers of Religion: Guidance Notes* (1996).

[112] Maintenance of Ministry Scheme (hereafter MMS), s. 1: all references in the Constitution to the Maintenance of Ministry Scheme or the Reconstruction Scheme must be construed as referring to this scheme; for schemes, see above Ch. 1.

[113] MMS, s. 24; see also Const. III.33: the Representative Body may reduce stipends or grants on three months' notice.

[114] MMS, s. 23. This is a subcommittee of the Finance and Resources Committee of the Representative Body: for composition, see COFC, 29.

[115] MMS, s. 2: the amounts must be printed in the Schedule to the scheme; the schedule need not be printed as part of the MMS, but the contents of the schedule must be printed at least annually by the Representative Body and delivered to its members and all serving clerics and deaconesses in the Church in Wales.

clerics in post at the beginning of each quarter.[116] In addition to the Maintenance of Ministry Fund, the Representative Body must make allocations to the dioceses arising from bequests.[117] The Diocesan Board of Finance, in conjunction with the bishop, is responsible for the administration of any grant made to it for the payment for duties in vacant curacies. Each board must submit to the Representative Body a statement of account at the end of each financial year showing the application of the grant.[118]

Charges on the Fund On the recommendation of the Diocesan Board of Finance,[119] the following are a proper charge against the Maintenance of Ministry Fund for the diocese concerned:[120] (1) the stipends and employer's National Insurance contributions of incumbents and assistant curates; (2) house allowances to incumbents;[121] (3) grants of a temporary nature to allow the bishop in special circumstances to provide additional assistance in the benefice;[122] (4) payments for any other purpose which would benefit an incumbent or a retired incumbent; (5) a grant to the widow, widower or other dependant[123] of an incumbent or an assistant curate immediately following his or her death; (6) a grant to a Diocesan Board of Finance to pay for duties in vacant curacies; (7) the removal expenses of an incumbent,[124] a widow, widower or other dependant of any deceased incumbent,[125] or an

---

[116] MMS, s. 3: the number of clerics must be increased by one fifth of the difference, if any, between the number of clerics in post at the beginning of each quarter, and the number of clerics stated by the Bench of Bishops to be required for each diocese, whenever the latter number exceeds the former.

[117] MMS, s. 4: this must be done in accordance with the Schedule.

[118] MMS, s. 22; see also s. 20: the contributions to the Diocesan Parsonage Board Account from each parsonage in the diocese within the Parsonages Scheme for the year commencing 1 January shall be at one of the rates selected by the Diocesan Parsonage Board, after consultation with the Diocesan Board of Finance from among those provided in the Schedule. For parsonages, see above Ch. 13.

[119] MMS, s. 5: the Diocesan Board of Finance must submit its recommendations in respect of stipends and allowances at least three months before the recommendations are to become effective, except in the case of a new appointment. At the commencement of the last month in each quarter, the Representative Body must inform the Diocesan Board of Finance of the estimated excess expenditure on the maintenance of the ministry over and above the quarterly sum. The Board of Finance must pay over to the Representative Body the sum so advised before the end of that quarter.

[120] MMS, s. 6(1).

[121] MMS, s. 6(2): 'incumbent' includes a cleric in charge of a suspended incumbency or conventional district and a vicar in a rectorial benefice.

[122] For example, where there is no vacancy in the incumbency but the incumbent is unable to officiate.

[123] MMS, s. 6(2): 'dependant' means a relative of a deceased cleric who, at the date of death, was residing and financially dependent on the cleric.

[124] This applies when the incumbent is moving into an incumbency in the diocese, moving when required by the diocese within an incumbency, or moving from an incumbency on retirement.

[125] This applies if the incumbent would have been entitled to removal expenses.

assistant curate;[126] (8) fees for services in vacant incumbencies;[127] (9) a travelling expenses allowance payable to clerics or deaconesses who, at the request of the diocesan bishop, exercise pastoral care in neighbouring vacant parishes; (10) the remuneration and expenses of archdeacons, canons, area deans and diocesan officers; (11) the remuneration and expenses of no more than three accredited lay ministers[128] in each diocese;[129] (12) augmentation of grants to a cathedral chapter;[130] (13) the expenses of the custodians of a parsonage in a vacant benefice;[131] and (14) contributions to the Parsonage Board Fund.[132] Except for reimbursement of expenses and fees for taking a service during a vacancy, these provisions do not apply to clerics in non-stipendiary ministry.[133]

Minimum Stipends for Parochial Clergy   The Diocesan Board of Finance must not, without the express approval of the Representative Body, recommend a stipend less than the minimum provided in the Maintenance of Ministry Scheme.[134] This rule applies to stipends for: an incumbent of a rectorial benefice; any other incumbent; a vicar in a rectorial benefice; a cleric in charge of a suspended incumbency or conventional district; and a cleric appointed to an extra-parochial office by episcopal licence under seal.[135] Similarly, a Diocesan Board of Finance must not, without the express approval of the Representative Body, recommend an allowance of less than

---

[126] This applies where the assistant curate takes up a first appointment, moves to another curacy, or is appointed to a benefice in the diocese; an assistant curate includes a cleric appointed to a full-time extra-parochial office and a deaconess (MMS, s. 6(2)).

[127] That is: (i) the fee, if any, for taking a service during a vacancy by a cleric or deaconess in full-time stipendiary ministry or undertaking service reckoned as pensionable service, or by a cleric in receipt of a pension by virtue of service in holy orders, or by a cleric in non-stipendiary ministry who is over seventy years of age; (ii) where a service is taken by a licensed reader, a fee must be paid to the Diocesan Association of Readers' Fund for each service; and (iii) the travelling allowance for any person taking services in a vacant cure.

[128] MMS, s. 6(2): an accredited lay minister is a lay person licensed by the bishop to engage in the work of mission and ministry in the diocese or a parish(es).

[129] The accredited lay ministers must be counted in the number of clerics in post in the diocese for the purposes of the quarterly apportionment effected under MMS, s. 3 (see above).

[130] That is, grants made under MMS, s. 19.

[131] Provision for this is contained in Const. X (see above Ch. 13).

[132] MMS, s. 6(1).

[133] MMS, s. 6(3).

[134] MMS, s. 7(1). The minimum stipends are set out in the Schedule to the Scheme.

[135] MMS, s. 7(1); but see also MMS, s. 7(2): when an incumbent or vicar in a rectorial benefice also holds an office or appointment other than in the ministry of the Church in Wales (for which a separate remuneration is received), the diocesan bishop may recommend to the Representative Body (acting through the Maintenance of Ministry Subcommittee) that the stipend to be paid is a sum (together with the separate stipend or payment received by the incumbent or vicar) not less than the appropriate minimum.

the minimum provided in the Scheme for an area dean.[136] These provisions do not apply in respect of non-stipendiary clerics.[137]

The Maintenance of Ministry Scheme also prescribes the minimum annual stipend for an assistant curate, cathedral chaplain or deaconess.[138] In special circumstances, a Diocesan Board of Finance may recommend a grant for an assistant curate or deaconess who, with the approval of the bishop, receives a stipend less than the prescribed minimum.[139] These provisions apply to any assistant curate or deaconess nominated by an incumbent to act as such in a parish with the permission of the bishop, and is undertaking full-time stipendiary duty.[140] The Diocesan Board of Finance may also recommend a grant payable to a parish for each full-time assistant curate or deaconess employed there, subject to them being in receipt of a prescribed stipend; the grant must not exceed the amount of the stipend paid by the parish.[141]

Dignitaries and Diocesan Clergy   The Representative Body must provide and pay the stipends and expenses of dignitaries and diocesan clergy.[142] For each diocesan bishop it must provide a personal stipend and an allowance towards the costs of the upkeep of his chapel and the maintenance of his robes. The diocesan bishop may claim further allowances in connection with prescribed items.[143] The archbishop, in addition to a stipend and allowances

---

[136] MMS, 7(3): the minimum is specified in s. 6 of Pt. I of the Schedule.

[137] MMS, s. 7(4).

[138] MMS, s. 9(1); for the minimum stipend, see MMS, Sched., Pt. I, s. 6.

[139] MMS, s. 9(2).

[140] MMS, s. 9(3).

[141] MMS, s. 8(1): the stipend must not be less than that laid down in MMS, s. 9(1); see also MMS, s. 8(2): special grants in lieu of curacy endowments existing prior to 31 March 1920 and the income from endowments given since that date continue to be paid in accordance with the endowment.

[142] MMS, s. 10.

[143] MMS, s. 11(1) and (2): claims may be made in respect of: reimbursement of the cost of duty travel by public transport and a travelling allowance for duty travel by car; the reimbursement of reasonable expenses of accommodation incurred on duty travel; subject to consultation with the Bishops Residences and Expenses Subcommittee, the reimbursement of the cost of wages, subsistence and National Insurance contributions in respect of a driver; the reimbursement of reasonable office expenses; within the Representative Body's salary scale for secretarial staff at 39 Cathedral Road, Cardiff, the reimbursement of the cost of salary and National Insurance contributions and other reasonable expenses in respect of his secretary; the reimbursement of reasonable expenses of hospitality; the reimbursement of expenses incurred in connection with ordinations; and the reimbursement of 75% of the cost of heating and lighting his residence. See also COFC, 35: the Bishops' Residences and Expenses Subcommittee is responsible to the Finance and Resources Committee of the Representative Body; it is composed of the chairman of the Representative Body (who acts as chair of the subcommittee), the archbishop (or his nominated alternate), the chairmen of the Property Subcommittee, the Investment Subcommittee, the Maintenance of Ministry Subcommittee and the Standing Committee (or another member of this nominated by him).

as a diocesan dishop, must receive a further allowance.[144] The Representative Body must provide a stipend for an assistant bishop who is appointed to serve in the diocese of the archbishop, but the stipend must be reduced by the amount of any other stipend payable to the assistant bishop by the Representative Body.[145]

The Representative Body must provide a stipend for a cathedral dean.[146] Similarly, it must provide a stipend for each full-time residentiary canon appointed under a cathedral scheme: its amount must be agreed between the diocesan bishop and the Chairman of the Maintenance of Ministry Subcommittee.[147] The Representative Body must make a grant to each cathedral chapter for any purpose in carrying out its cathedral scheme. Each cathedral chapter must furnish annually to the Representative Body audited accounts. These must include all monies received from the Representative Body as well as income from properties vested in the Representative Body and managed by the dean and chapter.[148] The Representative Body must also provide a stipend for each archdeacon.[149] The Representative Body must contribute towards the reasonable expenses of removal of dignitaries and their dependants, in such manner as must be decided by the Maintenance of Ministry Subcommittee.[150] Provision also exists for clerical gratuities.[151]

Incapacitated Incumbents

The canon law of the Church in Wales provides for the maintenance of the ministry in a parish during the incapacity of an incumbent, for meeting the cost of this, and for determining the remuneration of an incapacitated incumbent during illness. It also provides for a scheme by which an incapacitated incumbent may be required to appear before a medical board.[152]

---

[144] MMS, s. 11(3).

[145] MMS, s. 12.

[146] MMS, s. 13.

[147] MMS, s. 14: the stipend must not exceed that prescribed in rhe Schedule; see also s. 15: the Representative Body must provide a stipend for two chaplains in each cathedral.

[148] MMS, s. 19; it may also make an additional grant to a cathedral chapter of an amount equal to the stipend provided for a cathedral chaplain under s. 15 (for which see above).

[149] MMS, s. 16: the stipend must be reduced by the amount of any other stipend payable to the archdeacon by the Representative Body; and a stipend which has not been so reduced must not be paid to more than one archdeacon in each diocese; an archdeacon must also be provided with a residence, and may claim the further allowances for expenses in respect of his duties as an archdeacon (i.e. reimbursement of duty travel by public transport and a travelling allowance for duty travel by car, and reasonable expenses).

[150] MMS, s. 17: for the purposes of this section, 'dignitaries' means bishops, assistant bishops, deans, full-time residentiary canons, archdeacons and cathedral chaplains.

[151] MMS, s. 21: the scheme is contained in MMS, Sched.

[152] Can. 21–4–1982; para. 1: regulations appearing in the schedules to the canon apply

Notification of Incapacity   Immediately on becoming incapacitated, the incumbent must inform the body (or person) responsible for the payment of his stipend of the date on which he first became incapacitated and the nature of his incapacity.[153] On receiving this information, the authority responsible for payment of the stipend must forward to the incumbent a form of absence statement. This statement must be completed and returned by the incumbent when he is able to resume normal duties. If an incumbent's incapacity continues for more than seven days, an appropriate medical certificate must be sent to the stipend authority. Thereafter further medical certificates, as may be required by that authority, must be sent until the incapacity terminates.[154]

If an incumbent is incapacitated, the area dean must be notified.[155] When the incapacitated incumbent is an area dean, the archdeacon must be notified; and when the incapacitated incumbent is an archdeacon, the bishop must be notified.[156] During the first twenty-six weeks of incapacity, an incumbent is entitled to a full stipend and any regular payments made in respect of expenses, less any sickness benefits for which the incumbent is eligible during that period.[157] If incapacity continues beyond the twenty-six weeks, an incumbent is entitled to one-half of the stipend which would be applicable were he not incapacitated, less any sickness benefits for which he is eligible during that period.[158]

Maintenance of Ministry   If the incapacity of the incumbent so requires, the area dean must arrange for the maintenance of the ministry in the benefice concerned. When the incapacitated incumbent is an area dean, the archdeacon must arrange for his duties to be carried out. When the incapacitated incumbent is an archdeacon, the bishop must arrange for his duties to be carried out. At the end of every quarter, or at the termination of the incapacity, whichever is earlier, the area dean or the archdeacon (as the case may be) must submit to the Representative Body a schedule of the cost of the maintenance of the ministry. The cost must be borne by the Maintenance of Ministry Fund for the diocese concerned. The scale of fees and expenses payable for services must be that provided for vacant incumbencies.[159] The incumbent must, within the prescribed period, claim all statutory benefits for

to all incumbents, that is, incumbents in full-time stipendiary ministry; para. 2: the provisions of Sched. 2 do not apply to the archbishop or bishops.

[153] Can. 21–4–1982, Sched. 1, r.1(1): but information to this effect received from any other source and communicated in writing to the incumbent may be treated as coming from the incumbent.

[154] Can. 21–4–1982, Sched. 1, r.1(2) and (3).

[155] This does not apply if the cleric is incumbent of a benefice annexed to a cathedral.

[156] Can. 21–4–1982, Sched. 1, r.2.

[157] Ibid., r.3.

[158] Ibid., r.4.

[159] Ibid., r.5.

which he is eligible and, on request, inform the Representative Body of the amount of these.[160] The incapacity of an incumbent is deemed to terminate when either he is able to resume his normal duties,[161] or he retires, whichever happens first.[162]

The Medical Board   When an incumbent has been incapacitated by physical or mental ill-health for a continuous period exceeding four weeks, or for a total of twenty-eight days in any one period of three months, the bishop may require him to appear before a medical board. The board consists of an archdeacon and two lay persons, both of whom must be registered medical practitioners.[163] The board must advise the bishop as to whether in its opinion the incumbent is unable by reason of incapacity of mind or body temporarily or permanently to discharge the duties of his office.[164]

An incumbent required to appear before the board must be given at least fourteen days' prior written notice to that effect. The incumbent is entitled to be represented or accompanied before the board by one person. The findings of the board must, within fourteen days of its deliberations, be reported simultaneously to the bishop and to the incumbent. In the event of disagreement between any members of the board, the majority view prevails. The board is required to disclose reasons for its findings to the incumbent, if the incumbent so desires. An incumbent, if so required by the board, must ask his own medical adviser to produce to the board evidence of the incumbent's medical condition relevant to the incapacity. The board may require an incumbent to submit to an independent medical examination. All expenses of the board and incumbent are to be borne by the Representative Body.[165]

---

[160] Ibid., r.6.
[161] This must be evidenced by the completion and return of an absence statement and, if the period of incapacity has exceeded seven days, a medical clearance certificate (r.6).
[162] Ibid., r.6.
[163] Can. 21-4-1982, Sched 2: each bishop, from his diocese, must nominate to a provincial list an archdeacon and two lay persons who are registered medical practitioners. The names of the three persons must remain on the provincial list for three years and they are eligible for re-nomination. Any vacancy in the list must be filled by a further nomination for three years by the bishop. Anyone may resign from the list by written notice to the Secretary of the Representative Body.
[164] Can. 21-4-1982, Sched. 2, rr.1-3.
[165] Ibid., rr.6-8. when an incumbent is required to appear before the board, the Secretary of the Representative Body acts as secretary of the board. The secretary must select from the provincial list (see above) the members of the board for that occasion; but the board must not include anyone nominated from the diocese in which the incumbent concerned is then serving.

CLERGY PENSIONS

On retirement, as with most Anglican churches, clergy of the Church in Wales have a right to a pension.[166] Diocesan bishops, deans (including incumbents who are also deans), canons, prebendaries, and archdeacons must retire at seventy.[167] Similarly, clerics holding any other office and deaconesses must retire at seventy.[168] A diocesan bishop may retire between sixty-five and seventy. Any other cleric or a deaconess may retire between sixty-five and seventy on giving the bishop three months' previous written notice of their intention to do so.[169] The archbishop or a diocesan bishop may retire before reaching the age of sixty-five on grounds of permanent disability.[170] On like grounds, other clerics or deaconesses may retire before reaching sixty-five with the written consent of the bishop.[171]

Pensionable Service   On the retirement of clerics or deaconesses, pensions must be paid in accordance with the Clerics' and Deaconesses' Pensions Scheme.[172] Pensions are non-contributory, and must be paid by the Representative Body.[173] Claimants must satisfy the rules as to pensionable service, that is, years of service rendered by a cleric or deaconess in the full-time stipendiary ministry of the Church in Wales.[174] To calculate a pension, the maximum period of pensionable service is forty years, and the minimum is

---

[166] See generally CLAC, 335ff.
[167] Const. XII.1(1) and (2).
[168] Const., XII.1(3): however, they may postpone retirement for no more than three months if at least one month before reaching seventy they notify the bishop in writing of the later date on which they intend to retire; yet, the bishop, at his discretion, may allow the cleric (if not the rector of a rectorial benefice) or deaconess to continue for such period and to retire at such later date as the bishop thinks fit.
[169] Const. XII.2.
[170] Const. XII.3(1): the disability must be proved by medical certificate and other evidence.
[171] Const. XII.3(2): the disability must be proved by medical certificate and other evidence.
[172] Const. XII.4. Provisions for pensions are contained in the Maintenance of Ministry Scheme. See also MMS, Sched., Pt. II, s. 13: the rate of pensions in payment must be increased by the percentage by which minimum clerical stipends are increased in each year; ibid, s. 4: any matter relating to the scheme for which provision is not made shall be determined by the Representative Body.
[173] MMS, Sched., Pt. II, s. 1. See also *Guide to Your Church in Wales Pension*, issued by the Stipends Department of the Representative Body (1999).
[174] MMS, Sched., Pt. II, s. 5(1): pensionable service also includes full-time stipendiary ministry elsewhere as provided; but, in the case of persons retiring after 20 September 1983, every completed month counts as a twelfth part of a year in calculating the total period of service; s. 5(2): full-time stipendiary service in the Church in Wales, as a secretary of a provincial council or committee, or as a diocesan officer appointed to perform extra-parochial duties by licence under seal, is to be regarded as pensionable service; for s. 5(3), and the special case of clerics in part-time stipendiary service, see below. See also MMS, s. 25: no pension may be paid which exceeds the limits permitted by the Finance Act 1970, or any modification in this.

two years.[175] No pension can be paid without an application in the form prescribed by the Representative Body and signed by or on behalf of the applicant.[176] No pension may be assigned or surrendered.[177]

Pension Rates   The rate for the payment of pensions to clerics and deaconesses is, for each year of pensionable service, one-fortieth of sixty per cent of the minimum stipend of the highest pensionable office held at any time during the last five years of such service; for these purposes, the offices of archbishop, diocesan bishop, assistant bishop, dean, archdeacon and incumbent are pensionable offices.[178] A cleric who has not held one of the above pensionable offices, and a deaconess, are entitled to a pension as though he or she had been an incumbent.[179] No pension rights are deemed to accrue as a result of any allowance or additional stipend paid to a cleric by reason of serving in a non-pensionable office.[180] The rate of pensions in payment must be increased by the percentage by which minimum clerical stipends are increased in each year.[181]

Special Cases   The Representative Body may make an *ex-gratia* award to a cleric or deaconess who has less than two years' pensionable service to their credit. This may be done if the diocesan bishop so recommends, and on such conditions as the Representative Body thinks fit. The award may be reviewed at any time.[182] Before or during the payment of a pension to a cleric or deaconess suffering permanent disability,[183] the Representative Body may require the cleric or deaconess to undergo a medical examination by a doctor

---

[175] MMS, Sched., Pt. II, s. 6.
[176] MMS, Sched., Pt. II, s. 12: unless the applicant is the archbishop, a diocesan bishop or a person falling under MMS, Sched., Pt. II, s. 15(1) (see below), the application must be countersigned by the diocesan bishop; applications under s. 15(1) must be submitted directly to the Secretary of the Representative Body.
[177] MMS, Sched., Pt. II, s. 2: that is, no pension payable by the Representative Body under this pension scheme.
[178] MMS, Sched., Pt. II, s. 11(1) and (2). See also ibid., s. 27: notwithstanding s. 11, clerics serving as area deans any time between 1 January 1992 and 31 December 1996, or who retire within five years of holding that office during that period, must be paid a pension at one-fortieth of sixty per cent of the stipend of an area dean; this includes any allowance or additional stipend paid to the cleric by virtue of serving in that office.
[179] MMS, Sched., Pt. II, s. 11(3). However, the offices of a residentiary canon and of a rector (in a rectorial benefice) are deemed to be pensionable offices, for the purposes of the pension rate, in respect of clerics holding office on 31 December 2001 or who (having held such office on or before that date) retire from the full-time stipendiary ministry of the Church in Wales on or before 31 December 2006 (having held office during the five years prior to their retirement).
[180] MMS, Sched., Pt. II, s. 11(4). Special rules apply to a person, not in pensionable service, who attains the appropriate minimum retirement age after 5 April 1975 and who qualifies for a pension: MMS, Sched., Pt. II, s. 15.
[181] MMS, Sched., Pt. II, s. 13.
[182] MMS, Sched., Pt. II, s. 16.
[183] Under Const. XII.3 (see above).

selected by the Representative Body. If they recover their health and accept a stipendiary office, the Representative Body may review the amount of the pension.[184] When a cleric has been required to retire,[185] the amount of the pension is fixed by reference to years of pensionable service in the same way as if the cleric had retired on the attainment of the required age for retirement.[186]

Special rules also apply to the following: (1) when a diocesan bishop (with the consent of the Bench of Bishops), or any other cleric or a deaconess (with the written consent of the bishop), leaves Wales to serve in the mission field overseas or as a chaplain to a Welsh church in England; (2) when a cleric or deaconess serves for a period as a full-time Chaplain in Wales of the Missions to Seafarers; or (3) when a cleric or deaconess serves for a period as a full-time member of the teaching staff of listed institutions.[187] In these cases, service is deemed to be pensionable service. However, the service does not (of itself) carry consequent pension rights, and the Representative Body may determine whether any particular service overseas is in the mission field.[188]

Where the total income of any person in receipt of a pension under the Maintenance of Ministry Scheme is less than the maximum pension of an incumbent, the Representative Body may, if it thinks fit, augment the pension by way of a discretionary grant.[189] The Representative Body must decide in every case whether a cleric in part-time stipendiary service in the Church in Wales is to be allowed to accrue pension benefits proportional to those accrued by clerics in full-time stipendiary service.[190] The Representative Body may also decide that service rendered by a cleric or deaconess other than expressly referred to in the Maintenance of Ministry Scheme shall be deemed to be pensionable service.[191] A gratuity must be paid to each retiring cleric who is entitled to a pension payable by the Representative Body.[192]

Pensions for Surviving Spouses A surviving spouse, whose husband or wife died on or after 23 September 1994, is entitled to a pension as of right if:

---

[184] MMS, Sched., Pt. II, s. 14: a review takes place if the Representative Body thinks fit.
[185] Pursuant to Const. VII.46 or 47.
[186] MMS, Sched., Pt. II, s. 9.
[187] Namely: University of Wales, Lampeter; St Michael's College, Llandaff; or as a full-time warden or other member of the staff of a church hostel in Wales recognized as such by the Bench of Bishops.
[188] MMS, Sched., Pt. II, s. 7; for provisions relating to cases of clergy whose ordination was delayed because of war, see MMS, Pt. II, s. 8.
[189] MMS, Sched., Pt. II, s. 17. See also ibid., s. 26: all clerics who retired during the years 1978 to 1984 (inclusive) shall, in addition to their pensions, receive annually a prescribed augmentation for each year of pensionable service less than 40 years (subject to a maximum of 20 years).
[190] MMS, Sched., Pt. II, s. 5(3): the Representative Body may, if it thinks fit, decide that service, rendered by a cleric or deaconess, be deemed to be pensionable service, and also may resolve any other matter requiring a decision for the purposes of the church's pension scheme.
[191] MMS, Sched., Pt. II, s. 10.
[192] MMS, Sched., Pt. II, s. 18–21.

(a) the deceased, immediately before death, was a cleric who was either in receipt of a pension (including an *ex-gratia* pension) or a grant for service in the ministry of the church, payable by the Representative Body, or in pensionable service (and had at least two pensionable years of service to their credit); and (b) the surviving spouse was married to the deceased, if retired, at the time of retirement.[193] The rate of the pension is sixty per cent of the pension which the deceased cleric was receiving at the date of death, or would have been entitled to receive if the deceased had retired immediately before death.[194] In addition, surviving spouses, of prescribed classes of cleric,[195] are entitled to a pension as of right in respect of a cleric who died before 1 April 1966,[196] those who died on or after 1 April 1966 and before 1 January 1978,[197] and those who died on or after 1 January 1978 and before 23 September 1994.[198] The Representative Body, in exceptional circumstances, may also award an *ex-gratia* pension to persons whose deceased spouses fall into these categories.[199] Where the total income of any surviving spouse in receipt of a pension is less than sixty per cent of the maximum pension of an incumbent, the Representative Body may, if it thinks fit, augment such pension by way of a discretionary grant.[200] The Representative Body must make an annual grant to the Widows, Orphans and Dependants Society of the Church in Wales.[201]

---

[193] MMS, Sched., Pt. II, s. 22.

[194] MMS, Sched., Pt. II, s. 23(1); s. 23(2): for this purpose, save where a surviving spouse's pension is calculated on the deceased spouse's entitlement under s. 15(1) (see above), any increase in the rate of clergy pensions shall be deemed to be applicable to the surviving spouse's pension.

[195] The right is enjoyed by a surviving spouse whose deceased husband or wife was immediately before death a cleric who was either: (a) in receipt of a pension (including an *ex-gratia* pension) or a grant in respect of service in the ministry of the Church in Wales, payable by the Representative Body, or (b) would have been in receipt of a pension if a previous Pension Scheme had been in operation at the date of death, or (c) in pensionable service and with at least two pensionable years of service to his or her credit: MMS, Sched., Pt. II, s. 28.

[196] MMS, Sched., Pt. II, s.28(i): the right exists if the cleric, who died before 1 April 1966, had at least ten pensionable years of service to their credit; and the surviving spouse had been married to the deceased cleric for at least five years and was cohabiting with the cleric at the time of their death.

[197] MMS, Sched., Pt. II, s. 28(ii): the right exists if the cleric, who died on or after 1 April 1966 and before 1 January 1978, had at least five pensio able years of service to their credit; and the surviving spouse had been married to the deceased cleric for at least five years and was cohabiting with the cleric at the time of their death.

[198] MMS, Sched., Pt. II, s.28(iii): the right exists if the cleric, who died on or after 1 January 1978 and before 23 September 1994, had at least five pensionable years of service to their credit; and the surviving spouse had been married to the deceased cleric for at least five years and was cohabiting with the cleric at the time of their death.

[199] MMS, Sched., Pt. II, s. 24: i.e. those spouses qualified under MMS, Sched. Pt. II, s. 28, notwithstanding that they have not been married for least five years.

[200] MMS, Sched. Pt II., s. 25.

[201] MMS, s. 19.

APPENDIX

RULES OF THE CHURCH IN WALES DISCIPLINARY TRIBUNAL

1. The Tribunal shall hear and determine only such complaints alleged to fall within Chapter XI Section 18(1) as are considered appropriate to be referred to the Tribunal by any Diocesan Bishop.

2. Every reference by a Diocesan Bishop under Rule 1 shall be made in writing to the Registrar.

3. Every reference shall be accompanied by such letters, documents, statements or other material relied on by the Diocesan Bishop in making the reference.

4. Within fourteen days of receiving the reference the President shall nominate at least five members of the Tribunal to form an Investigatory Committee in accordance with Chapter XI Section 19 (4). The President shall have regard to the nature of the reference and the expertise needed to investigate. One member will be nominated to chair the Committee.

5. Five members shall form a quorum of the Committee and their decision or the decision of a majority of them shall be the decision of the Committee.

6. The Registrar shall forthwith notify the Respondent of the members of the Committee. The President shall consider any written objection made by the Respondent to the composition of the Committee.

7. Within fourteen days of nomination of the Committee the Chairman shall cause the Registrar to write to the Respondent specifying the relevant paragraphs of Chapter XI Section 18 (1). At the same time the Registrar shall send to the Respondent copies of all letters, documents, statements or other material which the Committee has received and a copy of these Rules.

8. The Respondent, if he or she so wishes, may within fourteen days of receiving the materials referred to in Rule 7 submit in writing to the Registrar such explanation and statements or other evidence which he or she wishes the Committee to consider at that stage.

9. If it appears that the Committee may wish to make an order suspending the Respondent under Chapter XI Section 27, the Chairman shall direct the Registrar to notify the Respondent accordingly and to enquire whether he or she wishes to appear before the Committee and be heard on the question of whether such order should be made.

10. If the Committee makes an order suspending the Respondent, the Registrar shall notify the Respondent's Bishop forthwith.

11. The Committee shall have power to direct that further evidence be sought from such sources and in such form as it thinks fit. All such evidence shall be disclosed to the Respondent who shall be entitled to place before the Committee such relevant evidence as he or she wishes. All such evidence must be disclosed not less than seven days before any hearing or adjourned hearing.

12. Subject to Rule 18 the Registrar shall notify the Respondent of the date and place on which the Committee intends to hold a hearing and the Respondent shall be entitled to attend. Not less than twenty-eight days' notice must be given of the date of such hearing.

13. The Committee shall meet in private.

14. The Registrar shall be Legal Adviser to the Committee.

15. The Committee will carry out its tasks with as little formality as is consistent with fairness and expeditious investigation of references.

16. The Respondent may be accompanied at any hearing before the Committee by such person, including any legal representative, as the Respondent thinks fit, subject only to the power of the Committee to control its own proceedings. Such person may only address the Committee with the specific consent of the Committee.

17. The Committee shall determine whether on the evidence there is a case to answer under Chapter XI Section 18 (1). If there is no case to answer, the Committee shall direct the Registrar to notify in writing forthwith both the Respondent and the Respondent's Bishop and any other person whom the Committee considers should be informed.

18. If the Committee finds a case to answer, it must first consider whether the matter can be resolved by reconciliation or other methods of resolving any conflict and shall take into account the views of any complainant or other person aggrieved.

19. In such cases as the Committee shall consider appropriate and with the consent of the Respondent, the Committee may exercise the Tribunal's power to order an absolute or conditional discharge or rebuke instead of transmitting the reference for hearing before the Tribunal.

20. In any case where the Respondent has been suspended and it appears to the Committee that the matter is of sufficient seriousness and that there is no prospect of reconciliation or other resolution by agreement, the reference shall immediately be transmitted for hearing before the Tribunal.

21. In each and every case the Chairman shall prepare a report of the Committee and such report shall be sent to the Respondent and to the Registrar. If the reference is not to be transmitted for hearing by the Tribunal, such report shall be sent to the Respondent's Bishop.

The Tribunal

22. When the Committee reports that there is a case to answer and transmits the reference to the Tribunal for hearing, the Registrar, after consultation with the Chairman of the Committee, shall within seven days nominate a solicitor or other suitably qualified person as Proctor to conduct the case before the Tribunal.

23. Within fourteen days after the nomination of the Proctor the President shall nominate at least five members in accordance with Chapter XI Section 19 (3) to form a Tribunal. One member shall be nominated to chair the Tribunal.

24. No member who sat on the Committee shall be nominated to sit on the Tribunal in the same reference.

25. The Registrar shall forthwith notify the Respondent and the Proctor of the members of the Tribunal. The President shall consider any written objection to the composition of the Tribunal.

26. The President, if he thinks fit, when nominating members and the Tribunal, after giving the Respondent an opportunity to make representations, shall at any stage have power to summon to its assistance one or more persons of skill and experience in the matter to which the proceedings relate to act as Assessors.

27. Within fourteen days after the nomination of the Chairman and members the Proctor shall file with the Registrar and serve on the Respondent written notice of the allegations against the Respondent. Such notice shall be called the Complaint.

28. The Complaint shall include:

(a) the name and address of the Respondent;

(b) the office (if any) which the Respondent holds in the Church in Wales and the date of appointment;

(c) particulars of the conduct or omissions alleged, including as far as possible the date upon which and the place where the matters relied on occurred;

(d) the relevant paragraphs of Chapter XI Section 18(1).

29. Within fourteen days after the date of the Complaint the Proctor shall file with the Registrar and serve on the Respondent written statements of the witnesses on whom he or she intends to rely at the hearing together with copies of all relevant documents.

30. The Chairman, after consultation with the members and after giving the Proctor and the Respondent the opportunity to make representations in writing, or if in his or her discretion he or she thinks it necessary, at an oral hearing may give the parties such directions for the just and expeditious management and hearing of the case as he or she thinks fit.

31. Any party may seek further directions from the Chairman by written application to the Registrar and serving a copy of such application upon the other party.

32. Not less than twenty-eight days' notice of the date of any final hearing shall be given to the parties.

33. The Respondent shall serve on the Proctor and file with the Registrar written statements of the witnesses on whom he or she intends to rely at the hearing together with all relevant documents not later than the date fixed by the Chairman's directions.

34. All parties shall within seven days after receiving notice of the hearing date lodge with the Registrar a list of the names and addresses of the witnesses the party wishes to call to give oral evidence at the hearing and the Registrar shall forthwith issue a summons to attend at the time and place fixed for the hearing to those persons on such lists who are members of the Church in Wales and to bring with them any relevant documents in their possession or power.

35. The hearing shall be in private unless the Tribunal, after giving the Proctor and the Respondent the opportunity to make representations, decides in the interests of justice to hold such hearing in public, in which case the Tribunal may during any part of the proceedings exclude such person or persons as it thinks fit.

36. The Respondent shall have the right to be represented by a cleric, solicitor or counsel before the Tribunal or by such lay person as the Tribunal may permit.

37. The burden of proof shall be upon the Proctor.

38. After hearing the evidence the Tribunal shall determine either to reject the Complaint or any part thereof or to find the Complaint or any part thereof proved.

39. After giving the Respondent an opportunity to make representations to the Tribunal and to call evidence in mitigation of penalty, the Tribunal shall pronounce such judgement, sentence or order as the Tribunal shall determine.

40. The determination of the Tribunal on the Complaint and any judgement, sentence or order made by the Tribunal shall be made public in such manner as the Tribunal after giving the Respondent an opportunity to make representations shall decide.

General

The following Rules shall apply to any proceedings before the Committee and the Tribunal.

41. Welsh may be spoken by any party, witness or other person and used in any document relied upon.

42. The standard of proof to be applied shall be the balance of probabilities always taking into account that the more serious the allegation, the more cogent is the evidence required to prove it.

43. Subject to the provisions of Chapter I Section 5 any document directed to be filed with the Registrar shall be sent to the Registry by recorded delivery post and any document directed to be served on any other party shall be sent by recorded delivery post to the last known address of the person to be served.

44. A certificate from a secular court of conviction for a criminal offence shall be conclusive proof that the acts therein specified were committed by the person named in the certificate.

45. The Chairman, after giving an opportunity to the Respondent to make representations, shall have power to enlarge the time appointed by these Rules for doing any act or taking any proceedings upon such terms as the circumstances may require and any such enlargement may be ordered although the application is not made until after the expiry of the time appointed.

46. All proceedings shall be recorded.

47. Save as otherwise expressly provided by these Rules the Tribunal and Committee shall determine their own procedure.

Interpretation

'Chapter' and 'Section' refer to the Constitution of the Church in Wales;

'Committee' means the Investigatory Committee of the Disciplinary Tribunal;

'President' means the President of the Disciplinary Tribunal appointed under Chapter XI Section 24 or such other member of the Tribunal authorized by the President to act in his place or if the President is unable to give such authority by a member of the Tribunal nominated by a majority of the membership;

'Registrar' means the Registrar or a Deputy Registrar appointed in accordance with Chapter XI Section 25;

'Respondent' means a member of the Church in Wales against whom complaint is made.

BIBLIOGRAPHY

For the legal texts of the Church in Wales, including ecclesiastical quasi-legislation, see the Table of Ecclesiastical Legislation.

PRIMARY SOURCES

Australia: *The Anglican Church of Australia, Constitution, Canons and Rules of the General Synod* (1995).

Brazil: Episcopal Anglican Church of Brazil: *Igreja Episcopal Anglicana do Brasil: Constituicao* (1994).

—— *Igreja Episcopal Anglicana do Brasil: Canones Gerais* (1994).

Burundi: Church of the Province of Burundi, *Constitution* (1991).

Canada: Anglican Church of Canada, *Handbook of the General Synod of the Anglican Church of Canada* (11th edn, 1996).

Central Africa: Church of the Province of Central Africa, *Constitution and Canons* (1996).

Chile: Diocese of Chile, Anglican Church of the Southern Cone of America, *Estatutos de la Corporación Anglicana de Chile* (1995) (this includes the Canons).

England: Church of England, *Canons of the Church of England* (1964–97).

Indian Ocean: Church of the Province of the Indian Ocean, *Constitution and Canons* (1973–94).

Ireland: *The Constitution of the Church of Ireland* (1988–96).

Japan: Holy Catholic Church in Japan (Nippon Sei Ko Kai), *Constitution and Canons* (1971–94).

Kenya: Church of the Province of Kenya, *Constitution* (1979).

Korea: *The Constitution and Canons of the Anglican Church of Korea* (1992).

Melanesia: Church of the Province of Melanesia, *Constitution and Canons* (1992).

New Zealand: Anglican Church in Aotearoa, New Zealand and Polynesia, *Constitution and Code of Canons* (1995).

Nigeria: Church of the Province of Nigeria, *Constitution* (1979).

North India: United Church of North India, *Constitution and Bye-Laws* (1986).

Papua New Guinea: Anglican Church of (the Province of) Papua New Guinea, *Provincial Constitution and Provincial Canons* (1996).

Philippines: Episcopal Church in the (Province of the) Philippines, *Constitution and Canons* (1996).

Port Moresby (Papua New Guinea), Diocese of: *The Diocesan Constitution and Canons* (1996).

Portugal: Lusitanian Church (Portuguese Episcopal Church), *Igreja Lusitana, Catolica, Apostolica, Evangelica, Canones* (1980).

Rwanda: Church of the Province of Rwanda, *Draft Constitution* (1996).

Scotland: Scottish Episcopal Church, *Code of Canons* (1996).

—— *Digest of Resolutions of General Synod* (1997).

South East Asia: Church of the Province of South East Asia, *Constitution* and *Regulations* (1997).

South India: *The Constitution of the Church of South India* (1992).

Southern Africa: Church of the Province of Southern Africa, *Constitution and Canons* (1994) (this includes *Acts* and *Resolutions* of the Provincial Synod up to 1992).

Southern Cone: Anglican Church of the Southern Cone of America, *Constitution and Canons* (1981).

Spain: Spanish Reformed Episcopal Church, *Bases Fundamentales de Denominacion, Doctrina, Personalidad, Gobierno y Disciplina y Canones Complementarios de las Mismas de la Iglesia Española Reformada Episcopal* (1993).

Sydney (Australia), Diocese of: *The 7th Handbook* (1994).

Tanzania: Church of the Province of Tanzania, *Katiba na Kanuni* (1970).

Uganda: Church of the Province of Uganda, *Provincial Constitution* (1972: as amended, 1994).

USA: *Constitutions and Canons for the Government of the Protestant Episcopal Church in the United States of America* (1994).

West Africa: Church of the Province of West Africa, *Constitution and Canons* (1989).

Western New York (ECUSA), Diocese of: *The Constitution, Canons and Directory*, in *Journal of the One Hundred and Fifty-Eighth Annual Convention* (1995).

West Indies: *Constitution and Canons of the Church of the Province of the West Indies* (1991).

Zaire: Church of the Province of Zaire, *Constitution* (1992).

REPORTS AND CONSULTATION DOCUMENTS

Anglican Marriage in England and Wales: A Guide to the Law for Clergy, issued by the Faculty Office of the Archbishop of Canterbury (1999).

A Workbook for Deaneries of the Church in Wales, Governing Body Deaneries Working Group (2001).

Bibliography on Dying, Death and Bereavement, issued by the Churches Group on Funeral Services at Cemeteries and Crematoria and circulated to the clergy of the Church in Wales by the Bench of Bishops (1994).

Disability Discrimination Act 1995, Consultation Draft, Council for the Care of Churches (2001).

Guide to Your Church in Wales Pension, issued by the Stipends Department of the Representative Body (1999).

Marriage and Divorce, a Statement by the Bench of Bishops of the Church in Wales (1998).

Official Report of the Proceedings of the Convention of the Church in Wales (Cardiff, 1917).

Report of the Review of Electoral College Procedure (February 2001).

The Canon Law of the Church of England, Report of the Archbishops' Commission on Canon Law (London, 1947).

The Cure of Souls: The Calling, Life and Practice of Clergy, being the Report of a Working Party set up in 1995 by the Archbishop of Wales (1996).

The Ecumenical Face of the Province, produced by the Division for Ecumenism and published by the (former) Board of Mission of the Church in Wales (1999).

The Report of the Standing Committee Working Group to Review Chapter V of the Constitution (June 2001).

The Taxation of Ministers of Religion: Guidance Notes, Churches Main Committee (1996).

The Virginia Report, The Report of the Inter-Anglican Theological and Doctrinal Commission, in *The Official Report of the Lambeth Conference 1998* (Harrisburg, Pennsylvania, 1999), 15.

BOOKS AND ARTICLES

Abraham-Williams, G. (ed.), *Towards Making an Ecumenical Bishop* (Penarth, 1997).

Bailey, D., 'Legal regulation of the appointment, ministry and episcopal oversight of army chaplains' (LL M dissertation, University of Wales, Cardiff, 1999).

Baldwin, R., and Houghton, J., 'Circular arguments: the status and legitimacy of administrative rules', *Public Law* (1986), 239.

Barber, P., 'Outrageous behaviour', 4 *ELJ* (1996), 584.

Barrow, J. (ed.), *St Davids Episcopal* Acta: *1085–1280* (Cardiff, 1998).

Bradney, A., *Religions, Rights and Laws* (Leicester, 1993).

Bray, G. (ed.), *The Historic Anglican Canons: 1529–1947* (London, 1998).

Brown, R., 'What of the Church in Wales?', 3 *ELJ* (1993), 20.

—— 'The disestablishment of the Church in Wales', 5 *ELJ* (1999), 252.

Brundage, J.A., *Medieval Canon Law* (London, 1995).

Burn, R., *Ecclesiastical Law* (5th edn, London, 1788).

Bursell, R. D. H., 'What is the place of custom in English canon law?', 1 *ELJ* (1989), 12.

—— 'The seal of the confessional', 1(7), *ELJ* (1990), 84.

—— *Liturgy, Order and the Law* (Oxford, 1996).

—— 'Digging up exhumation', 5 *ELJ* (1998), 18.

Cameron, G. K., 'The Church in Wales, the canons of 1604 and the doctrine of custom' (LLM dissertation, University of Wales, Cardiff, 1997).

Charles, R., 'Church schools and the law' (LLM dissertation, University of Wales, Cardiff, 1997).

Coleman, E. (ed.), *Resolutions of the Twelve Lambeth Conferences 1867–1988* (Toronto, 1992).

Coriden, J. A., *An Introduction to Canon Law* (London, 1990).

Cripps, H., *A Practical Treatise on the Law Relating to the Church and Clergy* (8th edn, London, 1937).

Cumper, P., 'The protection of religious rights under section 13 of the Human Rights Act 1998', *Public Law* (2000), 254.

Denning, A. T., 'The meaning of ecclesiastical law', 60 *Law Quarterly Review* (1944), 235.

Doe, N. (ed.), *Essays in Canon Law: A Study of the Law of the Church in Wales* (Cardiff, 1992).

—— 'Towards a critique of the role of theology in English ecclesiastical and canon law', 2 *ELJ* (1990–2), 328.

—— 'A facilitative canon law: the problem of sanctions and forgiveness', in N. Doe (ed.), *Essays in Canon Law* (Cardiff, 1992), 69.

——*The Legal Framework of the Church of England: A Critical Study in a Comparative Context* (Oxford, 1996).

—— 'Ministers of religion and employment law in the United Kingdom: recent judicial developments', 13 *Anuario de Derecho Eclesiastico del Estado* (1997), 349.

—— *Canon Law in the Anglican Communion: A Worldwide Perspective* (Oxford, 1998).

——, M. Hill and R. Ombres (eds), *English Canon Law* (Cardiff, 1998).

—— 'Ecclesiastical quasi-legislation', ibid., 101.

—— 'The principles of canon law: a focus of legal unity in Anglican–Roman Catholic relations', 5 *ELJ* (1999), 221.

—— 'Disestablishment and the legal position of the Church in Wales' (a paper delivered at a seminar to mark the eightieth anniversary of disestablishment (1920–2000), Cardiff, 29 March 2000).

—— 'Canon law and communion', a paper delivered to the meeting of the Primates of the Anglican Communion, Kanuga, North Carolina, USA, 6 March 2001, reproduced in 30 *The Anglican* (2001), 5.

—— and A. Jeremy, 'Justifications for religious autonomy', in R. O'Dair and A. Lewis (eds), *Law and Religion*, Current Legal Issues 2001, 4 (Oxford, 2001), 421.

Dulles, A. V., *Models of the Church* (Dublin, 1976).

Duncan, G. and Lankshear, D. W., *Church Schools: A Guide for Governors* (1996).

Edge, P. W., 'The employment of religious adherents by religious organisations', in P. W. Edge and G. Harvey (eds), *Law and Religion in Contemporary Society* (Aldershot, 2000), 151.

—— and Loughrey, J. M., 'Religious charities and the jurisdiction of the Charity Commission', 21 *Legal Studies* (2001), 36.

Edwards, A. J., 'Building a canon law: the contribution of Archbishop Green', in N. Doe (ed.), *Essays in Canon Law* (Cardiff, 1992), 49.

Elliott, D. W., 'An evidential privilege for priest–penitent communications', 3 *ELJ* (1995), 272.

Ferme, B. E., *Canon Law in Medieval England* (Rome, 1996).

Gainer, J., 'The *jus liturgicum* of the bishop and the Church in Wales', in N. Doe (ed.), *Essays in Canon Law* (Cardiff, 1992), 111.

—— 'John Sankey and the constitution of the Church in Wales' (LL M dissertation, University of Wales, Cardiff, 1994).

Godolphin, J., *Reportorium Canonicum* (3rd edn, London, 1687).

Green, C. A. H., *The Setting of the Constitution of the Church in Wales* (London, 1937).

Greenwood, R., *Practising Community: The Task of the Local Church* (London, 1996).

Griffiths, J. A., 'Cognitive faith and the position of mental handicap in canon law', in N. Doe (ed.), *Essays in Canon Law* (Cardiff, 1992), 89.

Halsbury, *Laws of England*, vol. 14, *Ecclesiastical Law* (4th edn, London, 1975).

Hamilton, C., *Family, Law and Religion* (London, 1993).

Harnack, A., trans. F. L. Pogson, *The Constitution and Law of the Church in the First Two Centuries* (London, 1910).

Harris, N. S., *The Law Relating to Schools* (2nd edn, 1995).

Harte, D., 'Religious education and worship in state schools', in N. Doe, M. Hill and R. Ombres (eds), *English Canon Law* (Cardiff, 1998), 115.

Hill, M., *Ecclesiastical Law* (2nd edn, Oxford, 2001).

—— 'Judicial review of ecclesiastical courts', in N. Doe, M. Hill and R. Ombres (eds), *English Canon Law* (Cardiff, 1998), 104.

—— 'Judicial approaches to religious disputes', in R. O'Dair and A. Lewis (eds), *Law and Religion*, Current Legal Issues 2001, 4 (Oxford, 2001), 409.

Holeton, D. R., 'Initiation', in S. Sykes and J. Booty (eds), *The Study of Anglicanism* (London, 1988), 261.

Jacob, J. (ed.), *Speller's Law Relating to Hospitals* (6th edn, London, 1978).

Jagger, P. J., *Christian Initiation: 1552–1969* (London, 1970).

James, D. G., 'The office of assistant bishop and the canon law of the Church in Wales' (LL M dissertation, University of Wales, Cardiff, 1994).

Jeremy, A. W., 'The framework, assessment and juridical basis of the parish quota in the Anglican Communion', in J. Fox (ed.), *Render unto Caesar: Church Property in Roman Catholic and Anglican Canon Law* (Rome, 2000), 113.

Jones, P., *The Governance of the Church in Wales* (Cardiff, 2000).

Langley, D., *Health Care Constitutions* (London, 1996).

Leeder, L., *Ecclesiastical Law Handbook* (London, 1997).

Legal Opinions Concerning the Church of England, Legal Advisory Commission (London, 1994).

Leigh, I., 'Towards a Christian approach to religious liberty', in P. R. Beaumont (ed.), *Christian Perspectives on Human Rights and Legal Philosophy* (Carlisle, 1998), 31.

Lewis, A., 'The case for constitutional renewal in the Church in Wales', in N. Doe (ed.), *Essays in Canon Law* (Cardiff, 1992), 175.

Lewis, E., *Prayer Book Revision in the Church in Wales* (Penarth, 1958).

McFarlane, A., 'Child protection: the Church of England and the law' (LL M dissertation, University of Wales, Cardiff, 1998).

Moffat, G., and Chesterman, M., *Trusts Law* (London, 1988).

Montgomery, J., *Health Care Law* (Oxford, 1997).

Nicholson, J., 'Male circumcision', Centre for Law and Religion, 1 (2) *Newsletter* (2000), 4.

Ogilvie, M. H., 'What is a church by law established?', *Osgoode Hall Law Journal*, 28 (1990), 179.

Ombres, R., 'Why then the law?', *New Blackfriars* (1974), 296.

Phillimore, R., *The Ecclesiastical Law of the Church of England*, 2 vols. (2nd edn, London, 1895).

Picarda, H., 'Religious observance and the element of public benefit', 2 *The Charity Law and Practice Review* (1993), 155.

Poulter, S., *Ethnicity, Law and Human Rights* (Oxford, 1998).

Price, W., *The Governing Body of the Church in Wales*, St David's Papers (Penarth, 1990).

Pryce, H., *Native Law and the Church in Medieval Wales* (Oxford, 1993).

Quint, F., and Spring, T., 'Religion, charity law and human rights', 5 *The Charity Law and Practice Review* (1999), 153.

Robbers, G. (ed.), *State and Church in the European Union* (Baden-Baden, 1996).

Roberts, E. P., 'The Welsh church, canon law and the Welsh language', in N. Doe (ed.), *Essays in Canon Law* (Cardiff, 1992), 151.

Smethurst, A. F., Wilson, H. R., and Riley, H. (eds.), *Acts of the Convocations of Canterbury and York* (London, 1961).

Smith, P., 'Points of law and practice concerning ecclesiastical visitation', 2 *ELJ* (1990–2), 189.

Urresti, T., 'Canon law and theology: two different sciences', 8 *Concilium* (1967), 10.

Walker, D. (ed.), *A History of the Church in Wales* (Penarth, 1976; reissued 1990).

Watkin, T. G., 'The vestiges of establishment: the ecclesiastical and canon law of the Church in Wales', 2 *ELJ* (1990), 110.

—— 'Disestablishment, self-determination and the constitutional development of the Church in Wales', in N. Doe (ed.), *Essays in Canon Law* (Cardiff, 1992), 25.

—— 'Consensus and the constitution', 3 *ELJ* (1994), 232.

—— 'Welsh church courts and the rule of law', 5 *ELJ* (2000), 460.

INDEX